T0135172

Lecture Notes in Computer Science   12676

More information about this subseries at http://www.springer.com/series/7410

Matthew Bernhard · Andrea Bracciali ·
Lewis Gudgeon · Thomas Haines ·
Ariah Klages-Mundt · Shin'ichiro Matsuo ·
Daniel Perez · Massimiliano Sala ·
Sam Werner (Eds.)

Financial Cryptography and Data Security

FC 2021 International Workshops

CoDecFin, DeFi, VOTING, and WTSC
Virtual Event, March 5, 2021
Revised Selected Papers

 Springer

Editors

Matthew Bernhard
University of Michigan–Ann Arbor
Ann Arbor, MI, USA

Lewis Gudgeon
Imperial College London
London, UK

Ariah Klages-Mundt
Ithaca College
Ithaca, USA

Daniel Perez
Imperial College London
London, UK

Sam Werner
Imperial College London
London, UK

Andrea Bracciali ⓘ
Computer Science and Mathematics
Stirling University
Stirling, UK

Thomas Haines
Norwegian University of Science
and Technology
Trondheim, Norway

Shin'ichiro Matsuo
Department of Computer Science
Georgetown University
Washington, WA, USA

Massimiliano Sala ⓘ
Dipartimento di Matematica
University of Trento
Trento, Trento, Italy

ISSN 0302-9743   ISSN 1611-3349 (electronic)
Lecture Notes in Computer Science
ISBN 978-3-662-63957-3   ISBN 978-3-662-63958-0 (eBook)
https://doi.org/10.1007/978-3-662-63958-0

LNCS Sublibrary: SL4 – Security and Cryptology

This Springer imprint is published by the registered company Springer-Verlag GmbH, DE part of Springer Nature
The registered company address is: Heidelberger Platz 3, 14197 Berlin, Germany

CoDecFin 2021 Preface

The Second Workshop on Coordination of Decentralized Finance (CoDecFin 2021) took place in conjunction with Financial Cryptography and Data Security 2021 on March 5, 2021. The CoDecFin workshop is focused on multi-disciplinary issues regarding technologies and operations of decentralized finance based on permissionless blockchain.

From an academic point of view, security and privacy protection are some of the leading research streams. The Financial Cryptography conference discusses these research challenges. On the other hand, other stakeholders than cryptographers and blockchain engineers have different interests in these characteristics of blockchain technology. For example, regulators face difficulty in tracing transactions in terms of anti-money laundering (AML) against privacy-enhancing crypto-assets. Another example is consumer protection in the case of cyberattacks on crypto-asset custodians. Blockchain business entities sometimes start their business before maturing technology, but the technology and operations are not transparent to regulators and consumers. The main problem is a lack of communication among stakeholders of the decentralized finance ecosystem. The G20 discussed the issue of insufficient communication among stakeholders in 2019. It concluded that there is an essential need for multi-stakeholder discussion among engineers, regulators, business entities, and operators based on the neutrality of academia.

The CoDecFin workshop was initiated in 2020 to facilitate such multi-stakeholder discussion in a neutral academic environment. The goals of CoDecFin were to have common understandings of technology and regulatory goals and to discuss essential issues of blockchain technology faced by all stakeholders mentioned above. It was a historic workshop because we could involve regulators and engineers in the discussion at the Financial Cryptography conference.

CoDecFin 2021 consisted of three parts: a keynote talk, presentations by all stakeholders, and roundtable discussions. The keynote talk by Peter Van Balkenburgh discussed "Your Right to DeFi". The presentations were selected based on the peer-review process. The topics included DeFi risks, AML/KYC, and privacy. As this workshop was held right after the Financial Crimes Enforcement Network (FinCEN) proposed a new draft regulation on AML/KYC and the treatment of un-hosted wallets, the AML/KYC and privacy session focused on the issues related to this proposal. In the third part, we invited panelists from all stakeholders, including blockchain businesses, regulators, engineers, and academia, on the AML/KYC session issues to join the roundtable discussions. Presentations and discussions are included as papers of this proceedings.

May 2021   Shin'ichiro Matsuo

CoDecFin 2021 Organization

Workshop Chair

Shin'ichiro Matsuo   Georgetown University, NTT Research, and
     BSafe.network, USA

Program Committee

Julien Bringer	Kallistech, France
Joaquin Garcia-Alfaro	Telecom SudParis, France
Arthur Gervais	Imperial College London, UK
Byron Gibson	Stanford Center for Blockchain Research, USA
Feng Chen	University of British Columbia, Canada
Shin'ichiro Matsuo (Chair)	Georgetown University, NTT Research, and BSafe.network, USA
Steven Nam	Stanford Journal of Blockchain Law & Policy, USA
Michele Benedetto Neitz	Golden Gate University, USA
Roman Danziger Pavlov	SafeStead Inc., USA
Robert Schwentker	DLT Education and BSafe.network, USA
Yonatan Sompolinsky	The Hebrew University of Jerusalema and DAGlabs, Israel
Shigeya Suzuki	Keio University
Ryosuke Ushida	JFSA and Georgetown University, USA
Robert Wardrop	University of Cambridge, UK
Pindar Wong	BSafe.network, Hong Kong
Aaron Wright	Cardozo School of Law, USA
Anton Yemelyanov	Base58 Association, Canada
Aviv Zohar	The Hebrew University of Jerusalem, Israel

DeFi 2021 Preface

These proceedings collect the papers accepted at the First Workshop on Decentralized Finance (DeFi 2021 - http://fc21.ifca.ai/defi/), held in association with the Financial Cryptography and Data Security 2021 conference (FC 2021) on March 5, 2021.

The focus of the DeFi workshop series is decentralized finance, a blockchain powered peer-to-peer financial system. This first workshop coincided with the early fruition of DeFi, and sought to solicit contributions from both academia and industry which focussed on addressing fundamental, timely, and important questions at the centre of DeFi.

This first workshop received 40 submissions, of which 22 were accepted either as a short paper (9) or as a talk (13). All of the short papers and a subset of the talks, as précis, appear in these proceedings. Overall, the organizers were extremely impressed by the quality of submissions received and were delighted by the strong attendance and lively discussion during the workshop. The workshop was conducted online as a result of the COVID-19 pandemic, but we look forward to future years where it can be conducted in person.

In addition to talks pertaining to submissions we had a guest speaker, Raphael Auer, from the Bank for International Settlements, and we would like to thank him for his talk. The workshop closed with a panel, featuring Tarun Chitra (Gauntlet), Robert Leshner (Compound), Andrew Miller (University of Illinois at Urbana-Champaign), and Jeremy Musighi (Balancer), which covered a wide range of topics from privacy in DeFi to the role of auditors. We would like to sincerely thank the panelists for taking part and for the lively discussion

The Organizing Committee would like to extend sincere thanks to all those who submitted their work, the Program Committee for their careful work, and all those who participated in the workshop. In addition, we would like to extend our thanks to Kevin McCurley and Kay McKelly, for their seamless organization of the online support needed to conduct this event virtually, and Rafael Hirschfeld for his flawless support, organization, and encouragement of this first workshop.

June 2021

Lewis Gudgeon
Ariah Klages-Mundt
Daniel Perez
Sam Werner

DeFi 2021 Organization

Workshop Chairs

Lewis Gudgeon   Imperial College London, UK
Ariah Klages-Mundt   Cornell University, USA
Daniel Perez   Imperial College London, UK
Sam Werner   Imperial College London, UK

Program Committee

Cuneyt Akcora   University of Manitoba, Canada
Raphael Auer   Bank for International Settlements, Switzerland
Tarun Chitra   Gauntlet Networks, USA
Martin Florian   Humboldt-Universität zu Berlin
Dominik Harz   Imperial College London, UK
William Knottenbelt   Imperial College London, UK
Jiasun Li   George Mason University, USA
Benjamin Livshits   Imperial College London and Brave Software, UK
Jun-You Liu   Cornell University, USA
Patrick McCorry   anydot, UK
Andrew Miller   University of Illinois at Urbana-Champaign, USA
Andreea Minca   Cornell University, USA
Daniel Moroz   Harvard University, USA
David Parkes   Harvard University, USA
Julien Prat   CNRS, France
Tim Roughgarden   Columbia University, USA
Alexei Zamyatin   Imperial College London, UK
Fan Zhang   Chainlink, USA

VOTING 2021 Preface

VOTING 2021 marks the 6th Workshop on Advances in Secure Electronic Voting associated with the Financial Cryptography and Data Security 2021 conference (FC 2021) held virtually due to the COVID-19 pandemic on March 5, 2021.

This year's workshop received 14 papers with 7 accepted. We are grateful for our Program Committee for their time and effort, and especially their flexibility when we extended the submission deadline. We also thank the authors of all submitted papers, and especially the presenters for joining the workshop online despite the ongoing COVID-19 crisis. We are also grateful to Ray Hirschfeld, Sergi Delgado Segura, and IFCA for organizing all the logistics of the event and the FC workshop chairs for their continued support of VOTING. For VOTING 2022 the tradition of staggered chairs is continued with Thomas Haines and Aleks Essex serving as program chairs.

April 2021

Matthew Bernhard
Thomas Haines

VOTING 2021 Organization

Program Chairs

Matthew Bernhard   VotingWorks, USA
Thomas Haines   Norwegian University of Science and Technology, Norway

Program Committee

Roberto Araujo   Universidade Federal do Pará, Brazil
Josh Benaloh   Microsoft Research, USA
Jeremy Clark   Concordia University, Canada
Chris Culnane   Independent Researcher, UK
Constantin Dragan   University of Surrey, UK
Jeremy Epstein   SRI International, USA
Aleksander Essex   Western University, Canada
Kristian Gjøsteen   Norwegian University of Science and Technology
Rajeev Gore   The Australian National University, Australia
Rolf Haenni   Bern University of Applied Sciences, Switzerland
Reto Koenig   Bern University of Applied Sciences, Switzerland
Ralf Kuesters   University of Stuttgart, Germany
Oksana Kulyk   IT University of Copenhagen, Denmark
Olivier Pereira   Université catholique de Louvain, Belgium
Peter Rønne   University of Luxembourg, Luxembourg
Peter Y. A. Ryan   University of Luxembourg, Luxembourg
Steve Schneider   University of Surrey, UK
Carsten Schuermann   IT University of Copenhagen, Denmark
Philip Stark   University of California, Berkeley, USA
Vanessa Teague   Thinking Cybersecurity, Australia
Poorvi Vora   The George Washington University, USA
Dan Wallach   Rice University, USA

WTSC 2021 Preface

These proceedings collect the papers accepted at the Fifth Workshop on Trusted Smart Contracts (WTSC21 - http://fc21.ifca.ai/wtsc/) associated with the Financial Cryptography and Data Security 2021 conference (FC 2021).

The WTSC series focuses on smart contracts, i.e., self-enforcing agreements in the form of executable programs, and other decentralized applications that are deployed to, and run on top of, (specialized) blockchains. These technologies introduce a novel programming framework and execution environment, which, together with the supporting blockchain technologies, carry unanswered and challenging research questions. Multidisciplinary and multifactorial aspects affect correctness, safety, privacy, authentication, efficiency, sustainability, resilience, and trust in smart contracts and decentralized applications.

WTSC aims to address the scientific foundations of Trusted Smart Contract engineering, i.e., the development of contracts that enjoy some verifiable "correctness" properties, and to discuss open problems, proposed solutions, and the vision on future developments amongst a research community that is growing around these themes and brings together users, practitioners, industry, institutions, and academia. This was reflected in the multidisciplinary Program Committee (PC) of this fifth edition of WTSC, comprising members from companies, universities, and research institutions from several countries worldwide, who kindly accepted to support the event. The association with FC 2021 provided, once again, an ideal context for our workshop.

This year's edition of WTSC received 30 submissions by about 90 authors, confirming a growing trend and increased interest. Given the high quality of submission, 16 papers were accepted after double-blind peer review. Thanks to the generous effort by the PC, each paper received an average of 3.3 reviews, providing constructive feedback to authors. Papers revised after the discussion at the workshop are collected in the present volume. These analyze the current state of the art of smart contracts and their development. Important aspects that were discussed at the workshop included security and verification, attacks' analysis, scalability, relationships of smart contracts and consensus, and privacy-preserving applications. An emerging theme received a lot of attention: decentralized finance (DeFi). Apart from the contributed talks, we had a final roundtable on DeFi jointly with the 2nd Workshop on Coordination of Decentralized Finance (CoDecFin 2021).

Generally speaking, the presentations made a full day of interesting talks and discussion. More detailed video presentations are made available online on a dedicated YouTube channel[1] that can be reached from the workshop's web page. Following our tradition of excellent invited speakers (Buterin, Breitman, Gutmann, Mishra, Artamonov, Grigg), our workshop started with a beautiful presentation by Darren Tapp, leading scientist in the cryptocurrency community DASH.

---

[1] https://www.youtube.com/watch?v=MvGnPhpkNlM&list=PL_aN0fSJkEsoopkLAivp89w5hH dF19W0A.

This year's edition was planned to take place in Granada, Spain, on March 5, 2021, but was held online due to the COVID-19 pandemic. Although we missed direct interaction a lot, we believe the community enjoyed the online presentations and discussions.

WTSC 2021's chairs would like to thank everyone for their usual, and this year extra, effort and valuable contributions: authors, Program Committee members and reviewers, and participants, as well as the support by IFCA, FC 2021 committees, Kevin McCurley and Kay McKelly for the online framework to run the conference, and Ray Hirschfeld for the usual exceptional organization of the event.

May 2021   Andrea Bracciali
                                                     Massimiliano Sala

WTSC 2021 Organization

Workshop Chairs

Andrea Bracciali   University of Stirling, UK
Massimiliano Sala   University of Trento, Italy

Program Committee

Monika di Angelo	Vienna University of Technology, Austria
Igor Artamonov	Ethereum Classic, UK
Daniel Augot	Inria, France
Surya Bakshi	University of Illinois, USA
Fadi Barbara	University of Turin, Italy
Massimo Bartoletti	University of Cagliari, Italy
Stefano Bistarelli	University of Perugia, Italy
Christina Boura	Versailles Saint-Quentin-en-Yvelines University, France
Andrea Bracciali	University of Stirling, UK
Daniel Broby	Strathclyde University, UK
James Chapman	IOHK, UK
Martin Chapman	King's College London, UK
Alexander Denzler	Lucerne University of Applied Sciences and Arts, Switzerland
Nicola Dimitri	University of Siena, Italy
Nadia Fabrizio	Cefriel, Italy
Murdoch Gabbay	Heriot-Watt University, UK
Oliver Giudice	Banca d'Italia, Italy
Davide Grossi	University of Groningen, The Netherlands
Yoichi Hirai	brainbot technologies AG, Denmark
Lars R. Knudsen	Technical University of Denmark, Denmark
Ioannis Kounelis	Joint Research Centre, European Commission, Italy
Pascal Lafourcade	University of Clermont Auvergne, France
Andrew Lewis-Pye	London School of Economics, UK
Carsten Maple	University of Warwick, UK
Michele Marchesi	University of Cagliari, Italy
Fabio Martinelli	IIT-CNR, Italy
Luca Mazzola	Lucerne University of Applied Sciences and Arts, Switzerland
Sihem Mesnager	University of Paris 8 Vincennes-Saint-Denis, France
Philippe Meyer	Avaloq, Switzerland
Bud Mishra	New York University, USA

Contents

DeFi – Formal Attack Analysis

DeFi – Economics and Regulation

DeFi – MEV and Illicit Activity

DeFi – Order Routing and Formal Methods

Voting

WTSC – Security and Verification

WTSC – Foundations

WWTSC – Attacks' Analysis

WTSC – DeFi and Tokens

CoDecFin – DeFi Risks

Risk Framework for Bitcoin Custody Operation with the Revault Protocol

Jacob Swambo[1,2]($\boxtimes$) and Antoine Poinsot[2]

[1] Department of Informatics, King's College London, London, England
jacob.swambo@kcl.ac.uk
[2] WizardSardine, Lisboa, Portugal
darosior@protonmail.com

Abstract. Our contributions with this paper are twofold. First, we elucidate the methodological requirements for a risk framework of custodial operations and argue for the value of this type of risk model as complementary with cryptographic and blockchain security models. Second, we present a risk model in the form of a library of attack-trees for Revault – an open-source custody protocol. The model can be used by organisations as a risk quantification framework for a thorough security analysis in their specific deployment context. Our work exemplifies an approach that can be used independent of which custody protocol is being considered, including complex protocols with multiple stakeholders and active defence infrastructure.

1 Introduction

While mainstream acceptance of Bitcoin as an asset appears to be increasing, advanced tools and methods for secure custody of bitcoins are slow to develop. Bitcoin custody encompasses the protection of assets through software, hardware, and operational processes. The foundation of Bitcoin custody is key-management, a well understood topic in the academic literature and in practice. However, Bitcoin custody, in particular multi-stakeholder custody, involves human processes, communication protocols, network monitoring and response systems, software, hardware and physical security environments. Given a secure cryptographic layer, there are still vulnerabilities introduced at the application layer by software developers, at the hardware layer throughout the supply chain, and at the operations layer by users. Without adequate risk management frameworks for custodial operations, Bitcoin users are likely to suffer unexpected losses whether they self-custody funds or employ a third-party custodian.

Open-source custody protocols are emerging [5,25,38,39] and are a critical ecosystem component for improving security standards. If a custody protocol stands to public scrutiny and offers a high-level of security without relying on proprietary processes, users, insurance companies and regulators can have more confidence in it. The emerging custody protocols are trying to reconcile the needs of traditional businesses and banking with Bitcoin's novel identity-less and

© International Financial Cryptography Association 2021
M. Bernhard et al. (Eds.): FC 2021 Workshops, LNCS 12676, pp. 3–20, 2021.
https://doi.org/10.1007/978-3-662-63958-0_1

irreversible transaction properties. A lack of available and accepted open-source custody protocols means that organisations are heavily relying on third-party custodians, or deploying their own custody protocol.

We propose an attack modelling technique as the basis for a risk framework for Bitcoin custody operations, using the Revault protocol[1] as a case-study [4,25]. While the process of model construction is intensive, the resultant framework is extensible and modular and some of its components can be re-used with different custody protocols. It is intended to be readily comprehensible, and, given sufficient validation, the framework can be used by any organisation intending to deploy Revault to better understand their risk posture.

Risk quantification frameworks address several ecosystem problems. Organisations that control bitcoins or other digital assets need accurate models to engage in realistic risk-management. The complexity of custodial risks leaves insurance companies guessing rather than systematically estimating when pricing their insurance offerings or assessing particular solutions for digital custody. Finally, emerging regulatory standards for custody [9,26] are simple and fail to capture advanced custody architectures or enable context-specific risk analyses that acknowledge the full security environment of a custody operation.

The remainder of this paper is structured as follows. Section 2 summarises the components and processes of the Revault protocol. Section 3 discusses our evaluation criteria for an operational risk framework, and introduces the attack-tree formalism on which our risk model is based. Section 4 presents our operational risk model for Revault. Section 5 concludes this paper.

2   Overview of Revault Custody Protocol

Revault is a multi-party custody protocol that distinguishes between *stakeholders* and fund *managers*. The primary protection for funds is a high-threshold multi-signature Script controlled by the stakeholders. The day-to-day operational overhead of fund management is simplified by enabling portions of funds to be delegated to fund managers. Stakeholders define spending policies in-line with traditional controls of expenses, and have automated servers to enforce their policies. In addition, a deterrent is withheld by each stakeholder to mitigate incentives to physically threaten the stakeholders. To achieve this, Revault makes use of sets of pre-signed transactions coupled with an active defence mechanism for detecting and responding to attempted theft transactions. In the following, we will outline the components of the Revault architecture, the transaction set, the stakeholders' routine signing process and the managers' spend process. Refer to [4] for the detailed specification of the open-source protocol.

---

[1] Specifically, the version identified as 609b40dda07155abe5cd4a5af77fc2211d11fbc1 which can be found on the open-source repository hosted on Github [4].

2.1   Revault Architecture Components

Each stakeholder and manager has a *hardware security module* (HSM) to manage their private keys and generate signatures for transactions. A backup of private keys is stored for each HSM in a separate protected physical environment.

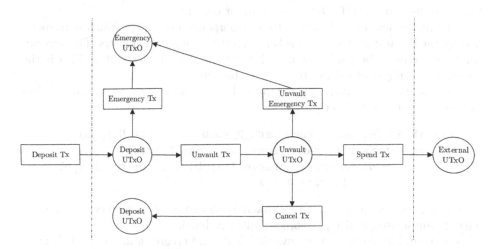

Fig. 1. Diagram of the transaction (Tx) set structure in the Revault protocol. An Unspent-transaction-output (UTxO) is created by a preceding Tx and is consumed by an input in a proceeding Tx.

Each stakeholder and manager uses a *wallet* software to track their co-owned bitcoins, craft transactions, store transaction signatures and communicate with each other through a *coordinator*. The coordinator is a proxy server that simplifies communication for the multi-party wallet. All communication uses Noise KK encrypted and authenticated channels [33].

Stakeholders each have one or more *watchtower*, an online server that enforces the stakeholder's spending policy limitations. Stakeholders each have an *anti-replay oracle* server.

2.2   Revault Transaction Set

The use of hierarchical deterministic wallets means that each participant in the Revault protocol has a tree of public and private keys [41]. To discuss ownership of bitcoins, we refer to a generalisation of a locking Script, called a *descriptor*. The wallet will have multiple addresses that correspond to a single abstracted descriptor. Funds are deposited into the multi-party wallet through a Deposit transaction (Tx) output that pays to the deposit descriptor, describing $N-$signatories locking Scripts derived from the stakeholders' (*stk*) extended public keys (*xpub*). In descriptors language formalisation [2] it is defined as:

```
thresh(N, stk_1_xpub, stk_2_xpub, ..., stk_N_xpub)
```

The set of transactions prepared with stakeholders' wallets and signed using their hardware security modules (HSM) include the Emergency Tx, Unvault Tx, Unvault-Emergency Tx and Cancel Tx. The managers can only prepare and sign a Spend Tx type. Figure 1 depicts these transactions and the essential unspent-transaction-outputs (UTxOs) they create or consume.

An Emergency Tx locks funds to an emergency descriptor which is unspecified by the Revault protocol and is kept private among stakeholders. The descriptor must however be harder to unlock than the deposit descriptor. This is the deterrent for physical threats to the stakeholders.

An Unvault Tx consumes the deposit UTxO and creates an unvault UTxO locked to the unvault descriptor,

```
or( thresh(N, stk_1_xpub, stk_2_xpub, ..., stk_N_xpub),
    and( thresh(K, man_1_xpub, ..., man_M_xpub),
        and( thresh(N, oracle_1_xpub, ..., oracle_N_xpub),
            older(X) ) ) ),
```

that is redeemable by either the N stakeholders *or* the M managers (*man*) along with N automated anti-replay oracles after X blocks.

A Cancel Tx consumes the unvault UTxO and creates a new deposit UTxO. The watchtowers' role is to broadcast the Cancel Tx if a fraudulent spend attempt is detected (either through an unauthorised attempt at broadcasting an Unvault Tx or if a Spend Tx does not abide by the spending policy). The time-lock gives watchtowers X blocks worth of time to broadcast a Cancel Tx. An Unvault-Emergency Tx consumes the unvault UTxO and locks funds to the emergency descriptor. It has the same purpose as the Emergency Tx, only it consumes the unvault UTxO rather than the deposit UTxO. A Spend Tx is used by managers to pay to external addresses.

2.3   Stakeholders' Signing Routine

Stakeholders' wallets routinely check for new deposits and each one triggers a signing routine. Figure 2 shows the connections and message types for an example Revault deployment enacting the signing routine. The wallet crafts an Emergency Tx and requests the stakeholder to sign it using their HSM. The stakeholder will verify the emergency descriptor on the HSM before authorising the signature generation[2]. The wallet then connects to the coordinator to push its signature and will fetch other stakeholders' signatures.

Optionally, stakeholders may also sign the Cancel, Unvault-Emergency, and Unvault Txs to securely delegate funds to the managers. In this case the signing

---

[2] This feature is not available with current HSMs, but integrating compatibility with descriptors (along with other security features) would improve the human-verification component of HSM security and is being discussed on the *bitcoin-dev* mailing list [24].

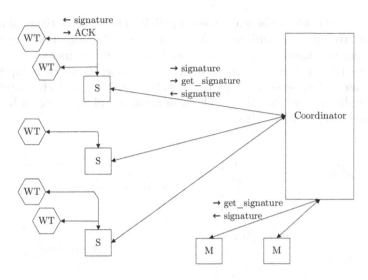

Fig. 2. Data flow diagram for the communication of the *stakeholders' signing routine* with an example Revault deployment. There are three stakeholders (S) who each have one or two watchtowers (WT). There are two managers (M) and a coordinator. Signature messages, signature requests and watchtower acknowledgements (ACK) are only shown once per connection type but apply to each connection of that type (e.g. there is {← signature, → ACK} between each WT and S).

process is the same but is carried out in two steps: first, the signatures for the Cancel and Unvault-Emergency Txs are exchanged with the other stakeholders through the coordinator and then shared with the watchtower(s), and only then are the Unvault Tx signatures shared with managers.

2.4 Managers' Spending Process

Most spending policies cannot be inferred from the Unvault Tx alone and so the Spend Tx must be known to the watchtower to validate an unvaulting attempt. In these cases the Spend Tx must be advertised to the watchtowers before unvaulting, otherwise it will be cancelled. The anti-replay oracle is required to avoid the Spend Tx being modified by the managers *after* the unvault time-lock expires and thus by-passing enforcement of the watchtowers' spending policies.

Any manager can initiate a spend. Figure 3 depicts the spend process. The initiator creates a Spend Tx, verifies and signs it using their HSM and passes it back to the wallet in the partially-signed Bitcoin Tx (PSBT) format [10]. It's exchanged with a sufficient threshold of the other managers to add their signatures and hand it back to the initiator. The initiator requests a signature from each of the anti-replay oracles and pushes the fully-signed Spend Tx to the coordinator. The initiator broadcasts the Unvault Tx, triggering a lookup from the watchtowers to the coordinator for the Spend Tx. If the Spend Tx is valid according to *all* of the watchtowers policies and none of them cancel this unvaulting attempt, the manager waits X blocks and broadcasts the Spend Tx.

If, during the unvaulting process, there's a significant increase in the fee-level required for a Spend Tx to be mined, a manager needs to bump the fee. Managers use a dedicated single-party fee wallet for this. Similarly, watchtowers use a fee wallet in the case there is high demand for block space to bump the fee for Cancel or emergency Txs.

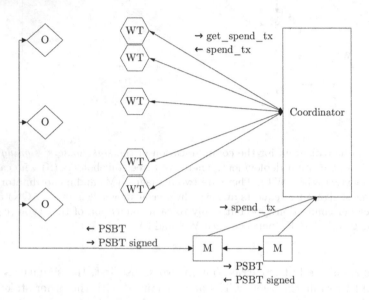

Fig. 3. Data flow diagram for the communication of the managers' spend process. In this example there are two managers (M), three anti-replay oracles (O), five watchtowers (WT) and a coordinator. A Partially-signed Bitcoin Tx (PSBT) is exchanged among managers and between a manager and the anti-replay oracles. A fully signed SpendTx is shared with the WTs through the coordinator.

3   Methodology

To see where this research fits in to the big picture, consider the key life-cycle of a custodial operation. There are three phases; initialization, operation, and termination. Initialization is where wallet and communication keys are generated, where software integrity is verified, hardware security modules are checked, and relevant public information is shared among participants. Operation encompasses the active fund management. Termination is the phase wherein the wallet is de-commissioned and all sensitive information destroyed. Initialization and termination are out of scope for this paper. Our risk model covers the operations phase. In the following we present our rationale for our chosen attack modeling formalism and explain how this can be used as a risk framework.

3.1   Operational Security Models

A framework for high-level risk analyses for the integration of custody into a multi-stakeholder context has not yet been presented. To-date the literature has focused primarily on cryptographic security modeling, dealing with low-level risks associated with cryptographic primitives, key-management protocols, HSMs and single-party wallets. The underlying cryptographic security is fundamental but should be complemented by an operational security model, which is much more likely to be the domain where participants create vulnerabilities for an attacker. Advanced custody protocols that use multi-layer access control with both static and active defences for insider and external attackers demand a whole-system approach to security analysis.

We present now several requirements for our modelling formalism: a) the ability to represent complex processes with numerous components and sequential events; b) supports qualitative risk analysis; c) supports automated quantitative methods for multi-attribute risk analysis; d) readily comprehensible and visual models that are more amenable to open-source intelligence; and e) extensible and modular models to support differential analysis and re-use of modules.

The two most popular attack modeling techniques in cyber-security literature are attack-trees and attack graphs [23]. In short, tools for attack graphs tend to produce graphs that aren't readily comprehensible due to the complexity of real-world attack scenarios [14]. That is, attack graphs don't scale well [35]. On the other hand, attack-trees seem to meet all of our requirements, at least when considered with the right structure and semantics (as described in Sect. 3.2) and thus we construct our risk model using this formalism.

While a statement such as 'our custody solution is based on an $m-$of$-n$ security model' can entail a lot for simple multi-signature custody protocols, it doesn't capture the reality nearly as well as our proposed methodology would. It is certainly not sufficient for a more complex custody protocol like Revault. What is the physical environment for those n private keys? Are any of those keys online? Are there key backups and, if so, what protections are in place for these? Too much depends on the broader security environment of a custody protocol for it to be left without scrutiny.

Application threat modelling has been used to harden the Revault protocol throughout both its theoretical development and implementation. For each application process (spend, routine signing, emergency, revault) a component-by-component and connection-by-connection analysis has been carried out to determine the consequences of outages, data tampering, component corruption, etc., and has resulted in the design specification [4] and the transaction flow threat model [25]. The application threat modeling approach is complementary and has informed us in enumerating the risks presented with the attack-trees. However, in contrast to attack-trees, it lacks a semantic structure which is amenable for automated risk quantification and thus isn't suitable as the basis of a risk framework.

3.2   Attack-Tree Formalism

The risk model is presented using the formalism of attack-trees [6, 36, 40]. Attack-trees have an attack at their root, and branches that capture alternate (OR) and complementary (AND) attack pathways comprised of intermediate attack goals as non-leaf nodes and basic attack steps as leaf nodes. As in numerous other works [11, 18, 22, 27–29], we extend the basic attack-tree to support sequential conjunction of branches (SAND) allowing us to model an attack where some sub-tree of an attack pathway has to occur before and in addition to another sub-tree. For brevity we depict our attack-trees as nested lists. The logical gates (OR, AND, SAND) shown with each node apply to the next node at the same depth. This means that at any given depth, a node with a SAND gate occurs *before* other nodes that are shown below it. Some aspects of the system are built to be resilient to attack and failure through redundancy. For example, an attacker needs to compromise all stakeholders' private keys to steal funds locked to the deposit descriptor. To be concise, rather than having several copies of the same sub-tree we write (X times) to note that the sub-tree has to happen X times. During an analysis, these sub-trees should be considered as X separate AND sub-trees, since they are contextually different (corresponding to different participants, remote and physical environments).

We provide a set of attack-trees, capturing prominent risks that have been enumerated primarily by considering tangible and intangible assets. Tangible assets (bitcoins) are distinguished by the access control structures determined by the set of descriptors. We consider operational privacy and business continuity as intangible assets.

Our work here is focused on security, rather than safety. In principle, the same methodology could be extended to an integrated security-safety model by constructing attack-fault-trees [22]. Another common extension to the attack-tree formalism is to include countermeasures, producing attack-defence-trees [16, 19]. The benefit of our modular modelling technique is that it enables future work to integrate these extensions and re-use results from this work. Hence, we prioritise constructing a strong foundation based only on attacks, and aim to incrementally improve on the model presented as new intelligence emerges.

3.3   On Risk Analysis

Our purpose in constructing the risk model presented in Sect. 4 is to provide a framework to support both qualitative and quantitative risk analyses for specific deployment instances of Revault custody. By determining costs, likelihoods, and other attributes for risks associated with custodial processes, an organisation can perform a differential analysis of countermeasures until their risk-tolerance is satisfied. An explicit framework not only helps an organisation deploying Revault with risk-management but could form a standard by which insurance companies and regulators consider specific deployments. As with any model of complex reality, attack-trees are imperfect and cannot capture every possible attack pathway, but the alternative—complete ignorance—is not better.

To perform a context-specific risk analysis, a set of estimates are made (using in-house empirical data, public research, and expert opinion) for each basic attack step on different attributes such as monetary cost, execution time, or likelihood. With that, a bottom-up procedure (from leaf nodes to the root) is used to compute aggregated attributes. Bayesian methods can be used to update prior estimates with more refined values as new data sources emerge. The process for generating estimates is critical and should be considered with care. In-depth research-based practical guidance on this topic is given by D. W. Hubbard and R. Seiersen in [17]. Given specific contextual information, estimations can be improved by further decomposing basic attack steps (e.g. 'steal keys backup') into multiple steps (e.g. 'bribe manager to determine backup location' SAND 'break into safe'). If a basic attack step has a highly uncertain estimate, then further decomposition into more explicit steps can be beneficial. On the other hand, decomposing into quantities that are more speculative than the first could compound uncertainty rather than reducing it.

Various methods for analysis can be used to compute aggregated attributes for attack-trees. Kordy et al. gave an overview [20]. Our purpose here is to provide the framework on which to perform analyses rather than to provide a specific analysis. We have not performed a comprehensive evaluation of analysis methods, but offer some suggestions based on a comparison in [21]. Two methods that support evaluating the attributes of cost, probability, and time are stochastic-model checking [22] and game-theoretic analysis [16]. Whichever methods are used must appropriately capture the constraints of our model (including SAND gates) and should be automated to enable rapid attribute-based queries for security metrics such as; the expected attack pay-off for the most likely attack, or the possible attack pathways given a budget of $10,000.

Our approach to constructing the risk model is centered on assets since these are clearly distinguished through Bitcoin descriptors, as continuity of a custodial process, or as operational privacy. However, when performing the risk analysis it can be insightful to consider attacker personas [37]: a crime syndicate; an opportunistic burglar; a nation state; a business competitor; or even an insider. If the organisation understands any of these personas well (arguably they should especially understand their competitors and employees) they can reduce the uncertainty in their aggregate risk estimates for these scenarios. Attacker-profiles are a useful way to prune attack-trees [21].

4   Risk Model

We have constructed the risk model with several assumptions that limit the scope of the analysis to the operational aspects of custody. Known risks from other protocol and environment dependencies that are discussed in other works should be considered as complementary but are, for the purpose of clarity, assumed to be benign here. First, we assume that the Bitcoin network is functional, realising its live-ness and availability properties [7,8,12,13,32]. We assume that there is significant hash-rate to prevent blockchain reorganisations of a depth higher than the Unvault Tx's relative lock-time. Next, we assume that Revault's Tx model is robust; with scripts that realise the access control structures we expect, without unintended consequences from Tx malleability and network propagation issues as described in [25]. We assume the initialization process was secure and safe; private keys and backups were correctly and confidentially constructed for each participant, software and hardware integrity were verified, relevant public key information for both the wallet and communication was shared among participants leading to a correct configuration for the wallet clients, watchtowers, anti-replay oracles and the coordinator. We assume that Revault's communication security model as described in [4] is robust. That is, where messages need to be authenticated or confidential, they are. We assume that the software development life-cycle of Revault is secure, such that any deployment is using an implementation that adheres to the protocol specification. Finally, we assume that entities constructing Deposit Txs don't succumb to a man-in-the-middle attack. That is, they lock funds to the deposit descriptor rather than to an attacker's address.

4.1   Common Attack Sub-Trees

These attack sub-trees are common to different attacks on Revault, and **a**, **b**, **c**, **d**, **e**, **f** and **g** are likely to be common to attacks on other custody protocols.

a : Compromise a participant (stakeholder or manager)
    1 : Coerce participant (OR)
    2 : Corrupt participant

Coercion and insider threats from corrupt participants must be considered. Legal defences for malicious employee behaviour can be effective deterrents here.

b : Compromise a participant's (stakeholder's or manager's) HSM
    1 : Physical attack of HSM (OR)
        1.1 : Determine location of participant's HSM (SAND)
        1.2 : Access the physical security environment of the participant's HSM (SAND)
        1.3 : Exfiltrate keys (either on premise or after stealing it) (OR)
        1.4 : By-pass PIN and make the HSM sign a malicious chosen message
    2 : Remote attack of HSM (OR)
        2.1 : Compromise a device that is then connected to the HSM (SAND)
            2.1.1 : (see **g**) Compromise the participant's wallet software (OR)
            2.1.2 : Trick participant into connecting their HSM to a compromised device via social engineering
        2.2 : Exploit a firmware vulnerability (OR)
        2.3 : Trick participant into compromising their own HSM with the user interface of the compromised device
    3 : (see **a**) Compromise a participant

c : Compromise a participant's (stakeholder's or manager's) keys backup
    1 : Physical Attack (OR)
        1.1 : Determine location of the keys backup (SAND)

    1.1.1 : Watch the participant between the custody initialization and the start of operations (OR)

    1.1.2 : Watch the participant during a backup check (OR)

   1.2 : Access the physical security environment of the keys backup (SAND)

   1.3 : Depending on backup format, steal or copy it

  2 : (see **a**) Compromise a participant

d : Compromise a server (watchtower, anti-replay oracle, or coordinator)

  1 : Remote attack (OR)

   1.1 : Exploit a software vulnerability (OR)

    1.1.1 : Determine the public interfaces of the server (SAND)

    1.1.2 : Exploit a vulnerability on one of the softwares listening on these interfaces

   1.2 : Exploit a human vulnerability (e.g. trick participant into performing a malicious update)

  2 : Physical attack (OR)

   2.1 : Determine server's location (SAND)

   2.2 : Access the physical security environment of the server (SAND)

  3 : (see **a**) Compromise the participant managing the server

An attacker who successfully completes **d** for a watchtower will be able to steal funds from the watchtower's fee wallet and will be able to force an emergency scenario by broadcasting all Emergency and Unvault-Emergency Txs it has stored. They can also prevent broadcast of a Cancel Tx from this watchtower either passively (*ACK* the secure storage of the signature to the stakeholder, but then drop the signature) or actively.

e : Shutdown a watchtower

  1 : Physical attack on the watchtower (OR)

   1.1 : Determine watchtower's location (SAND)

   1.2 : Sever the internet connection to the building in which the watchtower is located (OR)

   1.3 : Sever the power-line connection to the building in which the watchtower is located (OR)

   1.4 : Access the physical security of the watchtower and un-plug the machine

  2 : Remote attack on the watchtower

   2.1 : Determine public interfaces of watchtower (SAND)

   2.2 : Denial of Service attack through one of the public interfaces (OR)

   2.3 : Eclipse attack on the watchtower's Bitcoin node [15] (OR)

    2.3.1 : Slowly force de-synchronisation of watchtower with the true block height by delaying block propagation [34] (OR)

    2.3.2 : Prevent outgoing propagation of Cancel or Emergency Txs

   2.4 : Denial of Service attack on the fee-bumping UTxOs pool—not enough funds to pay competitive fees (OR)

f : Get signature from participant to unlock UTxO for Theft Tx

  1 : (see **a**) Compromise a participant (OR)

  2 : (see **b**) Compromise participant's HSM (OR)

  3 : (see **c**) Compromise participant's keys backup

g : Compromise a participant's wallet
    1 : Physical attack (OR)
        1.1 : Locate participant's device (SAND)
        1.2 : Access physical security environment of participant's device
    2 : Remote attack (OR)
        2.1 : Determine public interfaces of device (SAND)
        2.2 : Exploit a vulnerability
    3 : (see **a**) Compromise participant

Participant's wallet devices are expected to be used for day-to-day activities. With many vulnerabilities to exploit, the likelihood of success for **g** is high.

h : Determine the locking Script for a deposit or unvault UTxO (*Witness Script*)
    1 : (see **g**) Compromise any participant's wallet (OR)
    2 : (see **d**) Compromise a watchtower (OR)
    3 : (see **d**) Compromise an anti-replay oracle

Deposit and unvault descriptors are deterministic, but public keys are needed to derive UTxO locking Scripts. These are stored by all wallets, watchtowers and anti-replay oracles.

i : Satisfy an input in a Theft Tx that consumes an identified deposit UTxO or unvault UTxO (through $N-$of$-N$)
    1 : (see **h**) Determine the UTxO locking Script (*Witness Script*) (SAND)
    2 : Prevent the relevant Emergency Tx from being broadcast until the Theft Tx is confirmed (where $A + B = N$) (AND)
        2.1 : (see **d**) Compromise a watchtower (A times)
        2.2 : (see **e**) Shutdown a watchtower (B times)
        2.3 : (see **g**) Compromise stakeholder's wallet (N times)
    3 : (see **f**) Get signature from a stakeholder to unlock UTxO for Theft Tx (N times)

j : Satisfy an input in a Theft Tx that consumes an identified unvault UTxO (through $K-$of$-M$, anti-replay oracles and time-lock)
    1 : (see **h**) Determine the UTxO locking Script (*Witness Script*) (SAND)
    2 : Receive signatures for Theft Tx from all N anti-replay oracles (AND)
        2.1 : Compromise a manager's private communication keys and the set of anti-replay oracles' public communication keys (OR)
            2.1.1 : (see **g**) Compromise a manager's wallet (OR)
            2.1.2 : (see **a**) Compromise a manager
        2.2 : (see **d**) Compromise the anti-replay oracle
    3 : (see **f**) Get signature from a manager to unlock UTxO for Theft Tx (K times)

k : Satisfy an input in a Theft Tx that consumes an identified emergency UTxO
    1 : Determine the emergency descriptor policy (SAND)
    2 : Satisfy the emergency descriptor's locking conditions (may include waiting for time-locks, giving sufficient signatures, giving hash pre-images, *etc.*)

The details of the emergency descriptor are intentionally not specified with the Revault protocol, except that it is more difficult to access than the deposit descriptor. Stakeholders may compartmentalise and distribute the descriptor information to afford its privacy some resilience to attack.

4.2   Attack-Trees

The following attack-trees are the foundation for an operational risk framework for Revault.

A : Compromise privacy of the custody operation (determine the set of public UTxOs)
  1 : (see **d**) Compromise any of the servers (OR)
  2 : (see **a**) Compromise a participant (OR)
  3 : (see **g**) Compromise a participant's wallet (OR)
  4 : Traffic analysis of connections between servers and/or wallets (OR)
  5 : Blockchain analysis

Without privacy support for advanced descriptors (such as by using MuSig2 [30] or MuSig-DN [31] if the proposed Taproot [1] upgrade is activated by the Bitcoin network) Revault's operational privacy is brittle.

B : Broadcast Theft Tx(s) that consume all deposit UTxOs
  1 : (see **A**) Determine $\mathcal{D}$, the set of deposit UTxOs (SAND)
  2 : (see **h**) Determine the locking Script for deposit UTxO ($|\mathcal{D}|$ times)
  3 : (see **i**) Satisfy an input in a Theft Tx that consumes an identified deposit UTxO ($|\mathcal{D}|$ times)

A Theft Tx that consumes all available deposit UTxOs would be catastrophic since this comprises the majority of funds. We recommend a defence wherein each stakeholder is equipped with a panic button that is directly connected to their watchtower or dedicated emergency service. When triggered, all the signed Emergency and Unvault-Emergency Txs are broadcast, negating the pay-off for an attacker and thus acting as a deterrent.

C : Broadcast Theft Tx(s) that consume as many available unvault UTxOs as watchtower spending policies permit
  1 : Determine spending constraints of all watchtowers' policies (SAND)
    1.1 : (see **a**) Compromise a participant (OR)
    1.2 : (see **g**) Compromise a manager's wallet
    1.3 : (see **d**) Compromise a watchtower (N times)
  2 : Determine $\mathcal{U}$, the set of available unvault UTxOs (SAND)
    2.1 : (see **A**) Compromise privacy of the custody operation (determine the set of public UTxOs) (SAND)
    2.2 : (see **h**) Determine the locking Script for unvault UTxO ($|\mathcal{U}|$ times)
  3 : (see **i** OR **j**) Satisfy an input in a Theft Tx that consumes an identified unvault UTxO ($|\mathcal{U}|$ times)

C can be avoided if watchtowers have a white-list of addresses that Spend Txs can pay to.

D : Broadcast Theft Tx(s) that consume all available unvault UTxOs, bypassing watchtowers' spending policies
  1 : Prevent watchtower from broadcasting Cancel or Unvault-Emergency Txs before Theft Tx is confirmed (N times SAND)

      1.1 : (see **d**) Compromise a watchtower (OR)

      1.2 : (see **e**) Shutdown a watchtower

    2 : Determine $\mathcal{U}$, the set of available unvault UTxOs (SAND)

      2.1 : (see **A**) Compromise privacy of the custody operation (determine the set of public UTxOs) (SAND)

      2.2 : (see **h**) Determine the locking Script for unvault UTxO ($|\mathcal{U}|$ times)

    3 : (see **i** OR **j**) Satisfy an input in a Theft Tx that consumes an identified unvault UTxO ($|\mathcal{U}|$ times)

E : Broadcast a Theft Tx that by-passes watchtowers' spending policies

    1 : Determine $\mathcal{U}$, the set of available unvault UTxOs (SAND)

      1.1 : (see **A**) Compromise privacy of the custody operation (determine the set of public UTxOs) (SAND)

      1.2 : (see **h**) Determine the locking Script for unvault UTxO ($|\mathcal{U}|$ times)

    2 : (see **f**) Get signature from a manager to unlock $U \subseteq \mathcal{U}$, a subset of available unvault UTxOs for a valid Spend Tx (K times)

    3 : (see **i** OR **j**) Satisfy an input in a Theft Tx that consumes an identified unvault UTxO ($|U|$ times)

    4 : (see **d**) Compromise an anti-replay oracle to get a signature for the valid Spend Tx which consumes U, the UTxOs (N times SAND)

    5 : Advertise the valid Spend Tx to the watchtowers through the coordinator (SAND)

    6 : Broadcast all Unvault Txs that the valid Spend Tx depends on and wait for the time-lock to expire

F : Force emergency scenario

    1 : Broadcast the full set of signed Emergency and Unvault-emergency transactions

      1.1 : (see **d**) Compromise a watchtower (OR)

      1.2 : (see **a**) Compromise a stakeholder

The emergency deterrent results in better security from the most egregious physical threats to participants (particularly stakeholders who control the majority of funds) but also in a fragility to the continuity of operations that could be abused by an attacker. Attacks that rely on **E** may seek a pay-off other than fund theft, such as damaging the reputation of the organisation for having down-time and taking a leveraged bet on the likely market consequences. However, forced down-time attacks through power or internet outages or detainment of personnel are prevalent threats for organisations who aren't deploying Revault. In any case, with this risk model the consequence of not using an emergency deterrent can be considered by performing an analysis with pruned attack-trees.

G : Broadcast a Theft Tx which consumes all available UTxOs locked to the emergency descriptor

    1 : (see **F**) Force an emergency scenario (SAND)

    2 : Determine $\mathcal{E}$, the set of available emergency UTxOs (SAND)

      2.1 : (see **A**) Compromise privacy of the custody operation (determine the set of public UTxOs)

    3 : (see **k**) Satisfy an input in a Theft Tx that consumes an identified emergency UTxO ($|\mathcal{E}|$ times)

H : Broadcast a Theft Tx which spends from a manager's fee wallet
    1 : (see **g**) Compromise a manager's wallet

While this is a relatively simple attack, the fee wallet will never hold a significant portion of bitcoins and is considered external to the custody protocol.

I : Prevent Emergency, Unvault-Emergency, and Cancel Tx valid signature exchange
    1 : 1 of N stakeholders doesn't sign (OR)
        1.1 : Prevent stakeholder from accessing their HSM (OR)
        1.2 : Prevent stakeholder from accessing their wallet (OR)
        1.3 : (see **a**) Compromise a stakeholder
    2 : Shutdown coordinator (OR)
    3 : (see **e**) Shutdown a watchtower (N times) (OR)
    4 : Blockchain re-organization and Deposit Tx outpoint malleation.

J : Prevent Unvault Tx signature exchange
    1 : 1 of N stakeholders doesn't sign (OR)
        1.1 : Prevent stakeholder from accessing their HSM (OR)
        1.2 : Prevent stakeholder from accessing their wallet software (OR)
        1.3 : (see **a**) Compromise a stakeholder
    2 : Shutdown coordinator (OR)
    3 : Prevent all managers from accessing their wallet software

K : Prevent managers from broadcasting a Spend Tx
    1 : Prevent managers from signing the Spend transaction (OR)
        1.1 : (see **d**) Compromise an anti-replay oracle (OR)
        1.2 : Prevent sufficient threshold of managers from signing the Spend Tx (where $A + B + C = M - K + 1$) (OR)
            1.2.1 : (see **a**) Compromise a manager (A times)
            1.2.2 : Prevent manager from accessing their HSM (B times)
            1.2.3 : Prevent manager from accessing their wallet software (C times)
    2 : Force broadcast of Cancel Tx (OR)
        2.1 : (see **d**) Compromise a watchtower
    3 : Prevent broadcast of Unvault Tx
        3.1 : High demand for block space making the Unvault Tx not profitable to mine.[3]
        3.2 : (see **g**) Compromise manager's wallet (M times)

5   Conclusion

The rise of Bitcoin has led to a new commercial ecosystem, with market exchanges enabling its sale and purchase, companies and financial institutions offering secure custody services, and insurance brokers and underwriters willing to insure individuals, exchanges and custodians against loss or theft of their assets . In this paper we first posit that a methodology to better understand risks

---

[3] Manager's fee-bumping wallet can not cover this until a network policy such as Package Relay [3] is implemented.

in custodial operations is needed, something complementary to understanding blockchain and cryptographic security. We put forth requirements of the modelling technique and propose attack-trees as a formalism which satisfies those requirements. We exemplify the approach by presenting a library of attack-trees constructed for a multi-party custody protocol called Revault and explain how this framework can be used as a basis for risk-management in custodial operations. The next steps for this work are to: construct a set of defences to the prominent risks and incorporate them into the model; and to determine or build a suitable tool for automating computations for a specific analysis.

Acknowledgements. We thank Professor McBurney (King's College London), Kevin Laoec (WizardSardine) for insightful conversations and for reviewing the text.

Funding Information. Funding is gratefully acknowledged under a UK EPSRC-funded GTA Award through King's College London and from WizardSardine.

References

1. (Bitcoin Improvement Proposal) Taproot: SegWit version 1 spending rules. https://github.com/bitcoin/bips/blob/master/bip-0341.mediawiki. Accessed 29 Jan 2021
2. Output Script Descriptors: a language for abstracting out the spending conditions of a Bitcoin transaction output. https://github.com/bitcoin/bitcoin/blob/master/doc/descriptors.md. Accessed 26 Jan 2021
3. Package Relay design questions for the Bitcoin P2P network. https://github.com/bitcoin/bitcoin/issues/14895. Accessed 29 Jan 2021
4. Practical Revault: A specification for the initialization and operation of the Revault custody protocol. https://github.com/re-vault/practical-revault
5. Glacier design document (2017). https://glacierprotocol.org/assets/design-doc-v0.9-beta.pdf. Accessed 10 Jan 2021
6. Amoroso, E.G.: Fundamentals of Computer Security Technology. Prentice-Hall Inc, Hoboken (1994)
7. Badertscher, C., Garay, J., Maurer, U., Tschudi, D., Zikas, V.: But why does it work? A rational protocol design treatment of bitcoin. In: Nielsen, J.B., Rijmen, V. (eds.) EUROCRYPT 2018. LNCS, vol. 10821, pp. 34–65. Springer, Cham (2018). https://doi.org/10.1007/978-3-319-78375-8_2
8. Badertscher, C., Maurer, U., Tschudi, D., Zikas, V.: Bitcoin as a transaction ledger: A composable treatment, vol. 10401 LNCS (2017). https://doi.org/10.1007/978-3-319-63688-7_11
9. Capital Markets and Technology Association: Digital Assets Custody Standard (2020). https://www.cmta.ch/content/272/cmta-digital-assets-custody-standard-v1-public-consultation.pdf. Accessed 10 Jan 2021
10. Chow, A.: Partially signed bitcoin transaction format (2017). https://github.com/bitcoin/bips/blob/master/bip-0174.mediawiki. Accessed 18 May 2020
11. Gadyatskaya, O., Jhawar, R., Kordy, P., Lounis, K., Mauw, S., Trujillo-Rasua, R.: Attack Trees for Practical Security Assessment: Ranking of Attack Scenarios with ADTool 2.0. vol. 9826, pp. 159–162 (2016). https://doi.org/10.1007/978-3-319-43425-4_10

12. Garay, J., Kiayias, A., Leonardos, N.: The Bitcoin backbone protocol: Analysis and applications. Lecture Notes in Computer Science (including subseries Lecture Notes in Artificial Intelligence and Lecture Notes in Bioinformatics), vol. 9057, pp. 281–310 (2015). https://doi.org/10.1007/978-3-662-46803-6_10
13. Garay, J., Kiayias, A., Leonardos, N.: The bitcoin backbone protocol with chains of variable difficulty. In: Katz, J., Shacham, H. (eds.) CRYPTO 2017. LNCS, vol. 10401, pp. 291–323. Springer, Cham (2017). https://doi.org/10.1007/978-3-319-63688-7_10
14. Haque, M.S.: An evolutionary approach of attack graphs and attack trees: a survey of attack modeling (2017)
15. Heilman, E., Kendler, A., Zohar, A., Goldberg, S.: Eclipse attacks on bitcoin's peer-to-peer network. In: 24th USENIX Security Symposium (USENIX Security 15), pp. 129–144. USENIX Association, Washington, D.C. August 2015. https://www.usenix.org/conference/usenixsecurity15/technical-sessions/presentation/heilman
16. Hermanns, H., Krämer, J., Krcál, J., Stoelinga, M.: The value of attack-defence diagrams, vol. 9635, pp. 163–185 (2016). https://doi.org/10.1007/978-3-662-49635-0_9
17. Hubbard, D.W., Seiersen, R.: How to Measure Anything in Cybersecurity Risk (2016)
18. Jhawar, R., Kordy, B., Mauw, S., Radomirovic, S., Trujillo-Rasua, R.: Attack Trees with Sequential Conjunction. CoRR abs/1503.02261 (2015). http://arxiv.org/abs/1503.02261
19. Kordy, B., Mauw, S., Radomirovic, S., Schweitzer, P.: Foundations of attack-defense trees, vol. 6561, pp. 80–95 (2010). https://doi.org/10.1007/978-3-642-19751-2_6
20. Kordy, B., Piètre-Cambacédès, L., Schweitzer, P.: Dag-based attack and defense modeling: don't miss the forest for the attack trees. Comput. Sci. Rev. **13** (2013). https://doi.org/10.1016/j.cosrev.2014.07.001
21. Kumar, R.: Truth or Dare: Quantitative security risk analysis using attack trees. Ph.D. thesis (2018). https://doi.org/10.3990/1.9789036546256
22. Kumar, R., Stoelinga, M.: Quantitative Security and Safety Analysis with Attack-Fault Trees (2017). https://doi.org/10.1109/HASE.2017.12
23. Lallie, H., Debattista, K., Bal, J.: A review of attack graph and attack tree visual syntax in cyber security. Comput. Sci. Rev. **35**, 100219 (2020). https://doi.org/10.1016/j.cosrev.2019.100219
24. Loaec, K.: Hardware wallets and "advanced" Bitcoin features (2021). https://lists.linuxfoundation.org/pipermail/bitcoin-dev/2021-January/018352.html. Accessed 19 Jan 2021
25. Loaec, K., Poinsot, A.: Revault: a multi-party Bicoin vault architecture (2020). https://github.com/re-vault/practical-revault/blob/master/revault.pdf
26. Sato, M., Shimaoka, M., Nakajima, H.: General Security Considerations for Cryptoassets Custodians (2019). https://tools.ietf.org/html/draft-vcgtf-crypto-assets-security-considerations-05
27. Maynard, P., Mclaughlin, K., Sezer, S.: Modelling Duqu 2.0 Malware using Attack Trees with Sequential Conjunction, pp. 465–472 (2016). https://doi.org/10.5220/0005745704650472
28. Maynard, P., McLaughlin, K., Sezer, S.: Decomposition and sequential-AND analysis of known cyber-attacks on critical infrastructure control systems. J. Cybersecurity **6**(1) (2020). https://doi.org/10.1093/cybsec/tyaa020
29. Nguyen, H.N., Bryans, J., Shaikh, S.: Attack Defense Trees with Sequential Conjunction. IEEE (2019)

30. Nick, J., Ruffing, T., Seurin, Y.: Musig2: Simple two-round Schnorr multi-signatures. Cryptology ePrint Archive, Report 2020/1261 (2020). https://eprint.iacr.org/2020/1261
31. Nick, J., Ruffing, T., Seurin, Y., Wuille, P.: MuSig-DN: Schnorr multi-signatures with verifiably deterministic nonces. Cryptology ePrint Archive, Report 2020/1057 (2020). https://eprint.iacr.org/2020/1057
32. Pass, R., Seeman, L., Shelat, A.: Analysis of the blockchain protocol in asynchronous networks. In: Coron, J.-S., Nielsen, J.B. (eds.) EUROCRYPT 2017. LNCS, vol. 10211, pp. 643–673. Springer, Cham (2017). https://doi.org/10.1007/978-3-319-56614-6_22
33. Perrin, T.: The Noise Protocol Framework (2018). https://noiseprotocol.org/noise.pdf. Accessed 19 Jan 2021
34. Riard, A., Naumenko, G.: Time-dilation attacks on the lightning network (2020)
35. Schmitz, C., Sekulla, A., Pape, S.: Asset-Centric Analysis and Visualisation of Attack Trees, pp. 45–64 (2020). https://doi.org/10.1007/978-3-030-62230-5_3
36. Schneier, B.: Attack Trees (1999). https://www.schneier.com/academic/archives/1999/12/attack_trees.html. Accessed 12 Jan 2021
37. Shostack, A.: Threat Modeling: Designing for Security (2014)
38. Square: Subzero (2020). https://subzero.readthedocs.io/en/master/. Accessed 19 Jan 2020
39. Swambo, J., Hommel, S., McElrath, B., Bishop, B.: Custody protocols using bitcoin vaults (2020). https://arxiv.org/abs/2005.11776. Accessed 10 Jan 2021
40. Weiss, J.D.: A system security engineering process. In: Proceedings of the 14th National Computer Security Conference (1991)
41. Wuille, P.: Hierarchical deterministic wallets (2012). https://github.com/bitcoin/bips/blob/master/bip-0032.mediawiki. Accessed 18 May 2020

Regulatory Considerations on Centralized Aspects of DeFi Managed by DAOs

Ryosuke Ushida[1,2] and James Angel[2(✉)]

[1] Financial Services Agency Japan, Tokyo, Japan
[2] Georgetown University, Washington, D.C., USA
{ru64,angelj}@georgetown.edu

Abstract. This paper focuses on the centralized governance mechanisms of decentralized finance (DeFi) projects managed by Distributed Autonomous Organizations (DAOs) and discusses regulatory considerations. Unlike highly decentralized ecosystems such as Bitcoin, the degree of decentralization varies among DeFi projects. Centralized aspects such as concentrated ownership of governance tokens and admin keys have significant implications on their governance. Concerns include decision-making concentration risk and poor alignment of interests among stakeholders. From a regulatory viewpoint, centralized aspects could make it easier for regulators to impose requirements and therefore increase compliance costs. This might drive the DeFi community to seek further decentralization to avoid regulatory burdens. We conclude that the DeFi ecosystem should learn from the experience of both Internet governance as a partially decentralized system and from traditional corporate governance.

Keywords: Blockchain · DeFi · DAO · Decentralized financial system · Corporate governance · Regulation · On-chain governance · Off-chain governance · Governance token

1 Introduction

1.1 Background and Terminology

Decentralized Finance (DeFi), which generally refers to a decentralized form of financial applications executed by smart contracts on a public blockchain, is proliferating from $660M in TVL (Total Value Locked) in early 2020 to $14.5B at the end of December 2020. A wide range of financial products is available without KYC (Know Your Customers), including crypto-asset exchange, lending, derivatives, insurance, and decentralized stablecoins. In 2019, the Financial Stability Board [2] defined decentralized financial technology as "Technologies that have the potential to reduce or eliminate the need for one or more intermediaries or centralised processes in the provision of financial services" and defined financial systems as "new financial system that decentralized financial technology could bring". On the other hand, there is no widely-accepted definition of DeFi and

© International Financial Cryptography Association 2021
M. Bernhard et al. (Eds.): FC 2021 Workshops, LNCS 12676, pp. 21–36, 2021.
https://doi.org/10.1007/978-3-662-63958-0_2

Term	Definition	Example	Reference
Decentralized financial technology	Technologies that have the potential to reduce or eliminate the need for one or more intermediaries or centralised processes in the provision of financial services	Blockchain, DLT	FSB (2019)
Decentralized financial System	New financial system that *decentralized financial technology* could bring	Bitcoin, Ethereum	FSB (2019)
DeFi	Financial application that could consists a part of *decentralized financial system*	Maker, Compound, Uniswap	Defined in this paper
Decentralized Autonomous Organization (DAO)	Organization that is run through rules encoded as computer programs called "smart contracts"	MakerDAO, KyberDAO, Aragon	Chohan (2017)

Fig. 1. Terminology

the word seems to be used arbitrarily for marketing and other purposes. In this paper, we define DeFi as a "financial application that could consist of a part of a decentralized financial system". While underlying blockchain platforms such as Bitcoin and Ethereum could be categorized as DeFi in a broad sense, our analysis focuses on smart contract-based applications on such platforms. DeFi protocols are often developed and managed by so-called DAOs, Decentralized Autonomous Organizations. Although the DAO is also not strictly defined, we use Chohan's [15] definition: "an organization represented by rules encoded as a computer program that is transparent, controlled by the organization members and not influenced by a centralized entity." Typical DAOs include The DAO (2016), MakerDAO, and KyberDAO.

The degree of decentralization varies from one DeFi project to another, and many of them are quite centralized, especially in the bootstrapping stage. For example, specific individuals or groups have the authority to change the protocol or freeze locked assets. To mitigate the Single Point of Failure (SPoF) risk caused by dependence on such trusted parties, many communities are heading for bottom-up, decentralized governance by transferring management authority of the protocol to the DAO through on-chain voting. Given the incessant hacking incidents and increasing attention from regulatory authorities, the sound development of governance of the entire ecosystem is indispensable if they look ahead to mass adoption beyond niche use cases.

1.2   Related Works

The governance issues of decentralized financial systems are attracting many researchers' attention. Some explore to build sound governance of decentralized financial systems in light of the Internet governance lessons. De Filippi and Wright [5] discuss the applicability of the four regulatory tools (i.e., Law, Market, Norm, and Architecture/Code) in cyberspace proposed by Lessig [9] to control activities in decentralized financial systems. Takanashi et al. [14] points out the importance of developing an architecture/code that harmonizes with law/regulations, aligns with social norms, and is competitive in the market.

Another point of discussion is the comparison with corporate governance. Hacker [6] argues that complexity-induced uncertainty could be reduced, and stability and order could be strengthened by adapting a corporate governance framework to blockchain-based organizations. Blemus and Guegan [1] analyzes the opportunities and risks posed by tokenization and distributed ledger technology from the perspective of corporate governance. They raised issues related to the responsibility for decision-making by DAOs, which have no management team or board of directors and are determined by token holders without legal framework applicable to DAOs.

Corporate governance and Internet governance are very different in terms of the attributes of governance targets. Nabilou [10] argues that it is misleading to draw parallels between the highly decentralized governance of Bitcoin and corporate governance. On the other hand, Collomb and De Filippi [3] point out that "The DAO", the first DAO initiative that ended in hacking in 2016, was designed to mimic and improve on corporate governance, and the problems caused was rooted in the fact that The DAO was run like traditional corporations. Considering the centralized aspects of the current DeFi applications, an extensive analysis should be conducted from both Internet and corporate governance viewpoints with particular attention to the regulatory implications. However, the ecosystem is fast changing and there is no sufficient academic discussion on it.

1.3   Contributions

This paper has two contributions to the ongoing governance discussion about decentralized financial systems and DeFi. First, we identify and discuss key factors that affects the governance of individual DeFi project managed by DAO and the DeFi ecosystem based on the existing works related to Internet and corporate governance. An emphasis is placed on the difference between decentralized finance with and without DAO and how the centralized aspect of incorporating DAO could affect the governance mechanism of the overall system. Second, we discuss regulatory considerations on the centralized elements of the ongoing DeFi projects/ecosystem for regulators and policymakers to develop a better regulatory framework for its sustainable development.

2   Governance of DeFi Managed by DAO

This chapter elaborates on factors affecting the governance of individual DeFi projects, followed by the analysis of ecosystem governance. We stress the importance of understanding dynamic interactions among individual DeFi and the ecosystem at large. In many DeFi projects, relevant protocols are often managed by DAOs, with the community voting on critical decisions such as parameter changes and emergency response. In assessing the governance of the DAO-centered systems, it is vital to consider the direct participants in the project and the interrelationships among a wide range of relevant stakeholders in the whole DeFi ecosystem.

2.1 Corporate and Internet Governance as Dual Reference Points

Overall, a DeFi ecosystem is a complex structure composed of several elements and stakeholders, including:

– Individual DeFi projects managed by DAOs
– A public blockchain, including scaling solutions, as an underlying platform
– DeFi integrators such as oracle providers and custody solution providers
– DeFi aggregators and curators
– DAO software as a service such as Aragon DAO and OpenLaw
– Centralized financial service providers such as centralized exchanges
– Multiple DeFi ecosystems (i.e., Ethereum, EOS, Polkadot, etc.)

Several researchers indicate the usefulness of analyzing the DAO-based decentralized financial systems from corporate governance perspective. Among others, Hacker [6] argues that token-based venture capital often looks more like companies with principals (i.e., investors) and agents (i.e., managers) than open-source networks. He also mentions that many for-profit token applications share many characteristics with corporations and investment funds, rather than open-source networks. He also observes that token issuance could serve as an alternative way to funding entrepreneurial projects. Also, Kondova and Barba [8] pinpoints that OECD principles [11] on disclosure and transparency and DAO governance share similarities in the decision-making process. In a highly decentralized system such as Bitcoin, corporate governance, which assumes a centralized organization and typically discusses the principal-agency problems and the separation of ownership and management, may not necessarily be applicable. However, there could be a good applicability to the ongoing DeFi projects, which have multiple centralized aspects. In addition, to assess the significance of the factors as means of control in the "apparently" decentralized system, we discuss from the viewpoints of law, market, norm, and architecture presented by Lessig [9] as four regulatory tools in cyberspace and extended by De Filippi and Wright [5] and Takanashi et al. [14] to apply the framework in the decentralized financial system.

2.2 Individual DeFi Project Governance

A DeFi project typically consists of protocols (i.e., single or a set of smart contracts on the underlying public blockchain), foundation/developer team, initial investors, token holders, and a variety of types of users such as liquidity providers, lenders and borrowers. There is no "one-size-fits-all" solution as each DeFi project varies greatly in many ways such as decision-making mechanism, protocol upgradability, attributes of tokens and types of financial applications. A couple of factors likely influence the governance of many DeFi projects with DAOs. In this section, we elaborate on governance factors that would constrain the activities in the projects to discuss the regulatory implications in the following chapter.

2.2.1 On-Chain Voting by Governance Token Holders

In order to promote decentralized decision-making, more and more projects are adopting token-based governance. This community-driven bottom-up, decentralized mechanism could eliminate or mitigate the concentration risk of control by certain parties such as the developer team. Tokens can be designed in a variety of ways. Some tokens have not only voting rights and rights to create and submit proposals, but also the rights to receive a portion of the cash flow generated by the protocol. Some can be also used for specific purposes as utility tokens. In this paper, we define a governance token as a token that has a voting right for decision-making which influences the project, regardless of whether it has other rights/functions or not. Hacker [6] argues that token-based systems provide a clear designation of competences and procedures that breaks up the informal power structures and presents an opportunity to distribute power in a fairer and more transparent way. However, in "The DAO" case, the SEC [13] points out the limited influence of the token holders in decision making. While a "DAO Token" holder was given certain voting rights and ownership rights, the Curators, a group of individuals selected by The DAO's developer and a German company "Slock.it", have broad discretion in making investment proposals. Besides, proposals by token holders had to be reviewed by the Curators before they were voted on. As such, the structure was significantly centralized in favor of the Curators and Slock.it. Token-based voting is just a part of the decision-making process in the existing DeFi projects, and its authority can be restrictive depending on the token design and governance process. Regarding the viewpoint of architecture/code, token holders' degree of control largely depends on the upgradability of the deployed smart contracts.

The distribution of governance tokens is another important issue in assessing the influence of minority token holders on decision making. Governance tokens are distributed in a variety of ways. Some tokens, such as Maker's MKR, are distributed by a specific party, such as a foundation, to early investors and adopters in the form of private sales. Others, such as Compound's COMP[1] and Uniswap's UNI[2], are distributed as rewards or compensations for locking up a certain amount of crypto-assets into a relevant smart contract, which is generally called "liquidity mining". In the case of Uniswap, about 18% is distributed to investors, 21.2% to team members and future employees, 0.7% to team advisors, and the remaining 60% to community members such as liquidity providers over a four-year period. It should be noted that the timing, methods of distribution and distribution ratio are arbitrarily decided by a specific entity in many projects and a large number of voting rights are often granted to particular groups or individuals, the implication of which will be discussed in detail in the following chapter. This is not unlike the super-voting shares often retained by the founders of companies.

---

[1] https://medium.com/compound-finance/expanding-compound-governance-ce13fcd4fe36.

[2] https://uniswap.org/blog/uni/.

In terms of the effectiveness and validity of decision-making, the turn-out ratio is an important metric to assess whether token-based voting functions appropriately. Blemus and Gregan argues that decentralized governance is based on the idea of a flat hierarchy, with token holders devoting sufficient time to participate and vote in the community's best interests. In this regard, many DeFi projects are struggling to attract adequate attention from token holders. In the case of the MakerDAO, only 32 voters participated in the emergency voting following the liquidation failure in March 2020, and one address accounted for more than 50% of the total votes. Mechanisms to increase the participation ratio include delegation mechanisms, quadratic voting, and improved UX/UI. Further analysis and experimentation are required to justify the token-based voting system as an appropriate decision-making process for sustainable community development.

From the market mechanism perspective, governance token holders are incentivized to act to maximize their economic benefits. They generally benefit from the capital gain (i.e., appreciation of the token values in the secondary market) and income gain (e.g., distribution from the trading fees generated by the protocol). One concern is that they might prioritize their short-term interests and ruin the long-term development of the project. This is more likely if they have substantial control over the protocol and it is easy to exit by selling the token. For example, some token holders might vote for burning vast amounts of governance tokens and/or increase the distribution ratio of the generated incomes to the stakeholders without engaging in the discussion about long-term strategy. They would expect to benefit from an increase in the token value in the short term while they sell the tokens before deterioration. As Hirschman [7] argues, the easier exit is, the less likely "voice", or voting right, will be used.

2.2.2   Code Is Law/Governance Minimization

Blockchain and smart contract code is written in a formalized language and, unlike law and regulations that leave room for discretion, only actions that follow the rules set in the code are allowed. When the code is adopted as the primary constraint tool, little changes are made to the blockchain protocol except for technical maintenance. The ecosystem is built by relying solely on the original code to minimize human intervention via an on-chain or off-chain governance process. As mentioned in the previous section, the institutionalization of a specific governance process has the risk that the ecosystem could be captured by certain groups such as governance token holders. The ecosystem could be damaged by token holders' behavior that does not align with the incentive of others. In this regard, relying solely on the code could assure certain neutrality that mitigates the risks of SPoFs of specific entities. In a community with a norm that values this neutrality, a code-centric ecosystem will be created, and De Filippi and Loveluck [4] discuss that many in the blockchain community tend to believe that individuals and organizations cannot be trusted and social interactions should be managed solely by computer code.

On the other hand, as De Filippi et al. points out, a formalized rule is easily gamed or exploited by malicious actors. Computer code lacks the flexibility needed to respond to edge cases, such as hacking due to bugs or vulnerabilities in the code, or to comply with incessantly changing regulatory requirements. Zamfir [16], one of Ethereum's core developers, claims that the concept of governance minimization is based on a naive interpretation of how the code interacts with the existing legal system and stands by off-chain governance to intervene to resolve disputes. While computer code is certainly one of the powerful constraints, it is important to position it appropriately in interactions with other constraints such as law and social norms.

2.2.3   Off-Chain Consensus by Community

In the case of the Bitcoin ecosystem, Nabilou [10] describes that "various actors such as mining pools, node operators, users, developers, exchanges, custodians and wallet providers, and eventually the media and advocacy groups have their say and they ultimately decide over critical governance issues either by reaching a consensus or by forking". While some researchers like Nabilou acclaim that their existing governance arrangements have been largely successful in dealing with Bitcoin's major crises, others including Hacker [6] criticize the lack of proper governance mechanism, especially for protocol update for dispute resolution by pointing out that, as an example, the Github repository is maintained by a small group of developers and unpredictability in changes to the protocol result from the lack of an institutionalized process to accommodate dissent from a wide range of stakeholders. The Etherum community, which also does not have a formal governance process such as an on-chain voting mechanism, resorted to an off-chain consensus when they decided to undo the mess caused by "The DAO" hack via a controversial hard fork. Many researchers question the transparency of the undocumented decision-making process and the validity of the judgment. Conversely, Zamfir [16] is opposed to excessively institutionalized governance such as on-chain voting as it could force the community to choose what is against the social norm of the community captured by specific governing forces such as governments, corporates or cartel of specific groups of the community. It is worth noting that law and its potential enforcement could primarily affect the community's decision against the rule of code, as some of the community members would notice the increased attention from authorities.

Off-chain governance mechanisms are put in place even in DeFi projects incorporating token voting systems. The community usually spends quite some time discussing before proceeding to the formal on-chain voting process on their discussion fora such as Discord and website managed by foundation or developer team. Furthermore, some DeFi projects such as MakerDAO have implemented the ability to upgrade the protocol in emergencies without going through the possibly time-consuming voting processes[3]. What needs to be considered in designing governance mechanisms is to strike a better balance between transparency and security that fits the project's long-term goal in considering the distinct benefits and risks that on-chain/off-chain governance could bring.

2.2.4 Legal Compliance/Avoidance

One of the differentiating factors among DeFi projects could be the willingness of the community to comply or circumvent the existing legal framework applied to financial services in each jurisdiction. At present, it seems that the primary value proposition of many DeFi is not complying with regulatory requirements such as KYC/AML (Know Your Customer/Anti Money Laundering rules). This purportedly "democratizes" the financial services for financial inclusion while protecting users from the threat of government actions such as taxation and expropriation. In light of growing concerns and scrutiny from regulatory authorities, some of the DeFi projects might choose to further decentralize the project by, for example, dispersing the governance token ownership, anonymizing the developer and community members, or voiding administrative functions to lessen the control points that could be captured by regulators[4].

On the contrary, others might choose to closely work with regulators and other stakeholders outside of the blockchain ecosystem to ensure legal certainty. For that sake, whether or not it should be called "DeFi", they could choose to increase the centralized aspects of the DeFi project to be able to meet regulatory requirements in an effective manner as traditional organizations usually do. One example is Nexus Mutual, a P2P discretionary mutual on Ethereum offering a blockchain-based solution to cover against smart contract failure such as "The DAO" hack. It was established as a company limited in the UK and has received approval by the Financial Conduct Authority. KYC/AML requirements must be fulfilled to become a member of the community and the membership gives legal rights to the assets of the mutual. Residents in some jurisdictions are not able to become a member due to relevant local regulations[5]. Another eye-catching initiative is OpenLaw's LAO, a Limited Liability Autonomous Organization that enables its members to invest in Ethereum ventures projects and generate a profit in a legally compliant manner[6]. The LAO is an LLC (Limited Liability Company) set up in Delaware and it harnesses smart contracts to handle mechanics related to voting, funding, and allocation of collected funds. It intends to ensure legal

---

[3] Maker has a dark fix mechanism for handling critical vulnerabilities in the protocol where the trust to its specialist team is required, which has never happened as of the end of 2021 [Source: Presentation at BGIN https://www.youtube.com/watch?v=cD717AuLLJo].

[4] SEC charged the founder of EtherDelta with operating an unregistered exchange in November 2018. SEC points out the concentration of power to the founder exampled by his exclusive access to the private key for the "administrator account".

[5] https://nexusmutual.gitbook.io/docs/welcome/use-cases.

[6] https://medium.com/openlawofficial/the-lao-a-for-profit-limited-liability-autonomous-organization-9eae89c9669c.

certainty, limit the members' liability, and streamline complex tax issues. Similar example is the Flamingo, an NFT (Non fungible token)-focused DAO organized as a Delaware LLC that aims to explore emerging investment opportunities for ownable, blockchain-based assets.

In general, there exists a trade-off between regulatory compliance and openness of the project. In the case of the LAO, the maximum number of members is limited to 99, the minimum investment is 120 ETH, and the membership is limited to 9% or for 1,080 ETH. The Flamingo also limits its membership to accredited investors capped at a maximum of 100. Such limitations could curve some of the key value propositions of DeFi, such as composability upheld by its permissionless nature, while paving the way to mass adoption in complying with social requirements. It should be noted that they might need to meet not only securities regulation but also other regulatory requirements regarding AML/KYC and financial stability, which could further increase compliance costs.

2.3 Ecosystem Governance

Hacker [6] pinpoints that governance is generally recognized as a system that forms coordination between different actors. The BCBS [12] stated that the "primary objective of corporate governance for banks should be safeguarding stakeholders' interest in conformity with public interest on a sustainable basis, and shareholders' interest would be secondary to depositors' interest." Considering that complex financial products are being offered by DeFi protocols interacting with each other, regardless of the degree of decentralization, it is necessary to take into account the inter-relationships with diverse, relevant stakeholders to align what the DeFi ecosystem would achieve with public interests. In the following, we analyze the interactions with stakeholders that are considered to be particularly important in evaluating the ecosystem governance.

2.3.1 Interdependent DeFi Protocols

The DeFi ecosystem is often described as "money Legos" for its philosophical nature of composability, enabling a DeFi protocol to interact with other smart contracts deployed on the same or interoperable blockchain without any permissions or contracts. For instance, a DEX aggregator 1inch.exchange[7] offers the best exchange rate by discovering the efficient swapping routes across a bunch of DEXs on Ethereum, such as Uniswap and Aave. While the open and flexible nature would be competitive advantages against traditional financial services, inadequate security considerations result in a number of hacking incidents, as shown in the previous chapter. A quintessential example is the hack against a decentralized lending and margin lending platform bZx in February 2020. The attacker exploited its collateral pool by taking advantage of so-called flash loans, a technique that combines a complicated set of actions including lending, pooling and selling of tokens in just a single transaction. The hacker used dydx,

---

[7] https://1inch-exchange.medium.com/.

Compound, Uniswap and Kyber network protocols in the first attack and stole $350,000 followed by the $600,000 loss in the second attack after bZx's team updated its protocol using their admin keys after the initial attack[8]. The loss was compensated as the community happened to have enough resources for compensation, but the ecosystem should make clear who is responsible for what with legal certainties to brace for future incidents and dispute resolutions among DeFi projects and other stakeholders. In a simplified on-chain voting system, the opinions of different stakeholders are not reflected in the decision-making process, and there is a risk of decisions being made that are biased towards the interests of token holders. From the banking governance point of view, as BCBS [12] points out, what matters is having the right level of authority, responsibility, accountability, checks and balances among stakeholders. At present, there seems no agreement among stakeholders for the division of responsibilities and no mechanism is put in place to align the interests among stakeholders and fulfill obligations to the outside world. The way of making clear the responsibilities could be a smart contract-based agreement between protocols utilizing the tools such as OpenLaw, which creates and executes legal agreements on blockchain[9].

2.3.2   Underlying Blockchain Layer

When DeFi protocols are deployed on a blockchain, the security, scalability, native tokens, and governance of the infrastructure layer have a critical impact on the DeFi projects in respective ways. The expansion of the DeFi ecosystem frequently drives Gas prices due to the lack of scalability of Ethereum, and the high volatility of ETH often leads to collateral shortfall and liquidation failures.[10] Conversely, a single DeFi project could significantly affect the underlying layer as The DAO hack ended up in a hard fork of Ethereum to undo the fraudulent transactions. While a tremendous amount of effort is poured into addressing the scalability issues such as 2nd layer solutions and Sharding, the outcomes remain to be seen. Security and governance considerations need to be thoroughly discussed to mitigate the risks that could emerge from the resulting consequences, such as the migration of DeFi projects to the alternative layer. Some governance arrangements should be in place to fill the potential gaps between the blockchain and application layers, examples of which include having regular calls among core developers, working together to build a solution in critical need for the ecosystem such as digital identity, and sharing common financial resources to align the interest of each party.

2.3.3   Existing Financial System

The border between the DeFi and centralized finance is likely to become vague going forward. It is demonstrated by the fact that centralized exchanges such

---

[8] https://blog.coinbase.com/around-the-block-analysis-on-the-bzx-attack-defi-vulnerabilities-the-state-of-debit-cards-in-1289f7f77137.

[9] https://media.consensys.net/introducing-openlaw-7a2ea410138b.

[10] https://blog.makerdao.com/the-market-collapse-of-march-12-2020-how-it-impacted-makerdao/.

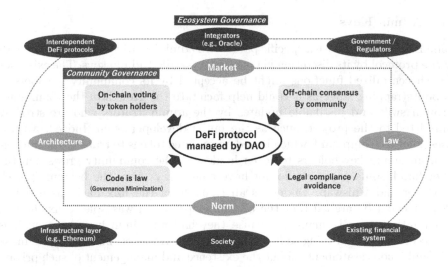

Fig. 2. DeFi governance overview

as Binance and FTX are active to list a wide range of DeFi tokens, including governance tokens, and by the re-centralization of some DeFi projects described in paragraph 2.2.4. An example of the DeFi and centralized finance interaction is Set Protocol, which automatically rebalances the tokenized assets based on customizable algorithmic strategy by tapping liquidity of almost anywhere, including DEXs and centralized exchanges and crypto OTC trading desks. Some governance arrangement should be established between the parties. The division of responsibilities between the decentralized and centralized organizations via smart contract agreement might benefit both if the division of roles fit for each economic purpose and legal requirements are adequately satisfied.

2.3.4   Other Governance Factors

In addition to the above, there exist several factors that should be considered in ecosystem governance. One of the most decisive factors is the governments and regulators, which will be discussed in detail in the next chapter. Besides, oracle governance is critical as many DeFi protocols rely on it as a price feeder. Furthermore, a variety of types of integrators and aggregators such as wallet providers, DEX aggregators also play an important role in this ecosystem. Digging deeper into these issues is an important research topic for the future.

3   Regulatory Considerations on Centralized Aspects

In this chapter, we demonstrate the multifaceted centralized aspects of the DeFi projects analyze regulatory implications on them.

3.1   Admin Keys

Some DeFi projects have a specific party with administrative authorities to modify the protocol by its discretion via private keys called admin keys. The existence of such centralized functions might be accepted by its community members in its bootstrapping stage as it could help facilitate the growth of the community through swift and justifiable updates by the administrators who are strongly committed to the project, such as the initial developer team. Indeed, we saw cases, such as Compound, which issued governance tokens to transfer the authority from admin key holders to token holders as the community grows. On the other hand, some protocols do not have admin keys from the beginning, such as Maker and Uniswap. Taking as an example of the bZx hack discussed in 2.2.1, it could be argued that the bZx developer team was able to fix the bug in a relatively timely manner because they had an admin key. As such, it is not necessarily a bad thing to hold an admin key. However, many projects make only ambiguous statements about the existence and management of such private keys, and even those who claim to be managing them properly have no verification at all. These custody risks are difficult to verify even with external audits, and participants of the ecosystem need to trust the key holders. It would be necessary to follow the security management standards such as ISO/TR 23576 from the operational security perspective. The administrators should strive for appropriate lifecycle management of private keys and transparent information disclosure. In addition, it should be pointed out that the admin key may act as a backdoor and threaten the security of the entire system.

3.1.1   Regulatory Considerations

The admin keys and their holders could be one of the control points for regulators as Takanashi et al. [14] argues that backdoor "could facilitate nearly perfect oversight from the government within the network". SEC [13] refers to the fact that eleven "high profile" individuals are selected "as holders of The DAO's Curator "Multisig" (or "private key")" in its investigation report. The EtherDelta examined in 2.1.4 is another proof that regulatory bodies take the admin keys seriously to assess whether the developer is liable for the unlawful financial service provision via smart contracts. If regulators are able to identify the admin key holders, the regulators might ask them to take necessary actions such as freezing of stolen tokens in case of theft or money laundering. As an example, when crypto assets were stolen from the hot wallet of a centralized exchange KuCoin, some ERC-20 token issuers such as USDT and Ocean (government tokens) restricted token movement by administrator's judgement. Though it is not clear whether there was an order or request from the authorities, it is conceivable that the authorities will take similar enforcement actions against future incidents. Moreover, depending on the type of financial product offered, authorities might require the admin key holders to comply with same regulations that existing financial institutions providing comparable services are required to abide by.

Taking a step further, the authorities may decide that uncontrollable projects are unacceptable in order to achieve their regulatory objectives and demand that the adoption of admin keys be required at the launch of the protocol despite the effectiveness of its enforceability. In the early 1990s, the United States National Security Agency (NSA) intended to force telecom companies to adopt a chipset with a backdoor called the Clipper chip so that law enforcement authorities could decode the intercepted voice and data transmissions. The attempt failed due to strong opposition from cryptographers and related groups, but it should be kept in mind that some authorities could have a strong motivation to have control over the protocol, as exemplified by the recent discussion on restricting end-to-end encryption. Since the admin key encompasses issues such as custody risk, as pointed out in the previous paragraph, both developers and authorities should at least conduct in-depth risk assessment analysis before making critical decisions.

3.2 Governance Token Holders

Blemus and Gregan [1] argue that one of the purposes of distributed governance is to minimize the risk of "tyranny of the majority". However, regarding the degree of concentration of decision-making, governance tokens could work towards increasing the concentration of control over the protocols. Observing the DeFi ecosystem, in many projects, the majority of the governance token is held by the developer team or early investors such as venture capital. For example, 40% of Uniswap's UNI is going to distribute to the inner members such as initial investors and developers, as seen in 2.1.1. Community members usually receive the token via retrospective distribution or as a reward for adding liquidity to the protocol pool. Still, many holders only hold a minority portion of the stake and play only a limited role in governance voting. As a result, large token holders occupy a dominant position in decision-making. It should also be noted that voting rights are often concentrated in specific holders through delegation function.

3.2.1 Regulatory Considerations

One of the major regulatory issues is the applicability of governance tokens as securities. While the holders of some governance tokens are entitled to receive a part of the fee income generated by the protocol, others have only voting rights and do not have the right to the treasury of the protocol directly. However, in many protocols, a portion of the tokens is burned as the cash flow to the protocol increases, which is equivalent to a share buyback in the case of ordinary stocks, and can be considered to have the same economic function as dividend. Collomb et al. argue that regulators should assess not only the original nature or function of the tokens being issued but also the underlying motivations of both token issuers and investors, as well as the risks that investors may incur in purchasing these tokens. Given the assumptions that token holders' primary motivation is capital and income gains that would be realized from the growth of the DeFi projects, it is conceivable that some of them are regarded as a kind of securities or investment contracts, especially for those that have specific centralized party to manage the protocol, though it needs to be examined in the context of the legal framework of relevant jurisdictions. As an example, the SEC [13] has concluded that The DAO token was a security at the time of the issuance, and charged Ripple Labs Inc. and two of its executives alleging that they raised over $1.3 billion through an unregistered, ongoing digital asset securities offering[11].

Given the similarity of the governance tokens to securities, disclosure requirements should be well considered, particularly for the minor token holder protection. In corporate governance, many jurisdictions have put various institutional frameworks in place, such as a requirement to submit statements of large-volume holdings, to mitigate the dominance by large investor regulation to protect minority shareholders' interest. While such regulatory frameworks are not in place as of now, some projects such as Nexus Mutua implement specific voting rules to curve the strong voting power of large holders by, as an example, limiting the maximum voting rights to 5% of the total voting rights. However, this kind of arrangement could also raise concerns about fairness among shareholders.

Another consideration is concerning the possibility of token-based voting mechanisms being captured by authorities. It is conceivable that the authorities could hold a large number of tokens and intervene in the DeFi community's decision-making.

3.3   Other Centralized Factors

3.3.1   Collateral
Even if the DeFi protocol itself is highly decentralized, there are cases where assets accepted as collateral or locked in its pools are managed in a centralized manner. Maker community decided to add the USDC, custodial stablecoins backed by US dollars, as one of the collateral assets in March 2020 to increase the pool's liquidity after the liquidation failure incidents[12]. As a US corporation, Circle manages the USDC. Enforcement officials may demand the company to freeze the USDC used as a collateral of Dai, a stablecoin issued by Maker protocol, to stop illegal financial transactions. Also, if the Maker community could intervene in the decision via on-chain voting, the voters against the request from authorities could have legal responsibilities. If there is no generally agreed extent of liability of voters, the token holders might choose not to join the voting to avoid getting involved into the complicated situation.

3.3.2   Aggregator
The need for aggregation services is growing as the DeFi ecosystem expands. DEX aggregators enable users to access multiple liquidity pools and offer the best trading price as explained in 2.3.1. Yearn Finance provides lending aggregation

---

[11] https://www.sec.gov/news/press-release/2020-338.
[12] https://forum.makerdao.com/t/proposal-for-collateral-onboarding-of-usdc/1588.

by which interest accrual process is optimized by shifting deposited funds automatically between lending pools such as Compound and AAVE. Yearn Finance also helps users to maximize their profit making via liquidity mining or yield firming. Whereas aggregators are yet another protocol like many other DeFi protocols and often do not custody the user's assets, it could be a point of centralization when a lot of users rely on the aggregation services and access the user-friendly front interface. The operators of the website might be deemed liable if it is evident that illegal activities are facilitated by the aggregation protocols.

3.3.3   Legal Entity

Chohan [15] discusses the legal indeterminacy of DAO and raises concern about the unlimited liability of the DAO participants if it is structured in the form of a general partnership as opposed to a corporation. As discussed in 2.2.4, legal arrangements lower the risks to investors in starting a business by making the investors have limited liability. Note that this freedom from liability is not affected by how shareholders vote. In addition, legal entity would be necessary to manage intellectual property rights of the community and to deal with jurisdictional-wise issues such as tax issues.

4   Conclusion and Future Works

There is no need to reinvent the wheel of governance. Whether it is Internet governance or corporate governance, useful mechanisms should be adopted in the DeFi ecosystem. Given the different degrees of decentralization of ongoing projects, the hybrid approach might hit the target. However, it is worth mentioning that it does not mean that we should ignore the existing governance arrangements already in place in the community. It should be also noted that the DeFi ecosystem is rapidly changing and each project seems to be exploring various directions toward further decentralization or re-centralization, which would affects the enforceability of regulation. This would make it much more difficult for regulators to properly assess the risk and implement tailored, risk-based regulatory approaches. Whereas this paper provides an overview of the governance mechanism and regulatory implications, an in-depth analysis should be done in consideration of complicated elements such as jurisdictional regulatory gaps and privacy-enhancing technologies. Besides, salient features of DeFi such as transparency should be examined from corporate governance point of view. It is also necessary to delve into the governance of organizations that are more similar to DAO, such as cooperative financial institutions. Since there is a wide range of issues to be discussed and solved, which neither the DeFi ecosystem participants nor the authorities alone could not sufficiently address, a multi-stakeholder approach should be taken to pave the way for the wider application of innovative financial products for social goods.

References

1. Blemus, S., Guegan, D.: Initial crypto-asset offerings (ICOs), tokenization and corporate governance (2019)

2. Financial Stability Board: Decentralised financial technologies: report on financial stability, regulatory and governance implications (2019). https://www.fsb.org/wp-content/uploads/P060619.pdf
3. Collomb, A., de Filippi, P., Sok, K.: Blockchain technology and financial regulation: a risk-based approach to the regulation of ICOs. Eur. J. Risk Regul. **10**(2), 263–314 (2019)
4. De Filippi, P., Loveluck, B.: The invisible politics of bitcoin: governance crisis of a decentralized infrastructure. Internet Policy Rev. **5**, 09 (2016)
5. De Filippi, P., Wright, A.: Blockchain and the Law: The Rule of Code. Harvard University Press, Cambridge (2018)
6. Hacker, P.: Corporate Governance for Complex Cryptocurrencies? A Framework for Stability and Decision Making in Blockchain-Based Organizations, pp. 140–166. Oxford University Press, Oxford (2017)
7. Hirschman, A.O.: Exit, Voice, and Loyalty: Responses to Decline in Firms, Organizations, and States (1972)
8. Kondova, G., Barba, R.: Governance of decentralized autonomous organizations. J. Mod. Account. Auditing **15**, 406–411 (2019)
9. Lessig, L.: Code and Other Laws of Cyberspace. Basic Books, New York (1999)
10. Nabilou, H.: Bitcoin governance as a decentralized financial market infrastructure (2020)
11. OECD. G20/OECD Principles of Corporate Governance (2015)
12. Basel Committee on Banking Supervision: Corporate governance principles for banks (2015). https://www.bis.org/bcbs/publ/d328.pdf
13. U.S. Securities and Exchange Commission: Report of investigation pursuant to section 21(a) of the securities exchange act of 1934: The dao (2017). https://www.sec.gov/litigation/investreport/34-81207.pdf
14. Takanashi, Y., Matsuo, S., Burger, E., Sullivan, C., Miller, J., Sato, H.: Call for multi-stakeholder communication to establish a governance mechanism for the emerging blockchain-based financial ecosystem, part 1 of 2. Stanford J. Blockchain Law Policy (2020)
15. WChohan, U.W.: The decentralized autonomous organization and governance issues. J. Cyber Policy 1–7 (2017)
16. Zamfir, V.: Against Szabo's law, for a new crypto legal system (2019). https://medium.com/cryptolawreview/against-szabos-law-for-a-new-crypto-legal-system-d00d0f3d3827

CoDecFin – AML/KYC and Privacy

Collaborative Deanonymization

Patrik Keller[1]([⊠]), Martin Florian[2], and Rainer Böhme[1]

[1] University of Innsbruck, Innsbruck, Austria
{patrik.keller,rainer.boehme}@uibk.ac.at
[2] Weizenbaum Institute, Humboldt University of Berlin, Berlin, Germany
martin.florian@hu-berlin.de

Abstract. Privacy-seeking cryptocurrency users rely on anonymization techniques like CoinJoin and ring transactions. By using such technologies benign users potentially provide anonymity to bad actors. We propose overlay protocols to resolve the tension between anonymity and accountability in a peer-to-peer manner. Cryptocurrencies can adopt this approach to enable prosecution of publicly recognized crimes. We illustrate how the protocols could apply to Monero rings and CoinJoin transactions in Bitcoin.

1 Introduction

"Anonymity loves company." [6] It is well-established that anonymity is co-created by the members of an anonymity set, who share the same intention and employ technical systems and protocols to make them appear indistinguishable to outside observers [16]. Inherently, benign members seeking privacy assist bad actors avoiding law enforcement.

Previously, the tension between privacy and law enforcement has been studied for mixes in communication networks [4,5,11]. The proposed solutions rely on putting backdoors into systems or the supporting cryptography, such that designated parties can revoke the anonymity in justified cases. Access to the backdoor is made transparent, which holds law enforcement accountable and impedes mass surveillance. With the advent of privacy-hardened cryptocurrencies, the tension is instantiated for money flows. While backdoors seem technically feasible, it is unlikely that they can be sustained in decentralized systems, whose raison d'être is the rejection of privileged parties with special access rights.

Another, more widely acceptable idea to combat money laundering specifically are threshold schemes. Small payments would enjoy unlinkability while larger transactions require identification or are traceable by design [10,19]. The downsides of this approach include the need to agree on a threshold and, more importantly, it would require strong identities in order to prevent "smurfing" attacks, which split a large sum into many small payments.

We explore a different approach. In many cases, the parties forming the anonymity set can retain some private information, which can help deanonymize other members of the set. Collaborative deanonymization means that some parties, henceforth called *witnesses*, share information on request for the purpose

M. Bernhard et al. (Eds.): FC 2021 Workshops, LNCS 12676, pp. 39–46, 2021.
https://doi.org/10.1007/978-3-662-63958-0_3

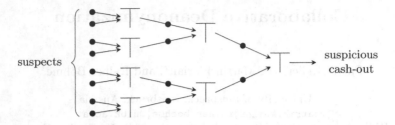

Fig. 1. Example entity graph of 7 ring-type transactions, $m = 2$. Dots are entities, arrows denote possible payments. Observe the exponential growth of suspects.

of solving a crime. In a nutshell, law enforcement publicly shares information requests for specific crimes. Then users check whether they are involved, decide whether the crime should be prosecuted, and potentially reveal private information to support deanonymization.

We argue that this approach is compatible with the peer-to-peer spirit of decentralized systems because every witness decides if she supports the investigation or not. This limits the method to felonies that are universally disapproved, such as extortion (ransomware) or the financing of child sexual abuse. For the method to be effective, it is not required that every witness collaborates. Every collaborating witness reduces the search space. Law enforcement might leverage a range of incentives to induce collaboration: alibi, altruism, bounties, and—in justified cases—force (e. g., seizure and use of a private key). Unlike traffic or blockchain analyses, collaborative deanonymization does not scale, hence the risk of secret mass surveillance is small. Moreover, as search requests are announced publicly, law enforcement can be held accountable. The very fact that anonymity is conditional can deter crime.

In the following we develop a scenario (Sect. 2), formulate desiderata, and sketch overlay protocols (Sects. 3 and 4) that enable collaborative deanonymization of two relevant privacy techniques, CoinJoin and Monero rings, without changing the target systems. Section 5 concludes.

2   Scenario and Model

Consider a scenario where a law enforcement agency (LEA) identifies a suspicious cash-out from a cryptocurrency address. The objective of an investigation is to find an identifiable source, i. e., *backtracking*. After employing known blockchain analysis methods, like state-of-the-art clustering [8], the LEA obtains an entity graph where backtracking is ambiguous only due to mixing transactions.

We model such transactions as collections of m inputs and n outputs. The LEA has no information about the relation.[1] Without loss of generality, we

---

[1] Conversely, if the LEA has some information (e. g. due to non-uniformly valued inputs and outputs), it can partition the transaction and proceed as described.

assume that each output of a transaction is funded by exactly one input. Back-tracking links the entity associated with the targeted t-th output to the entity of the funding input. Between transactions, each input references exactly one output of a previous transaction.

general		join-type		ring-type	
		1	$\psi(1)$	1	σ
		2	$\psi(2)$	2	
m	n	$\vdots$	$\vdots$	$\vdots$	
		m	$\psi(m)$	m	

We consider two of the most relevant types of mixing transactions: join-type as used in CoinJoin [12] and ring-type as used in Monero [7]. Join-type transactions are formed collaboratively by m parties, potentially facilitated by an intermediary such as JoinMarket [13]. We model this using m inputs, each funding a distinct output ($n = m$). A join-type transaction can then be expressed as a permutation ψ on $\{1, \ldots, m\}$. The LEA's problem is to find the funding input $\psi(t)$ of the t-th output. In practice, CoinJoin transactions vary in size. A study estimates the modal value of inputs for CoinJoins on Bitcoin at $m = 3$ [13]. Transactions with $m > 10$ are rare.[2]

In contrast to join-type transactions, ring-type transactions can be formed *without* the cooperation of other entities. Moreover, a ring-type transaction does not spend all outputs referenced on its input side. In our simplified model, ring transactions have m inputs and a single output ($n = t = 1$). The LEA's goal is to learn the true input σ.[3] At the time of writing, the Monero reference implementation fixes the number of inputs to $m = 11$.

For both types of mixing transactions, the anonymity of the participants is based on the observer's uncertainty about ψ and σ, respectively. If multiple mixing transactions are cascaded, the number of possible funding sources (*suspects*) increases exponentially in the number of layers (see Fig. 1). We propose protocols that allow the LEA to reduce the number of suspects in collaboration with a subset of the involved parties.

3   Collaborative Backtracking

We assume an authenticated one-way communication channel from the LEA to the protocol participants. The LEA uses this channel to announce inquiries on targeted transaction outputs. Each inquiry conveys enough information so that a potential witness can decide whether she supports the request, i.e., whether she approves prosecution of the specific case, or not.

We further assume an unauthenticated but confidential communication channel from the witnesses to the LEA and, for group testimonies, communication

---

[2] A CoinJoin with $m = 100$ made headlines in June 2019: https://www.coindesk.com/bitcoin-users-perform-what-might-be-the-largest-coinjoin-ever.

[3] We depart from Monero's terminology, which calls an entire ring "input.".

channels between the witnesses. Witnesses willing to support an inquiry use these channels to give testimonies that facilitate backtracking for a single transaction.

3.1 Individual Testimony

An individual testimony is a protocol between a single witness and the LEA. It results in ruling out one of the possible inputs. Formally speaking, the witness associated with the i-th input should prove that $\psi(t) \neq i$ or $\sigma \neq i$, respectively.

For join-type transactions, the witness can testify by signing a challenge with the private keys belonging to the i-th input and the j-th output (obviously $t \neq j$).

Ring-type transactions hide the true input using traceable ring signatures [7]. By design, these ring signatures reveal attempts to spend an input more than once. The spending of an input yields a transaction-independent *key image* that must be included in a valid signature—transactions attempting to spend the same input will contain identical key images [17]. Let o be the output of a *preceding* transaction that links the witness to the suspicious transaction T. The witness prepares a phantom transaction T' for the LEA. It has one input referencing o and one output. The output could be invalid in order to avoid accidental inclusion in the blockchain. For example, T' could spend more funds than available in o. Crucially, the phantom transaction unambiguously spends o. If the key image associated with T' is different to the key image of T, it must hold that $i \neq \sigma$.

3.2 Group Testimony

The LEA is interested in a single input to output relationship, but it learns one relationship per individual testimony. Group testimonies can avoid this unnecessary privacy loss. Multiple witnesses controlling the set of inputs S collaboratively testify $\psi(t) \notin S$ or $\sigma \notin S$, while maintaining their anonymity within S.

For join-type transactions, this can be realized by signing a challenge with all $2 \cdot |S|$ private keys belonging to the witnesses' inputs and outputs. In the best case, all $m - 1$ witnesses cooperate ($S = \{1, \ldots, m\} \setminus \{t\}$) and identify the true suspect. If $|S| < m$ witnesses participate in the protocol, for example because private keys are deleted or witnesses unreachable, the search space is reduced to $m - |S|$ suspects. Join-type group testimonies retain S as the anonymity set of witnesses. Cases where $S = \{1, \ldots, m\} \setminus \{t\}$ minimize the anonymity loss for witnesses when testifying that $\psi(t) \notin S$.

For ring-type transactions, it is possible to implement group testimonies with the construction of a provably spent set [18,20]. For example, each cooperating witness can individually form a new transaction T' like for an individual testimony, however this time referencing not only its own input but all inputs S of cooperating witnesses. Given $|S|$ transactions that all have the same set of inputs S and yet differing key images, the LEA gains evidence that $\sigma \notin S$. If an output o referenced by an input $i \in S$ is *unspent* at the time of the testimony, the respective witness can achieve an anonymity set of S for o by referencing all S when spending o. Conversely, if o has already been spent in a transaction T'' with input set S'', the anonymity set of the witness reduces to $S \cap S''$.

Notably, each of the cooperative protocols can be executed jointly for multiple mixing transactions. This testifies that the owners of S (now generalized to the enumeration of all inputs in all transactions involved) initiated none of these transactions. This approach is especially interesting for ring-type transactions, as larger S increase the overlap with the anonymity sets of outputs that have already been spent elsewhere.

3.3   Dealing with the Risk of False Testimonies

A general question is how much confidence the LEA can place in the testimonies. This calls for a closer look at how collaborative deanonymization can fail, and in the worst case produce false or misleading evidence. We observe crucial differences between join-type and ring-type transactions.

Monero stores σ on the blockchain, however in encrypted form. This should reduce the risk of false testimonies to the security of the cryptography used, even if private keys are leaked or stolen.

By contrast, CoinJoin does not commit ψ to the blockchain. Even computationally unbounded observers cannot decide about the relation. The resulting deniability bears a risk of false testimonies. For example, if the perpetrator has access to the private keys of a witness, he could obtain a false alibi by signing a false input–output relation. If the victim among the witnesses does not participate in the collaborative deanonymization, she is falsely accused. If she does participate, the LEA receives two conflicting statements. This concentrates the suspicion on both the perpetrator and the victim, hence perpetrators have little to gain from false statements—unless their victims are unavailable.

The sketched situation highlights that parties engaging in CoinJoins might be exposed to physical risks under collaborative deanonymization. A potential direction of research is to modify the protocols used for CoinJoin formation in such a way that ψ is committed to the blockchain at the time of the transaction. This would obviate false accusations and reduce the incentives to attack other witnesses. The key question to answer is under which conditions what part of ψ should be revealable. For example, should every party commit to one relation individually? Would a threshold scheme make sense? Moreover, it would be desirable to make the commitment coercion-resistant. Otherwise, the risk could reappear at the time of the CoinJoin formation, rather than be mitigated.

Another approach for increasing the credibility of testimonies could be based on witnesses proving that addresses belong to the same wallet, e.g., if their wallet generates addresses deterministically from a common secret. It is an open question how such a proof can efficiently be completed without revealing more information about the wallet than necessary.

4   Forward Tracking

A variant of the scenario presented in Sect. 2 is *forward tracking*. Here, the LEA has identified a suspicious origin and wishes to trace the money flow to its (current) destination or until it hits a known cash-out point. We sketch how our approach can be adapted to this case.

4.1   Testimonies for Forward Tracking

Due to the symmetry of join-type transactions, the backtracking protocols (Sect. 3) can be repurposed for forward tracking. Since ψ is bijective, testimonies which rule out assignments of ψ also rule out assignments of ψ^{-1}.

Ring-type transactions are less straightforward. The protocols given in Sect. 3 enable collaborating witnesses to testify that a set of inputs S does not contain the funding input for a given transaction T, i. e., $\sigma \notin S$. For the case of forward tracking, they must instead prove that only one specific suspicious input s is not a funding input, i. e., $\sigma \neq s$. Individual witnesses can accomplish this by creating a phantom transaction T', which include all but the suspicious input s. As T' and T share the same funding input i, they will produce identical key images. By comparing the key images of T and T', the LEA can verify that $\sigma \neq s$ without learning i.

4.2   Blacklisting and Cover Transactions

Forward tracking is related to transaction *blacklisting* previously proposed (and controversially debated) as a regulatory instrument [2,15]. Specifically the "poison" policy [14], where taint of a single input is propagated to all outputs, mimics the proliferation of a priori suspicion. An interesting question is whether the threat of blacklisting can foster collaboration. For example, the propagation policy could terminate at whitelisted transactions after sufficient evidence has been collected to disambiguate the entity graph (for forward and backtracking).

Forward tracking on Monero rings comes with two caveats. First, it might be hard to decide about when to terminate (unsuccessfully), because it is often unknown whether a given output has been spent at all. Second, the method is susceptible to cover transactions placed by a perpetrator. Such transactions reference the investigated money flow in order to increase the search space and with it the number of witnesses needed.

Blacklisting might be a defense against this behavior because it would devalue the funds in cover transactions and thus raise the cost of creating them. However, the effectiveness of this method as well as other defenses are open research questions. We note that backtracking is not affected by the threat of cover transactions because funding transactions cannot be added after the spending transaction.

5   Conclusion and Outlook

We have outlined a novel way to investigate criminal money flows in cryptocurrencies even if the perpetrators use anonymization techniques. Our approach requires collaboration of witnesses, which keeps the method costly enough to prevent mass surveillance or the prosecution of petty crimes. Specifically, we have given protocols for backtracking and forward tracking of CoinJoin transactions in Bitcoin as well as Monero rings. Several techniques ensure that the information shared with law enforcement can be limited to the necessary minimum. The new risk of false accusations has been discussed. A general consequence of collaborative deanonymization is that old private keys remain sensitive even if they do not control any funds anymore.

We shall also pinpoint future work. Obviously, the protocols for secure testimonies need to be further developed and their properties formalized and proven. A proof-of-concept implementation for the most relevant types of mixing transactions could demonstrate the practicality of our approach. Whether and under which condition LEAs can deploy collaborative deanonymization, must be subject of more interdisciplinary work with legal scholars. Adapting the approach to less common types of mixing transactions (see for instance Table 1 of [9] for an overview) would help to complete the picture.

The topic also lends itself to economic studies. One could investigate the incentives of witnesses to collaborate, presumably with cooperative game theory [3]. In addition, potential knock-on effects on the participation in mixing transactions call for a model in the tradition of competitive game theory [1].

Two broader technical directions are to explore collaborative deanonymization for anonymous communication systems, and to research deniable privacy techniques, which could protect potential witnesses from any pressure to testify or release deanonymizing information.

In summary, collaborative deanonymization appears not only under-researched, but also under-estimated for its potential to balance the conflicting goals of privacy and law enforcement in future digital currency systems. This short paper sets out to make a case for this promising tool.

Acknowledgements. We thank our colleagues Michael Fröwis, Malte Möser, Tim Ruffing, and a number of anonymous reviewers for helpful discussions of earlier versions of this work. Rainer Böhme's and Patrik Keller's work on this topic is supported by the Austrian FFG's KIRAS programme under project VIRTCRIME.

References

1. Abramova, S., Schöttle, P., Böhme, R.: Mixing coins of different quality: a game-theoretic approach. In: Brenner, M., et al. (eds.) FC 2017. LNCS, vol. 10323, pp. 280–297. Springer, Cham (2017). https://doi.org/10.1007/978-3-319-70278-0_18
2. Anderson, R., Shumailov, I., Ahmed, M.: Making bitcoin legal. In: Matyáš, V., Švenda, P., Stajano, F., Christianson, B., Anderson, J. (eds.) Security Protocols 2018. LNCS, vol. 11286, pp. 243–253. Springer, Cham (2018). https://doi.org/10.1007/978-3-030-03251-7_29
3. Arce, D.G., Böhme, R.: Pricing anonymity. In: Meiklejohn, S., Sako, K. (eds.) FC 2018. LNCS, vol. 10957, pp. 349–368. Springer, Heidelberg (2018). https://doi.org/10.1007/978-3-662-58387-6_19

4. Backes, M., Clark, J., Kate, A., Simeonovski, M., Druschel, P.: BackRef: accountability in anonymous communication networks. In: Boureanu, I., Owesarski, P., Vaudenay, S. (eds.) ACNS 2014. LNCS, vol. 8479, pp. 380–400. Springer, Cham (2014). https://doi.org/10.1007/978-3-319-07536-5_23
5. Claessens, J., Díaz, C., Goemans, C., Dumortier, J., Preneel, B., Vandewalle, J.: Revocable anonymous access to the Internet? Internet Res. **13**(4), 242–258 (2003)
6. Dingledine, R., Mathewson, N.: Anonymity loves company: usability and the network effect. In: Workshop on the Economics of Information Security (2006)
7. Fujisaki, E., Suzuki, K.: Traceable ring signature. In: Okamoto, T., Wang, X. (eds.) PKC 2007. LNCS, vol. 4450, pp. 181–200. Springer, Heidelberg (2007). https://doi.org/10.1007/978-3-540-71677-8_13
8. Goldfeder, S., Kalodner, H., Reisman, D., Narayanan, A.: When the cookie meets the blockchain: privacy risks of web payments via cryptocurrencies. Privacy Enhancing Technol. **4**, 179–199 (2018)
9. Heilman, E., AlShenibr, L., Baldimtsi, F., Scafuro, A., Goldberg, S.: TumbleBit: an untrusted bitcoin-compatible anonymous payment hub. In: Network and Distributed System Security Symposium. Internet Society (2017)
10. Jarecki, S., Shmatikov, V.: Probabilistic escrow of financial transactions with cumulative threshold disclosure. In: Patrick, A.S., Yung, M. (eds.) FC 2005. LNCS, vol. 3570, pp. 172–187. Springer, Heidelberg (2005). https://doi.org/10.1007/11507840_17
11. Köpsell, S., Wendolsky, R., Federrath, H.: Revocable anonymity. In: Müller, G. (ed.) ETRICS 2006. LNCS, vol. 3995, pp. 206–220. Springer, Heidelberg (2006). https://doi.org/10.1007/11766155_15
12. Maxwell, G.: CoinJoin: Bitcoin privacy for the real world. Forum post (2013)
13. Möser, M., Böhme, R.: Join me on a market for anonymity. In: Workshop on the Economics of Information Security (2016)
14. Möser, M., Böhme, R., Breuker, D.: Towards risk scoring of bitcoin transactions. In: Böhme, R., Brenner, M., Moore, T., Smith, M. (eds.) FC 2014. LNCS, vol. 8438, pp. 16–32. Springer, Heidelberg (2014). https://doi.org/10.1007/978-3-662-44774-1_2
15. Möser, M., Narayanan, A.: Effective cryptocurrency regulation through blacklisting. Preprint (2019)
16. Pfitzmann, A., Köhntopp, M.: Anonymity, unobservability, and pseudonymity — a proposal for terminology. In: Federrath, H. (ed.) Designing Privacy Enhancing Technologies. LNCS, vol. 2009, pp. 1–9. Springer, Heidelberg (2001). https://doi.org/10.1007/3-540-44702-4_1
17. van Saberhagen, N.: CryptoNote v2.0. Whitepaper (2013)
18. Wijaya, D.A., Liu, J., Steinfeld, R., Liu, D.: Monero ring attack: recreating zero mixin transaction effect. In: Trust, Security And Privacy In Computing And Communications, pp. 1196–1201. IEEE (2018)
19. Wüst, K., Kostiainen, K., Čapkun, V., Čapkun, S.: PRCash: fast, private and regulated transactions for digital currencies. In: Goldberg, I., Moore, T. (eds.) FC 2019. LNCS, vol. 11598, pp. 158–178. Springer, Cham (2019). https://doi.org/10.1007/978-3-030-32101-7_11
20. Yu, Z., Au, M.H., Yu, J., Yang, R., Xu, Q., Lau, W.F.: New empirical traceability analysis of CryptoNote-style blockchains. In: Goldberg, I., Moore, T. (eds.) FC 2019. LNCS, vol. 11598, pp. 133–149. Springer, Cham (2019). https://doi.org/10.1007/978-3-030-32101-7_9

Re: FinCEN Docket Number FINCEN-2020-0020; RIN 1506-AB47; Requirements for Certain Transactions Involving Convertible Virtual Currency or Digital Assets

Ryan Taylor[✉]

Dash Core Group, Scottsdale, USA
ryan@dash.org

Abstract. Dash is **NOT** an anonymity-enhanced cryptocurrency.

Keywords: Blockchain · KYC · AML · Compliance · Information security · Regulation awareness · Anonymity-enhanced cryptocurrency · AEC · FinCEN

1 Introduction

Dash Core Group ("DCG") appreciates the opportunity to submit this letter for consideration by the Financial Crimes Enforcement Network ("FinCEN") with respect to the Notice of Proposed Rulemaking ("NPR"), published on December 23, 2020, titled "Requirements for Certain Transactions Involving Convertible Virtual Currency or Digital Assets" See 85 FR 83840.

We offer this letter for a very specific purpose. The NPR describes at length the government's concerns that certain segments of the convertible virtual currency ("CVC") market create an illicit finance threat. In particular, the NPR's background section identifies anonymity-enhanced cryptocurrencies ("AECs") as a money laundering risk, and specifically names the Dash cryptocurrency as an AEC "that inhibit[s] investigators' ability both to identify transaction activity involving blockchain data and to attribute this activity to illicit activity conducted by natural persons" 85 FR 83844.

This characterization of the Dash cryptocurrency is wrong. It misunderstands how the Dash cryptocurrency works. It ignores public statements by neutral third party experts- including the prominent blockchain analysis company Chainalysis, which the U.S. government itself often uses in its investigations-that transactions involving the Dash cryptocurrency can be both identified and attributed. And this characterization is having a material, negative impact on the Dash network's operations, as cryptocurrency exchanges around the world

M. Bernhard et al. (Eds.): FC 2021 Workshops, LNCS 12676, pp. 47–53, 2021.
https://doi.org/10.1007/978-3-662-63958-0_4

have begun delisting the Dash cryptocurrency based on the U.S. government's repeated (and mistaken) assertions that Dash is a money
laundering risk.

DCG strongly opposes the use of cryptocurrencies for illicit purposes. Indeed,
we have worked productively with law enforcement agents when they have
approached us to advance their legitimate investigations. Moreover, we met with
officials at FinCEN in June 2020 to describe how the Dash network works, and
why any characterization of the Dash cryptocurrency as a money laundering
risk is flawed. Nonetheless, the mis-characterization of Dash in official U.S. government documents continues. This arbitrary and capricious state of affairs is
unacceptable, and it is significantly impacting the Dash network's operations.
**We respectfully ask you to strike any reference to Dash in any future
iterations of (or documents relating to) this Rule.**

2   Dash Is Not an Anonymity-Enhanced Cryptocurrency

Dash is a leading cryptocurrency network focused on payments.[1] A fork of Bitcoin's code, the Dash network is a user-operated network whose most typical
use case is as digital cash for everyday transactions. Payments are near-instant,
easy, and secure; users can purchase goods at thousands of merchants, and can
trade Dash at major exchanges and brokers around the world.

We should emphasize the most important point upfront: *Dash's network,
just like Bitcoin's, features a transparent, auditable blockchain that
does not have any hidden addresses or hidden transaction details. All
transactions list the complete set of inputs, outputs, addresses, and
amounts.*

We are, accordingly, at a loss for why official U.S. government documents
continue to mislabel Dash as an AEC that is routinely used as a vehicle for
money laundering and other illicit activity.[2] Most likely, those who view Dash
as a money laundering risk are basing their assumptions on old (and flawed)
information. It is true that Dash's founder-who is no longer associated with
the project, and has not been for almost four years-announced, shortly after

---

[1] DCG is distinct from the Dash network, and is one of the many entities serving
that network. DCG is the largest software development organization for the Dash
network and is primarily tasked with development of the protocol. We also engage in
business development and marketing efforts that benefit the network. Other software
development teams independent of DCG also perform work for the network.

[2] In addition to FinCEN's NPR, the U.S. Department of Justice recently issued an
influential report that publicly (and erroneously) named Dash as an AEC that
employs "non-public or private blockchains that make it more difficult to trace or
to attribute transactions," "may undermine the AML/CFT controls used to detect
suspicious activity by MSBs and other financial institutions, and may limit or even
negate a business's ability to conduct AML/CFT checks on customer activity and
to satisfy B[ank] S[ecrecy] A[ct] requirements." U.S. Department of Justice, Cryptocurrency Enforcement Framework (Oct. 2020) at 4, 41, available at: https://www.
justice.gov/ag/page/file/1326061/download.

Dash's launch in 2014, an initial focus on enhancing the pseudonymity of Bitcoin through an implementation of CoinJoin, and rebranded the coin (which then was called Xcoin) as "Darkcoin." This early decision branded Dash in a negative light and encouraged sensational press coverage depicting Dash as a cryptocurrency that facilitated illegal activities. Since mid-2014, however, the project focus has pivoted significantly. The coin was renamed "Dash" in March 2015 to reflect the network's new focus on providing its users with payment speed and efficiency (rather than privacy/anonymity), as embodied in its popular "InstantSend" feature. Speed, efficiency, and a superior user experience remain Dash's focus, but unfortunately the coin's legacy privacy/anonymity reputation lingers, particularly in the media.[3]

As we explained to representatives of FinCEN in June 2020, Dash is not an AEC because its privacy feature is simply a branded implementation of non-custodial CoinJoin, a privacy- enhancing technique that adds complexity to transactions that can be performed on any transparent blockchain. That is, unlike many other privacy solutions, CoinJoin transactions do not require any modifications to the Bitcoin protocol upon which Dash is based.

Notably, third-party experts agree with our assessment. For example, Chainalysis, a reputable company that both FinCEN and the Department of Justice use to combat money laundering, terrorist financing, and other illicit cryptocurrency uses, issued a statement (without any prompting from us) when, in mid-2020, it launched coverage of Dash. As Chainalysis declared:

"We just launched support for two notable cryptocurrencies in Chainalysis Reactor and KYT (Know Your Transaction): Dash and Zcash. As two of the most popular so-called "privacy coins"-cryptocurrencies with privacy enhancing features encoded into their protocols-they account for over 1.5 billion of reported daily trading volume.

You may be wondering how Chainalysis products could support privacy coins. Isn't the whole purpose of privacy coins to make transactions impossible to trace?

That's an oversimplification, in that it misunderstands both the privacy features coins like Dash and Zcash offer and how users actually utilize those features in everyday transactions."[4]

The statement goes on to explain that Dash's "most notable privacy modification [from Bitcoin] is its PrivateSend functionality." PrivateSend is "a branded implementation of the CoinJoin protocol . . . as a way to obscure the origin of

---

[3] For example, the popular Investopedia website lists Dash as the "#3" "privacy-oriented cryptocurrency," whose "PrivateSend feature" supposedly "obscur[es] the origin of your funds"-though the website does acknowledge that certain settings allow for users "to remain within their countries' regulatory standards." Investopedia, "Six Private Cryptocurrencies," available at: https://www.investopedia.com/tech/five-most-private-cryptocurrencies/ (last updated Dec. 24, 2020). For the reasons expressed in this letter, Investopedia's characterization is mistaken. We address the "PrivateSend" feature later in the text of this letter.

[4] Chainalysis, "Introducing Investigation and Compliance Support for Dash and Zcash," June 8, 2020, available at: https://blog.chainalysis.com/reports/introducing-chainalysis-investigation-compliance-support-dash-zcash.

funds." (As Chainalysis notes, however, "PrivateSend is optional," and "Dash transactions are unmixed by default.") The statement then describes how PrivateSend works from a technical perspective; the key takeaway point is this: "It's possible to perform mixing transactions that are functionally identical to PrivateSend on other technologically similar cryptocurrencies. This means from a technical standpoint, Dash's privacy functionality is no greater than Bitcoin's, making the label of 'privacy coin' a misnomer for Dash. In fact, independent wallet softwares provide more advanced forms of CoinJoin that are being used with major cryptocurrencies not labeled as privacy coins, such as Bitcoin, Bitcoin Cash, and Litecoin."[5] In other words, according to Chainalysis-the same company that the U.S. Department of Justice has publicly lauded on multiple occasions as a trusted private sector partner in the fight against illicit uses of cryptocurrency[6] -Dash's privacy features make it no harder, and in certain circumstances easier, to trace than Bitcoin. And, of course, no knowledgeable person would suggest that the use of Bitcoin raises insuperable challenges to law enforcement to confront and address the public safety and national security risks outlined in the NPR.

In an effort to demonstrate the similarities between the "digital trails" left by transactions conducted using Dash and those using Bitcoin, DCG in May 2019 took the initiative to conduct "PrivateSend" transactions on the Bitcoin network, and compared them to transactions using Dash. Here are links to the Bitcoin "PrivateSend" transactions.[7]

And here are links to the Dash "PrivateSend" transactions[8]

Each transaction block includes 20 publicly-displayed input and output addresses, and reflects identical transaction amounts. The blocks are identical in the information they reveal and there is absolutely no distinction between them!

In sum, Dash is a transparent, analyzable blockchain indistinguishable from Bitcoin in its functionality. Dash's PrivateSend feature is simply a branded implementation of non- custodial CoinJoin available on most public blockchains.

---

[5] Id. (emphasis added).

[6] See, e.g., U.S. Dep't of Justice, Press Release, "United States Files A Civil Action To Forfeit Cryptocurrency Valued At Over One Billion U.S. Dollars," Nov. 5, 2020, available at: https://www.justice.gov/usao-ndca/pr/united-states-files-civil-action-forfeit-cryptocurrency-valued-over-one-billion-us (thanking Chainalysis by name); U.S. Dep't of Justice, Press Release, "Global Disruption of Three Terror Finance Cyber-Enabled Campaigns," Aug. 13, 2020, available at: https://www.justice.gov/opa/pr/global-disruption-three-terror-finance-cyber-enabled-campaigns (same); U.S. Dep't of Justice, Press Release, "Three Individuals Charged For Alleged Roles In Twitter Hack," July 31, 2020, available at: https://www.justice.gov/usao-ndca/pr/three-individuals-charged-alleged-roles-twitter-hack.

[7] See Bitcoin Transaction through PrivateSend: https://btc.cryptoid.info/btc/tx.dws?2e9aa4e7c7aa704055adc7ce396533164a097515189a30f1e9c8fa73b21dc174.html.

[8] See links to Dash PrivateSend transactions for comparison to Bitcoin "PrivateSend" transactions here at: https://chainz.cryptoid.info/dash/tx.dws?a8656b7655c14445c652d8e5e27a6155e8a39aa792f99210607437737999a945.html.

All transaction inputs, outputs, addresses, and amounts are fully visible on the Dash blockchain for all transactions.

Of course, none of this is news to FinCEN; we covered these points in detail during our June 2020 meeting with nearly a dozen representatives across the agency's various divisions. Unfortunately, we have heard nothing from FinCEN since then. Instead, despite clear evidence to the contrary, the agency appears to have adopted the plainly erroneous view that Dash represents a money laundering risk.

3 Dash Is Rarely, if Ever, Used for Illicit Activities or in Connection with Darknet Marketplaces

Not only is Dash a transparent, analyzable blockchain indistinguishable from Bitcoin in its functionality; it actually poses a lower risk than Bitcoin when it comes to illicit usage. First, there is no evidence that Dash is used for illicit purposes. In a recent Rand Corporation analysis of DarkWeb cryptocurrency usage, for example, Dash accounted for only 0.05% of identified cryptocurrency wallets[9].

Second, Dash does not support advanced forms of CoinJoin such as Chaumian CoinJoin, which is present on the Bitcoin network. Finally, Dash does not support off- chain transactions that are not auditable on-chain. To reiterate the point once again: All transaction inputs, outputs, addresses, and amounts are fully visible on the Dash blockchain for all transactions.

4 The U.S. Government's Mischaracterization of Dash has had a Significant, Material, and Adverse Impact

The public naming and shaming of Dash as an AEC (or "privacy coin") in FinCEN's NPR (as well as earlier in the fall of 2020 in the Department of Justice's "Cryptocurrency Enforcement Framework") has had a hugely negative impact on the project. This impact is real, and it has affected multiple aspects of our users, DCG's business, and the individuals involved in the project.

---

[9] See Erik Silfversten, et al., Exploring the use of Zcash cryptocurrency for illicit or criminal purposes," Rand Corp., 2020, at 23 (Fig. 3.7), available at: https://www.rand.org/pubs/research_reports/RR4418.html. As this report observes, "[S]ome commentators believe that due to their privacy enhancing features, altcoins such as Zcash (as well as Monero, Dash and Litecoin) represent notable competitors for Bitcoin with illicit users on the dark web." Id. at 12. The report concludes, however, that "little empirical evidence or research exists in support of this claim." Id. While we would disagree with the ill-informed commentators referenced in the report, who believe, without evidence, that Dash is an "altcoin" whose users tend towards criminality, we concur fully with the report's assessment that the use of Dash on illicit darknet marketplaces is negligible.

First, regulators around the world look to the United States as a regulatory leader in the innovative space of cryptocurrencies. As the U.S. government continues to perpetuate a false narrative that Dash is a privacy coin that poses an unacceptable money laundering risk, other countries are following its lead without independently corroborating its conclusions or conducting primary research into the issue. Specifically, Canada's FINTRAC, in December 2020, leveraged the U.S. Department of Justice report to define Dash as a privacy coin, stating that the use of Dash indicates a heightened risk of money laundering or terrorist financing-language that is eerily similar to DOJ's.[10]

In addition, we have in recent weeks received inquiries from regulators from other countries to whom DCG has taken the time to explain our optional privacy feature. The regulators are asking DCG to comment on the categorization of Dash as an AEC, when we specifically presented materials to them demonstrating why Dash is not an AEC. With their off-the-cuff (mis)characterizations of Dash, both FinCEN and the DOJ have undermined detailed, time- consuming facts and arguments DCG has conveyed to regulators outside of the United States, thereby sowing confusion.

Second, the categorization has had a significant negative business impact on Dash. We have learned that cryptocurrency exchanges that currently list or are considering listing Dash are now reviewing their policies to ensure that they are in compliance with the U.S. government's regulatory guidance. Apparently, relying on DOJ's and FinCEN's recent pronouncements, a number of exchanges have taken the additional step of delisting Dash in order to "derisk" themselves. For example, on January 1, 2021, Bittrex, one of the world's leading cryptocurrency exchanges, announced that it would delist Dash as of January 15, 2021.[11] No official explanation was given, but public reporting suggests that Bittrex's action is part of a broader trend wherein "exchanges around the world have been moving to delist coins that seek to preserve the privacy of their users as a way to be compliant with know-your-customer (KYC) and anti-money laundering (AML) regulations that are spreading around the world."[12]

Completely overlooked in all of this is the fact that Dash is not a "privacy coin," and that its use is perfectly compatible with KYC and AML regulations. Meanwhile, it is Dash's users and the members of its network who are left holding the bag for the U.S. government's mistake: for example, Dash's price immediately dropped by approximately 15% on news of its Bittrex delisting.

---

[10] Financial Transactions and Reports Analysis Centre of Canada (FINTRAC), "Money laundering and terrorist financing indicators—Virtual currency transactions," Dec. 2020, available at: https://www.fintrac-canafe.gc.ca/guidance-directives/transaction-operation/indicators-indicateurs/vc_mltf-eng.

[11] Nasdaq, "Bittrex to Delist 'Privacy Coins' Monero, Dash and Zcash," Jan. 1, 2021, available at: https://www.nasdaq.com/articles/bittrex-to-delist-privacy-coins-monero-dash-and-zcash-2021-01-01; see also Bittrex, "Pending Market Removals 01/15/21," Jan. 1, 2021, available at: https://bittrex.zendesk.com/hc/en-us/articles/360054393492-Pending-Market-Removals-01-15-21.

[12] Id.

Finally, individuals associated with the Dash project have incurred significant reputational risk and harm as a result of the U.S. government's continued (mis)characterization of the Dash cryptocurrency. Compliance departments at certain financial institutions have interpreted the FinCEN and DOJ statements to mean that being associated with DCG indicates "high-risk activity that is indicative of possible criminal conduct . . . " We have learned that traditional bank account openings have been refused on the basis of a person's association with Dash-again, as a direct and express result of FinCEN's and DOJ's false characterization. These impacts are affecting all DCG members, to the extent employees and subcontractors of Dash have the option of receiving their salary in Dash cryptocurrency. Of course, as the recent news from Bittrex simply confirms, FinCEN's (and DOJ's) misinformed, off-the-cuff references to Dash as a money laundering risk in official U.S. government documents may lead to additional significant repercussions for DCG members, as mere association with a project deemed to support illicit purposes could (and, by all indications, likely will) lead to further unjustified blacklisting within the United States, and around the world.

5 Conclusion

DCG strongly objects to FinCEN's inclusion of Dash in the NPR as an AEC that poses a law enforcement and national security threat. It is unacceptable to reference Dash in this light, especially where we have-

- proactively reached out to FinCEN to describe how the Dash cryptocurrency works;
- where reputable third parties (with whom we have no connection) have independently confirmed our points;
- where there is no evidence that Dash is actually used in illicit ways;
- where we have received no clarification from FinCEN as to why the agency believes Dash to be an AEC, and where it has never articulated a response to our fact-based arguments.

Meanwhile, we continue to suffer real (and possibly irreversible) harm as a result of the U.S. government's actions.

DCG is available to resolve any questions and is happy to continue to engage with FinCEN. But we respectfully ask you to act quickly. There is simply no justification for the U.S. government's continued behavior in labelling the Dash cryptocurrency an AEC. Until the definitional issue is resolved, please remove any and all references to Dash in the pending Rule (and in any materials surrounding it).

Analyzing FinCEN's Proposed Regulation Relating to AML and KYC Laws

Aaron Wright[1]($^\boxtimes$) and Sachin Meier[2]

[1] Cardozo Law, Yeshiva University, New York City, USA
aaron.wright@yu.edu
[2] Georgetown University, Washington DC, USA

Keywords: FinCEN · Anti-money laundering · Financial crimes · NPRM · Privacy · Bitcoin · Cryptocurrency

1 Introduction

Questions related to anti-money laundering (AML) have pervaded policy conversations around blockchain technology for years. At their core, blockchains enable the rapid exchange of value, whether Bitcoin or other blockchain-based tokens, without the need to provide additional identity related information. With blockchains, value flows across the internet nearly as seamlessly as email and the technology is accessible to anyone with an Internet connection. Users of blockchain technology can remain pseudonymous, raising vexing questions related to the manner in which existing AML and related know-your-customer (KYC) compliance regimes should apply to this emerging technological ecosystem.

AML/KYC-related concerns have been long anticipated by proponents of technology involving strong cryptography, such as blockchains. For example, as far back as 1988, early cypherpunk and researchers Timothy May noted in his "Crypto Anarchist Manifesto" that "[t]he State will of course try to slow or halt the spread of . . . technology [involving strong cryptography], citing national security concerns, use of the technology by drug dealers and tax evaders, and fears of societal disintegration" [1].

As even acknowledged by May, however, "many of these concerns will be valid" [1]. Blockchains create opportunities for technologists to reimagine and improve existing financial systems and its underlying infrastructure. At the same time, they create risks for abuse and misuse.

As the value of digital assets has exploded over the past several years, governments around the globe have begun to increasingly grapple with the question as to how AML/KYC rules should apply to blockchain technology. One of the latest attempts at this question was put forward for public comment by the United States Financial Crimes Enforcement Network (FinCEN), on December 18, 2020, through a notice of proposed rulemaking (the Proposal) along with a short set of FAQs regarding proposed requirements for certain transactions

© International Financial Cryptography Association 2021
M. Bernhard et al. (Eds.): FC 2021 Workshops, LNCS 12676, pp. 54–62, 2021.
https://doi.org/10.1007/978-3-662-63958-0_5

involving convertible virtual currencies (CVC) or digital assets with legal tender status (LTDA).

As discussed below, under the Proposal, if adopted, banks and money service businesses (MSBs) would be required to submit reports, keep records, and verify the identity of customers participating in transactions above certain thresholds involving blockchain-based wallets[1] not hosted by a financial institution (often referred to as "unhosted wallets") or wallets hosted by a financial institution in certain jurisdictions identified by FinCEN.[2]

The purpose of this paper is to provide an overview of FinCEN's latest proposal, outline public comments to this proposal, as well as to highlight certain legal challenges that the Proposal may face if it is adopted in its current form.

2   Overview of FinCEN Proposal

FinCEN is no stranger to grappling with questions relating to digital assets and cryptocurrencies. Starting in 2019, FinCEN issued guidance consolidating regulations, rulings, and prior guidance about digital assets and MSBs under the Bank Secrecy Act. FinCEN has also released an advisory to assist financial institutions in identifying and reporting suspicious activity or criminal use of cryptocurrencies.

The latest proposed rulemaking states that it was created in response to perceived concerns related to criminal actors' use of–and the national security risks posed by–certain digital asset-related transactions, involving assets on public permissionless blockchains. FinCEN cited concern that digital assets were being used to "facilitate international terrorist financing, weapons proliferation, sanctions evasion, and transnational money laundering as well as to buy and sell controlled substances, stolen and fraudulent identification documents and access devices, counterfeit goods, malware and other computer hacking tools, firearms, and toxic chemicals," and engage in ransomware attacks. FinCEN also stated a secondary

---

[1] A "wallet" allows a user to store, send, and receive cryptocurrency.

[2] The Proposal was made pursuant to the Bank Secrecy Act (BSA) and the proposed reporting and recordkeeping rules are similar to the rules for transactions in currency and for bank wire transfers, respectively. Relying on the Administrative Procedure Act's exemption from the 60-day comment period, FinCEN originally provided 15 days for public comment, or until January 4, 2021. However, FinCEN noted that it will endeavor to consider any material comments received after the deadline as well. On January 15, FinCEN extended the comment period for an additional 15 days for comments on the proposed reporting requirements, and for 45 days for comments on the requirement to report counterparty information and the recordkeeping requirements. In so doing, FinCEN noted the volume of comments received, as well as the enactment of the Anti-Money Laundering Act of 2020 (Division F) of Public Law 116-283 (AML Act), which amended 31 USC § 5312(a)(3), the definition of "monetary instruments" in the BSA, on which FinCEN proposes to rely in determining that CVC/LTDA are monetary instruments.

goal for the Proposal to establish controls to protect US national security from various state-sponsored threats, including state-sponsored ransomware and cybersecurity attacks, sanctions evasion, and the financing of global terrorism.

The proposed reporting requirement applies to CVC and LTDA transactions between a bank or MSB and a counterparty where: (1) the transaction exceeds $10,000 in value and (2) the counterparty uses an unhosted or otherwise covered wallet. The Proposal defines "otherwise covered" wallets as those held at a financial institution that is not subject to the BSA and is located in a foreign jurisdiction identified by FinCEN as a jurisdiction of primary money laundering concern, including Burma, Iran, and North Korea.

Transactions between hosted wallets and transactions where the counterparty wallet is hosted by a foreign financial institution, except for a foreign financial institution in a jurisdiction listed on the Foreign Jurisdictions List, would be exempt from the requirements. FinCEN plans to issue a value transaction report form similar to, but distinct from, the existing currency transaction reporting (CTR) form that will require the reporting of information on the filer, transaction, hosted wallet customer, and each counterparty. Pursuant to the Proposal, banks and MSBs will have 15 days from the date on which a reportable transaction occurs to file a report with FinCEN. The Proposal also includes an aggregation requirement if the financial institution has knowledge that a transaction is one of multiple CVC/LTDA transactions involving a single person within a 24-h period that aggregate to value in or value out of greater than $10,000.

In its January notice extending the comment period, FinCEN reiterated that it is not modifying the regulatory definition of "monetary instruments" or otherwise altering existing BSA regulatory requirements applicable to "monetary instruments" in FinCEN's regulations, including the existing CTR requirement and the existing transportation of currency or monetary instruments reporting requirement.

2.1   Recordkeeping and Verification Requirement

If implemented, the Proposal would require banks and MSBs to keep records of a customer's CVC or LTDA transactions and counterparties, and verify the identity of their customers, if a counterparty uses an unhosted or otherwise covered wallet and the transaction is greater than $3,000. They would also be required to verify the identity of the person accessing the customer's account, which may be someone conducting a transaction on the customer's behalf.

Consistent with a bank's or MSB's AML/CFT program, a bank or MSB would need to establish risk-based procedures for verifying their hosted wallet customer's identity that are sufficient to enable the bank or MSB to form a reasonable belief that it knows the true identity of its customer. For example, financial institutions should check FinCEN for the registration of a counterparty that purports to be a regulated MSB and for foreign financial institutions, and "would need to apply reasonable, risk-based, documented procedures to confirm that the foreign financial institution is complying with registration or similar requirements that apply to financial institutions in the foreign jurisdiction."

In addition, banks and MSBs would be expected to incorporate policies tailored to their respective business models should a bank or MSB be unable to obtain the required information, such as by terminating its customer's account in appropriate circumstances. The proposed recordkeeping and verification requirements would not apply to transactions between hosted wallets (except for otherwise covered wallets). Such transactions are already covered under existing AML requirements.

Unlike other recordkeeping requirements, the recordkeeping requirement in the Proposal would require the electronic retention of information based on the fact that such recordkeeping is the practical way in which businesses engaged in CVC or LTDA transactions are likely to track their data and the most efficient form in which data can be provided to law enforcement and national security authorities. Furthermore, the information must be retrievable by the bank or MSB by reference to the name or account number of its customer, or the name of its customer's counterparty.

2.2 Additional Data Collection

Under the Proposal, FinCEN expects that banks and MSBs would be able to employ a single set of information collection and verification procedures to satisfy both the reporting and the recordkeeping requirements. The data to be collected would include the following:

- The name and address of the financial institution's customer
- The type of CVC or LTDA used in the transaction
- The amount of CVC or LTDA in the transaction
- The time of the transaction
- The transaction hash
- The assessed value of the transaction, in US dollars, based on the prevailing exchange rate at the time of the transaction
- Any payment instructions received from the financial institution's customer
- The name and physical address of each counterparty to the transaction of the financial institution's customer
- Other counterparty information the secretary of the US Department of the Treasury may prescribe as mandatory on the reporting form for transactions subject to reporting pursuant to Sect. 1010.316(b)
- Any other information that uniquely identifies the transaction, the accounts, and, to the extent reasonably available, the parties involved
- Any form relating to the transaction that is completed or signed by the financial institution's customer

Notably, the Proposal does not impact direct peer-to-peer (P2P) digital assets or other blockchain-based transactions; rather, it only imposes a reporting and recordkeeping burden on banks and MSBs. However, the requirement will indirectly affect all users of unhosted wallets that engage in any transactions with banks and MSBs, which will be required to gather information from such users in order to comply with the new rule.

FinCEN has said that these new reports will allow law enforcement agencies to protect national security by more quickly and accurately tracking money flows to identify and stop terrorist attacks, drug and human trafficking, and cybercrime. However, there are questions as to whether the rule as written will accomplish these goals when parties generally set up a new wallet even for transactions that are fully compliant with the law. This can make the records kept and reported essentially useless with regard to tracking patterns of money flows to identify and stop bad actors.

3   Analysis of Public Comments

During the comment period, FinCEN received a number of public comments in response to the Proposal, despite a truncated notice and comment period. Roughly 7,500 people and entities submitted comments, the most FinCEN has received on any proposed rulemaking. The comments constitute nearly 70% of all comments FinCEN has received on all rule-makings since 2008 combined. An overwhelming majority of the comments published by members of the blockchain technology industry and individuals strongly opposed to the proposed regulation. Comments poured in from companies, software developers, advocacy groups, and individuals around the globe.

3.1   Institutional Responses

Several well-established institutions provided lengthy comments opposing the Proposal. Organizations at the forefront of the blockchain technology sector, such as Square, River Financial, Coinbase, and Fidelity Digital Assets pushed back against the proposed rulemaking, often highlighting the burdens of increased regulation and accompanying data collection. They also questioned whether the regulation would achieve its stated objective, given a concern that the Proposal failed to account for the technical operation of a blockchain. As pointed out by several institutions and blockchain experts, public blockchain-based wallets are nothing more than an address, raising complex questions related to ownership and control.

In addition, several institutions, including River Financial and Square Crypto, argued that the heightened compliance requirements created a risk that well intentioned individuals off of regulated exchanges and brokerages and onto newer, more user friendly decentralized platforms, due to cost, privacy concerns, or simple ease of use.

The number of users of blockchain-based decentralized finance (DeFi) services, such as decentralized exchanges (DEXs) is expanding. And, the Proposal's additional compliance requirements existing and new users of blockchain technology to migrate over to these newer services. Additional compliance increases the cost of these services and degrades the user experience, creating a motivation for users to migrate to potentially harder to regulate decentralized platforms.

New DeFi protocols such as Uniswap and Sushiswap enable seamless peer-to-peer exchanges in as little as a few clicks. These platforms are permissionless and do not currently incorporate any AML/KYC-related compliance. Volumes on these platforms have grown considerably over the past six months and are beginning to rival centralized exchanges. If regulation creates impediments to the use of centralized exchanges, users could increasingly migrate to these alternative services.

Alternatively, Bitcoin and other digital assets are easy to self-custody, giving customers the power to abandon regulated platforms, if regulatory requirements grow too cumbersome. As a result, the Proposal if implemented, will do "very little to stop bad actors, who face only the minor inconvenience of moving funds to a 'rule-compliant' wallet before moving them again."

3.2 Blockchain Developers

Concern was not raised solely by established institutions. The technologists pioneering and driving the responsible development of blockchain technology raised passionate objections to the Proposal. For example, Matt Corallo, a contributor to Bitcoin Core[3] and an employee of Square Crypto, raised several points about technical difficulties in implementing this rule, due to the inner workings of blockchain tech. For example, the Proposal requires the collection of additional information, but blockchains "do not include built-in mechanisms for banks or other forms of money services businesses to easily retrieve information like names and physical addresses. Due to these limitations, "[t]he only practical way in which a regulated entity could retrieve the counterparty information" would be to "force users to input that information directly when making a transaction."

3.3 Individuals

Users and enthusiasts of blockchain technology submitted the bulk of the public comments, offering comments of varying length and focus. As with institutions and developers, an overwhelming majority of individual responses objected to the Proposal, due to the:

– Burden of compliance
– Data collection and security

---

[3] Bitcoin Core is the reference implementation for Bitcoin. It is the source code which contains the consensus parameters and rules that define the Bitcoin protocol. Nodes run Bitcoin Core software in order to participate in the Bitcoin network. Read more about Bitcoin Core here: https://river.com/learn/what-is-bitcoin-core/.

- Inefficacy of Regulation, and the
- Short comment period[4]

4   Potential Legal Challenges

As highlighted in several public comments, the Proposal may face significant legal challenge in the United States on substantive grounds. The Proposal arguably violates the Fourth Amendment and may fail to comply with international privacy standards by giving the US government access to sensitive financial data beyond what is contemplated by the regulation.

The proposed regulation requires that MSBs collect identifying information associated with wallet addresses and report that information to the government for transactions over a certain threshold. But when the government learns the identity associated with a particular blockchain-based wallet, it also gains the ability to learn the identity associated with all transactions for that address (which are publicly viewable on a given blockchain), even when the amounts of those transactions are far below the Proposal's contemplated reporting threshold. While the identity associated with the counterparties to those other transactions may not always be known, the government's database may well also contain that information because of the breadth of the proposed regulation. This could deanonymize all transactions on a blockchain, encroaching financial privacy.

In addition, any data collected by FinCEN could become a honeypot of information that tempts bad actors, or those who might misuse it beyond its original intended use. Indeed, thousands of FinCEN's own files were recently exposed to the public, raising questions as to FinCEN's security protocols. If sensitive data relating to blockchain users was made available to ill intentioned actors, blockchain users could face cybersecurity hacks, thefts, or other intrusions on financial privacy.

4.1   Fourth Amendment Concerns

The proposed regulation arguably violates the Fourth Amendment's protections for individual privacy. Historically, courts in the US have held that consumers lose their privacy rights in the data they entrust with third parties under the "third party doctrine". However, courts increasingly have become skeptical of these pre-digital decisions, reflecting evolving societal norms around privacy expectations.

---

[4] Institutions and individuals also complained about FinCEN's unusually short and poorly timed comment period. Coinbase published an entire comment solely dedicated to this issue, and requested that FinCEN extend the comment period to the traditional 60-day timespan. FinCEN initially released the 72-page Proposal in late December, such that the comment period would take place across Christmas Eve, Christmas Day, New Year's Eve, and New Year's Day. This circumstance provided minimal time for companies to digest the Proposal and formulate a proper, comprehensive response to the many flaws of the Proposal.

For example, the Supreme Court has begun to narrow the US's approach to the third-party doctrine, going so far as to note that "it may be necessary to reconsider the premise that an individual has no reasonable expectation of privacy in information voluntarily disclosed to third parties" [4]. Indeed, in California Bankers Association v. Shultz, the Supreme Court noted that, "[f]inancial transactions can reveal much about a person's activities, associations, and beliefs. At some point, governmental intrusion upon these areas would implicate legitimate expectations of privacy" [5].

Due to the public and traceable nature of public blockchain, the Proposal runs the risk of dramatically increasing the scope of the government's knowledge about US blockchain user's financial privacy, potentially raising Fourth Amendment concerns.

4.2 International Privacy Concerns

The expanded reach of the proposed regulation likely will create new tensions with existing privacy and data protection law outside the United States. As noted above, obtaining the identity of the owner of a wallet often provides sufficient information to identify the wallet owner's previous transactional records, enabling the holder of this information to glean a greater range of information about the private lives and financial habits of the individuals or entities concerned.

Due to the nature of a blockchain, the contemplated disclosures would enable the government to gain access to a wider set of financial data, more than the identity of a given wallet's owner. Government access to such broad ranging financial data may trigger legal safeguards under international and foreign laws, which may require independent judicial authorization or the only permit the collection of such information with judicial consent, additional notifications, or other requirements.

The current proposal does not outline how this regulation would seek to resolve such potential conflicts of law between the United States and other jurisdictions. Without such clarity, there is a risk that the enforcement of these broader regulations would lead to legal challenges in Europe and elsewhere creating further legal uncertainty.

5   Conclusion

FinCEN's Proposal aims to limit criminal and other socially undesirable activity through additional disclosure and reporting, in an attempt to create more reliable and trustworthy marketplaces where both blockchain technologists and existing entities can participate. However, as reflected in public comments, these additional requirements create practical challenges, due to the nature of the technology and the increased cost of compliance–both for covered entities and users. The Proposal may also face legal scrutiny in the US, given the potential breath of data collection available, and may create tensions with privacy and other data collection laws of other jurisdictions, requiring either further harmonization or creating a patchwork approach for entities operating globally.

Even if these practical and legal challenges are somehow addressed, users may choose to rely on more decentralized and emerging DeFi alternatives, due to simple ease of use, creating even more challenging regulatory concerns that would require an alternative approach to regulation. At the end, there would be a hard-to-navigate patchwork of legal rules and regulations that would not be consistent across different blockchain-related projects, companies, and use cases.

References

1. May, T.: The Crypto Anarchist Manifesto. https://www.activism.net/cypherpunk/crypto-anarchy.html
2. Scheiber, N., Flitter, E.: Banks Suspected Illegal Activity, but Processed Big Transactions Anyway, New York Times (2020). Available at https://www.nytimes.com/2020/09/20/business/fincen-banks-suspicious-activity-reports-buzzfeed.html
3. Nakamoto, S.: Bitcoin: a peer-to-peer electronic cash system. https://bitcoin.org/bitcoin.pdf (2008)
4. US v. Jones, 565 U.S. 400, 132 S. Ct. 945, 181 L. Ed. 2d 911 (2012)
5. California Bankers Assn. v. Shultz, 416 U.S. 21, 94 S. Ct. 1494, 39 L. Ed. 2d 812 (1974)

DeFi – Protocol Design

Optimal Fees for Geometric Mean Market Makers

Alex Evans[1(✉)], Guillermo Angeris[2], and Tarun Chitra[3]

[1] Bain Capital, Boston, MA 02116, USA
aevans@baincapital.com
[2] Stanford University, Stanford, CA 94305, USA
angeris@stanford.edu
[3] Gauntlet Network, New York, NY 11201, USA
tarun@gauntlet.network

Abstract. Constant Function Market Makers (CFMMs) are a family
of automated market makers that enable censorship-resistant decentralized exchange on public blockchains. Arbitrage trades have been shown
to align the prices reported by CFMMs with those of external markets. These trades impose costs on Liquidity Providers (LPs) who supply
reserves to CFMMs. Trading fees have been proposed as a mechanism
for compensating LPs for arbitrage losses. However, large fees reduce
the accuracy of the prices reported by CFMMs and can cause reserves to
deviate from desirable asset compositions. CFMM designers are therefore
faced with the problem of how to optimally select fees to attract liquidity.
We develop a framework for determining the value to LPs of supplying
liquidity to a CFMM with fees when the underlying process follows a
general diffusion. Focusing on a popular class of CFMMs which we call
Geometric Mean Market Makers (G3Ms), our approach also allows one to
select optimal fees for maximizing LP value. We illustrate our methodology by showing that an LP with mean-variance utility will prefer a G3M
over all alternative trading strategies as fees approach zero.

1 Introduction

Constant Function Market Makers (CFMMs) [2] are a family of automated market makers that enable censorship-resistant decentralized exchange on public
blockchains. In CFMMs, Liquidity Providers (LPs) supply assets (reserves) to
an on-chain smart contract. The smart contract makes reserves available for
swaps, executing a trade only if it preserves some function of reserves, known
as 'the invariant.' For example, Uniswap [1] only permits trades that preserve
the product of reserves (the product of reserve quantities must be the same
before and after a trade). Similarly, Balancer only permits trades that preserve
the weighted geometric mean of reserves. LPs are entitled to a pro-rata share of
the CFMM's reserves, as well as any trading fees that the CFMM collects. As
of this writing, CFMMs have attracted billions of dollars worth of reserves and
trade over \$1 Billion worth of cryptocurrency daily [12]. The rapid growth in

© International Financial Cryptography Association 2021
M. Bernhard et al. (Eds.): FC 2021 Workshops, LNCS 12676, pp. 65–79, 2021.
https://doi.org/10.1007/978-3-662-63958-0_6

the value deposited in CFMMs has allowed these protocols to regularly compete with established centralized exchanges on the basis of liquidity [6]. At the same time, this growth has raised questions of efficiency, including how to optimally utilize reserves and how to select parameters for attracting liquidity and trading volume.

Under fairly general conditions, the prices reported by CFMMs have been shown to closely track those of external, more liquid markets [2]. Because the price reported by a CFMM is a function of reserves, this "oracle" property requires an arbitrageur to maximize profit by adjusting reserves to align the CFMM's price with that of the external market. Because reserves are adjusted in response to price changes on the external market, the asset composition that Liquidity Providers (LPs) are entitled to is continually rebalanced. Protocols such as Balancer take advantage of this property to offer LPs payoffs that resemble constant-mix portfolios [16]. While LPs may benefit from rebalancing their portfolio to a target allocation, they also bear the cost of arbitrage transactions. In response, most CFMMs charge fees for incoming trades. However, fees make arbitrage less profitable, leading to only partial adjustment of reserves in response to price changes. This allows asset compositions to stray further from their desired allocations and reduces the accuracy of the prices reported by the CFMM. As a result, fees may in fact reduce the value LPs receive in certain cases. Given these trade-offs, CFMM designers are faced with the problem of how to assess the impact of fees on LP value and how to select optimal fees for attracting liquidity.

Our analysis focuses on Geometric Mean Market Makers (G3Ms), which include most popular CFMMs used in practice, including Uniswap, Sushiswap and Balancer [1,16]. G3Ms require that the reserves of the CFMM before and after each trade must have the same (weighted) geometric mean. As a by-product of arbitrage, the proportion of value deposited in the constant-mean CFMM for a given asset closely tracks the weight applied to the asset when calculating the weighted geometric mean [16]. This property resembles a constant-mix portfolio and simplifies the analysis of Liquidity Provider (LP) returns. G3Ms allow us to model weight dynamics directly in the presence of fees. It has recently been shown that G3Ms can replicate a wide variety of trading strategies, including options payouts, using dynamic weights [13]. Our analysis therefore extends naturally to a large class of LP payouts that can be represented by G3Ms.

Prior Work. Prior work on LP returns in CFMMs has primarily focused on the case where no fees are charged. In [13], it is shown LPs in G3Ms with no fees underperform equivalent constant-mix portfolios due to arbitrage. However, the case with fees is more involved as path independence is typically not satisfied. This question was addressed in [18] for the case of a Uniswap LP seeking to maximize the growth rate of wealth when the underlying price process follows a geometric Brownian motion. This model assumes a particular functional form of the fee and shows that LPs can generate positive geometric growth with any non-zero fee provided that the mean and volatility are bounded in a suitable manner. The result holds for the specific case where the objective of the LP is to maximize the expected logarithm of reserve value when the underlying price process follows a geometric Brownian motion with certain mean and volatility constants. Our approach extends this setting to general diffusions and LP objective functions.

A separate line of work has applied conventional microstructure models to the problem of LP profitability, positing a game between LPs and informed traders to estimate profitability conditions for Uniswap [5]. This framework is generalized to arbitrary CFMMs in [3], where it is shown that the curvature of the CFMM's trading function can be used to bound LP profitability. Our results apply to the case where the trader has perfect information and extracts risk-free profit at the expense of the LP. We show that there are general conditions under which the effect of arbitrage on the LP's value function approaches zero for small fees.

Optimal Control and Portfolio Optimization. While constant-mix portfolios produce excess growth due to rebalancing, no-fee G3Ms have been shown to divert this growth to arbitrageurs in order to incentivize continual rebalancing [13]. While arbitrage losses are limited by increasing the fee that the G3M charges, this also limits the amount of rebalancing that arbitrageurs are incentivized to perform. We seek to formalize the impact of this trade-off on the value LPs receive from the G3M.

The problem of optimal portfolio selection in continuous time is well-studied in financial optimization, starting with the classical investment-consumption of Merton [17]. There are numerous extensions to the classical model that incorporate the impact of proportional transaction costs [7, 11, 15]. In this setting, it is shown that the optimal investment policy involves a no-trade region around the optimal portfolio weight [8–10]. In a G3M, an LP does not have direct control over reserves and relies on an arbitrageur for rebalancing reserves to the target asset proportions. It is shown in [4] that the arbitrageur takes no action inside a no-arbitrage interval around the desired weight. However, the cost to the LP at the boundary is not proportional to the dollar value of rebalancing required.

The passive nature of LP rebalancing and non-proportional costs complicate the problem of optimal portfolio strategies for G3Ms. Classical rebalancing [15] assumes that the portfolio holder actively trades to adjust their portfolio weights. Unlike traditional portfolio optimization, G3M arbitrageurs adjust the portfolio with the aim of extracting a profit at the expense of LPs. In this work, we provide a solution to this problem by explicitly modeling the arbitrage costs incurred at the boundary of the no-trade region for different levels of the fee. Our approach is inspired by the stochastic control problems used in traditional portfolio optimization. These methods are often used in reinforcement learning, portfolio analysis, and recently in decentralized finance (DeFi) [14].

Summary. We study the value to LPs of contributing capital to a G3M with fees. We consider the dynamics of the portfolio proportions as a function of time and fees assuming arbitrageurs trade against the CFMM to maximize profit. We show that the proportion of G3M value held in a given asset fluctuates freely within an interval where arbitrage is unprofitable. If the state variable exits this interval, an arbitrage opportunity arises to return it a point in the interior of the interval. We explicitly calculate the cost of this adjustment and show that it vanishes to first order when the state process has continuous sample paths. The observation allows one to compute the value to the LP for a given choice of fee by solving a differential equation subject to two conditions that hold at the boundary of the no-arbitrage interval. We illustrate this approach for the specific example of maximizing mean-variance utility for a geometric Brownian motion and demonstrate how to optimize the resulting value.

2   Problem Description

In the arbitrage game, we have two players, each of whom trades in a two-asset economy: the liquidity provider, who is interested in minimizing some penalty function depending on the portfolio weights and an arbitrageur who trades against the liquidity provider's assets (and therefore, as a side effect, changes the portfolio weight).

Penalty Function. We will define the *penalty function* $\phi : \mathbf{R} \to \mathbf{R} \cup \{+\infty\}$ which depends on the portfolio weight $w \in [0,1]$ for a given coin. The penalty function maps the weight to a liquidity provider's loss; *i.e.*, we can view the function ϕ as the 'tracking error' common in the control literature. We will assume that ϕ has a minimizer $w^\star \in [0,1]$ such that $\phi(w^\star) \leq \phi(w)$ for all $w \in [0,1]$.

Portfolio Weight Dynamics. The portfolio weight is, in general, a stochastic process that evolves in time, which we will write as $w_t \in [0,1]$ at time t. We will assume a discretization in time, with steps of size $h > 0$ and later recover continuous results by taking the appropriate limits, such that $t = 0, h, 2h, \ldots$. In this case, we will assume a basic model with increments given by

$$\xi_t(w,h) = a(w)h + b(w)\varepsilon_t\sqrt{h}, \quad t = 0, h, \ldots,$$

where $\varepsilon_t \sim \{\pm 1\}$ with equal probability. (For example, if $a(w) = 0$ and $b(w) = 1$ for any w, then as $h \downarrow 0$ we have that $\sum_{n=1}^{\tau/h} \xi_{nh}$ converges weakly to a standard Brownian motion over time τ.) Then, the dynamics of the weights will be given by some function $F : \mathbf{R} \times \mathbf{R} \to \mathbf{R}$:

$$w_{t+h} = F(w_t, \xi_t(w_t, h)), \quad t = 0, h, \ldots,$$

where F is a function that models the arbitrage dynamics; *i.e.*, the arbitrageur sees a change in the portfolio weight of ξ_t and performs arbitrage which results in some new weight w_{t+h}. We will often abuse notation slightly by writing ξ_t instead of $\xi_t(w_t, h)$ to improve readability.

As a side note, we will be very informal regarding different types of convergence in the presentation and will freely switch expectations, limits, and derivatives, along with assuming that all functions are 'nice enough.' While we will mostly work with the discrete approximations, some limits taken at the end will require justification—a reader familiar with stochastic processes and basic analysis should be able to insert the corresponding theorems as necessary, but we will not discuss them further.

Arbitrage Loss and Total Expected Loss. By definition, the arbitrageur is guaranteed nonnegative profit at every time t by exploiting the change in portfolio weights from time t to $t+h$. We can (conversely) view this as a penalty incurred by the LP which we will call the *adjustment cost*, defined by a nonnegative function $C : \mathbf{R} \times \mathbf{R} \to \mathbf{R}_+$. A simple interpretation for $C(w_t, \xi_t) \geq 0$ is that it is the cost at time t, incurred by the LP, for adjusting the would-be portfolio weights $w_t + \xi_t$ to some different weight w_{t+h}.

This lets us write the expected loss for a liquidity provider, starting at weight $w \in [0,1]$:

$$J(w) = \mathbf{E}\left[\sum_{n=0}^{\infty} e^{-nhr}(\phi(w_{nh})h + C(w_{nh}, \xi_{nh})) \,\middle|\, w_0 = w\right], \tag{1}$$

where $w_{t+h} = F(w_t, \xi_t)$. Here, r is the continuous discounting rate, such that e^{-rt} is the amount discounted at time t.

A (Tight) Lower Bound. A simple lower bound on the expected loss J comes from the fact that $\phi(w_{nh}) \geq \phi(w^\star)$, by definition of $\phi(w^\star)$, and $C(w_{nh}, \xi_{nh}) \geq 0$ by definition of the adjustment cost C, which implies that the expected loss is bounded from below by:

$$J(w) \geq \sum_{n=0}^{\infty} e^{-nhr} \phi(w^\star) h.$$

If ϕ is normalized such that $\phi(w^\star) = 0$ (this can be done without loss of generality by replacing $\phi(w)$ with $\phi(w) - \phi(w^\star)$), this simplifies to:

$$J(w) \geq 0.$$

The remainder of the paper shows that, in fact, this simple bound becomes asymptotically tight as the fees approach, but do not equal, zero. (We will see soon how such fees connect to the problem.) This would immediately imply that the liquidity provider's losses are minimized by reducing the fees as much as possible, while ensuring they are not zero.

No-Fee Interval. In general, CFMMs have a *no-fee interval* (which is a function of the fees) where no possible weight adjustment is profitable for arbitrageurs [2, 4]. For most CFMMs, and, more specifically, for the G3Ms we study here, the no-fee interval $[w_D, w_U] \subseteq [0,1]$ has nonempty interior when the fee is nonzero; *i.e.*, $w_D < w_U$. This condition implies that, if the portfolio weight w_t lies in the interior of the interval, any vanishingly small change will not be adjusted and incurs no losses. More formally, if $w_D < w_t < w_U$, then

$$w_{t+h} = F(w_t, \xi_t) = w_t + \xi_t \quad \text{and} \quad C(w_t, \xi_t) = 0, \tag{2}$$

for all h small enough, since $\xi_t \sim O(h^{1/2})$ by definition. We will show this is true for all G3Ms in Sect. 3.

Differential Equation Limit. While (1) is a complete description of our problem, it is in general not easy to analyze directly. On the other hand, in a similar way to dynamic programming, we can write $J(w_t)$ in terms of the current cost at time t plus a discounted expectation of $J(w_{t+h})$ given w_t:

$$J(w) = \phi(w)h + \mathbf{E}[C(w, \xi_t) \mid w_t = w] + e^{-rh}\, \mathbf{E}[J(w_{t+h}) \mid w_t = w].$$

By rearranging and dividing both sides by h, we find that

$$e^{-rh}\, \mathbf{E}\left[\frac{J(w_{t+h}) - J(w)}{h} \,\bigg|\, w_t = w \right] + \phi(w) \tag{3}$$

$$+ \frac{\mathbf{E}[C(w, \xi_t) \mid w_t = w]}{h} - \frac{1 - e^{-rh}}{h} J(w) = 0.$$

Note that, if w lies in the interior of the no-arbitrage integral, $w_D < w < w_U$, then the limit as $h \downarrow 0$ implies that $C(w, \xi_t)/h = 0$, since $\xi_t \downarrow 0$ and $C(w, \xi_t) = 0$ for all ξ_t small enough, from (2). Similarly, since $w_{t+h} = w_t + \xi_t$ for all ξ_t small enough, we have

$$\lim_{h \downarrow 0} \mathbf{E}\left[\frac{J(w_{t+h}) - J(w)}{h} \,\bigg|\, w_t = w \right] = a(w)J'(w) + \frac{b(w)^2}{2} J''(w),$$

which follows from Taylor expanding $J(w_{t+h}) = J(w + \xi_t)$ into its linear and quadratic terms, as ξ_t is on the order of $h^{1/2}$, and taking the corresponding expectation. This means that the final limit of (3) as $h \downarrow 0$, is the following differential equation:

$$a(w)J'(w) + \frac{b^2(w)}{2} J''(w) + \phi(w) - rJ(w) = 0, \tag{4}$$

whenever $w_D < w < w_U$. In order to solve this differential equation, we will also need appropriate boundary conditions which will depend on the specifics of the CFMM we are considering. In our case, we will show that

$$J'(w_D) = J'(w_U) = 0, \tag{5}$$

is satisfied.

3   Fees for G3Ms

In this section, we will provide a specific application of the framework provided in Sect. 2 in order to show that a G3M with appropriately chosen weights will always have an optimal fee that is as small as possible without being zero.

Constant Function Market Makers. A constant function market maker is defined by its reserves $R_\alpha(t)$ of coin α and $R_\beta(t)$ of coin β at time t. Traders can trade with the CFMM (and therefore liquidity providers' funds) by proposing a trade $\Delta_\alpha \geq 0$ of coin α and $\Delta_\beta \leq 0$ of coin β to the CFMM. The trade is accepted if the CFMM's *trading function* defined by $\psi : \mathbf{R}_+ \times \mathbf{R}_+ \to \mathbf{R}$ satisfies

$$\psi(R_\alpha(t) + \gamma_2 \Delta_\alpha, R_\beta(t) + \Delta_\beta) = \psi(R_\alpha(t), R_\beta(t)).$$

(*i.e.*, it is 'kept constant.') Here $(1 - \gamma)$ is the fee, which must satisfy $0 < \gamma \leq 1$. If, instead, we wish to trade $\Delta_\alpha \leq 0$ for $\Delta_\beta \geq 0$, we would instead switch the fee to the incoming coin β, *i.e.*, the trade is accepted if

$$\psi(R_\alpha(t) + \Delta_\alpha, R_\beta(t) + \gamma_1 \Delta_\beta) = \psi(R_\alpha(t), R_\beta(t)).$$

If the trade $(\Delta_\alpha, \Delta_\beta)$ satisfies either equation, then the CFMM takes Δ_α from the trader (if $\Delta_\alpha \geq 0$, otherwise it pays out Δ_α) and pays out $\Delta_\beta \geq 0$ (as before), updating its reserves to

$$R_\alpha(t + h) = R_\alpha(t) + \Delta_\alpha \quad \text{and} \quad R_\beta(t + h) = R_\beta(t) + \Delta_\beta.$$

For more information on CFMMs see, *e.g.*, [2].

In the special case of G3Ms, which is the case we consider in the remainder of the paper, we have the specific trading function:

$$\psi(R_\alpha, R_\beta) = R_\alpha^{1-\theta} R_\beta^\theta,$$

where $0 < \theta < 1$ is called the weight parameter. We derive explicit formulas for w_U, w_D and the adjustment costs in this case in Appendix § A.

Portfolio Value and Weight. The definition of the *portfolio value* of liquidity providers for the CFMM is the total present market value of reserves. If asset β has some market value $S(t)$ at time t, then the portfolio value is given by

$$R_\alpha(t) + S(t) R_\beta,$$

and the *portfolio weight* (of coin β) of the liquidity providers is defined as

$$w_t = \frac{R_\beta(t) S(t)}{R_\alpha(t) + R_\beta(t) S(t)}.$$

In other words, w_t is the total proportion of wealth allocated to asset β with respect to the complete porfolio.

Price Process. We will compute the optimal fees when the price of the risky asset follows

$$S(t + h) = S(t) \left[(\mu - r)h + \sigma \varepsilon_t \sqrt{h} \right], \tag{6}$$

where $\varepsilon_t \sim \{\pm 1\}$ is uniform and μ, r and σ are constants that represent the growth rate, discounting rate, and volatility, respectively. (We will later take $h \downarrow 0$ such that $S(t)$ converges to a geometric Brownian motion.)

When no adjustments occur by the arbitrageur, there is no trade performed and so $R_\alpha(t) = R_\alpha$ and $R_\beta(t) = R_\beta$ are constant from t to $t + h$. So, the corresponding dynamics of w_t can be derived in the limit of small h:

$$w_{t+h} - w_t = w_t(1 - w_t)(\mu - r - w_t\sigma^2)h + w_t(1 - w_t)\sigma\varepsilon_t\sqrt{h} + O(h^{3/2}). \quad (7)$$

Through a discrete approximation, we prove the boundary conditions (5) for these weight dynamics in Appendix § B.

Penalty Function. We assume the penalty function is given by

$$\phi(w_t) = \frac{1}{2}\lambda\sigma^2(w_t - w^*)^2 \quad (8)$$

for some constant w^*. This functional form is used in [15] and conforms with the assumption that LP has mean-variance preferences over rates of return to wealth with risk aversion parameter λ. In particular, we note that this expression generalizes the setting considered in [18] where one seeks to maximize the growth rate of LP wealth. To see this, note the expected logarithm of wealth satisfies

$$\frac{1}{T}\mathbf{E}[\ln(W(T)/W(0)] = \frac{1}{T}\int_0^T (w_s(\mu - r) - \frac{1}{2}\sigma^2 w_s)ds.$$

Through a standard procedure, this expectation can be shown to be maximized by fixing $w^* = \frac{\mu - r}{\sigma^2}$. Substituting this value when taking the difference between the growth rate at w^* and w,

$$[(\mu - r)w^* - \frac{1}{2}\sigma^2(w^*)^2]dt - [(\mu - r)w_t - \frac{1}{2}\sigma^2 w_t^2]dt = \frac{1}{2}\sigma^2(w - w^*)^2 dt,$$

which (8) for the special case of $\lambda = 1$.

Approximation. We consider the case when $w_t \approx w^*$ which will provide a close approximation for small fees. When this is true, we can approximate (7) by

$$w_{t+h} - w_t = w_t a h + w_t b d\varepsilon_t\sqrt{h},$$

where

$$a = (1 - w^*)(\mu - r - w^*\sigma^2), \qquad b = (1 - w^*)\sigma.$$

The equation in (4) simplifies to Euler-Cauchy form and has an explicit solution given in [15],

$$J(w, \gamma_1, \gamma_2) = \frac{1}{2}\lambda\sigma^2\left[\frac{w^2}{r - 2a - b^2} - \frac{2ww*}{r - a} + \frac{(w^*)^2}{r}\right] + C_1 w^{z_1} + C_2 w^{z_2}. \quad (9)$$

where

$$z_1 = \frac{\frac{b^2}{2} - a + \sqrt{(a - \frac{b^2}{2})^2 + 2b^2 r}}{b^2}, \qquad z_2 = \frac{\frac{b^2}{2} - a - \sqrt{(a - \frac{b^2}{2})^2 + 2b^2 r}}{b^2}$$

Determining Optimal Values. Note that (4) and (5) will hold for all values of γ_1 and γ_2. For the optimal values, we show in Sect. C that

$$J_{11}(w_U, \gamma_1, \gamma_2) = J_{11}(w_D, \gamma_1, \gamma_2) = 0. \tag{10}$$

Using the conditions in (5) and (10), we will determine the values of the coefficients C_1, C_2 in (9) as well as the optimal values for γ_1 and γ_2. One can check that the (numerical) maxima happen when γ_1 and γ_2 both approach 1 (zero fee). However, the system of equations has no solution as C_1 and C_2 are undefined for $\gamma_1 = \gamma_2 = 1$. Taking the limit as $(\gamma_1, \gamma_2) \rightarrow (1^-, 1^-)$, one can show that $J(w, \gamma_1, \gamma_2)$ approaches zero, implying that no cost is incurred relative to the optimal strategy (Fig. 1).

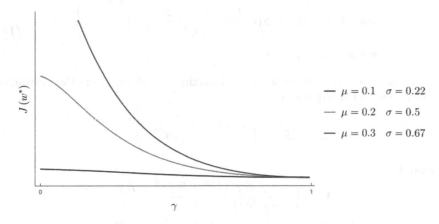

Fig. 1. Cost function for $J(w^\star)$ when the LP seeks to minimize the penalty on the rate of wealth growth ($\lambda = 1$) and fees are equal regardless of trading direction $\gamma = \gamma_1 = \gamma_2$. We plot different mean-variance pairs that each satisfy $w^\star = \frac{1}{2}$. Higher volatility increases the relative cost incurred for higher values of the fee, for every choice $J(w^\star)$ is brought close to zero as the fee approaches zero (while the function is not continuous at $\gamma = 1$)

4   Conclusion

Fees are a critical component of LP value in CFMMs. Fees offset the cost of arbitrage, but also reduce the extent of rebalancing performed. We formalize this trade-off through a control-inspired approach that allows us to explicitly derive a solution for LP value for given fee choices. This solution also allows us to make the optimal choice of fees for maximizing value for the LP. In the example where the LP faces a quadratic tracking error for asset prices following geometric Brownian motion, we show that costs are minimized as fees approach zero. Our result applies to all G3Ms and allows one to derive results for general LP objective functions when the underlying asset price dynamics are governed by a continuous process.

A G3M Arbitrage Results

When the arbitrageur adds reserves of the risky asset, we have the following constant geometric mean formula,

$$(R_\alpha - \Delta_\alpha)^{1-\theta}(R_\beta + \gamma_1 \Delta_\beta)^\theta = R_\alpha^{1-\theta} R_\beta^\theta.$$

Solving for Δ_β,

$$\Delta_\beta = \frac{1}{\gamma_1} R_\beta \left(\left(\frac{R_\alpha}{R_\alpha - \Delta_\alpha} \right)^{\frac{1-\theta}{\theta}} - 1 \right)$$

The aribtrageur's problem is therefore

$$\text{maximize} \quad \Delta_\alpha - S(t)\frac{1}{\gamma_1} R_\beta \left(\left(\frac{R_\alpha}{R_\alpha - \Delta_\alpha} \right)^{\frac{1-\theta}{\theta}} - 1 \right) \tag{11}$$

$$\text{subject to} \quad \Delta_\alpha \geq 0$$

As in [4], we note that the unconstrained maxima are those where the derivative of (11) is zero. This happens when

$$\Delta_\alpha = R_\alpha - \left(\frac{1-\theta}{\gamma_1 \theta} S(t) R_\beta R_\alpha^{\frac{1-\theta}{\theta}} \right)^\theta. \tag{12}$$

This implies

$$\Delta_\beta = \left(\frac{\theta}{1-\theta}\frac{R_\alpha}{S(t)} \right)^{1-\theta} \left(\frac{R_\beta}{\gamma_1} \right)^\theta - \frac{R_\beta}{\gamma_1}.$$

Substituting this back into the objective of (11) and simplifying, we get that the total arbitrage profit for the trader

$$R_\alpha - \frac{1}{\theta^\theta(1-\theta)^{1-\theta}} R_\alpha^{1-\theta} \left(\frac{S(t)R_\beta}{\gamma_1} \right)^\theta + \frac{S(t)R_\beta}{\gamma_1}$$

Scaling to total LP wealth $S(t)R_\beta + R_\alpha$,

$$C_d = (1 - w(t)) - \frac{1}{\theta^\theta(1-\theta)^{1-\theta}} \left(\frac{w(t)}{\gamma_1} \right)^\theta (1 - w(t))^{1-\theta} + \frac{w(t)}{\gamma_1}, \tag{13}$$

where $w(t) = \frac{S(t)R_\beta}{S(t)R_\beta + R_\alpha}$, the fraction of LP wealth in the risky asset prior to rebalancing. No-arbitrage requires that $\Delta \leq 0$ in (12), which implies

$$w(t) \geq \frac{\gamma_1 \theta}{1 - \theta + \gamma_1 \theta} = w_D$$

After this adjustment, the quantities are updated to $R_\alpha \mapsto R_\alpha - \Delta_\alpha$ and $R_\beta \mapsto R_\beta + \Delta_\beta$. The weight after the adjustment is given by

$$w_d(t) = \frac{(R_\beta + \Delta_\beta)S}{(R_\beta + \Delta_\beta)S + R_\alpha - \Delta_\alpha}$$

Which we can rewrite as

$$w_d(t) = \frac{1 + \gamma_1^\theta \left(\frac{1-\theta}{\theta} \frac{w(t)}{1-w(t)} \right)^{1-\theta} (1 - \gamma_1^{-1})}{\frac{1}{\theta} + \gamma_1^\theta \left(\frac{1-\theta}{\theta} \frac{w(t)}{1-w(t)} \right)^{1-\theta} (1 - \gamma_1^{-1})} \tag{14}$$

When adding units of the numéraire in exchange for the risky asset, the constant geometric mean gives

$$(R_\alpha + \gamma_2 \Delta_\alpha)^{1-\theta} (R_\beta - \Delta_\beta)^\theta = R_\alpha^{1-\theta} R_\beta^\theta.$$

Through a similar procedure, it is possible to show

$$C_u = \frac{1}{\gamma_2}(1 - w(t)) - \frac{1}{\theta^\theta (1-\theta)^{1-\theta}} \left(\frac{1}{\gamma_2}(1 - w(t)) \right)^{1-\theta} w(t)^\theta + w(t), \tag{15}$$

and

$$w(t) \le \frac{\theta}{\gamma_2(1 - \theta) + \theta}.$$

The weight after the adjustment is given by

$$w_u(t) = \frac{1}{\frac{1}{\theta} + \left(\gamma_2 \frac{1-\theta}{\theta} \right)^{1-\theta} \left(\frac{1-w(t)}{w(t)} \right)^\theta (1 - \gamma_2^{-1})}.$$

B   Proof of Boundary Conditions

We proceed by a discrete approximation of the problem and derive the associated boundary conditions at the limit. Analogous to [8,9], we divide time into discrete intervals of length τ and state into steps of size ξ. In what follows, we will approximate the weight variable in a slightly different way, but will still recover (3) at the limit; here, for each i, we will have

$$w_{i+1} - w_i = \xi.$$

We approximate the unadjusted weight process with a random walk. Starting from w_i, the next step after τ units of time have passed will be w_{i-1}, with probability p, and w_{i+1}, with probability $q = 1 - p$. If we suppose these probabilities satisfy

$$aw_i\tau = q\xi + p(-\xi),$$

then this implies

$$p = \frac{1}{2}(1 - aw_i\tau/\xi), \qquad q = \frac{1}{2}(1 + aw_i\tau/\xi).$$

The variance is given by

$$b^2 w_i^2 \tau = q(\xi - aw_i\tau)^2 + p(\xi + aw_i\tau)^2 = \xi^2 - a^2 w_i^2 \tau^2.$$

Keeping only the leading term, $b^2 w_i^2 \tau = \xi^2$, and taking the limit as τ and ξ tend to zero, we recover the process in (3). From §A, we have the boundaries of the no-arbitrage interval,

$$\frac{\gamma_1 w^*}{1 - w^* + \gamma_1 w^*} = w_D, \qquad \frac{w^*}{\gamma_2(1 - w^*) + w^*} = w_U.$$

The random walk proceeds unadjusted on the states $i = D + 1, .., U - 1$. If the process is at D and takes a step to the right, again no arbitrage adjustment occurs. If, however, the process moves to $D - 1$, then arbitrage instantaneously adjusts the weight to w_d in (14). At $i = D$ the next step will be w_{D+1}, with probability p, and w_d with probability $q = 1 - p$. Similarly, at the upper boundary, we will have w_{U-1} with probability p, and w_u, with probability $q = 1 - p$. Therefore, at the boundary point w_U, we have

$$J(w_U) = f(w_U)\tau + e^{-r\tau} p J(w_{U-1}) + e^{-r\tau} q J(w_u(\xi)) - q C_u(\xi),$$

where

$$C_u(\xi) = \frac{1}{\gamma_2}(1 - w_U - \xi) - \frac{(1 - w_U - \xi)^{1-w^*}}{\gamma_2(w^*)^{w^*}(1 - w^*)^{1-w^*}}(w_U + \xi)^{w^*} + w_U + \xi, \quad (16)$$

and

$$w_u(\xi) = \frac{1}{\frac{1}{w^*} + \left(\gamma_2 \frac{1-w^*}{w^*}\right)^{1-w^*} \left(\frac{1-W_U-\xi}{W_U+\xi}\right)^{w^*} (1 - \gamma_2^{-1})}.$$

Rearranging terms and multiplying by $e^{r\tau}$

$$e^{r\tau} J(w_U) - p J(w_{U-1}) - q J(w_u(\xi)) = e^{r\tau} f(w_U)\tau - e^{r\tau} q C_u(\xi)).$$

Expanding on the right side and noting that τ is $o(\xi)$,

$$\tau[1 + r\tau + o(\tau)]f(w_U) - \frac{1}{2}(1 + a\xi/(w_U b^2))[1 + r\tau + o(\tau)]C_u(\xi)$$

$$= -\frac{1}{2}(1 + a\xi/(w_U b^2))C_u(\xi) + o(\xi).$$

Expanding on the left side,

$$[1 + r\tau + o(\tau)]J(w_U) - p[J(w_U) - J_1(w_U)\xi + o(\xi)] + q J(w_u(\xi))$$
$$= q[J(w_U) - J(w_u(\xi))] + p J_1(w_U) + o(\xi)$$
$$= \frac{1}{2}(1 + a\xi/(w_U b^2))[J(w_U) - J(w_u(\xi))] + \frac{1}{2}(1 - a\xi/(w_U b^2))J_1(w_U)\xi + o(\xi)$$
$$= \frac{1}{2}\left([J(w_U) - J(w_u(\xi))] + \frac{a\xi}{w_U b^2}[J(w_U) - J(w_u(\xi))] + J_1(w_U)\xi\right) + o(\xi).$$

Next, we divide both sides by ξ and take the limit as ξ tends to zero. From (16), one can check that

$$C_U(\xi) = \frac{(\gamma_2(1 - w^\star) - w)^3}{2\gamma_2^2(1 - w^\star)w^\star}\xi^2 + o(\xi^2)$$

Therefore, the right-hand side is zero. For the left-hand side, noting that $w_u(0) = w_U$ we have

$$\lim_{\xi \to 0} \frac{1}{2}\left[[J(w_U) - J(w_u(\xi))] + \frac{a\xi}{w_U b^2}[J(w_U) - J(w_u(\xi))] + J_1(w_U)\xi + o(\xi)\right]$$

$$= \lim_{\xi \to 0} \frac{1}{2}\left[\frac{J(w_U) - J(w_u(\xi))}{\xi} + J_1(w_U)\right]$$

By the Mean Value Theorem, there exists $\zeta \in (w_U, w_u(\xi))$ such that

$$\lim_{\xi \to 0} \frac{1}{2}\left[\frac{J(w_U) - J(w_u(\xi))}{\xi} + J_1(w_U)\right] = \lim_{\xi \to 0} \frac{1}{2}\left[\frac{J_1(\zeta)[w_U - w_u(\xi)]}{\xi} + J_1(w_U)\right]$$

$$= \lim_{\xi \to 0} \frac{1}{2}\left[-\frac{J_1(\zeta)[w_u'(0)\xi + o(\xi)]}{\xi} + \frac{1}{2}J_1(w_U)\right] = \frac{1}{2}J_1(w_U)(1 - w_u'(0))$$

$$= \frac{\gamma_2(1 - w^*) - w^*}{2\gamma_2}J_1(w_U)$$

Noting $\frac{\gamma_2(1-w^*)-w^*}{2\gamma_2}$ is non-zero and finite for $0 < \gamma_2 \le 1$ completes the proof of (5). For $\gamma_2 = 0$, the boundary condition does not apply as no adjustment occurs and this holds for all $w > w_D = 0$. The proof for the lower boundary is similar.

C   Optimality Conditions

Substituting the boundary condition (5) into the general solution (9) we have

$$J_1(w_U, \gamma_1, \gamma_2) = \frac{1}{2}\lambda\sigma^2\left[\frac{2w_U}{r - 2a - b^2} - \frac{2w^*}{r - a}\right] + C_1 z_1 w_U^{z_1 - 1} + C_2 z_2 w_U^{z_2 - 1}.$$

Taking the derivative with respect to γ_1

$$J_{12}(w_U, \gamma_1, \gamma_2) = \frac{\partial C_1}{\partial \gamma_1} z_1 w_U^{z_1 - 1} + \frac{\partial C_2}{\partial \gamma_1} z_2 w_U^{z_2 - 1} = 0.$$

We note that for $b \ne 0$ and $r > 0$, z_1 and z_2 will have opposite signs. Since $w^{z_1 - q}$ and $w^{z_2 - q}$ are positive, we conclude that $\frac{\partial C_1}{\partial \gamma_1}$ and $\frac{\partial C_2}{\partial \gamma_1}$ have the same sign. So,

$$J_2(w, \gamma_1, \gamma_2) = \frac{\partial C_1}{\partial \gamma_1} w^{z_1} + \frac{\partial C_2}{\partial \gamma_1} w^{z_2}.$$

Again w^{z_1} and w^{z_2} are positive and the derivatives have the same sign. This implies that changing γ_1 either increases or decreases the total cost for all values of w. The first-order condition for optimality is therefore $J_2(w, \gamma_1, \gamma_2) = 0$. We conclude that

$$\frac{\partial C_1}{\partial \gamma_2} = \frac{\partial C_2}{\partial \gamma_2} = 0.$$

Taking the derivative of (5) with respect to γ_1 gives

$$J_{12}(w_D, \gamma_1, \gamma_2) = 0$$

$$\frac{\partial C_1}{\partial \gamma_1} z_1 w_D^{z_1-1} + \frac{\partial C_2}{\partial \gamma_1} z_2 w_D^{z_2-1} +$$

$$\frac{w^*(1-w^*)}{(1+(\gamma_1-1)w^*)^2}[C_1 z_1(z_1-1)w_D^{z_1-2} 2C_2 z_2(z_2-1)w_D^{z_2-2} + \frac{\lambda \sigma^2}{r-2a-b^2}] = 0$$

$$\frac{w^*(1-w^*)}{(1+(\gamma_1-1)w^*)^2} J_{11}(w_D, \gamma_1, \gamma_2) = 0,$$

which gives the desired result for the second derivative at the lower boundary. The proof is identical for the upper boundary.

References

1. Adams, H.: Uniswap whitepaper. Technical report (2018)
2. Angeris, G., Chitra, T.: Improved price oracles: constant function market makers. In: Proceedings of the 2nd ACM Conference on Advances in Financial Technologies, AFT 2020, pp. 80–91. Association for Computing Machinery, New York (2020). https://doi.org/10.1145/3419614.3423251. https://doi-org.stanford.idm.oclc.org/10.1145/3419614.3423251
3. Angeris, G., Evans, A., Chitra, T.: When does the tail wag the dog? Curvature and market making. arXiv preprint arXiv:2012.08040 (2020)
4. Angeris, G., Kao, H.T., Chiang, R., Noyes, C., Chitra, T.: An analysis of uniswap markets. Cryptoeconomic Syst. J. (2019, to appear)
5. Aoyagi, J.: Lazy liquidity in automated market making. Available at SSRN 3674178 (2020)
6. Cermak, L.: Uniswap's monthly trade volume exceeded coinbase's in september, October 2020. https://www.theblockcrypto.com/linked/79775/uniswap-coinbase-monthly-volume-september
7. Davis, M.H.A., Norman, A.R.: Portfolio selection with transaction costs. Math. Oper. Res. **15**(4), 676–713 (1990). https://EconPapers.repec.org/RePEc:inm:ormoor:v:15:y:1990:i:4:p:676--713
8. Dixit, A.: The Art of Smooth Pasting. Fundamentals of pure and applied economics. Harwood Academic Publishers (1993). https://books.google.com/books?id=nmoUDNfYK2sC
9. Dixit, A.: A simplified treatment of the theory of optimal regulation of Brownian motion. J. Econ. Dyn. Control **15**(4), 657–673 (1991)
10. Dumas, B.: Super contact and related optimality conditions. J. Econ. Dyn. Control **15**(4), 675–685 (1991). https://EconPapers.repec.org/RePEc:eee:dyncon:v:15:y:1991:i:4:p:675--685
11. Dumas, B., Luciano, E.: An exact solution to a dynamic portfolio choice problem under transactions costs. J. Financ. **46**(2), 577–95 (1991). https://EconPapers.repec.org/RePEc:bla:jfinan:v:46:y:1991:i:2:p:577--95
12. Dune: Dune analytics decentralized exchange dashboard (2020). https://explore.duneanalytics.com/public/dashboards/c87JEtVi2GlyIZHQOR02NsfyJV48eaKEQSiKplJ7

13. Evans, A.: Liquidity provider returns in geometric mean markets. arXiv preprint arXiv:2006.08806 (2020)
14. Kao, H.T., Chitra, T.: Feedback control as a new primitive for DeFi (2020). https://medium.com/gauntlet-networks/feedback-control-as-a-new-primitive-for-defi-27b493f25b1
15. Leland, H.E.: Optimal portfolio management with transactions costs and capital gains taxes. Working Paper RPF-290, IBER, UC Berkeley, December 1999. SSRN: https://ssrn.com/abstract=206871
16. Martinelli, F., Mushegian, N.: Balancer: A non-custodial portfolio manager, liquidity provider, and price sensor (2019)
17. Merton, R.: Lifetime portfolio selection under uncertainty: the continuous-time case. Rev. Econ. Stat. **51**(3), 247–57 (1969). https://EconPapers.repec.org/RePEc:tpr:restat:v:51:y:1969:i:3:p:247--57
18. Tassy, M., White, D.: Growth rate of a liquidity provider's wealth in $xy = c$ automated market makers, November 2020. https://math.dartmouth.edu/~mtassy/articles/AMM_returns.pdf

Market Based Mechanisms
for Incentivising Exchange Liquidity
Provision

W. Gawlikowicz[1(✉)], B. Mannerings[1], T. Rudolph[1], and D. Šiška[1,2]

[1] Vega Protocol, Gibraltar, UK
[2] School of Mathematics, University of Edinburgh, Edinburgh, Scotland

Abstract. A key problem for order book exchanges is how to attract liquidity providers and retain their support in all market conditions. This is commonly approached through individual business agreements with market makers whereby a bespoke contract is negotiated for specific obligations and rewards. Such approaches require a central intermediary that profits from liquidity provision to administer, and typically fail to align the incentives of exchanges and liquidity providers as markets grow. This is costly, slow, and scalability is limited by the exchange's resources, contacts, and expertise.

This paper develops mechanisms for creating open, automated and scalable *liquidity markets*. We describe formal methods to quantify liquidity and discuss various approaches to determine its price. In so doing, we introduce a novel way to structure liquidity commitments, along with a mechanism based on a financial bond with penalties for under-provision to maximise market makers' adherence to their obligations. We also investigate mechanisms to allocate rewards derived from trading fees between market makers, so as to incentivise desirable-but-risky behaviours such as market creation and early commitment of liquidity. We complement this work with several agent based simulations exploring the proposed mechanisms.

1 Introduction

Since the advent of electronic computers in the last century, more and more aspects of running a financial exchange have been automated. Indeed, for most of us the idea of keeping a limit order book[1] by hand seems absurd. Additionally, more and more of the actual trading, including market making[2], is carried out algorithmically, confirming what Black wrote some fifty years ago [1].

However, there are aspects of financial exchanges that have so far eluded full automation. In particular the contractual relationship between exchanges and

---

[1] A record of outstanding buy and sell orders set to trade at a specified (or better) price. Once the prices (and volumes) of buy and sell orders match a trade is generated and the associated orders get removed from the book).

[2] The act of supplying both buy and sell prices to the market with the intention of making a profit on the price difference.

© International Financial Cryptography Association 2021
M. Bernhard et al. (Eds.): FC 2021 Workshops, LNCS 12676, pp. 80–96, 2021.
https://doi.org/10.1007/978-3-662-63958-0_7

market makers still relies on bespoke legal agreements [10]. This reduces the pool of liquidity available to compete for the provision of market making as a service and increases the cost of running the exchange. Both of these in turn decrease the efficiency of the market (the exchange needs to collect higher fees to cover these costs).

If the whole mechanism of the exchange is automated (it is all software) then a significant portion of its revenue (generated by charging fees for trading) should be split between two types of participants: those running the software (operators) and those providing liquidity (market makers). Determining the relative apportioning of incentives between market makers should take into account the value that their specific provision of liquidity has provided, both in terms of its timing, competitiveness, and longevity.

1.1 Motivation

A key problem for exchanges is attracting and rewarding liquidity providers. The entrenched model is to establish business partnerships with market makers, and negotiate obligations (provision of order book volume at some bid/ask) and rewards; typically in the form of fee rebates [12]. It has been shown that such direct liquidity incentives can be highly effective in boosting liquidity, especially for new and small cap markets [11,14,15], as well as following exogenous price shocks [13].

These relationships are governed by business contracts making them a non-scalable and expensive solution limited by the business development capacity of the exchange. Construction of such contracts is non-trivial as they need to comply with market regulations and be build so as to not distort incentives for other market participants which would be counterproductive as far as improving liquidity is concerned [16].

Furthermore, these agreements are typically non-transferable, have limited responsiveness to market conditions and do not align the incentives of owners/operators of a market and liquidity providers [10]. This is particularly noticeable in the case where market makers (akin to early venture in a startup) invest resources into bootstrapping a new market's liquidity, yet typically gain no explicit benefit from the market's commercial success.

This paper develops mechanisms for creating automated and scalable *liquidity markets*. We describe various price determination methods for liquidity provision and how to divide rewards between market makers so as to incentivise desirable behaviours such as early commitment of liquidity to a market. We further outline various ways to measure liquidity provision on an order book, and in so doing introduce a novel way to structure liquidity obligations, along with an automated financial method for penalising market makers who fail to meet the obligations.

We have built our framework assuming that attracting liquidity is occurring in a competitive environment where each market (for a single financial product) is competing with other markets to attract liquidity supply. To put it in a different way, each liquidity provider has the choice of markets to which they supply liquidity and are therefore going to rationally select markets that reward them more highly. We also assume that each market may have multiple market makers and that the rewards are derived from the *all fee income* paid by traders of that market.

To optimally incentivise liquidity providers it is essential to understand the value, to a given market, of liquidity provision on an order book. The authors know of no established way to do this and this paper explores multiple approaches. Black [1] defines a liquid market as one that is both continuous and efficient. Intuitively, these characteristics increase when order book volume is supplied closer to the "true market price". This paper develops various approaches to evaluating relative liquidity profiles on an order book. We extend this to consider various levers that may be tailored according to a market's liquidity requirements, e.g. firmness, valuing long term provision, etc.

It is crucial to note that there are at least two classes of markets that one should consider: spot markets and derivatives[3] markets (by the latter we mean any markets that allow trading on margin, e.g. short positions). For a spot market, liquidity is important in attracting business, efficient price discovery and aiding information flows. However, a market that allows margin trading needs to also protect itself against potentially insolvent participants. See e.g. [7, Section 6]. One of the key parts of the protection is the ability to close out an insolvent participant while protecting the position of their counterparty. In order to be able to do this there must be sufficient volume on the order book to execute such a trade (albeit possibly at a loss). Thus for a derivatives market, sufficient liquidity provision is key for safe operation.

1.2 Literature Review

Existing academic research on liquidity focuses on modelling the impact of information flow and interactions between market participants on order book composition.

Grossman and Stiglitz [3] model a market consisting of a risk-free asset with a known, constant return and a risky asset with a return modelled as a sum of two random variables, one of which can be observed at a fixed cost. There are two types of agents in the market: informed traders who choose to incur the cost to reduce variance of the risky asset as observed by them, and uninformed traders who make decisions solely based on observed prices. Furthermore, the agents observe returns realised by the other market players and decide if they want to switch from being informed to uninformed or vice versa. In [3], the authors have shown that, for a special case of agents with constant absolute risk-aversion utility functions and normally distributed random variables, the equilibrium price distribution exists and can be calculated, and that a number of conjectures that they have formulated can be shown formally. These relate to the impact of the information content of the system on the market price and traded volumes.

---

[3] Financial instruments deriving their value from the future value of other financial assets.

Kyle [4] prescribes a similar type of market with one notable addition - market maker is modelled as a separate type of agent. The market is modelled as a sequence of two step auctions. In the first step, informed trader submits the market order with the quantity based on private observation of the liquidation value of the asset and own trading history. Uninformed traders submit market orders that are uncorrelated with that of the informed agent or own trading history. In the second step, market maker sets prices conditional on quantities traded by other market participants such that the market clears. Market maker is unable to distinguish between the two other types of traders. Market making is assumed to be perfectly competitive - market maker chooses a pricing rule such that the expected profit is zero. The authors in [4] show that a pricing rule linear in the observed traded quantities is optimal and leads to the existence of the equilibrium price. One of the measures of liquidity that the authors consider is the market depth - the order flow required to move a price by one unit of measure. They show that it's proportional to the ratio of quantity traded by uninformed traders to the value of the information held by the informed traders.

Glosten and Milgrom [5] model interaction between price asymmetry, the size of the bid-ask spread and the volumes traded. The model assumes that market maker sets a single bid and a single ask price per unit of stock. Once the prices are set one of the traders arrives at the market at a random time and decides whether to buy or sell one unit, or do nothing. The market maker is then free to revise the prices and the process continues. Like in the models described above, there are both informed and uninformed traders in the market. All agents are assumed to be risk-neutral. Additionally, market maker is perfectly competitive and incurs no transaction costs - expected profit from each trade is zero. The authors in [5] show that even with the above assumptions the bid-ask spread still arises under their model as a purely informational phenomenon. The bid prices will decrease and ask prices will increase as the proportion of informed traders increases. Moreover, the authors were able to derive a bound on the size of the spread and show that there can be occasions when all trading ceases as no uniformed traders are willing to trade in the presence of too much insider information. Lastly, it's been shown that on average the spread in the model decreases as the traded volume increases.

While the above academic publications were important stepping stones in the analysis of market liquidity, they do not offer any explicit solution to the problem that we're trying to solve.

The recent rise of DeFi, decentralised financial system based on blockchain technology placing a lot of emphasis on interoperability between its various components and encapsulating market mechanics in clear-cut rules and governance actions, seems to offer a fertile ground for rethinking and formalising liquidity incentives found in traditional markets.

Gudgeon et al. [17] analyse protocols for loanable funds, namely Compound, Aave and dYdX. These protocols provide overcollateralised loans between various cryptoassets. The protocols use interest rate models to programmatically set lending and borrowing rates so as to balance the demand between the two. Part of the spread between borrowing and lending rates is set aside for periods of market stress, whereas the rest is kept in profit. Authors have shown that periods of illiquidity are common and often happen simultaneously in the protocols considered. The liquidity reserves can often be unbalanced since it's not uncommon for just a few accounts to control majority of protocol's funds. Authors also point to some evidence of market inefficiency suggesting that agents are not necessarily responding optimally to the interest rate incentives. While these protocols remain popular and fulfill an important function within the broader DeFi ecosystem, the liquidity incentives that they rely on are not fit for adoption in more general, order book based markets. It has also been shown that combination of large amount of debt maintained within a lending protocol with periods of low liquidity can relatively quickly lead to the insolvency of the protocol further implying that market mechanisms employed by those protocols likely do not offer a robust alternative to the existing financial system [18].

An interesting approach towards rationalising and automating liquidity provision has been put forward by Hummingbot [8].

The authors propose a liquidity marketplace built around the *Spread Density Function*. The liquidity buyer specifies a monotonically decreasing function $\rho(s)$ of spread supported on $[0, s_{max}]$, where s_{max} is the maximum spread at which rewards for market makers will still be provided. Additionally, the total monthly budget B and number of seconds T defining the frequency with which order book snapshots will be taken get specified.

The total payout available per snapshot is then:

$$b := \frac{B \cdot T \cdot 12}{365.25 \cdot 24 \cdot 3600}.$$

The sum of weighted orders per snapshot is given by $W := \sum_{|s| < s_{max}} \nu_s \rho(s)$, where ν_s is the aggregate volume of all orders at the spread level s. The payout for market maker m at that spread level is then

$$R_{s,m} := b \frac{\nu_{s,m} \rho(s)}{W}.$$

The total compensation for market maker m per snapshot is thus given by

$$b_m := \sum_{|s| < s_{max}} R_{s,m}.$$

The approach outlined above provides clear rules for interaction between market makers and exchanges and as such is a noteworthy innovation. While the frequent order book sampling and market making reward attribution addresses the problem of market makers withdrawing liquidity at times of high volatility to some extent, it does not fully preclude it. As already mentioned, while it may be an acceptable, albeit undesirable state of affairs for spot exchanges, it is potentially fatal for derivatives exchanges which rely on liquidity for their risk management measures. Thus, we proceed with our analysis of the liquidity provision problem and ways addressing it.

2 Dynamic Liquidity Rewards

The goal is to set up a market mechanism that optimises the amount of liquidity provision such that liquidity incentives increase when liquidity is under-supplied, and decrease when there is sufficient liquidity in the market. Markets are assumed to potentially have multiple market makers, each of whom can decide which market to supply liquidity to. The mechanism is based on rewards and penalties outlined below.

Market makers are rewarded from the revenue derived by an exchange through the fees charged on trades. Typically both sides of a trade are charged a fee and then rebates are given to market makers if they are involved in the trade. This fee amount is usually expressed in either basis points (bps) or as a percentage of the trade's notional value[4] at the point of trade. One way or another, the fee has cash value and the amount can be split between various participants to motivate desired behaviour.

A spot exchange will highly value market makers who are involved in trades. Hence the mechanism should reward limit orders that are hit resulting in a trade. This rewards market makers for the competitiveness of their pricing.

An exchange allowing margin trading (derivatives exchange) will rely on liquidity depth[5] for closing out delinquent traders. Thus it will choose to reward providing guaranteed liquidity at all times, based on an appropriate measure, see Sect. 4.

While legal contracts can be used to enforce the obligations, we propose an economic approach where market makers commit a financial bond (or stake) for providing liquidity, which is slashed if they fail to meet their liquidity obligations. The size of the stake will imply a level of liquidity provision commitment.

These commitments may be to provide prices and/or to respond to prices on the order book. For example, a market maker may be required to maintain an amount of volume, proportional to their stake bid and offered within 15% of the best bid/offer/mid price for 85% of the time. In some illiquid markets, the market makers may be required to simply respond to a price placed on the order book with an appropriately competitive counter price.

Here we propose to first fix a measure of liquidity λ - see Sect. 4 for details. A market maker committing to provide the liquidity level $\lambda_{committed}$ will then have to deposit a bond (stake) with the exchange typically calculated as

$$S = \lambda_{commtited} \cdot \text{scaling constant},$$

where the scaling constant will depend on the liquidity measure and the market in question.

The exchange will then fix a time period τ which could be anything from several seconds to hours or days. If at any time during that period volume of limit orders provided by the market maker results in liquidity $\lambda_{provided}$ which is lower than $\lambda_{committed}$ a penalty will be applied to market makers' stake. A

---

[4] Total value of the position.

[5] Order book volume at different price levels around the mid-price.

number of reasonable penalisation strategies can be devised based on the specific market. Typically the penalty should be a fraction of the stake

$$\text{Penalty} = \text{Penalty fraction} \cdot S$$

with $0 < \text{Penalty fraction} < 1$.

Compliance could be further assured by requiring liquidity providers to submit a set of pegged orders[6] with relative weightings per each order book side. These orders would then get automatically deployed in case the orders manually maintained by a given liquidity provider do not fulfil the liquidity commitment $\lambda_{\text{committed}}$. The volumes of those orders would be set so that the commitment is met. Weightings set by the liquidity provider would be taken into account to give them a degree of control over the resulting order structure. It will also be impacted by the choice of liquidity measure discounting (requiring higher volume) orders that provide less liquidity in that measure (e.g. orders placed far away from the mid price). If the margin account maintained by a liquidity provider is insufficient to support those orders the bond account balance can be used to cover the shortfall (with the appropriate penalty applied).

The overall income from trading on a given market at an instant of time is the volume at the time multiplied by the trading fee. Market makers will choose to participate (commit a bond and provide liquidity) if the share of the return they are getting is sufficient reward for the capital they are contributing and risk they are taking. In what we are proposing, the market makers are rewarded by obtaining a fraction of the entire fee income. Thus to increase their income they would like to increase the fee or increase the traded volume. However an increase in fee is likely to lead to a decrease in volume and vice versa. We see that the key is then to allow the market makers to jointly set the fee at an appropriate level. It is also clear that different market makers are likely going to have different opinions on what the appropriate level is.

2.1 Voting Based Mechanism

Each market maker can submit their desired fee: f_i for $i = 1, \ldots, n$ with n the number of market makers. Each market maker also has a stake committed S_i (with the resulting liquidity commitment $\lambda_i^{\text{committed}} = S_i/\text{scaling constant}$).

The trading fee is then a simple weighted average

$$f = \frac{1}{S} \sum_{i=1}^{N} f_i \cdot S_i,$$

where S is the total committed stake i.e. $S = \sum_{i=1}^{n} S_i$.

---

[6] Pegged order has its priced derived from a reference price and an offset, e.g. and order to buy at two ticks from the mid price. The price gets updated each time the reference price moves.

2.2 Radical Market Method

Upon inception of a market there is only one market maker, providing stake S_{old} and setting the market fee f_{old}. During each time period τ the fee either stays as before, or if another market maker chooses to enter the market by providing an additional stake ΔS, then we have $S_{new} = S_{old} + \Delta S$ and the fee is adjusted as

$$f_{new} = \frac{S_{new} - \Delta S}{S_{new}} \cdot f_{old}.$$

A possible stake and fee evolution is given in Table 1. A more complete agent based simulation is provided in Sect. 3.1.

Table 1. Possible fee evolution responding to stake in the radical market method.

Period index	Added stake	Total stake	Fee
1	100	100	1%
2	0	100	1%
3	100	200	0.5%
4	300	500	0.2%
5	−200	300	0.33%
6	−200	100	1.0%
7	−50	50	2%

2.3 Offer Stack Meeting Liquidity Demand

Let us start by trying to estimate liquidity demand in a given market. The simplest way to do this is to consider recent trading activity. One could, for instance, use a moving weighted average of volume of recent trades.

However, lack of trading should not necessarily be equated with low liquidity demand. Markets that have very wide pricing (and no trading) may be demonstrating a need for more competitive liquidity provision, since that which is provided is not priced where the demand is.

In the case of derivatives markets, the open interest captures the potential size of defaulting positions that the exchange is bearing at a point in time. The exchange may require immediate access to liquidity in order to close out traders when they approach a risk of bankruptcy. Hence, in this situation, open interest can be taken as an estimate of liquidity demand. Again there is a problem: a derivative market with no open interest doesn't necessarily imply that there is no demand for liquidity. However, if the aim of the exchange in attracting liquidity is primarily to mitigate risk then this may be a very reasonable measure.

Once the liquidity demand has been established, we then have the following relationship

Liquidity demand $\longrightarrow$ Required committed liquidity $\longrightarrow$ Required market making stake.

Translating required committed liquidity into required stake is just a multiplication using scaling factor. We propose that translating "liquidity demand" (in whichever measure) into "required committed liquidity" is best achieved via an affine transformation:

$\lambda^{\text{required}}$:= Required committed liquidity = Scaling factor $\cdot$ Liquidity demand + Additive factor.

The n different market makers now submit bids with stake and proposed fee: (S_i, f_i). Assume we have sorted so that they are increasing in f_i (so f_1 is the lowest offered trading fee, f_n the highest). Since stake can be directly translated into committed liquidity we may view this also as $(\lambda_i^{\text{committed}}, f_i)$. Let us define

$$\lambda_k^{\text{cumulative}} := \sum_{i=1}^{k} \lambda_i^{\text{committed}}, \quad k = 1, \ldots, n.$$

The market trading fee is then set by first calculating $k^* := \min\{k = 1, \ldots, n : \lambda^{\text{required}} \leq \lambda_k^{\text{cumulative}}\}$ and then taking the fee to be $f = f_{k^*}$. In other words: we take the liquidity offers of the market makers willing to provide the most competitive trading fees, then we start adding up their committed liquidity and the trading fee is that proposed by the market maker whose committed liquidity meets or just exceeds the required liquidity.

The liquidity demand can also be used to only allow liquidity providers to reduce their stake if doing so would not cause $\lambda_n^{\text{cumulative}} < \lambda^{\text{required}}$. If on the other hand the liquidity demand were to rise so as to exceed the liquidity supplied by all active liquidity providers the market could be put into temporary auction mode. During the auction mode new orders will still be accepted, but no trades would get generated. Once enough additional stake gets committed to the market the auction would uncross generating trades from orders with overlapping bid and ask prices at a price that would maximise the traded volume.

2.4   Distributing Fees

We have mentioned earlier that the trading fees should be distributed between those providing the market infrastructure (operators) and those who provide liquidity (market makers). Since creating a new liquid market where there was none before is typically expensive, the market makers who provide liquidity since inception should receive higher rewards than those who join a liquid and successful venture. On the other hand, having more market making capital committed is generally a good thing (it may drive down fees, and it will increase market resilience). So late entrants need to be incentivised to join.

Time-Based Weighting. Hence we propose that the share of fees going to various market makers so that each market maker $i = 1, \ldots, n$ gets proportion p_i given by

$$p_i := \frac{\phi(t - T_i) \cdot S_i}{\sum_{j=1}^{n} \phi(t - T_j) \cdot S_j},$$

where t is the current time,[7] S_i is the stake committed by a market maker i at time T_i (in the past) and where $s \mapsto \phi(s)$ is a bounded, increasing function of time e.g. logistic

$$\phi(s) = \frac{1}{1 + e^{-k \cdot (s-s_0)}}.$$

Here k fixes the steepness of the curve and s_0 the time it takes to go from 0 the midpoint value of $\frac{1}{2}$. The reason to take a bounded function is to make sure that late entrants will, eventually, be assigned enough weight. If we allowed an unbounded function then the late entrants will never catch-up with the early ones - and so they will not have any incentive to join.

Figure 1 shows the resulting fee split between four market makers staking the same overall amount in annual, semi-annual, quarterly and monthly arrears over the course of one year. The example uses a logistic function with parameters $k = 8, s_0 = 0.5$.

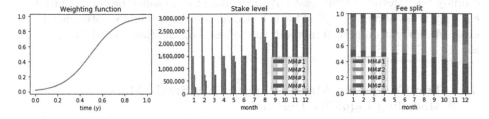

Fig. 1. Fee split for a 1y market with $k = 8, s_0 = 0.5$ and four market makers following different staking schedules.

Equity-Like Market Share. Alternatively, fees could be split based on some measure of market's value over time. This might have the added benefit of rewarding liquidity providers not only for joining early, but also for joining at times of lower market value.

Assume all market maker fees are collected in a separate account and periodically distributed among all liquidity providers. Define the "equity" liquidity provider i holds in the period m as:

$$\text{Equity}_i(m) = S_i \cdot \frac{\text{market value proxy}(t_m)}{\text{market value proxy}(t_0)},$$

where t_m is the time corresponding to the end of period m, t_0 is the time when liquidity provider i posted their stake and:

$$\text{market value proxy}(t_m) = \max(\sum_{j=1}^{n} S_j, \text{factor} \cdot \text{traded value in period m}).$$

---

[7] We write a difference in our notation but could in principle count time using various conventions e.g. ignoring periods when a market is shut.

The share of the market maker fees accrued in period m is distributed between the eligible liquidity providers as:

$$\text{Equity share}_i(m) = \frac{\text{Equity}_i(m)}{\sum_{j=1}^n \text{Equity}_j(m)}.$$

3   Agent Based Models

We now consider two different agent-based models. One model, in Sect. 3.1, models a mechanism where the trading fee increases if both agents want to decrease their commitment and conversely the trading fee decreases if both agents are willing to increase their bonded commitment. The other model, in Sect. 3.2, models liquidity demand.

It is worth noting that for either of the models we cannot compute Nash equilibrium explicitly and so we resort to numerical approximation. In this paper we employ the "Method of Successive Approximations" to solve the control problem each agent is solving, see [2]. This is based on the Pontryiagin's optimality principle. A different numerical method can be based on the Bellman/HJB equation, see [6] and [9].

3.1   Two Competing Market Makers in a Single Market - Not Modelling Liquidity Demand

We have two agents and each has different beliefs about the market, which is captured by the volume response function V^i, $i = 1, 2$. We have $(f, S) \mapsto V^i(f, S)$ where $f \in (0, 1)$ denotes the trading fee and $S \in (0, \infty)$ is the total market making stake committed to the market. We assume that $S \mapsto V^i(f, S)$ is increasing for every f (the more stake on a market the more volume it can support) while $f \mapsto V^i(f, S)$ is monotone decreasing (higher fee leads to less trading volume).

The market makers share the income from trading proportionally to their stake size. For a period of time dt this is given by $fV(f, S) \, dt$. Using S^i to denote the stake of market maker (MM) i she obtains $\frac{S^i}{S^1 + S^2} fV(f, S) \, dt$ in that time period. On the other hand, they have to maintain liquidity above a certain level and if they fail they are penalised by the amount $\sigma_\lambda^i S^i$. The other cost would be the cost of capital, which can easily be included, but we omit it for brevity. Finally the market maker is penalised (with $\delta > 0$ small) by $\delta |\alpha^i|^2$ with α^i denoting how quickly they change their stake. At first sight this might look strange but it promotes predictability for other participants, since it prevents the MM from pulling out liquidity immediately.

The MM i adjusts their stake at rate α_t^i and the trading fee is determined by the enthusiasm of MMs to increase their stake - the more they increase the stake the more the fee decreases:

$$dS_t^1 = \gamma_S \alpha_t^1 \, dt, \quad dS_t^2 = \gamma_S \alpha_t^2 \, dt \quad \text{and} \quad df_t = -\gamma_f(\alpha_t^1 + \alpha_t^2) \, dt. \tag{1}$$

The optimisation problem agent i is solving is to maximise

$$J^i(f, S^1, S^2, \alpha^i, \alpha^{j,*}) = \int_0^T \left[\frac{S^i}{S_t^1 + S_t^2} f_t V^i(f_t, S_t^1 + S_t^2) - \sigma_\lambda^i S_t^i \right] dt.$$

over all (admissible) strategies $\alpha^i = (\alpha_t^i)$ with the strategy of the other agent assumed to be fixed (and optimal for the other agent). Please refer to Appendix B.1[8] for the outline of the solution to the problem.

Simulation Results: To run a simulation we need to choose the volume response function, the details can be found in the IPython notebook[9]. Figure 2 displays this function for agents 1 and 2. Agent 2 assumes the same response but higher maximum trading volume.

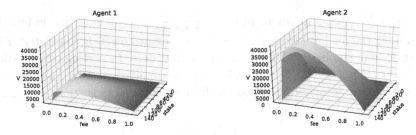

Fig. 2. The function $(f, S) \mapsto f V^1(f, S)$ (left) and $(f, S) \mapsto f V^2(f, S)$ (right).

To test, we create a setting where Agent 1 is staking a market but she thinks that there won't be too much trading (for whatever reason) while Agent 2 starts with almost no stake but has much higher belief in the volume. What we see is that Agent 1 reduces her stake (which on its own would lead to an increase in fees) but Agent 2 increases her stake aggressively, so overall the fees fall. The results are in Fig. 3.

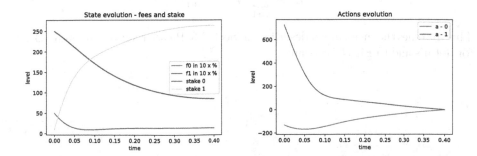

Fig. 3. Fees and stake evolution (left) and agents' actions evolution (right).

[8] Available at: https://papers.ssrn.com/sol3/papers.cfm?abstract_id=3651085.
[9] Available at: https://github.com/vegaprotocol/research/.

3.2   Multiple Competing Market Makers - Basic Liquidity Demand Model

We will have $i = 1, \dots, N$ market makers. Each market maker uses two controls: $\theta_t^i = \left[\alpha_t^{i,f}, \alpha_t^{i,S}\right]$ which fix the speed of change in their desired fee and stake respectively:

$$df_t^i = \alpha_t^{i,f} dt \text{ and } dS_t^i = \alpha_t^{i,S} dt.$$

We fix constants $\kappa_D > 0$ (volume response to liquidity demand), $\kappa_f > 0$ (volume response to fee level) and $\mathrm{LD}_F^* > 0$ (market liquidity demand). The trading volume in the market evolves as

$$dV_t = \kappa_D \left(\mathrm{LD}_F^* - \frac{V_t}{\bar{S}_t} \right) V_t dt - \kappa_f L(\bar{f}_t) V_t dt, \quad V_0 = v_0,$$

where $\bar{S}_t = \sum_{i=1}^N S_t^i$ and where $L(f) = \frac{1}{1+\exp(-(f-\mathrm{FP}^{\mathrm{mid}}))}$ is a logistic function determining the fee level from $\bar{f}_t$. Let us now look at how $\bar{f}_t$ is calculated. First we sort f_t^i from smallest to largest (we use π to denote the sorting permutation) $: f_t^{\pi(1)} \leq f_t^{\pi(2)} \leq \dots \leq f_t^{\pi(N)}$. We calculate the cumulative stake corresponding to market makers providing fees, sorted from smallest to largest:

$$C_t^i := \sum_{j=1}^i S_t^{\pi(j)}.$$

We check the index of the last market maker providing commitment needed to meet current liquidity demand:

$$i^* := \max\left\{ i = 1, \dots, N : \kappa_C C^i \leq \frac{V_t}{\bar{S}_t} \right\}.$$

Finally we set

$$\bar{f}_t := \sum_{j=1}^{i^*+1} f_t^{\pi(i)} \frac{S_t^{\pi(i)}}{C^{i^*+1}}.$$

This matches the mechanism described in Sect. 2.3. Please refer to Appendix B.2[10] for details and to Fig. 4 for results.

---

[10] Available at: https://papers.ssrn.com/sol3/papers.cfm?abstract_id=3651085.

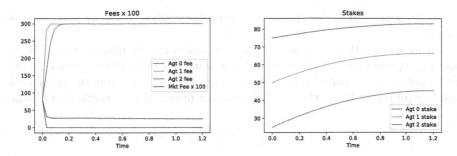

Fig. 4. Fees and stake evolution (left) and agents' actions evolution (right).

4   Measuring Liquidity Provision

In this section we consider a possible way of measuring liquidity. An alternative method is proposed in Appendix A(See footnote 10)

Limit Order Book Description

At any time, the state of orders on the order book can be described in terms of the volume $V(t, p)$ of orders waiting at price level p on a grid with mesh size given by the "tick" size θ. When time is fixed or plays no role then we will write simply $V(p)$. Following the usual convention we will use negative volumes (i.e. $V < 0$) for *buy* orders and positive volumes for *sell* orders. The best bid price (best buy offer) is $s^b(V) := \max\{p > 0, V(p) < 0\}$. The best ask price (best sell offer) is $s^a(V) := \min\{p > 0, V(p) > 0\}$. We will assume that $0 < s^b(V) < s^a(V) < \infty$. This give the *mid price* $S = \frac{1}{2}\left(s^a(V) + s^b(V)\right)$ and the *bid-ask spread* $s^a(V) - s^b(V)$.

We can also take an alternative but related view which describes the order book as volume U at a distance x from the mid-price so that

$$U(x) = V(S + x).$$

If the tick-size θ is small then we can also adopt a continuous approximation to the order book which is now described in terms of *density* $v = v(p)$ given by

$$v(p) \approx \frac{V(p)}{\theta} \quad \text{and} \quad u(x) = v(S + x).$$

Note that we assume that $p \in (-\infty, \infty)$ as on some order books p would not be a price but instead for example a bond yield which can be negative.

Probabilistically Weighted Volume

A simplest possible measure of liquidity would be to calculate $\int_{-\infty}^{\infty} |u(x)| \, dx$ i.e. to sum up the entire volume on the book. The problem with this naive approach is that it counts equally all the volume regardless of how far away from the mid price it is.

Let us assume that we have a stochastic model for the mid price at a future time $\tau > 0$, denoted S_τ, which provides us with the probability density for S_τ. Let us denote the density by $f_S = f_S(x)$. Then we could measure the order book liquidity (or equivalently the liquidity amount provided by a single participant) as

$$\lambda(u) := \int_{-\infty}^{\infty} |u(x)| f_S(x) \, dx.$$

This could however report high liquidity even if there were e.g. only sell orders on the book. A more sensible measure of order book liquidity is thus

$$\lambda(u) := \min\left(\int_{-\infty}^{0} |u(x)| f_S(x) \, dx, \int_{0}^{\infty} |u(x)| f_S(x) \, dx \right). \tag{2}$$

On a market where at a certain (large and unlikely) price movement triggers an auction[11] one may only wish to account for volume that is not as far away as to trigger an auction. Specifically if $x_{\min} < 0$ and $x_{\max} > 0$ are the levels that trigger the auction then

$$\lambda(u) := \min\left(\int_{x_{\min}}^{0} |u(x)| f_S(x) \, dx, \int_{0}^{x_{\max}} |u(x)| f_S(x) \, dx \right). \tag{3}$$

Notice that as long as at two points x and x' we have $f_S(x) = f_S(x')$ then equal volume at x and x' provides equal amount of liquidity according to this measure, regardless of the distance of x and x' from the mid. This is counterintuitive to most peoples' understanding of liquidity and hence most likely undesirable. To rectify this let us write F_S for the cumulative density function[12] and let

$$p_S(x) := \begin{cases} \displaystyle\int_{x}^{\infty} f_S(y) \, dy = 1 - F_S(x), & \text{if } x > 0, \\[2mm] \displaystyle\int_{-\infty}^{x} f_S(y) \, dy = F_S(x), & \text{if } x \leq 0. \end{cases}$$

A moment reflection reveals that $p_S(x)$ is the probability that volume at point x traded at the next time step τ (according to the model given by f_S). Thus another reasonable way to measure liquidity is

$$\lambda(u) := \min\left(\int_{x_{\min}}^{0} |u(x)| p_S(x) \, dx, \int_{0}^{x_{\max}} |u(x)| p_S(x) \, dx \right). \tag{4}$$

---

[11] When market is in auction trades are no longer generated as soon as there's a match in price between a buy and sell order, instead orders keep getting added to the order book, possibly resulting in a crossed state - an overlap between bids and offers - until the auction concludes and associated trades are generated so as to maximise the traded volume (subject to additional rules should a few price levels result in the same maximum volume).

[12] i.e. $F_S(x) = \int_{-\infty}^{x} f_S(y) \, dy$.

Liquidity Across Time

Since market-makers are to be rewarded for providing liquidity we must have a way of considering how the liquidity available exists over time. There are two basic ways to see this. First is to consider the average liquidity provided by a participant over a time interval $[0,T]$: $\frac{1}{T}\int_0^T \lambda(u_t)\,dt$. This allows market makers to completely withdraw liquidity for brief periods and compensate by providing more during calm periods. This will generally be undesirable from the point of view of the exchange. The other is the minimum liquidity provided: $\min_{t\in[0,T]} \lambda(u_t)$.

5   Conclusion

We have reviewed existing approaches to measuring liquidity, its impact on market efficiency and established ways of incentivising it which spanned both traditional finance and the emerging DeFi system.

The main contribution of this paper is to propose market-based, scalable mechanism for building liquidity provision incentives into the exchange mechanics that can be fully automated. This is particularly useful for derivatives exchanges due to its ability to guarantee a predefined level of liquidity irrespective of market conditions and behaviour of other market participants. Finally, we used agent-based models to simulate some of the mechanisms we proposed. They demonstrate that the intuition used to design the mechanisms is correct and the design leads to the desired outcomes.

References

1. Black, F.: Toward a fully automated stock exchange. Financ. Anal. J. **27**(4), 28–35+44 (1971)
2. Chernousko, F.L., Lyubushin, A.A.: Method of successive approximations for solution of optimal control problems. Optimal Control Appl. Methods **3**, 101–114 (1982)
3. Grossman, S.J., Stiglitz, J.E.: On the impossibility of informationally efficient markets. Am. Econ. Rev. **70**(3), 393–408 (1980)
4. Kyle, A.S.: Continuous auctions and insider trading. Econometrica **53**(6), 1315–1335 (1985)
5. Glosten, L.R., Milgrom, P.R.: Bid, ask and transaction prices in a specialist market with heterogeneously informed traders. J. Financ. Econ. **14**, 71–100 (1985)
6. Gyöngy, I., Šiška, D.: On finite-difference approximations for normalized Bellman equations. Appl. Math. Optim. **60**(3), 297–339 (2009)
7. Danezis, G., Hrycyszyn, D., Mannerings, B., Rudolph, T., Šiška, D.: Vega Protocol: a liquidity incentivising trading protocol for smart financial products. Vega research paper (2018)
8. Feng, M., Bhat, R., Las Marias, C.P.: Liquidity Mining: A marketplace-based approach to market maker compensation, Hummingbot research paper (2019)

9. Kerimkulov, B., Šiška, D., Szpruch, L.: Exponential convergence and stability of Howards's policy improvement algorithm for controlled diffusions. SIAM J. Control Optim. **58**(3), 1314–1340 (2020)

10. Dolgopolov, S.: Linking the securities market structure and capital formation: incentives for market makers? Univ. Pennsylvania J. Bus. Law **16**(1), 1–56 (2013)

11. Clapham, B., Gomber, P., Lausen, J., Panz, S.: Liquidity provider incentives in fragmented securities markets. J. Empir. Financ. **60**, 16–38 (2021)

12. Malinova, K., Park, A.: Subsidizing liquidity: the impact of make/take fees on market quality. J. Financ. **70**(2), 509–536 (2015)

13. Das, S.: The effects of market-making on price dynamics. In: Proceedings of the 7th International Joint Conference on Autonomous Agents and Multiagent Systems, vol. 2, pp. 887–894 (2008)

14. Menkveld, A., Wang, T.: How do designated market makers create value for small-caps? J. Financ. Markets **16**(3), 571–603 (2011)

15. Venkataraman, K., Waisburd, A.C.: The value of the designated market maker. J. Financ. Quant. Anal. **42**(3), 735–758 (2007)

16. Calzolari, G., Denicolò, V.: Exclusive contracts and market dominance. Am. Econ. Rev. **105**(11), 3321–3351 (2015)

17. Gudgeon, L., Werner, S.M., Perez, D., Knottenbelt, W.J.: DeFi protocols for loanable funds: interest rates, liquidity and market efficiency. arXiv:2006.13922v3 (2020)

18. Gudgeon, L., Perez, D., Harz, D., Livshits, B., Gervais, A.: The decentralized financial crisis. arXiv:2002.08099v2 (2020)

Understand Volatility of Algorithmic Stablecoin: Modeling, Verification and Empirical Analysis

Wenqi Zhao[✉], Hui Li, and Yuming Yuan

Huobi Research, Hainan, China
{zhaowenqi,lihui0729,yuanyuming}@huobi.com

Abstract. An algorithmic stablecoin is a type of cryptocurrency managed by algorithms (*i.e.*, smart contracts) to dynamically minimize the volatility of its price relative to a specific form of asset, *e.g.*, US dollar. As algorithmic stablecoins have been growing rapidly in recent years, they become much more volatile than expected. In this paper, we took a deep dive into the core of algorithmic stablecoins and shared our answer to two fundamental research questions, *i.e.*, Are algorithmic stablecoins volatile by design? Are they volatile in practice? Specifically, we introduced an in-depth study on three popular types of algorithmic stablecoins and developed a modeling framework to formalize their key design protocols. Through formal verification, the framework can identify critical conditions under which stablecoins might become volatile. Furthermore, we performed a systematic empirical analysis on real transaction activities of the **Basis Cash** stablecoin to relate theoretical possibilities to market observations. Lastly, we highlighted key design decisions for future development of algorithmic stablecoins.

Keywords: Stablecoins · Modeling framework · Empirical analysis

1 Introduction

As cryptocurrencies on blockchain are notoriously known as volatile, *i.e.*, Their prices often fluctuate rapidly, stablecoins are proposed to peg their value to some external assets, *e.g.*, US dollar. In contrast to "unstable" cryptocurrencies, *e.g.*, Bitcoin [19], Ethereum [24], a stablecoin is able to minimize the volatility of its price relative to the pegged asset based on different mechanisms. The most common kind of stablecoin is backed-stablecoin, *i.e.*, The value of a stablecoin is backed by external assets, *e.g.*, commodity, fiat money or cryptocurrency as collateral. For example, the USDC stablecoin is backed by US dollar [5]. Unlike backed-stablecoins, algorithmic stablecoins, which are commonly not backed by other assets, have been gaining an increasing level of popularity in recent years due to the capability to stabilize its price via decentralized algorithms (*i.e.*, smart contract) without degrading too much capital efficiency. In general, this

© International Financial Cryptography Association 2021
M. Bernhard et al. (Eds.): FC 2021 Workshops, LNCS 12676, pp. 97–108, 2021.
https://doi.org/10.1007/978-3-662-63958-0_8

is realized by controlling the money supply of algorithmic stablecoins, which is similar to printing and destroying money in central banks. In this paper, we mainly focus on algorithmic stablecoins and will use the term interchangeably with "stablecoin" (Backed-stablecoins are not the main target in this work.).

Assuming that a stablecoin is pegged to US dollar, a smart contract is designed to dynamically manage its supply to minimize price volatility. We simply explain the algorithm as follows and will further the discussion later. When the price of the stablecoin exceeds one US dollar, the contract "produces" more coins and distributes them to the market. As a result, the price of the stablecoin should accordingly drop. In cases where the price of the stablecoin is lower than one US dollar, the smart contract decreases the supply of it in order to gradually lift its price back to one dollar. In practice, the aforementioned general algorithm can be instantiated by different models to achieve a more robust control over stablecoins. While many interesting research attempts aim at inventing such models, there is relatively little study on the other side, *i.e.*, Do they really work?

In this paper, we described a fundamental analysis on the volatility of algorithmic stablecoins, both theoretically and empirically. Our attempt of this study is to answer two fundamental research questions, which are:

Research Question 1: Are algorithmic stablecoins volatile *by design*?
Research Question 2: Are algorithmic stablecoins volatile *in practice*?

Our goal of the analysis described in this paper is to provide a more comprehensive understanding on the protocols of stablecoins (at both design and implementation level) with a specific focus on their volatility, which we believe is critical in the optimization of existing stablecoins and creation of potential future designs. We summarize our main contributions as follows.

– We introduced an in-depth protocol analysis on the designs of three popular types of algorithmic stablecoins. Moreover, we developed a general formal modeling and verification framework for stablecoins, which can be used to identify specific hidden criteria under which stablecoins might become volatile.
– We further conducted a systematic empirical study of the `Basis Cash` stablecoin based on real transaction activities on Ethereum and managed to relate theoretical possibilities (that stablecoins might be volatile) to market observations (unexpected volatile prices) between Dec 2020 to Jan 2021.

Paper Organization. The rest of the paper is organized as follows. Section 2 gives a systematic introduction of algorithmic stablecoins. Section 3 presents a formal modeling and verification framework designed for understanding and analyzing the volatility of algorithmic stablecoins in general. Furthermore, Sect. 4 describes an empirical study on one popular project and explains important observations based on real market transactions. In Sect. 5, we discuss related works in the literature and Sect. 6 concludes the whole paper.

2   Background

We classify algorithmic stablecoins into three categories, *i.e.*, rebase-style, seigniorage share and partial-collateral. In this section, we briefly explain key designs of all three types of stablecoins with popular projects as examples.

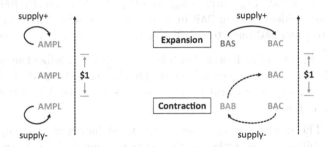

Fig. 1. The algorithmic stablecoins of `Ampleforth` and `Basis Cash`.

2.1   Rebase (`Ampleforth`)

The rebase-style stablecoins manage price-elastic ERC20 tokens, *i.e.*, The total supply of a stablecoin is non-fixed and adjusted adaptively on a routine basis. More specifically, the adjustment is automatically realized via the "rebase" process, which gradually stabilize the price of a target stablecoin near a specific peg, *e.g.*, one US dollar. We use `Ampleforth` [1] as an example for illustration, as shown in the left part of Fig. 1.

By design, the rebasing of `Ampleforth` is activated at 2am UTC on a daily basis. At the time of rebase, new coins are minted and distributed to all accounts proportionally based on their corresponding balances when the price of `Ampleforth` is higher than its peg. Given that the price of `Ampleforth` is $1.2 with its peg to be $1 (*i.e.*, 20% relate to peg), an account with 100 coins is rebased to own 120. On the other hand, holding coins might be automatically proportionally burned when the price falls below the peg.

2.2   Seigniorage Share (`Basis Cash`)

The seigniorage share model for algorithmic stablecoins commonly introduces two types of cryptocurrencies, *i.e.*, *coins* as a stablecoin and *shares* as ownership of seigniorage. In principle, shares are used to increase the supply of coins when the price of a coin is above its intended peg. In addition to these two cryptocurrencies, seigniorage-style stablecoins often issue a redeemable bond as an incentive for buyers when the price goes down below the peg. We use the `Basis Cash` [2] stablecoin for further explanation, as shown in the right part of Fig. 1. `Basis Cash` introduces three types of cryptocurrencies:

– BAC. BAC is the stablecoin and issued by the `Basis Cash` with a peg of $1.

- BAS. BAS stands for Basis Shares, which is a seigniorage ERC20 token and provides inflationary gains of BAC. The design purpose of BAS is to prevent the price of BAC from going too high via dynamically increasing its supply. Currently, BAS can be earned via participating in yield farming, *i.e.*, deposit liquidity in decentralized finance platforms (*e.g.*, Uniswap [6]).
- BAB. BAB refers to Basis Bond whose price P_{bab} is mathematically determined by the price of BAC P_{bac}, *i.e.*, $P_{bab} = (P_{bac})^2$. Particularly, BAB offers an incentive for holders to earn BAB in a cost-effective way. The design purpose behind is to push BAC back to one dollar when its price falls below \$1.

The general protocol of Basis Cash is designed to stabilize the price of BAC via adaptively controlling the supply of it. This is realized based on the two key mechanisms, *i.e.*, *expansion* and *contraction*, respectively. We simply describe the processes as below.

Expansion. The mechanism of expansion aims at increasing the supply of BAC in order to stabilize its price when it rises over the one dollar peg. In the design of Basis Cash, expansion is automatically activated in two settings. First, BAC will be minted and distributed as a reward to BAS holders. That said, for anyone who owns a specific amount of BAS, the expansion process proportionally assigns new BAC to his or her account. In the second case, owners of BAB are allowed to redeem BAC with their BAB at a 1:1 price, which also result in a quantity growth of BAC. Due to the increased supply in both situations, the expansion is expected to gradually make the price of BAC to decrease.

Contraction. In contrast to the process of expansion, contraction is designed to shrink the supply of BAC. To this end, an incentive is introduced in Basis Cash to encourage buyers to exchange BAB with BAC when the price of BAC is below one dollar. In the particular situation, one BAC is guaranteed to generate more than one BAB based on their price dependency as aforementioned. Moreover, the protocol of Basis Cash ensures that a specific amount of BAB is able to redeem the same amount of BAC when the price of BAC grows above \$1 and required conditions are met. Based on the design of contraction, th price of BAC is anticipated not to fall too far from its peg. Compared to the design of rebase-style algorithmic stablecoins, the contraction mechanism of seigniorage share ones is commonly optional rather than automatically enforced. As shown in the right part of Fig. 1, the two dashed lines indicate that investors are allowed to participate in the contraction phase, or not.

2.3 Partial-Collateral (Frax)

In contrast to the two types of algorithmic stablecoins, an emerging class called fractional-algorithmic protocol is recently proposed as a combination of fully-collateral and fully-algorithmic ones. Compared to existing collateral-style stablecoins, *e.g.*, DAI, partial-collateral protocols introduce less custodial risks and avoid over-collateralization. On the other hand, it is designed to enforce a relatively tight peg with higher level of stability than purely algorithmic designs. We use the Frax project [4] below for illustration.

Particularly, Frax is the first attempt to implement the partial-collateral protocol of stablecoins. It introduces a two-token system, *i.e.*, FRAX as a stablecoin pegged to \$1 and FXS as a governance token, respectively. A collateral ratio $0 \leq r \leq 1$ is dynamically determined very hour with a step of 0.25% in the protocol to control at what percentage of peg the collateral is required to take to stabilize the value of FRAX. In cases where $r = 0.5$, \$0.5 must be in other types of stablecoins as collateral to mint a new FRAX. It becomes fully collateral when $r = 1.0$ and a pure algorithmic stablecoin if $r = 0$.

The collateral ratio r is 1.0 at genesis. In principle, minting a specific amount n of FRAX involves placing $n \times r$ of the value as collateral and burning $n \times (1 - r)$ of the value with FXS. As the price goes above its peg, the protocol provides the incentive for investors to mint new FRAX. Accordingly, the increased supply of FRAX is expected to gradually enforce the price to decrease. In cases where the price falls below the peg, the protocol allows investors to swap a combination of collateral and FXS valued \$1 with a single FRAX whose value is lower than \$1. Such incentives can potentially produce FRAX purchases and rise its price as well.

3 Modeling and Verification

3.1 Modeling of Stablecoin

We highlighted a formal modeling framework $\mathcal{M}$ for stablecoins. More formally, $\mathcal{M} := \langle \mathcal{P}, \mathcal{E}, \mathcal{C}, \mathcal{S}, \mathcal{B}, \mathcal{X} \rangle$ is a network consisting of six types of timed automata [7], each of which is a tuple $Q := \langle S, s_0, X, A, T, I, S_n \rangle$. S is the finite set of states. $s_0 \in S$ is the initial state. X is a set of non-negative real numbers as clock variables. $S_n \subseteq S$ is a set of accepting states. A is a set of actions and I is a set of invariants assigned to states. Given that Φ is constraint function, $T \subseteq S \times \Phi(X) \times 2^X \times A \times S$ is a collection of state transitions $\langle s, a, g, R, s' \rangle$, where s and s' are source and destination states, a is an action, g is the condition to enable the transition and R is the set of clocks to be reset.

Moreover, $\mathcal{M}$ provides communication through four classes of synchronized channels $\Omega := \{\omega_e, \omega_c, \omega_x, \omega_u\}$. Specifically, ω_e and ω_c are designed to trigger *expansion* and *contraction* procedures. ω_x simulates market trading activities and generates a new price of stablecoin. ω_u synchronizes updates between $\mathcal{E}$, $\mathcal{C}$ and $\mathcal{X}$. Particularly, we presented a formal model of Basis Cash in Fig. 2. The framework is general to other types of stablecoins. Due to page limits, we selected Basis Cash because it manifests a typical model and was one of the most popular markets at the time of writing.

- $\mathcal{P}$ models the main protocol with five states, *i.e.*, initial state, Pre_Expansion and Expanded states when price is above the peg, Pre_Contraction and Contracted states when price is below the peg. The channels of expand (ω_e) and contract (ω_c) are activated on two transitions to enable the processes of expansion and contraction.
- $\mathcal{E}$ automata defines a process with a clock t and three states. $\mathcal{E}$ responds to expansion requests from $\mathcal{P}$. An expanding transition is executed to grow the

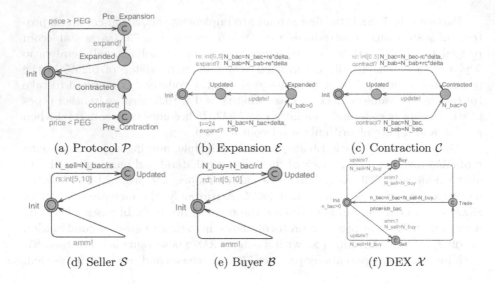

Fig. 2. Timed automata model of `Basis Cash` stablecoin.

supply of stablecoins (*i.e.*, global variable N_bac). The transition is allowed if t is at an expansion point (*e.g.*, 24:00 UTC). For `Basis Cash`, $\mathcal{E}$ creates two expansion transitions and synchronizes with $\mathcal{X}$ via the **update** channel (ω_u).

- $\mathcal{C}$ automata abstracts the contraction process. Similar to $\mathcal{E}$, a transition is provided to refine the decrease of supply via updating a global variable. Another transition is designed to model that the supply stays unchanged (investors can choose not to swap `BAB` with `BAC`).
- $\mathcal{S}$ and $\mathcal{B}$ are designed to model the behavior of sellers and buyers in an exchange. They generate random trading requests through the ω_x channel.
- $\mathcal{X}$ introduces an abstract model of decentralized exchanges (DEX) with automatic market making (AMM), *e.g.*, `Uniswap` [6]. $\mathcal{X}$ defines `Sell` and `Buy` states to indicate whether it is a buyer's market (*i.e.*, more sellers than buyers) or seller's market (the other way around). New prices are computed based on AMM and its pool of stablecoins.

3.2 Formal Verification

We further highlight important formal specifications to define stability properties (or non-volatility) of stablecoins with temporal logic [21]. Specifically, stability (non-volatility) is specified through the following two properties (A and G are quantifiers, *i.e.*, for all paths and for all states of a path in the state space [21]).

$$\text{AG } (\mathcal{P}.\texttt{Expanded} \wedge \mathcal{E}.\texttt{Updated}) \implies !\mathcal{X}.\texttt{Buy} \qquad \text{(expansion-validity)}$$

$$\text{AG } (\mathcal{P}.\texttt{Contracted} \wedge \mathcal{C}.\texttt{Updated}) \implies !\mathcal{X}.\texttt{Sell} \qquad \text{(contraction-validity)}$$

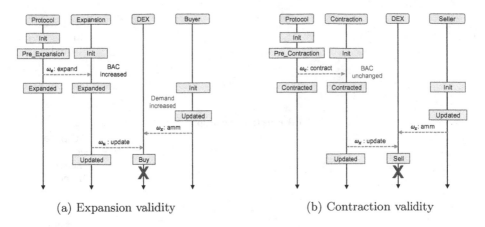

(a) Expansion validity (b) Contraction validity

Fig. 3. Counter-examples on non-volatility properties of `Basis Cash` stablecoin.

Specifications of Stability (Non-Volatility). Two properties are specified as in expansion-validity and contraction-validity to formalize the resilience against price fluctuation (with `Basis Cash` as an example). As formalized by expansion-validity, in cases where $\mathcal{P}$ is at state `Expansion` and $\mathcal{E}$ is at `Updated` (*i.e.*, expansion has been enforced), $\mathcal{X}$ must not stay at the state of `Buy` for the price to fall, *i.e.*, buyer's market. Similarly, when $\mathcal{P}$ is at `Contraction` and $\mathcal{C}$ is at `Updated`, $\mathcal{X}$ must not be at the state of `Sell`, *i.e.*, seller's market.

Counter-Example Analysis. We verified the model of `Basis Cash` with the `Uppaal` model checker for timed automata [16]. Figure 3 shows two counter-examples of the stability properties, *i.e.*, conditions under which `Basis Cash` might become volatile. Figure 3a describes a trading scenario where expansion validity is violated. Specifically, a demand growth of `BAC` occurs when the expansion process is started to mint and distribute new stablecoins. As a result, DEX goes to the state of `Buy` instead of `Sell` to trigger a counter-example. In terms of contraction-validity, Fig. 3b demonstrates another potential volatility of `Basis Cash`. When the price of `BAC` goes down below its peg, the contraction allows investors to swap `BAB` with `BAC`. However, in cases where the swap does not happen therefore supply of `BAC` stays unchanged, the contraction-validity is violated since DEX goes to the state of `Sell` instead of `Buy` as expected.

4 Empirical Analysis

Based on the formal modeling and verification of `Basis Cash`, we now describe an empirical analysis with real market observations, as shown in Fig. 4. More specifically, the empirical analysis was based on data at the time of writing from `Dune Analytics` [3]. We open-sourced all the data-retrieving queries at `https://explore.duneanalytics.com/dashboard/winky`.

Normal Cases. The first pair of figures, *i.e.*, Fig. 4a and 4b, shows two cases where expansion and contraction worked well to stabilize the price of `BAC`.

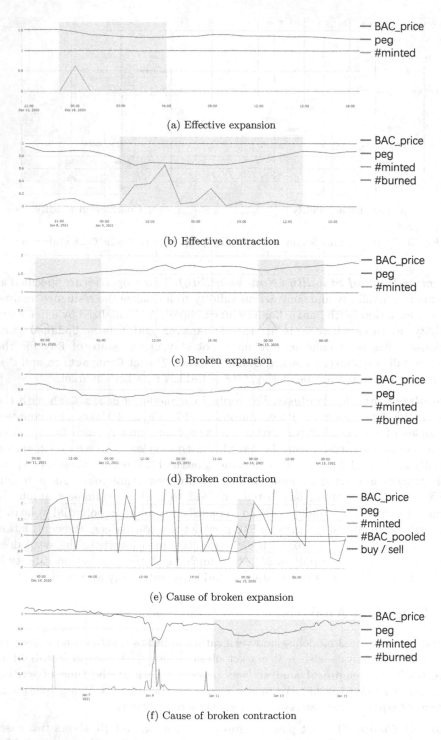

(a) Effective expansion

(b) Effective contraction

(c) Broken expansion

(d) Broken contraction

(e) Cause of broken expansion

(f) Cause of broken contraction

Fig. 4. Empirical analysis of `Basis Cash`. Unit: 10 million. (Color figure online)

As highlighted in Fig. 4a, as new BAC were minted (indicated by the green hump in the shaded area), its price gradually went down (blue line). Similarly, as a number of BAC were burned (indicated by the purple line) for contraction in Fig. 4b, its price started to rise. Such normal cases perfectly satisfied the design intent of Basis Cash and are different instances of traversing the state space as modeled in Fig. 2.

Broken Expansion. Unfortunately, Basis Cash might manifest an abnormal market as alarmed in Fig. 3 where the price of BAC becomes highly volatile. In our preliminary analysis, we found that such possibilities became real activities. Specifically, Fig. 4c and 4e have explained a broken expansion as inferred in Sect. 3.2 on Dec 14 and 15, 2020. In Fig. 4c, the expansion started at 00:00 with a collection of new BAC minted (green hump). However, its price increased in 7 h from \$1.35 to \$1.56 (Dec 14) and from \$1.62 to \$1.76 (Dec 15) instead of sticking to the peg, which amounted to a total growth of 15.72% and 8.40%. Based on Fig. 4e, the broken expansion was attributed to a rapid increase of demand as marked in Fig. 4e (brown line). As a measurement of purchase divided by sales, the brown line stayed above 1 in the most of the time. That said, there were more buyers of BAC in the market than sellers. Back at that time, *i.e.*, a relatively early stage of Basis Cash, yield-farming on BAC-DAI was very popular and led to a extremely high yield rate. Consequently, the demand of BAC was rapidly lifted even at an expansion point. Furthermore, the popularity of BAC was also reflected by the fact that 92% of the newly minted BAC on Dec 14, 2020 went to the yield-farming pool within 2 h after expansion (purple line in Fig. 4e).

Broken Contraction. In further, the potential volatility due to broken contraction was also confirmed in Fig. 4d and 4f. From Jan 11, 2021 to the time of writing, the price of BAC has been staying below its one US dollar peg as displayed in Fig. 4d despite that entries of contraction were continuously open during that period. That said, the mechanism of contraction failed to pull BAC back to or slightly over its peg price. The reason behind was the low participation in contraction at that time, *i.e.*, Many investors were unwilling to burn BAC for BAB due to the fear that they might never be able to redeem. As shown in Fig. 4f, the number of burned BAC (purple humps in the specific shaded area) during that period was much smaller than several days ago.

Design Decisions. Based on the aforementioned empirical analysis, we summarize two high-level important design decisions for algorithmic stablecoins in the future, especially for those adopting a similar design of Basis Cash.

- Compared to the design of extraction or similar mechanism where the supply of an algorithmic stablecoin goes up, the design of contraction is fundamentally more important and challenging. This is because cryptocurrencies are naturally easier to fall than rise. Therefore, a robust design of contraction should be well incentivized with investors' fear and reluctance taken into consideration.
- As two of the important parameters in algorithmic stablecoins, the quantity and cycle of intervention, *i.e.*, by how much adjustment an algorithm should

enforce and how frequent it needs to be triggered, might be potential improvements in the future. While a strong intervention might drive the stablecoin into another polar, a subtle one is probably ineffective. Similar balance is also required when it comes to the cycle of an algorithmic intervention. More reliable and flexible models are highly desired in this context.

5   Related Work

Stablecoins are cryptocurrencies with computing economic designs to achieve a relative stable market value and purchasing capability as well. Research on stablecoins have been attracting both economic and computer science researchers in recent years. Saito *et al.* proposed to stabilize blockchain cryptocurrencies via automatically controlling their supply to absorb both positive and negative demand shocks [22]. From the view of economics, Iwamura *et al.* suggested a new monetary policy for cryptocurrencies to stabilize their values [14]. Caginalp *et al.* argued that existing valuation frameworks were not compatible with cryptocurrencies which hold no underlying value thus new models were needed to the design of stablecoins [11]. To further develop this idea, they proposed a model of cryptocurrencies based on asset flow equations and investigated their stability with different parameterized configurations [10]. The resulting system was able to provide linear stability under specific market conditions. In the context of algorithmic stablecoins, Ametrano described a preliminary design in 2014 called *Hayek Money* which has been implemented by many projects nowadays [8]. In this specific design, price stability is achieved by dynamically rebasing the amount of cryptocurrency. A new paradigm was introduced to control the number of money units in all digital wallets instead of making each unit change its value. To further avoid unanticipated fluctuation of cryptocurrency prices, Sams designed *seigniorage shares* to include an elastic supply rule which adjusts the quantity of coins adaptively according to the changes of market value [23]. Compared to cryptocurrencies like Bitcoin whose supply growth is determined in advance, such scheme is more resilient against the intrinsic uncertainty of cryptocurrencies.

Design review and classification of stablecoins were al discussed in several research papers and industry reports [9,12,13,15,17,18,20]. Pernice *et al.* explored the landscape of stablecoins by proposing a taxonomy based on three types of collateralization, *i.e.*, direct, proxy and self-collateralization [20]. They further highlighted important implications and open questions based on the current development of stablecoins. From the viewpoint as decentralized payment systems, Mita *et al.* presented a similar discussion where stablecoins were categorized based on different types of collateral and intervention [17]. They pointed out that although algorithmic stablecoins introduced decentralization, they were weakly standardized to become practical payment tools. Moin *et al.* decomposed stablecoins in the literature into important building blocks [18]. They analyzed pros and cons of different designs and identified potential future trends as well. Klages *et al.* characterized stablecoins based on their functional risks related with incentive security and economic stability [15].

6   Conclusion

In this paper, we presented an in-depth theoretical and empirical analysis on the volatility of algorithmic stablecoins. We highlighted a formal modeling framework for stablecoins to identified important market criteria under which they might become volatile. Moreover, we related our theoretical findings to transaction activities on stablecoins via a further empirical analysis with real market data. Empirical results showed that potential possibilities predicted in the proposed model were confirmed in practice. Lastly, we highlighted important design decisions for the future development of stablecoin. All data used in this work are available at `https://explore.duneanalytics.com/dashboard/winky`.

References

1. Ampleforth. https://www.ampleforth.org/ (2021)
2. Basis Cash. https://basis.cash/ (2021)
3. Dune Analytics. https://duneanalytics.com/ (2021)
4. Frax. https://frax.finance/ (2021)
5. Tether. http://tether.to (2021)
6. Uniswap. http://uniswap.io (2021)
7. Alur, R., Dill, D.L.: A theory of timed automata. Theor. Comput. Sci. **126**(2), 183–235 (1994)
8. Ametrano, F.M.: Hayek money: the cryptocurrency price stability solution. Available at SSRN 2425270 (2016)
9. Bullmann, D., Klemm, J., Pinna, A.: In search for stability in crypto-assets: are stablecoins the solution? ECB Occasional Paper (230) (2019)
10. Caginalp, C.: A dynamical systems approach to cryptocurrency stability. arXiv preprint arXiv:1805.03143 (2018)
11. Caginalp, C., Caginalp, G.: Opinion: Valuation, liquidity price, and stability of cryptocurrencies. Proc. Nat. Acad. Sci. **115**(6), 1131–1134 (2018)
12. Clark, J., Demirag, D., Moosavi, S.: SoK: demystifying stablecoins. Available at SSRN 3466371 (2019)
13. Hileman, G.: State of stablecoins (2019). Available at SSRN (2019)
14. Iwamura, M., Kitamura, Y., Matsumoto, T., Saito, K.: Can we stabilize the price of a cryptocurrency?: Understanding the design of bitcoin and its potential to compete with central bank money. Hitotsubashi J. Econ. **60**, 41–60 (2019)
15. Klages-Mundt, A., Harz, D., Gudgeon, L., Liu, J.Y., Minca, A.: Stablecoins 2.0: economic foundations and risk-based models. In: Proceedings of the 2nd ACM Conference on Advances in Financial Technologies, pp. 59–79 (2020)
16. Larsen, K.G., Pettersson, P., Yi, W.: Uppaal in a nutshell. Int. J. Softw. Tools Technol. Transf. **1**(1–2), 134–152 (1997)
17. Mita, M., Ito, K., Ohsawa, S., Tanaka, H.: What is stablecoin?: A survey on price stabilization mechanisms for decentralized payment systems. In: 2019 8th International Congress on Advanced Applied Informatics (IIAI-AAI), pp. 60–66. IEEE (2019)
18. Moin, A., Sekniqi, K., Sirer, E.G.: SoK: a classification framework for stablecoin designs. In: Financial Cryptography (2020)
19. Nakamoto, S.: Bitcoin: a peer-to-peer electronic cash system. Tech. rep, Manubot (2019)

20. Pernice, I.G., Henningsen, S., Proskalovich, R., Florian, M., Elendner, H., Scheuermann, B.: Monetary stabilization in cryptocurrencies-design approaches and open questions. In: 2019 Crypto Valley Conference on Blockchain Technology (CVCBT), pp. 47–59. IEEE (2019)
21. Pnueli, A.: The temporal logic of programs. In: 18th Annual Symposium on Foundations of Computer Science (sfcs 1977), pp. 46–57. IEEE (1977)
22. Saito, K., Iwamura, M.: How to make a digital currency on a blockchain stable. Future Gener. Comput. Syst. **100**, 58–69 (2019)
23. Sams, R.: A note on cryptocurrency stabilisation: seigniorage shares. Brave New Coin, pp. 1–8 (2015)
24. Wood, G., et al.: Ethereum: a secure decentralised generalised transaction ledger. Ethereum Proj. Yellow Pap. **151**(2014), 1–32 (2014)

Measuring Asset Composability
as a Proxy for DeFi Integration

Victor von Wachter[1]([✉]), Johannes Rude Jensen[1,2], and Omri Ross[1,2]

[1] University of Copenhagen, Copenhagen, Denmark
victor.vonwachter@di.ku.dk
[2] eToroX Labs, Copenhagen, Denmark

Abstract. Decentralized financial (DeFi) applications on the Ethereum blockchain are highly interoperable because they share a single state in a deterministic computational environment. Stakeholders can deposit claims on assets, referred to as 'liquidity shares', across applications producing effects equivalent to rehypothecation in traditional financial systems. We seek to understand the degree to which this practice may contribute to financial integration on Ethereum by examining transactions in 'composed' derivatives for the assets DAI, USDC, USDT, ETH and tokenized BTC for the full set of 344.8 million Ethereum transactions computed in 2020. We identify a salient trend for 'composing' assets in multiple sequential generations of derivatives and comment on potential systemic implications for the Ethereum network.

Keywords: DeFi · Blockchain · Asset composability · Integration risks

1 Introduction

Smart contracts on the Ethereum blockchain share a single state in a deterministic execution environment [1], a feature which introduces a high level of interoperalility between decentralized financial (DeFi) applications. This novelty has thus far, resulted in a rich ecosystem of financial applications, primarily lead by borrowing/lending money markets [2,3] and constant function market makers (CFMM) [4,5]. At the time of writing, crypto assets valued in excess of \$39 billion is managed by some 75[1] DeFi applications on the Ethereum blockchain.

From the consumers' perspective, interoperability between financial applications is a desirable feature, resulting in a vibrant and highly competitive marketplace of increasingly exotic financial products. Yet, if left unsupervised, interoperability between liquidity reserves may lead to dependencies amongst applications, as techniques equivalent to the practice of rehypothecation in the traditional financial system [6] become normalized.

When allocating assets to a CFMM such as Uniswap, Curve or Balancer, liquidity providers receive 'liquidity provider shares' (LP shares) [7] redeemable

---

[1] defipulse.com, as of 31st Jan 2020.

© International Financial Cryptography Association 2021
M. Bernhard et al. (Eds.): FC 2021 Workshops, LNCS 12676, pp. 109–114, 2021.
https://doi.org/10.1007/978-3-662-63958-0_9

for a proportional share of the liquidity pool with the unrealized returns of the position. LP shares are typically computed as transferable, fungible tokens which has led to the emergence of new secondary markets in which applications offer liquidity and lending pools for LP shares themselves. Supplying LP shares to these pools results in the issuance of meta LP shares. This process is, in some cases, repeated recursively as stakeholders seek to maximize yield or functionality across a diverse set of applications. While LP shares are often treated by market participants as simple IOUs, they do in fact represent a complex payout function, as shown in the literature by [7,8]. Further complicating matters, the practice of 'yield farming', i.e. allocating assets across DeFi applications to maximize returns [9], has introduced a competitive environment in which applications seek to attract additional liquidity by rewarding LP shareholders with 'governance tokens' [10].

We approach Ethereum as a financial ecosystem with structural properties comparable to those of a single market [11,12]. For this work, we examine the degree to which a crypto asset can be utilized in a sequence of increasingly complex 'wrapping' operations, guiding our research question: *Can we measure assets composability as a proxy for financial integration on the Ethereum Blockchain?* Informed by the process proposed by [13], we measure the degree to which crypto assets in smart contracts may contribute towards effects equivalent to financial integration on the Ethereum blockchain. We approach transaction data on Ethereum with an asset oriented perspective, in contrast to previous studies of financial activity on Ethereum, sorting by addresses [13] or applications [14].

2   Method

We measure asset composability by identifying the number of derivatives produced from an initial root asset I. We extend work presented in [13] by proposing an algorithm for unwrapping crypto assets. The algorithm builds a tree structure of derivatives from the initial asset I (Fig. 1). We measure the distance δ to the initial asset $\delta_A = \sum_{i=0}^{N} |w_i|$ as a proxy for the degree to which an asset contributes towards integration on Ethereum. That is, the sum of relevant wrapping operations, where $w := (w_1, \ldots, w_n)$ is the vector of all adjustments for the composed asset A.

In the example (Fig. 1), an asset is allocated to a CFMM liquidity pool, triggering the issuance of the corresponding LP shares. At this point, we consider the initial asset as wrapped once, resulting in a distance of 1. Subsequently allocating the LP share to another application would trigger the issuance of another LP share, which amounts to a distance of $\delta = 2$. We target five popular crypto assets: DAI, USDT, USDC, ETH, and tokenized BTC[2] for the duration of 2020 (Table 1). Collectively, the selected assets amounted to over 70% of the

---

[2] Bitcoin (BTC) is a non-native asset on Ethereum, represented by 'wrapped bitcoin' locked on the original blockchain. We compile the three largest representations of Bitcoin on Ethereum into a single category, assigning the category an initial distance of one.

```
1: repeat
2:          T <- all transactions of initial assets from block #9193266 to #11565018
3:                     draw 10,000 random transactions t in T
4:                 for each t:
5:                         identify erc20 tokens in transaction
6:                             if token A is wrapped version of initial asset
7:                                 if A less than 100 transfers ignore
8:                                 else wᵢ +1 and calculate distance δ_A
9:                             end if
10:                end for
11: until no relevant new wrapped assets
```

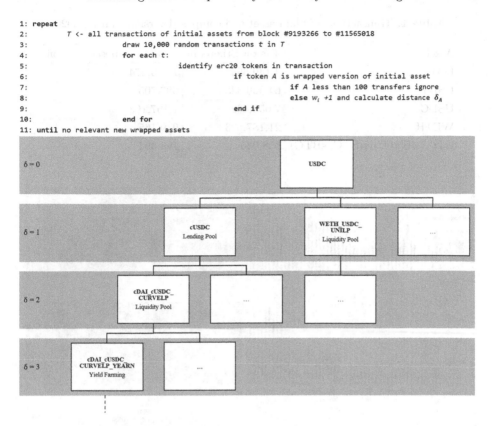

Fig. 1. Method and exemplary asset tree structure for USDC

total value administered within DeFi applications (see Footnote 1) at the end of the sample period.

3 Results

We find derivatives of the five initial assets among all 344.8 million Ethereum transactions in 2020 (block #9193266 to #11565018). For each initial asset we compare the number of transactions in the 'plain' version of the asset, against the number of transactions in its derivatives (Fig. 2).

For the first 6 months plain DAI transfers amounted between 82%–91% (blue) of all DAI asset transfers and composed DAI with $\delta = 1$ amounted between 9%–18% (orange) respectively. The data indicates a clear trend towards increasingly complex wrapping operations peaking in the third quarter of 2020, a period colloquially referred to as 'DeFi Summer' due to a high volume of governance tokens issued at the time [10]. The tendency is especially salient in 'DAI', for which to up to 84% of all transactions involved a 'wrapped' derivative of the initial asset. Curiously, the asset with the largest market cap on Ethereum,

Table 1. Transactions of plain asset and composed versions during 2020

Asset	Txs on Ethereum	Txs of composed version
DAI	4,149,654	1,033,674
USDT	64,956,383	687,705
USDC	7,053,402	1,167,163
WETH	21,187,823	919,165
BTC (wBTC, renBTC, sBTC)	658,035	193,394

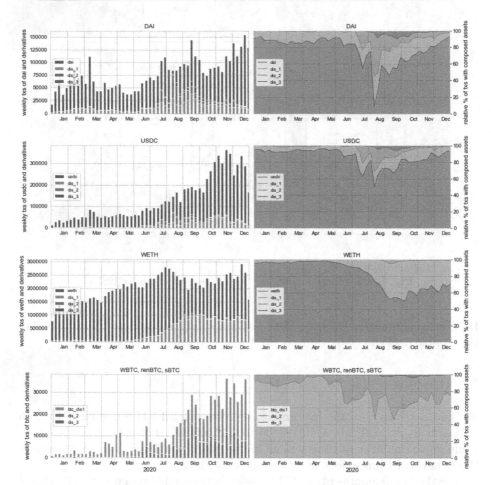

Fig. 2. Asset composability of popular Ethereum assets during 2020 (Color figure online)

USDT, appears to be the least popular with an insignificant 687,705 transactions in 'wrapped' derivatives, compared to 64,956,383 transactions in the plain asset.

4   Discussion and Conclusion

Computing fractional ownership claims in a deterministic, single state environment introduces a large set of new opportunities for innovation in the financial sector. Because transactions on permissionless blockchains, such as Ethereum, settles atomically, the role for central clearing counterparties in mitigating counterparty risk is largely mitigated for simple transactions. Yet, to date, little is understood about the systemic implications of the design of these applications and how novel concepts like LP shares, may exacerbate the impact of shocks triggered by exploits [15,16].

A quantifiable approach to the study of financial integration on the Ethereum net-work will facilitate a better understanding how shocks travel through tightly inter-connected webs of DeFi applications, which may provide guidance towards promoting resilience and protecting investors against systemic risk. In this work, we present initial indicators by examining the degree to which transactions in 'wrapped' derivatives of an asset, representing increasingly complex payout functions, may offer an indication of the degree of financial integration on the network. We position this contribution within the broader literature on the quantification of 'composability risk' for the DeFi ecosystem, a critical gap raised by [6].

To provide actionable insights for market participants and regulators, this and future studies must expand the scope by considering all relevant factors for the transmission of shocks, including smart-contract design and default risk for the individual DeFi application.

 This project has received funding from the European Union's Horizon 2020 research and innovation programme under the Marie Skłodowska-Curie grant agreement No 801199

References

1. Antonopoulos, A., Wood, G.: Mastering Ethereum: Building Smart Contracts and DApps. O'Reilly Media, Sebastopol (2018)
2. Bartoletti, M., Chiang, J.H., Lluch-Lafuente, A.: SoK: Lending Pools in Decentralized Finance (2020). http://arxiv.org/abs/2012.13230
3. Kao, H.-T., Chitra, T., Chiang, R., Morrow Gauntlet, J.: An Analysis of the Market Risk to Participants in the Compound Protocol (2019). https://scfab.github.io/2020/FAB2020_p5.pdf
4. Angeris, G., Kao, H.-T., Chiang, R., Noyes, C., Chitra, T.: An Analysis of Uniswap Markets (2019). http://arxiv.org/abs/1911.03380
5. Angeris, G., Chitra, T.: Improved Price Oracles: Constant Function Market Makers (2020). https://arxiv.org/abs/2003.10001
6. Werner, S.M., Perez, D., Gudgeon, L., Klages-Mundt, A., Harz, D., Knottenbelt, W.J.: SoK: Decentralized Finance (DeFi) (2021). https://arxiv.org/abs/2101.08778
7. Evans, A.: Liquidity Provider Returns in Geometric Mean Markets (2020). https://arxiv.org/abs/2006.08806

8. Jensen, J.R., Pourpouneh, M., Nielsen, K., Ross, O.: The Homogeneous Properties of Automated Market Makers (2021). https://www.ssrn.com/abstract=3807820
9. Angeris, G., Evans, A., Chitra, T.: When does the tail wag the dog? Curvature and market making (2020). https://arxiv.org/abs/2012.08040
10. von Wachter, V., Jensen, J.R., Ross, O.: How Decentralized is the Governance of Blockchain-based Finance? Empirical Evidence from four Governance Token Distributions (2020). https://arxiv.org/abs/2102.10096
11. Castiglionesi, F., Feriozzi, F., Lorenzoni, G.: Financial integration and liquidity crises. Manag. Sci. **65**(3), 955–975 (2019). https://doi.org/10.1287/mnsc.2017.2841
12. Somin, S., Altshuler, Y., Gordon, G., 'Sandy' Pentland, A., Shmueli, E.: Network dynamics of a financial ecosystem. Sci. Rep. **10**(1), 1–10 (2020). https://doi.org/10.1038/s41598-020-61346-y
13. Nadler, M., Schär, F.: Decentralized Finance, Centralized Ownership? An Iterative Mapping Process to Measure Protocol Token Distribution (2020). http://arxiv.org/abs/2012.09306
14. Tolmach, P., Li, Y., Lin, S.-W., Liu, Y.: Formal Analysis of Composable DeFi Protocols (2021). https://arxiv.org/abs/2103.00540
15. Wright, T.: (2020). https://cointelegraph.com/news/akropolis-defi-protocol-paused-as-hackers-get-away-with-2m-in-dai. Accessed 20 Dec 2020
16. Turley, C.: (2020). https://defirate.com/imbtc-uniswap-hack/. Accessed 20 Dec 2020

Demystifying Pythia: A Survey of ChainLink Oracles Usage on Ethereum

Mudabbir Kaleem[(⊠)] and Weidong Shi

University of Houston, Houston, TX, USA
{mkaleem,wshi3}@uh.edu

Abstract. Smart contracts are dependent on oracle systems for their adoption and usability. We perform an empirical study of oracle systems' usage trends and adoption metrics to provide better insight into the health of the smart contract ecosystem. We collect ChainLink usage data on the Ethereum network using a modified Ethereum client and running a full node. We analyze the collected data and present our findings and insights surrounding the usage trends, adoption metrics, oracle pricing and service quality associated with ChainLink on the Ethereum network. We infer that ChainLink's usage and growth are dominated by the DeFi ecosystem and for its demand for decentralized price feeds.

Keywords: Oracles · DeFi · Smart contracts · Blockchain · Ethereum · ChainLink

1 Introduction

Since the launch of the Ethereum [3] network in 2015, smart contracts [16] have become one of the central features of blockchain-based systems. Although initially limited in usage to token control and on-chain data access, smart contracts today are rapidly expanding their domain of applications [12] due to the availability of oracles [2]. Oracles provide the interface between the blockchain's isolated execution environment and external off-chain data sources, enabling smart contracts to retrieve and post real-world data and events. Consequently, the potential utility and future mass adoption of smart contract platforms is inextricably tied to the oracle service providers within the ecosystem.

Bearing that in mind, the motivation of this study was to survey oracle usage in the smart contract ecosystem. Currently, different projects like ChainLink [10], Provable [15] and Augur [14] are offering third party oracle services to smart contracts. These projects have adapted a decentralized approach for collecting and aggregating oracle data, thereby addressing "the oracle problem" [9] of having centralized points of failures in blockchain environments. For our survey, we target ChainLink, which evidently captures the majority share of the oracle middleware market at the time of writing. To establish this, we surveyed the top forty DeFi projects by market capitalization [8] and found all among them which had a use case for external oracles to be using ChainLink except two projects.

© International Financial Cryptography Association 2021
M. Bernhard et al. (Eds.): FC 2021 Workshops, LNCS 12676, pp. 115–123, 2021.
https://doi.org/10.1007/978-3-662-63958-0_10

ChainLink provides a comprehensive list of their project integrations on their website [7] and it includes major DeFi projects such as Aave, Ampleforth, Chiliz, Polygon, Kyber Network and 0x among others. Although ChainLink provides its oracle services over multiple chains, we concern our study with ChainLink oracle usage on Ethereum since it is the most widely adopted smart contract platform at this time. We believe that ChainLink oracle usage on Ethereum represents the significant bulk of oracle traffic on smart contract platforms. Our study finds that Chainlink's growth and usage is strongly centered around the DeFi ecosystem where a few projects have been responsible for most of the oracle service traffic for price feeds. We also show that Chainlink's price feeds feature has seen a steady growth since its inception whereas the external API feature has seen negligible traffic. The oracle traffic statistics and trends provided by this survey can be used to gauge the adoption and health of the smart contract ecosystem in general. At the time of writing, we are not aware of any other formal study providing oracle usage insights in the smart contract environment.

2   ChainLink Overview

ChainLink is an oracle service provider for smart contracts that is currently live on three platforms: Ethereum, Binance Chain and the Matic Network. ChainLink went live in May 2019 and is currently the most popular oracle service provider for smart contracts. ChainLink maintains a decentralized oracle network and aggregates data from multiple oracle nodes on the network to provide data feeds that do not rely on a single oracle node or data source [4]. ChainLink employs an ERC-20 and ERC-677 compliant token called LINK which is used by oracle consumers to pay the oracle nodes for data provision. ChainLink currently provides three features for consumer smart contracts on the Ethereum mainnet.

Price Feeds: are a ChainLink feature to provide different market prices and conversion rates data in the blockchain environment for usage by smart contracts. ChainLink achieves this by having a decentralized price feed for each of these data points, which is fed price data through multiple oracle nodes using different sources. This is implemented by having an aggregator contract for each feed on-chain which is fed data by multiple oracle nodes through their interface contracts. The feed aggregator contract then aggregates all the nodes' answers to provide a final answer to any consumer contract via public Solidity functions. Consumers of the price feeds data call these aggregator contracts when the data is desired. The ChainLink documentation lists the aggregator contract addresses for the available price feeds [5]. The price feeds are sponsored by various projects and currently available for public usage without any LINK token charge.

External APIs: is a ChainLink feature that allows smart contracts in the blockchain environment to perform external API calls through ChainLink oracle nodes. These API calls can be HTTP Get Requests on the web or other APIs provided by the oracle node for different use cases. ChainLink API requests are currently handled 1:1 by an oracle and ChainLink currently does not provide decentralization benefits by default for API calls although a user might implement it on their own. The consumers of ChainLink's API feature have to pay their request servicing oracle node in LINK tokens for the service. The cost varies depending on the node and the nature of the request but is around 0.1 LINK on average and the highest being 1 LINK at the time of writing. Commonly used public API endpoints are available as "jobs" in ChainLink which allows user to only specify the job ID and not having to specify the URL, format etc. This makes the consumer side code more succinct and the implementation easier.

Verifiable Random Numbers (VRF): is a ChainLink feature to provide verifiable random number generation functionality on-chain. ChainLink achieves this by having off-chain random number verifier contracts which verify the randomness of the number generated by an oracle node in response to a consumer request. VRF feature allows for provable random numbers, which protects the consumer from attacks even if the node servicing the request has been compromised.

3   Study Design

3.1   Data Collection

For both the Price Feeds and the External APIs we collected data from the launch of ChainLink mainnet in May 2019 up till the end of October 2020 (Ethereum block 11167816). The VRF feature data was not collected and is not part of this study since it only went live at the end of October 2020 and the resulting data was insufficient for a formal study.

Modified Ethereum Client: For collecting the Price Feed usage data, we looked at the price feed addresses available on the ChainLink website [5]. There were 88 price feed addresses at the time of writing which are proxy aggregator addresses. ChainLink has also, since its launch, made upgrades to the aggregator contracts. The current version of aggregators are labeled as v3. We used the wayback machine web archives [17] to retrieve old aggregator addresses and had a total of 169 addresses for our study (88 v3, 80 v2, 1 v1). The ChainLink team also later provided us with historical addresses which we used to verify our list. For capturing the price feed data we could not use the Web3 API since all price feed consumer requests were direct calls or "internal transactions". Hence we modified the Golang Ethereum client code to log data when internal function calls were made to these 169 addresses. We captured the block number, calling address, opcode, value and input data parameters for these internal calls to these addresses and stored them in a local MySQL database.

Ethereum Full Node and Web3: For collecting data related to ChainLink API usage we used the Web3 API with an Ethereum full node that we ran locally. ChainLink implements the API feature using the CallAndTransfer() functionality of the ERC-677 token standard. Every time a consumer requests an oracle, it generates a ChainlinkRequest event and sends the LINK to the oracle node along with data describing the API to fetch, the job ID, the format of the output, the callback address and function which the oracle must respond to and other data if required. The oracle node interface contract generates an OracleRequest event upon receiving the LINK and data and the external node listens to this event. It responds with the result after some time and makes a transaction to the callback function with the data response. The consumer contract then raises a ChainlinkFulfilled event. We use the Web3 APIs to capture these events and extract the required data which includes: the block number of the request, the requesting address, the oracle node requested, the job ID specified, the callback function and address provided, the LINK token paid, the ChainLink request ID, the request transactions hash, any additional data provided, the response block number, the response and the response transaction hash. We store the results in our local MySQL database for all such oracle service request-response cycles on ChainLink.

We used Etherscan [11] to verify various samples of our collected data to ensure that our data collection process was performed correctly.

3.2   Study Objectives

The study was aimed at providing insights into the usage of ChainLink oracles on Ethereum. For this purpose we looked at the following five aspects:

- **Oracle usage trends and demographics**
- **Oracle Adoption**
- **Oracle Pricing**
- **Oracle Servicing Delays**

4   Results

4.1   Usage Trends and Demographics

After the data collection was completed and the required data was populated into our MySQL server, we had the quantitative information summarized in Table 1. A total of 2,717,049 API requests were made to Oracles during the entire duration of our study and in total 2,409,074 price feed calls were made to ChainLink's public price feed contracts for fetching the market place data. Although the numbers appear encouraging at first sight, upon further investigation, we found that 99.75% of API requests to ChainLink oracle nodes were made by ChainLink price feed aggregator addresses themselves. This is because prior to the v3 aggregator release in August 2020 [6], all price feed aggregator contracts made API requests to oracle nodes to fetch prices. After removing these

API requests, we are only left with 6634 API requests performed on ChainLink for the entire 18 month period! We also see that the number of distinct users that made use of these features is very low.

Next, we present a list of the most popular price feeds based on their share of the historical price-feed traffic in Fig. 1. We also present the corresponding consumer projects/contracts of these price feeds ordered by their share of the historical price-feed traffic. To get the corresponding projects/contracts, we grouped the most regular consumer addresses (Top 26 addresses, which represent more than 90% of all price-feed traffic) by their public tags available on Etherscan [11]. Our results show that Synthetix [1], which is a blockchain-based derivatives trading platform, is responsible for more than 47% of the historic price feed traffic. If we subtract ChainLink's internal traffic from the numbers, Sythetix's share of the historical price feed traffic rises to 75%.

Table 1. Price Feeds and API: collected data summary.

Feature	Total requests	Excluding ChainLink internal requests	Distinct Caller/consumer addresses	Distinct Callee addresses (price-feeds/oracle nodes)
Price Feeds	2409074	N/A	294	129
External APIs	2717049	6634	271	159

Feed Name	Percentage of Traffic		Consumer Tag	Percentage of Price Feed Requests
ETH / USD	10.5993		Synthetix	57.4234
EUR / USD	6.6621		ChainLink Proxy Price Provider	17.0403
AUD / USD	6.6246		Unknown	12.8212
XAG / USD	6.2909		ChainLink Aggregator Facade	6.1165
XAU / USD	6.2669		CREAM Finance	3.5961
GBP / USD	5.7996		ENS	1.0431
CHF / USD	5.7952		Nexus Mutual	0.9570
JPY / USD	5.4070		ChainLink Adapter	0.5170
USDC / ETH	4.4811		BZX	0.4854
DAI / ETH	3.2655			

Fig. 1. Leaderboards: price feeds attracting the most traffic and projects generating the most price feed traffic.

4.2 Oracle Adaption in the Market

To study ChainLink oracles' adaption trends in the market, we look at the historical data for the average number of price-feed and API requests made to ChainLink oracles per month Fig. 2. Plotting the data, we can see that the price-feed feature appears to be far more popular among users and has been rapidly

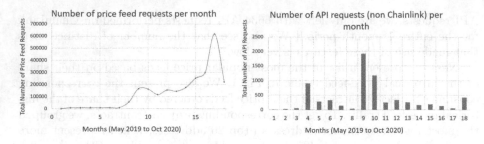

Fig. 2. Number of price feed and API requests on ChainLink by month.

gaining more traffic volume. The API feature does not appear to have a large demand among the users. We believe that this can be attributed to the fact that most projects and use-cases are able to fulfill their data needs using the ChainLink provided price feeds and do not have to employ a custom API. We also show in Fig. 3 that ChainLink has continuously increased the number of price feeds being offered to users. The increase in price feed offerings has kept up with the increase in adaption as evidenced in these figures. In contrast to the price-feeds, Oracle nodes have not seen a marked increase in the variety of API calls and jobs being requested.

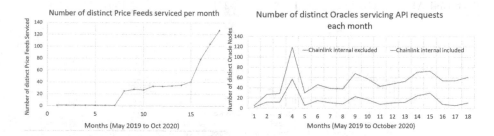

Fig. 3. Number of distinct price feeds serviced and active oracles by month.

4.3   Oracle Pricing

ChainLink is currently providing the price feeds feature to all smart contract users on the Ethereum chain without cost. These price feeds are sponsored by various blockchain projects using these feeds in their contracts. A user does need to pay an Oracle node in LINK token if they make a direct API request. The current cost of ChainLink API usage varies and can be as high as 1 LINK depending on the oracle and the data being requested. We look at the historical price paid for running a single API request in Fig. 4. We also look at the historical average income which the data providing oracle nodes from these requests. We see the average LINK paid for oracle requests on ChainLink is increasing of late, and that coupled with the increase in the LINK token price is bound to discourage the use of oracle APIs for trivial use cases.

4.4   Oracle Servicing Delays

Different smart contract use cases require their oracle service requests to be processed within a time constraint. For the wide adoption of smart contracts, it is essential that the oracle system is able to service time-critical requests. We analyze our available API data in Fig. 5 to determine the historical average delay experience on ChainLink API requests. Due to a small number of outliers, the average obtained was around six hundred blocks. After filtering out these outliers and only keeping the requests that were serviced within one hundred blocks, we obtained the data shown in our figures. We can see that for ChainLink oracles most API requests are serviced within the next four to five blocks with the historical average block delay being close to four Ethereum blocks which corresponds to roughly one minute.

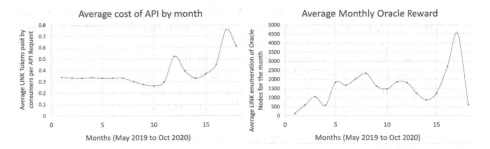

Fig. 4. Average cost of a single API request and the average fees collected in LINK by oracle nodes.

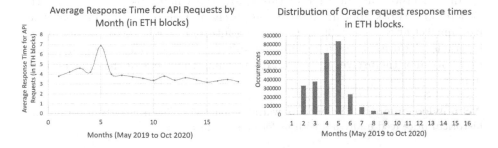

Fig. 5. Average response time and response time distribution for API requests.

5   Analysis and Conclusion

Based on our analysis of the collected data, we obtained the following important insights regarding Chainlink usage on Ethereum in particular and the trends for Oracle systems in general:

- The number of individual users of the ChainLink platform is not very high. Currently, it is mostly being used by DeFi(Decentralized Finance) projects and applications to provide market prices to its contracts. This is perhaps indicative of a trend in the smart contract ecosystem in general.
- Currently, a single DeFi project, Synthetix has been responsible for almost 75% of the historic price-feed traffic in the ChainLink network (given that we ignore ChainLink's self-generated traffic). Synthetix uses various commodity and currency ratio feeds on ChainLink which are among the feeds that have serviced the most traffic. This dominance of Synthetix related traffic might fade with ChainLink increasingly integrating with new projects.
- The data shows that there is currently not a big market of people wanting to use oracles to connect smart contracts to the external world for trivial use cases. Whether it is the genuine lack of market demand for these applications or whether high Ethereum gas prices and ChainLink API fees discourage people from doing so will require further investigation.
- While ChainLink's API feature has not seen increased use with the rise of DeFi, ChainLink's price feeds have seen increasing usage since the project's launch. ChainLink has also managed to provide an increasing variety of price feeds to cater to the demands of new DeFi projects integrating with Chain-Link.
- The rising average API cost seen on the network might be attributed to the increased LINK token price which forces people to only make Oracle API usage for non-trivial cases.
- The average response time of ChainLink's API feature is seen to remain steady between 4 and 5 blocks which might not be good enough for time-sensitive applications.

In conclusion, at the time of this study, the ChainLink ecosystem on the Ethereum network appears to be driven purely by DeFi's demand for decentralized market price feeds [13]. In the coming future, it would be interesting to see if Oracle platforms like ChainLink take initiatives to attract other segments of users or tailor themselves more towards fulfilling the needs of the growing DeFi market.

Acknowledgements. The authors warmly thank the ChainLink team for sharing historical price feed addresses with us for cross-verification.

References

1. Synthetix (2019). https://www.synthetix.io

2. Al-Breiki, H., Rehman, M.H.U., Salah, K., Svetinovic, D.: Trustworthy blockchain oracles: review, comparison, and open research challenges. IEEE Access **8**, 85675–85685 (2020)
3. Buterin, V., et al.: Ethereum: a next-generation smart contract and decentralized application platform (2014). https://github.com/ethereum/wiki/wiki
4. ChainLink: Chainlink developer documentation. https://docs.chain.link
5. ChainLink: Ethereum price feeds. https://docs.chain.link/docs/ethereum-addresses
6. ChainLink: Developer communications, August 2020. https://docs.chain.link/docs/developer-communications
7. ChainLink: Ecosystem, March 2021. https://chainlinkecosystem.com/ecosystem
8. Coinmarketcap: DeFi category, March 2021. https://coinmarketcap.com/defi
9. Egberts, A.: The oracle problem-an analysis of how blockchain oracles undermine the advantages of decentralized ledger systems (2017)
10. Ellis, S., Juels, A., Nazarov, S.: Chainlink: a decentralized oracle network (2017). https://link.smartcontract.com/whitepaper
11. Etherscan: The Ethereum block explorer (2017)
12. Kehrli, J.: Blockchain 2.0-from bitcoin transactions to smart contract applications. Niceideas, November 2016. https://www.niceideas.ch/roller2/badtrash/entry/blockchain-2-0-frombitcoin
13. Liu, B., Szalachowski, P., Zhou, J.: A first look into DeFi oracles. arXiv preprint arXiv:2005.04377 (2020)
14. Peterson, J., Krug, J., Zoltu, M., Williams, A.K., Alexander, S.: Augur: a decentralized oracle and prediction market platform (2019)
15. Provable. https://provable.xyz. Accessed 10 Sept 2020
16. Szabo, N.: Formalizing and securing relationships on public networks. First Monday (1997)
17. Wayback Machine: The internet archive. https://archive.org/web/

On Stablecoin Price Processes
and Arbitrage

Ingolf Gunnar Anton Pernice[⊠]

Weizenbaum Institute, 10623 Berlin, Germany
`ingolf.ga.pernice@hu-berlin.de`

Abstract. This study applies the Caginalp and Balenovic (1999) model for asset flow dynamics to fully collateralized stablecoins. The analysis provides novel insights on how trend-reversion and reactions to peg deviations work together to keep stablecoin prices close to the price they are targeting. A fixed-effects panel regression indicates that the model's abstraction of trading motivations indeed fits stablecoin price processes well. The results convey first indication that theoretic stablecoin models might benefit from modeling price dynamics to switch between two market regimes: one for day-to-day price formation and limited arbitrage activity; and one for extraordinary market situations.

Keywords: Stablecoins · Arbitrage · Price formation

1   Introduction

Stablecoins are being increasingly adopted as bridge to trade traditional cryptocurrencies [3,8,38,45], marketed as medium-of-exchange for decentralized finance and smart contracts [39,40] and have recently been approved by US regulators as payment method for federally chartered banks [1]. Increasing practical relevance fosters the demand for understanding economic properties of such instruments. The majority of projects simply tokenize the asset their tokens are stabilized against (e.g. the USD, EUR or gold) or store a third asset in the respective amount [43]. Assuming that traders trust governance, collateral and technology, and their trust is justified, there is little room for disagreement on the token's fundamental values. If there were any structured deviation, efficient-market theorists might argue that market participants would seize the resulting opportunity of arbitrage, closing the gap [26].[1] Stablecoin prices would then

---

[1] In a strict sense, arbitrage opportunities can be defined as "investment strategy that guarantees a positive payoff in some contingency with no possibility of a negative payoff and with no net investment" [25, p.57]. In this paper the term is used in a wider sense, describing the trader's perceptions.

I thank Gunduz Caginalp for his invaluable input and enlightening conversations. I also thank Martin Florian and Anna Almosova for their constructive feedback.

ⓒ International Financial Cryptography Association 2021
M. Bernhard et al. (Eds.): FC 2021 Workshops, LNCS 12676, pp. 124–135, 2021.
https://doi.org/10.1007/978-3-662-63958-0_11

merely reflect the value of the collateral and random noise. If, however, price adjustments are restricted by incomplete arbitrage, interesting patterns might emerge that reflect the trader's decisions [10,22]. This paper explores and quantifies such dynamics.

My empiric approach is based on a recent theoretical approach from asset pricing literature proposed first in [18] and refined by [14] which opens up asset pricing to dynamic systems modeling known from thermodynamic physics. In the following, the latter will be called the "Caginalp and Balenovic (1999) asset flow" (CBAF) approach. In a nutshell, the authors model price determination by abstracting trading decisions as flows from asset-to-cash and vice versa. As such, traders are abstracted as being driven by price trends and the deviation of the asset's market price from its fundamental value. Exploring theoretic approaches to the instability of price processes, a first application to the field of cryptocurrencies has been attempted by [12]. Applying the CBAF model to stablecoin arbitrage promises to offer a convincing model for the interplay of trend following and peg deviations. In contrast to most models for cryptocurrency pricing, the above model requires few assumptions.[2] Exploring early trading data for 11 fully collateralized stablecoins, this study evaluates the appropriateness of the intuitive trader abstraction adopted by the CBAF approach and offers insights into stablecoin price dynamics in general. My empirical setup couples variables approximating trend-following with a measure for peg deviations in a dynamic coin-fixed-effects (coin-FE) panel data regression. The study engages in rigorous robustness checking by testing the models for the influence of seasonal dummies, interaction terms for the direction of trends, sign of peg deviations and different parameters in data preprocessing. I find a striking difference between results being based on data with—and without outlier treatment even for merely truncating price changes exceeding 5 standard deviations. For data including extreme price changes, the CBAF model approximates price formation well. Deviations from the peg and trend following are strong determinants of coming price changes. For outlier-free data, however, the effects seem to blend in with other price-determinants (the stablecoin's token supply and Bitcoin's price volatility). This result indicates that apart from very few occasions arbitrage activity is weak. This poses the questions, whether costs of arbitrage might be prohibitive high except for extreme but rare market situations. It might be considered to model price formation by switching between two regimes: a first one offering profits for large trades towards the peg, and a second one being characterized by limited levels of arbitrage activity.

The paper is organized as follows: Sect. 2 outlines related work, Sect. 3 introduces the theoretic backgrounds of arbitrage and the CBAF model, Sect. 4 discusses data and econometric approach. Sect. 5 describes the results and Sect. 6 concludes the study.

---

[2] Compared with, for example, game-theoretic approaches [13] and consumer demand models [2,4,7].

2   Related Work

Studies investigating the asset class and its manifestations include [19,23,41,43] and [11]. The user perception in the adoption of stablecoins has been studied in [32], while [5] analyzed the suitability of stablecoins as save-haven investment. The relation between cryptocurrency prices and stablecoin trading has been focused on by [3,8,45] and [27]. Adopting a risk-oriented approach, [33,34] and [35] suggest theoretic models to study stability and resilience of stablecoins. While the latter focuses on extreme events, [38] not only offers a theoretic model for day-to-day arbitrage but also provides, to my knowledge, the first extensive empirical analysis of the drivers of stablecoin prices. This paper differs in perspective and econometric approach: Instead of peg deviations, this paper analyzes price processes and tests the *CBAF* model for applicability. While [38] relies on an auto-regressive distributed lag model with a rich database, however, just for *Tether*, this paper adopts a dynamic coin-FE panel data regression on market data for 11 stablecoins.

3   Stablecoin Arbitrage and the CBAF Model

Stablecoin arbitrage uses primary and secondary markets [38]. On the primary market, coins are created and redeemed against collateral with the issuer. On the secondary market, stablecoins are traded against fiat and cryptocurrencies. If market prices deviate from the peg, arbitrage traders might decide to either trade against peg deviations directly on the secondary market or involve the stablecoin issuer. In the first case, arbitrage traders simply trade towards the peg. They would buy when prices are below—and sell when prices are above the peg. In the second case, abstracting from technical details,[3] arbitrage traders would purchase coins from the markets and redeem them with the issuer when prices are below the peg. When prices are above the peg, traders would first create coins with the issuer and subsequently sell them on secondary markets.

The *CBAF* approach as presented in [14] models traders as switching from cash to asset or vice versa with a certain probability k. Variable k is modeled to include motivations based on past price changes ζ_1 and the market discount relative to the asset's fundamental value ζ_2. These components are modeled using the trader's memory with respect to price trends and deviations from fundamental values (c_1 and c_2) and their focus on these two respective components (q_1 and q_2). Core component of ζ_1 is the relative price trend $f(\tau) = \frac{1}{P(\tau)}\frac{dP(\tau)}{d\tau}$ over period τ on time scale τ_0. ζ_2 is constructed around deviations $g(\tau) = \frac{P_a(\tau)-P(\tau)}{P(\tau)}$ of market price $P(\tau)$ from fundamental value P_a. Thus, the two components can be expressed as

$$\zeta_1(t) = q_1 c_1 \int_{-\infty}^{t} e^{\frac{-(t-\tau)}{c_1}} \cdot f(\tau)\, d\tau \qquad (1)$$
$$\zeta_2(t) = q_2 c_2 \int_{-\infty}^{t} e^{\frac{-(t-\tau)}{c_2}} \cdot g(\tau)\, d\tau. \qquad (2)$$

---

[3] Models for more complex stablecoins can be found e.g. in [33] and [34].

Limiting k to values between 0 and 1, k is constructed as $k = \frac{1}{2} + \frac{tanh(\zeta_1 + \zeta_2)}{2}$. For ζ_1 and ζ_2 equal to zero, the probability of flows from cash to asset and vice versa are thus equally likely. Demand D and supply S of the asset are modeled using k and the fraction already invested into the asset B. Their relation can be expressed as $D = k(1 - B)$ and $S = (1 - k)B$ and thus $\frac{D}{S} = \frac{k}{1-k}\frac{1-B}{B}$. Prices P are assumed to change logarithmic with excess demand, leading to

$$\frac{1}{P}\frac{dP}{dt} = \delta \cdot log\left(\frac{D}{S} - 1\right) = \delta \cdot log\left(\frac{k}{1-k}\frac{1-B}{B}\right) \tag{3}$$

with δ representing an amplitude that scales with time. For a deeper discussion of the model and its applications see [14,16,17,44] and [12]. While this paper will not be offering estimates for the individual parameters, the study gathers evidence supporting the basic intuition of the model: Under the efficient market hypothesis, fluctuations of $P(t)$ around the peg, assumed to equal P_a, would merely be random.[4] Obviously, in this case, neither of the two components ought to be reflected in market data of stablecoins. If, however, evidence of ζ_1 or ζ_2 is present, it is of considerable interest to understand how the two components are jointly driving stablecoin prices.

4   Data and Econometric Approach

The following paragraphs will discuss data preprocessing and the economic approach for testing the applicability of the *CBAF* model.

Data was gathered from www.coingecko.com. Similar to www.coinmarketcap. de the data provider currently crawls 382 cryptocurrency exchanges but offers hourly data over a well-documented API for free.[5] The full dataset comprises 19 cryptocurrencies. The sample includes projects that are listed at www.coingecko. com, promise stability of their exchange rates in their whitepapers and collateralize their tokens to at least 100%. The study considers designs that use the asset-pegged-to as collateral but also includes tokens that use a third asset, often a crypto-asset, in a quantity reflecting at least full collateralization. Some of the 19 cryptocurrencies are quite young and immature. Shallow markets with low volumes and few trades per measurement period might in part be driven by market microstructure effects which could lead to biased regressions. To reduce noise, this study thus excludes months for that the stablecoin shows a market capitalization of under USD 10 m or daily trading volumes of under USD 1 m. Coins have been dropped completely if the remaining dataset included less then $24 \cdot 31$ hourly observations. This restricted the dataset to 11 stablecoins with 767 to 16970 trading hours leading to 101,243 observations in total. Table 6 of Appendix 7.3 in the full paper shows that the results hold as well if market capitalization thresholds of USD 100 m and USD 5 m—and thresholds for

---

[4] This study assumes that traders rightfully trust in the peg as a correct estimate of the tokens fundamental value. This fails when doubts about the stablecoins collateral or security arise.

[5] As of 2020-08-17.

daily trading volumes of USD 50 m and USD 50k are chosen. To understand the effect of extreme values on the estimated models, price changes diverging over 5 standard deviations (SD) from the mean have been truncated. Table 1 in Appendix B gives an overview over cutoff points and the relative and absolute number of classified outliers. The threshold was chosen deliberately high to correct only the most extreme values. Such might have a disproportionate effect on ordinary-least-squares (OLS) regression results [6]. To make the estimated coefficients comparable, all variables apart from the dummies have been standardized based on Z-scores $X^{stand} = \frac{X - \mu(X)}{\sigma(X)}$, with mean $\mu(\cdot)$ and standard deviation $\sigma(\cdot)$. To verify the applicability of the $CBAF$ model, a linear panel regression in conjunction with squared and cubed trend variables to model nonlinear relationships has been applied to exchange-traded funds [17] and stocks [15]. Now this framework is applied to stablecoins by adjusting it slightly to the characteristics of the dataset and adding a variety of robustness checks. Traditional linear modeling might fail to pick up the complex relations in price formation. In contrast to linear models, polynomials allow for very strong negative (positive) past returns to induce positive (negative) bounce-back effects. Mixing up relations between strong and weak price changes, simple auto-regressive price regressions abstaining from the above step might miss potential information on prices. As a remedy, following [15] and [17], this study includes variables to the power into a fixed-effects panel data approach.[6] To capture price trends, in accordance to [15], this paper uses a simple weighted aggregation of past price changes. The prior might be expressed using prices P and smoothing factor s over a look-back window d as

$$T_t = \frac{1}{\sum_{k=1}^{d} e^{sk}} \sum_{k=1}^{d} \left(\frac{P_{t-k+1} - P_{t-k}}{P_{t-k}} \cdot e^{sk} \right). \tag{4}$$

The smoothing term ensures that older observations of variable changes are entering the sum with lower weights ($s = -0.25$ and $d = 10$). Trends in prices have been shown to explain variation in future returns for cryptocurrencies in [20,30] and [28]. To calculate the distance D of market price P from the peg P_a, simply $D_t = P_t - P_{a,t}$ is formed. As control variables the token supply and Bitcoin's price-volatility are used. Controlling for the volatility of the second and third largest traditional cryptocurrencies by trading volume (*Ether* and *Ripple*) or for the *Ethereum Gas* price turned out to yield insignificant coefficients. Regressions are formed denominating cryptocurrency price changes as ΔP, the trend as T and peg deviations as D. Moreover ΔS and ΔV^{BTC} are the first differences of token supply and Bitcoin's price-volatility respectively. Dummy variables include seasonal ones (Z_t^{hour}, Z_t^{day}, Z_t^{month}) and others that account for the sign of the peg deviation ($Z_t^{D>0}$) and the direction of the trend ($Z_t^{T>0}$). The unobserved coin effect is denominated as a_i while b_t gives the unobserved

---

[6] Robustness against multicollinearity among the regressors is ensured by checking the respective Variance Inflation Factors (VIF) (compare Appendix 7.2 Table 3 of the full paper).

time effect and the remaining residual errors are given as u_{it}. A parsimonious base-line regression can thus be based on unobserved-effects equation

$$
\begin{aligned}
\Delta P_{i,t+1} =& \beta_2 T_{i,t} + \beta_3 T_{i,t}^2 + \beta_4 T_{i,t}^3 + \beta_5 D_{i,t} + \beta_3 D_{i,t}^2 + \beta_4 D_{i,t}^3 \\
& + \beta_5 \Delta S_{i,t} + \beta_6 \Delta V^{\text{BTC}} + a_i + b_t + u_{it},
\end{aligned} \tag{5}
$$

while the full general regression is based on

$$
\begin{aligned}
\Delta P_{i,t+1} =& \beta_2 T_{i,t} + \beta_3 T_{i,t}^2 + \beta_4 T_{i,t}^3 + \beta_5 D_{i,t} + \beta_6 D_{i,t}^2 + \beta_7 D_{i,t}^3 \\
& + \beta_8 \Delta S_{i,t} + \beta_9 \Delta V_{i,t}^{\text{BTC}} + Z_t^{\text{hour}} + Z_t^{\text{day}} + Z_t^{\text{month}} + \beta_{10} T_{i,t} \cdot Z_t^{T>0} \\
& + \beta_{11} T_{i,t} \cdot Z_t^{D>0} + \beta_{12} D_{i,t} \cdot Z_t^{D>0} + \beta_{13} D_{i,t} \cdot Z_t^{T>0} + a_i + b_t + u_{it},
\end{aligned} \tag{6}
$$

where t is the time- and i the coin index.

While two-way fixed-effects regression are applied to eliminate time and entity effects in the original framework [15,17], recent research indicates that this approach might lead to mostly uninterpretable coefficients [29,36] and biased inferences in most general applications [31]. This study thus settles on eliminating a_i by coin-fixed-effects but models common time effects by including seasonal dummies and control variables. Treatment of the Nickel bias and other issues related to panel data regressions with long time series dimensions (e.g. heteroskedasticity, non-stationarity and serial correlation) are treated in line with state-of-the-art approaches. For more information refer to Appendix A.

5   Results

Table 1 supplies estimates of the coefficients given in Eq. 4. As suggested by the applied asset pricing theory, not only current deviations from the peg but also price trends show significant relations with the coming hour's price change. Also, the adopted nonlinear regression framework has proven useful. Most of the variables that are raised to the second and third power show high significance and our models explain roughly 20% of the variance in the one-hour-ahead price changes.
[7] However, coefficient estimates vary with the way outliers are treated. For the model based on data for which no outlier treatment has been implemented (compare Column 1 Table 1), the polynomial of significant coefficients for the estimated price change is $\widehat{\Delta P}_{t+1} = -0.160D_t + 0.085D_t^2 - 0.417D_t^3$. This polynomial is displayed in Fig. 1, which relates peg deviations and trends to the coming hours price change. Even relative small peg deviations are associated with moderate price changes. Large peg deviations, however, precede extreme price changes forcefully driving prices back to the peg. The coefficients related to price trends display nonlinearity as well and form $\widehat{\Delta P}_{t+1} = -0.266D_t + 0.178D_t^3$. Weak price trends seem to be reverted, while stronger ones lead to trend following. In other

---

[7] Price changes are infamously noisy [9]. Regressing daily order flows on price changes for *Tether* [38] arrive at R-squares up to 13%.

Table 1. Coin-FE regression based on Eq. 4.

	Dependent variable:	
	ΔP_{t+1}	
	(1)	(2)
D_t	$-0.160^{***}(0.008)$	$-0.259^{***}(0.008)$
D_t^2	$0.085^{***}(0.027)$	$0.046^{***}(0.006)$
D_t^3	$-0.417^{***}(0.046)$	$0.056^{**}(0.023)$
T_t	$-0.266^{***}(0.009)$	$-0.184^{***}(0.005)$
T_t^2	$-0.009(0.023)$	$-0.005(0.008)$
T_t^3	$0.178^{***}(0.053)$	$-0.011(0.037)$
ΔS_t	$0.208^{***}(0.077)$	$0.394^{***}(0.144)$
$\Delta V_t^{\mathrm{BTC}}$	$-0.070(0.050)$	$-0.308^{***}(0.089)$
Observations	101,243	101,243
R^2	0.200	0.198
Adjusted R^2	0.200	0.198
F Statistic	$3,162.209^{***}$	$3,123.468^{***}$
(df = 8; 101224)		

Note: $^{*}p < 0.1$; $^{**}p < 0.05$; $^{***}p < 0.01$
Variable denominations are given in Sect. 4 under Eq. 4.
Column (1) for untreated- and column (2) for outlier free
data. Standard errors given in brackets.

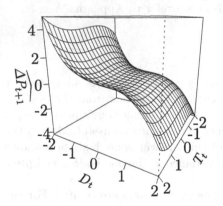

Fig. 1. Coefficient interplay for untreated data   **Fig. 2.** Coefficient interplay for outlier-free data

words, series of consecutive strong price changes of the same direction are prolonged. This might be a result of consecutive hours of price jumps after large deviations. In comparison to price trends, but also all other tested variables, the joint influence of the coefficients for peg deviations seems be the largest by far. Their influence is roughly symmetric for positive and negative price deviations. For the model based on data for which price changes in excess of 5 SD have been truncated (Column 2 of Table 1), the joint estimated effect of price trends and peg deviations on coming price changes is displayed in Fig. 2. For peg deviations, the polynomial of significant coefficients is $\widehat{\Delta P}_{t+1} = -0.259D_t + 0.046D_t^2 + 0.056D_t^3$ with roots roughly at -2.6, 0 and 1.8. The effect of smaller peg deviations is in line with expectations: The relation of peg deviations and the coming price change is positive for $-2.6 \leq D \leq 0$ and negative for $0 \leq D \leq 1.8$ and would thus lead to mean-reverting prices. For positive deviations $D > 1.8$ and negative deviations $D < -2.6$, however, signs turn and peg deviations are associated with price changes leading away from the peg. The reason for this seemingly counter-intuitive result might be that the majority (95.37%) of observed price changes lie within the 2 SD displayed in Figs. 1 and 2. Rather than avoiding rare but large errors from outliers, the coefficients seem to be optimized to fit smaller fluctuations around the peg. Not only the results for peg deviations—but also price trends differ. The latter, estimated based on outlier free data, show a linear, negative relation to coming price changes. In other words, series of price changes of equal sign revert soon. The size of the coefficients for trend and peg deviations are relatively low, though. For instance, a peg deviation of 2 SD in negative direction is associated merely with an increase in prices of 0.1 SD. A negative price trend of 1 SD is associated with an increase of prices of around 0.2 SD. Arbitrage is estimated to have a very limited effect in the outlier-free dataset. With coefficients of 0.394 and -0.308 respectively, the change in token supply and the change in the Bitcoin's price volatility seem to be equally important price determinants, at least. This contrast is surprising, given that they are caused by the truncation of merely 363 of 101243 observations. Table 2 of Appendix B gives coefficients for the same model but complemented by dummy representations accounting for hours, weekdays, months as well as interaction terms for the sign of the peg deviation and the direction of the price trend. The results differ only negligibly.

6   Conclusion

The stark contrast of the importance of peg deviations in the fitted models with—and without outlier treatment is striking. For data including extreme price changes, peg deviations and trend dynamics seem to approximate price formation well. For stablecoins, the intuitive *CBAF* approach to model trader behavior might thus be seen as a good approximation for the determinants of price changes. For outlier-free data, however, the effects seem to blend in with other price-determinants. The above results pose the question of whether stablecoin markets might not best be modeled as switching between a first regime characterized by limited arbitrage, and a second one setting in when markets promise sufficient profits for large trades towards the peg. While the most obvious candidate for explaining such results might be costs of arbitrage, at least short-term variation of the *Ethereum Gas* price turned out to yield insignificant coefficients when adopted as control variable. Future research might employ cointegration analysis capable of unvailing also longterm relationships.

A   Robustness

The dataset applied in this study combines 11 timeseries of differing lengths and might thus be described as an unbalanced timeseries panel. While a large T dimension is generally beneficial, simple panel data approaches might be mis-specified. A first issue is serial correlation. In most financial time series prior realizations affect coming ones. Including lagged data might thus be useful to capture serial correlation in the data - this is usually referred to as dynamic panel modeling. Instead of including lagged data explicitly, in this study, the trend variable is carrying auto-regressive information.Using simple fixed-effects models jointly with lagged variables, however, induces the so-called Nickell bias as the lagged variable causes endogeneity in the regressors [42]. As argued by [21, p.163], including fixed-effects into dynamic specifications of panel data regres-sions, even for simple OLS estimates, can mitigate the issue to some degree. Their coefficients, however, are still seriously biased for small T. In our case, including coin-fixed-effects and considering that T is very large, Nickell's bias should be negligible.[8] There are other issues known from time-series analysis, though. [46] warned about relying on the above for inference for non-stationary data (which might lead to spurious regression results) and suggested to check the error term for heteroskedasticity, serial correlation and nonnormality. To counter this problem, this study ensures stationarity using the Levin-Lin-Chu unit root test [37]. As the test does not reject the presence of a unit root for token supply and volatility, we take first differences of these variables.

As discussed earlier, we apply coin-FE panel regressions based on simple OLS-estimation. As a consequence, several assumptions are to be ensured. Resid-uals ought to display a mean of zero and be free of heteroscedasticity, cross-sectional, and serial correlation. Breusch-Pagan Lagrange Multiplier tests and Pesaran cross-sectional dependence tests are used to test for cross-sectional dependence in the residuals. Additionally, Student's t-tests have been applied to check the residuals for a mean of zero. Breusch-Godfrey/Wooldridge tests have been applied to test for serial correlation. Breusch-Pagan tests are used for detecting heteroskedasticity. While a deviation from zero for the residuals is strongly rejected, unfortunately, the remaining tests reveal heteroscedasticity, serial, and also cross-sectional correlation. In other words, residuals are showing variance clusters and are depending on their own- and even lags across coins. As a consequence, the simple OLS estimator is biased. To still draw robust infer-ences from the estimated model, spacial correlation consistent (SCC) estimators introduced in [24] are used. The approach adapts Newey-West estimators to the panel setting and leads to robust standard errors even in the presence of heteroscedasticity and cross-sectional and serial correlation.

For tables and further details on the above robustness checks, please refer to the full paper.

---

[8] In fact, following [46], the bias for the fixed-effects estimator approaches zero with rate $1/T$.

B   Tables

Table 1. Outliers.

Cutoff	Outliers as defined by cutoff in percent	
(in Std. Dev.)	N	%
1	18839	18.6
2	4686	4.63
3	1563	1.54
4	683	0.67
5	363	0.36

Fraction of data classified as outliers.

Table 2. Coin-FE regression.

	Dependent variable: ΔP_{t+1}	
	(1)	(2)
D_t	$-0.111^{***}(0.010)$	$-0.230^{***}(0.014)$
D_t^2	$0.089^{***}(0.027)$	$0.047^{***}(0.007)$
D_t^3	$-0.472^{***}(0.047)$	$0.032(0.025)$
T_t	$-0.248^{***}(0.012)$	$-0.180^{***}(0.009)$
T_t^2	$-0.010(0.023)$	$-0.006(0.009)$
T_t^3	$0.162^{***}(0.054)$	$-0.015(0.038)$
ΔS_t	$0.202^{***}(0.074)$	$0.392^{***}(0.142)$
ΔV_t^{BTC}	$-0.063(0.051)$	$-0.304^{***}(0.089)$
Z_t^{hour}	$-0.0003(0.0003)$	$-0.0003(0.001)$
Z_t^{day}	$-0.0002(0.0003)$	$-0.001(0.001)$
Z_t^{month}	$-0.003^{***}(0.0003)$	$-0.006^{***}(0.001)$
$D \cdot Z_t^{D>0}$	$-0.018^{***}(0.002)$	$-0.006(0.009)$
$D \cdot Z_t^{T>0}$	$-0.003^{**}(0.001)$	$-0.011(0.007)$
$T \cdot Z_t^{D>0}$	$0.003^{***}(0.001)$	$-0.005(0.008)$
$T \cdot Z_t^{T>0}$	$0.0001(0.001)$	$0.009(0.007)$
Adjusted R^2	0.208	0.199
F Statistic	$1{,}769.824^{***}$	$1{,}681.830^{***}$
(df = 15; 101217)		

Note: $^*p < 0.1$; $^{**}p < 0.05$; $^{***}p < 0.01$
This table gives the results of a coin-FE regression for the
full model specified in Eq. 4. Column (1) for untreated-
and column (2) for outlier free data. Coefficient's standard
errors given in brackets.

References

1. Federally chartered banks and thrifts may participate in independent node verification networks and use stablecoins for payment activities. https://www.occ.gov/news-issuances/news-releases/2021/nr-occ-2021-2.html. Accessed 7 Jan 2021
2. Almosova, A.: A monetary model of blockchain (2018)
3. Ante, L., Fiedler, I., Strehle, E.: The influence of stablecoin issuances on cryptocurrency markets. Finance Res. Lett. **41**, 101867 (2020)
4. Athey, S., Parashkevov, I., Sarukkai, V., Xia, J.: Bitcoin pricing, adoption, and usage: theory and evidence (2016)
5. Baumöhl, E., Vyrost, T.: Stablecoins as a crypto safe haven? Not all of them! (2020)
6. Belsley, D.A., Kuh, E., Welsch, R.E.: Regression Diagnostics: Identifying Influential Data and Sources of Collinearity, vol. 571. John Wiley & Sons (2005)
7. Biais, B., Bisiere, C., Bouvard, M., Casamatta, C., Menkveld, A.J.: Equilibrium bitcoin pricing. Available at SSRN (2018)
8. Bianchi, D., Iacopini, M., Rossini, L.: Stablecoins and cryptocurrency returns: evidence from large Bayesian vars. Available at SSRN (2020)
9. Black, F.: Noise. J. Finance **41**(3), 528–543 (1986)
10. Britten-Jones, M., Neuberger, A.: Arbitrage pricing with incomplete markets. Appl. Math. Finance **3**(4), 347–363 (1996)
11. Bullmann, D., Klemm, J., Pinna, A.: In search for stability in crypto-assets: are stablecoins the solution? ECB Occasional Paper (230) (2019)
12. Caginalp, C.: A dynamical systems approach to cryptocurrency stability. arXiv preprint arXiv:1805.03143 (2018)
13. Caginalp, C., Caginalp, G.: Establishing cryptocurrency equilibria through game theory. Mathematics (AIMS), Forthcoming (2019)
14. Caginalp, G., Balenovich, D.: Asset flow and momentum: deterministic and stochastic equations. Philos. Trans. R. Soc. A Math. Phys. Eng. Sci. **357**(1758), 2119–2133 (1999)
15. Caginalp, G., Desantis, M.: Stock price dynamics: nonlinear trend, volume, volatility, resistance and money supply. Quant. Finance **11**(6), 849–861 (2011)
16. Caginalp, G., DeSantis, M.: Nonlinear price dynamics of s&p 100 stocks. Physica A Statist. Mech. Appl. **547**, 122067 (2019)
17. Caginalp, G., DeSantis, M., Sayrak, A.: The nonlinear price dynamics of us equity ETFs. J. Econometrics **183**(2), 193–201 (2014)
18. Caginalp, G., Ermentrout, G.: A kinetic thermodynamics approach to the psychology of fluctuations in financial markets. Appl. Math. Lett. **3**(4), 17–19 (1990)
19. Clark, J., Demirag, D., Moosavi, S.: SoK: demystifying stablecoins. Available at SSRN 3466371 (2019)
20. Corbet, S., Eraslan, V., Lucey, B., Sensoy, A.: The effectiveness of technical trading rules in cryptocurrency markets. Finance Res. Lett. **31**, 32–37 (2019)
21. Croissant, Y., Millo, G., et al.: Panel data econometrics with R. Wiley Online Library (2019)
22. Delbaen, F., Schachermayer, W.: The Mathematics of Arbitrage. Springer (2006). https://doi.org/10.1007/978-3-540-31299-4
23. Dell'Erba, M.: Stablecoins in cryptoeconomics from initial coin offerings to central bank digital currencies. NYUJ Legis. & Pub. Pol'y **22**, 1 (2019)
24. Driscoll, J.C., Kraay, A.C.: Consistent covariance matrix estimation with spatially dependent panel data. Rev. Econ. Statist. **80**(4), 549–560 (1998)

25. Deutsch, H.-P., Beinker, M.W.: Arbitrage. In: Derivatives and Internal Models. FCMS, pp. 97–106. Springer, Cham (2019). https://doi.org/10.1007/978-3-030-22899-6_6
26. Fama, E.F.: Random walks in stock market prices. Financ. Anal. J. **51**(1), 75–80 (1995)
27. Griffin, J.M., Shams, A.: Is bitcoin really untethered? J. Finance **75**(4), 1913–1964 (2020)
28. Grobys, K., Ahmed, S., Sapkota, N.: Technical trading rules in the cryptocurrency market. Finance Res. Lett. **32**, 101396 (2020)
29. Hill, T.D., Davis, A.P., Roos, J.M., French, M.T.: Limitations of fixed-effects models for panel data. Sociol. Perspect. **63**(3), 357–369 (2020)
30. Hudson, R., Urquhart, A.: Technical trading and cryptocurrencies. Ann. Oper. Res. **297**(1), 191–220 (2019). https://doi.org/10.1007/s10479-019-03357-1
31. Imai, K., Kim, I.S.: On the use of two-way fixed effects regression models for causal inference with panel data. Harvard University, Unpublished paper (2019)
32. Kimmerl, J.: Understanding users' perception on the adoption of stablecoins-the libra case. In: PACIS, p. 187 (2020)
33. Klages-Mundt, A., Harz, D., Gudgeon, L., Liu, J.Y., Minca, A.: Stablecoins 2.0: economic foundations and risk-based models. In: Proceedings of the 2nd ACM Conference on Advances in Financial Technologies, pp. 59–79 (2020)
34. Klages-Mundt, A., Minca, A.: (in) stability for the blockchain: Deleveraging spirals and stablecoin attacks. arXiv preprint arXiv:1906.02152 (2019)
35. Klages-Mundt, A., Minca, A.: While stability lasts: a stochastic model of stablecoins. arXiv preprint arXiv:2004.01304 (2020)
36. Kropko, J., Kubinec, R.: Why the two-way fixed effects model is difficult to interpret, and what to do about it. Available at SSRN 3062619 (2018)
37. Levin, A., Lin, C.F., Chu, C.S.J.: Unit root tests in panel data: asymptotic and finite-sample properties. J. Econometrics **108**(1), 1–24 (2002)
38. Lyons, R.K., Viswanath-Natraj, G.: What keeps stablecoins stable? Tech. rep, National Bureau of Economic Research (2020)
39. Misc.: Centre whitepaper. https://www.centre.io/pdfs/centre-whitepaper.pdf. visited on 30 Nov 2018
40. Misc.: Stably whitepaper. https://s3.ca-central-1.amazonaws.com/stably-public-documents/whitepapers/Stably+Whitepaper+v6.pdf (2018). Visited on 16 July 2018
41. Moin, A., Sekniqi, K., Sirer, E.G.: SoK: a classification framework for stablecoin designs. In: Financial Cryptography (2020)
42. Nickell, S.: Biases in dynamic models with fixed effects. Econometrica J. Econometric Soc. **46**, 1417–1426 (1981)
43. Pernice, I.G., Henningsen, S., Proskalovich, R., Florian, M., Elendner, H., Scheuermann, B.: Monetary stabilization in cryptocurrencies-design approaches and open questions. In: 2019 Crypto Valley Conference on Blockchain Technology (CVCBT), pp. 47–59. IEEE (2019)
44. Porter, D.P., Smith, V.L.: Stock market bubbles in the laboratory. Appl. Math. Finance **1**(2), 111–128 (1994)
45. Wang, G.J., Ma, X.Y., Wu, H.Y.: Are stablecoins truly diversifiers, hedges, or safe havens against traditional cryptocurrencies as their name suggests? Res. Int. Bus. Finance **54**, 101225 (2020)
46. Wooldridge, J.M.: Introductory econometrics: a modern approach. Nelson Education (2016)

Red-Black Coins: Dai Without Liquidations

Mehdi Salehi$^{(\boxtimes)}$, Jeremy Clark, and Mohammad Mannan

Concordia University, Montreal, Canada

Abstract. A number of Ethereum projects for stablecoins and synthetic assets use the same core mechanism for fixing the price of an asset. In this paper, we distil this shared approach into a primitive we call red-black coins. We use a model to demonstrate the primitive's financial character-istics and to reason about how it should be priced. Real world projects do not use the red-black coin primitive in isolation but lay on other mechanisms and features to provide fungibility and to reduce exposure to price drops. One mechanism is called liquidation, however liquidation is hard to analyze as it relies on human behaviour and could produce unintended economic consequences. Therefore we additionally develop a design landscape for extending the red-black coin primitives and put forward a research agenda for alternatives to liquidation.

1 Introductory Remarks

Cryptocurrencies like Bitcoin (BTC) and Ether (ETH) are marked by extreme volatility in price relative to the US dollar (USD). As decentralized finance (DeFi) services mature on Ethereum, a critical component to their success is letting users choose between holding ETH and holding a stablecoin that targets USD (or some other metric of stability) in price.

Some stablecoins work like a hypothetical vending machine [3]: Alice deposits two 'coins' from a volatile currency (*e.g.,* a cryptocurrency like ETH) into the machine and it returns to her two new coins—a 'black' coin that is stable and a 'red' coin that is even more volatile in price than the original coins Alice put in. Together, the red and black coins are equal in value to the two input coins. The machine cannot reduce overall price volatility, but it can push volatility from the black coin onto the red coin.

Consider the following example of such a stability mechanism. An asset is chosen that is considered stable by definition (*e.g.,* the US dollar). The vending machine is implemented as a decentralized app (DApp; *a.k.a.,* smart contract) on a blockchain (*e.g.,* Ethereum). Alice deposits an amount of ETH worth $1.50 USD into the DApp. The DApp references a trusted oracle service for the current ETH/USD exchange rate to enforce this. The DApp holds the ETH as a deposit for future redemption, and returns to Alice a red coin and a black coin (*e.g.,* as ERC-20 tokens). Alice can sell one or both coins. In the future, the owner of the black coin can redeem it for ETH from the DApp, and receive the equivalent

© International Financial Cryptography Association 2021
M. Bernhard et al. (Eds.): FC 2021 Workshops, LNCS 12676, pp. 136–145, 2021.
https://doi.org/10.1007/978-3-662-63958-0_12

of $1.00 USD. This assumes the initial deposit of $1.50 USD worth of ETH is still worth at least $1.00 USD at redemption time—if not, the black coin owner receives all of the collateral. The red coin holder receives any remaining ETH after the black coin holder is paid.

The key idea is that the black coin will nearly always be worth the equivalent of $1.00 USD. This is true when ETH/USD increases in value, stays the same, or declines moderately. Only if it declines significantly does the black coin start to experience volatility in price—its redemption value will decrease at the same rate as ETH/USD itself. For the red coin, the redemption value increases and decreases as ETH/USD itself increases and decreases, however the gains and losses are amplified. This is an overview; we return to these details below.

Synthetic Assets. The red-black coin primitive can be generalized to produce black coins that match the price of any financial asset, not just a currency like the USD, simply by changing the price that the oracle references. For example, a black coin for one share of the company Apple (APPL) would use an ETH/APPL price feed (possibly constructed by bridging ETH/USD and APPL/USD prices) and otherwise be exactly the same. These black coins are "synthetic assets" because they expose the holder to the price movements of the asset but do not afford the holder any other benefits of holding the financial instrument (*e.g.*, shareholder votes or dividends for equities; physical delivery for futures; or the ability to settle a loan, or option contract on the asset). What a red coin represents in this example is less natural than for a stablecoin: it is a bet that ETH will increase in price faster than APPL.

Relation to Dai. At the time of writing, the stablecoin Dai has (i) a market cap of $800M (the largest of all non-centralized stablecoins); (ii) its parent service, Maker, locks $1.2B worth of ETH (the third largest DeFi service, and the largest stablecoin); and (iii) it is the most supplied and most borrowed asset on the DeFi lending service Compound.[1] Dai uses the red-black coin primitive—black coins are called Dai and a red coin is a Vault (*née* collateralized debt position or CDP). However the system is immensely more complicated because it adds a number of features that the basic red-black coin primitive lacks: (1) interchangeability (fungibility) of black coins across multiple producers, (2) a liquidation process to incentivize red coin holders to increase the collateralized ETH as ETH/USD declines or face an auction that automatically settles a red-black pair, and (3) fees to balance supply/demand of black and red coins that are adjustable through a distributed governance. Other projects built on the red-black primitive (for both stablecoins and synthetic assets) include Synthetix's sUSD,[2] Kava's USDX,[3] UMA,[4] and BitUSD.[5]

---

[1] https://compound.finance/markets.
[2] https://docs.synthetix.io/litepaper/.
[3] https://www.kava.io/.
[4] https://docs.umaproject.org/.
[5] https://github.com/bitshares.

Liquidations. The worst-case scenario for a red-black coin is a decline in the value of ETH/USD. As a primitive, red-black coins simply force the holders to take on this risk. By contrast, liquidations are the main preventative mechanism used by full-fledged systems like Dai. Liquidations are controversial: many vault holders have lost ETH due to liquidations, they require special monitoring tools (*e.g.,* DeFiSaver.com), any analysis includes assumptions about how humans behave and how fast market actions can be taken, and maligned incentives (*e.g.,* return DAI for ETH when ETH/DAI is in decline) can lead to economic crises and deleveraging spirals [5,9]. Liquidations failed Dai on Ethereum's "Black Thursday" event in March 2020 and required a bail-out. In this paper, red-black coins can be thought of as "Dai without liquidations". Since liquidations have a downside, it is important to weigh these against what they contribute. To understand what they contribute, we must first thoroughly understand red-black coins and their shortcomings. Further it might be possible that liquidations are not the best tool to address any shortcomings—we consider alternatives in Sect. 3.

1.1 Contributions and Related Work

We reference some financial instruments and terminology throughout the paper; we refer the reader elsewhere for full explanations of these [6]. Several systemization of knowledge papers cover stablecoins [3,7,10,11]. Our notion of a red-black coin is inspired by the 'indirectly-backed' classification from [3] and they are categorized as 'non-custodial' stablecoins with 'exogenous collateral' [7]. The stability mechanism is often described as allowing a user to 'borrow' USD from themselves using their ETH as collateral [10,11]. We find this framing less intuitive than one of a simple derivative contract [3]. None of the SoKs provide modelling of the stability mechanism in this paper, and instead focus on surveying several different types of stablecoins. Maker is considered a decentralized finance (DeFi) project and it (and other DeFi projects) has been studied from orthogonal angles including attacks/measurements on governance and oracles, attacks using flash loans, and modelling liquidity crises [4,5,7,9,12].

In this paper, we isolate and study the red-black coin primitive to better understand its characteristics, which seems prudent before analyzing more complex systems. We use the ETH price model from [5] to model how risky red and black coins are under different scenarios. We then examine the necessity of the extra infrastructure projects like what Maker adds to the red-black coins—precisely what does the added complexity (*e.g.,* stability fees, liquidation, global shutdown, *etc.*) achieve and what are the design alternatives for the same functionality? We assume that the market for red and black coins are perfectly liquid to have a simple model to analyze. Others have explored the effect of supply and demand and the possibility of market collapse due to the feedback effects on liquidity and volatility from deleveraging effects during crises [8,9]. The key difference is these other works consider liquidations to be an inherent building block in their analysis, whereas we study an even simpler stablecoin without liquidations to better understand the parameters of what liquidations are supposed to

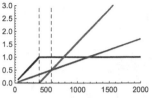

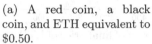

(a) A red coin, a black coin, and ETH equivalent to $0.50.

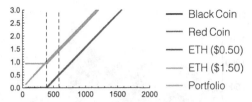

(b) A red coin, ETH equivalent to $1.50, and a portfolio of a red coin and $0.94.

Fig. 1. Redemption value in USD (y-axis) as the price of ETH (x-axis) changes. (Color figure online)

provide (and critically consider if these provisions could be better provider by alternative mechanisms).

In addition to our work, there are other stablecoins that issue one stablecoin and one volatile coin but provide stability through a different mechanism, such as algorithmically expanding and contracting supply [14]. Cao *et al.* frame their stablecoin as a financial instrument and use traditional option theory models to analyze their system [2].

2   Financial Characteristics

In this section, we answer questions about the financial characteristics of the red-black primitive. Consider a black coin that targets $1 USD when 1 ETH is $381.56 USD, and the DApp holds 0.00393126 ETH (worth $1.5 USD). Assume for now that (i) a red-black coin is a (non-fungible) contract between two individuals, (ii) it has a fixed maturity date, and (iii) no one intervenes when ETH/USD declines enough that black coins starts to lose value (no liquidations). Figure 1(a) shows how much a black coin is worth (y-axis) as the price of ETH varies (x-axis). The starting point ($381.56 USD) is marked and if the price of ETH increases (rightward), the black coin is always worth $1. If the value of ETH decreases (leftward), the black coin is still stable until the value of ETH hits $254.37 (marked)—at this point, 0.00393126 ETH starts to become worth less than $1 and the black coin 'breaks the buck.'

Figure 1(a) also shows the redemption value of a red coin. When created, a red coin is redeemable for $0.50 USD. A user with $0.50 USD can choose between purchasing a red coin or purchasing ETH (also shown). In both cases, the user profits when ETH increases and loses when ETH decreases in price. However the slope of red coin is greater. This indicates it is a *leveraged* position in ETH.

2.1   How Much Should You Pay for a Black Coin?

Consider a black coin that is purchased today when ETH is $381.56 USD. How much will it be worth in 100 days? In most future worlds, the black coin will

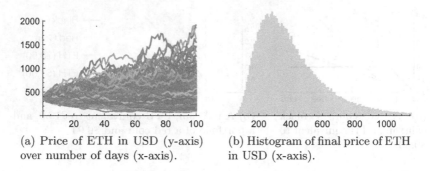

(a) Price of ETH in USD (y-axis) over number of days (x-axis).

(b) Histogram of final price of ETH in USD (x-axis).

Fig. 2. ETH/USD Monte Carlo simulation results.

be worth \$1. In some future worlds (when ETH is worth less than \$254.37), the black coin will break the buck. But even here, it takes a 'haircut' on value as opposed to being worthless (*e.g.*, it can be redeemed for, say, \$0.90).

The average value of a black coin for different possible outcomes can be estimated if we have a statistical model for ETH price movements. In finance, many statistical models have been proposed for many assets. Pricing ETH remains an open research problem. Until future research from the finance community advocates for the most appropriate model, we will sketch in some concrete numbers using Geometric Brownian Motion (GBM), which underlies the Black-Scholes model for pricing options [1] and has been used for ETH in other work [5]. We omit the details of the model itself (covered in nearly every financial textbook [15]). We fit the model to the historical 'closing' prices of ETH for 1000 days prior to 18 Sept 2020[6] and obtain $\mu = 0.000744754$ (an upward drift in price over time) and $\sigma = 0.0524172$ (a measure of volatility). If we simulate the next 100 days using Monte Carlo, we obtain the results in Fig. 2. For the parameters of this example, the average value of the black coin is \$0.94 USD at the maturity date. Our model can be adjusted for the initial price, over-collateralization ratio (Sect. 2.2), and days until redemption. It is available in Python and Mathematica.[7]

As shown in Fig. 2(b), the expected return is log-normal. When we model more than 100 days, the variance increases and the average redemption value of a black coin decreases: \$0.94 USD after 100 days, \$0.85 USD after 200 days, and \$0.80 after 1 year. This does not mean the black coin is worth less over time, it means the risk it falls out-of-the-money increases the more time you give it.

2.2 Why Would You Want a Red Coin?

While a stablecoin has utility to the holder, it is less clear what the utility of a red coin is. A red coin is a *leveraged* position in ETH, which means that both gains and losses are amplified—compare the slope of the red coin value with a \$0.50

---

[6] CoinGecko API: https://api.coingecko.com.

[7] GitHub: https://github.com/GreatSoshiant/Monte-Carlo/tree/master/Code.

ETH investment at the same starting point ($381.56 USD) in Fig. 1(a). Leverage is popular with investors. Investing in a red coin is equivalent to investing $0.50 along with borrowing 2 × $0.50 in ETH (*i.e.*, 3:1 leverage). If the over-collateralization ratio is decreased from 1.50 to 1.10, then leverage for the red coin increases to 11:1. However, the black coin becomes riskier and its 100-day average value drops from $0.94 to $0.86. For a $2.00 collateralization, red coin leverage is 2:1, and the black coin average value is $0.98.

Speculators seek out red coins but what about a user that wants to hold ETH without any leverage? She seemingly has no interest in red (or black) coins. Consider two scenarios: (a) she holds $1.50 worth of ETH; and (b) she takes her $1.50 worth of ETH, issues and sells a black coin (*e.g.*, for $0.97 USD), and holds the red coin. She actually has a small portfolio of a red coin and close to $1 USD. The redemption value of (a) and (b) are depicted in Fig. 1(b), along with the red coin by itself. The portfolio is actually an attractive investment— she has 'insurance' against catastrophic loss during a devaluation of ETH for a small fixed 'fee'—the $0.03 USD difference between what she received for the black coin ($0.94) and what the DApp pays out to the black coin holder ($1.00). Additionally, she produced a stable black coin, which has external benefit to the decentralized economy.

3   Research Agenda: Extending Red-Black Coins

Red-black coins are primitives. Before deploying them, other aspects of their design should to be considered. Design decisions include the maturity/redemption policy, how to make black and red coins fungible, and interventions to prevent the black coin from breaking the buck. One path through the decision tree leads to a design like Dai, however there are many other decisions that could result in very different stablecoins that have not been thoroughly explored by academics or the DeFi community to our knowledge. We do not propose a specific alternative but see our contribution as setting a research agenda.

3.1   Fungibility

Assume Alice creates a red/black coin, selling the red coin to Carol. Later, Bob creates a red/black coin, selling the red coin to David. Alice's black coin is not identical to Bob's black coin. Because they were created at different times, the ETH/USD exchange rate is different, and thus the amount of collateral in ETH in the DApp will be different. The more collateral, the more a black coin is worth (recall Sect. 2.2). Such coins are not interchangeable or *fungible* which adds effort to valuation and exchange.

One design option is to (1) **forgo fungibility** and have each coin pair be its own individual contract between two counter-parties (*a.k.a.*, over-the-counter (OTC) contracts). This is the difference between, say, a forward and futures contract [6]. A second option is to (2) **pool the collateral** of the red coins so that each black coin is a claim against the pool. A pool can be unfair: the losses are democratized to all black coin holders. When pooled, Alice might obtain a black coin before an ETH/USD price bubble; all the black coins issued during the rising bubble are backed by significantly less collateral and when the bubble bursts (consider the case that it reverts to the pre-bubble price), the pool could become under-collateralized, impacting Alice. Had Alice used an OTC contract instead, her red coin would acquire and lose value with the bubble but not be under-collaterialized after bursting.

A third option is to additionally offer **(3) red coin fungibility**. Since red coins have variable collateral (based on when they were created), two conditions need to be added to its transfer function: (i) red coins with less than a specified collateral are not transferable, and (ii) red coins with more than the specified collateral will transfer the surplus to the seller's address while transferring it. While this is not possible with vaults in Dai currently, it seems feasible to add.

3.2   Redemption

A policy for redeeming the collateralized ETH is the next design decision. Note that the DApp can autonomously distribute the collateral without the participation of the red or black coin holder, however someone needs to trigger a function call against the DApp to finalize the process.

Red-black coins could **(1) mature on a pre-specified date** (*e.g.*, the first day of a specified month). At any given time, red/black coins in circulation would have one of a few different expiration dates, while still allowing some degree of fungibility. Coin holders would shorten or extend their coins by trading for a coin with a different maturity date. This is precisely how futures mature [6], and yTokens are based on the same principle [13]. After maturity, the DApp would lock all transfer functions and only allow withdrawal by the coin holders. The first to ask for a withdrawal would trigger the DApp to look up the ETH/USD price as of the maturity date and split the collateral accordingly.

Alternatively, red-black coins could be redeemed at any time **(2) on demand by the black coin holder**, or **(3) red coin holder**, **(4) either**, or **(5) both**. Options (in the US style) work on the principal of (2) or (3) [6,15]. Allowing either to redeem is unlike anything we could find in traditional finance—we speculate it would add uncertainty without any clear gain. Requiring both to agree to redemption could be done by agreement, or (consistent with futures contracts [6]), a red coin holder could acquire a (fungible) black coin and redeem the (netted-out) pair.

3.3   Under-Collateralization

When the ETH/USD exchange rate drops enough that under-collateralization is possible, the system could **(1) do nothing** and let the black coin holder price the risk of this into the coin. If the design attempts further mitigation, the DApp could operate like a margin trading account and require red coin holders to top-up their collateral. If they do not, it is **(2) liquidated** (*e.g.*, sold by auction for black coins). The challenge is incentivizing users to sell USD-pegged black coins for ETH when ETH/USD is in decline (a counter-cyclic investment). In Dai, because collateral is pooled, liquidation is essential because under-collateralized red coins hurt all black coin holders. When collateral is not pooled, liquidation is useless for black coin holders because both ETH and black coins decrease in value at the same rate (recall Fig. 1) so it is simpler to do nothing.

Liquidation does not incentivize topped-up collateral unless it is accompanied by a **(3) punishment** (otherwise red coin holders might try to buy their liquidated assets from themselves at a discount). Beyond charging a fee, a stablecoin system might also withhold rewards (some systems used a secondary token for providing governance and providing rewards) or block red coin transfers until collateral is restored. In traditional financial markets, it is also the case that a trader's margin is inadequate to settle their account, they are still legally liable for the difference. A stablecoin accompanied by a **(4) reputation system** could mandate that red coin holders settle any obligation, however the potential loses for a red coin holder becomes unbound. A different approach is to obtain **(5) insurance** or financial coverage for the event of a decline in ETH/USD. This could be actual insurance, whether decentralized or from a traditional brokerage, or an offsetting financial investment that hedges the currency exchange risk.

The last approach is **(6) bail out** any losses through sales of a secondary token. This was used recently by Maker for Dai holders when its normal procedures of (2) and (3) were not adequate for dealing with a sharp, unexpected decline in the price of ETH on 12 March 2020 ('black Thursday'). While the auction was successful and recollateralized the pool, it cannot be guaranteed that minting new tokens will be adequate for offsetting any incurred debt. This event also exposed the lack of understanding and underestimation of risk by many vault (*i.e.,* red coin) holders who faced losses under (3), and raises the question of whether a system should be designed that is more forgiving to red coin holders in turbulent markets.

3.4   Autonomy

A design based on the red-black coin primitive that is OTC and does not liquidate is entirely autonomous. It can be instantiated in a DApp and operate without human intervention. While black coins are price-stable under most market conditions, traders who are time-sensitive may forgo obtaining a good price in order to trade quickly. This particularly is influential for stablecoins which provide a low-friction avenue in and out of speculative positions on the price of ETH. Since red and black coins are issued in the same proportion, supply/demand imbalances between them could also add volatility to the black coin price. This could potentially be addressed in the design.

A non-interventionist approach would let the red and black coin price **(1) float freely**. This avoids adding complexity to the design—in fact, a design goal might be to design a system that traders can easily understand and grasp the risk of. This could thwart potential lawsuits, such as a recent class action suit against Dai.[8] An alternative is to further stabilize prices by **(2) setting rates and fees** at various points in the system. For example, if black coin holders can redeem at any time, a fee could be charged to the black coin holder and paid to the red coin holder. If redemption requires both a red and black coin, the fee could be collected by the DApp. This principle is used by central banks for targeting interest rates, and is used in Maker to control the spot market for Dai. It is a struggle to set fees in the context of a decentralized and autonomous organization—while allowing decisions to be voted on is a first step, it does not guarantee that token holders are independent, informed, and not unduly influenced by the 'expert' recommendations.

4   Concluding Remarks

In this paper, we distil complex stablecoin systems into one of their core primitives, the red-black coin and provide a detailed study of its characteristics and possible extensions. It would be useful to have research results on the most suitable financial model for the ETH/USD price rate (*e.g.,* drift-diffusion or GARCH) for us to use in work like this paper. Future work could also examine the benefits of building a Dai alternative, still based on red-black coins but using different design parameters. Two examples that seem interesting are: (a) a more understandable system that reduces the amount of intervention, and (b) a system with fungible red coins that can be traded freely. Finally, while our paper answers the question of how much you should pay for a black coin, the analysis is much more complicated for Dai—with pooled collateral, liquidation, and bailouts, Dai is less risky than a simple black coin but the risk that these countermeasures systemically fail is not zero.

Acknowledgements. We thank the reviewers who helped to improve our paper. J. Clark acknowledges support for this research project from the National Sciences and Engineering Research Council (NSERC), Raymond Chabot Grant Thornton, and Catallaxy Industrial Research Chair in Blockchain Technologies, and the AMF (Autorité des Marchés Financiers). J. Clark and M. Mannan further acknowledge NSERC funding through Discovery Grants.

References

1. Black, F., Scholes, M.: The pricing of options and corporate liabilities. J. Polit. Econ. **81**(3) (1973)
2. Cao, Y., Dai, M., Kou, S., Li, L., Yang, C.: Designing stable coins. Technical report, Duo Network Whitepaper (2018)
3. Clark, J., Demirag, D., Moosavi, S.: Demystifying stablecoins. Commun. ACM. **63** (2020)
4. Gu, W., Raghuvanshi, A., Boneh, D.: Empirical measurements on pricing oracles and decentralized governance for stablecoins. In: Cryptoeconomic Systems (2020)

---

[8] https://www.coindesk.com/28m-makerdao-class-action-lawsuit-arbitration.

5. Gudgeon, L., Perez, D., Harz, D., Livshits, B., Gervais, A.: The decentralized financial crisis. In: CVCBT (2020)
6. Harris, L.: Trading and Exchanges: market Microstructure for Practitioners. Oxford (2003)
7. Klages-Mundt, A., Harz, D., Gudgeon, L., Liu, J.Y., Minca, A.: Stablecoins 2.0: Economic foundations and risk-based models. In: Proceedings of the 2nd ACM Conference on Advances in Financial Technologies, pp. 59–79 (2020)
8. Klages-Mundt, A., Minca, A.: (In) stability for the blockchain: Deleveraging spirals and stablecoin attacks. arXiv preprint arXiv:1906.02152 (2019)
9. Klages-Mundt, A., Minca, A.: While stability lasts: a stochastic model of stablecoins. Technical report, arXiv (2020)
10. Moin, A., Sekniqi, K., Sirer, E.G.: SoK: a classification framework for stablecoin designs. In: Financial Cryptography (2020)
11. Pernice, I.G.A., Henningsen, S., Proskalovich, R., Florian, M., Elendner, H.: Monetary stabilization in cryptocurrencies: Design approaches and open questions. In: CVCBT (2019)
12. Qin, K., Zhou, L., Livshits, B., Gervais, A.: Attacking the DeFi ecosystem with flash loans for fun and profit. Technical report, arXiv:2003.03810v2 (2020)
13. Robinson, D., Niemerg, A.: The yield protocol: on-chain lending with interest rate discovery. Technical report, Yield.is, April 2020
14. Sams, R.: A note on cryptocurrency stabilisation: Seigniorage shares (2015)
15. Seydel, R.U.: Tools for Computational Finance, 4th edn. Springer, Heidelberg (2009). https://doi.org/10.1007/978-3-540-92929-1

DeFi – Formal Attack Analysis

Formal Analysis of Composable DeFi Protocols

Palina Tolmach[1,2]([✉]), Yi Li[2], Shang-Wei Lin[2], and Yang Liu[2]

[1] Institute of High Performance Computing, Agency for Science,
Technology and Research, Singapore, Singapore
[2] Nanyang Technological University, Singapore, Singapore
{palina001,yi_li,shang-wei.lin,yangliu}@ntu.edu.sg

Abstract. Decentralized finance (DeFi) has become one of the most successful applications of blockchain and smart contracts. The DeFi ecosystem enables a wide range of crypto-financial activities, while the underlying smart contracts often contain bugs, with many vulnerabilities arising from the unforeseen consequences of composing DeFi protocols together. In this paper, we propose a formal process-algebraic technique that models DeFi protocols in a compositional manner to allow for efficient property verification. We also conduct a case study to demonstrate the proposed approach in analyzing the composition of two interacting DeFi protocols, namely, Curve and Compound. Finally, we discuss how the proposed modeling and verification approach can be used to analyze financial and security properties of interest.

1 Introduction

With more than \$12 billions currently locked inside, decentralized finance (DeFi) becomes one of the most prominent applications of the blockchain technology [10]. DeFi protocols implement various financial applications, including analogs of traditional-finance use cases, such as lending [21], exchange [4,12], investment [2], etc. These protocols give users access to digital assets, e.g., *tokens*, and expose them to the cryptocurrency market. As an example, stablecoins are cryptocurrencies providing minimum volatility by pegging their prices to fiat money, real-world commodity, or a more "stable" cryptocurrency, such as ETH [29].

At the same time, billions of dollars stored in DeFi stimulate the invention of new security attacks. Unlike other smart contracts applications, the security of DeFi protocols can be compromised by not only software vulnerabilities but also unforeseen movements in the cryptocurrency market or arbitrage and speculation opportunities. For example, an attacker drained \$2M of funds from the (twice audited) Akropolis DeFi platform [14] through a well-studied reentrancy vulnerability [15,27,35]. As another example, in March 2020, the network congestion caused by market instability led to major disruptions and losses in some of DeFi protocols during the events of so-called "Black Thursday" [31].

© International Financial Cryptography Association 2021
M. Bernhard et al. (Eds.): FC 2021 Workshops, LNCS 12676, pp. 149–161, 2021.
https://doi.org/10.1007/978-3-662-63958-0_13

A distinctive feature of DeFi applications is their similarity to the pieces of so-called *Money Legos* [40]. In other words, the design of DeFi protocols often facilitates interoperability between them including the support of tokens issued by different DeFi platforms. While the composability of DeFi applications enables the construction of a decentralized financial ecosystem, integrations between protocols contribute to the creation of new attack vectors. For example, a recent attack on the Harvest yield aggregation protocol [1] was made possible due to its dependence on the prices reported by the Curve decentralized exchange protocol [12]. By performing a $17M trade in Curve, the attacker could indirectly manipulate the price of tokens in Harvest, obtaining $24M of protocol funds [13]. An established way to rigorously verify correctness of safety-critical systems, including smart contracts, is to employ formal analysis [43]. In the field of DeFi, security audits often involve formal analysis, but usually focusing only on the verification of individual protocols. Yet, the "money-lego" structure of the DeFi ecosystem demands compositional analysis, which allows reasoning about the possible interplay between DeFi protocols and their impact on each other.

To model and analyze the behaviors of composable DeFi protocols, we formulate general formal models of components of DeFi protocols, particularly, *tokens* and *pools*. Based on their actual implementations, we develop process-algebraic models of two widely used DeFi protocols: a decentralized exchange—Curve Finance [12], and a lending protocol—Compound [21]. In addition, we formally model the behavior of the USDC stablecoin. Using the developed model, we formally verify some of the (already stated) relevant properties of the protocols under consideration. Finally, we formulate safety and correctness properties that are expected to hold throughout the interactions between the considered protocols.

2   Background

In this section, we provide necessary background for the rest of the paper.

2.1   DeFi Protocols

We consider two common types of DeFi protocols: *decentralized exchanges* (DEX) and *protocols for loanable funds* (PLF), a.k.a. *lending protocols*.

Decentralized Exchanges. DEX is one of the first and most popular DeFi applications. While a centralized exchange has to match a seller with a specific buyer, a typical DEX uses smart contracts to execute trades asynchronously [5,11]. A *pool*, implemented using smart contracts, stores the reserves of two or more types of tokens and automatically determines the exchange rate between these tokens.

A common way to determine the exchange rate between assets within a DEX pool is by maintaining a *constant-product* and/or *constant-sum* invariant between the values of the tokens contained in the pool. Essentially, the invariant implies that if a user trades t_1 for t_2, the price of t_1 in the pool goes down, while the price of t_2 increases. This model, therefore, provides an arbitrage opportunity for the users of DEXes, encouraging them to deposit or sell tokens of type t_2 at a higher price, which thereby restores the balance between tokens.

Lending Protocols. PLFs [17,30] rely on smart contracts to mediate token lending and borrowing. Different from DEXes, lending pools collect assets of (usually) one token type from liquidity providers. In return, the depositors are given pool tokens with the value constantly increasing from the interest fees paid by borrowers. The interest rate for borrowers depends on a chosen interest rate model and is usually decided by the utilization rate—the ratio between the supply and demand of the pool. To protect a protocol from the cryptocurrency volatility, the borrower is also supposed to supply a collateral (e.g., in ETH or a stablecoin) that is bigger than the amount of borrowed funds by at least a collateralization ratio.

2.2 Formal Modeling and Verification

Communicating Sequential Process (CSP) [18] is a formal language for describing patterns of interaction for concurrent systems [34]. A CSP model contains a set of synchronized or interleaving processes, each of which consists of a sequence of ordered events. For instance, a process P, with an event a followed by another event b, can be written as "$P = a \rightarrow b$". Multiple processes can be composed either sequentially or in parallel. Sequential composition of two processes P and Q (denoted by P; Q) acts as P first, and acts as Q upon the termination of P. The two processes can also be composed in parallel and synchronized on an event X ($P \mid [X] \mid Q$), or asynchronously ($P \mid\mid\mid Q$). Finally, a process Q can interrupt another process P when event e happens ($P \bigtriangledown e \rightarrow Q$). The detailed syntax are summarized as follows.

$$
\begin{aligned}
P := \quad & STOP \quad \mid SKIP & \mid e \rightarrow P & \quad \mid P \,\Box\, P \\
\mid \quad & P \sqcap P \quad \mid P \mid\mid\mid P & \mid P \mid [X] \mid P & \quad \mid P \setminus X \\
\mid \quad & P; \ P \quad \mid \text{if } b \text{ then } P \text{ else } P & \mid P \bigtriangledown P &
\end{aligned}
$$

CSP# [28,38] is an extension to CSP with embedding of data operations. CSP# combines high-level compositional operators from process algebra with program-like codes, which makes the language much more expressive. The models and properties specified in CSP# can be checked using Process Analysis Toolkit (PAT) [28,36,37], which is a framework for specification, simulation, and verification of concurrent and real-time systems. PAT supports event-based compositional models and efficient LTL model checking with various fairness assumptions. Model checking [9] is widely used to verify state-transition systems of one or several interacting smart contracts against a temporal logic specification [39]. In this work, we use the model checker of PAT to verify the properties of individual and interacting DeFi protocols, as described in Sect. 4.

One unique feature of PAT is that it allows users to define static functions and data types as C# libraries. These user-defined C# libraries are built as

DLL files and are loaded during execution, which compensates for the common deficiencies of model checkers on complex data operations and data types. We utilize this capability and implement complex mathematical computations underlying the token price calculation in C#. Finally, the translation from high-level smart contract programming languages, such as Vyper and Solidity, to C# is straightforward.

3   Methodology

To reason about a system of interconnected protocols, we use a *process-algebraic* approach to model various components of the DeFi ecosystem. First, we formally define the main components of DeFi applications along with the environment models. Then, we model two widely used Ethereum DeFi protocols and their interactions using CSP#, by translating the major smart contract functions into CSP, in a similar fashion to some of the previous work [22,33].

3.1   Protocol Formal Modeling

In this section, we propose formal definitions for the two key constituents of lending and exchange DeFi protocols: *token* and *pool*.[1] The behaviors of the aforementioned objects can be formalized as state transition systems, and we focus on their states here.

We model the *states* of users, smart contracts and the environment variables (e.g., `block.number`) as global variables in the CSP# model. Functions, on the other hand, are translated into *processes*. Inspired by [6], we assume a set of blockchain *users* ($\mathbb{U}$) and a set of *tokens* ($\mathbb{T}$). Tokens are programmable assets managed by smart contracts [8]. The majority of tokens used in DeFi protocols, except the native platform cryptocurrency ETH, are implemented in the form of a contract conforming to the ERC20 standard [41]. ERC20 regulates the development of fungible tokens by specifying the interface of the corresponding smart contract, i.e., public functions and events that it should emit during executions. In accordance with the standard, we define tokens in Definition 1.

Definition 1 (Token). *A token $t \in \mathbb{T}$ is a tuple $(\mathbb{U}, TS, B, A, \mathbb{F})$, where $\mathbb{U}$ is a set of users, $TS \in \mathbb{Z}_{\geqslant 0}$ is the total supply, $B : \mathbb{U} \mapsto \mathbb{Z}_{\geqslant 0}$ is the mapping from users to their token balances, $A : \mathbb{U} \times \mathbb{U} \mapsto \mathbb{Z}_{\geqslant 0}$ specifies the allowances, i.e., amounts of token that a user is allowed to spend from another user's balance, and $\mathbb{F}$ is the set of state-changing functions modifying the state of the token.*

Given a token $t \in \mathbb{T}$, we use $t.TS$ to denote its total supply and $t.A$ to denote its allowances, and so on. The balance invariant of t satisfies the formula: $t.TS = \sum_{u \in \mathbb{U}} t.B(u)$. $\mathbb{F}$ includes functions changing the values of A, B, and TS, e.g., `approve()`, `transfer()`, `transferFrom()`, `mint()`, `burn()`, etc. Figure 1 demonstrates a partial implementation of the state of the USDC token in a

```
var USDC_balances[N]:{0..} = [b₁,b₂,...,b_N];
var USDC_allowed[N][N]:{0..};
var USDC_totalSupply = ts;
...
```

Fig. 1. USDC token state implementation in CSP#.

```
Curve_addLiquidity(uamounts, min_mint_amount, sender) = atomic {
    ...
    USDC_transferFrom(user, curveDeposit, uamounts, ...);
    ...
    cUSDC_mint(uamounts, curveDeposit);
    ...
    cUSDC_approve(curveSwap, cAmounts[USDC], curveDeposit);
    Curve_swap_addLiquidity(cAmounts, min_mint_amount, sender);
    cCrv_transfer(user, cCrv_mintAmount, curveDeposit);}
```

Fig. 2. CSP# process for the add_liquidity() function of a Curve pool.

model with N participants. Formally, the state of a user account u is the set of balances of tokens in the user's possession, i.e., $\{t.B(u) \mid u \in \mathbb{U} \text{ and } t \in \mathbb{T}\}$.

Definition 2 specifies pools, which are smart contracts used to aggregate a number of tokens.

Definition 2 (Pool). *A pool P is a tuple $(\mathbb{T}_P, \mathbb{T}_P^R, \mathbb{F}_P)$, where $\mathbb{T}_P \subset \mathbb{T}$ is a set of pool tokens of P,[2] $\mathbb{T}_P^R \subset \mathbb{T}$ is a set of liquidity tokens supported by P, and $\mathbb{F}_P$ is a set of functions $\{(\mathbb{T}_P \times \mathbb{T}_P^R) \mapsto (\mathbb{T}_P \times \mathbb{T}_P^R)\}_i$ changing the state of P.*

Depending on the protocol application, liquidity tokens $\mathbb{T}_P^R \subset \mathbb{T}$ are used to facilitate decentralized token exchange, lending, investments, or other DeFi use cases. Liquidity pools in DEX usually hold liquidity in two or more types of tokens [3,4,12], while lending protocol [21] or yield aggregator [2] pools typically accept a single type of token as input. In both cases, the users depositing tokens (a.k.a. *liquidity providers*) receive a certain amount of pool tokens ($\mathbb{T}_P$), which represent user's share and can be used to redeem the deposit with the earned interests from the pool. $\mathbb{F}_P$ is a set of functions that can change the state of a pool. Figure 2 illustrates the process-algebraic encoding of a state-changing function that implements adding liquidity to a pool from the Curve protocol. To mimic the atomic transaction execution model in Ethereum, we mark state-changing processes as *atomic*, so that their executions cannot be interrupted by an interleaving.

3.2 Protocol Composition

Now, we illustrate how interactions between users and DeFi protocols (*user-protocol*) as well as interactions among different protocols (*protocol-protocol*) can

---

[1] Depending on the application, pools are also referred to as *markets*, *vaults*, or *pairs*.

[2] Most of the pools in DeFi support a single pool token.

be modeled formally. In both cases, the initiator of a transaction sends a certain amount of tokens to a receiving DeFi protocol and/or receives some tokens from it in return.

In the case of *user-protocol* interaction, we model the behavior of a user by a *sequential composition* (denoted by ';') of one or more processes. These processes correspond to the public state-changing functions of DeFi protocols and tokens invoked by the user. For example, the behavior of a depositor in Curve (i.e., Curve_Depositor) is demonstrated in Fig. 3.

```
Curve_Depositor() = USDC_approve(curveDeposit, suppliedTokens, user);
  Curve_addLiquidity(suppliedTokens, minMintTokens, user);
  ...
  cCrv_approve(curveDeposit, add, user);
  Curve_remove_liquidity_one_coin(add, 0, user, true);
```

Fig. 3. The implementation of Curve depositor behavior in CSP#.

The subject system is then modeled by an *interleaving* (denoted by '|||') of such user processes. For instance, Fig. 4 shows the depositor, exchanger, and borrower processes composed asynchronously, which simulates possible state changes in interacting protocols caused by concurrently acting users. The processes simulating state-changing functions are atomic, i.e., executing without interruption so that the interleaving between user processes can only happen after a state-changing process is finished. We simulate the block mining using a process that increases the value of the block number variable.

```
System() = Curve_Depositor() ||| Curve_Exchanger() |||
Compound_Depositor() ||| Compound_Borrower() ||| IncreaseBlockNum();
```

Fig. 4. The analyzed user composition.

The *protocol-protocol* interactions in DeFi smart contracts are external calls to a function of another protocol. Following a similar approach, we model smart contract functions with external calls to other DeFi applications and token contracts as an *atomic sequential composition* of corresponding processes. The sequential composition of two processes ensures that the former process has to finish before the latter can start, so that the model operates similarly as the execution of internal transactions in blockchain. The CSP# representation of a function that implements adding liquidity to a pool of the Curve DeFi protocol is shown in Fig. 2. The communication among users, tokens, and different protocols is simulated via shared global variables, such as token balances shown in Fig. 1.

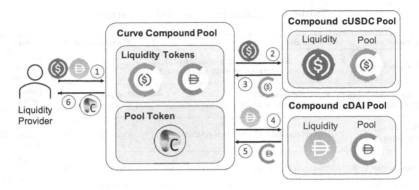

Fig. 5. A scheme of token transfers between Curve Compound pool participants.

4   Evaluation

In this section, we evaluate our modeling approach by checking a set of relevant properties on Compound pool of the Curve DEX[3] using PAT and report on the results of property verification. We performed the evaluation on a virtual machine with Windows 10, 8 GB RAM and 1 CPU core, using PAT version 3.5.0. The virtual machine is running on MacOS Catalina v.10.15.7, 32 GB RAM and 2 GHz quad-core Intel Core i5 processor.

The Curve Compound pool allows trading between a pair of stablecoins: USDC and DAI. Under the hood, the Curve pool transfers its USDC and DAI to a lending platform Compound, in exchange for the corresponding Compound's pool tokens—cUSDC and cDAI. cUSDC and cDAI are, therefore, used for all the operations within the Curve Compound pool. Figure 5 outlines the process of adding liquidity to the Curve Compound pool: ① a liquidity provider sends USDC and/or DAI to the pool; ② Curve supplies the received USDC to the USDC Compound pool and ③ receives an appropriate amount of cUSDC in return; ④-⑤ the same process is repeated for DAI/cDAI; ⑥ the user receives a certain amount of cCrv—a pool token of the Curve Compound pool.

State-changing actions of interest include providing and removing liquidity in both Curve and Compound, exchanging tokens in Curve, and taking/repaying a loan in Compound. In this paper, we mostly concentrate on the operations that involve USDC: in our model, a liquidity provider on Curve adds and withdraws liquidity in USDC, while Compound depositors and borrowers also perform the corresponding actions with the USDC Compound pool. To model slippage and front-running that can occur in the pool of a DEX, the token exchanges between cUSDC and cDAI in Curve can happen in both directions. We assume that the modeled trading activity reflects the possible changes in the USDC/DAI exchange rate, which we do not explicitly consider otherwise. In addition, since we focus on the operations involving the USDC stablecoin, we simplify the implementation of DAI to basic ERC20 functionality and do not consider the underly-

---

[3] https://www.curve.fi/compound.

Table 1. A summary of verified properties.

#	Properties	LTL Formulae	Protocols	Results	Stats
(1)	Balance Invariants	□((sum(cCrv_balances) == cCrv_totalSupply) && sum(cDAI_accountTokens) == cDAI_totalSupply)...)	All Tokens	Valid	Time (s): 275.5 s #State: 127337 #Transition: 133763
(2)	Proportional Token Exchange	□((suppliedTokens > 0) → ◇((mintedCTokens > 0) && (mintedCCrvTokens > 0)))	Curve Compound	Valid	Time (s): 277.7 s #State: 127367 #Transition: 133821
(3)	Non-decreasing Exchange Rate	□(prevExchangeRate ≤ newExchangeRate)	Compound	Valid	Time (s): 277.9s #State: 127337 #Transition: 133763
(4)	Non-negative Profit	□ (Mint.cUSDC → □(depositorProfit ≥ 0))	Compound	Invalid	Time (s): 1.0 s #State: 430 #Transition: 453
(5)	Bounded Loss	□ (AddLiquidity → □(depositorLoss ≤ ADMISSIBLE_LOSS)	Curve	Invalid	Time (s): 0.5s #State: 177 #Transition: 196

ing stabilizing mechanism implemented by MakerDAO. We modeled pools and tokens by manually translating their source code written in Solidity or Vyper to CSP# and C# languages supported by PAT. While the translation between high-level languages (e.g., Solidity/C#) is straightforward, data operations and programming constructs supported by CSP# also facilitate translation to a modeling language. The source code of the model can be found in a repository: https://github.com/polinatolmach/DeFi-csp-models/.

Based on the defined model, we formulated and verified properties for tokens, individual DEX and lending DeFi applications as well as their composition. LTL formulae and verification results for the properties are demonstrated in Table 1. The first property in Table 1 is the *Balance Invariant* [39]—an important property related to tokens, which we verify for all the tokens involved in the modeled composition: stablecoins (USDC and DAI) and pool tokens (cCrv, cUSDC, etc.). Property (2) in Table 1 is a token-related requirement for a composition of protocols stating that *the positively-valued tokens should never produce zero tokens* (Proportional Token Exchange) [7]. We verified that this requirement holds for all pairs of tokens involved in the process of adding liquidity to the Curve Compound pool (Fig. 5).

Among the properties of individual protocols, our model allows verification of *the exchange rate of the pool token in Compound being non-decreasing*, meaning that a liquidity provider always receives a guaranteed interest on her deposit (Property (3) in Table 1). For a liquidity provider on Compound, we additionally checked whether her *profit from providing and then redeeming liquidity can only be non-negative* (Property (4) in Table 1). While this requirement holds under normal conditions, it does fail in the event of *overutilization*, i.e., if the pool does not have enough liquidity to repay the depositor. To model *overutilization*, we defined a user who borrows all the available liquidity from the Compound pool. For simplicity, we omitted the collateralization requirements in our model—each loan is assumed to be collateralized using the token that is not considered in the current model (e.g., ETH). Although the simplifications assumed in our model allow reaching overutilization easier than it is in reality, it remains one of the main risks associated with lending protocols [6].

Overutilization in a Compound pool causes a violation of an analogous property defined for a Curve liquidity provider, showing the potentially harmful effects of composability. In other words, the users of both Compound and Curve are not always able to redeem their original deposit back. Considering that a liquidity provider in a DEX can legitimately suffer losses from the *impermanent loss*, the property (5) in Table 1 requires *the loss to be bounded by a certain value*, which we set to 20% of the original deposit. This requirement can also be violated in an anticipated way due to *front-running* and *slippage* caused by massive trades made by other users. The violations of both properties are identified by PAT in sub-second time. Being an on-the-fly model checker, PAT stops constructing and exploring the state space after detecting the violation, which explains the time discrepancy between the verification of properties (1)–(3) and (4), (5). For both violated properties, the reachability analysis in PAT also helps identify the maximum possible losses and profits for both Curve and Compound depositors. Finally, we confirmed the violation of properties on a locally deployed Ethereum network, assuming the same set of simplifications to smart contracts as in the model.

The performed evaluation demonstrates the suitability of applying process algebra CSP for modeling concurrently acting users and DeFi protocols on blockchain. The results also confirm that model checking can automatically reveal undesirable conditions in the operation of a single DeFi protocol or a composition of those. However, with expanding the composition of modeled users and protocols, the number of states grows exponentially. To combat the state explosion problem, we consider utilizing techniques from the area of compositional verification, such as assume-guarantee reasoning [23–25], which we leave for future work.

5 Related Work

The analysis of DeFi protocols is a relatively new field. The existing works often focus on specific types of DeFi protocols or investigate abnormal behaviors observed in the wild. For example, Liu and Szalachowski explored the usage of *oracles* in four major DeFi platforms [26], revealing the operational issues inherent in oracles and common deviations between the real and reported prices.

A number of articles analyze the attack vectors that involve a *flash loan* [16, 32], while Wang et al. [42] proposed a framework that allows the identification and classification of flash loan transactions. Their technique is able to detect speculative usage of flash loans and other potentially harmful behaviors.

Several studies explore the operation and properties of DeFi *lending protocols* [6,17,19,30]. Kao et al. [19] utilized agent-based simulations to analyze the market risks faced by the Compound lending protocol users. Stress-tests were performed to demonstrate the scalability of the protocol on a larger borrow size under reasonably volatile conditions. Formal models of lending protocols and their pools were formulated in two recent publications [6,30]. Bartoletti et al. [6] also formulated the fundamental properties of lending pools and typical ways of their interaction with other DeFi protocols. Meanwhile, Perez et al. [30] utilized the abstract formal model of Compound to explore the possibility of liquidations of undercollateralized positions. Different from the discussed publications, this paper formulates a more general formal model of a pool, which can be used to formalize both lending and DEX protocols.

In addition, Klages-Mundt et al. [20] proposed a framework for modeling and classifying stablecoins. The authors also formulated and examined the risks associated with stablecoins and their use in the DeFi ecosystem. The formal model of a token considered in this paper is of a higher level and does not cover its underlying economical mechanism.

Finally, a recent publication by Bernardi et al. [7] proposed a set of invariants that are relevant for individual DeFi protocols, including DEXes and lending platforms. While our study involves verification of some of the invariants proposed in this article, we further extend them to the system of interacting DeFi protocols.

6   Conclusion and Future Work

In this paper, we proposed formal definitions for the main components of DeFi protocols and an approach to model their implementations and interactions in a process-algebraic modeling language. We demonstrated how model checking can automatically verify correctness properties for a composition of DeFi protocols and tokens. The proposed technique successfully identifies the DeFi-specific conditions that cause the violations of these properties.

As future work, we plan to enrich the models to account for functionality related to liquidity-mining and governance mechanisms in the considered DeFi protocols. We would also like to extend the set of properties to cover both security vulnerabilities and the cryptoeconomical aspects of DeFi executions. Finally, to address the state explosion problem, we plan to integrate techniques from the area of compositional verification.

Acknowledgements. This research is partially supported by the Ministry of Education, Singapore, under its Academic Research Fund Tier 1 (Award No. 2018-T1-002-069) and Tier 2 (Award No. MOE2018-T2-1-068), and by the National Research Foundation, Singapore, and the Energy Market Authority, under its Energy Programme (EP Award No. NRF2017EWT-EP003-023). Any opinions, findings and conclusions or recommendations expressed in this material are those of the authors and do not reflect the views of National Research Foundation, Singapore and the Energy Market Authority.

References

1. Harvest Finance (2020). https://harvest.finance/. Accessed 12 Oct 2020
2. Introduction to Yearn - yearn.finance (2020). https://docs.yearn.finance/. Accessed 12 Nov 2020
3. Whitepaper - Balancer (2020). https://balancer.finance/whitepaper/. Accessed 12 Oct 2020
4. Adams, H., Zinsmeister, N., Robinson, D.: Uniswap v2 Core Whitepaper (2020). https://uniswap.org/whitepaper.pdf. Accessed 12 Oct 2020
5. Angeris, G., Kao, H.T., Chiang, R., Noyes, C., Chitra, T.: An analysis of uniswap markets (2020). https://arxiv.org/abs/1911.03380
6. Bartoletti, M., Chiang, J.H., Lluch-Lafuente, A.: SOK: lending pools in decentralized finance (2020). https://arxiv.org/abs/2012.13230
7. Bernardi, T., et al.: WIP: finding bugs automatically in smart contracts with parameterized invariants (2020). https://www.certora.com/pubs/sbc2020.pdf. Accessed 14 July 2020
8. Chen, W., Zhang, T., Chen, Z., Zheng, Z., Lu, Y.: Traveling the token world: a graph analysis of Ethereum ERC20 token ecosystem. In: Proceedings of The Web Conference 2020. WWW 2020, pp. 1411–1421. ACM (2020). https://doi.org/10.1145/3366423.3380215
9. Clarke, E.M., Grumberg, O., Peled, D.A.: Model Checking. MIT Press, Cambridge (2000)
10. Coingape: DeFi success story continues as TVL peaks yet again; hits \$12 billion (2020). https://coinmarketcap.com/ru/headlines/news/defi-success-story-continues-as-tvl-peaks-yet-again-hits-12-billion. Accessed 18 Nov 2020
11. Daian, P., et al.: Flash boys 2.0: Frontrunning, transaction reordering, and consensus instability in decentralized exchanges (2019). https://arxiv.org/abs/1904.05234
12. Egorov, M.: StableSwap - efficient mechanism for Stablecoin liquidity — Curve. fi Whitepaper (2020). https://www.curve.fi/stableswap-paper.pdf. Accessed 18 Nov 18 2020
13. Finance, H.: Harvest Flashloan Economic Attack Post-Mortem (2020). https://medium.com/harvest-finance/harvest-flashloan-economic-attack-post-mortem-3cf900d65217. Accessed 18 Nov 2020
14. Foxley, W.: DeFi project Akropolis drained of \$2m in DAI (2020). https://www.coindesk.com/defi-project-akropolis-token-pool-drained. Accessed 14 Nov 2020
15. Grossman, S., et al.: Online detection of effectively callback free objects with applications to smart contracts. Proc. ACM Program. Lang. pp. 1–28 (2017). https://doi.org/10.1145/3158136
16. Gudgeon, L., Perez, D., Harz, D., Livshits, B., Gervais, A.: The decentralized financial crisis (2020). https://arxiv.org/abs/2002.08099
17. Gudgeon, L., Werner, S.M., Perez, D., Knottenbelt, W.J.: DeFi protocols for loanable funds: interest rates, liquidity and market efficiency (2020). https://arxiv.org/abs/2006.13922
18. Hoare, C.A.R.: Communicating Sequential Processes. International Series on Computer Science, Prentice-Hall (1985)
19. Kao, H.T., Chitra, T., Chiang, R., Morrow, J.: An Analysis of the Market Risk to Participants in the Compound Protocol (2020). https://scfab.github.io/2020/FAB2020_p5.pdf. Accessed 18 Nov 2020

20. Klages-Mundt, A., Harz, D., Gudgeon, L., Liu, J.Y., Minca, A.: Stablecoins 2.0. In: Proceedings of the 2nd ACM Conference on Advances in Financial Technologies, October 2020. https://doi.org/10.1145/3419614.3423261

21. Leshner, R., Hayes, G.: Compound: The Money Market Protocol — Whitepaper (2020). https://compound.finance/documents/Compound.Whitepaper.pdf. Accessed 18 Nov 2020

22. Li, X., Su, C., Xiong, Y., Huang, W., Wang, W.: Formal verification of BNB smart contract. In: Proceedings of the BIGCOM, pp. 74–78, August 2019. https://doi.org/10.1109/BIGCOM.2019.00021

23. Lin, S., Andre, E., Liu, Y., Sun, J., Dong, J.: Learning assumptions for compositional verification of timed systems. IEEE Trans. Software Eng. (02), 137–153 (2014). https://doi.org/10.1109/TSE.2013.57

24. Lin, S.-W., Liu, Y., Sun, J., Dong, J.S., André, É.: Automatic compositional verification of timed systems. In: Giannakopoulou, D., Méry, D. (eds.) FM 2012. LNCS, vol. 7436, pp. 272–276. Springer, Heidelberg (2012). https://doi.org/10.1007/978-3-642-32759-9_24

25. Lin, S.W., Sun, J., Nguyen, T.K., Liu, Y., Dong, J.S.: Interpolation guided compositional verification. In: Proceedings of the 30th IEEE/ACM International Conference on Automated Software Engineering. ASE 2015, pp. 65–74. IEEE Press (2015). https://doi.org/10.1109/ASE.2015.33

26. Liu, B., Szalachowski, P.: A first look into DeFi oracles (2020). https://arxiv.org/abs/2005.04377

27. Liu, C., Liu, H., Cao, Z., Chen, Z., Chen, B., Roscoe, B.: ReGuard: finding reentrancy bugs in smart contracts. In: Proceedings of the 40th International Conference on Software Engineering: Companion Proceedings, pp. 65–68. ACM (2018). https://doi.org/10.1145/3183440.3183495

28. Liu, Y., Sun, J., Dong, J.S.: Pat 3: An extensible architecture for building multi-domain model checkers. In: 2011 IEEE 22nd International Symposium on Software Reliability Engineering, pp. 190–199 (2011). https://doi.org/10.1109/ISSRE.2011.19

29. Moin, A., Sirer, E.G., Sekniqi, K.: A classification framework for stablecoin designs (2019). https://arxiv.org/abs/1910.10098

30. Perez, D., Werner, S.M., Xu, J., Livshits, B.: Liquidations: DeFi on a knife-edge (2020). https://arxiv.org/abs/2009.13235

31. Pulse, D.: DeFi status report post-black thursday (2020). https://defipulse.com/blog/defi-status-report-black-thursday. Accessed 18 Nov 2020

32. Qin, K., Zhou, L., Livshits, B., Gervais, A.: Attacking the DeFi ecosystem with flash loans for fun and profit (2020). https://arxiv.org/abs/2003.03810

33. Qu, M., Huang, X., Chen, X., Wang, Y., Ma, X., Liu, D.: Formal verification of smart contracts from the perspective of concurrency. In: Qiu, M. (ed.) SmartBlock 2018. LNCS, vol. 11373, pp. 32–43. Springer, Cham (2018). https://doi.org/10.1007/978-3-030-05764-0_4

34. Roscoe, A.W.: The Theory and Practice of Concurrency. Prentice Hall (1997). iSBN 0-13-674409-5

35. Samreen, N., Alalfi, M.H.: Reentrancy vulnerability identification in Ethereum smart contracts. In: 2020 IEEE International Workshop on Blockchain Oriented Software Engineering (IWBOSE), pp. 22–29 (2020). https://doi.org/10.1109/IWBOSE50093.2020.9050260

36. Sun, J., Liu, Y., Dong, J.S., Pang, J.: PAT: towards flexible verification under fairness. In: Bouajjani, A., Maler, O. (eds.) CAV 2009. LNCS, vol. 5643, pp. 709–714. Springer, Heidelberg (2009). https://doi.org/10.1007/978-3-642-02658-4_59

37. Sun, J., Liu, Y., Dong, J.S.: Model checking CSP revisited: introducing a process analysis toolkit. In: Margaria, T., Steffen, B. (eds.) ISoLA 2008. CCIS, vol. 17, pp. 307–322. Springer, Heidelberg (2008). https://doi.org/10.1007/978-3-540-88479-8_22
38. Sun, J., Liu, Y., Dong, J.S., Chen, C.: Integrating specification and programs for system modeling and verification. In: Proceedings of the 2009 Third IEEE International Symposium on Theoretical Aspects of Software Engineering, pp. 127–135 (2009). https://doi.org/10.1109/TASE.2009.32
39. Tolmach, P., Li, Y., Lin, S.-W., Liu, Y., Li, Z.: A survey of smart contract formal specification and verification. ACM Comput. Surv. **54**(7), 38 p. (2021). Article no. 148. https://doi.org/10.1145/3464421
40. Totle: Building with Money Legos (2020). https://medium.com/totle/building-with-money-legos-ab63a58ae764. Accessed 17 Nov 2020
41. Vogelsteller, F., Buterin, V.: ERC-20 token standard (2015). https://eips.ethereum.org/EIPS/eip-20. Accessed 14 July 2020
42. Wang, D., et al.: Towards understanding flash loan and its applications in DeFi ecosystem (2020). https://arxiv.org/abs/2010.12252
43. Woodcock, J., Larsen, P.G., Bicarregui, J., Fitzgerald, J.: Formal methods: practice and experience. ACM Comput. Surv. **41**(4), 1–36 (2009). https://doi.org/10.1145/1592434.1592436

How to Exploit a DeFi Project

Xinyuan Sun[1]([✉]), Shaokai Lin[2], Vilhelm Sjöberg[1], and Jay Jie[1]

[1] CertiK, New York, NY 10018, USA
{sxysun,vilhelm.sjoberg,jay.jie}@certik.io
[2] University of California, Berkeley, Berkeley, CA 94720, USA
shaokai@berkeley.edu

Abstract. The growing adoption of decentralized finance poses new security risks, as designing increasingly complex financial models is error-prone. We have witnessed numerous DeFi projects hacked (for tens of millions of dollars) because of unsound liquidation conditions, asset pricing, or position management, etc. To address these issues, we present a systematic way of finding vulnerabilities in DeFi projects based on automatically extracting financial models from smart contracts and reasoning about them symbolically using either a model checker or an interactive theorem prover. Specifically, we (i) formalized the concept of soundness in the financial model of a DeFi project which captures an interesting class of exploits (flash-loan attacks), and (ii) built a domain-specific language to automatically extract models from smart contracts and search possible exploits or prove their soundness. To demonstrate the capability of our approach, we model variants of most DeFi projects with a TVL (total value locked) larger than 20M USD (totaling about 8B USD TVL) and check their soundness. The result showed that we can automatically find both previous exploits and potential new flaws in DeFi.

Keywords: Decentralized finance · Model checking · Formal verification

1 Overview

In the past year, there have been so many decentralized finance project breaches to the point that million-dollar hacks don't make the news anymore. We reviewed 31 exploit incidents happened to DeFi in 2020 and found that they in total caused a capital loss of 315.95M USD (Appendix A, Table 1), with the highest attack resulting 50M USD of lost funds. The inability to find and prevent those hacks resulted from the complexity of the DeFi "money Lego"—we not only have to consider contract implementation correctness but also, more importantly, the soundness of interleaved financial models. To quote an experienced auditor: "If you go into a DEX audit without a full understanding of how options or derivatives work, you are probably going about it all wrong."

Challenges. To systematically study DeFi exploits, we face two challenges:

© International Financial Cryptography Association 2021
M. Bernhard et al. (Eds.): FC 2021 Workshops, LNCS 12676, pp. 162–167, 2021.
https://doi.org/10.1007/978-3-662-63958-0_14

(i) We lack a classification of past financial security-related exploits on DeFi projects. Earlier attack vectors like re-entrancy or access control only concern simple semantics, and other functional correctness related hacks are well defined with respect to the specifications. However, there has been little work in the formalization of a DeFi exploit. People often argue if some exploit is a hack or an arbitrage, especially in communities where decentralization is valued (smart contract code is deemed as law for every trader to follow).

(ii) From the 31 DeFi attacks we studied, we found that 20 of them concern high-level financial model details (e.g., token bonding curve economics, AMM's self-balancing mechanism, etc.,) hidden in the footnotes of the project whitepaper or, worse, tens of thousands of lines of smart contract codes. The complex nature of DeFi protocols makes it infeasible for us to reason directly about the implementation. The truth is, current smart contract security solutions [3–5,10] like pattern-based vulnerability matching or SMT-based verification, though well-studied, are not tailored to formally reason about assets and derivatives.

Attack Patterns. To address challenge (i), we studied 31 past "attacks"[1] on DeFi projects and found that they fall into three categories: unsound financial models, arbitrages, or insecure implementations. The arbitrage case is unavoidable as arbitrage is necessary for decentralized exchanges to align their prices with the real market price. The best thing we can do is to write a community arbitrage bot on-chain and distribute revenue to liquidity providers (who are usually losing money in arbitrage actions). If we consider priority gas auctions where miners extract the most value with a consensus-level advantage, then there is no way to stop this kind of "attacks" unless we devise a fairer auction mechanism [1]. Furthermore, arbitrage has the smallest impact out of the three categories in Table.1, with an average of 70k USD weekly profit and about 4M USD gain over one year [12], consisting less than 2% of the total capital loss. Insecure implementations of smart contracts (e.g., re-entrancy caused by inclusion of ERC777 tokens [6]) are already well-addressed by previous work [3–5,10]. While these attacks can be caught by existing tools, they still happened because some projects didn't go through a proper audit, so these kind of attacks are more of an engineering problem.

Scope. In this work we focus on unsound financial models, that is, we limit our scope to exploits where the attacker can mint, hold or burn assets (tokens, or positions representing a certain amount of token) at the expense of everyday traders and liquidity provider's interests, thus damaging the entire ecosystem's health. We emphasize on damaging the entire ecosystem's health because in cases like arbitrage or high slippage, *reasonably-knowledgeable* users should take responsibility for their own bad trades, while in a financial model flaw situation, the attacker can profit off users even if no one makes mistakes (even though some people might argue that by using flash-loans to manipulate the spot market for greater income in the derivatives constitutes an hack but is a necessary evil to

---

[1] see appendix A.

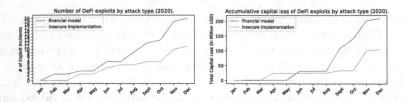

Fig. 1. DeFi exploit trends in 2020.

cool the market down by deleveraging). From Fig. 1, we can see that financial models have been consistently attacked more than insecure implementations all year, but exploits related to them only started to contribute a dominant amount of capital losses since August, reaching a 66.48% at the end of year. This demonstrates that financial model exploits has been increasingly more damaging than insecure implementation exploits due to the mass adoption of DeFi since summer 2020. By *reasonably-knowledgeable*, we mean having knowledge of common sense finance. For example, users know that they can make a profit by arbitraging different spot prices at different exchanges, or that when using a self-balancing automated market maker, they should trade with the optimal price calculated from the reserves. But a reasonably-knowledgeable user would not be expected to know things that require detailed analysis of DeFi, e.g., that they can profit from manipulation of token inflation models using some exchanges' trading mechanism [11]. Additionally, we say a user is *maximally-rational* if they are reasonably-knowledgeable and rational, i.e., they trade in a way that maximizes their profits using their reasonable amount of knowledge. For example, if there is a spot arbitrage opportunity created by their own trades, they will arbitrage within the same transaction as their initial trade to front-run everybody else. Another example would be taking liquidation reward of an under-collaterized debt position on lending platforms (e.g., Compound).

Soundness. Formally, we model DeFi exploits in a model checking fashion. We say that the application starts with an initial state s_0 and transition functions $F = \{f_1, f_2 \ldots f_n\}$, each abstracted from an actual state changing function in the project's smart contracts (e.g., `borrow` from AAVE [9]). If a state s_j is derivable from a state s_i by at most m arbitrary transactions which each can involve up to n contract calls, we write $s_i \Rightarrow_{m,n} s_j$. Note that each of the n contract calls within one transaction have a single caller, sequential execution semantics and deterministic ordering, while the m transactions have a non-deterministic ordering (decided by miners). If in those m transactions and n contract calls all users are *maximally-rational*, we write the transition relation as $\Rightarrow_{\mathcal{R}\ m,n}$. We define a state s_i as *consistent* if the state is the result of a series of interactions between multiple *maximally-rational* traders. Intuitively, *consistent* states can be understood as a state where spot and futures price of every trading pair is uniform across all DEXs and CEXs within a reasonable bound (e.g., less than the transaction fees). We say there is a hack of the financial model in a DeFi project if there exists such s_i, a *consistent* state derivable from the initial state

s_0 by relation $\Rightarrow_{*,*}$, from where the attacker can take an arbitrary amount of interleaved (across different transactions) contract calls and reach a state s_j where the asset of the attacker at s_j is strictly greater than his/her asset at s_i while everybody else acts maximally-rationally. Therefore, we define the ideal-soundness of a DeFi project as the absence of a hack: $\neg \exists s_i, s_j, h, s.t. s_0 \Rightarrow_{*,*} s_i \rightarrow consistent(s_i) \rightarrow s_i \Rightarrow_{\mathcal{R} \ *,*} s_j \rightarrow \varXi(h, s_i) < \varXi(h, s_j)$, where $\varXi(h, s_i)$ is the total value of address h's capital denoted in ETH, if liquidated, at state s_i.

k-soundness. The ideal-soundness property is infeasible to express or check (for limitations of current automated reasoning techniques) in reality. For example, what kind of knowledge is reasonable for a DeFi user to be assumed to know is disputed, and the maximally-rational constraint on relation $\Rightarrow_{\mathcal{R} \ m,n}$ is hard to express. Therefore, we make three refinements to the previous definition: (1) we limit transaction transition from the sound state s_i to one, i.e., $\Rightarrow_{\mathcal{R} \ 1,*}$, so that no other users can interact with the contract except for the attacker. This means everyone is trivially maximally-rational as they do not operate. (Equivalently, you can imagine this as only considering "flash loan"-style attacks, in the sense that every operation within a flash-loan is deterministic and packed into one transaction). (2) we further limit the number of possible contract calls within that one transaction on s_i to a finite number k, i.e., $\Rightarrow_{\mathcal{R} \ 1,k}$. This enables us to use bounded model checking to traverse the state space symbolically so that we can prove there are no possible exploits within k steps. (3) we drop the requirement that state s_i has to be derivable from the initial state and we arbitrarily start from a state s_i with concrete values generated under the constraint *consistent*. Altogether, we define this changed property as k-soundness. We say a DeFi project is k-sound with respect to s_i if and only if given a concrete contract state s_i that is *consistent*, there exists no address that can statically (symbolically) find a way to increase its total asset within k interactions with the contract: $\neg \exists s_j, h, s.t. consistent(s_i) \rightarrow s_i \Rightarrow_{\mathcal{R} \ 1,k} s_j \rightarrow \varXi(h, s_i) < \varXi(h, s_j)$.

Model Extraction. We address challenge (ii) by providing a domain specific language to model assets in DeFi projects. We built the DSL using DeepSEA [8], which can automatically extract the financial model we annotated into (1) the UCLID5 [7] model checker and check for k-soundness, or (2) compile it to a Coq specification so that we can prove stronger correctness like ideal-soundness by manually. To make future usage easier, we provide a decentralized finance model library written in our DSL that covers all popular services (liquidity farming, interest-bearing tokens, automated market makers, etc.). Moreover, since DeepSEA has a certified compiler backend, we can emit executable EVM/eWasm code for those asset-related functions after verifying their correctness. In the future, we could also extend the model checker into checking liveness properties like eventual governance to prevent failures like yam.finance [2].

Case Study. We used our language to model a past attack[2] of the bZx project which happened because of an incorrect liquidation check (the short position hacker opened did not liquidate despite under-collateralization). Specifically, we

---

[2] the bZx attack on Feb.15th, 2020, shown in appendix A.

wrote simplified versions of the bZx and Uniswap contracts in DeepSEA and our DSL automatically extracted them into UCLID5 models, we checked against k-soundness ($k = 5$ in our setup) of the contract and it successfully gave us the exploit pattern.

Acknowledgement. We would like to acknowledge the contribution of many colleagues on various related projects at CertiK, especially Ronghui Gu, Dan She, Jialiang Chang, Junhong Chen and Zhaozhong Ni.

A   Past Exploits on DeFi Projects

Table 1. Exploits on DeFi projects happened in 2020

Platform	Attack type[1]	Reason	Loss[2]	Date
bZx	financial model	liquidation check	830k	2020.2.15
bZx	financial model	oracle synchronization	642k	2020.2.18
Uniswap	insecure implementation	ERC777 re-entrancy	220k	2020.4.18
Lendf.Me	insecure implementation	ERC777 re-entrancy	24.7M	2020.4.22
Hegic	financial model	frozen funds	29k	2020.4.23
Bancor	insecure implementation	access control	131.9k	2020.6.19
Atomic Loans	insecure implementation	front-running	N/A	2020.6.24
Balancer	financial model	deflation model	500k	2020.6.29
Balancer	financial model	reserve synchronization	2.7k	2020.6.29
Synthetix	financial model	oracle synchronization	30M	2019.6.30
VETH	insecure implementation	access control	900k	2020.7.1
Uniswap BZRX	arbitrage	bonding curve	531k	2020.7.14
Opyn	financial model	option exercise	371k	2020.8.4
Uniswap & Curve	arbitrage	spot arbitrage	43k	2020.8.10
NUGS	financial model	token inflation	N/A	2020.8.12
Yam.finance	financial model	token inflation	60M	2020.8.12
SYFI	financial model	exchange rate	250k	2020.9.10
bZx	insecure implementation	double dipping	8M	2020.9.14
Soda	financial model	loan liquidation	160k	2020.9.20
Eminence	financial model	burning mechanism	15M	2020.9.29
Harvest.finance	financial model	interest model	33.8M	2020.10.26
Akropolis	insecure implementation	re-entrancy	20M	2020.11.12
Value DeFI	financial model	oracle manipulation	7.4M	2020.11.14
Cheese Bank	financial model	oracle manipulation	3.3M	2020.11.16
OUSD	insecure implementation	re-entrancy	7M	2020.11.17
88mph	financial model	token burning	N/A	2020.11.19
Pickle.finance	insecure implementation	whitelist	20M	2020.11.22
Compound	financial model	oracle manipulation	N/A	2020.11.26
Pickle.finance	insecure implementation	whitelist	20M	2020.11.22
Sushiswap	financial model	token conversion	15k	2020.11.30
Saffron Finance	financial model	frozen funds	50M	2020.11.30
Warp finance	financial model	oracle manipulation	7.7M	2020.12.18
Cover Protocol	insecure implementation	outdated cache	4.4M	2020.12.28
total	N/A	N/A	315.95M	N/A

[1] We do not include centralization issues (rug pulls)
[2] Capital loss calculated using corresponding cryptocurrencies' prices at time of exploit

References

1. Daian, P., et al.: Flash boys 2.0: Frontrunning, transaction reordering, and consensus instability in decentralized exchanges. arXiv preprint arXiv:1904.05234 (2019)
2. Georgiev, G.: Yam finance crashes over 90%, founder admits his failure (2020). https://cryptopotato.com/yam-finance-crashes-over-90-founder-admits-his-failure/
3. Hajdu, Á., Jovanović, D.: Solc-verify: a modular verifier for solidity smart contracts. arXiv preprint arXiv:1907.04262 (2019)
4. Luu, L., Chu, D.H., Olickel, H., Saxena, P., Hobor, A.: Making smart contracts smarter. In: Proceedings of the 2016 ACM SIGSAC Conference on Computer and Communications Security, pp. 254–269. ACM (2016)
5. Permenev, A., Dimitrov, D., Tsankov, P., Drachsler-Cohen, D., Vechev, M.: Verx: Safety verification of smart contracts. Security and Privacy 2020 (2019)
6. Riley, D.: $25m in cryptocurrency stolen in hack of lendf.me and uniswap (2020). https://siliconangle.com/2020/04/19/25m-cryptocurrency-stolen-hack-lendf-uniswap/
7. Seshia, S.A., Subramanyan, P.: Uclid 5: Integrating modeling, verification, synthesis and learning. In: 2018 16th ACM/IEEE International Conference on Formal Methods and Models for System Design (MEMOCODE). pp. 1–10, October 2018. https://doi.org/10.1109/MEMCOD.2018.8556946
8. Sjöberg, V., Sang, Y., Weng, S.c., Shao, Z.: Deepsea: a language for certified system software. In: Proceedings of the ACM on Programming Languages 3(OOPSLA), pp. 1–27 (2019)
9. Team, A.: Aave developers doc (2020). https://docs.aave.com/developers/
10. Wang, Yuepeng, et al.: Formal verification of workflow policies for smart contracts in azure blockchain. In: Chakraborty, Supratik, Navas, Jorge A.. (eds.) VSTTE 2019. LNCS, vol. 12031, pp. 87–106. Springer, Cham (2020). https://doi.org/10.1007/978-3-030-41600-3_7
11. Williams, M.: Rising defi protocol balancer loses $500,000 to hacker in pool exploit (updated) (2020). https://www.bitcoininsider.org/article/89413/rising-defi-protocol-balancer-loses-500000-hacker-pool-exploit-updated
12. Zhou, L., Qin, K., Cully, A., Livshits, B., Gervais, A.: On the just-in-time discovery of profit-generating transactions in defi protocols. arXiv preprint arXiv:2103.02228 (2021)

DeFi – Economics and Regulation

DeFi as an Information Aggregator

Jiasun Li[✉]

George Mason University, Fairfax, VA 22030, USA
jli29@gmu.edu
https://sites.google.com/site/jiasunlihome/

Abstract. This paper aims to draw attention to the information aggregation role of DeFi, which has not received as much attention in community discussions as many other DeFi topics yet. A study in this direction
seems important, however, given that DeFi intends to rebuild financial
markets based on smart contracts, while a large literature in financial
economics has studied information aggregation via the market. In those
papers, investors submit demand schedules for a risky asset during the
trading process: Equilibrium trading quantities are contingent on the
realized price, which is an implicit function of all investors' information,
determined by market clearing. Similarly, when agents with dispersed
private information interact in a more general setting, they may also
want to have their actions contingent on others', as the aggregate action
profile in equilibrium is also an implicit function of everyone's information. For example, investors in a risky project may want to have individual investment amounts contingent on their total investment amount. A
well-designed smart contract that appropriately divides payoffs may thus
induce contingent actions that efficiently use the aggregated information,
leading to efficient allocations. Therefore, DeFi may improve the information aggregation role of financial markets, in addition to streamlining
operations or cutting out the middle-man.

1 Introduction

There have been many efforts in recent years to replicate traditional financial
market functionalities via smart contracts, commonly known as decentralized
finance (DcFi). Much of the focus has been on streamlining the operational
processes or "cutting out the middle-man". What seems to be missing from
community discussions, however, is the informational role of DeFi (and smart
contracts in general).

On the contrary, the information role of market prices has long been highlighted in the finance and economics literature. For example, that market price
can aggregate information is the central pillar of the celebrated efficient market
hypothesis [1] and rational expectation theory in financial economics [2,3] (and
more generally [4,5], etc.), as well as the discussion on the role of the market
economy in general [6,7]. Given that DeFi attempts to replicate traditional market functionalities, it is timely to ask whether, and if so, how can smart contracts

M. Bernhard et al. (Eds.): FC 2021 Workshops, LNCS 12676, pp. 171–176, 2021.
https://doi.org/10.1007/978-3-662-63958-0_15

play a similar information aggregating role. Furthermore, since the celebrated "invisible hand" argument for markets only works under no informational frictions or externalities, can smart contracts further improve the allocational efficiency of traditional market functions?

This paper provides a positive answer, inspired by recent theoretical findings in economics [8]. In short, using smart contracts to execute "contingent actions" (conditional on actions of other people in the market) aggregates dispersed private information among market participants, just like price aggregates information in familiar discussions on market efficiency and rational expectation. In other words, smart contracts could significantly expand the applicability of the "invisible hand" argument and improve both informational and allocative efficiency over existing market solutions. This perspective points out a role smart contracts could play which has so far been largely neglected. This paper thus attempts to draw the community's attention to this potentially important role of DeFi.

To better understand the argument above, we first briefly review the role of traditional financial markets. Generally speaking, financial markets have at least two major functions: First, to improve allocations (e.g. transfer of assets from sellers with lower valuations to buyers with higher valuations); Second, to aggregate information (since everyone's trading behavior is a function of his/her own private information, the equilibrium market price, which by itself is a function of all agents' trading behaviors, is thus in turn a function of all agents' information).

Typically, in a market with relatively small frictions, the above two market functions tend to perform well. Nevertheless, when externalities are present (for example, if one market participant has monopoly power), market allocations are often not optimal. In such scenarios, forces outside the market are often needed to correct the externalities (such as the introduction of taxes). Smart contracts may be able to do better than the market because 1) regarding allocations, one may be able to make the allocations by smart contracts directly integrate both market allocations and external corrections; 2) regarding how investors can benefit from information aggregation, note that in classic finance discussions on how market prices aggregate information, say, Grossman and Stiglitz's rational expectations model [3], investors submit a series of limit orders at different prices so that their specific transactions are functions of the final market price. Because the price itself integrates all market participants' information, investors can make their specific transactions benefit from other market participants' overall information through a series of limit orders. Smart contracts, which allows investors to make decisions directly contingent on others' actions (rather than indirectly through the price), are thus expected to achieve a similar goal.

The intuitive reasoning above hints that smart contracts may correct externalities in traditional finance markets and substitute the information aggregation function of the equilibrium market price. Formally, the next section proves that a well-designed smart contract can produce a Pareto optimal equilibrium outcome under fairly general conditions. In this way, the smart contract enables the well-known invisible hand to obtain a wider reach.

2   Analytical Results

We consider an economy with n agents who represent some market participants. Each agent $i \in \{1, \cdots, n\}$ has a utility function $u_i(\cdot)$ and a private signal s_i of a random state variable ω. We assume $u_i'(\cdot) > 0$, $u_i''(\cdot) < 0$, $u_i'(-\infty) \to +\infty$, $u_i'(+\infty) \to 0$, and $(\tilde{\omega}, \tilde{s})$ follows a general joint distribution. There is a production technology characterized by a profit function $\pi(\omega, \sum_{i=1}^{n} y_j)$ where y_i is agent i's choice of action and $\frac{\partial}{\partial Y}\pi(\omega, Y) > 0$. For example, the joint investment from a group of n investors in a constant-return-to-scale project has ω being the project's net return, y_i being i's amount of dollar investment, and $\pi(\omega, \sum_{i=1}^{n} y_j) = \omega \times \sum_{i=1}^{n} y_j$. We first define contingent actions:

Definition 1 (contingent action). *Agent i's contingent action $y_i(s_i, \{y_j\}_{j \neq i})$ is defined as a mapping from i's private signal s_i and others' actions $\{y_j\}_{j \neq i}$ to i's own action y_i.*

We can interpret contingent actions as generalizations of demand schedules in a market economy, which are mappings from prices to one's actions, to a broader game theoretical setting. When agents are allowed to choose contingent actions, we have the following result:

Proposition 2. *In general, $\exists$ a contract (an ex ante profit division rule among all agents) under which an equilibrium of contingent actions has an interim Pareto optimal outcome.[1]*

Proof. We first note an observation that will be useful later in the proof:

$$\forall k \neq i, \frac{\partial}{\partial y_k}\pi(\omega, \{y_j\}_{j=1}^n) = \frac{\partial}{\partial y_i}\pi(\omega, \{y_j\}_{j=1}^n). \tag{1}$$

An interim Pareto optimal allocation is characterized by the solution to the problem faced by a planner who knows the entire signal profile s and specifies actions $\{y_j^*(s)\}_{j=1}^n$ and allocations $\{q_i(\omega, \{y_j\}_{j=1}^n)\}_{i=1}^n$ to maximize some social welfare function. That is,

$$\{y_j^*(s)\}_{j=1}^n = \arg\max_{\{y_j\}_{j=1}^n} \mathbb{E}\left[\sum_{i=1}^n a_i(\tilde{\omega}, s) \cdot u_i(q_i(\tilde{\omega}, \{y_j\}_{j=1}^n)) \Big| s\right] \quad \text{(interim efficiency)}, \tag{2}$$

where $\{a_i(\tilde{\omega}, s)\}_{i=1}^n$ are Pareto weights and $\forall(\omega, \{y_j\}_{j=1}^n)$, $\{q_i(\omega, \{y_j\}_{j=1}^n)\}_{i=1}^n$ are given by

$$\begin{cases} \{q_i(\omega, \{y_j\}_{j=1}^n)\}_{i=1}^n = \arg\max_{\{q_i\}_{i=1}^n} \sum_{i=1}^n a_i(\omega, s) \cdot u_i(q_i(\omega, \{y_j\}_{j=1}^n)) & \text{(ex post efficiency)}, \tag{3} \\ \sum_{i=1}^n q_i(\omega, \{y_j\}_{j=1}^n) = \pi(\omega, \{y_j\}_{j=1}^n) & \text{(feasibility)}. \tag{4} \end{cases}$$

---

[1] By "in general", we exclude ill-behaved utility/profit functions and distributions under which either the equilibrium or the Pareto optimal allocation for a given set of Pareto weights does not uniquely exist.

We are interested in interim Pareto optimal allocations where Pareto weights do not depend on realized states and signals, that is, $\{a_i(\tilde{\omega}, s)\}_{i=1}^n = \{a_i\}_{i=1}^n$.

We proceed by first characterizing $\left\{q_i(\omega, \{y_j\}_{j=1}^n)\right\}_{j=1}^n$ for a given $(\omega, \{y_j\}_{j=1}^n)$. Denote the Lagrangian multiplier of (4) as $L(\omega, \{y_j\}_{j=1}^n)$, then $\forall i \in \{1, \cdots, n\}$,

$$q_i(\omega, \{y_j\}_{j=1}^n) = (u_i')^{-1}\left(\frac{L(\omega, \{y_j\}_{j=1}^n)}{a_i}\right), \tag{5}$$

where $(u_i')^{-1}$ denotes the inverse function of u_i', and $L(\omega, \{y_j\}_{j=1}^n)$ is implicitly defined by

$$\sum_{i=1}^n (u_i')^{-1}\left(\frac{L(\omega, \{y_j\}_{j=1}^n)}{a_i}\right) = \pi(\omega, \{y_j\}_{j=1}^n). \tag{6}$$

Plug (4) and (5) into the FOC of (2) with respect to y_k, we get

$$\mathbb{E}\left[L(\omega, \{y_j\}_{j=1}^n)\frac{\partial}{\partial y_k}\pi(\tilde{\omega}, \{y_j\}_{j=1}^n)\Big| s\right] = 0.$$

Thus for a given signal profile s, the first-best action profile $\{y_j^*(s)\}_{j=1}^n$ is characterized by a set of n equations: $\forall k \in \{1, \cdots, n\}$,

$$\mathbb{E}[L(\tilde{\omega}, \{y_j^*(s)\}_{j=1}^n)\left(\sum_{i=1}^n \frac{\frac{1}{a_i}}{u_i''((u_i')^{-1}(\frac{L(\tilde{\omega}, \{y_j^*(s)\}_{j=1}^n)}{a_i}))}\right)\frac{\partial}{\partial y_k}L(\tilde{\omega}, \{y_j^*(s)\}_{j=1}^n)|s] = 0. \tag{7}$$

Equilibrium. We proceed to characterize the equilibrium under a contract that gives $Q_i(\omega, \{y_j\}_{j=1}^n) \equiv (u_i')^{-1}(\frac{L(\omega, \{y_j\}_{j=1}^n)}{a_i})$ to agent i. By (6) we have that $\forall r$ and $\{y_j\}_{j=1}^n$, $\sum_{i=1}^n Q_i(\omega, \{y_j\}_{j=1}^n) = \pi(\omega, \{y_j\}_{j=1}^n)$, therefore $\{Q_i\}_{i=1}^n$ is a feasible allocation.

Agent i's contingent action $y_i(s_i, \{y_j\}_{j\neq i}) = \arg\max_{y_i} \mathbb{E}\left[u_i(Q_i(\tilde{r}, \{y_j\}_{j=1}^n))\right.$ $\left.|\{y_j\}_{j\neq i}, s_i\right] = \arg\max_{y_i} \mathbb{E}\left[u_i((u_i')^{-1}(\frac{L(\omega, \{y_j\}_{j=1}^n)}{a_i}))\Big|\{y_j\}_{j\neq i}, s_i\right]$, and FOC gives that at equilibrium

$$\mathbb{E}\left[L(\omega, \{y_j\}_{j=1}^n)\frac{\frac{1}{a_i^2}}{u_i''((u_i')^{-1}(\frac{L(\omega, \{y_j\}_{j=1}^n))}{a_i}))}\frac{\partial}{\partial y_i}L(\omega, \{y_j\}_{j=1}^n)\Big|\{y_j\}_{j\neq i}, s_i\right] = 0. \tag{8}$$

By (1), $\forall k \neq i$, $\frac{\partial}{\partial y_k}\pi(\omega, \{y_j\}_{j=1}^n) = \frac{\partial}{\partial y_i}\pi(\omega, \{y_j\}_{j=1}^n)$, taking partial derivatives on both sides of (6) gives that $\forall k \neq i$, $\frac{\partial}{\partial y_k}L(\omega, \{y_j\}_{j=1}^n) = \frac{\partial}{\partial y_i}L(\omega, \{y_j\}_{j=1}^n)$. Plug in (8) we get

$$\mathbb{E}\left[L(\omega, \{y_j\}_{j=1}^n)\frac{\frac{1}{a_i^2}}{u_i''((u_i')^{-1}(\frac{L(\omega, \{y_j\}_{j=1}^n))}{a_i}))}\frac{\partial}{\partial y_k}L(\omega, \{y_j\}_{j=1}^n)\Big|\{y_j\}_{j\neq i}, s_i\right] = 0. \tag{9}$$

FOCs for different agent i-s gives n equations like (9). Multiple each by a_i and sum over, we get that the equilibrium is characterized by a set of n equations: $\forall k \in \{1, \cdots, n\}$,

$$
\mathbb{E}\left[L(\omega, \{y_j\}_{j=1}^n) \sum_{i=1}^n \left(\frac{\frac{1}{a_i}}{u_i''((u_i')^{-1}(\frac{L(\omega,\{y_j\}_{j=1}^n))}{a_i})} \right) \frac{\partial}{\partial y_k} L(\omega, \{y_j\}_{j=1}^n) \bigg|\{y_j\}_{j \neq i}, s_i \right] = 0.
$$

(10)

Since the n equations together pin down the solution $\{\hat{y}_j(s)\}_{j=1}^n$, the expectations in (10) is effectively conditional on s. Then compared to the equation set of (7), it is immediately that as long as (7) has a unique solution, the equilibrium and Pareto optimal action profiles $\{\hat{y}_j(s)\}_{j=1}^n$ and $\{y_j^*(s)\}_{j=1}^n$ must be identical.

Further Discussions. Implementing contingent actions à la Proposition 2 requires infrastructures to simultaneously 1) accommodate contingency plans, 2) enforce commitments to chosen decisions, and 3) ensure mutually best responses. To this end, smart contracts, which accommodate all three requirements particularly well, may come in handy: As computer codes executing pre-specified "if-then" logic, they fulfill Requirement 1 by definition. Running on immutable blockchains (Requirement 2), they enjoy "atomic" executions, that is, they allow executions of related operations to "either all occur or all abort". Hence, a set of contingent actions can be programmed to iterate toward equilibrium and be taken only when all optimization conditions are met (Requirement 3).

While Bitcoin's Script supports limited smart contract functionalities, Ethereum popularized general-use smart contracts that can act as "legal persons" to send and receive transactions under pre-programmed conditions. Many new blockchains also support smart contracts (e.g. Facebook's Diem via its Move language). Given these technological advancements, our information aggregation perspective may open the door to inspiring more future applications beyond replicating traditional financial market functions.

On the other hand, despite rapid growth, smart contract applications are still in their early days right now, with many likely suboptimal specifications. Our theory may thus also guide their further improvements. For example, over the past couple of years, smart contracts have enabled token sales, many of which effectively implement crowdfunding with the intermediary platforms replaced by smart contracts. These applications as well as more general investment settings can readily use our suggested contracts to improve capital allocation, thanks to smart contracts' programming flexibility and low deployment cost. Separately, there have also been many discussions on decentralized autonomous organizations (DAOs), which envision to organize businesses as "nexus of smart contracts" in an apparent reference to the "nexus of contracts" theory of the firm [9]. The general results from Proposition 2 may offer guidance on this front.

That said, for our theory to reach its full potential, we still need a few technological breakthroughs in smart contracts. First, we look for solutions to trustlessly bring off-chain data onto the blockchain (i.e. the so-called oracle problem).

While there are partial solutions for some specific settings (e.g. Chainlink), general-purpose oracles are still under active research. We also look for further optimizations on gas costs for smart contract executions, especially if we implement our Proposition 2 with iterations. Finally, smart contract integrity is another area that calls for improvements to prevent bugs such as those seen in the hack of the first decentralized autonomous organization (commonly know as *The DAO*) that led to Ethereum's fork.

References

1. Fama, E.F.: Efficient capital markets: a review of theory and empirical work*. J. Fin. **25**(2), 383–417 (1970)
2. Grossman, S.: On the efficiency of competitive stock markets where trades have diverse information. J. Fin. **31**(2), 573–585 (1976)
3. Grossman, S.J., Stiglitz, J.E.: On the impossibility of informationally efficient markets. Am. Econ. Rev. **70**(3), 393–408 (1980)
4. Lucas, R.E.: Expectations and the neutrality of money. J. Econ. Theory **4**(2), 103–124 (1972)
5. Lucas, R.E., Jr.: Econometric policy evaluation: a critique. In: Carnegie-Rochester Conference Series on Public Policy, vol. 1, pp. 19–46. North-Holland (1976)
6. Hayek, F.: The Road to Serfdom. University of Chicago Press and Routledge Press (1944)
7. Hayek, F.: The use of knowledge in society. Am. Econ. Rev. **35**(4), 519–30 (1945)
8. Li, J.: Information aggregation via contracting. SSRN 3682883 (2020)
9. Alchian, A.A., Demsetz, H.: Production, information costs, and economic organization. Am. Econ. Rev. **62**, 777–795 (1972)

A Game-Theoretic Analysis
of Cross-ledger Swaps with Packetized
Payments

Alevtina Dubovitskaya[1,2](✉)(iD), Damien Ackerer[3](iD), and Jiahua Xu[4,5](iD)

[1] Lucerne University of Applied Sciences and Arts, Lucerne, Switzerland
`alevtina.dubovitskaya@hslu.ch`
[2] Swisscom, Bern, Switzerland
[3] Covario, Zug, Switzerland
`damien.ackerer@covar.io`
[4] UCL Centre for Blockchain Technologies, London, UK
`jiahua.xu@ucl.ac.uk`
[5] École Polytechnique Fédérale de Lausanne (EPFL), Lausanne, Switzerland

Abstract. We propose a game-theoretic framework to study the outcomes of packetized payments, a cross-ledger transaction protocol, with strategic and possibly malicious agents. We derive the transaction failure rate and demonstrate that without disciplinary mechanisms, packetized payments are likely to be incomplete. Our analysis suggests that collateral deposits can prevent malicious agents from taking advantage of the protocol. We further infer that the deposit amount should depend on the underlying asset price volatility or that it should be dynamically adjusted as the price changes.

Keywords: Blockchain · Packetized payments · Atomic swaps

1 Introduction

1.1 Background

HTLCs. Hashed Time Lock Contracts (HTLCs) have been recently proposed [3] to achieve atomicity of a cross-ledger transaction without any connections between the ledgers, and are often employed in decentralized exchanges (DEX)[1] to complete peer-to-peer exchange [1,6].

An atomic swap with HTLCs starts with one transactional agent, say Alice, randomly generating a secret key. Alice then locks her asset in an HTLC that will transfer the asset to her counterparty, say Bob, upon verification of the secret key. Bob subsequently locks his asset in an HTLC that will transfer the asset to Alice upon verification of the same secret key. The swap completes

---

[1] Cross-ledger DEX protocols are not to be confused with DEX protocols operated within one chain, such as automated market makers (AMM) on Ethereum [16].

© International Financial Cryptography Association 2021
M. Bernhard et al. (Eds.): FC 2021 Workshops, LNCS 12676, pp. 177–187, 2021.
https://doi.org/10.1007/978-3-662-63958-0_16

when Alice unlocks Bob's asset with the secret key generated by herself, which simultaneously exposes the secret key, allowing Bob to also unlock Alice's asset. Should Alice fail to unlock Bob's asset with her secret key, the two HTLCs will respectively send the locked asset to their original owners when the time locks expire.

One problem of HTLCs is that they create a free option for Alice, who can ultimately choose when and whether or not to expose the secret key, thus delaying the completion of the swap or even causing it to fail. Bob also has the option not to lock his asset, which leads to blocking of Alice's funds for nothing [15].

Packetized Payments (PP). Robinson [12] underlines the aforementioned problems associated with HTLCs, and proposes an alternative approach for cross-ledger atomic swaps: packetized payments (PP). Originally developed as part of the Interledger Protocol [5] named *Hyperledger Quilt*,[2] a cross-ledger swap with packetized payments is conducted with a series of alternating transactions.

First, the total asset amounts to be traded are split into N "economically-insignificant" amounts (Fig. 1a Step A). Next, these small portions of assets will be sent on one and then on another blockchain sequentially: Steps B and C are to be repeated N times in order to complete the transaction.

Note that, at each iteration, the protocol may require the agent to match and extend the previous transfer such that the agents are alternately exposed to counterparty risk (Fig. 1b). Otherwise, the payment initiator would have to agree to always bear the risk of abandonment from the other agent. If one agent behaves maliciously and does not execute the transfer when it is his or her turn, the counterparty loses *only* a fraction of the asset they would be willing to trade. Therefore, PP caps the amount of assets that can be lost at a fraction of the asset determined at Step A and prevents the whole amount of assets being blocked for a long period of time. It also prevents a potential loss of the whole amount of assets, while requiring only simple transfer transactions.

1.2   Contribution

Our framework builds on finite extensive-form games with imperfect information [9], where the only known unknown information is the counterparty's type, which can be either honest or malicious. We study agents' strategies and derive preference parameter conditions consistent with their actions. We also derive the transaction failure rate as a function of the percentages of honest and malicious agents.

We show that in a swap game with packetized payments, it is impossible to enforce malicious agents to complete the transaction without an additional disciplinary mechanism. We illustrate that the "biased" preferences of agents for completed transactions have to be economically large, which motivates the necessity of alternative contracting mechanisms such as collateral deposits. Still,

---

[2] https://github.com/hyperledger/quilt.

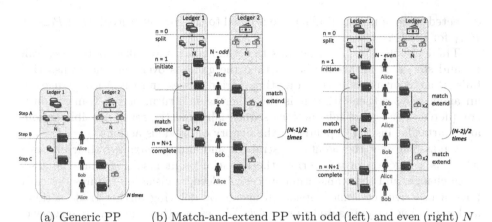

(a) Generic PP   (b) Match-and-extend PP with odd (left) and even (right) N

Fig. 1. Packetized payment (PP) schemas.

we infer that the initial collateral amount should depend on the asset price volatility, or that it should be dynamically adjusted as the asset price fluctuates. As the first cross-chain packetized payment protocol *Hyperledger Quilt* is yet to be launched and empirical evidence is absent, our work provides the first simulation result that can facilitate further development of the protocol.

We focus on packetized payments, yet our approach can be extended to other cross-ledger transaction protocols.

2   A Game-Theoretic Analysis

2.1   Framework

Two agents, Alice and Bob, or a and b, want to exchange one unit of asset 1, say one Altcoin, from a for some units of asset 2, say Tether (USDT), from b. We assume that asset 2 is the reference asset in which the agents value their goods. We denote P_t the time-t price of asset 1 expressed in units of asset 2, for example the price of one Altcoin in USDT. We assume for simplicity that there is no interest rate or coin staking, meaning that the asset quantities do not increase by themselves whenever locked in a special wallet or account. Therefore, only the price of asset 1 is stochastic in our framework.

There are three possible times t at which the agents may take actions: 0, 1, and 2. The price dynamics of asset 1 is given by

$$P_t = P_{t-1} \pm \delta \tag{1}$$

for $t = 1, 2$ with equal probability of up and down moves, for some initial price $P_0 > 0$ and some constant $\delta > 0$ such that $\delta \leq \frac{P_0}{2}$ so that the price remains non-negative during the game. Note that the asset price is a martingale, that is the expected value of next period's price is equal to the current price, $\mathbb{E}\left[P_t \mid P_{t-1}\right] = P_{t-1}$ for $t = 1, 2$.

There are three types of actions that the agents may take: continue c, wait w, and stop s. If an agent plays s then the game is over and the transaction fails. If an agent plays w then one time period passes and the price changes. If an agent plays c then either it is the other agent's turn, or the transaction is completed. The agents take actions sequentially and the set of possible actions at a particular instant depends on the history of previous actions.

We assume that the agents are strategic and aim to maximize their interests which is a function of two terms: the financial profit resulting from the asset price change, and the transaction success. Indeed, transaction failures typically have a negative economic impact on agents by delaying further trade actions, and increasing the exposure to price risk. We assume that there are two types of agents: the honest or high type h, and the malicious or low type l. We formalize the two types in the following definition.

Definition 1 (Agent types). *An agent of type h, namely* honest, *always chooses to play continue c. An agent of type l, namely* malicious, *satisfies the parameter condition $\alpha_{i,l} = 0$ for $i = a, b$.*

We model the agent incentives using a utility function as follows:

$$\mathcal{U}(i, j) = \alpha_{i,j} X + \beta_i XY \tag{2}$$

for any agent $i \in \{a, b\}$ of type $j \in \{h, l\}$, and where $X = 1$ indicates transaction success and $X = -1$ transaction failure, and Y is the profit and loss resulting from the asset price change and transfer. The constant $\alpha_{i,j} \geq 0$ measures the extent to which an agent is willing to complete the transaction. For example, if $\alpha_{i,j}$ is large then the agent will most likely prefer to complete the transaction despite an adverse price change. We set $\beta_b = 1$ and $\beta_a = -1$ modeling the agent's opposite exposures to price changes. Note that if the transaction fails, that is $X = -1$, then Alice is positively exposed to Y because asset 1 was not transferred to Bob as $\beta_a X = 1$ in this case.

In Sect. 2.2, we derive the optimal strategy of the malicious agent, and the conditions on $\alpha_{i,h}$ such that an agent is *willingly honest*.

We denote μ_i the fraction of honest agents i and, thus, $1 - \mu_i$ the fraction of malicious agents i for $i \in \{a, b\}$. The agents meet at random, and each does not know whether the other agent is malicious or not. Furthermore, the agents have full information about their environments. We write $\mathbb{E}\left[\mathcal{X} \mid \mathcal{Y}\right]$ the expected value of the variable $\mathcal{X}$ given the history of actions and other possible refinements $\mathcal{Y}$. We write $\mathcal{T}(i)$ the type of agent i, for example $\mathcal{T}_a = h$ means that Alice is honest. We denote $\mathcal{A}(j, \mathcal{H})$ the best response, or action taken, by an agent of type j following the history $\mathcal{H}$, which is defined as the action maximizing their expected utility.

Note that Alice and Bob must take into account the likelihood that they can be trading with either a malicious or an honest agent. For example, the expected utility of a type j Bob conditioned on the history of actions $\mathcal{H}$ is given by

Table 1. Summary of notations

Notation	Description
a and b	Alice and Bob
h and l	Honest and malicious
c, w, and s	Actions: continue, wait, and stop
$\mathcal{T}_i$	Agent i type
μ_i	Honest agent i percentage, $\mathbb{P}[\mathcal{T}_i = h]$
$\mathcal{A}(j, \mathcal{H})$	Agent type j action after $\mathcal{H}$
X	Swap success (1) or failure (-1)
Y	Financial profit and loss
$\alpha_{i,j}$	Agent preference parameter for swap success
β_i	$\beta_a = -1$ and $\beta_b = 1$ indicate the asset price exposure direction
P_t	Time-t price of asset 1 denominated in asset 2
δ	One-period price change of asset 1 denominated in asset 2

$$\mathbb{E}\left[\mathcal{U}(b, j) \mid \mathcal{H}\right] = \mu_a \mathbb{E}\left[\mathcal{U}(b, j) \mid \mathcal{H}, \mathcal{T}_a = h\right]$$
$$+ (1 - \mu_a)\mathbb{E}\left[\mathcal{U}(b, j) \mid \mathcal{H}, \mathcal{T}_a = l\right]$$

where $\mathbb{E}\left[\mathcal{U}(b, j) \mid \mathcal{H}, \mathcal{T}_a = l\right]$ denotes the expected utility of type j Bob under the assumption that Alice is malicious, and so on.

We use brackets to denote the history of actions, for examples $\{\emptyset\}$ for no action taken and $\{c, w, c\}$ for continue–wait–continue actions. Which agent played a particular action and whose turn it is to play next will be clear from the game descriptions. Notations are summarized in Table 1.

2.2 A Short Packetized Payment Game

Packetized payments split the transaction into small transfers where each agent exposed herself or himself to a one-way transfer alternately. At any point in time, one agent may decide not to transfer furthermore and stop the transaction. As a consequence, the variable Y depends on the exit time and is given by

$$Y_n = \begin{cases} 0 & n = 0, \\ \frac{n}{N}P_{t_n} - \frac{n-1}{N}P_0 & n \text{ is odd and } 0 < n \leq N \\ \frac{n-1}{N}P_{t_n} - \frac{n}{N}P_0 & n \text{ is even and } 0 < n \leq N \\ P_{t_n} - P_0 & n = N+1 \end{cases} \tag{3}$$

where the subscript n indicates the current step of the transaction, $\frac{1}{N}$ is the granularity amount of the PP, and t_n indicates the time at which the n-th step takes place.

For clarity of exposition, we study a swap performed in 3 payment transactions in total so that $t_n = n$ for $n = 0, 1, 2$ (see Fig. 2a). Still, this setup is sufficient to illustrate the functioning of packetized payments.

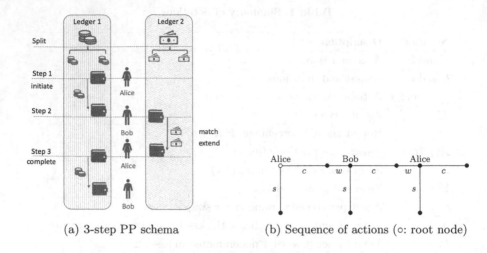

(a) 3-step PP schema   (b) Sequence of actions (∘: root node)

Fig. 2. Match-and-extend PP in 3 steps

The sequence of actions for the packetized payment game are described in Fig. 2b. In summary, Alice transfers half of the asset to Bob, then Bob makes the whole P_0 payment, and finally Alice transfers the remaining half of the asset. The agents can only decide to continue c or stop s. However, when an agent continues, i.e. plays c, we assume that the transaction also waits, i.e. plays w, for a short time period over which the asset price changes. Note that the game resembles the *centipede game* from [13], however there are important differences: the agents have partial information, and the payoffs are stochastic. Indeed, each agent does not know the other agent type, honest or malicious, and the payoff they get depends on the asset price which is stochastic.

Remark 1. We assumed that Bob matches Alice's payment of $\frac{1}{N}$ and sends an additional $\frac{1}{N}$ payment at the same time (match and extend). This is a fairer mechanism as the agents alternately expose themselves to a loss of $\frac{1}{N}$. Indeed, the alternative would be to let Bob only match while Alice initiates all the payments. This would however result in Alice being the only one exposed to counterparty risk and would require $2N$ transfers instead of $N+1$.

The first and striking result is that malicious agents, either Bob or Alice, will never complete the transaction. Indeed, there is no incentive for an agent who only cares about its financial profit to complete the transaction, as shown in Proposition 1. All proofs can be found in Appendix.

Proposition 1 (Malicious Alice and Bob). *We have that* $\mathcal{A}(l, \{c, w\}) = s$ *and* $\mathcal{A}(l, \{c, w, c, w\}) = s$.

From this result we can also infer the percentage of failed transactions.

Corollary 1 (Transaction failure probability). *Assuming that both malicious and honest agents participate in the transaction, then the percentage of incomplete transactions is* $1 - \mu_b \mu_a$.

As it is always best for the malicious type to stop, the transaction will only be completed if the two agents are honest. We derive a necessary condition so that Bob is honest and continues the transaction.

Proposition 2 (Honest Bob). *Assume that Alice of either type plays c at the initial step. Then Bob is honest if and only if*

$$\mu_a > \frac{2P_0}{4\alpha_{b,h} + P_0 - \delta}$$

Note that this result holds only if Bob did not update his prior that Alice is honest with probability μ_a, which is the case when both Alice types play c at step 0. We observe that if the price is more volatile, meaning larger δ, then a larger fraction of honest a agents is required. Interestingly, even with no price movement $\delta = 0$ and only honest a agents, we see that Bob's preference parameter for a completed transaction must be fairly large in value, $\alpha_{b,h} > \frac{P_0}{4}$.

We now derive conditions necessary for Alice to be honest.

Proposition 3 (Honest Alice). *Alice is honest if and only if*

$$\alpha_{a,h} > \frac{P_0 + 2\delta}{4} \quad and \quad \mu_b > \frac{P_0}{4\alpha_{a,h} + P_0}. \tag{4}$$

We see that the conditions for Alice to be honest are more stringent than for Bob even in a setup without any malicious agents, that is when $\mu_a = \mu_b = 1$. Notably if the percentage of honest Bob becomes very small, $\mu_b \to 0$, then there cannot exist any honest Alice unless $\alpha_{a,h} \to +\infty$.

3   Discussion

Our game-theoretic analysis shows that there is no incentive for malicious agents to complete a PP transaction. As a consequence, the transaction failure rate should be large and the economic incentive for agents to behave honestly would need to be enormous. Importantly, a malicious agent can enter multiple PP transactions in parallel with different counterparties for larger profits.

From a practical perspective, PPs are relatively simple, but require many transfers, whose total cost is therefore uncertain. Lightning networks [11] can be employed for micropayments needed for packetized payments without incurring high transaction fees. However, this reintroduces the problem of the assets being locked and, in this case, in the form of collateral deposit on the escrow accounts of each agent on each blockchain: Alice and Bob will need to create two micropayment channels, one on top of each blockchain, and lock the collateral on each channel. In addition, if an honest agent does not receive a payment from a counterparty, and is willing to close the micropayment channel, the funds on the escrow account will be blocked for a certain blockchain-specific period of time [7]. It is also worth noticing that there may be small delays between transfers for network validation, which in turn lead to price fluctuations, as described in the PP game. Importantly, PPs cannot be used to exchange non-fungible assets such as CryptoKitties[3] or "digital twins" of physical goods [12].

3.1 Collateral Deposit

Using collateral deposits to reduce the risk of agents exposed to adverse behavior of other agents is not new. For example, applying collateral to disincentivize aborting a fair exchange has been discussed in works on rational fair exchange [14]. Zamyatin et al. [17] suggest using collateral at least equal to the assets locked on the blockchain for a trade. They also propose overcollateralization and a liquidation mechanism to mitigate extreme price fluctuations for short- and long-term cross-ledger transactions. While this ensures that economically rational agents have no incentive to misbehave, a disadvantage of this solution is that if an agent would like to transfer all their assets of one kind, they will be obliged to execute multiple transactions, each with an amount (approximately) equal to a half of the amount of the asset they currently possess.

Based on the proposed game-theoretic model, it can be shown that a marginal amount of collateral is sufficient to prevent agents from behaving maliciously. We modify the frameworks of Sect. 2 so as to require agents to place collateral which will be lost if they exit the transaction without completing it. The following Proposition shows that this extinguishes malicious behaviors in our framework.

Proposition 4 (PP with collateral). *Assume that Bob places a collateral larger than $\frac{P_0+\delta}{2}$, and Alice places a collateral larger than $\frac{P_0+2\delta}{2}$, then it is optimal for malicious agents to continue the transaction in the packetized payment game described in Sect. 2.2.*

Two relevant observations can be made for real-world applications. First, both expressions for the minimum collateral requirement involve the term δ which suggests that collateral demand should be a function of the asset price volatility, which is known to be time varying. Second, for the packetized payment, the initial collateral involves the fractional transfer value $\frac{P_0}{2}$, or $\frac{P_{t_n}}{N}$ in general, which suggests that the collateral requirement can be small, with N large, but should be adjusted dynamically as the asset price changes. Indeed, the price can vary up or down to $P_0 \pm N\delta$ in extreme scenarios, but will in general fluctuate significantly less.

3.2 Reputation Mechanism

We have always assumed that an agent cannot predict the strategy of their counterparty ex-ante as the agent types, malicious or honest, are not observable.

---

[3] https://www.cryptokitties.co/.

However, in reality, if an agent trades regularly with another agent that it can identify, or if an agent has some information on the previous behavior of another agent, then a self-selected agent matching can occur instead of a random one.

In principle, as all the transactions executed on a ledger can generally be seen, the transaction history of an agent can be analyzed to build his or her reputation. However, computation of such reputation value is problematic in a case of permissionless blockchains for several reasons. First, an agent can create multiple accounts and attempt to preserve their anonymity. Even though de-anonymization is possible [2], one cannot guarantee a perfect mapping between one user and all his or her transactions, in the case of multiple accounts. Second, it may not always be possible to distinguish a cross-ledger transaction from a single-chain transaction. However, if these two challenges are addressed, thanks to the book-keeping property [4] and immutability of a ledger, using a reputation mechanism can complement existing protocols.

4 Conclusion and Future Work

We introduce a game-theoretic approach to model agent behaviors in cross-ledger transactions with packetized payments. We derive conditions for agents to behave honestly or maliciously, as well as different measures of economic and transaction success. We propose to dynamically compute and adjust the collateral amounts in order to enforce honest behaviors among agents, and we discussed the implementation challenges of reputation systems as a disciplinary mechanism.

An important observation is that trustless cross-ledger swap protocols should use disciplinary mechanisms such as collateral deposit. The implementation, cost, performance, and complexity of various protocols on permissionless blockchains supporting smart contracts – e.g. Ethereum, EOS, Tezos [10], and Neo [8] – thus merit future research.

Appendix

Most of the arguments in the proofs below follow the hypothesis that an agent always takes the actions which maximize their expected utility, taking into account future and possibly adversarial actions from the other agent. We always describe the key conditions (inequalities) to be verified but provide limited details on the derivations as they can be long and tedious.

Proof of Proposition 1. At time 2 if $T_a = l$, then Alice loses $\frac{P_2}{2}$ in utility by playing c instead of s. Similarly, at time 1 if $T_b = l$, then Bob gets $\frac{P_1}{2}$ in utility by playing s whereas he expects to receive $\mathbb{E}\left[\mathcal{U}(b,l) \mid \{c,c\}\right] = \mu_a(P_1 - P_0) + (1-\mu_a)(\frac{P_1}{2} - P_0)$ if he plays c. We have $\mathbb{E}\left[\mathcal{U}(b,l) \mid \{c,c\}\right] < \frac{P_1}{2}$ since $\delta < \frac{P_0}{2}$ and $\mu_a \leq 1$, hence a malicious Bob plays s.

Proof of Corollary 1. The transaction succeeds only if Alice and Bob are honest which happens with probability $\mathbb{P}[T_a = T_b = h] = \mu_a\mu_b$.

Proof of Proposition 2. We have $\mathbb{E}\left[\mathcal{U}(b,h) \mid \{c,w,c\}\right] = \mu_a(P_1 - P_0 + \alpha_{b,h}) + (1 - \mu_a)(-\alpha_{b,h} + \frac{P_1}{2} - P_0)$ and $\mathbb{E}\left[\mathcal{U}(b,h) \mid \{c,w,s\}\right] = -\alpha_{b,h} + \frac{P_1}{2}$. We obtain that $\mathcal{A}(b,\{c,w\}) = c$ by taking $P_1 = P_0 - \delta$.

Proof of Proposition 3. We have $\mathcal{A}(h,\{c,w,c,w\}) = c$ if and only if $\alpha_{a,h} + P_0 - P_2 > -\alpha_{a,h} + P_0 - \frac{P_2}{2}$ which is equivalent to $\alpha_{a,h} > \frac{P_0 + 2\delta}{4}$. Then, with $\mathcal{A}(h,\{c,w,c,w\}) = c$, we have that $\mathbb{E}\left[\mathcal{U}(a,h) \mid \{c\}\right] = \mu_b\alpha_{a,h} + (1 - \mu_b)(-\alpha_{a,h} - \frac{P_0}{2})$ and $\mathbb{E}\left[\mathcal{U}(a,h) \mid \{s\}\right] = -\alpha_{a,h}$. Therefore, for agent a to be honest it must also be that $\mu_b > \frac{P_0}{4\alpha_{a,h} + P_0}$.

Proof of Proposition 4. This is immediate as malicious agents would never be able to make any profit by exiting prematurely the transaction.

References

1. Decred-compatible cross-chain atomic swapping (2018). https://github.com/decred/atomicswap/
2. Biryukov, A., Khovratovich, D., Pustogarov, I.: Deanonymisation of clients in bitcoin P2P network. In: The ACM Conference on Computer and Communications Security, pp. 15–29. ACM (2014). https://doi.org/10.1145/2660267.2660379
3. Herlihy, M.: Atomic cross-chain swaps. In: Proceedings of the 2018 ACM Symposium on Principles of Distributed Computing, pp. 245–254. ACM, Association for Computing Machinery, July 2018. https://doi.org/10.1145/3212734.3212736
4. Ibañez, J.I., Bayer, C.N., Tasca, P., Xu, J.: REA, triple-entry accounting and blockchain: converging paths to shared ledger systems. SSRN Electron. J. (2021). https://doi.org/10.2139/ssrn.3602207
5. Interledger: Interledger Protocol (2020). https://interledger.org/rfcs/0027-interledger-protocol-4/
6. Komodo: Komodo's Atomic-Swap Powered, Decentralized Exchange: Barterdex (2021). https://docs.komodoplatform.com/whitepaper/chapter6.html
7. Luu, L., Narayanan, V., Zheng, C., Baweja, K., Gilbert, S., Saxena, P.: A secure sharding protocol for open blockchains. In: Proceedings of the 2016 ACM SIGSAC Conference on Computer and Communications Security, pp. 17–30. ACM (2016)
8. Neo: Neo White Paper (2020). https://docs.neo.org/docs/en-us/basic/whitepaper.html
9. Osborne, M.J., Rubinstein, A.: A Course in Game Theory. MIT Press, Cambridge (1994)
10. Perez, D., Xu, J., Livshits, B.: Revisiting transactional statistics of high-scalability blockchains. In: The ACM Internet Measurement Conference, pp. 535–550, October 2020. https://dl.acm.org/doi/10.1145/3419394.3423628
11. Poon, J., Dryja, T.: The bitcoin lightning network: Scalable off-chain instant payments (2016)
12. Robinson, D.: HTLCs considered harmful. In: Stanford Blockchain Conference (2019). http://diyhpl.us/wiki/transcripts/stanford-blockchain-conference/2019/htlcs-considered-harmful/
13. Rosenthal, R.W.: Games of perfect information, predatory pricing and the chainstore paradox. J. Econ. Theory **25**(1), 92–100 (1981). https://linkinghub.elsevier.com/retrieve/pii/0022053181900181

14. Syverson, P.: Weakly secret bit commitment: applications to lotteries and fair exchange. In: The 11th IEEE Computer Security Foundations Workshop, pp. 2–13. IEEE Computing Society (1998). http://ieeexplore.ieee.org/document/683149/
15. Xu, J., Ackerer, D., Dubovitskaya, A.: A game-theoretic analysis of cross-chain atomic swaps with HTLCs. In: IEEE 41st International Conference on Distributed Computing Systems (ICDCS) (2021)
16. Xu, J., Vavryk, N., Paruch, K., Cousaert, S.: SoK: decentralized exchanges (DEX) with automated market maker (AMM) protocols, March 2021. http://arxiv.org/abs/2103.12732
17. Zamyatin, A., Harz, D., Lind, J., Panayiotou, P., Gervais, A., Knottenbelt, W.: XCLAIM: trustless, interoperable, cryptocurrency-backed assets. In: IEEE Symposium on Security and Privacy, pp. 193–210. IEEE, May 2019. https://ieeexplore.ieee.org/document/8835387/

DeFi – MEV and Illicit Activity

Wendy Grows Up: More Order Fairness

Klaus Kursawe[(✉)]

Vega Protocol, RUE Antoine Carteret 3, 1202 Geneve, CH, Switzerland
klaus@vega.xyz

Abstract. Transaction order related issues such as MEV (Miner Extractable Value) and frontrunning in blockchain networks stemming from the ability of validators to reorder transactions. This can not only extract a tax on honest users, but also skew the validator economy by making it harder to control financial inactivation of validators, and might even lead to regulatory issues. We present a pre-protocol that allows a blockchain application to combine different forms of order fairness with causal order to prevent such issues on the level of the blockchain, and that can be combined with various blockchain implementations.

1 Introduction

In recent years, blockchain applications have increased in complexity and utility, allowing more advanced financial tools such as exchanges and trading markets to be decentralized, thus highlighting new challenges for consensus protocols. Especially, it is no longer sufficient for a consensus layer protocols to only guarantee consistency of the blockchain. While additional requirements have been investigated in the past – for example causal order or censorship resilience – very little attention has been given to the fairness of the order of events, making it possible to execute frontrunning or rushing attacks. Several such attacks have been observed in the wild already, with more issues to be expected with increasingly sophisticated usecases. Some blockchains attempt to make such attacks somewhat harder, for example through special protection for the leader, rapid leader change [1] or a completely leaderless approach [3], while others can be easily manipulated by a single corrupt validator or a well targeted denial of service attack.

In a previous paper [5], we introduced Wendy, a pre-protocol to blockchains that can assure fairness. We now present further development of Wendy.

- The protocol is now divided into a framework and the fairness enforcement. The definition of fairness, as well as some assumptions on the adversary strength, are affecting only the fairness enforcement part. Thus, the framework can work with several different definitions of fairness, and easily switch between them as well as using different definitions of fairness for different applications or markets on the same blockchain. This approach also makes it easier to analyse properties of a new fairness definition, as the analysis can focus on a small part of the overall protocol.

M. Bernhard et al. (Eds.): FC 2021 Workshops, LNCS 12676, pp. 191–196, 2021.
https://doi.org/10.1007/978-3-662-63958-0_17

- We integrated the possibility to combine the order fairness with commit and reveal, which means that commit and reveal schemes can rely on the order fairness to reveal at an earlier point in time.
- We have built an implementation of Wendy running on a simulated network and blockchain. This now allows us to provide first numbers on the performance overhead caused by Wendy, and can be used to test different fairness definitions.

The aim of Wendy is to integrate with many existing blockchains without significant change or non-standard assumption on the blockchain implementation. The main requirement is that there is some set of parties (resp. validators) known to each other through which fairness is defined. This comes naturally to most voting based protocols, while longest-chain based protocols with an undefined set of participants will need to use a mixed model approach to be compatible with our model, as done for example in finality gadgets [2].

2   The Framework Protocol

Wendy focuses on block order fairness, i.e., if a transaction t_1 is required to precede another transaction t_2, Wendy guarantees that t_1 is in the same or an earlier block than t_2. The exact order is then implemented by a post-protocol given the data Wendy provides with a transaction.

We allow for the underlying blockchain can be a multi-purpose chain, where not all transactions necessarily need to be fair to each other (or follow the same fairness rules with respect to each other). To this end, all transactions have one (or several labels). Each label has its own fairness definition, and transactions that do not share a label do not affect each other. Transactions can also be unlabeled, in which case they bypass Wendy altogether. We also allow a label to define conditions that can switch to another definition of fairness. This could be temporary – e.g., to break a loop or resolve a deadlock, or a more permanent, coordinated switch, e.g. to adapt to network load.

Clients can send transactions to a single validator, or to several (or all) of them. While Wendy does assure that all transactions gets seen by all validators, this can of course only be guaranteed if at least one honest party is aware of the transaction – a client who sends a transaction only to one validator that then turns out to be malicious can not expect any guarantees.

Finally, the framework combines causal order (commit and reveal) [3,6] with order fairness. For the scope of this paper, we assume that a causality mechanism - i.e., the ability of client to threshold-encrypt transactions, and of validators to generate and reveal appropriate decryption shares. Due to the fairness properties of Wendy, the shares can be revealed at an earlier state, namely, once a newly generated transaction cannot front-run the revealed one due to the fairness rules. This is especially useful for a non-finalizing blockchain, as Wendy can assure that order properties hold in every possible fork.

Pre-Protocol Wendy for protocol instance ID

All voting parties:

    let i be the counter of incoming transactions, starting at 0.

    on receiving a transaction or vote message **do**

        if the transaction in the message is (weakly) revealable, and marked for (weak) causality,

            multicast the decryption share of the request to all participants if that hasn't already happened

        if the message contains a transaction $\hat{t} \notin \mathcal{U} \cup \mathcal{D}$,

            if the transaction is labeled for no fairness, add it to $\mathcal{D}$ and $\mathcal{Q}$

            else send the message ("VOTE",ID,b,i, timestamp$(\hat{t})$,$H(\hat{t})$,$\hat{t}$) to all parties, where i is the sequence number of that request

            add $\hat{t}$ to $\mathcal{U}$

    on receiving a valid delivered block **B** from the underlying blockchain **do**

        put all elements from **B** into $\mathcal{D}$ and remove them from $\mathcal{U}$ and $\mathcal{Q}$

        postprocess **B**

All potential leaders:

    on receiving a vote message with a correct sequence number **or** changing $\mathcal{U}$ **do**

        for all transactions $t \in \mathcal{U}$, set $\mathcal{B}_t$ to $\{t\}$

        while for any $\mathcal{B}_t \neq \emptyset$ any transaction $t' \notin \mathcal{B}_t$ blocks a transaction $t'' \in \mathcal{B}_t$

            add t' to $\mathcal{B}_t$

        end while

        for all t for which no transaction in $\mathcal{B}_t$ is blocked,

            add $\mathcal{B}_t$ to the $\mathcal{Q}$, validated by all signed votes for requests in $\mathcal{B}_t$

            add all $t' \in \mathcal{B}_t$ to $\mathcal{D}$, and remove them from all sets $\mathcal{B}_x$ and $\mathcal{U}$

    if a *fairness-switch condition for label l* is satisfied

        Switch to the appropriate new definition for fairness

        Add the proof of the switch condition to the next block

        Recompute all $\mathcal{B}_x$

There are three core functions to the protocol that define both what is considered fair and impose most of the model. For the case of description, we assume here that validators postpone out of sequence votes, i.e., if a vote with sequence number s is accepted, all votes with sequence numbers smaller than s have been seen.

3   Fairness Functions

To illustrate the functions, we use the concept of block-order fairness, i.e., if all honest parties see tx_1 before tx_2, then tx_1 must be in the same or an earlier block than tx_2 (and, where decidable, scheduled before tx_2 in the post-processing).

isBlocked(tx)

The function isBlocked (tx) identifies if it is possible that a so-far-unknown transaction might be scheduled with priority to tx. If this is the case, tx cannot be consumed by the blockchain. A transaction usually is blocked due to missing votes from other validators concerning transactions may have priority over tx.

In the order-fairness definition, tx is blocked if it has received t or less votes; this implies that it is still possible that $n - t$ votes come in that report to have seen a transaction before tx that currently has not been seen.

depends(tx_1, tx_2)
This function determines if tx_2 might have priority over tx_1, i.e., if (assuming all still missing votes are worst case for tx_1, by the fairness rules tx_2 must come in an earlier or the same block as tx_1. We also say that tx_2 is blocked by tx_1.

In the order fairness model, tx_1 is **not** blocked by tx_2 if there are $t + 1$ votes reporting tx_1 before tx_2, i.e., at least one honest party saw tx_1 before tx_2.

isRevealable(tx_1)
A transaction is *revealable*, if, given the current information, it blocks all newly generated transactions. It is *weakly revealable*, if it is not blocked, and cannot be blocked by any newly generated transaction. For simplicity, we assume a $t + 1$ threshold here; if we have an $n - t$ threshold, a transaction may become revealable at an earlier stage, at the price of a slightly more complicated analysis.

In the block order fairness, a transaction is revealable if it has been voted on by all parties or finalized.

Efficient Computeability. We assume that, in the chosen model of the fairness function (i.e., taking into account byzantine failures and asynchrony), all information to compute the three fairness functions will be both measurable securely and available 'soon', or trigger a switch in fairness definitions. The precise definition of soon is not trivial [3] and out of scope for this paper.

Loop Freeness. Ideally, a fairness rule does not create loops, i.e., a scenario where both t_1 depends on t_2 and t_2 depends on t_1. However, the framework can handle loops relatively well by putting the entire loop into one block and letting the application sort out what to do with it.

Efficient Termination. Efficient termination requires transactions to be delivered 'soon'. This would be violated by the possibility of unlimited sized fairness loops [4,5], or because the fairness function requires input that it does not get through byzantine behavior or the network asynchrony. To mitigate this, Wendy allows to switch the fairness definition if a predefined condition arises - this could be measured by the number of blocked transaction, transaction waiting time, etc.

Monotony. Monotony essentially means that once a transaction is unblocked, it stays unblocked. A fairness function that lacks monotony is not reliably implementable, as a transaction can be finalized in a block based on available information, and afterwards a transaction is seen that would get precedence over it. Nevertheless, it can make sense to have a non-monotonous fairness function. For example, if the fairness function wants to prioritize by paid fees, it is always possible that a currently unseen transaction offers more fees than any transaction that a validator has seen so far. In this case, it does make sense for a validator to make a 'best-effort' attempt.

4   Other Example Fairness Definitions

4.1   Timed Order Fairness

All parties have local (not necessarily synchronized) clocks. If there is a time τ such that all honest parties see tx_1 before τ and tx_2 after τ, then tx_1 must be scheduled before tx_2.

A transaction tx is blocked, if less than t+1 valid votes are received. Now one honest party has reported all transactions it saw up to tx. Any unknown transaction will get a bigger timestamp from it and thus cannot have precedence.

Consider a time τ' such that at least one honest party saw tx before and one after τ'. Let's call that $tau(tx)$. A transaction tx_1 does not depend on tx_2, if $tau(tx_1) < tau(tx_2)$. If tx_2 had to be scheduled before tx_1 by above rule, then its tau value would have to be smaller.

A transaction tx is revealable, if n parties have reported tx as well as a transaction with a timestamp larger than the maximum of the timestamps on tx. Thus, the maximal timestamp on tx is the τ w.r.t to any new transaction.

A transaction tx is weakly revealable, if t+1 valid votes have arrived for tx This means tx is no longer blocked, and it is not possible anymore that any other vote gets precedence

4.2   Capitalist Fairness with Social Security

For each block, schedule the highest paying known transactions at the time the block is prepared. Transactions get a bonus for waiting, so no transaction needs to wait forever.

A transaction tx is blocked, if less than $t + 1$ valid votes are received.

Let $f(tx)$ be the fee paid for transaction tx and $w(tx)$ the number of blocks tx waited since being unblocked. A transaction tx_1 depends on tx_2, if t+1 valid votes have arrived for tx_1 and tx_2, and $f(tx_2) * 1.1^w(tx_2) > f(tx_1) * 1.1^w(tx_1)$

The blocking function is the minimum delay after which it is assured that an honest party received a transaction. The dependency function sorts all unblocked transactions by paid fee, while applying a multiplier for waiting transactions.

As the dependency function lacks the monotony property, a transaction tx can only be is (weakly) revealable once it is finalized.

5   Implementation Notes

The primary performance impact of Wendy is that some transaction are delayed through going through the protocol, and thus end up in a later block than they would otherwise. In our simulations, the main factor (relatively independent of the fairness definition) is the additional delay to gather the input from a set of validators to evaluate the fairness rules. The ratio of delayed transactions is roughly the ration of message transmission time to block-delivery time - thus, Wendy will have a measurable impact on very low latency blockchains, and be

almost unnoticeable on slower ones like Ethereum. An additional factor is the
increased communication ans computation; however, the impact of this highly
depends on how much validators are already on their limit, and thus can't be
quantified in a generic way.

References

1. Buchman, E., Kwon, J., Milosevic, Z.: The latest gossip on BFT consensus. CoRR
   http://arxiv.org/abs/1807.04938 (2018)
2. Buterin, V., Griffith, V.: Casper the friendly finality gadget. CoRR http://arxiv.
   org/abs/1710.09437 (2017)
3. Cachin, C., Kursawe, K., Petzold, F., Shoup, V.: Secure and efficient asynchronous
   broadcast protocols. In: Kilian, J. (ed.) CRYPTO 2001. LNCS, vol. 2139, pp. 524–
   541. Springer, Heidelberg (2001). https://doi.org/10.1007/3-540-44647-8_31
4. Kelkar, M., Zhang, F., Goldfeder, S., Juels, A.: Order-Fairness for Byzantine Consensus. In: Micciancio, D., Ristenpart, T. (eds.) CRYPTO 2020. LNCS, vol. 12172, pp.
   451–480. Springer, Cham (2020). https://doi.org/10.1007/978-3-030-56877-1_16.
   https://eprint.iacr.org/2020/269
5. Kursawe, K.: Wendy, the good little fairness widget: achieving order fairness for
   blockchains. In: AFT 2020: 2nd ACM Conference on Advances in Financial Technologies, 21–23 October, 2020, pp. 25–36. ACM (2020). https://doi.org/10.1145/
   3419614.3423263
6. Reiter, M.K., Birman, K.P.: How to securely replicate services. ACM Trans. Program. Lang. Syst. **16**(3), 986–1009 (1994) https://doi.org/10.1145/177492.177745

Measuring Illicit Activity in DeFi: The Case of Ethereum

Jiasun Li[1], Foteini Baldimtsi[1(✉)], Joao P. Brandao[1], Maurice Kugler[1],
Rafeh Hulays[2], Eric Showers[2], Zain Ali[1], and Joseph Chang[1]

[1] George Mason University, Fairfax, USA
foteini@gmu.edu
[2] Blockchain Intelligence Group, Vancouver, Canada

Abstract. We analyze the magnitude of illicit activities in the Ethereum
ecosystem. Using proprietary labeling data from the Blockchain Intelligence Group (BIG), we investigate the characteristics of a number
of *"malicious"* Ethereum addresses. We first calculate the total number of transactions involving these addresses and the total amount of
funds transferred through them, and then characterize smart contract
addresses for ERC-20 tokens or DeFi applications, that the malicious
addresses interact with. Finally, we apply machine learning techniques
to identify additional "malicious" addresses by conducting a network
clustering analysis within all Ethereum addresses from transactional relationships with the initial set of malicious addresses.

1 Introduction

Since the introduction of Bitcoin [1], the first cryptocurrency back in 2008, there
has been an explosive growth in the number of circulating cryptocurrencies. By
2020, more than 2000 different cryptocurrencies [2] have made up an estimated
market capitalization of more than $900 billion [3]. These cryptocurrencies form
one of the largest unregulated markets in the world, and there has been a widely-
held impression that cryptocurrencies serve as havens for criminals, used either
as a medium of exchange for illicit goods or as a means of hiding the source of
(i.e., laundering) dirty money. However, calculating the actual volume of illicit
activities in the cryptocurrency space remains a difficult research question.

A recent study focused on Bitcoin estimates that approximately one-quarter
of Bitcoin users are involved in illegal activity [4]. The authors find that Bitcoin
users who are involved in illegal activities differ from other users in several characteristics: illegal users tend to incur more frequent yet smaller transactions,
and tend to repeatedly transact with a small set of counterparties. Despite a
high number of transactions, illegal users tend to hold less bitcoin, consistent
with the risk they face in having their bitcoin holdings seized by authorities.
Users are more likely to be involved in illegal activities when there are many
darknet marketplaces in operation [5], few shadow coins in existence, and immediately following darknet marketplaces seizures or scams [6]. Finally, users are

M. Bernhard et al. (Eds.): FC 2021 Workshops, LNCS 12676, pp. 197–203, 2021.
https://doi.org/10.1007/978-3-662-63958-0_18

more likely to be involved in illegal activity if they use "mixing services" or "tumblers" [7] to conceal their identity.

Although [4] presents an interesting analysis on the state of illicit activities in Bitcoin, the rest of the cryptocurrencies space, especially the emerging DeFi universe that is built on smart contracts and their potential use for illegal activity [8], remains unexplored. In order to bridge this gap, we are looking at other cryptocurrencies and DeFi systems.

Our research thus focuses on the following question:

To what extent are illicit activities present among cryptocurrencies other than Bitcoin, as well as smart contract applications?

In this work, we start by investigating Ethereum (the second largest cryptocurrency which has a market capitalization of over USD 120 billion as of January 2021). Given the rich characteristics of Ethereum (which comes equipped with a smart contract functionality as opposed to Bitcoin), we wish to explore the illicit activity done on the system and also look at the special cases of smart contracts and ERC-20 tokens.

2   Ethereum Basics

Ethereum is a blockchain system that was proposed by Vitalik Buterin in 2013 [9] and became available in 2015. Similar to Bitcoin, Ethereum operates as a cryptocurrency but it's main philosophy goes beyond typical cryptocurrency transactions as it allows developers to build and store new applications (or else *smart contracts* on the blockchain.

Ethereum Blockchain Architecture. The Ethereum blockchain, similar to most blockchain systems, consists of *blocks* which are linked to each other via the use of cryptographic hash functions. *Miners* collect and validate user transactions and group them in blocks that are included in the blockchain and are paid for their effort via transaction *fees*. Participants decide on the current view of the blockchain (i.e. which are the included blocks/transactions and in which sequence) via a *consensus* mechanism. Currently, similar to Bitcoin, Ethereum employs a proof-of-work based consensus mechanism, which allows easy participation to the consensus mechanism while avoiding sybil attacks by using the computational power of participants to weight their power in the consensus voting process. Ethereum is projected to move to a different consensus mechanism, called proof-of-stake, in 2021.

Accounts and Transactions. Ethereum's transaction structure is *account based* (as opposed to Bitcoin's UTXO/transaction based model) which is very similar to a traditional banking system. The native cryptocurrency token is called *ether* (ETH). An Ethereum account is a 20-byte *address* which stores the state of ownership of ether tokens. As described in Ethereum's whitepaper [9], an account contains four fields: (1) a nonce (counter of how many transactions this account has created/sent), (2) the account's current ether balance, (3) the account's contract code, if present and (4) the account's storage (empty by default). In practice, there exist two types of Ethereum accounts: "regular" accounts (or else externally owned accounts) which are free to create, are used for transactions of ETH and they are controlled by the owner of the private key that corresponds to the account address; and, "contract" accounts controlled by code as we will explain in more details below.

A transaction between regular accounts includes: the address of the recipient, a digital signature from the sender (authorizing the transfer), the amount of ETH to be transferred and some auxiliary information such as fee information and optional data.

Smart Contracts. As explained above, smart contracts are a type of Ethereum accounts. One can simply think of smart contracts as a piece of software code that runs on the Ethereum blockchain. Every smart contract, consists of a piece of code (its functions) and data (its state) and also has a balance, i.e. can send transactions over the network. The main characteristic of smart contracts is that they're not controlled by a user, instead they are deployed to the network and run as programmed. Regular accounts can interact with a smart contract by submitting transactions that execute a function defined on the smart contract.

3   Our Methodology

To quantify illicit activities on Ethereum we identify a set of addresses/ transactions that have been marked as "malicious" using an initial set of labeled Ethereum addresses, graciously provided to us by the Blockchain Intelligence Group (BIG)[1], which we refer to as our original *malicious set* (MS). We then analyze how this set interacts with the rest of all Ethereum addresses via a network clustering analysis explained below.

Since the original data from BIG contains detailed labeling flags for all addresses, in order to determine MS, we need to ask *what types of labels characterize illicit activities?* In collaboration with BIG and based on previous work [4] we focus on a number of flags that involve scams, phishing attacks, and darknet transactions. Table 1 provides detailed descriptions of these labels.

We obtain a total of 3559 addresses marked as malicious under the flag descriptions given above. Of these 3559 addresses only 2628 appear in the Ethereum blockchain. The remaining ones are addresses that are known to be malicious, but do not have any funds transferred to them. For instance, an address might have been posted in a known scam, but no funds were ever transferred to it, so it will not actually appear on the blockchain.

Given the set of malicious addresses described above, we go through the entire Ethereum blockchain database between July 2015 and December 2020 to analyze illicit behaviors. Specifically, we looked at blocks in the Ethereum

---

[1] https://blockchaingroup.io/.

Table 1. Flag description

Label/flag	Description
scam	An activity that is associated with a fraudulent or deceptive act
phishing	A type of scam in which a user is tricked into revealing personal or confidential information which the scammer can use illicitly
github-darklist	GitHub is a platform that allows developers to host and version control their code using git
seen_on_paste_bin	The paste bin allows users to share information in plain text
exchange_client	An address controlled by the client of an exchange
seen_on_dark_web	The dark web is defined as "the portion of the Internet that is intentionally hidden from search engines, uses masked IP addresses, and is accessible only with a special web browser
hack_parity_perpetrator	Parity Wallet was breached which allowed hackers to steal cryptocurrencies
seen_on_dark_market	A transaction associated with or using mixing and tumbling services, suggesting an intent to obscure the flow of illicit funds between known wallet addresses and darknet marketplaces

blockchain between Tue May 26 16:23:22 2020 UTC. The first block on database was mined on Thu Jul 30 15:26:13 2015 UTC.

As of December 2020, the malicious set (MS) *currently* owns 326,443.71 Eth. Table 2 presents a number of summary statistics. The first row counts (a) how many transactions have been done by the malicious set (MS), (b) what was the total value of these transactions (in both Ether and USD - using the conversion rate of January 13th 2021), and (c) the total number of receiving addresses (i.e. with how many addresses has the malicious set interacted with). Since certain Ethereum transactions are "regular" ones, i.e. spending ether only, while others are token-transfers or more generally transactions to trigger smart contract state updates, the 2nd and 3rd rows look at "regular" transactions originating from the malicious set (MS) and token transfers, respectively. Rows 4–6 focus on transactions *within* the malicious set (i.e. both sending and receiving address are in MS) and rows 7–9 are the complementary set, i.e. transactions from MS to non MS addresses. Finally, rows 10–12 look at the number of ERC-20 transactions within the malicious set.

4   Robustness: Expanding the Malicious Set

Beyond analyzing MS, we further conduct a network clustering analysis to identify whether additional Ethereum addresses should be marked as malicious. Fol-

Table 2. Statistics of malicious addresses

Statistics detail	Transaction (tx)	Value (Eth)	Value (USD)	Addresses
Total out from MS	370,553	1,314,539.20	1,410,316,526.11	183,502
Total out from MS with Eth	341,635	1,314,539.20	1,410,316,526.11	182,046
Total out from MS as token transfers	28,918	0	0	1,513
Total out from MS to MS	1347	221,566.95	237,710,317.98	347
Total out from MS to MS with Eth	908	221,566.95	237,710,317.98	336
Total out from MS to MS as token transfers	439	0	0	16
Total out from MS to non-MS	369,206	1,092,972.25	1,172,606,208.14	183,155
Total out from MS to non-MS with Eth	340,727	1,092,972.25	1,172,606,208.14	181,710
Total out from MS to non-MS as token transfers	28,479	0	0	1497
Total out ERC-20 from MS	13,714	-	-	35,210
Total out ERC-20 from MS to MS	3,428	-	-	111
Total out ERC-20 from MS to non-MS	10,286	-	-	35,099

lowing [4] we further exploit the Ethereum transaction network to identify potentially malicious users. The underlying assumption works as follows: If a set S of users are known to be involved in illicit activity given the flags provided by BIG, a user X that trades exclusively or predominantly with users in S is likely to also be involved in illicit activity. Similarly, a user Y that trades predominantly with users that are not in S is likely to be a compliant user. This intuition drives the classification of users into compliant and illicit on the basis of their transaction partners.

More formally, the method we apply is a network cluster analysis algorithm that takes as inputs the set of users ("nodes" in network terminology) and the trades between users ("edges" or "links" in network terminology). The output of the algorithm is an assignment of users to groups such that the "modularity" of the groups (density of links within groups and sparsity of links between groups) is maximized. The method labels a user as illicit (compliant) if the disproportionate share of their transactions is with members of the illicit (compliant) group. The method does not assume that users only engage in either compliant or illicit activity—users can do both. Therefore, there will be some trades between the compliant and illicit groups.

We apply the same methodology as in [4]: a variant of the smart local moving (SLM) algorithm developed by [10], adapted to our specific application. The algorithm's name ("smart moving") comes from the fact that the algorithm finds the underlying group structure in the network by moving nodes from one group to another, if such a move improves the model fit. Applied to our data, the algorithm is as follows:

- Step 1: Assign all the flagged illicit users to the illicit group and all of the remaining users to the compliant group.
- Step 2: Loop through each user, performing the following operation on each:
  - If the user disproportionately transacts with members of the user's currently assigned group, then leave the user in that group;
  - Otherwise, move the user to the other group (if the user is assigned to the illicit group, move the user to compliant group, and vice versa).
- Step 3: Repeat Step 2 until, in a complete loop through all users, no user switches between groups. At that point the assignment to groups is stable and ensures that each member trades disproportionately with other members of the same group.

Due to the iterative nature of the algorithm, not all of the "flagged" illicit users will necessarily remain in the illicit group. For example, it is possible that some of the users that had been flagged by BIG but were mainly using ether for compliant purposes. This will be recognized by the algorithm in Step 2 and the user will be moved to the compliant group.

The resulting malicious set after the expansion algorithm is 23,638 addresses and converged after 2 iterations. An interesting finding is that although the malicious set grew by a lot, the total amount of ETH in outgoing transactions was only marginally increased to reach 1,316,153.44 ETH.

5   Conclusion

The goal of this paper is to spark some discussion on what quantifies as illicit activity on Ethereum and other DeFi systems and how can we possibly detect and analyze it. We present our original set of findings for the case of Ethereum and discuss our observations.

Acknowledgements. The GMU authors of this paper were supported by a US Department of Homeland Security award #205187 through the Criminal Investigations and Network Analysis Center (CINA).

References

1. Nakamoto, S.: Bitcoin: a peer-to-peer electronic cash system, vol. 2012, p. 28 (2008). https://bitcointalk.org/index.php?topic=321228.0
2. Coinmarket (2019). https://coinmarketcap.com/all/views/all/

3. Coincodex - crypto market overview (2019). https://coincodex.com/market-overview/
4. Foley, S., Karlsen, J.R., Putniņš, T.J.: Sex, drugs, and bitcoin: how much illegal activity is financed through cryptocurrencies? Rev. Financ. Stud. **32**(5), 1798–1853 (2019)
5. Christin, N.: Traveling the silk road: a measurement analysis of a large anonymous online marketplace. In: Proceedings of the 22nd International Conference on World Wide Web, WWW 2013, pp. 213–224 (2013)
6. Buskirk, J., Naicker, S., Roxburgh, A., Bruno, R., Burns, L.: Who sells what? Country specific differences in substance availability on the agora dark net marketplace. Int. J. Drug Policy **35**, 16–23 (2016)
7. Bestmixer (2019). https://bestmixer.io/en
8. Juels, A., Kosba, A., Shi, E.: The ring of Gyges: investigating the future of criminal smart contracts. In: Proceedings of the 2016 ACM SIGSAC Conference on Computer and Communications Security, pp. 283–295 (2016)
9. Buterin, V.: Ethereum whitepaper (2015)
10. Waltman, L., van Eck, N.J.: A smart local moving algorithm for large-scale modularity-based community detection. Eur. Phys. J. B **86**(11), 1–14 (2013). https://doi.org/10.1140/epjb/e2013-40829-0

DeFi – Order Routing and Formal Methods

Global Order Routing on Exchange Networks

Vincent Danos[1]([✉]), Hamza El Khalloufi[1], and Julien Prat[2]

[1] CNRS, DI ENS, PSL-ENS, INRIA, Paris, France
[2] CNRS, CREST, École Polytechnique, Barcelona, Spain

Abstract. We propose an abstract notion of networks of exchanges with an eye to modelling the global money market of DeFi (decentralised finance). We formalise routing and arbitrage on such networks as convex optimisation problems. We provide bounds with closed formulas in the specific case of Uniswap-like automated markets and a restricted form of cyclic arbitrage. We compute the associated lower bounds on actual data derived from the Ethereum blockchain.

1 Introduction

The global money market of DeFi (decentralised finance) allows traders to exchange assets represented by ERC20 tokens on the Ethereum blockchain. Each money market on a specific pair of tokens A/B can be seen as a 2-sided platform where liquidity providers transact with liquidity consumers. There are several implementations of such platforms. Some use the traditional form of the limit order book [1], but most use the so-called constant function automated market makers (e.g. Uniswap v2 [2]) which compute prices algorithmically as a function of their current reserves in A and B. The intense competition for liquidity and high clonability of the said platforms has given rise to a dense and complex network (a tiny subgraph of which is shown in Fig. 5). Prior academic work on such networks [3,4] focusses on local questions, with the exception of the recent Ref. [6] which looks at cyclic arbitrage (about which more later). Our contribution explores two global questions centred on liquidity consumers (also known as takers or traders).

The first question is *routing*: eg "Here I have a 100 ETH, how should I best convert them to DAIs". Unsurprisingly, direct routes may not always be best, and convex combination of routes may dominate any particular path. Figure 1 gives an actual example of routing a 100 ETH in order to maximise the amount of DAIs obtained. One sees that the order is split among 7 distinct money markets.

The second question is *arbitrage* (aka price consistency): eg in a given state of the network "Is there any way I can chain operations leading to certain non-zero profit". We define in this paper a class of convex optimisation problems which encompasses both the global routing problem and the arbitrage problem. We show that problems in this class always have solutions. We also show that optimal arbitrage eliminates price inconsistencies. One can construe this result

© International Financial Cryptography Association 2021
M. Bernhard et al. (Eds.): FC 2021 Workshops, LNCS 12676, pp. 207–226, 2021.
https://doi.org/10.1007/978-3-662-63958-0_19

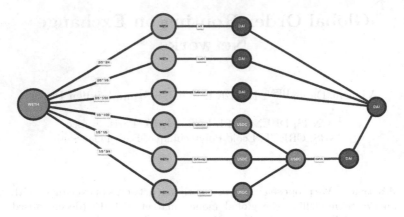

Fig. 1. A transfer plan using 7 distinct money markets (blue edges). Notice that a third of the original 100 ETH travels through an indirect path. (Color figure online)

as saying that the global network 'learns' a consistent set of prices under optimal arbitrage.

For both questions we introduce tractable sub-problems. Specifically, we demonstrate that arbitraging along cycles, while sub-optimal in general can be efficiently tested and solved. This leads to computationally cheap lower bounds on profit. For Uniswap price functions, we derive a closed formula to compute the maximal extractible profit on any given cycle. Putting the two results together (cyclic arbitrage detection and explicit max profit), we look at actual Ethereum data and efficiently find lower bounds for several arbitrage opportunities. For routing we introduce the convex subproblem where one restricts to convex combinations of a given set of independent paths. It is possible to derive a simple algorithm for optimal convex combinations of Uniswap price functions, which is of independent interest and that we will publish elsewhere.

2   Prices, Plans, Profits

Many price functions have been considered to define prices in algorithmic exchanges. We will use the specific Uniswap function (defined right below) to obtain closed form solutions for cyclic arbitrage. Up to that point all our development is generic and relies only on the following abstract definition.

Definition 1. *A price function is a map $f : \mathbb{R}_+ \to \mathbb{R}_+$ such that $f(0) = 0$, f is monotonically increasing, strictly concave, bounded, and continuous.*

We also sometimes suppose our price functions are differentiable. It will be clear when we do.

The requirements encapsulated in Definition 1 are natural for prices: $f(0) = 0$ means one gets nothing for nothing, increasing means one gets more for more, concave means returns decrease, and boundedness expresses the fact that liquidity reserves are finite.

Notice that a (half) order-book on an A/B pair -ie a price-sorted list of discrete offers (p_i, V_i) where V_i is an amount of Bs and p_i the unit price to pay in A to take that offer- also defines a price function. It just happens to be piecewise affine (hence is not everywhere differentiable). Boundedness holds whether liquidity is provided via an order book or a constant function market-maker.

A simple example of price function is the Uniswap one. For an A/B pair it reads:

$$f(x) := [B](\gamma x)/(\gamma x + [A]) \tag{1}$$

where $[A]$, $[B] > 0$ are the local reserves (or pools) in tokens A and B. The γ parameter is such that $0 \leq 1 - \gamma < 1$, and $1 - \gamma$ represents the fee extracted by the liquidity providers for every transaction. It is easy to see that $0 \leq f(x) < [B]$. Hence a Uniswap pair never pays out more than the reserve however small.[1] This function satisfies all the requirements of a price function as defined above. The dual price function which specifies how many As one gets for a given amount of Bs is obtained simply by exchanging the roles of $[A]$, $[B]$ (not to be confused with f^{-1} which specifies how many As one needs to spend to obtain a given amount of Bs).

The reserves $[A]$, $[B]$ are modified by every transaction and therefore induce a modification of the price function -also known as the price impact of the transaction.[2]

The class of price functions is closed under: sum, composition, pre- and post-composition by positive scalar multiplication.

Definition 2. *An* exchange network *consists of:*

- *an undirected multi-graph $G = (V, E)$, without loops*
- *a fixed chosen orientation for each edge e in E*
- *a family of price functions $(f_e; e \in E)$*

We write $s(e), t(e) \in V$ for the source and target of an edge e. Hence both s and t have type $E \to V$; and for $A \in V$, $s^{-1}(A)$ is the set of edges emanating from A, while $t^{-1}(A)$ is the set of edges pointing to A.

Given $\phi = e_1, \ldots, e_n$ a simple path in G, set:

$$f_\phi = f_{e_n} \circ \cdots \circ f_{e_1}$$

f_ϕ is a price function (by composition). The path has to be simple, else the first visit to an edge may change the reserves, and the second one will find an

---

[1] Actually one could redefine f as $f(x) = f(\infty)(xf'(0))/(xf'(0)+f(\infty))$ as $f(\infty) = [B]$ the total reserve in $[B]$, and $f'(0) = \gamma[B]/[A]$ the marginal price of A in B.

[2] One could call the Uniswap price function a 'price state machine' as it defines a price function for every state of its internal reserves.

updated price function. In this paper, we only rarely consider specific update mechanisms, and almost always work with a given fixed state of the network of abstract price functions.

An example of such a structure is a snapshot of the Uniswap network. Nodes are ERC20s, edges are pairs with a chosen orientation. The level of reserves in each pair determines the price function f_e. In reality, the graph part also changes slowly as new nodes and pairs are added.

We now define our main object of interest:

Definition 3. *A transfer plan τ is an element of the standard cone $E \to \mathbb{R}_+$ (hence convex). The support of τ is the subset of E where τ is non-zero.*

For each e, $\tau(e) \geq 0$ specifies the amount of $s(e)$ injected in the price function f_e.

There are implicit restrictions in Definition 3 which are worth discussing. We do not consider sliced orders, i.e. repeated swaps on the same directed edge. It is known for constant function aMMs that slicing leads to sub-optimal plans [3]. Also, we do not consider backtracking, i.e. transfer plans where an underlying edge is used twice with opposite orientations. This is because each edge is directed.[3] Finally, we do not incorporate in our notion of transfer plan the very real possibility which DeFi agents have, namely to modify the reserves (eg by depositing or withdrawing liquidity in the various pools of aMMs) and therefore the price functions while trading. It seems unlikely that backtracking or liquidity modifications could improve transfer plans relative to the objectives given below, but it remains to be seen.

A plan τ translates directly in a concrete Ethereum transaction. Because of the existence of flash loans, at least for most liquid tokens, the order in which each elementary swaps are performed is irrelevant. We neglect in this model gas costs and flash loan fees.

Given (G, f) we can now define the profit map Ψ which maps a transfer plan (an E-vector), to its resulting balance (a V-vector):

Definition 4. *The profit map $\Psi : \mathbb{R}_+^E \to \mathbb{R}^V$ derives from the data as follows:*

$$\Psi(\tau)(A) := \Psi_+(\tau)(A) - \Psi_-(\tau)(A)$$
$$\Psi_+(\tau)(A) := \sum_{e \in t^{-1}(A)} f_e(\tau(e))$$
$$\Psi_-(\tau)(A) := \sum_{e' \in s^{-1}(A)} \tau(e')$$

The first component $\Psi_+(\tau)(A)$ is the amount of A returned by τ, while the second $\Psi_-(\tau)(A)$ is the amount of A invested by τ. The difference $\Psi(\tau)(A)$ is the balance change of A as a result of executing τ -ie the profit (which can be negative!).

---

[3] To express backtracking plans and allow sequences of swaps on e with alternating orientations, one could use the larger cone of finite sequences $E \to \sum_n \mathbb{R}_+^n$.

We see that:

- $\Psi_+(\_)(A)$ is concave, non-decreasing, bounded, differentiable (if edges are); it is only increasing and strictly concave in those components τ_e such that $t(e) = A$.
- $\Psi_-(\_)(A)$ is a linear function $\mathbb{R}_+^E \to \mathbb{R}_+$;
- $\Psi(\_)(A)$ is a concave function bounded above by $\sum_{e \in t^{-1}(A)} f_e(\infty)$ (sum of A's liquidities available in the network) and $\Psi(0_E) = 0_V$.

Say a node A is:

- a *source* in τ if $\Psi_+(\tau)(A) = 0$, $\Psi_-(\tau)(A) > 0$,
- a *sink* if $\Psi_+(\tau)(A) > 0$, $\Psi_-(\tau)(A) = 0$,
- an *intermediate* if $\Psi_+(\tau)(A) = \Psi_-(\tau)(A) > 0$.

For differentiable price functions we can compute Ψ's Jacobian:

$$\Psi(\tau + h)(A) - \Psi(\tau)(A) = \sum_{e \in t^{-1}(A)} (h_e f_e'(\tau(e)) + o(h_e)) - \sum_{e' \in s^{-1}(A)} h_{e'}$$

So the Jacobian matrix of Ψ of dimension $V \times E$ is:

$$J\Psi(\tau)(A, e) = \begin{cases} f_e'(\tau(e)) & \text{if } e \in t^{-1}(A) \\ -1 & \text{if } e \in s^{-1}(A) \\ 0 & \text{else} \end{cases}$$

(Note that as G is loopless, no e is both in $s^{-1}(A)$ and $t^{-1}(A)$.)

As said, a transfer plan also has a side effect (here a monoid action) on the price functions which we denote by $f_e \mapsto^\tau \tau(e) \cdot f_e$; that is to say if f_e is the price function of edge e, and the amount $\tau(e)$ is injected in e, we write $\tau(e) \cdot f_e$ for the new price function. We also write more generally $\tau \cdot \Psi$ for the new profit function induced by the execution of plan τ. We leave this action implicit and just ask that it verifies the *no-slicing* property:

$$\Psi(\tau_1 + \tau_2) \geq \Psi(\tau_1) + \tau_1 \cdot \Psi(\tau_2)$$

This inequality expresses the fact that no profit can be made by simply slicing a plan in two parts. It is easy to see that Uniswap price functions satisfy no-slicing, and, therefore, so do profit functions derived from Uniswap price functions.

We can represent some of the plans defined above in a more diagrammatic way. Figure 1 (retrieved from the 1inch price aggregator web site) gave an example with a unique source ETH and unique sink DAI and one intermediate node USDC (with zero balance). The plan τ invests at ETH and collects the returns at DAI: $\Psi_-(\tau)(\text{ETH}) = x$, $\Psi_+(\tau)(\text{ETH}) = 0$; $\Psi_-(\tau)(\text{DAI}) = 0$, $\Psi_+(\tau)(\text{DAI}) = y$; y can be computed as the composite function of x indicated by the diagram.

Diagrams are convenient ways to represent those plans that have only sources, sinks, and intermediates. Every diagram gives rise to a plan. Not every plan is a diagram, but with respect to some of the objectives functions presented in the next section, optimal ones will be.

3   Orders, Routes, Arbitrage

We define now a number of convex problems for transfer plans in standard form [5, §4.2.1]. In each case we ask whether the problem is feasible and has a bounded objective function. At the end of the section, we prove the existence of solutions for these problems (provided they are feasible). As profit functions are not strictly concave in all coordinates, the solutions may not be unique in general.

3.1   Smart Order Routing

Recall the routing question in the introduction: "what is the maximum amount of DAI I can get for 100ETH using all aMMs and dexes available?"

This question can be recast as the *forward routing problem* with $A \neq B$, $a \in \mathbb{R}_+$:

$$sor(a : A, B) = \begin{array}{l} \max \ \Psi(\tau)(B) \\ \text{with } \Psi(\tau)(A) \geq -a \\ \Psi(\tau)(C) \geq 0, \ C \neq A, B \end{array} \tag{2}$$

For a plan to satisfy the constraints (aka be feasible), it should not cost more than $a : A$ (but could invest more), and have non-negative balance for Cs which are neither A nor B. The zero plan 0_E satisfies the constraints, so the problem is feasible.

An optimal τ will have $\Psi(\tau)(A) = -a$, iff A and B are connected in G. One says the constraint is active in this case. Indeed, pick any path ϕ from A to B in G, if there is some unspent A in τ, i.e. $\Psi(\tau)(A) > -a$ one can push the remainder $a' > 0$ through ϕ to obtain $f_\phi(a') > 0$ additional Bs. Conversely, if there is no possible way to use some A to get some B, the amount of A spent is indifferent. Likewise, the C constraints will be active for optimum τ if connected to B.

We also see that for the routing problem to be sensible, there must be a compatibility with the orientation of G in the sense that directed paths must exist between inputs and outputs of the problem. Else the problem is degenerate.

As the user may have several types of tokens on hand, it makes senses to generalise the above allowing for multiple inputs (but still one output):

$$sor(a_1 : A_1, \ldots, a_n : A_n, B) = \begin{array}{l} \max \ \Psi(\tau)(B) \\ \text{with } \Psi(\tau)(A_i) \geq -a_i \\ \Psi(\tau)(C) \geq 0, \ C \neq A_i, B \end{array} \tag{3}$$

What about the inverse question "what is the minimum amount of ETH I need to spend to get 100DAI?". This question can also recast as the *backward routing problem* with $A \neq B$, with $b \in \mathbb{R}_+$:

$$sor(A, b : B) = \begin{array}{l} \max \ \Psi(\tau)(A) \\ \text{with } \Psi(\tau)(B) \geq b \\ \Psi(\tau)(C) \geq 0, \ C \neq A, B \end{array} \tag{4}$$

A feasible plan is one that pays $\geq b$ tokens of type B and has positive balance on all Cs. Differently from the forward problem, the backward feasibility set may be empty. Suppose the only edge in G joins A to B and $b > f_e(\infty)$. No matter how much money one injects on the A side, it will never obtain b. If the feasibility set is not empty, an optimum plan will strive to minimise the expense in A. Note that $\Psi(\tau)(A)$ will be negative at optimum, unless there is an arbitrage opportunity (which user could take, see below).

So far the objectives only concern one output. To generalise to multi-output plans, we can set a reference price $p \in \mathbb{R}_+^V$ and use it to scalarise the problem [5, §4.7.4].

For $a \in \mathbb{R}_+$, $\psi_0 \leq 0_V$, we define:

$$sor(p, a : A) = \begin{array}{c} \max \; \langle p, \Psi(\tau) \rangle \\ \text{with } \Psi_-(\tau)(A) \leq a \\ \Psi(\tau) \geq \psi_0 \end{array} \tag{5}$$

Here a feasible plan must invest no more than $a : A$, and respect an overall budget limit ψ_0. Hence there is always the zero plan.

3.2 Arbitrage

On to the price consistency problem:

$$arb(A) = \begin{array}{c} \max \; \Psi(\tau)(A) \\ \text{with } \Psi(\tau) \geq 0 \end{array} \tag{6}$$

A feasible plan is any that results in a non-negative balance for all tokens. It is feasible as 0_E satisfies constraints. The optimal value will therefore also be non-negative. Of course the interesting question is qualitatively whether there is a non-zero solution, and quantitatively how to compute it. As above one can prove that any solution will activate the constraints $\Psi(\tau)(B) = 0$ for $B \neq A$.

As in the routing problem, one can scalarise the multi-output version of this problem by maximising $\langle p, \Psi(\tau) \rangle$ under the free-lunch constraint $\Psi(\tau) \geq 0_V$.

Assuming that Ψ satisfies no-slicing:

Proposition 1. *The arbitrage problem (6) is idempotent.*

Proof: Let $\tau_1^\star$, $\tau_2^\star$ be two successive optimal plans. We compute:

$$\Psi(\tau_1^\star + \tau_2^\star) \geq_{nsl} \Psi(\tau_1^\star) + \tau_1^\star \cdot \Psi(\tau_2^\star) \geq 0$$

where recall $\tau \cdot \Psi$ is the profit function after the execution of τ. The sum $\tau_1^\star + \tau_2^\star$ represents the fused plan. The first inequality is the no slicing condition defined earlier (joining orders on the same edge is always better). By definition, both terms on the rhs of this inequality are positive, and, therefore, so is the lhs. In other words $\tau_1^\star + \tau_2^\star$ is feasible. It also follows that $\Psi(\tau_1^\star + \tau_2^\star) \geq \Psi(\tau_1^\star)$, and, therefore, by optimality of $\tau_1^\star$, it must be that $\tau_2^\star = 0$. $\qquad\square$

In the differentiable case it is enough to look near the zero plan to detect non-zero arbitrage.

Proposition 2. *There is a non-zero solution to the arbitrage problem iff there exists $\epsilon \geq 0_E$, such that $J\Psi(0)(\epsilon) \geq 0$ with at least one coordinate $J\Psi(0)(\epsilon)(A) > 0$.*

Proof: The if part is clear. The only if part follows from the fact that Ψ is concave. To see this pick a τ (not necessarily optimal) such that $\Psi(\tau)(A) > 0$, and choose $t \in (0, 1)$:

$$\Psi(t\tau) = \Psi((1-t)0_E + t\tau) \geq (1-t)\Psi(0_E) + t\Psi(\tau) = t\Psi(\tau)$$

where we use the fact that Ψ is concave (in each argument) and $\Psi(0_E) = 0_V$.

By definition of the Jacobian:

$$\Psi(t\tau) = J\Psi(0)(t\tau) + o(\|t\|_1)$$

It follows that for $t > 0$ small enough, $J\Psi(0)(\epsilon)(A) > 0$, with $\epsilon = t\tau$.   □

The criterion implies that at least one $\epsilon_e > 0$. Keep in mind that the arbitrage may be very small (see lower bound examples later). The criterion says nothing about its magnitude; it merely gives a direction ϵ in the cone of plans in which to look for one.

Using the expression obtained earlier for $J(\Psi)$, we can rephrase the criterion as follows:

Corollary 1. *Problem (6) has a non-zero solution iff there is $\epsilon \in \mathbb{R}_+^E$ such that for all $A \in V$:*

$$\sum_{e \in t^{-1}(A)} f'_e(0)\epsilon_e \geq \sum_{e' \in s^{-1}(A)} \epsilon_{e'}$$

and for at least one A the inequality is strict.

For concrete price functions such as Uniswap's with derivatives at zero which are 0-homogenous in the reserves, a rescaling of these reserves by a positive coefficient leaves the criterion invariant.

3.3   Existence

Except for problem (5), problems considered so far have the following form:

$$\begin{aligned} \max\ & h(\Psi(\tau)) \\ \text{with}\ & \Psi(\tau) \geq \psi_0 \end{aligned} \tag{7}$$

with $h : \mathbb{R}^V \to \mathbb{R}$ a continuous function, $\psi_0 \leq 0_V$.

Proposition 3. *The feasible set $C = \{\tau \mid \Psi(\tau) \geq \psi_0\}$ of problem (7) is compact and non-empty in $\mathbb{R}_+^E$; therefore problem (7) has solutions.*

Proof:

First C is non-empty as 0_E is in C.

Second $C = \cap_A \Psi(\tau)(A)^{-1}[\psi_0(A), \infty)$ is closed in $\mathbb{R}_+^E$, as $\Psi(\tau)(A)$ is continuous.

Suppose C is not bounded. Pick a sequence $\tau_n \in C$ such that $\|\tau_n\|_\infty \geq n$, and $e_n \in E$ such that $\|\tau_n\|_\infty = \tau_n(e_n)$. As E is finite, there must a subsequence of e_n which is constant and equal to some e_0 with source A. Let τ'_m be the associated subsequence of plans. By construction $\tau'_m(e_0) \to \infty$.

For general reasons, we have:

$$\Psi(\tau)(A) \leq \sum_E f_e(\infty) - \tau(e_0)$$

hence $\Psi(\tau'_m)(A) \to -\infty$ which contradicts the budget constraint $\Psi(\tau)(A) \geq \psi_0(A)$.

As $h \circ \Psi$ is continuous, the second point follows. $\square$

4   Lower Bounds

The problems considered in the preceding section may have solutions, but the proof hardly tells us how to find them. In this section, we add new feasibility constraints and derive simpler and tractable subproblems which will give lower bounds to the original ones.

In the appendix we further specialise to Uniswap's price functions and obtain closed formulas.

4.1   Routing on Independent Paths

Let us return to the forward routing problem with source A and target B. Fix $(\phi_i;\ 0 \leq i < n)$ a family of independent paths in G from A to B with underlying edge and node sets $E' \subseteq E$, $V' \subseteq V$, and strictly concave price functions.

We restrict the forward A/B routing problem (2) by restricting plans to have their support included in E'. This subproblem is again convex, evidently. All nodes $C \in V'\backslash\{A, B\}$ have non-negative balance by definition, but we have noticed already that optimal solutions of the original problem satisfy $\Psi(\tau^\star)(C) = 0$ (Cs are intermediates). This leads us to an alternative and equivalent formulation of the subproblem:

$$sor(a : A, \phi_1, \ldots, \phi_n) := \frac{\max \sum_i f_{\phi_i}(t_i a)}{\text{with } (t_i) \in \Delta_n} \tag{8}$$

with Δ_n the simplex of dimension $n-1$, where n is the number of support paths. The quantity t_i represents the fraction of the original budget a allocated to path ϕ_i.

Write $\hat{\Psi}_a(t) := \sum_i \phi_i(t_i a)$ for the new objective function.

For any convex combination $u + v = 1$, $u, v > 0$:

$$\hat{\Psi}_a(u(t_1, \ldots, t_n) + v(s_1, \ldots, s_n)) = \sum_i f_{\phi_i}((ut_i + vs_i)a)$$
$$= \sum_i f_{\phi_i}(ut_i a + vs_i a)$$
$$\geq \sum_i uf_{\phi_i}(t_i a) + \sum_i vf_{\phi_i}(s_i a)$$
$$= u \sum_i f_{\phi_i}(t_i a) + v \sum_i f_{\phi_i}(s_i a)$$
$$= u\hat{\Psi}_a(t_1, \ldots, t_n) + v\hat{\Psi}_a(s_1, \ldots, s_n)$$

hence $\hat{\Psi}_a$ is strictly concave, as the ϕ_is are.

We have proved that for any choice of a family of paths:

Proposition 4. *The restricted forward routing problem (8) has a unique solution t^*; moreover, its optimum is a lower bound to that of the unrestricted forward routing problem (2).*

Not every plan can be expressed as a sum of independent paths. There seems to be a natural intermediate and possibly tractable subproblem, where one maximises over diagrams. This is a larger subproblem as is evident from the example Fig. 1 which is not a sum of independent paths (because of the last USDC/DAI leg). Extending this proposition to diagrams would improve the lower bound. However, it is unclear how to do this as diagrams (say with one source, and one sink) do not form a convex subset of the plans.

4.2   Arbitraging Simple Cycles

Let us return to the arbitrage problem (6) with source A. Similarly to the routing problem, we restrict the arbitrage one. Specifically, we ask for plans which are supported by a given simple cycle going through A. The restricted problem is still convex as are all subproblems based on restriction on the support. Also, it is clear that the original problem has solutions that are not supported by a cycle, so this approach will only provide lower bounds, in general.

Let ϕ be a directed cycle in G. One needs only to direct edges in the cycle all in one direction or the other. As constraints will be active for solutions of the subproblem, we have an alternative and equivalent formulation:

$$arb(a : A, \phi) := \frac{\max f_\phi(a) - a}{\text{with } a \in \mathbb{R}_+} \tag{9}$$

Note that $f_\phi(a) - a$ is the profit function associated to the unique plan τ with $\tau(e) = a$ for the only edge e in ϕ with source A, which induces a zero profit at every other node of the cycle.

The only optimisation variable is now a. As f_ϕ is a strictly concave price function:

Proposition 5. *The cyclic arb subproblem has a unique solution (possibly trivial).*

The arbitrage criterion simplifies to:

Proposition 6. *The cyclic arbitrage problem (9) has a non-zero solution iff:*

$$f'_\phi(0) = \prod_{e \in \phi} f'_e(0) > 1$$

Using the argument of the proof of Proposition 2, one can show that the set of a such that $f_\phi(a) \geq a$ is a compact interval of the form $[0, a_0]$. The solution is somewhere in between and is non-trivial iff $0 < a_0$.

5   Cyclic Arbitrage: The Uniswap Case

Consider again the Uniswap graph, where nodes are ERC20 tokens, edges are pairs of reserve pools with fees $0 \leq 1-\gamma \ll 1$ (possibly different in each direction). As above the reserves of an A/B edge are written $[A]$, $[B]$ and we define the ratio $\rho_{AB} = [B]/[A]$ -so that the marginal price of A in B is $\gamma_{AB}\rho_{AB}$.

5.1   Closed Formulas for Arbitrage

To simplify notations we consider triangular cycles on tokens A, B and C.
We have a profitable triangular arbitrage if:

$$a_0 \xrightarrow{Swap} b \xrightarrow{Swap} c \xrightarrow{Swap} a_1, \text{ with } a_0 < a_1$$

We can specialise the arbitrage criterion of the main text as follows:

Lemma 1. *(cyclic arbitrage): A triangular cycle is arbitrage-free iff:*

$$\gamma_{AB}\gamma_{BC}\gamma_{CA} \leq \rho_{AB}\rho_{BC}\rho_{CA} \leq (\gamma_{AB}\gamma_{BC}\gamma_{CA})^{-1} \tag{10}$$

Although we have already proven this result, it is instructive to redo the proof in this special case, as composition of Uniswap price functions can be computed explicitely. Specifically, we have:

$$a_1 = \frac{\rho_{CA}}{\frac{\rho_{CB}\rho_{BA}}{\gamma_{CA}\gamma_{BC}\gamma_{AB}}\frac{1}{a_0} + \frac{\rho_{CB}\rho_{BA}}{\gamma_{CA}\gamma_{BC}[A]_{AB}} + \frac{\rho_{CB}}{\gamma_{CA}[B]_{BC}} + \frac{1}{[C]_{CA}}}$$

To have a non-zero arbitrage we need to have $a_0 < a_1$:

$$a_1 = \frac{\rho_{CA}}{\frac{\rho_{CB}\rho_{BA}}{\gamma_{CA}\gamma_{BC}\gamma_{AB}}\frac{1}{a_0} + \frac{\rho_{CB}\rho_{BA}}{\gamma_{CA}\gamma_{BC}[A]_{AB}} + \frac{\rho_{CB}}{\gamma_{CA}[B]_{BC}} + \frac{1}{[C]_{CA}}} > a_0$$

Equivalently:

$$0 < a_0 < \frac{\gamma_{AB}\gamma_{BC}\gamma_{CA}\rho_{AB}\rho_{BC}\rho_{CA} - 1}{\frac{\gamma_{AB}}{[A]_{AB}} + \frac{\gamma_{BC}\gamma_{AB}\rho_{AB}}{[B]_{BC}} + \frac{\gamma_{CA}\gamma_{BC}\gamma_{AB}\rho_{AB}\rho_{BC}}{[C]_{CA}}}$$

which can always be achieved by choosing a_0 small enough, provided $\gamma_{AB}\gamma_{BC}\gamma_{CA}\rho_{AB}\rho_{BC}\rho_{CA} > 1$, and the conclusion follows.   □

One sees that arbitrage can only exist in one orientation of the cycle.

In case of no fees, ($\gamma_{AB} = \gamma_{BC} = \gamma_{CA} = 1$), in order for the triangular cycle to be arbitrage-free, we need to have $\rho_{AB}\rho_{BC}\rho_{CA} = 1$, meaning that the product of marginal prices should be equal to 1. In the presence of fees the no-arbitrage zone is 'thicker' so to speak.

The explicit calculation shows that the arbitrage condition itself is homogeneous (invariant under a rescaling of the reserves). Next, we compute the max extractable profit and will se that the actual reserve sizes do matter (Fig. 2).

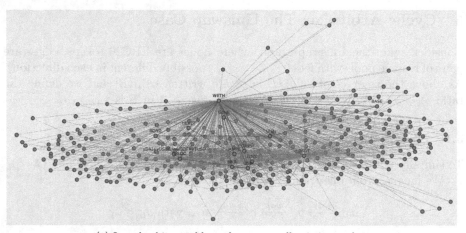

(a) In red arbitrageable cycles among all existing cycles.

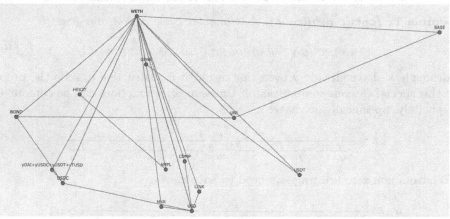

(b) Isolated arbitrageable cycles.

Fig. 2. Example of arbitrageable cycles in Uniswap. (Color figure online)

Proposition 7. *In case of the existence of a triangular arbitrage, we obtain the following:*

- *The **optimal input** a_0^* that maximises the arbitrage profit is:*

$$\max_{a_0}(a_1 - a_0) = \max_{a_0}(\frac{\gamma_{CA}\gamma_{BC}\gamma_{AB}\rho_{AB}\rho_{BC}\rho_{CA}a_0}{(\frac{\gamma_{AB}}{[A]_{AB}} + \frac{\gamma_{BC}\gamma_{AB}\rho_{AB}}{[B]_{BC}} + \frac{\gamma_{CA}\gamma_{BC}\gamma_{AB}\rho_{AB}\rho_{BC}}{[C]_{CA}})a_0 + 1} - a_0)$$

$$a_0^* = \frac{\sqrt{\gamma_{CA}\gamma_{BC}\gamma_{AB}\rho_{AB}\rho_{BC}\rho_{CA}} - 1}{\frac{\gamma_{AB}}{[A]_{AB}} + \frac{\gamma_{BC}\gamma_{AB}\rho_{AB}}{[B]_{BC}} + \frac{\gamma_{CA}\gamma_{BC}\gamma_{AB}\rho_{AB}\rho_{BC}}{[C]_{CA}}} \qquad (11)$$

- *The **optimal output** a_1^* that maximises the arbitrage profit obtained from this arbitrage operation is:*

$$a_1^* = \frac{\gamma_{CA}\gamma_{BC}\gamma_{AB}\rho_{AB}\rho_{BC}\rho_{CA} - \sqrt{\gamma_{CA}\gamma_{BC}\gamma_{AB}\rho_{AB}\rho_{BC}\rho_{CA}}}{\frac{\gamma_{AB}}{[A]_{AB}} + \frac{\gamma_{BC}\gamma_{AB}\rho_{AB}}{[B]_{BC}} + \frac{\gamma_{CA}\gamma_{BC}\gamma_{AB}\rho_{AB}\rho_{BC}}{[C]_{CA}}} \qquad (12)$$

- *The **maximum profit** obtained from this arbitrage operation is:*

$$Profit^* = a_1^* - a_0^* = \frac{(\sqrt{\gamma_{CA}\gamma_{BC}\gamma_{AB}\rho_{AB}\rho_{BC}\rho_{CA}} - 1)^2}{\frac{\gamma_{AB}}{[A]_{AB}} + \frac{\gamma_{BC}\gamma_{AB}\rho_{AB}}{[B]_{BC}} + \frac{\gamma_{CA}\gamma_{BC}\gamma_{AB}\rho_{AB}\rho_{BC}}{[C]_{CA}}} \qquad (13)$$

The above results can be obtained by straightforward computations. There are few things worth observing. If one rescales each reserves by a coefficient $\lambda \geq 0$, the arbitrage profit is also multiplied by the same coefficient. In other words the max arbitrage profit is homogeneous of degree 1 in the size of the reserves.

Closed formulas for max profit for Uniswap price functions give explicit lower bounds on optimal values for the corresponding original problems. One would also think that lifting solutions of the subproblems may give good initialisers to the original ones.

If there is an arbitrage, the arbitrageur can choose to start from any origin of the cycle. One may wonder whether the relative variation of the arbitrageur's portfolio depends on this choice.

Proposition 8. *If the external prices of the tokens present in the cycle do not change before and after the execution, then the maximum profit is independent from the origin.*

Proof: We position ourselves from an arbitrageur perspective. We suppose as above that the cycle is a triangle to simplify the notations. We also suppose that the arbitrageur possesses in her/his portfolio a sufficient quantities of tokens A, B and C, greater than a_0^*, b_0^* and c_0^* respectively. Initially, we also assume the existence of an external liquid market where the arbitrageur can exchange its tokens against a reference token R (it can be euros or a stable coin for example).

We suppose the existence of arbitrage, let X be one of A, B, C, x_0^* the optimal input quantity that maximises the arbitrage profit and p_R^X the price of X in R.

We can express the value in R of the portfolio part containing X before and after the arbitrage execution (V_{0R}^X and V_{1R}^X respectively), as follows:

$$V_{R_0}^X = x_0^* p_{R_0}^X \text{ and } V_{R_1}^X = x_1^* p_{R_1}^X$$

The percentage variation in the value of the portfolio part containing X is given by:

$$\Delta = \frac{V_{1R}^X - V_{0R}^X}{V_{0R}^X} = \frac{x_1^*}{x_0^*}\pi_{p_R^X} - 1$$

where $\pi_{p_R^X} := p_{R_1}^X / p_{R_0}^X$ measures the change of price of X before and after the arbitrage.

From the preceding proposition we have:

$$\frac{x_1^*}{x_0^*} = \frac{\gamma_{CA}\gamma_{BC}\gamma_{AB}\rho_{AB}\rho_{BC}\rho_{CA} - \sqrt{\gamma_{CA}\gamma_{BC}\gamma_{AB}\rho_{AB}\rho_{BC}\rho_{CA}}}{\sqrt{\gamma_{CA}\gamma_{BC}\gamma_{AB}\rho_{AB}\rho_{BC}\rho_{CA}} - 1}$$

Hence we can derive explicitly the relative change in wealth of the optimal arbitrageur:

$$\Delta = \sqrt{\gamma_{AB}\gamma_{BC}\gamma_{CA}\rho_{AB}\rho_{BC}\rho_{CA}}\,\pi_{p_R^X} - 1$$

which is positive if $p_{R_1}^X \geq p_{R_0}^X$, and, if prices stay the same, is indeed independent of the choice of the origin X.   □

5.2   Some Empirical Results

As of the 15th of December 2020, Uniswap contained 26139 pairs (WETH being connected to more than 12365 tokens) and more than 965 triangular cycles. We analyzed the data obtained from Etherum blockchain from block 11299400 to 11360599 (from 21/11/2020 to 30/11/2020) for the 200 most liquid pairs. We selected 11 triangular cycles that generated the maximum profits per block during this period on Uniswap:

[WETH, AKRO, USDC]

[WETH, DAI, HEGIC]

[WETH, sUSD, BASED]

[WETH, USDC, TOMOE]

[WETH, DAI, USDC]

[WETH, DAI, USDT]

[USDT, USDC, TOMOE]

[WETH, USDT, TOMOE]

[WETH, USDT, USDC]

[WETH, WBTC, USDC]

[WETH, USDT, YFV]

For each block we look for arbitrageable triangular cycles. Once detected, we compute the maximum profit per cycle and per block during the whole period. We plot the maximum profit (measured in USD) per block for each of the 11 selected triangular cycles. One can see that some of the optimal arbitrage profits disappear instantly (i.e. have a one block life time). Others last longer. A key difference with Ref. [6] is coverage. Their data covers Uniswapv2 for a much longer larger period of time and does not look for prediction of cyclic arbitrage on restricted set of tokens, as we do, but for detection thereof. And indeed, their findings show larger actual profits than the potential ones which our small scale data experiment predicts (Figs. 3 and 4).

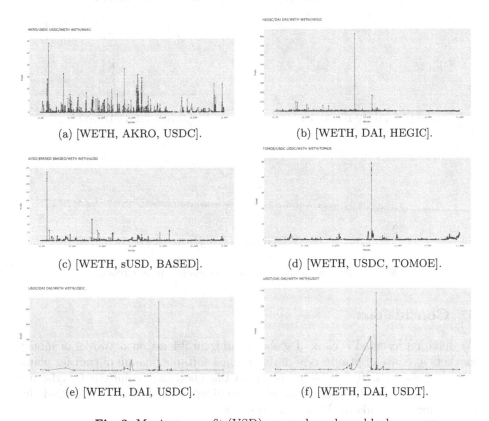

(a) [WETH, AKRO, USDC].

(b) [WETH, DAI, HEGIC].

(c) [WETH, sUSD, BASED].

(d) [WETH, USDC, TOMOE].

(e) [WETH, DAI, USDC].

(f) [WETH, DAI, USDT].

Fig. 3. Maximum profit (USD) per cycle and per block.

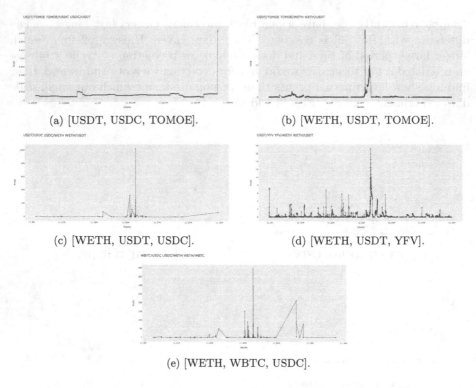

(a) [USDT, USDC, TOMOE].   (b) [WETH, USDT, TOMOE].

(c) [WETH, USDT, USDC].   (d) [WETH, USDT, YFV].

(e) [WETH, WBTC, USDC].

Fig. 4. Maximum profit (USD) per cycle and per block.

6   Conclusions

We have represented a class of global routing problems on networks of money markets as convex optimisation problems on a suitable domain of transfer plans. We have shown that feasible problems in this class have solutions (maybe not unique). We have also built tractable subproblems which allow one to find efficiently lower bounds to the original problems.

Preliminary data analysis shows the presence of non-trivial cyclic arbitrage opportunities (see appendix), and *a fortiori* general ones. There is also evidence of substantial gains from non-trivial routing (Fig. 1). So there is undeniably a practical interest in solving exactly or approximately, and efficiently, these global problems. All the more so if liquidity continues to fragment in DeFi, increasing the complexity of optimal routing. Substantial liquidity migrations on DeFi's money markets have happened, and it is unclear if and when liquidity will aggregate.

One limitation of our approach is that the problems before and after executing a given plan are related but here we do not exploit that information. So there is room for designing on-line versions of the above problems of which the amortised cost could be vastly improved - compared to resolving anew the problem at each update. A minimal way to exploit that relation would be to use a former optimum as initial data for a new gradient descent on the updated problem.

Also we have ignored gas fees as well as the uncertainty generated by the asynchrony inherent on blockchain-based smart contracts: the state of the world at the time the problem is solved, may be very different from the state at the time the corresponding instructions are executed. It would be interesting to include both aspects of this uncertainty (gas costs and asynchrony) in the problem for more robustness.

Acknowledgments. The authors wish to thank Saad Bouhoud, Ayman Elyahmidi, and Vincent Bernardoff for data-related discussions, and for sharing code to obtain the relevant Uniswap data from an Ethereum node. The authors also wish to thank Jérôme de Tychey for numerous interesting discussions on the matters of this paper, and Ye Wang and co-authors for sharing an early version of their paper on cyclic arbitrage [6].

A   The Uniswap Graph

Figure 5 proposes a view of the global Uniswap money market [2] restricted the top 64 ERC20 tokens and their 283 Uniswap pairs. It is worth stressing that

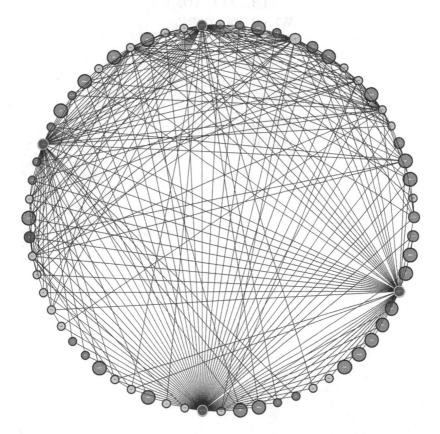

Fig. 5. The top 64 ERC20s (in market cap) and their pairs on Uniswapv2: there is an edge between two nodes if there exists a Uniswap pair between them (Nov 2020).

the actual graph of interest for routing and arbitrage is far more complex as it includes many more automated market makers (sometimes with considerable liquidity) as well as other forms of decentralised exchanges.

B   Some Empirical Results

As of the 15th of December 2020, Uniswap contained 26139 pairs (WETH being connected to more than 12365 tokens) and more than 965 triangular cycles. We analyzed the data obtained from Etherum blockchain from block 11299400 to 11360599 (from 21/11/2020 to 30/11/2020) for the 200 most liquid pairs. We selected 11 triangular cycles that generated the maximum profits per block during this period on Uniswap (Fig. 6):

[WETH, AKRO, USDC]

[WETH, DAI, HEGIC]

[WETH, sUSD, BASED]

[WETH, USDC, TOMOE]

[WETH, DAI, USDC]

[WETH, DAI, USDT]

[USDT, USDC, TOMOE]

[WETH, USDT, TOMOE]

[WETH, USDT, USDC]

[WETH, WBTC, USDC]

[WETH, USDT, YFV]

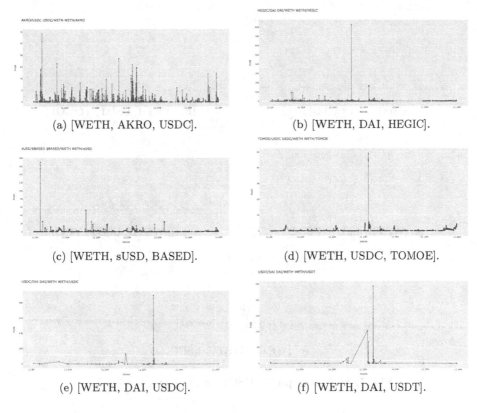

(a) [WETH, AKRO, USDC].

(b) [WETH, DAI, HEGIC].

(c) [WETH, sUSD, BASED].

(d) [WETH, USDC, TOMOE].

(e) [WETH, DAI, USDC].

(f) [WETH, DAI, USDT].

Fig. 6. Maximum profit (USD) per cycle and per block.

For each block we look for arbitrageable triangular cycles. Once detected, we compute the maximum profit per cycle and per block during the whole period. We plot in Fig. 7 the maximum profit (measured in USD) per block for each of the 11 selected triangular cycles. One can see that some of the optimal arbitrage profits disappear instantly (i.e. have a one block life time). Others last longer.

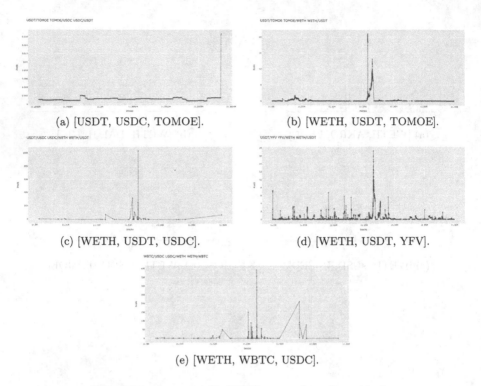

(a) [USDT, USDC, TOMOE].

(b) [WETH, USDT, TOMOE].

(c) [WETH, USDT, USDC].

(d) [WETH, USDT, YFV].

(e) [WETH, WBTC, USDC].

Fig. 7. Maximum profit (USD) per cycle and per block.

References

1. Abergel, F., Jedidi, A.: A mathematical approach to order book modeling. Int. J. Theor. Appl. Finance **16**(05), 1350025 (2013)
2. Adams, H., Zinsmeister, N., Robinson, D.: Uniswap v2 core, March 2020
3. Angeris, G., Kao, H.-T., Chiang, R., Noyes, C., Chitra, T.: An analysis of uniswap markets. Cryptoecon. Syst. J. **1**, 1 (2019)
4. Angeris, G., Chitra, T.: Improved price oracles: constant function market makers. arXiv preprint arXiv:2003.10001, June 2020
5. Boyd, S.P., Vandenberghe, L.: Convex Optimization. Cambridge University Press (2004)
6. Wang, Y., et al.: Cyclic arbitrage in decentralized exchange markets. In: Presented at the 1st Workshop on Decentralized Finance (DeFi) (2021)

Towards a Theory of Decentralized Finance

Massimo Bartoletti[1], James Hsin-yu Chiang[2(✉)], and Alberto Lluch Lafuente[2]

[1] Università degli Studi di Cagliari, Cagliari, Italy
[2] Technical University of Denmark, DTU Compute, Copenhagen, Denmark
jchi@dtu.dk

Abstract. Decentralized Finance (DeFi) has brought about decentralized applications which allow untrusted users to lend, borrow and exchange crypto-assets. Many of such applications fulfill the role of markets or market makers, featuring complex, highly parametric incentive mechanisms to equilibrate interest rates and prices. This complexity makes the behaviour of DeFi applications difficult to understand: indeed, ill-designed incentive mechanisms could potentially lead to emergent unwanted behaviours. We argue that theories, techniques and tools rooted in formal methods can provide useful instruments to better understand, specify and analyze DeFi systems. We summarize in this paper our first steps towards a theory of DeFi based on formal methods, and we overview the open challenges and opportunities for formal methods in DeFi.

1 DeFi Archetypes and Their Formalization

The emergence of permissionless, public blockchains has given birth to an entire ecosystem of *crypto-tokens* representing digital assets and derivatives. Facilitated and accelerated by smart contracts and standardized token interfaces [1], these so-called *decentralized finance* (DeFi) applications promise an open alternative to the traditional financial system. Prior foundational research in the domain of DeFi has been thoroughly summarized in [24].

To study properties emerging from the interaction between users and DeFi applications, we have initiated our line of research towards a theory of DeFi by focusing on the identification of *archetypal* DeFi applications and on the development of *executable specifications* for them, based on manual inspection of the underlying implementations of mainstream implementations. Our formal specifications encompass (abstractions of) the underlying economic incentive mechanisms [5,15,16] and pave the way towards a generalized theory of DeFi archetypes and their interactions, which may be intractable from analysis at the implementation level alone. These executable semantics represents a first step towards *domain-specific languages* for decentralized finance, where DeFi contracts are composed from formally specified primitives and thus exhibit well-defined, analyzable behaviour inferred from the language semantics. The main

© International Financial Cryptography Association 2021
M. Bernhard et al. (Eds.): FC 2021 Workshops, LNCS 12676, pp. 227–232, 2021.
https://doi.org/10.1007/978-3-662-63958-0_20

archetypes we have considered so far are *Lending Pools* (LPs) [7] and *Automatic Market Makers* (AMMs) [8].

Lending Pools. Lending pools are decentralized applications which allow mutually untrusted users to lend and borrow crypto-assets. In [7], we formalize all interactions between users and LPs, thereby providing a complete specification for the economic functionality of LPs. Our model allows to formally state and specify fundamental properties of LPs, like e.g. correct accounting of *minted* tokens and preservation of the supply of *deposited* tokens, which are crucial to ensure consistency in exchange and distribution of tokens enabled by LPs. Furthermore, our model allows one to reason about rational agents, which are incentivized to liquidate loans in return for discounted collateral or perform deposits immediately prior to interest accrual. We also provide solid arguments for the design of incentives of LPs, for example by formally proving that depositors can potentially redeem more tokens than they deposited, and by identifying the conditions under which redeems are not possible. In this regard, we formalize notions of *utilization safety,* which represents a utility trade-off between borrow and redeem actions, moderated by a dynamic interest rate. In LPs, loans are secured by collateral: yet, there exist LP states in which the borrower is no longer incentivized to return loan should the agent's collateralization drop below a certain threshold. We formally characterize such *collateral-safe* states. Finally, we exploit both notions of safety to illustrate attacks on utilization and collateralization, aimed at undermining the incentive mechanisms of LPs.

Automatic Market Makers. Automatic market makers allow users to exchange units of different types of crypto-assets, without the need to find a counter-party. In [8], we develop a theory for AMMs, specifying their possible interactions and their economic mechanisms. One of the results we provide is a concurrency theory for AMM actions. In particular, we show that sequences of *deposit* and *redeem* actions can be ordered interchangeably, resulting in observationally equivalent AMM states. We prove fundamental preservation properties for our AMM specification, like e.g. the preservation of deposited token supplies, and *token liquidity*, which ensures that deposited tokens cannot be *frozen* in an AMM application. Furthermore, we introduce a formal notion of *incentive-consistency*: AMM's rely on a dynamic exchange rate governed by a so-called *trading invariant*. Notably, we formalize the key incentive mechanism, the arbitrage game, for all trading invariants which are *incentive-consistent*, thus facilitating formal analysis of AMM behaviour which can be generalized beyond the mainstream constant-product AMMs.

2   Next Steps, Challenges and Opportunities

The identification and formalization of DeFi archetypes is only the first step towards a general theory of DeFi. There are many steps ahead, and new avenues for future research, full of challenges and opportunities. We discuss some of them, focusing mostly on issues that arise when considering DeFi ecosystems as composed by a set of collaboration or competing agents, interacting through possibly separate contract execution environments enabled by miners, who may have transaction ordering privileges and their own goals.

Agent Strategies. The formal methods toolbox provides a plethora of specification tools and languages to specify systems composed of concurrent actors [21,25]. In order to formally analyze the emergent behaviour of such a system, a specification of all user strategies must be defined or synthesised. Here we distinguish between *rational* strategies, which are risk-free actions increasing the user's net wealth and strategies which are *speculative*, driven by an agent's *expectation* of a future system state which is not guaranteed: attempting a liquidation action, for example, is a rational strategy as the actor will obtain collateral at a discounted rate or at worst, fail to execute any action at all if the transaction fails. On the other hand, depositing funds in a LP is speculative, as it is based on an expectation of future interest, regulated by future actions of borrowers and depositors.

Whereas there appears to be a clear path towards formal specification of rational strategies in DeFi systems, the specification of speculative agent behaviour in DeFi remains an open question. For individual DeFi archetypes, agent-based models have been proposed [2,17] with a focus on rational behaviour, yet the specification of economically speculative strategies in a wider, composition of DeFi application remains an open research challenge.

Classical agent-based models from economic disciplines feature specification techniques of economically (speculative) agent behaviour: here, we also observe that stochastic model checking tools from formal methods are increasingly deployed [22] in the economic research community and suggest that stochastic model checking of agent-based models of DeFi systems may provide a path forward towards the automatic analysis of agent strategies.

A Model of Transaction Concurrency. Actions performed in DeFi systems are generally not concurrent: this is observable with AMMs, for example, where an actor with transaction ordering privileges can benefit from ordering its own transaction before and after that of the victim [18,26]. More generally, the ability of miners to extract value beyond transaction fees from specific sequences of DeFi interactions has been denoted miner-extractable-value (MEV) [13]. Thus, a formal model of a DeFi system composed by different DeFi applications must also feature a notion of *incentive-consistent* action sequences in the presence of rational agents with transaction ordering privileges.

Such analysis is further complicated by atomic chains of transactions, such as those obtained by nested contract calls in Ethereum. Here, the sequencing of individual actions within the call-chain is determined by the authorizing user: this can result in DeFi exploits amplified by flash loans [10,19,23]. As transactions, call-chains must also exhibit consistency with miner transaction ordering incentives: here, we note a lack of formal models to integrate call-chain semantics with formal models of MEV.

A model of transaction ordering may ultimately facilitate the automated analysis of a DeFi system specification, given that it narrows the set of *valid* interaction sequences. Given sufficiently specified agent strategies, such a theory may pave the way towards novel model checking techniques in DeFi.

Cryptographic Protocol Composition. Cryptographic protocols play an increasingly central role in DeFi systems, as they allow DeFi applications to keep private selected parts of the application state: public execution introduces incentives (MEV) which challenge DeFi security, but the public execution of user actions also compromises privacy. The popularity of crypto-asset mixers [4] powered by ZK-SNARK proofs on the Ethereum blockchain foreshadows the emergence of privacy-focused DeFi applications, which in turn, may open new approaches to mitigate MEV. Private order-matching has been proposed with multi-party-computation techniques [11], and we foresee similar techniques for DeFi applications. Furthermore, advanced cryptographic protocols improve scalability: many DeFi applications have migrated to ZK-rollups [3] in order to absorb the increased user demand on the Ethereum blockchain.

For the secure composition of cryptographic protocols deployed for both privacy and scalability, the formal methods community may contribute both classical information flow [12] analysis techniques and cryptographic protocol composition analysis [14]: as a multitude of privacy-focused and scalable applications are composed in a single system, we highlight the formal analysis of safe cryptographic protocol composition in DeFi as an new research frontier.

Domain-Specific Languages. Since the analysis of security aspects of DeFi applications will invariably involve specifications of agents and miners, higher abstractions of DeFi specification will arguably be of interest to the DeFi and formal methods communities. Domain-specific languages with formal semantics (e.g. [6,9,20]) provide suitable specification means for such abstractions. Moreover, they fulfill two purposes: firstly, they enable formal reasoning and security proofs. Secondly, DeFi-specific languages can provide built-in security guarantees, given a foundational theory of the underlying DeFi system.

3   Concluding Remarks

We thank the organizing committee of the first edition of the DeFi workshop for the fruitful exchange of research ideas on the topic of decentralized finance and encourage the DeFi community to join us in extending the formal methods toolkit in addressing the open security challenges in decentralized finance present today and those emerging on the horizon.

Acknowledgements. The second author is supported by the PhD School of DTU Compute. The third author is partially supported by the EU H2020-SU-ICT-03-2018 Project No. 830929 CyberSec4Europe (cybersec4europe.eu).

References

1. ERC-20 token standard (2015). https://github.com/ethereum/EIPs/blob/master/EIPS/eip-20.md

2. Uniswap oracle template (2020). https://github.com/Uniswap/uniswap-v2-periphery/blob/dda62473e2da448bc9cb8f4514dadda4aeede5f4/contracts/examples/ExampleOracleSimple.sol
3. Starkware (2021). https://starkware.co/
4. Tornado (2021). https://tornado.cash/
5. Angeris, G., Evans, A., Chitra, T.: When does the tail wag the dog? Curvature and market making. arXiv preprint arXiv:2012.08040 (2020)
6. Arusoaie, A.: Certifying findel derivatives for blockchain. J. Logical Algebraic Methods Program. **121** (2021). https://doi.org/10.1016/j.jlamp.2021.100665
7. Bartoletti, M., Chiang, J.H., Lluch-Lafuente, A.: SoK: lending pools in decentralized finance. In: 5th Workshop on Trusted Smart Contracts (2021). (to appear). https://arxiv.org/abs/2012.13230
8. Bartoletti, M., Chiang, J.H., Lluch-Lafuente, A.: A theory of automated market makers in defi. arXiv preprint arXiv:2102.11350 (2021)
9. Bartoletti, M., Zunino, R.: BitML: a calculus for Bitcoin smart contracts. ACM CCS (2018). https://doi.org/10.1145/3243734.3243795
10. Cao, Y., Zou, C., Cheng, X.: Flashot: a snapshot of flash loan attack on DeFi ecosystem. arXiv preprint arXiv:2102.00626 (2021)
11. Baum, C., David, B., Frederiksen, T.: P2DEX: privacy-preserving decentralized cryptocurrency exchange. Cryptology ePrint Archive, Report 2021/283 (2021). https://eprint.iacr.org/2021/283
12. Cecchetti, E., Yao, S., Ni, H., Myers, A.C.: Compositional security for reentrant applications. arXiv preprint arXiv:2103.08577 (2021)
13. Daian, P., et al.: Flash boys 2.0: frontrunning in decentralized exchanges, miner extractable value, and consensus instability. In: IEEE Symposium on Security and Privacy, pp. 910–927. IEEE (2020). https://doi.org/10.1109/SP40000.2020.00040
14. Dolev, D., Yao, A.: On the security of public key protocols. IEEE Trans. Inf. Theory **29**(2), 198–208 (1983)
15. Evans, A., Angeris, G., Chitra, T.: Optimal fees for geometric mean market makers (2021). https://web.stanford.edu/~guillean/papers/g3m-optimal-fee.pdf
16. Gudgeon, L., Werner, S., Perez, D., Knottenbelt, W.J.: Defi protocols for loanable funds: interest rates, liquidity and market efficiency. In: ACM Conference on Advances in Financial Technologies, pp. 92–112 (2020). https://doi.org/10.1145/3419614.3423254
17. Kao, H.T., Chitra, T., Chiang, R., Morrow, J.: An analysis of the market risk to participants in the compound protocol. https://scfab.github.io/2020/FAB2020_p5.pdf
18. Qin, K., Zhou, L., Gervais, A.: Quantifying blockchain extractable value: how dark is the forest? (2021). https://arxiv.org/pdf/2101.05511
19. Qin, K., Zhou, L., Livshits, B., Gervais, A.: Attacking the DeFi ecosystem with flash loans for fun and profit. In: Financial Cryptography (2021). (to appear). https://arxiv.org/pdf/2003.03810
20. Lamela Seijas, P., Thompson, S.: Marlowe: financial contracts on blockchain. In: Margaria, T., Steffen, B. (eds.) ISoLA 2018. LNCS, vol. 11247, pp. 356–375. Springer, Cham (2018). https://doi.org/10.1007/978-3-030-03427-6_27
21. Tolmach, P., Li, Y., Lin, S.W., Liu, Y.: Formal analysis of composable DeFi protocols. In: 1st Workshop on Decentralized Finance (2021). (to appear). https://arxiv.org/abs/2103.00540
22. Vandin, A., Giachini, D., Lamperti, F., Chiaromonte, F.: Automated and distributed statistical analysis of economic agent-based models. arXiv preprint arXiv:2102.05405 (2021)

23. Wang, D., et al.: Towards understanding flash loan and its applications in DeFi ecosystem. arXiv preprint arXiv:2010.12252 (2020)
24. Werner, S.M., Perez, D., Gudgeon, L., Klages-Mundt, A., Harz, D., Knottenbelt, W.J.: SoK: decentralized finance (DeFi) (2021)
25. Zhao, W., Li, H., Yuan, Y.: (2021). (to appear). https://arxiv.org/abs/2101.08423
26. Zhou, L., Qin, K., Torres, C.F., Le, D.V., Gervais, A.: High-frequency trading on decentralized on-chain exchanges. arXiv preprint arXiv:2009.14021 (2020)

Voting

Auditing Hamiltonian Elections

Michelle Blom[1], Philip B. Stark[2], Peter J. Stuckey[3],
Vanessa Teague[4]([✉]), and Damjan Vukcevic[5,6]

[1] School of Computing and Information Systems, University of Melbourne,
Parkville, Australia
michelle.blom@unimelb.edu.au
[2] Department of Statistics, University of California, Berkeley, USA
[3] Department of Data Science and AI, Monash University, Clayton, Australia
[4] Thinking Cybersecurity Pty. Ltd., Melbourne, Australia
vanessa@thinkingcybersecurity.com
[5] School of Mathematics and Statistics, University of Melbourne, Parkville, Australia
[6] Melbourne Integrative Genomics, University of Melbourne, Parkville, Australia

Abstract. Presidential primaries are a critical part of the United States Presidential electoral process, since they are used to select the candidates in the Presidential election. While methods differ by state and party, many primaries involve proportional delegate allocation using the so-called Hamilton method. In this paper we show how to conduct risk-limiting audits for delegate allocation elections using variants of the Hamilton method where the viability of candidates is determined either by a plurality vote or using instant runoff voting. Experiments on real-world elections show that we can audit primary elections to high confidence (small risk limits) usually at low cost.

1 Introduction

Presidential primary elections are a critical part of the United States electoral process, since they are used to select the final candidates contesting the Presidential election for each of the major parties. For that reason it is important that the result of these primaries be trustworthy. While the method used for primary elections differs by party and state, the majority of such elections use delegate allocation by proportional representation, the so-called Hamilton method, named after its inventor, Alexander Hamilton.

Risk-limiting audits (RLAs) [9] require a durable, trustworthy record of the votes, typically paper ballots marked by hand, kept demonstrably secure. RLAs end in one of two ways: either they produce strong evidence that the reported winners really won, or they result in a full manual tabulation of the paper records. If a RLA leads to a full manual tabulation, the outcome of the tabulation replaces the original reported outcome if they differ, thus correcting the reported outcome (if the paper trail is trustworthy). The probability that a RLA fails to correct a reported outcome that is incorrect before that outcome becomes official is bounded by a "risk limit." An RLA with a risk limit of 1%, for example, has at

© International Financial Cryptography Association 2021
M. Bernhard et al. (Eds.): FC 2021 Workshops, LNCS 12676, pp. 235–250, 2021.
https://doi.org/10.1007/978-3-662-63958-0_21

most a 1% chance of failing to correct a reported election outcome that is wrong; equivalently, it has at least a 99% chance of correcting the reported outcome if it is wrong. RLAs are becoming the de-facto standard for post-election audits. They are required by statute in Colorado, Nevada, Rhode Island, and Virginia,[1] for some government elections (not primaries which are party elections), and have been piloted in over a dozen US states and Denmark. They are recommended by the US National Academies of Science, Engineering, and Medicine and endorsed by the American Statistical Association. Risk-limiting audits of limited scope have begun to be applied to US primary elections; our methods here would allow RLAs of the full elections.

In this paper we describe the first method that we are aware of for conducting an RLA for delegate allocation by proportional representation elections, which we call *Hamiltonian elections*. In addition to primary elections in some states in the USA, this type of election is used in Russia, Ukraine, Tunisia, Taiwan, Namibia and Hong Kong. We do so by adapting auditing methods designed for plurality and instant runoff voting (IRV) elections for auditing the viability of candidates, and generating a new kind of audit for proportional allocation.

A delegate allocation election by proportional representation is a complex form of election. Rather than simply electing candidates, the result of the election is to assign some number of delegates to some of the candidates. In the first stage of the election, the process determines the subset of candidates that are eligible or *viable* (for Democratic primaries, candidates need to receive at least 15% of the vote). In the second step, delegates are awarded to these viable candidates in approximate proportion to their vote. An RLA must determine the correctness of both the set of viable candidates and the number of delegates assigned to each viable candidate.

The first stage of the election uses either simple plurality voting, where each ballot is a vote for at most one candidate, or IRV, where each ballot is a ranking of some or all candidates. In IRV, candidates with the fewest first-choice ranks are eliminated and each ballot that ranked them first is reassigned to the next most-preferred ranked candidate on that ballot.

There is considerable work on both comparison audits and ballot-polling audits for plurality elections [6,11], but few for more complex election types. Sarwate et al. [8] consider IRV and some other preferential elections. Kroll et al. [5] show how to audit the overall US electoral college outcome, but not the allocation of individual delegates. Stark and Teague [12] devise audits for the D'Hondt method for proportional representation, which is related to but distinct from Hamiltonian methods. Blom et al. [2,3] describe efficient audits for IRV. As far as we know, there is no other auditing method for Hamiltonian Elections, nor any that combines a proportional representation method with IRV.

---

[1] Virginia's audit does not take place until after the outcome is certified, so it cannot limit the risk that an incorrect reported outcome will become final: technically, it is not a RLA.

Candidate	Votes	Proportion
Ann	57,532	76.1%
Bob	15,630	20.6%
Cal	1,600	2.1%
Dee	846	1.1%
Total Votes	**75,608**	**100.0%**

(a)

Candidate	Votes	Proportion
Ann	57,532	78.6%
Bob	15,630	21.4%
Qualified Votes	**73,162**	**100.0%**

(b)

Fig. 1. (a) Votes and (b) Qualified Votes in a Hamiltonian election with plurality-based exclusion.

2 Hamiltonian Elections

We have a set of n candidates C, a set of cast ballots[2] B, and a number of delegates D to be awarded to the candidates based on the votes. The *Hamilton* or *largest remainder* method, invented by Alexander Hamilton in 1792, allocates the delegates in approximate proportion to the votes the candidates received.

In a *pure Hamiltonian election*, also known as the *Hamilton method*, delegates are directly allocated based on the proportion of the vote. But most delegate elections use some form of *exclusion* of some candidates before the delegates are apportioned.

A *Hamiltonian election with exclusion* first determines which candidates in C are *viable*—eligible to be awarded one or more delegates. Typically, exclusion involves a plurality vote. Each ballot is a vote for at most one candidate. If a candidate receives a threshold proportion τ of the valid votes, the candidate is considered viable.[3] The votes cast for viable candidates are referred to as *qualified votes*. The qualified votes are used to allocate delegates, as described later in this section.

Example 1. Consider an example Hamiltonian election with exclusion with 4 candidates, Ann, Bob, Cal, and Dee and a viability threshold of $\tau = 15\%$. Figure 1(a) shows the tally of votes for each candidate, and the percentage of the overall vote that each candidate received. Ann and Bob received more than 15% of the vote and are viable candidates.

For elections with many candidates, a plurality exclusion might eliminate all of them. In an *instant-runoff Hamiltonian election* the viable candidates are determined by a form of IRV. Each ballot is now a partial ranking of the candidates, and the viable candidates are determined as follows:

1. Initialize the set of candidates. Each ballot is put in the pile for the candidate ranked highest on that ballot.

---

[2] We do not distinguish between ballots and ballot cards; in general, ballots consist of one or more cards, of which at most one contains any given contest.

[3] There are more complicated alternate rules for the case where no candidate reaches τ; we do not consider this case here.

2. If every (remaining) candidate has $\geqslant \tau$ of the votes in their pile, we finish the candidate selection process. All of these remaining candidates are viable.
3. Otherwise, the candidate with the lowest tally (fewest ballots in their pile) is eliminated, and each of their ballots is moved to the pile of the next ranked remaining candidate on the ballot. A ballot is *exhausted* if all further candidates mentioned on the ballot have already been eliminated.
4. We then return to step 2.

Example 2. Consider an instant-runoff Hamiltonian election with the same four candidates as Example 1, the same threshold, and 50,000 ballots with ranking [A,D,C,B] (that is, Ann followed by Dee, then Cal, then Bob), 9,630 of [B,C], 6,000 of [C,B], 1,600 of [C], 7,532 of [D,A,C], and 846 of [D,C]. The IRV election proceeds as follows. In the first round Cal has the lowest tally, 7,600 votes, which is 10.052% of the total vote, and hence less than 15%. Cal is eliminated: the 6,000 ballots [C,B] are transferred to Bob, and the 1,600 ballots [C] are exhausted (removed from consideration). In the next round Dee has the lowest tally, 8,378 votes which is 11.080%, so Dee is eliminated. The 7,632 [D,A,C] ballots are transferred to Ann, and the remaining 836 [D,C] ballots are exhausted. In the final round, Bob has the lowest tally, 20.672% of the vote, and the process ends since this is greater than 15%. The election is summarized in Fig. 2.

Cand.	Round 1			Round 2			Final Result		
		Ballot Number	Prop.		Ballot Number	Prop.		Ballot Number	Prop.
Ann	[**A**,D,C,B]	50,000	66.1%	[**A**,D,C,B]	50,000	66.1%	[**A**,D,C,B]	50,000	
							[**D**,**A**,C]	7,532	76.1%
Bob	[**B**,C]	9,630	12.7%	[**B**,C]	9,630		[**B**,C]	9,630	
				[**C**,**B**]	6,000	20.7%	[**C**,**B**]	6,000	20.7%
Cal	[**C**,B]	6,000		—			—		
	[**C**]	1,600	10.1%	—		—	—		
Dee	[**D**,A,C]	7,532		[**D**,A,C]	7,532		—		
	[**D**,C]	846	11.1%	[**D**,C]	846	11.1%	—		—
Total		**75,608**	100.0%		73,738	98.6%		73,162	96.8%

Fig. 2. IRV election for four candidates showing the elimination of first Cal, and then Dee, and the final round results.

The second stage in the process is to assign delegates to candidates on the basis of their tallies. We first compute, for each viable candidate c, the proportion of the *qualified votes* in their tally, p_c. Recall that we refer to ballots belonging to viable candidates as *qualified* votes. We denote the number of qualified votes as Q. In the context of IRV, ballots are qualified if they end up in the tally of a viable candidate. Non-qualified ballots result from exhaustion: every candidate in the ballot ranking has been eliminated (is non-viable). Where a plurality contest determines viability, all votes for a viable candidate are qualified.

We denote the set of viable candidates as $\mathcal{V}$. Delegates are awarded to viable candidates as follows:

1. We compute for each viable candidate c their *delegate quota*, $q_c = D \times p_c$ where p_c is the proportion of the qualified vote given to c (their final tally divided by Q).
2. We assign $i_c = \lfloor q_c \rfloor$ delegates to each candidate $c \in \mathcal{V}$.
3. At this stage, there are $r = D - \sum_{c \in \mathcal{V}} i_c$ remaining delegates to assign. We assign these delegates to the r candidates with the largest value of the remainder $q_c - i_c$. One delegate is given to each of these r candidates.
4. At this stage, each viable candidate c has received a_c total delegates, where a_c is q_c rounded either up or down.

Example 3. The end result of Examples 1 and 2 is the same. The qualified vote is $Q = 73,162$. The proportions of the qualified vote in viable candidates' tallies are: $p_{Ann} = 0.786$; and $p_{Bob} = 0.214$. Assuming there are $D = 5$ delegates to allocate, we find $q_{Ann} = 3.932$ and $q_{Bob} = 1.068$. We initially allocate 3 delegates to Ann and 1 to Bob. By comparing the remainders 0.932 and 0.068, we allocate the last delegate to Ann. So $a_{Ann} = 4$ and $a_{Bob} = 1$.

3 Auditing Fundamentals

A risk-limiting audit is a statistical test of the hypothesis that the reported outcome is incorrect. (In the current context, the reported outcome is the number of delegates finally awarded to each candidate.) If that hypothesis is not rejected, there is a full hand tabulation, which reveals the true outcome. If that differs from the reported outcome, it replaces the reported outcome. The significance level of the test is called the *risk limit*. A risk-limiting audit of a trustworthy paper trail of votes limits the risk that an incorrect electoral outcome will go uncorrected.

Two common building blocks for audits are to compare manual interpretation of randomly selected ballots or groups of ballots with how the voting system interpreted them (a *comparison* audit [10]), and to use only the manual interpretation of the randomly selected ballots (a *ballot-polling* audit [7]). Ballot polling requires less infrastructure (some voting systems do not generate or cannot export the data required for a comparison audit) but generally requires inspecting more ballots.

Recent work [11] shows that audits of most social choice functions can be reduced to checking a set of *assertions*. If all the assertions are true, the reported election outcome is correct. Each assertion is checked by conducting a hypothesis test of its logical negation. To reject the hypothesis that the negation is true is to conclude that the assertion is true. Each hypothesis is tested using a statistic calculated from the audit data. Larger values of the statistic are unlikely if the corresponding assertion is false. If the statistic takes a sufficiently large value, that is statistical evidence that the assertion is true, because such a large value would be very unlikely if the assertion were false. The statistic is generally calibrated to give *sequentially valid* tests of the assertions, meaning that the sample of ballots can be expanded at will and the statistic can be recomputed from the expanded sample, while controlling the probability of erroneously concluding that the assertion is true if the assertion is in fact false.

The initial sample size is generally chosen so that there is a reasonable chance that the audit will terminate without examining additional ballots if the reported results are approximately correct. If the initial sample does not give sufficiently strong evidence that all the assertions are correct, the sample is augmented and the condition is checked again.[4] The sample continues to expand until either all the assertions have been confirmed[5] or the sample contains every ballot, and the correct result is therefore known. At any point during the audit, the auditor can choose to conduct a full manual tabulation. If the audit leads to a full manual tabulation, the outcome of that tabulation replaces the reported outcome if they differ.

The basic assertions for Hamiltonian elections are:

(Super/sub) majority $p > t$, where p is the proportion of ballots that satisfy some condition (usually the condition is that the ballot has a vote for a particular candidate) among ballots that meet some validity condition, and t is a proportion in $(0, 1]$.

Pairwise majority $p_A > p_B$, where p_A and p_B are the proportions of ballots that meet two mutually exclusive conditions A and B, among ballots that meet some validity condition. (Typically, among the ballots that contain a valid vote, A is a ballot with a vote for one candidate, and B is a ballot with a vote for a different candidate).

Pairwise difference $p_A > p_B + d$, where p_A and p_B are the proportions of ballots that meet two mutually exclusive conditions among ballots that meet some validity condition, and d is a constant in the range $(-1, 1)$. This is a new form of assertion not previously used, that extends pairwise majority assertions. It is necessary for auditing delegate assignment in Hamiltonian elections.

In the SHANGRLA approach to RLAs [11], each assertion is transformed into a canonical form: the mean of an *assorter* (which assigns each ballot a nonnegative, bounded number) is greater than $1/2$. The value the assorter assigns to a ballot is generally a function of the votes on that ballot and others and the voting system's interpretation of the votes on that ballot and others.

For majority assertions, a ballot that satisfies the condition is assigned the value $1/(2t)$; a valid ballot that does not satisfy the condition is assigned the value 0; and an invalid ballot is assigned the value $1/2$. For pairwise majority assertions, a ballot for class A counts as 1 and a ballot for class B counts as 0. Ballots that fall outside both classes count as $1/2$.

---

[4] For sequentially valid test statistics, the sample can be augmented at will; for other methods, there may be an escalation schedule prescribing a sequence of sample sizes before conducting a full manual tabulation.

[5] In other words, the hypothesis that the assertion is false has been rejected at a sufficiently small significance level.

For pairwise difference assertions, we define the assorter g which assigns ballot b the value:

$$g(b) \equiv \begin{cases} 1/(1+d), & b \text{ has a vote of class A} \\ 0, & b \text{ has a vote of class B} \\ 1/(2(1+d)), & b \text{ has a valid vote in the contest that is not in A or B} \\ 1/2, & b \text{ does not have a valid vote in the contest.} \end{cases}$$

Let $\bar{g}$ be the mean of g over the ballots. We have that $0 \leqslant g(b) \leqslant 1/(1+d)$, and $\bar{g} > 1/2$ iff $p_A > p_B + d$. When $d = 0$ this reduces to the pairwise majority assorter if the "valid" category is the same.

The *margin* m of an assertion a is equal to 2 times the mean of its assorter (when applied to all ballots $\mathcal{B}$) minus 1. An assertion with a smaller margin will be harder to audit than an assertion with a larger margin.

3.1   Estimating Sample Size and Risk

The sample size required to confirm an assertion depends on the sampling design and the auditing strategy (e.g., sampling individual ballots or batches of ballots, using ballot polling or comparison); the "risk-measuring function" (see [11]); and the accuracy of the tally, among other things. Because it depends on what the sample reveals, it is random.

There is some flexibility in selecting a set of assertions to confirm IRV contests [1], so the set can be chosen to minimize a measure of the anticipated workload. We will estimate the workload on the assumption that the assertion is true but the reported tallies are not exactly correct. We will use the expected sample size as a measure of workload.[6]

Our auditing approach is applicable to any style of auditing. The workload, given a set of assertions, varies depending on the style of audit (e.g., ballot-level comparison, batch-level comparison, ballot-polling, or a combination of those) and the sampling design (e.g., with or without replacement, Bernoulli, stratified or not, weighted or not). For the purpose of illustration, in the examples and experiments in this paper, we assume that the audit will be a ballot-level comparison audit using sampling with replacement.

Because the sample is drawn with replacement, the same ballot can be drawn more than once. Given an assertion a, let $ASN(a, \alpha)$ denote the expected number of draws required to verify a to risk limit α, and if $\mathcal{A}$ is a set of assertions, let $ASN(\mathcal{A}, \alpha)$ denote the expected number of draws required to verify every assertion a in $\mathcal{A}$ to risk limit α. ASN depends on several factors: the risk limit α; the expected rate of errors (discrepancies) between paper ballots and their electronic records of various signs and magnitudes (in the context of comparison auditing); and the margins of the assertions.

---

[6] One might instead seek to minimize a quantile of the sample size or some other function of the distribution of sample size, for instance, to account for fixed costs for retrieving and opening a batch of ballots and per-ballot and per-contest costs.

We estimate $ASN(\mathcal{A}, \alpha)$ by simulation. We simulate the sampling of ballots, one at a time.[7] An "overstatement" error is introduced with a pre-specified probability e. If the sample reveals one or more overstatements, the measured risk (i.e., the P-value of the hypothesis that the assertion is false) increases by an amount that depends on margin m. Otherwise, the measured risk decreases by an amount that depends on m. We continue to sample ballots until the measured risk falls below α or until every ballot has been manually reviewed, in which case the outcome based on the manual interpretations replaces the original reported results. We take the median of the number of ballots sampled over N simulations as an estimate of $ASN(\mathcal{A}, \alpha)$. Inaccuracy of this estimate affects whether the selected assertions result in the smallest expected workload, but does not affect the risk limit. For the examples and experiments in this paper, we use $e = 0.002$ (equivalent to 2 errors per 1,000 ballots), $N = 20$, and a risk limit of 5%.

4   Auditing Viability

The first stage of the election identifies the viable candidates. We introduce notation for the assertions we will use to audit viability, as follows:

- *Viable*(c, E, t): Candidate c has at least proportion t of the vote after the candidates in set E have been eliminated. This amounts to a simple majority assertion $p_c > t$ after candidates in E are eliminated.
- *NonViable*(c, E, t): Candidate c has less than proportion t of the vote after candidates E have been eliminated. This amounts to a simple majority assertion $\bar{p}_c > 1 - t$ where $\bar{p}_c$ is the proportion of valid votes for candidates other than c after candidates E are eliminated.
- *IRV*(c, c', E): Candidate c has more votes than candidate c' after candidates E have been eliminated. This amounts to a pairwise majority assertion.

If the first stage is a plurality vote, $E \equiv \emptyset$: the elimination in the first stage only occurs for *IRV*.

Consider an election $\mathcal{E} = \langle \mathcal{C}, \mathcal{B}, \tau \rangle$ with candidates $\mathcal{C}$, cast ballots $\mathcal{B}$, and viability threshold τ ($\tau = 0.15$ for the primary elections we will examine). The outcome of this election is a set of viable candidates, $\mathcal{V} \subseteq \mathcal{C}$, together with, in the case of instant runoff Hamiltonian elections, a sequence of eliminated candidates, π. To check that the set of candidates reported to be viable really are the viable candidates, we test assertions that rule out all other possibilities. Consider the subset $\mathcal{V}' \subseteq \mathcal{C}$, where $\mathcal{V}' \neq \mathcal{V}$. We can demonstrate that $\mathcal{V}'$ is not the true set of viable candidates by showing that some candidate $c \in \mathcal{V}'$ does not belong there. We can also rule out $\mathcal{V}'$ as an outcome by showing that there is a candidate $c \notin \mathcal{V}'$ that does in fact belong in the viable set. We aim to find the 'least effort' set of assertions $\mathcal{A}$ that, if shown to hold in a risk-limiting audit, confirm that (i) each candidate in $\mathcal{V}$ is viable, and (ii) no candidate $c' \notin \mathcal{V}$ is viable.

---

[7] The procedure used to calculate the ASN for an assertion with margin m is available in the public repositories https://github.com/michelleblom/primaries and https://github.com/pbstark/SHANGRLA.

4.1   Viability: Plurality Hamiltonian Elections

For each viable candidate $v \in \mathcal{V}$ we need to verify the assertion $Viable(v, \emptyset, \tau)$. For each non-viable candidate $n \in \mathcal{C} \backslash \mathcal{V}$ we need to verify the assertion $NonViable(n, \emptyset, \tau)$. Let $\mathcal{A}$ be the union of these two sets of assertions. Note that $\mathcal{A}$ rules out any other set of viable candidates $\mathcal{V}' \neq \mathcal{V}$.

Example 4. To audit the first stage of the election of Example 1, we verify the assertions $\mathcal{A} = \{ Viable(\text{Ann}, \emptyset, 0.15), \ Viable(\text{Bob}, \emptyset, 0.15), \ NonViable(\text{Cal}, \emptyset, 0.15), \ NonViable(\text{Dee}, \emptyset, 0.15) \}$. The margins associated with these assertions are 4.073, 0.378, 0.152, and 0.163, respectively. The expected number of ballots we need to compare to the corresponding cast vote records to audit these assertions, assuming an overstatement error rate of 0.002 and a risk limit of $\alpha = 5\%$, are, respectively 1, 17, 46, and 42. The overall ASN for the audit is 46 ballots.

4.2   Viability: Instant-Runoff Hamiltonian Elections

Efficient RLAs for IRV have been devised only recently [1]. To audit the first stage of an IRV Hamiltonian election we must eliminate the possibility that a different set of candidates is viable. This means that we need to look at every other set of candidates, and propose an assertion that will show that set is not viable.

In contrast to auditing a simple IRV election, where there are $|\mathcal{C}| - 1$ potential winners other than the reported winner, a Hamiltonian election typically has many more. Let $M = \lfloor 1/\tau \rfloor$ be the maximum possible number of viable candidates. The number of possible winner sets O is

$$O \equiv \binom{|\mathcal{C}|}{M} + \binom{|\mathcal{C}|}{M-1} + \cdots + \binom{|\mathcal{C}|}{1}.$$

We can show that a subset of candidates $\mathcal{V}'$ is not the set of viable candidates in a number of ways:

- we could show that the tally of at least one $c \in \mathcal{V}'$ does not reach the required threshold assuming all candidates not mentioned in $\mathcal{V}'$ have been eliminated
- we could show that there is a candidate $c' \notin \mathcal{V}'$ that is viable on the basis of their first preferences, so any potential set of viable candidates must include c'
- we could show that the unmentioned candidates could not have been eliminated in a sequence that would result in $\mathcal{V}'$.

Reducing the Set of Subsets. While there are many possible alternate winner sets $\mathcal{V}'$, we can rule out many of these easily. We examine the assertions $Viable(w, \emptyset, \tau)$ for any candidate $w \in \mathcal{C}$ who had more than the proportion τ of the vote initially. This assertion will be easy to verify, as long as the proportion is not too close to τ. This assertion rules out any subset $\mathcal{V}'$ where $w \notin \mathcal{V}'$. Let $\mathcal{W}$ be the set of candidates where this assertion is expected to hold.

Next we examine the assertions $NonViable(l, \mathcal{C} \setminus \mathcal{W} \setminus \{l\}, \tau)$ for those candidates l who are not mentioned in at least τ of the ballots, when all but the definite winners $\mathcal{W}$ and l are eliminated. In this case candidate l can never reach τ proportion of the votes. Again this assertion is easy to verify as long as the proportion of such votes is not close to τ. This assertion removes any subset $\mathcal{V}'$ where $l \in \mathcal{V}'$. Let $\mathcal{L}$ be the set of candidates where this assertion is expected to hold.

We collect together $\mathcal{A} = \{ Viable(w, \emptyset, \tau) \mid w \in \mathcal{W} \} \cup \{ NonViable(l, \mathcal{C} \setminus \mathcal{W} \setminus \{l\}, \tau) \mid l \in \mathcal{L} \}$. If these assertions hold, we only need to consider subsets of viable candidates $\mathbf{V} = \{ \mathcal{V}' \subseteq \mathcal{C} \mid \mathcal{W} \subseteq \mathcal{V}', \mathcal{V}' \cap \mathcal{L} = \emptyset \} \setminus \{ \mathcal{V} \}$. There are only $|\mathbf{V}|$ subsets to further examine, where

$$|\mathbf{V}| = \binom{|\mathcal{C} \setminus \mathcal{W} \setminus \mathcal{L}|}{M - |\mathcal{W}|} + \cdots + \binom{|\mathcal{C} \setminus \mathcal{W} \setminus \mathcal{L}|}{1} - 1$$

Selecting Assertions for the Remaining Subsets. We now need to select a set of assertions that rule out any alternate set of viable candidates $\mathcal{V}' \in \mathbf{V}$. To form these assertions, we visualise the space of alternate election outcomes as a tree. We use a branch-and-bound algorithm to find a set of assertions that, if true, will prune (invalidate) all branches of this tree. At the top level of this tree is a node for each possible $\mathcal{V}' \in \mathbf{V}$. Each node defines an (initially empty) sequence of candidate eliminations, π, and a set of viable candidates, $\mathcal{V}'$. These nodes form a frontier, F.

Our algorithm maintains a lower bound LB on the estimated auditing effort (EAE) required to invalidate all alternate election outcomes, initially setting LB $= 0$. For each node $n = (\emptyset, \mathcal{V}')$ in F, we consider the set of assertions that could invalidate the outcome that it represents. Two kinds of assertion are considered at this point:

- $Viable(c', \mathcal{L}, t)$ for each candidate $c' \in \mathcal{C}$ that does not appear in $\mathcal{V}'$, and whose first preference tally exceeds t proportion of the vote when only candidates in $\mathcal{L}$ are eliminated;
- $NonViable(c, \mathcal{C} \setminus \mathcal{V}', t)$ for each candidate $c \in \mathcal{V}'$ whose tally, if all candidates $c' \in \mathcal{C} \setminus \mathcal{V}'$ have been eliminated, falls below t proportion of the vote.

We assign to n the assertion a from this set with the smallest EAE (EAE$[n] = ASN(\{a\}, \alpha)$) where we use the method for estimating ASN previously described. If no such assertion can be formed for n, we give n an EAE of ∞, EAE$[n] = \infty$. We then select the node in F with the highest EAE to expand.

To expand a node $n = (\pi, \mathcal{V}')$, we consider the set of candidates in $\mathcal{C}$ that do not currently appear in π or $\mathcal{V}'$. We denote this set of 'unmentioned' candidates, $\mathcal{U}$. For each candidate $c' \in \mathcal{U}$, we form a child of n in which c' is appended to the front of π. For instance, the node $([c'], \mathcal{V}')$ represents an outcome in which c' is the last candidate to be eliminated, after which all remaining candidates, $c \in \mathcal{V}'$, have at least $t = T$ proportion of the cast votes. All unmentioned candidates are assumed to have been eliminated, in some order, before c'. For each newly created node, we look for an assertion that could invalidate the corresponding outcome. Two kinds of assertion are considered to rule out an outcome $n' = ([c'|\pi'], \mathcal{V}')$:

- $Viable(c', \mathcal{U} \setminus \{c'\}, t)$ for each candidate $c' \in U$ that has at least t proportion of the vote in the context where candidates $\mathcal{U} \setminus \{c'\}$ have been eliminated. Candidate c' thus cannot have been eliminated at this point;
- $IRV(c', c, \mathcal{U} \setminus \{c'\})$ for each candidate $c' \in U$ that has a higher tally than some candidate $c \in \pi' \cup \mathcal{V}'$ in the context where candidates $\mathcal{U} \setminus \{c'\}$ have been eliminated. Candidate c' thus cannot have been eliminated at this point.

We assign to each child of n the assertion a from this set with the smallest $ASN(\{a\}, \alpha)$, and replace n on our frontier with its children. If neither of the above two types of assertion can be created for a given child of n, the child is labelled with an EAE of ∞ ($EAE[n'] = \infty$). We continue to expand nodes in this fashion until we reach a leaf node, $l = (\pi, \mathcal{V}')$, where $\pi \cup \mathcal{V}' = \mathcal{C}$ (all candidates are mentioned either in the elimination sequence π or in the viable set $\mathcal{V}'$). We assign to l an invalidating assertion of the above two kinds, if possible. We consider all the nodes in the branch that l sits on, and select the node n_b associated with the least cost assertion a. We add a to our set of assertions to audit $\mathcal{A}$, prune n_b and all of its descendants from the tree, and update our lower bound on audit cost LB to $\max(LB, EAE[a])$. We then look at all nodes on our frontier that can be pruned with an assertion that has an EAE $\leqslant$ LB. We add those assertions to $\mathcal{A}$, and prune the nodes from the frontier. The algorithm stops when the frontier is empty. If we discover a branch whose best assertion has an EAE of ∞, the algorithm stops in failure—indicating that a full manual count of the election is required.

This branch-and-bound algorithm is a variation of that described by [1,4] for generating an audit specification for an IRV election. It has been altered for the context where the ultimate outcome is a set of winning candidates—the viable candidates—and not one winner, left standing after all others are eliminated.

5 Auditing Delegate Assignment

The Hamilton method for proportional representation is used to assign delegates to viable candidates. It might appear that auditing the Hamilton method requires checking some delicate results, for instance, whether candidate A received at least 2 delegate quotas when candidate A actually received 2.001 delegate quotas. However, this is not necessary, because candidate A can receive 2 delegates without having at least 2 delegate quotas. For example, if A receives 1.999 quotas A may still end up with 2 delegates. Our auditing method avoids checking such things.

The audit instead examines all pairs of viable candidates, including those receiving no delegates. For each pair of viable candidates n and m we check whether $(q_n - (a_n - 1)) < 1 + (q_m - (a_m - 1))$ which requires that the quota of n is not 1 more than the quota for m, after removing all received delegates but the last. This can be equivalently rewritten as

$$p_m > p_n + \frac{a_m - a_n - 1}{D}, \quad n, m \in \mathcal{V}, n \neq m. \tag{1}$$

In the case that q_m was rounded up and q_n was rounded down, this captures that the remainder for m was greater than the remainder for n: $p_m D - (a_m - 1) > p_n D - a_n$.

We show that if the delegates are wrong with respect to the true votes, then one of these assertions is violated.

Theorem 1. *Suppose the number of assigned delegates a_c to each viable delegate c is incorrect, then one of the assertions of Eq. 1 will be violated.*

Proof. Suppose a'_c is the *true* number of delegates that should have been awarded to each candidate c. Since $\sum_{c \in \mathcal{V}} a_c = D$ and $\sum_{c \in \mathcal{V}} a'_c = D$, and they differ, there must be at least one candidate $m \in \mathcal{V}$, where $a_m \geqslant a'_m + 1$, who was awarded too many delegates, and at least one $n \in \mathcal{V}$, where $a_n \leqslant a'_n - 1$, who was awarded too few.

Since a'_m is the true number of delegates awarded to m we know that the (*true*) proportion of the vote for m, p_m, must be (a) $p_m D < a'_m \leqslant a_m - 1$ if m was rounded up or (b) $p_m D < a'_m + 1 \leqslant a_m$ if m was rounded down. Similarly, since a'_n is the true number of delegates awarded to n we know that either (c) $p_n D \geqslant a'_n - 1 \geqslant a_n$ if n was rounded up, or (d) $p_n D \geqslant a'_n \geqslant a_n + 1$ if n was rounded down.

If we add these two inequalities for combinations (a)+(c) or (b)+(d) we get $p_m D + a_n < p_n D + a_m - 1$. For the combination (a)+(d) we get $p_m D + a_n + 1 < p_n D + a_m - 1$. Any of these cause the assertion $p_m > p_n + \frac{a_m - a_n - 1}{D}$ to be falsified. For the last case (b)+(c) we need a stricter comparison, which we obtain by comparing the remainders. Since m was rounded down and n was rounded up, we know that remainder for m was less than the remainder for n, i.e., $p_m D - a'_m < p_n D - (a'_n - 1)$. Hence $p_m D < p_n D + a'_m - (a'_n - 1) \leqslant p_n D + (a_m - 1) - a_n$. Again the assertion $p_m > p_n + \frac{a_m - a_n - 1}{D}$ is falsified. $\quad\square$

Example 5. Consider the delegate allocation of Example 3. Recall that the proportions of the qualified vote are $p_{Ann} = 0.7836$ and $p_{Bob} = 0.2136$. We audit that $p_{Ann} < p_{Bob} + 4/5$ and $p_{Bob} < p_{Ann} - 2/5$. These facts require much less work to prove, than for example auditing that $p_{Bob} > 1/5$. The margins associated with the above pairwise difference assertions are 1.1 and 0.12, respectively. Assuming an error rate of 0.002, and a risk limit of $\alpha = 5\%$, the ASNs associated with these assertions are 5, and 59, ballots.

6   Experiments

We consider the set of Hamiltonian elections conducted as part of the selection process for the 2020 Democratic National Convention (DNC) presidential nominee. Most of these primaries determine candidate viability via a plurality vote.

Several states, including Wyoming and Alaska, use IRV. We estimate the number of ballots we would need to check in a comparison audit of these primaries. For each of these primaries, we audit the viability of candidates on the basis of the statewide vote, and that each viable candidate deserved the delegates that were awarded to them. We consider only the delegates that are awarded on the basis of statewide vote totals (PLEO[8] and at-large) as these are readily available.[9] In each proportional DNC primary, viable candidates must attain at least 15% of the total votes cast.

The full code used to generate the assertions for each DNC primary, and estimate the ASN for each audit, is located at:

https://github.com/michelleblom/primaries

Table 1 reports the expected number of ballot samples required to perform three levels of audit in each plurality and IRV-based primary conducted for the 2020 DNC.[10] Level 1 checks only that the reportedly viable candidates have at least 15% of the vote, and all other candidates do not. Level 2 checks candidate viability and that each viable candidate c, with a_c allocated delegates, deserved at least $a_c - 1$ of them. We introduce this level because, as the table shows, sometimes the complete auditing of the final delegate counts is difficult. Level 3 checks candidate viability and that each viable candidate deserved all of their allocated delegates. The assertions required to check the allocation of a candidate's final delegate are the hardest to audit.

Of the primaries in Table 1, Maine (ME), New Hampshire (NH), Washington (WA), Texas (TX), Idaho (ID), Massachusetts (MA), California (CA), and Minnesota (MN), were considered to be close with differences of less than 10% in the statewide vote between the two leading candidates. In Maine, the difference in the statewide vote for Biden and Sanders was less than 1% of the cast vote. Auditing the Maine primary, however, is expected to require only a sample of 189 ballots. The Rhode Island (RI) primary, in contrast, requires a full manual recount. In RI, Sanders narrowly falls below the 15% threshold with 14.93% of the vote to Biden's 76.67%. The margins that determine the complexity of these audits are the extent to which a candidates' vote falls below or exceeds the relevant threshold, and the relative size of the remainders in candidates' delegate quotas as a proportion of the number of delegates available.

Table 2 contrasts several of the hardest primaries of Table 1 to audit with some of the easiest. We record, for each of these primaries: the number of at-large delegates being awarded; the delegate quotas computed for each viable candidate; the difference between the decimal portion of these quotas (the remainder)

---

[8] Party Leaders and Elected Officials.

[9] Data for plurality-based primaries was obtained from www.thegreenpapers.com/P20. Data for IRV-based primaries we consider was provided by the relevant state-level Democrats.

[10] A small number of DNC 2020 primaries that did not use proportional allocation of delegates were not considered, in addition to those for which we could not obtain data.

Table 1. Estimated sample size required to audit viability and delegate distribution (PLEO and at-large) in all proportional (plurality or IRV-based) DNC primaries in 2020 for which data was available. Levels 1, 2, and 3 audit candidate viability, that each viable candidate deserved almost all of their allocated delegates, and that they deserved all of their delegates, respectively. An error rate of 0.002 (an expectation of 1 error per 1,000 ballots) was used in the estimation of sample sizes. The symbol '–' indicates that a full recount is required. The number of candidates ($|\mathcal{C}|$) and total number of cast ballots ($|\mathcal{B}|$) is stated for each election.

Plurality-based primaries

State	$|\mathcal{C}|$	$|\mathcal{B}|$	ASN ($\alpha = 5\%$)			State	$|\mathcal{C}|$	$|\mathcal{B}|$	ASN ($\alpha = 5\%$)		
			Level 1	Level 2	Level 3				Level 1	Level 2	Level 3
AL	15	452,093	182	182	1,352	NC	16	1,332,382	350	350	808
AR	18	229,122	121	121	1,154	NE	4	164,582	925	925	925
AZ	12	536,509	71	71	120	NH	34	298,377	104	104	155
CA	21	5,784,364	395	1,258	3,187,080	NJ	3	958,202	4,514	4,515	4,514
CO	13	960,128	42	42	–	NM	7	247,880	1,812	1,812	1,812
CT	4	260,750	174	174	174	NY	11	752,515	56	731	486,495
DC	5	110,688	334	334	334	OH	11	894,383	61	334	–
DE	3	91,682	80	80	80	OK	14	304,281	649	649	649
FL	16	1,739,214	91	208	766	OR	5	618,711	111	111	191
GA	12	1,086,729	107	218	218	PA	3	1,595,508	48	167	642
ID	14	1,323,509	143	143	143	PR	11	7,022	412	412	412
IL	12	1,674,133	44	140	620	RI	7	103,982	–	–	–
IN	9	474,800	391	391	391	SC	12	539,263	165	165	34,546
KY	11	537,905	209	209	209	SD	2	52,661	13	13	216
LA	14	267,286	79	98	98	TN	16	516,250	235	235	1,203
MA	18	1,417,498	185	185	832	TX	17	2,094,428	1,282	1,282	2,133
MD	15	1,050,773	83	170	170	UT	15	220,582	262	262	781
ME	13	205,937	189	189	189	VA	14	1,323,509	143	204	1,309
MI	16	1,587,679	57	118	–	VT	17	158,032	289	289	508
MN	16	744,198	309	309	6,195	WA	15	1,558,776	103	127	617
MO	23	666,112	44	130	–	WI	14	925,065	44	144	878
MS	10	274,391	–	–	–	WV	12	187,482	213	213	213
MT	4	149,973	5,159	5,159	5,159						
IRV-based primaries											
AK	9	19,811	88	88	88	WY	9	15,428	66	87	452

divided by the number of available delegates; and the estimated auditing effort (ASN) for the primary. For the first four primaries in the table, the last awarded at-large delegate is the hardest to audit.

The use of IRV for determining candidate viability does not make a Hamiltonian election more difficult to audit. While more assertions are created to audit an IRV-based primary, the difficulty of any audit is based on the cost (ballot samples required) of its most expensive assertion. Since all assertions are tested on each ballot examined, the principle cost is retrieving the correct ballot. The audit specifications generated for the Wyoming and Alaskan primaries contain 78 and 89 assertions, respectively. The number of assertions formed for a plurality-based primary is proportional to the number of candidates. NH, involving the most candidates at 34, has 48 assertions to audit.

Table 2. Hard (top) and relatively easy (bottom) primaries for which to audit the last assigned at-large delegate to each candidate. The number of at-large delegates D; the delegate quotas for Biden and Sanders; and the difference between the remainder of their quotas (divided by D) is reported, since this corresponds to the tightness of Eq. (1).

State	D	Quotas		Rem.	ASN
		Biden	Sanders	Diff./D	
CA	90	50.688	39.312	0.004	3.2×10^6
MO	15	9.524	5.476	0.003	–
NY	61	47.629	13.371	0.004	486,495
SC	12	8.533	3.467	0.006	34,546
ME	5	2.050	1.993	0.19	189
AZ	14	8.010	5.990	0.07	120
OR	13	9.948	3.052	0.07	191

The computational cost of generating these audit specifications is not significant. On a machine with an Intel Xeon Platinum 8176 chip (2.1 GHz), and 1 TB of RAM, the generation of an audit specification for Wyoming and Alaska takes 0.3 s and 0.4 s, respectively. The time required to generate an audit for each of the plurality-based primaries in Table 1 ranges from 0.2 ms to 0.24 s (and 0.03 s on average).

7   Conclusion

We provide an effective method for auditing delegate allocation by proportional representation (the Hamilton method), the first we know of for elections of this kind. Usually the audit only requires examining a small number of ballots. This could be used for primary elections in the USA and other elections in Russia, Ukraine, Tunisia, Taiwan, Namibia and Hong Kong.

We provide a version suitable for Democratic primaries in Alaska, Hawaii, Kansas, and Wyoming, which use a modified form where viability is decided using IRV.

To audit these elections we defined a new assertion for pairwise differences and corresponding assorter, which may be useful for auditing other methods.

References

1. Blom, M., Stuckey, P.J., Teague, V.J.: Ballot-polling risk limiting audits for IRV elections. In: Krimmer, R., Volkamer, M., Cortier, V., Goré, R., Hapsara, M., Serdült, U., Duenas-Cid, D. (eds.) E-Vote-ID 2018. LNCS, vol. 11143, pp. 17–34. Springer, Cham (2018). https://doi.org/10.1007/978-3-030-00419-4_2
2. Blom, M., Stuckey, P.J., Teague, V.J.: Computing the Margin of Victory in preferential parliamentary elections. In: Krimmer, R., Volkamer, M., Cortier, V., Goré, R., Hapsara, M., Serdült, U., Duenas-Cid, D. (eds.) E-Vote-ID 2018. LNCS, vol. 11143, pp. 1–16. Springer, Cham (2018). https://doi.org/10.1007/978-3-030-00419-4_1
3. Blom, M., Teague, V., Stuckey, P.J., Tidhar, R.: Efficient computation of exact IRV margins. In: European Conference on Artificial Intelligence (ECAI), pp. 480–488 (2016)
4. Blom, M.L., Stuckey, P.J., Teague, V.: Risk-limiting audits for IRV elections. CoRR abs/1903.08804 (2019). http://arxiv.org/abs/1903.08804
5. Kroll, J.A., Halderman, J.A., Felten, E.W.: Efficiently auditing multi-level elections. In: Krimmer, R., Volkamer, M. (eds.) Proceedings of Electronic Voting 2014 (EVOTE 2014), pp. 93–101. TUT Press (2014)
6. Lindeman, M., Stark, P.: A gentle introduction to risk-limiting audits. IEEE Secur. Priv. 10, 42–49 (2012)
7. Lindeman, M., Stark, P., Yates, V.: BRAVO: ballot-polling risk-limiting audits to verify outcomes. In: Proceedings of the 2011 Electronic Voting Technology Workshop/Workshop on Trustworthy Elections (EVT/WOTE 2011). USENIX (2012)
8. Sarwate, A., Checkoway, S., Shacham, H.: Risk-limiting audits and the margin of victory in nonplurality elections. Politics Policy 3(3), 29–64 (2013)
9. Stark, P.: Conservative statistical post-election audits. Annals of Applied Statistics (2008)
10. Stark, P.: Super-simple simultaneous single-ballot risk-limiting audits. In: Proceedings of the 2010 Electronic Voting Technology Workshop/Workshop on Trustworthy Elections (EVT/WOTE 2010). USENIX (2010)
11. Stark, P.B.: Sets of half-average nulls generate risk-limiting audits: Shangrla. In: Bernhard, M., Bracciali, A., Camp, L.J., Matsuo, S., Maurushat, A., Rønne, P.B., Sala, M. (eds.) Financial Cryptography and Data Security, pp. 319–336. Springer International Publishing, Cham (2020)
12. Stark, P.B., Teague, V.: Verifiable European elections: risk-limiting audits for D'Hondt and its relatives. USENIX J. Election Technol. Syst. (JETS) 1(3), 18–39 (2014). https://www.usenix.org/jets/issues/0301/stark

Cast-as-Intended: A Formal Definition and Case Studies

Peter B. Rønne[✉], Peter Y. A. Ryan, and Ben Smyth

DCS & Interdisciplinary Centre for Security, Reliability and Trust,
Esch-sur-Alzette, Luxembourg

Abstract. Verifiable voting systems allow voters to check whether their ballot is correctly recorded (individual verifiability) and allow anyone to check whether votes expressed in recorded ballots are correctly counted (universal verifiability). This suffices to ensure that honest voters' votes are correctly counted, assuming ballots are properly generated.

Achieving ballot assurance, i.e., assuring each voter that their vote is correctly encoded inside their ballot, whilst ensuring privacy, is a challenging aspect of voting system design. This assurance property is known as *cast-as-intended*. Unlike many properties of voting systems, it has yet to be formalised. We provide the first formal definition and apply our definition to MarkPledge, Prêt à Voter, Selene, ThreeBallot, and schemes based upon Benaloh challenges.

1 Introduction

End-to-end Verifiable (E2E V) voting systems produce evidence of correct operation: Cast ballots (which contain the vote in encrypted or encoded form) are published on a public bulletin board (ledger), so voters can check whether their ballot is collected (individual verifiability), and tallies are coupled with proofs, so anyone can check whether votes expressed in collected ballots are correctly counted (universal verifiability). By additionally providing means to check whether votes are correctly encoded in ballots, we achieve end-to-end verifiability. This is not yet enough to guarantee that the outcome is correct, for this we need extra measures such as eligibility verifiablity to prevent ballot stuffing and clash attacks[1] etc., but this is beyond the scope of this paper.

For many end-to-end verifiability systems (but not all, e.g., [29,30]), ballots are constructed using cryptographic operations, which are typically beyond the mathematical capabilities of even the most studious scholar. Moreover, assurance of correct encoding has to be provided without undermining privacy. Arguably, providing ballot assurance, in the face of coercion threats, is the most challenging aspect of End-to-end verifiability. Nonetheless, various ingenious methods have been devised to provide voters with suitable, non-transferable assurance.

One notion of checking whether ballots correctly encode votes is known as *cast-as-intended* (aka *ballot assurance*).

---

[1] Where more than one voter gets assigned the same ballot.

© International Financial Cryptography Association 2021
M. Bernhard et al. (Eds.): FC 2021 Workshops, LNCS 12676, pp. 251–262, 2021.
https://doi.org/10.1007/978-3-662-63958-0_22

– *Cast-as-intended.* A voter can check whether their ballot correctly expresses their vote.

Discussion of cast-as-intended originates from Chaum [7,8] and was taken further by Neff [27], Adida & Neff [1], and Benaloh [3,4]. Yet, formal study of cast-as-intended is limited: Unlike other properties of voting systems, a definition of cast-as-intended has yet to be formalised. (Cf. the rich literature on formal definitions of verifiability [10,18,20–22,24,36,38,39] and privacy [5,6,11,13,15, 16,20,21,25,26,34,37,40].). Here, we formalise cast-as-intended as a game in the computational model of cryptography, thus filling a gap in the literature.

In this paper we consider two categories of End-to-End Verifiable voting system: *conventional*, wherein each voter checks that a *protected ballot*[2] that represents their vote, typically an encryption of their vote, appears on the bulletin board, and *tracker-based*, where each voter checks their (plaintext) vote appears in the election outcome, using a private tracker. Examples of the former include Prêt à Voter, Helios, and Belenios. Examples of the latter, Selene [32] and sElect [23]. Cast-as-intended is achieved very differently across these categories, so we apply our definition to examples in each. In the first category, voters cast ballots that are encryptions of their votes and tallies should correspond votes embedded in those ballots. Since voters cannot compute ciphertexts, they rely on a device or process to encrypt. Assuring the voter that the resulting ballot correctly encodes their vote without undermining privacy, and in a manner that is usable and understandable, is highly non-trivial, and various techniques have been presented in the literature.

The second category provides verifiability in a more direct and transparent fashion: the voter is able to identify their (plaintext) vote in the tally. In fact, such systems provide *tallied as intended* verification and, in contrast to the conventional schemes, cast as intended is not strictly necessary. Some subtleties nonetheless remain. For example, each voter should be assured that their tracker is unique. We discuss the details later.

For conventional voting systems, in contrast to tracker-based schemes, it is essential that the voter be able to verify that their vote is correctly embedded in the ballot. This is typically achieved via some form of cut-and-choose mechanism: the device is required to commit to one or more encryptions of the voter's vote and all but one of these are randomly selected then audited to confirm that the correct vote was encoded. The remaining, non-audited ballot can then be cast.

Benaloh proposed a mechanism, in effect a sequential cut-and-choose, to provide such assurance [3, §4.2]: A voter inputs a vote into a device, the device computes an encryption of the vote, and commits to the resulting ciphertext, by printing the ciphertext or digitally signing it, for instance. Next, the voter chooses to audit or cast the ciphertext. For the former, if auditing fails, the voter should raise an alarm, otherwise (auditing succeeds), the audit or cast process repeats, until the voter chooses to cast.

Auditing typically reveals coins used to construct ciphertexts, enabling ciphertext reconstruction, which suffices to convince a voter that their ballot

---

[2] To use Rivest's terminology.

expresses their vote, assuming they can reconstruct the ciphertext themselves (using a system they trust) or a trusted third party can. Thus, cast-as-intended can be unconditionally achieved, assuming perfect correctness of the underlying encryption scheme.

Reliance on a trusted system or trusted third party to perform ballot audits may seem disingenuous; after all, trust is contrary to the goal of verifiability. However, ciphertexts can be reconstructed by multiple systems, third parties, or both, thereby removing the need to trust any individual device or service.

Most schemes that reveal coins do not allow audited ballots to be cast, to avoid compromising receipt-freeness. (A notable exception is Neff's Mark-Pledge [28].) A consequence of this observation is that ballot assurance is probabilistic rather than deterministic.

Sidebar 1. Preliminaries: Games and notation

Games are probabilistic algorithms that output booleans. An adversary *wins* a game by causing it to output true ($\top$) and the adversary's *success* in a game $\mathsf{Exp}(\cdot)$, denoted $\mathsf{Succ}(\mathsf{Exp}(\cdot))$, is the probability that the adversary wins, i.e., $\mathsf{Succ}(\mathsf{Exp}(\cdot)) = \Pr[\mathsf{Exp}(\cdot) = \top]$. Adversaries are *stateful*, i.e., information persists across invocations of an adversary in a game.

We let $A(x_1, \ldots, x_n; r)$ denote the output of probabilistic algorithm A on inputs $x_1, \ldots, x_n$ and coins r, and we let $A(x_1, \ldots, x_n)$ denote $A(x_1, \ldots, x_n; r)$, where coins r are chosen uniformly at random from the coin space of algorithm A. Moreover, we let $x \leftarrow T$ denote assignment of T to x, and we write $(x_1, \ldots, x_{|T|}) \leftarrow T$ for $x \leftarrow T$; $x_1 \leftarrow x[1]; \ldots; x_{|T|} \leftarrow x[|T|]$, when T is a vector.

---

2 Security Definition

For schemes in the conventional category, cast-as-intended requires ballots be correctly constructed. For many schemes, correct ballot construction simply requires computing a valid encryption of the vote, with respect to the public key of the tabulation process. For universally-verifiable voting systems, it follows that if a voter's ballot correctly encodes the voter's vote, and that ballot is correctly tallied, then the voter's vote will be correctly included in the tally.

We formalise cast-as-intended in the syntax proposed by Smyth, Frink & Clarkson [38]: Construction is defined by a probabilistic polynomial-time algorithm Vote, wherein

> Vote takes as input a public key pk, a voter's vote v, some number of candidates nc, and a security parameter κ, and outputs a ballot b or error symbol $\bot$, where vote v should be selected from a sequence $1, \ldots, nc$ of candidates.

Universal verifiability assures us that votes expressed in ballots constructed using algorithm Vote will be correctly counted, and cast-as-intended enables voters to check that their vote is expressed in a ballot constructed using algorithm Vote.

Ballot construction differs between systems. In some cases, the ballot may be generated by software on the voter's computer. Other cases may be more elaborate, e.g., Prêt à Voter involves authorities generating and distributing blank two-column paper ballots, and voters physically marking their selections before discarding the left column. Yet further systems (e.g., code-voting, PunchScan, Scantegrity, and PGD) encode votes by means other than encryption, using material from an initialisation phase. For example, in code voting, a correspondence between vote options and codes is committed in print on the code sheets, and this should be consistent with the mapping of codes to votes that is committed to the bulletin board. Some verifiable schemes even avoid cryptography, e.g., Randell/Ryan [29] and ThreeBallot [30].

Formalising cast-as-intended involves defining what it means for a ballot to be correctly constructed and the means to verify this, which can be captured as a game that challenges an adversary to achieve the opposite: To dupe a voter into believing their ballot encodes their vote, when it does not. We model ballot construction as an algorithm $\mathcal{A}$ parametrised by a public key pk, some number of candidates nc, and a security parameter κ, and we model the voter as an algorithm $\mathcal{V}$ that takes a vote v and a distinct security parameter $\hat{\kappa}$ as input. The latter security parameter determines the probability of breaking cast-as-intended, whereas the former determines the probability of breaking other security properties, such as individual and universal verifiability. We use distinct security parameters, because the complexity of algorithm $\mathcal{V}$ should be upper-bounded by the capability of a voter's mind, whereas algorithm $\mathcal{A}$ should be computable by machine.

The system is assumed to be adversarial and, to achieve cast-as-intended, some trustworthy device is also required. (Alternatively, a multitude of devices may be used, only one of which need be trustworthy.) We model such a device as an algorithm $\mathcal{T}$ that takes the same parameters as algorithm $\mathcal{A}$. Hence, ballot construction is modelled by the computation $b \leftarrow \mathcal{V}^{\mathcal{T},\mathcal{A}}(v, \hat{\kappa})$, where algorithm $\mathcal{T}$ is parameterised by pk, nc, and κ. If cast-as-intended is achieved, then such computations should result in a ballot $b = \mathsf{Vote}(pk, v, nc, \kappa; r)$ for some coins r or the error symbol $\bot$ (representing a voter detecting malice), which leads to our security definition (Definition 1). In that definition, we extend algorithm $\mathcal{A}$ with the capabilities of a malicious administrator that defines the public key, the voter's vote, and the number of candidates, when parametrised by security parameters κ and $\hat{\kappa}$.

Definition 1 (Cast-as-intended). *Let $\mathcal{V}$, $\mathcal{T}$, Vote, and $\mathcal{A}$ be probabilistic polynomial-time algorithms, κ and $\hat{\kappa}$ be security parameters, and* Cast-As-Intended *be the following game.*

Cast-As-Intended$(\mathcal{V}, \mathcal{T}, \mathsf{Vote}, \mathcal{A}, \kappa, \hat{\kappa})$
$\quad = (pk, v, nc) \leftarrow \mathcal{A}(\kappa, \hat{\kappa})$
$\quad b \leftarrow \mathcal{V}^{\mathcal{T}(pk,nc,\kappa),\mathcal{A}}(v, \hat{\kappa})$
$\quad$ **return** $\forall r \,.\, b \neq \mathsf{Vote}(pk, v, nc, \kappa; r) \wedge b \neq \bot \wedge 1 \leq v \leq nc$

We say $\mathcal{V}, \mathcal{T},$ Vote *satisfies* $\delta(\hat{\kappa})$-*cast-as-intended, if for all probabilistic polynomial-time adversaries* $\mathcal{A}$, *there exists a function* δ *and for all security parameters* κ *and* $\hat{\kappa}$, *we have* Succ(Cast-As-Intended($\mathcal{V}, \mathcal{T},$ Vote, $\mathcal{A}, \kappa, \hat{\kappa}$)) $\leq$ $\delta(\hat{\kappa}) +$ negl(κ).

An adversary $\mathcal{A}$ that wins Cast-As-Intended is able to identify a strategy, including choosing a public key pk, a vote v, and a number of candidates nc, such that a voter $\mathcal{V}$ will be deceived into casting a ballot b that does not express their vote v. That is, winning signifies an attack against cast-as-intended.

An election scheme satisfying cast-as-intended guarantees that a voter can check whether their ballot is an output of algorithm Vote, parametrised with their vote v along with public key pk, number of candidates nc, and security parameter κ, for some coins r. Supposing universal verifiability, a voter can check whether the election outcome corresponds to votes expressed in tallied ballots.

Our definition assumes that each voter performs verification steps correctly. Beyond the definition's scope, we must consider the practicality of voters correctly performing verification. Thus, even when a voting system satisfies cast-as-intended, that system may still be vulnerable to attacks arising from voter error or negligence (possibly attacker induced).

Let us finally remark on an important point, namely, that the definition depends crucially on the protocol description for the honest voter $\mathcal{V}$. If we have a protocol that always aborts the casting, then this would reduce the adversary's advantage to zero and we would claim it satisfies cast-as-intended. Hence, we also require a soundness condition asserting that $\mathcal{V}$ should only abort if the ballot is ill-formed, or more exactly, that this should only occur with bounded probability: We assume that $\mathcal{V}$ only aborts when indeed she has detected the b is ill-formed. In practice, whether we can check if a voter is maliciously aborting enters into the territory of *dispute resolution*.

3   Examples

3.1   Prêt à Voter

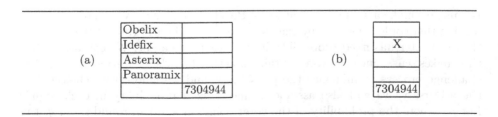

Fig. 1. Prêt à Voter ballot (a) and receipt (b) for vote "Idefix"

In Prêt à Voter [9] the voter gets a ballot with a left and right hand side (see Fig. 1). The candidates are listed in plaintext in a random order on the left hand side (LHS) and this order is embedded cryptographically in a value on the right hand side (RHS). In the privacy of the booth, the voter marks their selection on the right hand side against the candidate(s) as indicated on the LHS. Once they have made their mark(s) they detach and destroy the LHS, i.e. removes the plaintext list of candidates, thus concealing the selection and creating the receipt.

The universal verifiability of the scheme will afterwards guarantee that the vote is processed according to the encrypted order. The ballot is thus correctly constructed, if the encrypted candidate order on the RHS matches the one displayed in plaintext on the LHS. To check this the voter can perform ballot audits to verify this, but cannot verify the actual cast ballot. Additionally, ballots can be randomly audited by observers. Note that for Prêt à Voter ballot auditing can be delegated and is entirely privacy preserving and indeed dispute resolving.

Let us first consider the case where voters are instructed to choose $\hat{\kappa}$ ballots and audit all of these but one. In a worst case scenario, the adversary is able to inject a chosen number of maliciously created ballots into this selection $\hat{\kappa}$ ballots. The adversary obtains the best advantage by injecting precisely one ballot and wins if this is used for vote-casting, i.e. $P_{\text{Adv succ}} = 1/\hat{\kappa}$, i.e. $\delta \geq 1/\hat{\kappa}$.

We can also consider the case, where a voter audits a ballot with a probability p. We further assume that the probability that a ballot is audited by observers is q. We then find

$$P_{\text{Adv succ}} = (1 - q) \cdot (1 - p).$$

Using the arguments for Benaloh challenges below, this also holds if the voter audits multiple times with the same probability.

Here we are assuming that the random audits are unpredictable and that chain-of-custody of the set of ballot forms is guaranteed, i.e. fake ballot forms cannot be injected after the observer audits are performed. In fact, observer audits can be performed before, during and after voting, so this assumption is quite mild.

3.2   Benaloh

Let us now make a simplified analysis of Benaloh challenges. We ignore all information that could be leaked by the vote choice used by the voter. Let us assume that the voter has fixed probability in each round to audit. We can argue that this makes sense since the voter obtains no other knowledge during the Benaloh challenge process to influence the probability, and we ignore vote choices. For the adversary, we will also assume he has a fixed probability in each round. Let p_i denote the probability of the voter doing an audit in round i and q_i the probability that the adversary changes a vote in this round.

The probability that the adversary is successful is obtained by sum of the probabilities that he is successful in round i which is the probability that the voter challenges all earlier rounds, that the adversary was honest in all of these, and then he cheated in round i. That is

$$P_{\text{Adv succ}} = \sum_{i=1}^{\infty} p_1 \cdots p_{i-1}(1-q_1)\cdots(1-q_{i-1})(1-p_i)q_i.$$

We only aim to make a simplified analysis and we do this by assuming that the probabilities will not depend on the rounds. For the voter this could happen if we specify to the voter to make an audit with a certain probability. Then we get

$$P_{\text{Adv succ}} = \sum_{i=1}^{\infty} p^{i-1}(1-q)^{i-1}(1-p)q = \frac{(1-p)q}{1-p(1-q)}.$$

This function is increasing in cheat probability q. Thus if the adversary wants to maximise this, he chooses $q = 1$ i.e. to always cheat. The winning probability is then

$$P_{\text{Adv succ}} = 1 - p,$$

corresponding to the probability that the voter casts in the first round. That is we have $\delta \geq 1 - p$. Note that the average number of challenge rounds in the vote casting is $1/(1-p)$ (without an adversary present). Abusing notation, we thus have that $\delta \geq 1/\hat{\kappa}$ where $\hat{\kappa}$ is the number of challenge rounds.

Note however, that if the voter is not prescribed a certain audit probability p and doesn't care about the effort of doing the audits, then $P_{\text{Adv succ}}$ is a decreasing function in p i.e. the voter would choose $p \approx 1$, i.e. to almost always audit. A full analysis should be done via game theory, see also [12].

3.3 MarkPledge

MarkPledge [27], is of particular interest in the context of cast-as-intended as it provides assurance of correctness of the ballot that is actually cast. This is in contrast to cut-and-choose style ballot assurance, e.g. Benaloh challenges, where an audited ballot cannot be cast.

At a very high level, MarkPlegde involves the voter interacting with a device in the booth to perform an interactive zero-knowledge proof of correctness of the ballot. In essence, this proof serves to convince the voter that a 1 is encrypted against the candidate of choice and a transcript of this proof is printed on the receipt. As part of this interactive ZK proof, the voter provides a random challenge, e.g. a string of k digits.

This alone would not of course be receipt-free, so the chosen vote is masked by the device constructing fake ZK proof transcripts that an encryption of 1 against the other candidates. The device also provides a ZK proof that there is exactly one encryption of 1 and the other encryptions are of 0. Anyone later seeing the receipt cannot distinguish the real and fake proofs and hence cannot identify which candidate was selected. Only the voter will know for which candidate they executed the real, interactive proof.

During tabulation, the candidates with an encryption of zero are weeded out, exploiting the homomorphic properties of the encryption, leaving just those with the encryption of 1.

The ballot assurance provided by MarkPledge is therefore dependent on the size of the challenge space. So if the challenges are strings of k^* digits, we get a bound on the chance of the device being about to cheat the voter of $p = 1/10^{k^*}$.

3.4 ThreeBallot

In the ThreeBallot scheme by Rivest [30] a voter distributes their vote intent over three ballots. The scheme is interesting in this context as it does not employ cryptography, and voter can tell directly whether the (three)ballot is correctly constructed. We will also assume here that mechanisms are in place to ensure that the (three)ballot is well formed, i.e. obeys the rules (two votes for the chosen candidate and one for the others).

The ballots contain unique serial numbers. These are sent to a Bulletin Board, but the voter chooses one of the single ballots and gets a copy of it. The voter's choice of which of the three ballots should be concealed from the system. At home, the voter checks that the single ballot with the corresponding serial number appears online and that the partial vote choice in that ballot is correctly stored.

Note that this example is special since this verification step is also a stored-as-cast verification. With a malicious authority involved the serial numbers might not be unique, and could give rise to clash attacks. In this case it is not really meaningful to say that the displayed ballot is the voters ballot, since it will be assigned to one or more voters. However, in the scope of cast-as-intended, we will focus on a single voter setting, and leave such problems to other parts of verifiability.

If we assume that the voter chooses the receipt slip uniformly at random and the adversary is unaware of this choice, then the adversary can try to change one single ballot of three, and will succeed with an undetected change of the ballot with probability 2/3. Thus $\delta \geq 2/3$

Table 1. The different cast-as-intended protocols and their respective cast-as-intended δ-value. $\hat{\kappa}_1 = (1 - p) \cdot (1 - q)$, $\hat{\kappa}_2 = (1 - p)$. We also note if the verification checks, or parts thereof, are delegable.

Scheme	Prêt à Voter	Benaloh	MarkPledge	ThreeBallot	Selene
δ	$1/\hat{\kappa}_1$	$1/\hat{\kappa}_2$	$1/10^{\hat{\kappa}}$	2/3	0
Delegable	✓	✓	✗	✓	✗

4   Tracker-Based Schemes

Ryan, Rønne, & Iovino recently [32] introduced an orthogonal approach in which the cast-as-intended is first established after tallying. For traditional voting systems, voters perform a cast-as-intended check to ensure their ballot correctly expresses their vote, an individual-verifiability check to ensure their ballot is collected, and a universal-verifiability check to ensure their vote is counted. By comparison, Ryan, Rønne, & Iovino propose that voters simply check whether their plaintext vote is present in the tally, using a private tracker—the standard early cast-as-intended and individual-verifiability checks are not necessary; a more direct, more transparent form of verification is achieved. Voting systems Selene [32] and sElect [23] achieve this new form of tracker-based verifiability, with the main difference being that Selene first releases the tracker to the voter after tallying to provide coercion-mitigation - the voter can equivocate the tracker to a tracker for another vote.

4.1   Example: Selene

Selene, [32] is an example of a tracker-based verifiable scheme in which the voter can confirm directly that their vote is included in the tally. The mechanism can be applied to various forms of e-voting schemes [2,17,31,33], has been studied formally [19,42], and has been studied from a usability viewpoint [14,41]. In Selene the voters hold secret trapdoor keys. After the end of election and after the tally has been made public, the voters will receive an cryptographic term, called the *alpha* term. This is combined with a public beta term which is available on the bulletin board to form an ElGamal encryption of the tracker under the voter's trapdoor key. The voter can now decrypt this to retrieve their tracker. The tracker is then used to check the plaintext vote on the final tally board.

The authorities could send a fake alpha term to the voter, however, as is proven in [32] the chance of such an alpha term opening to an existing tracker is negligible assuming that the authorities do not know the voter's trapdoor key and under a computational assumption (hardness of computing g^{x^2} given g^x without knowing x). Thus if the voter's trapdoor key is not leaked and the computational assumption holds, then δ is negligible. This presupposes that the proofs and verifiable computations on the bulletin board are verified, which can be done by the voter herself, or any third party.

In a tracker based scheme, traditional cast-as-intended and individual- and universal-verifiable checks are all bundled into a single tallied-as-cast check.

5   Outlook

Verifiability has emerged as a means to ensure integrity of elections. Several aspects of verifiability have been identified: well studied notions of individual- and universal-verifiability, and the seemingly less well understood notion of cast-as-intended. We propose the first formal definition of cast-as-intended, closing a gap in the literature and enabling analysis of systems purporting to achieve cast-as-intended.

Future work could flesh out and make more rigorous the arguments we sketch for MarkPledge, Prêt à Voter, Selene, ThreeBallot, and schemes based upon Benaloh challenges. Other voting systems could also be analysed, e.g., Pretty Good Democracy and Bingo Voting. It would also be interesting to analyse any relation between cast-as-intended and dispute resolution, privacy during ballot construction, or both. Perhaps most importantly: A suitable security notion to bridge the gap between individual verifiability and cast-as-intended should be sought, see also [35] which points out that individual- and universal-verifiability plus cast-as-intended does not yield end-to-end verifiable voting systems, e.g. clash attacks are not captured. It would also be interesting to see to which extent trust can be removed from the cast-as-intended verification [18].

Another interesting future path is to relate the parameter $\hat{\kappa}$ more tightly to usability in order to compare the achieved level of security to the amount and complexity of user-interaction required. We already did a preliminary attempt of this with the values shown in Table 1 where $\hat{\kappa}$ represents the number of inter-actions or the number of digits a voter needs to handle, but comparing and understanding the usability, especially across systems, will require actual user studies.

Acknowledgements. This work received financial support from the Luxembourg National Research Fund (FNR) under the PolLux/CORE project STV (12685695) and the FNR CORE project EquiVox (13643617).

References

1. Adida, B., Andrew Neff, C.: Ballot casting assurance. In: EVT 2006: Electronic Voting Technology Workshop. USENIX Association (2006)
2. Alsadi, M., Schneider, S.: Verify my vote: voter experience. In: E-Vote-ID 2020, p. 280 (2020)
3. Benaloh, J.: Simple verifiable elections. In: EVT 2006: Electronic Voting Technology Workshop. USENIX Association (2006)
4. Benaloh, J.: Ballot casting assurance via voter-initiated poll station auditing. In: EVT 2007: Electronic Voting Technology Workshop. USENIX Association (2007)
5. Bernhard, D., Cortier, V., Galindo, D., Pereira, O., Warinschi, B.: SoK: a comprehensive analysis of game-based ballot privacy definitions. In: S&P 2015: 36th Security and Privacy Symposium, pp. 499–516. IEEE Computer Society (2015)
6. Blanchet, B., Smyth, B.: Automated reasoning for equivalences in the applied pi calculus with barriers. J. Comput. Secur. **26**(3), 367–422 (2018)
7. Chaum, D.: Secret-ballot receipts and transparent integrity. Better and less-costly electronic voting at polling places. IEEE S&P **4** (2004)
8. Chaum, D.: Secret-ballot receipts: true voter-verifiable elections. IEEE Secur. Privacy **2**(1), 38–47 (2004)
9. Chaum, D., Ryan, P.Y.A., Schneider, S.: A practical voter-verifiable election scheme. In: di Vimercati, S.C., Syverson, P., Gollmann, D. (eds.) ESORICS 2005. LNCS, vol. 3679, pp. 118–139. Springer, Heidelberg (2005). https://doi.org/10.1007/11555827_8

10. Cortier, V., Galindo, D., Küsters, R., Mueller, J., Truderung, T.: SoK: verifiability notions for e-voting protocols. In: S&P 2016: 37th IEEE Symposium on Security and Privacy, pp. 779–798. IEEE Computer Society (2016)
11. Cremers, C., Hirschi, L.: Improving automated symbolic analysis for e-voting protocols: a method based on sufficient conditions for ballot secrecy. arXiv, Report 1709.00194, September 2017
12. Culnane, C., Teague, V.: Strategies for voter-initiated election audits. In: Zhu, Q., Alpcan, T., Panaousis, E., Tambe, M., Casey, W. (eds.) GameSec 2016. LNCS, vol. 9996, pp. 235–247. Springer, Cham (2016). https://doi.org/10.1007/978-3-319-47413-7_14
13. Delaune, S., Kremer, S., Ryan, M.D.: Verifying privacy-type properties of electronic voting protocols. J. Comput. Secur. **17**(4), 435–487 (2009)
14. Distler, V., Zollinger, M.-L., Lallemand, C., Rønne, P.B., Ryan, P.Y.A., Koenig, V.: Security - visible, yet unseen? In: Brewster, S.A., Fitzpatrick, G., Cox, A.L., Kostakos, V., (eds.) Proceedings of the 2019 CHI Conference on Human Factors in Computing Systems, CHI 2019, Glasgow, Scotland, UK, 04–09 May 2019, p. 605. ACM (2019)
15. Fraser, A., Quaglia, E.A., Smyth, B.: A critique of game-based definitions of receipt-freeness for voting. In: Steinfeld, R., Yuen, T.H. (eds.) ProvSec 2019. LNCS, vol. 11821, pp. 189–205. Springer, Cham (2019). https://doi.org/10.1007/978-3-030-31919-9_11
16. Haines, T., Smyth, B.: Surveying definitions of coercion resistance. Cryptology ePrint Archive, Report 2019/822 (2020)
17. Iovino, V., Rial, A., Rønne, P.B., Ryan, P.Y.A.: Using selene to verify your vote in JCJ. In: Brenner, M., et al. (eds.) FC 2017. LNCS, vol. 10323, pp. 385–403. Springer, Cham (2017). https://doi.org/10.1007/978-3-319-70278-0_24
18. Iovino, V., Rial, A., Rønne, P.B., Ryan, P.Y.A.: Universal unconditional verifiability in e-voting without trusted parties. In: 33rd IEEE Computer Security Foundations Symposium, CSF 2020, Boston, MA, USA, 22–26 June 2020, pp. 33–48. IEEE (2020)
19. Jamroga, W., Knapik, M., Kurpiewski, D.: Model checking the SELENE e-voting protocol in multi-agent logics. In: Krimmer, R., et al. (eds.) E-Vote-ID 2018. LNCS, vol. 11143, pp. 100–116. Springer, Cham (2018). https://doi.org/10.1007/978-3-030-00419-4_7
20. Juels, A., Catalano, D., Jakobsson, M.: Coercion-resistant electronic elections. In: Chaum, D., et al. (eds.) Towards Trustworthy Elections. LNCS, vol. 6000, pp. 37–63. Springer, Heidelberg (2010). https://doi.org/10.1007/978-3-642-12980-3_2
21. Kiayias, A., Zacharias, T., Zhang, B.: End-to-end verifiable elections in the standard model. In: Oswald, E., Fischlin, M. (eds.) EUROCRYPT 2015. LNCS, vol. 9057, pp. 468–498. Springer, Heidelberg (2015). https://doi.org/10.1007/978-3-662-46803-6_16
22. Kremer, S., Ryan, M., Smyth, B.: Election verifiability in electronic voting protocols. In: Gritzalis, D., Preneel, B., Theoharidou, M. (eds.) ESORICS 2010. LNCS, vol. 6345, pp. 389–404. Springer, Heidelberg (2010). https://doi.org/10.1007/978-3-642-15497-3_24
23. Küsters, R., Müller, J., Scapin, E., Truderung, T.: sElect: a lightweight verifiable remote voting system. In: 2016 IEEE 29th Computer Security Foundations Symposium (CSF), pp. 341–354. IEEE (2016)
24. Küsters, R., Truderung, T., Vogt, A.: Accountability: definition and relationship to verifiability. In: CCS 2010: 17th ACM Conference on Computer and Communications Security, pp. 526–535. ACM Press (2010)

25. Küsters, R., Truderung, T., Vogt, A.: A game-based definition of coercion-resistance and its applications. J. Comput. Secur. **20**(6), 709–764 (2012)
26. Moran, T., Naor, M.: Receipt-free universally-verifiable voting with everlasting privacy. In: Dwork, C. (ed.) CRYPTO 2006. LNCS, vol. 4117, pp. 373–392. Springer, Heidelberg (2006). https://doi.org/10.1007/11818175_22
27. Andrew Neff, C.: Practical high certainty intent verification for encrypted votes. Unpublished manuscript (2004)
28. Andrew Neff, C.: Practical high certainty intent verification for encrypted votes (2004)
29. Randell, B., Ryan, P.Y.A.: Voting technologies and trust. IEEE Secur. Privacy **4**(5), 50–56 (2006)
30. Rivest, R.L.: The threeballot voting system (2006)
31. Rønne, P.B., Ryan, P.Y.A., Zollinger, M.-L.: Electryo, in-person voting with transparent voter verifiability and eligibility verifiability. In: E-Vote-ID 2018, p. 147 (2018)
32. Ryan, P.Y.A., Rønne, P.B., Iovino, V.: Selene: voting with transparent verifiability and coercion-mitigation. In: Clark, J., Meiklejohn, S., Ryan, P.Y.A., Wallach, D., Brenner, M., Rohloff, K. (eds.) FC 2016. LNCS, vol. 9604, pp. 176–192. Springer, Heidelberg (2016). https://doi.org/10.1007/978-3-662-53357-4_12
33. Sallal, M., et al.: Augmenting an internet voting system with selene verifiability using permissioned distributed ledger. In: 40th IEEE International Conference on Distributed Computing Systems, ICDCS 2020, Singapore, 29 November–1 December 2020, pp. 1167–1168. IEEE (2020)
34. Smyth, B.: Ballot secrecy: security definition, sufficient conditions, and analysis of Helios. Cryptology ePrint Archive, Report 2015/942 (2018)
35. Smyth, B.: Mind the gap: individual- and universal-verifiability plus cast-as-intended don't yield verifiable voting systems. Technical Report 2020/1054, Cryptology ePrint Archive (2020)
36. Smyth, B.: Surveying global verifiability. Inf. Process. Lett. **163**, 106000 (2020)
37. Smyth, B., Bernhard, D.: Ballot secrecy and ballot independence coincide. In: Crampton, J., Jajodia, S., Mayes, K. (eds.) ESORICS 2013. LNCS, vol. 8134, pp. 463–480. Springer, Heidelberg (2013). https://doi.org/10.1007/978-3-642-40203-6_26
38. Smyth, B., Frink, S., Clarkson, M.R.: Election verifiability: cryptographic definitions and an analysis of Helios and JCJ. Cryptology ePrint Archive, Report 2015/233 (2017)
39. Smyth, B., Ryan, M., Kremer, S., Kourjieh, M.: Towards automatic analysis of election verifiability properties. In: Armando, A., Lowe, G. (eds.) ARSPA-WITS 2010. LNCS, vol. 6186, pp. 146–163. Springer, Heidelberg (2010). https://doi.org/10.1007/978-3-642-16074-5_11
40. Unruh, D., Müller-Quade, J.: Universally composable incoercibility. In: Rabin, T. (ed.) CRYPTO 2010. LNCS, vol. 6223, pp. 411–428. Springer, Heidelberg (2010). https://doi.org/10.1007/978-3-642-14623-7_22
41. Zollinger, M.-L., Distler, V., Roenne, P., Ryan, P., Lallemand, C., Vincent, K.: How mental models align with security mechanisms, user experience design for e-voting (2019)
42. Zollinger, M.-L., Rønne, P.B., Ryan, P.Y.A.: Short paper: mechanized proofs of verifiability and privacy in a paper-based e-voting scheme. In: Bernhard, M., et al. (eds.) FC 2020. LNCS, vol. 12063, pp. 310–318. Springer, Cham (2020). https://doi.org/10.1007/978-3-030-54455-3_22

Mobile Voting – Still Too Risky?

Sven Heiberg[1], Kristjan Krips[2,3], and Jan Willemson[3,4](✉) (iD)

[1] Smartmatic-Cybernetica Centre of Excellence for Internet Voting, Tartu, Estonia
[2] Institute of Computer Science, University of Tartu, Tartu, Estonia
[3] Cybernetica, Tartu, Estonia
[4] Software Technology and Applications Competence Center, Tartu, Estonia

Abstract. This paper studies the challenges of creating a mobile device based voting client. We discuss the issues related to standalone and mobile browser based voting applications. In both cases we discuss the problems of vote privacy, integrity and voting channel availability. We conclude that neither of the options can currently achieve the level of security PC-based voting clients can provide, with the attack surface being larger in the case of mobile browser based voting application.

1 Introduction

Voting is the core method of delegating public power in modern democratic societies. However, in the contemporary increasingly mobile world, relying only on polling stations to vote is less and less of an option.

Physical polling station based elections were put into a completely new light due to the SARS-CoV-2 virus outbreak in early 2020 when it suddenly became strongly non-recommended for people to gather in small spaces. For example, there were local elections in France on March 15th which were held under a severe risk of spreading the virus [4]. A straightforward alternative is postal voting (that was heavily used e.g. in 2020 US presidential elections).

History of postal voting goes back a long time. Voters in the Swiss canton of St. Gallen are reported as having sent their ballots via mail as early as 1673; however, postal voting became more widely used only in late 19th/early 20th century [17]. Still, this method is not perfect. It is hard to remotely authenticate the voter, reliability of postal services varies a lot across the world, there are no good measures against vote selling, etc. Even the international postal service can have severe disruptions as illustrated by the US Postal service temporarily stopping its service to 102 countries during the pandemic in spring 2020[1]. Thus, it is important to study alternatives for remote voting.

Recent decades have given us fast development in both computerized networks and strong electronic identification mechanisms. These together lay a foundation for vote casting over Internet. And indeed, this approach has been tried

---

[1] https://newjerseyglobe.com/campaigns/with-102-countries-not-receiving-mail-from-u-s-military-and-overseas-voters-might-not-get-primary-election-ballots/.

© International Financial Cryptography Association 2021
M. Bernhard et al. (Eds.): FC 2021 Workshops, LNCS 12676, pp. 263–278, 2021.
https://doi.org/10.1007/978-3-662-63958-0_23

out in several parts of the World (e.g. Estonia, Norway, Switzerland, Australia, etc.) using either a PC- or browser-based voting client software.

In addition, mobile technology has been used in several countries for the purposes of democratic inclusion (e.g. campaigning and polling) since early 2000s [12]. The rise in mobile platforms usage has put forward a natural question whether casting votes from mobile devices would be a viable option.

For example, in a number of African countries more people have mobile phones than access to continuous electric supply [27]. At the same time, long distances and poor transportation make remote voting a necessity in order to achieve universal suffrage. Thus, the options for mobile voting have been studied in Africa for a decade already [6,7,15]. However, the security issues of smartphone based voting clients haven't gotten much attention by the research community.

The paper is organised as follows. Section 2 gives an overview of the used methodology. Next, Sect. 3, describes the issues of browser based voting. It is followed by Sect. 4, which highlights the issues faced by a standalone voting application on the two most popular mobile platforms – iOS and Android. Finally, Sect. 5 offers some discussion and conclusions.

2 Methodology

Voting software has to adhere to the security principles of the corresponding election system and jurisdiction. As a result, the list of requirements set for the elections varies a bit between different authors and sources (see e.g. [3,10,21,25]).

In this paper we concentrate on the client side security of remote electronic voting, hence we will focus on the following subset of general requirements.

1. **Vote privacy** is a measure to guarantee the freedom of choice.
2. **Vote integrity** in our setting means that the vote should reach the (digital) ballot box in a way that corresponds to the voter's real preference.
3. **Availability** means that voters should have access to the voting methods and channels to guarantee both uniformity and generality of elections.

Some aspects remain outside of the scope of the current paper, most notably tally integrity and verifiability issues. Eligibility verification and guaranteeing uniformity are typically solved via voter authentication, and this is a vast area of research on its own. Due to space limitations, we also leave mobile authentication out of scope of the current paper.

To further focus our field of interest, we will concentrate on solutions where the mobile device is used to directly implement the standard voting workflow including proving eligibility, presenting the candidates, recording the voter preference, submitting it and presenting any information required for individual verification of the vote. Under the hood, the voting software must also perform security-related operations like establishing authenticated, secrecy-and-integrity-protected channel to the server, protecting the vote from manipulation etc.

We note that in our setting, the voting application participates in the cryptographic protocol as a voter's tool to cast her preference as a vote, and to submit it into the digital ballot-box. This is different from e.g. code voting [11], where the voting application is a mere transparent transportation channel of anonymous pre-encrypted data. As a consequence, the client application learns both voter's identity and her preferences, and is in the position to change the vote. This problem can be mitigated by the voting protocol providing verifiability.

Given these limitations, we study two main alternative architectural solutions – implementing the voting client based on a browser platform, or as a standalone mobile application. In both cases, we will take a more detailed look at how the three main requirements identified above can be satisfied, and what are the residual risks given today's level of mobile platforms and their security features.

3   Issues with Browser Based Voting

We consider the voting application to be implemented as a dynamic webpage using HTML, JavaScript and CSS. The application is deployed to a web server and the URL is published. Voters use browsers of their choice to visit the webpage.

Browser is responsible for downloading the application files and creating a representation of the Document Object Model (DOM), which is made available to JavaScript via standardised APIs. In the voting workflow, the voter's actions activate JavaScript implementation of the protocol, which affect the DOM, changing what is rendered to the voter. The voting application is executed in the browser context and has limited access to the system level APIs.

While standalone applications can be analysed relative to the OS they are running on, web applications are not tied to a single platform. Thus, the security and privacy aspects of both mobile and desktop browsers have to be reviewed.

Usability. In the context of voting, the lack of screen size creates challenges for designing the user interface. For example, a desktop browser may display the full list of candidates, while a mobile version can not. Thus, a question arises which candidates should have the advantage of being displayed first.

The limitations on screen size have prevented mobile browsers from fully adapting some standard functionalities of their desktop counterparts. For example, it is common for mobile browsers to optimize the way how URL and URL bar are displayed. In addition, mobile browsers usually do not allow the users to view detailed information about the TLS connection. Such optimizations increase the risk of voters being tricked by a phishing website.

Mobile Browser Issues. Distributing the voting client as a standard web application has the potential to simplify deployment to both desktop and mobile platforms, unify user interface, and provide an option for easy hot-fixing. At the same time, this introduces a middleman (browser) between the voting application and the operating system, vastly increasing the attack surface.

Luo, Nikiforakis *et al.* published two longitudinal studies on security features of mobile browsers [19, 20]. They showed that, in general, mobile browsers lag behind their desktop counterparts in the adoption of new security features.

Thus, web applications used via mobile browsers are more vulnerable to a variety of attacks (e.g. phishing, malicious scripts, etc.). In the context of mobile voting this may create issues related with both ballot privacy and ballot integrity.

3.1 Privacy

Sandboxing. The voting application has to be isolated from other web pages and third party software. Browsers isolate content from different origins with the help of Same-Origin Policy (SOP). However, vulnerabilities can be used to bypass SOP[2]. Thus, some desktop browsers provide additional sandboxing by launching different web sites in different processes. Google Chrome does this since version 67 by relying on Site Isolation, which provides protection against multiple classes of attacks [23]. This feature was added to Android based Google Chrome for devices that have at least 2 GB of RAM, but it only works on web sites where users enter passwords[3]. While Firefox does not yet have a similar functionality, a project to add the feature is ongoing[4].

Even the extra measures do not provide absolute isolation. For example, malicious browser extensions could violate ballot privacy by reading page contents, as described in Sect. 3.2.

Telemetry. A 2020 report by Leith gave an overview of the telemetry mainstream browsers send back to the vendor or third parties [18]. The comparison showed that Brave Browser did the best when considering user's privacy, while Microsoft Edge and Yandex Browser were in the opposite end of the scale. Chrome, Firefox and Safari all sent information about the query that was typed to the URL bar to their respective vendors.

Google Chrome, Firefox and Safari rely on Google's Safe Browsing service to identify phishing sites and malware, while Microsoft Edge relies on Microsoft Defender SmartScreen for the same features. While Google's Safe Browsing uses k-anonymity mechanism and local filtering, Microsoft's SmartScreen uses local filtering only for top traffic sites and known phishing sites. The rest of the URL-s are sent to be analysed by the SmartScreen service[5].

In the context of voting, even the leakage of indirect information about the voting habits of users may cause security issues. This kind of information could be used in coercion attacks to detect whether a voter has abstained or re-voted.

Metadata about voters' behaviour is also visible to Internet service and DNS providers. Such data could be used to list eligible voters who abstain from voting. The list could be used for targeted attacks in order to submit votes on behalf of

---

[2] https://cve.mitre.org/cgi-bin/cvekey.cgi?keyword=Same+Origin+Policy+bypass.
[3] https://www.chromium.org/Home/chromium-security/site-isolation.
[4] https://wiki.mozilla.org/Project_Fission.
[5] https://docs.microsoft.com/en-us/microsoft-edge/privacy-whitepaper.

the abstained voters. This threat could be mitigated if all eligible voters would get notifications when a vote has been submitted on their behalf. However, such notifications would have organisational and privacy issues of their own.

Man-in-the-Middle Attacks. Real world examples show that TLS is often the only defensive measure that protects submitted ballots [2]. In case of a standalone voting application, the TLS certificate of the voting server can be *pinned*, i.e. the application can be built to accept a limited set of certificates. To bypass pinning, either the application or the operating system would have to be modified.

Mainstream browsers no longer support HTTP Public Key Pinning (HPKP). As a replacement, it is recommended to rely on Certificate Transparency (CT)[6] and DNS Certificate Authority Authorization (CAA)[7]. However, CT is not mandatory for locally issued certificates.

Thus, there is no straightforward way for pinning certificates for a browser based voting application. This makes it difficult to prevent man-in-the-middle (MITM) attacks by corporate middleboxes and anti-viruses that monitor the messages exchanged inside TLS sessions. A study published in 2017 found that such interception rate is in the range of 4–11% [5]. In 2019, Cloudflare reported that this rate has significantly increased since the 2017 study was published[8].

TLS traffic is often monitored via a local MITM approach, affecting the security guarantees provided by HTTPS [5]. Thus, in addition to the privacy risks, there are also risks to the integrity of the vote.

A voter is also able to set up a proxy to intercept and modify API calls. Thus, when designing API-s, it should be assumed that the queries may be intercepted.

3.2 Integrity

One of the main issues with online voting is the untrustworthiness of voter's device, which can affect the integrity of the ballot. The risks are even higher when votes are cast through a web application. Browsers introduce an extra layer that has to be protected in addition to the rest of the operating system.

Fortunately, security of mainstream browsers has improved over the years [19]. While zero-day vulnerabilities can not be ruled out, delivering patches to the end users is easy due to the browsers getting automatic updates either directly from the vendors or via the operating system. This holds both for mainstream desktop browsers and for mobile browsers running on iOS and Android.

Web Application Integrity. While the identity of a website can be verified by inspecting its certificate, there is no assurance that the web content distributed by the server is the one that was deployed by the election organizer. There are no straightforward ways for voters to verify integrity of the JavaScript

---

[6] https://tools.ietf.org/html/rfc6962.
[7] https://tools.ietf.org/html/rfc8659.
[8] https://blog.cloudflare.com/monsters-in-the-middleboxes/.

code. However, there are some mechanisms that provide partial solutions to the problem.

Scytl has proposed a tool (`wraudit`) to remotely verify that a proper web-application is distributed by the web server [24]. However, it does not prevent local tampering, and the voter can still access a tampered with web application.

W3C recommendation of Subresource Integrity (SRI)[9] defines a checksum-based mechanism by which user agents may verify that a fetched resource has been delivered without unexpected manipulation. However, SRI does not protect against tampering caused by a compromised web server or a MITM attack.

Cross-Origin Resource Sharing (CORS)[10] allows web servers to tell browsers which resources can be shared cross-origin. A voting server could inform browsers that it only accepts requests from the official voting web page. This would prevent a fake voting application from sending messages to the real back-end. The restriction could be circumvented by also using a fake back-end, either by proxying queries to the true back-end or disenfranchising voters completely.

Browser Extensions. Browser behaviour can be modified by extensions that may be able to interfere with web applications' control flow and visuals. Most mobile browsers do not support extensions, but there are a few exceptions[11].

Extensions can both read and modify the content of websites via DOM. There are some methods to ensure DOM integrity[12], but this far they are still experimental.

The current permission model for mainstream browsers allows extensions to ask for far-reaching access. When installing an extension, the user has to either accept the requested permissions, or retract from installing it altogether. While Firefox does not allow to turn off permissions, Google Chrome lets the user to configure on which web sites certain permissions may be used. However, the option may not be available for extensions installed using an enterprise policy.

Firefox extensions can ask the permission to "Access your data for all websites" and with other permissions it is also possible to change the content on selected pages. A Google Chrome extension can ask for a permission to "Read and change all your data on the websites you visit".

The latter has significant side-effects for browser based voting applications. It is a non-trivial task to protect the integrity and privacy of the ballot while a browser has been augmented with extensions. To mitigate the implied risks, the voter would have to make sure that browser extensions would not have access to the content on the vote casting website. This is infeasible for an average user.

---

[9] https://www.w3.org/TR/SRI/.

[10] https://fetch.spec.whatwg.org/.

[11] The Android version of Firefox supports extensions and there exist third-party mobile browsers (e.g. Kiwi) that support Google Chrome extensions.

[12] https://toreini.github.io/projects/domtegrity.html.

3.3 Availability

It is common for vendors to bundle browsers with their devices. This results in tens of browsers being used only by a small fraction of users.

Additionally, it was recently shown by Kondracki *et al.* that data saving browsers can affect both privacy and integrity of the transmitted content [16]. However, only some of these browsers intercepted TLS connections. This illustrates the need for separately validating browsers that can be used for voting.

On the other hand, monitoring the security of all marginally used browsers is not realistic. Thus, in the context of voting, supporting only a limited number of browsers seems unavoidable. At the same time, correctly detecting a browser on server-side is not 100% reliable as browsers may lie about their identity.

Authenticity of the Voting Application. A voter would have to check the TLS certificate of the web site to validate its authenticity. However, it may not be possible to view the full certificate on mobile browsers. By testing multiple browsers on Android and iOS (Google Chrome, Firefox, Brave, Microsoft Edge, UC Browser, Samsung Browser, Opera Mini/Touch, Safari), we discovered that only Google Chrome, Brave and Samsung Browser running on Android display detailed information about the certificate. Google Chrome on iOS and Firefox on Android allowed the user to only view the issuer of the certificate. The rest of the tested browsers only displayed a padlock icon on the URL bar. As it is trivial to get a valid TLS certificate for one's own domain, relying on the padlock icon can create a false sense of security about the website's trustworthiness [8].

URL Bar Visibility. Browsers on smartphones are optimised to increase the available screen area and thus limit the information displayed on the URL bar. We tested multiple browsers on Android and iOS (Google Chrome, Firefox, Brave, Microsoft Edge, UC Browser, Samsung Browser, Opera Mini/Touch, Safari) to see how their URL bar behaves.

It turned out that there is no common behaviour in this respect. Most of the tested browsers hide the URL bar while scrolling or changing page orientation. Only the iOS version of Chrome always displayed at least part of the URL.

It has been observed that some mobile browsers have issues with displaying long URL-s [20], which can be abused by phishing attacks. To prevent confusion, browsers should always display the domain name of the visited web site. Our testing revealed that Safari, Firefox, Edge, Opera Touch and UC Browser on iOS prioritize subdomains when using vertical layout as illustrated in Fig. 1. Testing the same layout in Android showed that Google Chrome, Firefox and Samsung Browser display the domain name of the visited website, while Microsoft's Edge, Opera Mini, UC Browser and Brave prioritize the left side of the URL. Surprisingly, UC Browser on Android showed the title of the web page instead of the URL, thereby making phishing attacks trivial, see Fig. 1.

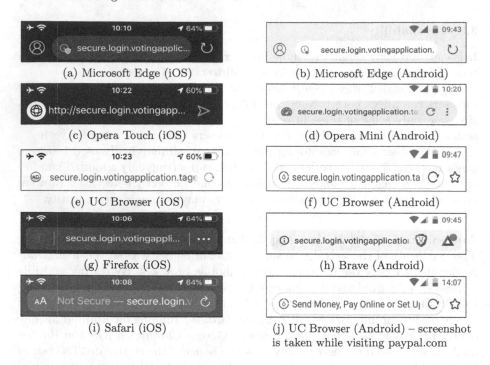

Fig. 1. URL bars of mobile browsers that do not display the domain of the website. The screenshots were taken in June 2020.

Such behaviour can be exploited by running targeted phishing campaigns to trick voters into using a fake voting website. A successful attack could reveal how these voters vote. It may also allow an attacker to block or change the vote that is going to be cast, or interfere with the vote verification processes.

4   Issues with a Standalone Voting Application

The main alternative to the browser-based approach is to have a standalone mobile application as a voting client. In this Section we will identify the main issues that can be caused by running a voting client in either iOS or Android.

In the following we assume that a standalone voting application is implemented as a native executable application, packaged for the given platform and distributed via the mainstream appstore. Thus, the applications are distributed as digitally signed packages (APK in Android, IPA in iOS).

Both Android and iOS applications are executed as isolated processes on the OS level; tampering with these processes requires system level access. The OS level APIs give fine-grained control over the voting application development and enable e.g. certificate pinning for TLS connections.

Usability. A standalone application can use slightly more screen area compared to a browser, but still has the issue of being unable to display the full list of candidates. In addition, smartphone applications are used in portrait mode by default, whereas PC based applications are mostly used in landscape mode.

Users interact with smartphone applications via tapping and gestures, which are not precise actions. Thus, the relative size of the UI elements has to be bigger compared to desktop applications. Therefore, complex interactions presented in a single view on a PC need to be restructured into multiple views for smartphones.

4.1 Privacy

Sandboxing. To protect the integrity and secrecy of the ballot, the voting application should be isolated from non-system software. Such behaviour can be provided by sandboxes isolating applications from each other. Unfortunately, relying just on a sandbox is insufficient as malware with root access can influence it.

Android and iOS sandbox all user installed applications while setting restrictions to getting root access. As a result, non-rooted mobile applications can not significantly influence or monitor execution of the voting application.

Android isolates applications in the kernel level by assigning a unique user ID to each application and running them in separate processes[13]. In addition, SELinux is used to enforce mandatory access control over Android processes.

iOS application sandbox is built on top of a mandatory access control system [29]. Contrarily to Android, regular applications do not run as separate users, instead they are executed as a user named `mobile`, while system processes can run as root. iOS applications are isolated into `chroot` style jails, such that each application is only able to access its own directory and has limited access to system resources. While jailbreaking does not automatically disable the application sandbox, it breaks the security model by allowing applications to get root access and thereby influence other applications [29].

Third-Party Applications. Privacy issues can also be caused by side-channel leakages from legitimate applications. For example, it is common for Android applications to silently request the list of other installed applications [26]. This is usually done by the advertisement libraries by using an official Android API.

Information about the voting or vote verification app can be abused by an attacker. When a user has not installed a voting application, an attacker may attempt to cast a vote on voter's behalf with a lower risk of the voter getting a potential "You have already voted" message. In case an attacker can predict which voters do not verify their votes, it is possible to run targeted vote manipulation attacks without the risk of being caught by verification.

Another Android specific risk is non-removable bloatware pre-installed into the device by the vendor. The risks of pre-installed applications were recently

---

[13] https://source.android.com/security/features.

studied by Gamba *et al.* by gathering 424,584 unique firmware samples [9]. They found that 74% of the non-public pre-installed applications did not get security updates, and 41% were not patched for at least 5 years. They also stated that bloatware poses a threat to user's privacy as it often contains third-party libraries and custom permissions, which are not explained to the users.

Man-in-the-Middle Attacks. We mentioned in Sect. 3.1 that MITM attacks pose a threat to the voting systems that rely on TLS to protect ballots [2]. However, in iOS and Android such attacks can be mitigated by certificate pinning.

In order to bypass certificate pinning in iOS, the device has to be jailbroken [29]. The common way to bypass pinning is to use the tool SSL Kill Switch 2, which patches the API that is used for certificate validation[14].

Before Android 7, third-party VPN applications often violated user's privacy [13]. Once an Android application had requested the BIND_VPN_SERVICE permission, it was able to break sandboxing and redirect the traffic of other applications. There were also examples of VPN applications doing TLS-interception.

However, since the release of Android 7, root access is required to add new root certificates that are trusted system-wide[15]. After that change, malicious TLS interception become significantly more difficult on Android devices.

4.2   Integrity

Risks somewhat similar to installing third party extensions to browsers (see Sect. 3.2) also occur on the OS level where third party apps can be installed. However, special attention is needed for applications that run in root privileges.

Rooting and Malicious Applications. Applications running with root access are a potential threat for the voting application. First, such malware can influence how other programs behave and thereby either drop or modify the ballot. Second, by getting access to the voter's credentials, it could cast a vote on behalf of her. Third, by intercepting information, ballot privacy could be violated.

iOS has strict rules for installing applications, allowing installation only from Apple's App Store. This restriction can be bypassed by acquiring superuser credentials on the device (jailbreaking). However, jailbreaking is non-trivial and may not be available for all iOS versions.

In Android, getting root access is easier. However, rooting is not even necessary in order to install third party application stores and applications on an Android device. Third party application stores, in turn, have fewer restrictions for uploading applications and provide a good distribution channel for malware.

On desktop platforms, anti-virus software can detect some types of malware. Anti-virus-like solutions also exist for Android and iOS, but ironically, their capabilities are limited as both of the OSes sandbox applications quite strictly.

---

[14] https://github.com/nabla-c0d3/ssl-kill-switch2.
[15] https://android-developers.googleblog.com/2016/07/changes-to-trusted-certificate.html.

A safer execution environment could be provided for the voting application by not supporting rooted devices. While various heuristics can be used to detect rooting, they are generally easy to circumvent [14]. Due to the threat of malware, absolute ballot privacy can not be guaranteed unless code voting is used [11]. However, that would significantly complicate the voting process for the voters.

Update Policy and Legacy Operating Systems. Android's update policy differentiates it from the other mainstream OSes. There is a problem of issuing software updates due to multiple dependencies between the software vendor, device manufacturers and the chip producer. Additionally, the business model of many device manufacturers is built around short product lifetime. As a result, updates and security patches are delayed or not available at all for many devices.

The situation with Android update policy has slightly improved during the last few years due to the separation of hardware specific code from the rest of Android[16] and introduction of the Android Enterprise Recommended program[17]. The former makes it easier for the vendors to create updates, but it does not force devices to be updated. The latter gives vendors the option to assign a special label to the devices which are guaranteed to get regular security patches.

A significant percentage of Android devices run old Android versions that contain severe vulnerabilities. While it would be preferable not to offer voting software for such devices, in practice this is not possible (iOS devices without jailbreaks being available being an exception). When an official voting application is not offered, it is still possible to create an independent voting client that follows the official API to communicate with the back-end server. The API can be found either from the documentation or by reverse engineering the official voting application as demonstrated e.g. for Voatz [28].

Authenticity and Integrity of the Voting Application. On desktop platforms, the voting application can in principle be distributed via an unreliable channel as the integrity and authenticity of the application can be verified post-transit. It can be done by relying on checksums or signatures, given that the information about how to verify is distributed over reliable channels. Windows and macOS automatically verify integrity of the signed binaries at the load time.

Android applications have to be signed before being distributed through Google Play Store. While the signature binds an application along with its updated versions to a certain key, it does not give assurance about the identity of the application developer as the signature can be issued with a self-signed certificate[18]. In addition, Android supports legacy signature schemes to provide backward compatibility. A recent study by Yoshida *et al.* showed that apps signed using MD5 and 512-bit RSA can still be found on Google Play Store [30].

---

[16] https://source.android.com/devices/architecture#hidl.
[17] https://www.android.com/enterprise/recommended/.
[18] https://source.android.com/security/apksigning.

Android allows new applications signed with APK Signature scheme v2 (or v3) to use RSA1024, although stronger alternatives are supported[19]. However, as RSA1024 provides only 80-bit security level, it is no longer recommended for even mid-term applications; at least RSA3072 should be used instead [1]. Unfortunately, the issues with weak signatures do not seem to disappear as applications uploaded to Google Play Store must be signed with a key that is valid at least until October 22nd 2033.[20] While key rotation functionality was added to APK Signature scheme v3 in August 2018,[21] it does not resolve issues with older signature schemes. There is no straightforward way to replace the signing key of an application that is signed with an older signature scheme[22].

iOS applications have to be signed with a developer key certified by Apple. The digital identity used for signing must be available through keychain. The macOS certificate assistant tool allows for requesting certificates with RSA (bitlengths 2048 to 8192) and ECC (bitlengths 256 to 521) keys.

4.3   Availability

On desktop platforms, the easiest solution to distribute an application is to allow it to be downloaded directly from its web page. In case of mobile platforms, installing apps from non-official sources is either impossible or not recommended due to security concerns. Thus, an official voting application would have to be distributed via the application store, but this can cause unexpected side-effects.

There is a risk of installing a bogus voting application as the app stores are not able to identify and remove all copycat applications. Counterfeit applications exist both in Google Play and in Apple's App Store[23]. A recent study analysed 1.2 million Google Play applications and detected 49,608 that were similar to one of the top 10,000 most popular applications in Google Play Store [22]. The potential counterfeits were scanned by VirusTotal and out of these, 2040 were classified to be malicious by at least 5 independent antivirus tools.

It should not be possible for third parties to issue updates for the voting application. However, Google is promoting an app signing functionality that allows application developers to out-source handling of the signing key to Google.[24] Although the developer can also use an upload key, this can be reset by Google. Thus, when releasing an official voting application, the signing key must not be disclosed to third parties and such functionality must not be used.

Additional risk lies in the limited control over the distribution channel. The application stores decide which applications to host and thus it is not guaranteed that a voting application is accepted in time. Similar problems may arise in case a hot-fix is needed due to a reported bug or vulnerability.

---

[19] https://source.android.com/security/apksigning/v2.

[20] https://developer.android.com/studio/publish/app-signing.

[21] https://source.android.com/security/apksigning/v3.

[22] http://support.google.com/googleplay/android-developer/answer/9842756.

[23] https://www.nytimes.com/2016/11/07/technology/more-iphone-fake-retail-apps-before-holidays.html.

[24] https://developer.android.com/studio/publish/app-signing.

Another aspect that may need to be considered is the leakage of app store profiles of voters who have downloaded the voting application. When a malicious actor gets access to such information, it may be possible to conduct targeted attacks against eligible voters who have not installed a voting application similarly to the attacks described in Sects. 3.1 and 4.1.

5   Discussion, Conclusions and Future Work

Several recent developments like increased migration and SARS-CoV-2 virus spreading have increased the motivation to introduce options for remote voting. There are two main alternatives for absentee ballot delivery – postal system and Internet – with both having their benefits and shortcomings.

In case remote voting is implemented via Internet, the main candidates for the voting client platform are PCs and mobile devices. This paper focused on the latter option, giving an overview of the arising issues in two main scenarios – browser based and standalone voting application on mobile platforms. Although mobile platforms are becoming more mature, they still have several shortcomings when considering them for remote electronic voting.

Firstly, there are a lot of legacy OS versions around that the vendors have no incentive to update, particularly in case of Android. However, in order to provide the voting option for a significant part of the electorate, there would be pressure to also support out-of date mobile OSes.

Second, smaller screen size makes it necessary to display only part of the content. This is a challenge from both the voting application UI and security point of view (as e.g. certificates and URLs can be displayed only partly).

When considering browser-based voting client as an alternative to a standalone app, one has to take into account that browsers extend the attack surface significantly. Mobile browsers also lag behind their PC counterparts in adoption of new security features. There is no standard way for users to check the integrity of web applications, and browser behaviour can be easily changed by third-party extensions that the users install without giving it much consideration.

As many of the shortcomings do not affect only voting, but have impact on a much wider variety of use cases, they can be expected to be fixed over time. It will be interesting to re-assess the situation in a few years to see if the situation will have been improved.

There are also several areas that remained outside of the scope of current paper and are left as subject for further research.

Voter authentication is likely to differ between desktop and mobile platforms. Smartphones tend to have relatively high quality cameras and the integration of fingerprint readers is becoming more widespread. As a negative side, it is difficult to interface a smartphone with a smart card based electronic identity solution. In addition, the mobile device itself is often used as a second authentication factor, which may exclude some authentication methods.

When running cryptographic protocols, access to high-quality randomness is important. While cryptographically strong random number generators are increasingly available on mobile platforms, their usability by mobile browsers still requires future research.

Acknowledgements. This paper has been supported by the Estonian Research Council under the grant number PRG920 and European Regional Development Fund through the grant number EU48684 and EXCITE centre of excellence. The authors are grateful to the Estonian Information System Authority and State Electoral Office for their support to the research process.

References

1. Abdalla, M., et al.: Algorithms, key size and protocols report. Tech. rep. ECRYPT CSA (2018). https://www.ecrypt.eu.org/csa/documents/D5.4-FinalAlgKeySizeProt.pdf
2. Cardillo, A., Essex, A.: The threat of SSL/TLS stripping to online voting. Proc. E-Vote-ID **2018**, 35–50 (2018)
3. Cetinkaya, O.: Analysis of security requirements for cryptographic voting protocols (extended abstract). In: Proceedings ARES 2008, pp. 1451–1456. IEEE Computer Society (2008)
4. Corbet, S.: France Holds Local Elections Despite COVID-19 Outbreak Fears. Time, March 2020. https://time.com/5803469/france-local-elections-coronavirus/
5. Durumeric, Z., et al.: The security impact of HTTPS interception. In: Proceedings of NDSS 2017. The Internet Society (2017)
6. Eilu, E., Baguma, R.: Designing reality Fit M-voting. In: Proceedings of the 7th International Conference on Theory and Practice of Electronic Governance. ICE-GOV 2013, pp. 326–329. ACM (2013)
7. Ekong, U.O., Ekong, V.: M-voting: a panacea for enhanced e-participation. Asian J. Inf. Technol. **9**(2), 111–116 (2010)
8. Felt, A.P., et al.: Rethinking connection security indicators. In: Twelfth Symposium on Usable Privacy and Security (SOUPS 2016), Denver, CO, pp. 1–14. USENIX Association, June 2016. https://www.usenix.org/conference/soups2016/technical-sessions/presentation/porter-felt
9. Gamba, J., Rashed, M., Razaghpanah, A., Tapiador, J., Vallina-Rodriguez, N.: An analysis of pre-installed android software. In: 2020 IEEE Symposium on Security and Privacy (SP), pp. 197–213, May 2020
10. Heiberg, S., Willemson, J.: Modeling threats of a voting method. In: Design, Development, and Use of Secure Electronic Voting Systems, pp. 128–148. IGI Global (2014)
11. Helbach, J., Schwenk, J.: Secure internet voting with code sheets. In: Alkassar, A., Volkamer, M. (eds.) Vote-ID 2007. LNCS, vol. 4896, pp. 166–177. Springer, Heidelberg (2007). https://doi.org/10.1007/978-3-540-77493-8_15
12. Hermanns, H.: Mobile democracy: mobile phones as democratic tools. Politics **28**(2), 74–82 (2008)
13. Ikram, M., Vallina-Rodriguez, N., Seneviratne, S., Kâafar, M.A., Paxson, V.: An analysis of the privacy and security risks of android VPN permission-enabled apps. Proc. IMC **2016**, 349–364 (2016)

14. Kellner, A., Horlboge, M., Rieck, K., Wressnegger, C.: False sense of security: a study on the effectivity of jailbreak detection in banking apps. In: Proceedings of IEEE EuroS&P 2019, pp. 1–14. IEEE (2019)
15. Kogeda, O.P., Mpekoa, N.: Model for a mobile phone voting system for South Africa. In: Proceedings of 15th Annual Conference on World Wide Web Applications, Cape Town, South Africa (2013)
16. Kondracki, B., Aliyeva, A., Egele, M., Polakis, J., Nikiforakis, N.: Meddling middlemen: empirical analysis of the risks of data-saving mobile browsers. In: 2020 IEEE S&P, pp. 1678–1692. IEEE, May 2020
17. Krimmer, R.: The evolution of e-voting: why voting technology is used and how it affects democracy. Ph.D. thesis, Tallinn University of Technology (2012)
18. Leith, D.J.: Web browser privacy: what do browsers say when they phone home? (2020), SCSS Technical Report, 24th February 2020
19. Luo, M., Laperdrix, P., Honarmand, N., Nikiforakis, N.: Time does not heal all wounds: a longitudinal analysis of security-mechanism support in mobile browsers. In: Proceedings of NDSS 2019. The Internet Society (2019)
20. Luo, M., Starov, O., Honarmand, N., Nikiforakis, N.: Hindsight: understanding the evolution of UI vulnerabilities in mobile browsers. In: Proceedings of the 2017 ACM CCS, CCS 2017, pp. 149–162. ACM (2017)
21. Mitrou, L., Gritzalis, D., Katsikas, S.K.: Revisiting legal and regulatory requirements for secure e-voting. In: Ghonaimy, A., El-Hadidi, M.T., Aslan, H.K. (eds.) Security in the Information Society: Visions and Perspectives, IFIP TC11 17th International Conference on Information Security (SEC2002), 7–9 May 2002, Cairo, Egypt. IFIP Conference Proceedings, vol. 214, pp. 469–480. Kluwer (2002)
22. Rajasegaran, J., Karunanayake, N., Gunathillake, A., Seneviratne, S., Jourjon, G.: A multi-modal neural embeddings approach for detecting mobile counterfeit apps. In: The World Wide Web Conference, WWW 2019, San Francisco, CA, USA, 13–17 May 2019, pp. 3165–3171. ACM (2019)
23. Reis, C., Moshchuk, A., Oskov, N.: Site isolation: process separation for web sites within the browser. In: 28th USENIX Security Symposium (USENIX Security 19), Santa Clara, CA, pp. 1661–1678. USENIX Association, August 2019. https://www. usenix.org/conference/usenixsecurity19/presentation/reis
24. Salvador, D., Cucurull, J., Julià, P.: wraudit: a tool to transparently monitor web resources' integrity. In: Groza, A., Prasath, R. (eds.) MIKE 2018. LNCS (LNAI), vol. 11308, pp. 239–247. Springer, Cham (2018). https://doi.org/10.1007/978-3-030-05918-7_21
25. Schryen, G.: Security aspects of internet voting. In: 37th Hawaii International Conference on System Sciences (HICSS-37 2004), CD-ROM/Abstracts Proceedings, 5–8 January 2004, Big Island, HI, USA. IEEE Computer Society (2004)
26. Scoccia, G.L., Kanj, I., Malavolta, I., Razavi, K.: Leave my apps alone! a study on how android developers access installed apps on user's device. In: Proceedings of the 7th IEEE/ACM International Conference on Mobile Software Engineering and Systems (2020). http://www.ivanomalavolta.com/files/papers/MOBILESoft_iam_2020.pdf
27. Shapshak, T.: Africa not just a mobile-first continent - it's mobile only (2012), CNN Business. https://edition.cnn.com/2012/10/04/tech/mobile/africa-mobile-opinion/index.html
28. Specter, M.A., Koppel, J., Weitzner, D.: The Ballot is Busted Before the Blockchain: A Security Analysis of Voatz, the First Internet Voting Application Used in US Federal Elections (2020)

29. Thiel, D.: iOS Application Security: The Definitive Guide for Hackers and Developers. No Starch Press (2016). https://nostarch.com/iossecurity
30. Yoshida, K., Imai, H., Serizawa, N., Mori, T., Kanaoka, A.: Understanding the origins of weak cryptographic algorithms used for signing android apps. J. Inf. Process. **27**, 593–602 (2019)

New Standards for E-Voting Systems: Reflections on Source Code Examinations

Thomas Haines[1](✉) and Peter Roenne[2]

[1] Norwegian University of Science and Technology, Trondheim, Norway
thomas.haines@ntnu.no
[2] Université du Luxembourg, Luxembourg, Luxembourg
peter.roenne@uni.lu

Abstract. There is a difference between a system having no known attacks and the system being secure—as cryptographers know all too well. Once we begin talking about the implementations of systems this issue becomes even more prominent since the amount of material which needs to be scrutinised skyrockets. Historically, lack of transparency and low standards for e-voting system implementations have resulted in a culture where open source code is seen as a gold standard; however, this ignores the issue of the comprehensibility of that code.

In this work we make concrete empirical recommendations based on our, and others, experiences and findings from examining the source code of e-voting systems. We highlight that any solution used for significant elections should be well designed, carefully analysed, deftly built, accurately documented and expertly maintained. Until e-voting system implementations are clear, comprehensible, and open to public scrutiny security standards are unlikely to improve.

Keywords: Voting · Implementation · Standards

1 Introduction

The theoretical foundations of verifiable electronic voting are fairly mature. Simple schemes such as Helios [Adi08], using homomorphic tallying, are well-known and theoretically easy to construct. Helios and other end-to-end verifiable schemes draw on a number of techniques to make the election software-independent [Riv08]. The idea of software-independence is that system should produce evidence which shows the election result was correct regardless of any flaws in the software used during the election. However, the term is perhaps slightly misleading because there is still a fundamental reliance on the software that checks the evidence.

We are now seeing small but critical bugs in the implementation of even theoretical simple schemes. For instance, the Swiss Post system contained many components which were broken despite extensive review [HLPT20]. This is the tip of the proverbial iceberg in terms of failures and issues in allegedly end-to-end verifiable systems; other examples have included the iVote system [HT15]

© International Financial Cryptography Association 2021
M. Bernhard et al. (Eds.): FC 2021 Workshops, LNCS 12676, pp. 279–289, 2021.
https://doi.org/10.1007/978-3-662-63958-0_24

deployed in the Australian state of New South Wales, the e-voting system used in national elections in Estonia [SFD+14], the Moscow voting system [GG20], and the issues with Voatz [SKW20] and Democracy Live [SH20].

The reason that these bugs slipped through varies but in many cases it is due to their nature. These bugs are not standard programming bugs which might be caught by standard best practice techniques. Rather, the code does not correctly capture the logical flow of the cryptographic protocol—possibly undermining the security guarantees which the cryptographic primitives were supposed to provide. Compounding these issues is that many of the bugs were present in the specification as well as the code. The bugs that we know of, were revealed when the systems were open sourced and experts in the field were able to examine the source. However, in none of these cases did the experts suggest that the list of bugs they found was exhaustive.

There is work underway to construct verifiers for e-voting schemes which are machine checked to be cryptographically secure [HGT19, HGS21]. However, these approaches cover only the publicly verifiable aspects of integrity. For deployed schemes we wish to ensure, in addition to universal verifiability, that the source code follows best practice and does not allow any obvious privacy attacks. The privacy of the deployed scheme is far more brittle than integrity and far harder to check. While we may hope that in future the code used to run elections has been machine checked to have many of the security properties we want, that day seems far off.

In this work we will discuss our, and others, experiences with examining the source code of deployed systems. We highlight problems with the processes which hampered the inspection of the systems. Based on these problems we highlight key recommendations; following these recommendations seems essential to allow the meaningful scrutiny of deployed systems.

1.1 The Problem

The aim of experts examining a system is not to find bugs but rather to ascertain that the system is reasonable free of bugs. While at present there is no issue with finding bugs the later aim—as we have noted—is rarely, if ever, achieved. In this paper we will discuss what steps vendors and election management bodies can take to enable better scrutiny of their systems.

Many of the lessons we will draw in this paper are related to those recently drawn by Haenni et al. [HDKL20]. However, the CHVote system they refer to was built from the ground up for a specific election system which is somewhat unusual; most vendors reuse their code in several different systems. The result of this is that several of the lessons we draw, while satisfied by CHVote, are not mentioned by Haenni et al.

Though we only use a single case study in the paper, the recommendations made in Sect. 3 are based on the authors' experiences in examining over a dozen different e-voting schemes, including:

- The iVote system used in the Australian states of New South Wales and Western Australia.

- The SwissPost system used in Switzerland.
- The CHVote system from Switzerland.
- The Helios system used by the International Association for Cryptologic Research.
- The Zeus system by GRNET.
- The Verify My Vote by the University of Surrey.
- The EVACS system used in the Australian Capital Territory.
- The STARVote system used in Travis county Texas.
- The UniCrypt system by the Bern University of Applied Sciences.
- The Verificatum Mixnet used in several systems.
- The ElectionGuard library by Microsoft.
- The vVote system used in the Australian state of Victoria.

In addition we draw upon the findings of other with respect to the following system:

- The Civitas system.
- The Norwegian system.

We will for each recommendation give an example of something that went wrong in practice when the recommendation was not followed and in many places also include a positive example. The examples are drawn partial from our own experience and partial from the experiences of others.

1.2   Outline of the Paper

By now, we have hopefully convinced the reader of the need to change the status quo if secure electronic voting is to be realised. We will in Sect. 2 take a case study of one particular flaw in the Scytl JavaScript ElGamal implementation. This flaw is not exploitable in the context of the system in which the JavaScript library is deployed; nevertheless, it will help us to demonstrate the gap between exploitable bugs and a system which is clearly reasonable free of bugs. In Sect. 3 we will provide recommendations on that concrete steps vendors and election management bodies should take before concluding in Sect. 4.

2   The Case Study

We will now give a case study which highlights the difficulties of examining systems. As we have already hinted, a major obstacle in examining system is the time constraints in relation to the complexity of the system; in general, *the simpler the system the better*. One common problem with deployed systems is that sub-components do not achieve clear security properties. This leaves reviewers chasing potential attacks throughout the system. In many cases, reviewers are unable to find an attack which will not be detected but given the degree of malleability the flaws in the sub-components allow, it is not possible to check that no such attack exists.

We have deliberately chosen a case study where a sub-component did not satisfy the claimed security but which did not break the overall system. We did this to emphasise the importance of clear and correct claims and documentation.

2.1 Introduction

In February 2020, we were given access to the released source code repository of the iVote system from the Australian state of New South Wales. The system is developed by the state electoral commission in collaboration with the vendor Scytl. The released documents include very little documentation and large amounts of code. In the recommendations below, we will talk about several problems with this repository but in this section we will focus on one particular flaw.

The encryption scheme ElGamal is commonly used in electronic voting protocols, including iVote, to provide privacy for the votes. ElGamal relies on a hardness assumption called the Decisional Diffie–Hellman problem which holds only for certain parameters of the system; in addition, the messages must be of the correct form (in the correct subgroup). If the parameters are chosen incorrectly or the messages are not of the correct form, then privacy of the votes is impacted.

Ensuring the messages are of the correct form can either be done at the application level or at the level of the crypto library. In response to our initial disclosures, Scytl indicated that they intend the checks to be performed at the application level; which they are. In examining the Scytl crypto library called cryptolib, we discovered incorrectly implemented checks that claim to ensure that the message was of the correct form. The result of which was that the code appeared to be making these checks without any actual security guarantees being achieved.

Scytl's claim that these checks belong at the application layer not in cryptolib seems inconsistent with the presence of such checks in cryptolib. It is problematic when reviewers find mistakes in the system and are expected to ignore them because they do not break the system in its current configuration, especially when this happens at the library level which is likely to be reused.

Summary of Details

- The method newZpGroupElement in cryptolib-js-mathematical service.js marks elements as belonging to the correct subgroup without checking.
- The method encrypt in cryptolib-js-elgamal encrypter.js checks that the message is marked as being in the correct subgroup but does not check that it is.
- These two flaws mean that, despite appearances, no checks that the messages belong to the message space are done before encrypting.
- These flaws do not appear to directly impact the privacy of iVote since the ivote-javascript-client-api follows the specification and maps the messages into the message space.

2.2 Background

iVote uses ElGamal encryption over the group of quadratic residues modulo a safe prime p. This group is of prime order q where $p = 2q + 1$. Care must be taken that both ciphertexts and messages belong to this group and not just the integers modulo p otherwise the semantic security of ElGamal will be broken.

ZpGroupElement. The library stores values using a class called ZpGroupElement which has three values:

p: The modulus of the Zp subgroup to which this Zp element belongs.
q: The *order* of the Zp subgroup to which this Zp group element belongs.
value: The value of the group element.

NewZpGroupElement. The method newZpGroupElement in the cryptolib-js-mathematical service.js is responsible for converting a BigInteger (or JSON) into a ZpGroupElement. In the case of a BigInteger, it performs the following three checks:

– That p is positive and greater than 3.
– That q is positive and less than p.
– That the value of the element is positive and less than p.

Having completed these checks it creates a ZpGroupElement (new ZpGroupElement(p, q, value)) which is marked as belonging to the subgroup of order q.

Problem. The checks suffice to ensure the value is in the multiplicative subgroup of $\mathbb{Z}_p$ but do not suffice to ensure that it belongs to the subgroup of order q.

Encrypt. The method *encrypt* in cryptolib-js-elgamal encrypter.js creates the ElGamal ciphertexts. Before it does this, it runs checkEncryptionData which in turn calls validator.checkZpGroupElements passing the group as a parameter. This function, which is defined in cryptolib-js-elgamal input-validator.js says

> "@param Zpsubgroup [group] Optional parameter pertaining to a Zp sub-group. If this option is provided, the modulus and order of the element will be checked against those of the group."

As we have noted the group is passed so the documentation says that the order of the element will be checked. The method then checks that the value q of the ZpGroupElement matches the value q of the group, but the order of the group element is not checked.

Problem. When they are created, all elements are marked as belonging to the subgroup without check, which makes the subgroup check meaningless.

2.3 Case Study Recommendation

There are two distinct solutions to the highlighted flaw in the case study.

Alternative A. The first solution is to remove the claims and incorrectly implemented checks from cryptolib which would align the code with the Scytl's claim that such checks belong at the application layer. At the very least the code needs to be clearly documented to reflect the fact that the checks do not provide the guarantees they claim.

Alternative B. The second solution is to correctly implement the checks. For example, for a message x check that:

1. $1 \leq x \leq p$
2. $x^q \bmod p = 1$

We note that there are more efficient ways to perform the check for quadratic residues using the Legendre symbol.

Summary. As we have stated, the problems above do not break the privacy of iVote because the application only calls the library on messages which are in the correct group.

The specific issues raised in this case study are related to a larger issue; the code of e-voting systems, and the applications in which they are used, are inadequately documented. Looking at the interactions of various academics with e-voting vendors, a trend can be observed from the vendors response to vulnerability discourses; they (at least from the public's perspective) retroactively define the security goals and in some cases engage in punitive measures which stifle public transparency. An important area of future improvement for e-voting vendors is to clearly document their code and specifications so that those examining system are aware of the intent.

3   Recommendations

To ensure e-voting systems are secure it is important the vendors and election management bodies engage with researches in an open, transparent and collaborative process. Below we give concrete recommendations of how this needs to be reflected in the process, documentation, and source code. We have split our recommendations into groups based on what phase of the project they correspond to. In practice most systems are developed in an agile not waterfall process but the phases will anyway serve as a convenient structure.

3.1   Design and Analysis Phase

1. Clear claims: The documentation accompanying the system should be clear about what security properties the system—and its sub-components—claim to achieve.

Clear claims are absolutely paramount to a transparent system. Claims of security which rapidly degrade into a very patchy set of trust assumptions as attacks are noticed are of little use when building secure systems.

Designing the system so that sub-components and phases of the protocol claim (and provide) clear security properties allows designers and examiners to structure their thinking. Further, it helps to ensure malicious behaviour is caught early.

Positive Example: The clear and high standards in Switzerland meant the bugs in the SwissPost system were clearly understood as failing to provide adequate security. Further, the presence of some many bugs at such a late stage revealed the inadequacy in the proceeding review processes. Switzerland has now refined its process to designing and reviewing system.

Negative Example: In contrast the lack of security requirements in many other countries such as Australia and Canada allows much weaker systems to operate.

2. Thorough documentation: The documentation—and source code comments—should be comprehensive, clear, correct and consistent.

Most of the systems include vast quantities of codes. A clear description of the protocol and intended functionality is crucial to understanding the system. One best practice for this, which was highlighted by the CHVote project, is the use of Pseudocode in the documentation.

Positive Example: The CHVote project[1] provides thorough documentation including pseudocode algorithms for its protocol. This allows programmers to more accurately implement the protocol and has allowed many examiners to notify the designers of major and minor findings.

Negative Example: In response to V. Teague's recent disclosures on mistakes in Sigma protocols in the iVote system, the vendor responded with a long response.[2] The response relies on saying that the mistakes do not matter because of how the protocol is realised, however, the details of the protocol used in the document are missing in the public documentation.

3.2 Build Phase

3. Minimality: The source code provided should be minimal; it should contain only code related to the system under review.

This issue is very important since more code takes longer to scrutinise. In addition, the more irrelevant code contained in the code base, the harder it is to understand the intended flow. While we understand the difficult in releasing only the code that is used, rather than the entirety of the supporting libraries, it seems some progress in this direction is required to achieve security.

Negative Example: The Swiss Post system included a broken implementation of a disjunctive Schnorr proof [HLPT20] despite no such proof being needed by the system in violation of minimalism.

---

[1] https://eprint.iacr.org/2017/325.pdf.
[2] https://www.scytl.com/wp-content/uploads/2019/11/Scytl_response-
_VT_NSW_iVote_Oct2019.pdf.

4. Buildable: The released source code should be easy to build. Preferable it should come with a configuration using a standard tool, such as Maven. The system should not depend on proprietary libraries which have not been released.

Examining and testing the system is best done not only by looking at the code but also by running it. In some cases the system is not buildable because it is incomplete in which case it is not possible to even look a the code.

Negative Example: The source code released for the iVote system is not buildable and indeed at certain key points the cryptographic code relies on proprietary libraries which have not been open sourced.

5. Executable: The system, once built, should be executable. The intended execution flow of the code should be clear either from the documentation or tests.

Particularly in JavaScript, methods can be heavily overloaded and do very different things based upon the type of input they receive. This makes it very hard to ascertain if the code behaves correctly on the input it is given during execution.

Negative Example: The Swiss Post system was not easily executable which significantly delayed the researchers examining the system.

6. Exportable: It should be possible to export test vectors into a well defined format for testing with an independent verifier.

While most systems support some form of export, many only export the information which is strictly necessary. Zero-knowledge proofs by design are incredible brittle to mistakes which makes debugging hard. We recommend systems to also include a complete export, including (at least some) intermediary values, which would form a better test vector.

Positive Example: The ElectionGuard system by Microsoft includes a reference implementation with a utility to run demo elections and export the resulting data. The resulting data is exported as a valid JSON file in a well defined format.

Negative Example: The election system used in the Estonian national election implements a custom hash function (based on SHA256) for use in its proofs. Including the challenge in the test vectors would ease the difficulties in assessing why an independent verifier was failing.

7. Consistent documentation and source: The source code and the documentation should correspond to each other.

As already elaborated, the review time is substantially increased by high levels of inconstancy in the source and documentation.

Negative Example: The ElectionGuard system's specification[3] required a group which was incompatible with the original reference implementation. We note that the original reference implementation was depreciated on the 15th of June 2020.

---

[3] https://github.com/microsoft/electionguard.

3.3 Maintain Phase

8. Regularly Updated: The open source variant of the system should be regularly updated so that experts can check that previous bugs are correctly fixed.

Most e-voting systems are regular updated with new features and patches. Every change may break the security of the system or fail to properly patch the intended vulnerability.

Negative Example: While Scytl has said they will fix the issue with the decryption proofs in iVote (that V. Teague discovered), at the time of writing the issue is still present in the semi-public repository. This prevents experts from checking the validity of the fix.[4]

9. Minimal restrictions on disclosure: The restrictions on the disclosure of vulnerabilities should be minimal.

The infrequency with which e-voting systems are used means vulnerability disclosure has difference incentives than in other areas. If a system is not being used nor is about to be used than why should disclosure be limited at all? On the other hand, if an election is running, or about to run, the parties involved have–in many cases–a very limited legally mandated time-frame to challenge the election result and withholding disclosure through that periods seems ethically dubious at best.

Negative Example: Prominent experts were offered access to the iVote system in Australia under an agreement which forbade them from disclosing vulnerabilities publicly for five years; they understandable declined to sign the agreement. The agreement has since been updated to restrict disclosure for 45 days which has resulted in much greater engagement.

4   Conclusion

In this paper we have discussed how the flaws in the code and documentation of systems opened to scrutiny by e-voting vendors and election management prevents meaningful analysis. We have given a case study from the iVote system which demonstrates that scrutineers are expected to overlook flaws in the code and documentation; cryptographic code which does not meets its security claims should not be included even if it does not break the current configuration.

Based on this and other experiences we provide 9 recommendations to vendors and election management bodies which would enable better scrutiny of e-voting systems:

1. Clear claims: Make clear claims about the security of the system

---

[4] A previous version of this paper erroneously claimed that an incorrect fix had been implemented in the semi-public repository; no fix has been implemented in the repository.

2. Thorough documentation: Provide comprehensive, clear, correct and consistent documentation
3. Minimality: The source code should be minimal and only contain code relevant to the system under review
4. Buildable: The source code should be easily buildable
5. Executable: The built system should be executable
6. Exportable: It should be possible to export test vectors for independent verification
7. Consistent documentation and source: The documentation should correspond to the source code
8. Regularly Updated: The open source system should be updated regularly to reflect the fixes of previously found bugs
9. Minimal restrictions on disclosure: Avoid long vulnerability disclosure times

All of our recommendations seem obvious but are still regularly violated in practice. We hope that by providing them in a single resource, it will help to serve as a checklist for vendors and election management bodies.

Acknowledgements. This work was supported by the Luxembourg National Research Fund (FNR) and the Research Council of Norway for the joint project SUR-CVS.

Disclaimer. This paper contains praises and critiques of the actions taken by a number of different e-voting vendors. Our evaluations are given for the purpose of clarifying what ought to be done; these examples are not intended to single out any particular vendor nor to suggest that all vendors exhibit all the issues discussed.

References

[Adi08] Adida, B.: Helios: web-based open-audit voting. In: van Oorschot, P.C., (ed.) USENIX Security Symposium, pp. 335–348. USENIX Association (2008)

[GG20] Gaudry, P., Golovnev, A.: Breaking the encryption scheme of the Moscow internet voting system. In: Bonneau, J., Heninger, N. (eds.) FC 2020. LNCS, vol. 12059, pp. 32–49. Springer, Cham (2020). https://doi.org/10.1007/978-3-030-51280-4_3

[HDKL20] Haenni, R., Dubuis, E., Koenig, R.E., Locher, P.: CHVote: sixteen best practices and lessons learned. In: Krimmer, R., et al. (eds.) E-Vote-ID 2020. LNCS, vol. 12455, pp. 95–111. Springer, Cham (2020). https://doi.org/10.1007/978-3-030-60347-2_7

[HGS21] Haines, T., Goré, R., Sharma, B.: Did you mix me? Formally verifying verifiable mix nets in voting. In: 2021 IEEE Symposium on Security and Privacy, SP 2021, San Jose, CA, USA, 23–27 May 2021. IEEE (2021)

[HGT19] Haines, T., Goré, R., Tiwari, M.: Verified verifiers for verifying elections. In: ACM Conference on Computer and Communications Security, pp. 685–702. ACM (2019)

[HLPT20] Haines, T., Jamie Lewis, S., Pereira, O., Teague, V.: How not to prove your election outcome. In: Oprea, A., Shacham, H. (eds.) 2020 IEEE Symposium on Security and Privacy, SP 2020, San Jose, CA, USA, 17–21 May 2020, pp. 784–800. IEEE (2020)

[HT15] Halderman, J.A., Teague, V.: The New South Wales iVote system: security failures and verification flaws in a live online election. In: Haenni, R., Koenig, R.E., Wikström, D. (eds.) VOTELID 2015. LNCS, vol. 9269, pp. 35–53. Springer, Cham (2015). https://doi.org/10.1007/978-3-319-22270-7_3

[Riv08] Rivest, R.L.: On the notion of 'software independence' in voting systems. Philos. Trans. R. Soc. A Math. Phys. Eng. Sci. **366**(1881), 3759–3767 (2008)

[SFD+14] Springall, D., et al.: Security analysis of the Estonian internet voting system. In: Proceedings of the 2014 ACM SIGSAC Conference on Computer and Communications Security, pp. 703–715. ACM (2014)

[SH20] Specter, M., Halderman, J.: Security analysis of the democracy live online voting system (2020)

[SKW20] Specter, M.A., Koppel, J., Weitzner, D.J.: The ballot is busted before the blockchain: a security analysis of voatz, the first internet voting application used in U.S. federal elections. In: USENIX Security Symposium, pp. 1535–1553. USENIX Association (2020)

Post-quantum Online Voting Scheme

Guillaume Kaim[1,2], Sébastien Canard[1], Adeline Roux-Langlois[2],
and Jacques Traoré[1(✉)]

[1] Orange Labs, Applied Crypto Group, Caen, France
`jacques.traore@orange.com`
[2] Univ Rennes, CNRS, IRISA, Rennes, France

Abstract. We propose a new post-quantum online voting scheme whose security relies on lattice assumptions. Compared to the state-of-the-art, our work does not make use of homomorphic primitives nor mix-nets, that are more traditional ways to build electronic voting protocols. The main reason is that zero-knowledge proofs, mandatory in the two afore-mentioned frameworks, are far to be as efficient as in "classical" cryptography, leading us to explore other approaches.

We rather base our work on a framework introduced by Fujioka et al. at Auscrypt 1992 that makes use of a blind signature scheme as the main building block. We depart however from this seminal work by allowing threshold issuance of blind signatures (to prevent ballot stuffing by malicious authorities) and by using a threshold post-quantum public key encryption scheme (rather than a commitment scheme) to allow voters to "vote and go" and to prevent "partial results". We instantiate all the required primitives with lattice-based constructions leading to the first online voting scheme that simultaneously provides post-quantum public verifiability and everlasting privacy (information-theoretic ballot anonymity). Another advantage of our protocol is that it can, contrary to recent proposals, efficiently handle elections with multiple candidates or with complex ballots (and not only referendums or single member plurality voting) without weakening the whole voting protocol by increasing the parameters size as with previous post-quantum voting schemes.

1 Introduction

The notion of online voting is appealing since the emergence of remote communications. However until now, there is no online voting protocol that fulfills all the properties (security, efficiency ...) required for such a sensitive topic. Still there exists some interesting constructions that have been used in real-world elections such as Votopia [KKLA01] or Helios [Adi08] which was trialed during student elections, for example in Princeton and the Catholic University of Louvain. The International Association of Cryptographic Researcher (IACR) also adopted Helios to elect its Board.

In this work we investigate the construction of a post-quantum online voting system built from a framework introduced by Fujioka et al. in Auscrypt 1992, which mainly relies on the well-known cryptographic primitive called a blind

© International Financial Cryptography Association 2021
M. Bernhard et al. (Eds.): FC 2021 Workshops, LNCS 12676, pp. 290–305, 2021.
https://doi.org/10.1007/978-3-662-63958-0_25

signature scheme. This framework contrasts from the current trend that makes use of homomorphic encryption, or mix-nets system to improve the efficiency of the tallying phase in addition to offer strong verifiability and privacy properties thanks to zero-knowledge proofs. However in post-quantum settings, a lack of efficiency of some of the primitives used in the two frameworks cited above lead us to investigate on new options for a practical online voting protocol. Indeed since the groundbreaking work of Shor [Sho97], we know that the arrival of quantum computers will harm most of the current cryptosystem used in practice, this is why it is important to replace them with quantum resistant constructions, among them lattice-based cryptography seems to be the most promising.

Post-Quantum Constructions. To the best of our knowledge, there exists only 2 post-quantum constructions, both built from lattice-based primitives. The first scheme is based on fully-homomorphic encryption by Chillotti et al. [CGGI16]. The second one uses zero-knowledge proofs on top of homomorphic commitments by del Pino et al. [dPLNS17].

Concerning the scheme of Chillotti et al. [CGGI16], the key idea is that they get rid of the zero-knowledge proofs that are inefficient in lattice-based settings. Indeed, their work is inspired by the online voting protocol of Helios [Adi08] which however requires zero-knowledge proofs to allow the voters to prove that their ballots are correctly formed, but also to permit the tally authority to prove that the result of the election is correct. In a nutshell, [CGGI16] uses a fully-homomorphic encryption scheme to replace the zero-knowledge proofs on the voter's side, while they use publicly verifiable ciphertext trapdoors to overcome the absence of zero-knowledge proofs on the authority side. However, using fully-homomorphic encryption makes the resulting voting scheme quite inefficient as pointed by del Pino et al. [dPLNS17]. This problem of efficiency may explains why implementations for the [CGGI16] scheme are lacking.

Concerning the construction of del Pino et al. [dPLNS17], the most important difference is that they make use zero-knowledge proofs contrary to [CGGI16]. In fact, the study of lattice-based zero-knowledge proofs has been intensive in the past five years with several advances in particular regarding their efficiency. This allows them to rely on a construction that makes a trade-off between efficiency and security. In short, their construction focuses on the Fiat-Shamir framework of [Lyu12], in order to prove the knowledge of the multiple of a short element instead of the element itself. In addition to the zero-knowledge primitive, they use a commitment scheme that benefits of an additive homomorphic property, which is very appealing in the online voting context. Finally, as said above, they provided an implementation of their voting scheme, that permits to analyze the efficiency of their construction in a real-world scenario. Indeed, generating and casting ballot is about 8.5 ms, and the time needed on the authority side as well as for the verification step takes about 0.15 s. However, their implementation only considers two candidates, while if we want to add more candidates, the globals parameters get bigger. Indeed, for 2^k possible candidates, the number of proofs needed is multiplied by a factor k, then the size of the vote increases from a logarithmic factor in the number of candidates.

Framework of Fujioka et al. and Adaptations. We base our construction on the framework of Fujioka et al. [FOO92] (FOO). In such framework, the anonymity is granted by a cryptographic primitive called blind signature, while everyone can verify that the outcome of the election is correct since all the elements that are necessary to the tally are made public at the end of the election. Blind signatures allow a user to obtain a signature on a message by interacting with a signing authority. At the end of the protocol, the authority has never seen the message and is not able to link a signature to the interactions that led to this signature. Therefore, the main building blocks of this framework are a blind signature scheme and a commitment scheme. The first one allows to preserve the anonymity of each voter, a requirement that is mandatory for any election, while it forbids voters from voting twice. The commitment scheme prevents any partial result to leak before the end of the election.

Concretely to generate his vote, any voter begins by computing a commitment of its voting choice, in order to conceal it from other voters until the end of the election. Then, he authenticates to the voting authority in order to obtain a blind signature on the commitment of his vote. Both the commitment and the (blind) signature constitute the voter's ballot which is then sent to the Bulletin Board (BB) via here again a perfectly anonymous channel. The later only stores signed ballots and discard invalid ones (i.e. either ballot that are not signed or ballot with an invalid signature). At the end of the election, all the voters have to open their commitment (they have to reveal their voting option and the random value used to generate the commitment), and to send both values (voting choice and random value) to the BB. However thanks to the blindness property and the use of a perfectly anonymous channel, the anonymity is preserved since no one will be able to link a signed ballot to the voter who requested the corresponding signature (and therefore no one will be able to link a voter to his vote). Finally anyone can tally the result of the election, by counting the votes and verifying the validity of the blind signatures associated to the opened commitments.

The FOO voting scheme suffers from several major drawbacks. The main one is that all voters have to participate to the ballot counting process, having to open their commitment at the end of the election: their scheme is not "vote and go" and would be unsuitable for real-life elections. Worse, the blind signature private key is held by a single authority who could easily stuff the BB by generating as many blind signatures (meaning valid but illegitimate ballots) as he wishes.

Our Contribution. Our main contribution is a new post-quantum online voting scheme whose security relies on lattice assumptions. Compared to the state-of-the-art, our work does not make use of homomorphic primitives nor zero-knowledge proofs of knowledge, that are more traditional ways to build electronic voting protocols. One interest of our construction is also that its efficiency does not depend on the number of candidates considered. Our construction can in particular handle complex ballots and could be used for example for preference voting or for elections with multiple candidates or voting options (for instance to select the most valuable players of a tournament as Votopia [KKLA01] did).

Our scheme uses of the FOO framework, with two main modifications.

- First, we use an encryption scheme instead of a commitment scheme so that the voting choices are now encrypted. At the end of the election, the decryption key will be made public so that anyone can decrypt the ballots and compute the election's result. With such modification, voters won't have to come back at the end of the election to open their commitment. Moreover, thanks to the indistinguishability property of the encryption scheme, the votes will remain hidden until the end of the election.
- Second, we transform the encryption and the blind signature schemes into threshold variants which allows to share the secret key between several authorities. Indeed the private key of the blind signature scheme is given to a single authority in [FOO92], who could generate as many ballots as he wants and stuff the Bulletin Board with them. The same problem would arise for the encryption scheme if we give the private decryption key to a single authority. It means that if the authority owning this private decryption key is corrupted, then he can get partial results by decrypting the ciphertexts before the end of the election, which is not desirable for most elections.

We then instantiate the needed building blocks in the lattice setting. We first chose to use the ring version of Dual-Regev [GPV08,LPR13] as our encryption scheme. The threshold transformation we considered turns it into a slight version of a threshold encryption scheme. Indeed, we just need to avoid that the secret key is given to a single authority, then only the key generation mechanism is impacted. The idea is that at the end of the election, at least a threshold of T authorities publish their shares, so that anyone can reconstruct the whole private key and decrypt the ciphertexts of the valid ballots included in the bulletin board.

We then use the lattice-based blind signature scheme given in [BCE+20] that we also adapt as a threshold variant. This second transformation is heavier, since the whole blind signature protocol is impacted. We start by using the result of Bendlin et al. [BKP13] that exhibits a generic transformation of a trapdoor based signature scheme [MP12] into a threshold variant[1]. Since the security of this transformation is proven using the universally composable (UC) model [Can01], then by composability our threshold variant remains secure. The two operations on the signer's part (the commitment and the signing step) are finally done in a threshold way by communicating with, at least, t signing authorities. We would like to emphasize that a recent paper [HKLN20] pointed out several issues in the one-more unforgeability proofs of previous lattice-based blind signature schemes. It leads to the fact that one-more unforgeability of [BCE+20] is only conjectured, while it proposes a better efficiency than the construction of [HKLN20].

---

[1] The basic threshold transformation of [BKP13] makes use of a trusted setup. A variant without such trusted setup is also given but needs the use of non-mature multilinear maps [GGH13]. In practice, it is not suitable to have an authority owning the complete secret keys, as implied by the trusted setup. However we would like to emphasize that the parameters of a voting scheme can be set a long time before election day and then we decided to focus on the operations performed by voters and the authority on the election day.

2   Preliminaries

Notation. The vectors are written in bold lower-case letters, and matrices in bold upper-case letters. The euclidean norm of a vector is denoted by $\|\mathbf{b}\|$, and the norm of a matrix $\|\mathbf{T}\| = \max_i \|\mathbf{t}_i\|$, where the $\mathbf{t}_i$'s are its column vectors. We denote by D a distribution over some countable support S and $x \hookleftarrow D$ the choice of x following the distribution D.

2.1   Lattices

We define a m-dimensional full rank lattice Λ as a discrete additive subgroup of $\mathbb{R}^m$. A lattice is the set of all integer combinations of some linearly independent basis vector $\mathbf{B} = \{\mathbf{b}_1, \ldots, \mathbf{b}_m\} \in \mathbb{R}^{n \times m}$: $\Lambda(\mathbf{B}) = \{\sum_{i=1}^m z_i \mathbf{b}_i, z_i \in \mathbb{Z}\}$.

We consider n a power of two, such that the polynomial ring $R = \mathbb{Z}[x]/(x^n + 1)$ is isomorphic to the integer lattice $\mathbb{Z}^n$. Then a polynomial $f = \sum_{i=0}^{n-1} f_i x^i$ in R corresponds to the integer vector of its coefficients $(f_0, \ldots, f_{n-1})$ in $\mathbb{Z}^n$. The notation norm of a polynomial $\|f\|$ means that we consider the norm of its coefficient vector, and as for the integer, the norm of a vector of polynomial $\|\mathbf{f}\| = \max_i \|f_i\|$. For the rest of the paper we will work with polynomials over R, or $R_q = R/qR = \mathbb{Z}_q[x]/(x^n + 1)$, where q is a prime verifying $q = 1 \pmod{2n}$.

Computational Problems. We consider Ring-SIS, a variant of the Short Integer Solution problem (SIS), proven to be at least as hard as the Shortest Independent Vectors Problem (SIVP) problem on ideal lattices [LM06,PR06].

Definition 1 (Ring-SIS$_{q,m,\beta}$). *Given* $\mathbf{a} = (a_1, \ldots, a_m)^T \in R_q^m$ *a vector of m uniformly random polynomials, find a non-zero vector of small polynomials* $\mathbf{x} = (x_1, \ldots, x_m)^T \in R^m$ *such that* $f_\mathbf{a}(\mathbf{x}) = \sum_{i=1}^m a_i \cdot x_i = 0 \bmod q$ *and* $0 < \|\mathbf{x}\| \leqslant \beta$.

We also define Ring-LWE that is similar to the Learning With Errors problem (LWE) [Reg05] but on a polynomial ring:

Definition 2 (Ring-LWE$_{q,D_{\mathbb{R},\alpha q},m}$). *Given a uniformly chosen vector* $\mathbf{a} \in R_q^m$ *and a polynomial* $\mathbf{b} = \mathbf{a} \cdot s + \mathbf{e} \bmod q$, *with* $s \leftarrow_\$ R_q$ *and* $\mathbf{e} \leftarrow D_{R^m,\alpha q}$, *the search Ring-LWE problem asks to find s. The decisional version asks to distinguish if a pair* $(\mathbf{a}, \mathbf{b}) \in R_q^m \times R_q^m$ *has been generated from the uniform distribution on* $R_q^m \times R_q^m$ *or if it has been generated as a Ring-LWE sample* $(\mathbf{a}, \mathbf{b} = \mathbf{a} \cdot s + \mathbf{e})$.

Gaussian Distribution. The Gaussian function of center $\mathbf{c} \in \mathbb{R}^n$ and width parameter σ is defined as $\rho_{\sigma,\mathbf{c}}(\mathbf{x}) = \exp(-\pi \frac{\|\mathbf{x}-\mathbf{c}\|^2}{\sigma^2})$, for all $\mathbf{x} \in \mathbb{R}^n$. A positive definite covariance matrix is defined as $\mathbf{\Sigma} = \mathbf{B}\mathbf{B}^T$: $\rho_{\sqrt{\Sigma},\mathbf{c}} = \exp(-\pi(\mathbf{x} - \mathbf{c})^T \mathbf{\Sigma}^{-1}(\mathbf{x}-\mathbf{c}))$. The discrete Gaussian distribution over a lattice Λ is defined as $D_{\Lambda,\sigma,\mathbf{c}}(\mathbf{x}) = \frac{\rho_{\sigma,\mathbf{c}}(\mathbf{x})}{\rho_{\sigma,\mathbf{c}}(\Lambda)}$ where $\rho_{\sigma,\mathbf{c}}(\Lambda) = \sum_{x \in \Lambda} \rho_{\sigma,\mathbf{c}}(\mathbf{x})$. The vectors sampled from $D_{\Lambda,\sigma}$ are short with overwhelming probability.

Lemma 1 ([Ban93], lemma 1.5). *For any lattice* $\Lambda \subseteq \mathbb{R}^n, \sigma > 0$ *and* $\mathbf{c} \in \mathbb{R}^n$, *we have* $Pr_{\mathbf{x} \hookleftarrow D_{\Lambda,\sigma,\mathbf{c}}}[\|\mathbf{x} - \mathbf{c}\| \leqslant \sqrt{n}\sigma] \geqslant 1 - 2^{-\Omega(n)}$.

Trapdoors. As introduced in [Ajt96] and widespread in [GPV08], a trapdoor for $\mathbf{A} \in \mathbb{Z}_q^{n \times m}$ is a short basis of the lattice $\Lambda_q^{\perp}(\mathbf{A}) := \{\mathbf{v} \in \mathbb{Z}^m \text{ such that } \mathbf{Av} = 0 \bmod q\}$. A trapdoor allows to sample short Gaussian vectors solutions to the Inhomogeneous Small Integer Solution (ISIS) problem: $\mathbf{Av} = \mathbf{x} \bmod q$ with $\mathbf{x} \in \mathbb{Z}_q^n$. This technique is called *Preimage Sampling*. In this work we make use of the trapdoor construction of [MP12]. *Construction.* In [MP12], the construction of the gadget-based trapdoor uses a gadget vector $\mathbf{g} = (1, 2, 4, \ldots, 2^{k-1})^T \in R_q^k$, with $k = \lceil \log_2 q \rceil$, takes as input the modulus q, the Gaussian parameter τ, and an optional $\mathbf{a}' \in R_q^{m-k}$ and $h \in R_q$. If no $\mathbf{a}'$ is given it is chosen uniformly in R_q^{m-k} and if no h is given, $h = 1$. The construction outputs a matrix $\mathbf{a} = (\mathbf{a}'^T \| h\mathbf{g} - \mathbf{a}'^T \mathbf{T})^T$ with $\mathbf{T} \in R^{(m-k) \times k}$ its trapdoor associated to the tag h, generated as a Gaussian of parameter τ.

Preimage Sampling. The construction given in [MP12] enables the use of the PreSample algorithm. Given $\mathbf{a} \in R_q^m$, such algorithm computes a short vector solution $\mathbf{v} \in R^m$ of a Ring-SIS problem $f_{\mathbf{a}}(\mathbf{v}) = \sum_{i=1}^m a_i \cdot v_i = 0 \bmod q$, available only thanks to a trapdoor $\mathbf{T} \in R_q^{(m-k) \times k}$ for $\mathbf{a}$.

Hash Function. We use the hash function family developed in [LM06], denoted $\mathcal{H}(R_q, m)$. Let R_q be a ring and $m \geqslant 1$ a positive integer. The hash function $h_{\mathbf{a}} : R_q^m \to R_q$ for $\mathbf{a} \in R_q^m$ is defined as: $\mathbf{x} \mapsto \langle \mathbf{a}, \mathbf{x} \rangle = \sum_{i=0}^{m-1} a_i \cdot x_i$.

Definition 3 (inspired by [Rüc10], definition 2.1). *Let $D \subset R$, the collision problem $Col(\mathcal{H}(R_q, m), D)$ asks to find a distinct pair $(\mathbf{x}, \mathbf{x}') \in D^m \times D^m$ such that $h(\mathbf{x}) = h(\mathbf{x}')$ for $h \leftarrow \mathcal{H}(R_q, m)$.*

Rejection Sampling. The construction of blind signature we consider, makes a significant use of the rejection sampling technique from [Lyu12]. Such rejection sampling is used in the case we have a distribution depending on a secret we want to hide. The main idea is to "reject" the elements of this distribution using a distribution probability not depending on the related secret. In case we can not perform any rejection sampling, the following lemma also allows to hide the center of a gaussian distribution.

Lemma 2 ([GKPV10], Lemma 3). *Let $v \in R$ be arbitrary. The statistical distance between the distributions $D_{R,\sigma}$ and $D_{R,\sigma,v}$ is at most $\frac{\|v\|}{\sigma}$.*

2.2 Online Voting Definition and Security Properties

We now give the definition of an online voting system, first talking about entities.

- First we get a set of N eligible voters V_i for $i \in [N]$.
- We also need a set of p authorities A_j for $j \in [p]$, that will share the private election keys.
- Finally we need a bulletin board BB, that will collect the (valid) ballots cast by the voters. At the end of the election, the valid ballots will be tallied.

We take as a basis the definition of an online voting protocol by Cortier et al. [CGGI14]. However, we voluntarily omit the credential phase, in which eligible voters obtain their voting credentials. We also modify some parts to manage the fact that our online voting framework needs interactiveness between voters and authorities.

Security. We discuss the security properties a secure online voting protocol should fulfill. Concerning **correctness**, we fit in with the definition of [CGGI14]. The idea is that a genuinely generated ballot is always accepted into the bulletin board, and for an election where all parties behave honestly, the result of the tally always corresponds to the votes cast by the voters.

The **verifiability** property is a fundamental security property needed in online voting schemes which has been the subject of several papers in the voting literature (see [CGK+16]). However, we also rely on the verifiability property introduced in [CGGI14]. Before describing it, we would like to emphasize that we only consider "partial tallying online voting protocols", which means that the tallying phase is not performed in a single computation, but each ballot is open separately, then the resulting tally is computed step by step. Verifiability asks the tallying result to be consistent with the votes cast by honest voters.

Vote secrecy is another fundamental security property. It asks that the voting choice of a voter remains private during and after the end of the election. In our definition, called **ballot anonymity** we depart from the classical ballot privacy requirement, that has been the subject of an intensive research (summarized in [BCG+15]). Indeed in our online voting protocol, each ballot will be anonymous, that is, it does not identify the voter who casts it. This contrasts with most of other voting protocols, where each ballot is directly linked to the voter who casts it, leading to the fact that in the tally procedure each individual ballot could not be open (or decrypt) otherwise this would leak for whom a voter voted. Our ballot anonymity requirement is very close to the privacy property defined in [KR05]. A voting protocol satisfies our ballot anonymity requirement if an attacker cannot link a ballot to the voter who casts it.

3   Our Construction

In this section, we first briefly recall the main tools that we are using: blind signature schemes and the ring version of the dual Regev encryption scheme. Then, we transform them in a distributed variant where the private key is shared among several authorities using the result from Bendlin et al. [BKP13]. Finally, we present our scheme and discuss its security.

3.1   Cryptographic Primitives

Blind Signatures. We first recall the blind signature described in [BCE+20].

- **Setup.** We consider the polynomial ring $R_q = \mathbb{Z}_q[X]/(X^n + 1)$. Two families of hash functions are necessary in this protocol, first a generic one H $\leftarrow_\$$

$\mathcal{H}(1^n) : \{0,1\}^* \to R_2$ (modelled as a random oracle), and a second one on the specific ring R_q, typically $h \leftarrow_\$ \mathcal{H}(R_q, m)$ as defined in the preliminaries. Table 1 shows up the different sizes of the parameters: n is a power of 2, in order to have the polynomial $X^n + 1$ irreducible, m ensures the worst-case to average case reduction of the scheme. The others parameters are set such that the rejection sampling and security arguments work.

- **Key Generation.** The key generation algorithm BS.Keygen(1^n) selects a secret key $\mathbf{s} \in R_3^m$ and a vector of polynomial $\mathbf{a} = (\mathbf{a}'^T \| h\mathbf{g} - \mathbf{a}'^T \mathbf{T_a})^T \in R_q^m$, along with a trapdoor $\mathbf{T_a}$ on $\mathbf{a}$, such that the hash function $h_\mathbf{a} \in \mathcal{H}(R_q, m)$ is built with this polynomial vector $\mathbf{a}$. Finally the public key $p = h_\mathbf{a}(\mathbf{s})$ is made public. BS.Keygen(1^n) outputs $s_k = (\mathbf{s}, \mathbf{T_a})$, $p_k = (p, \mathbf{a})$.

- **Signature.** The interactive blind signature protocol BS.Sign(Signer($\mathbf{s}, \mathbf{T_a}$), User(p, M)) is composed of 3 exchanges:
  - The signer generates $\mathbf{y} \hookleftarrow D_{R,\sigma}^m$ and sends $\mathbf{x} = h_\mathbf{a}(\mathbf{y})$ to the user.
  - The user generates two ephemeral vectors $\mathbf{t}_1 \hookleftarrow D_{R,\alpha}, \mathbf{t}_2 \hookleftarrow D_{R,\beta}^m$, such that if $\|\mathbf{t}_2\| > t\sqrt{n \cdot m} \cdot \beta$ it generates a fresh $\mathbf{t}_2 \hookleftarrow D_{R,\beta}^m$ until the test succeeds. He then generates the hashing values $\mathbf{e} = \mathrm{H}(\mathbf{x} - p \cdot \mathbf{t}_1 - h_\mathbf{a}(\mathbf{t}_2), M)$ and $\mathbf{e}^* = \mathbf{e} - \mathbf{t}_1$ and applies the rejection sampling test on $\mathbf{e}^*$. If this test passes, it sends $\mathbf{e}^*$ and otherwise, it restarts this whole step.
  - The signer generates the signature $\mathbf{z}^* = \mathbf{e}^* \cdot \mathbf{s} \mid \mathbf{y}$, it applies the rejection sampling test and sends $\mathbf{z}^*$ if the test passes and uses its trapdoor $\mathbf{T_a}$ to generate a presample on $\mathbf{e}^* \cdot p + \mathbf{x}$ with parameter σ if not. Finally if $\|\mathbf{z}^*\| > t\sqrt{n \cdot m} \cdot \sigma$ it generates fresh $\mathbf{z}^*$ with its trapdoor until this test passes. He sends $\mathbf{z}^*$ to the user.

  The user computes $\mathbf{z} = \mathbf{z}^* - \mathbf{t}_2$ and outputs the blind signature $(M, (\mathbf{z}, \mathbf{e}))$.
- **Verification.** The verification procedure BS.Verif($p, M, (\mathbf{z}, \mathbf{e})$) outputs 1 iff $\|\mathbf{z}\| \leqslant D$ and $\mathrm{H}(h_\mathbf{a}(\mathbf{z}) - p \cdot \mathbf{e}, M) = \mathbf{e}$.

Encryption Scheme. Concerning the encryption scheme, we use the Dual-Regev encryption scheme [GPV08,LPR13] on a polynomial ring R_q. However, any post-quantum encryption scheme would fit into our voting protocol.

- **Setup.** The set-up algorithm PK.Setup chooses integers n, m, q and two real α, β such that the dual-Regev encryption scheme on the polynomial rings is secure (see [LPR13]).

Table 1. Parameters of [BCE+20].

Parameter	Value	Asymptotic
n	Power of 2	–
m	$\lfloor \log q \rfloor + 1$	$\Omega(\log n)$
γ	$n\alpha$	$O(n\sqrt{n})$
α	$\omega(k\sqrt{\log n})$	$O(\sqrt{n})$
β	$2^{\omega(\log n)}\sigma\sqrt{n}$	$O(n^3 \, 2^{\omega(\log n)})$
σ	$\omega((n\sqrt{n}\alpha)\sqrt{\log n})$	$O(n^2\sqrt{n})$
D	$t\sqrt{n \cdot m}(\beta + \sigma)$	$O(n^3\sqrt{n} \, 2^{\omega(\log n)})$
q	$\geqslant 4mn\sqrt{n}\log(n)D.\text{prime}$	$\Theta(n^6 \, 2^{\omega(\log n)})$

- **KeyGen.** The Key generation algorithm PK.KeyGen(1^n) starts by sampling $\mathbf{s} \hookleftarrow D_{\mathbf{R}^m,\alpha}$, $\mathbf{a} \leftarrow_\$ \mathbf{R}_q^m$ uniformly at random and computes $u = \mathbf{a}^T\mathbf{s} \in \mathbf{R}_q^m$. It outputs (e_k, m_k) where $e_k = \mathbf{s} \in \mathbf{R}_q^m$ is the secret key and $m_k = (\mathbf{a}, u) \in \mathbf{R}_q^m \times \mathbf{R}_q$ is the public key.
- **Encrypt.** Given a message $m \in \mathbf{R}_2$, and a public key m_k, the encryption algorithm PK.Encrypt(m, m_k) chooses a vector $v \in \mathbf{R}_q$ uniformly at random, and outputs the ciphertext $(\mathbf{b} = \mathbf{a}v + \mathbf{e}, c = u \cdot v + e' + \lfloor q/2 \rfloor m) \in \mathbf{R}_q^m \times \mathbf{R}_q$ where $\mathbf{e} \hookleftarrow D_{\mathbf{R}^m,\beta}$, $e' \hookleftarrow D_{\mathbf{R},\beta}$.
- **Decrypt.** Given a ciphertext $(\mathbf{b}, c) \in \mathbf{R}_q^m \times \mathbf{R}_q$ and a private key $e_k = \mathbf{s} \in \mathbf{R}_q^m$, PK.Decrypt($(\mathbf{b}, c), e_k$) computes $\mu = c - \mathbf{b}^T\mathbf{s} = -\mathbf{e}^T \cdot \mathbf{s} + e' + \lfloor q/2 \rfloor m$. To recover the message m, it suffices to look after each coordinate of μ, if the i-th coordinate is closer to 0 than to $\lfloor q/2 \rfloor$ then the i-th bit of m is equal to 0 and 1 otherwise.

3.2   Threshold Functionalities

Threshold Tools and Variants. In the original version of a blind signature scheme, there is only one signer who could easily, in the context of online voting, stuff the Bulletin Board by adding as many valid (but illegitimate) ballots as he wishes. We therefore transform it into a threshold one, using the generic transformation of a trapdoor based signature scheme with strong trapdoor of [MP12], into a threshold trapdoor based signature scheme by [BKP13]. The construction of [BKP13] is built on the integer ring $\mathbb{Z}_q$, but the blind signature of [BCE+20] relies on polynomial ring $\mathbf{R}_q$. However the strong trapdoor construction can be adapted to this ring setting [MP12], and the Shamir secret sharing [Sha79] still works on this type of rings. Then the whole construction of [BKP13] can be adapted to the polynomial ring setting.

As our transformation is applied on a blind signature scheme and not on a signature scheme, we have several modifications to provide. The signer's part of the blind signature is composed of two steps. At first, it has to generate a commitment, which one can be transformed in a threshold manner using Shamir secret sharing and a trusted setup to share a Gaussian vector. The second step consists in a classic "Fiat-Shamir with abort" signature, which can easily be transformed into a threshold one by means of homomorphic properties of the Shamir secret sharing. In case of abort, the signer performs a GPV-like signature which is a generic signature scheme and can be transformed using the generic transformation of [BKP13] into a threshold scheme.

The proofs of the various protocols from [BKP13] are realized in the UC model [Can01], so that we just have to plug the threshold functionalities into the blind signature scheme, to obtain, by composability, a secure threshold variant of the blind signature scheme. Below we describe the two main protocols, which are the KeyGen and the SampleZ protocol. Moreover we choose to give an informal description of the functionalities involved for these two protocols. The full construction can be found in the paper of [BKP13].

We consider p authorities, such that a threshold of t authorities is mandatory to execute the various functions developed below. Let $\mathbf{a}' \in \mathbf{R}_q^{m-k}$ be a uniformly distributed vector of polynomial and $\mathbf{T} \in R_q^{(m-k)\times k}$ be a Gaussian-distributed matrix. Let $\{[\mathbf{T}]^i\}_{i\in[p]}$ be the shares of the polynomial matrix $\mathbf{T}$. Let us denote by $\mathbf{a}_1 = \mathbf{a}'^T \cdot \mathbf{T} \bmod q$ and $\mathbf{a} = [\mathbf{a}'|\mathbf{a}_1]$.

- $\mathcal{F}_{\text{Blind}}$: This functionality takes as input shares of an arbitrary value x and output fresh shares $[x]^i$ of this same value.
- $\mathcal{F}_{\text{SampZ}}$: This functionality takes as input dimensions $h \times d$ and a gaussian variance z. It outputs shares $[\mathbf{Z}]^i$ of a gaussian distributed matrix $\mathbf{Z} \leftarrow D_z^{h\times d}$.
- Threshold KeyGen protocol: The KeyGen protocol is realised in the $\mathcal{F}_{\text{Blind}}$, $\mathcal{F}_{\text{SampZ}}$ model. On input the tuple $(\mathbf{a}', h^* \in \mathbb{R}_q, z \in \mathbb{Z})$, each party i does:
  1. call $\mathcal{F}_{\text{SampZ}}((m - k) \times k, z)$, then receive $[\mathbf{T}]^i$;
  2. call $\mathcal{F}_{\text{Blind}}(-\mathbf{a}'^T[\mathbf{T}]^i)$, then receive $[\mathbf{a}_1]^i$;
  3. broadcast $[\mathbf{a}_1]^i$ and reconstruct $\mathbf{a}_1 = \mathbf{a}'^T \cdot \mathbf{T} \bmod q$ from other shares;
  4. output $\mathbf{a} = [\mathbf{a}'|h^* \cdot \mathbf{g} + \mathbf{a}_1]$ as the public key and $[\mathbf{T}]^i$ as the private key of the authority i.
- $\mathcal{F}_{\text{Gadget}}$: It takes as input a coset value $v \in R_q$ and outputs shares $[\mathbf{u}]^i \in R^k$ of a gaussian distributed polynomial vector such that $\mathbf{g}^T \cdot \mathbf{u} = v$.
- $\mathcal{F}_{\text{Correct}}$: This functionality generates for each $j \in [k]$ and $v \in R_q$ queues $Q_{j,v}$ of at least B values in each queue, that will allow the signer to perform at least B pre-image of each vector $v \in R_q$. Each queue $Q_{j,v}$ is composed by using the gadget functionality developed above and the shares $[\mathbf{T}]^i$ of the trapdoor such that each authority gets a share of $\mathbf{y}_{j,v} = \begin{bmatrix} \mathbf{T} \\ \mathbf{I} \end{bmatrix} (\mathbf{e}_j \otimes \mathbf{z}_{j,v})$ for $\mathbf{z}_{j,v} \in \Lambda_v^{\perp}(\mathbf{g}^T)$, with $\mathbf{e}_j$ the vector composed of 0 elements except the j-th coordinate which is equal to 1.
  Then, in the sampling algorithm of [MP12], when we have to correct a perturbation to get a correct sample for a given syndrom $v \in R_q$, the authorities recover a value in the corresponding queue $Q_{j,v_1}, \cdots, Q_{j,v_n}$.
- $\mathcal{F}_{\text{Perturb}}$: The perturb algorithm in the threshold setting, is the same as in the standard setting, but the perturbation vector is then shared between the p authorities using the functionality $\mathcal{F}_{\text{SampZ}}$. then it takes as inputs a dimension $h \times d$ and a gaussian parameter z, it outputs $[\mathbf{P}]^i$ with $\mathbf{P} \leftarrow D_z^{h\times d}$.

SampleZ Protocol. Using $\mathcal{F}_{\text{Perturb}}$ and $\mathcal{F}_{\text{Correct}}$ defined above (threshold counterparts of the steps composing the **Preimage sampling** protocol introduced in [MP12]), the SampleZ protocol generates a presample in the same way, but with the threshold variants of the subalgorithms perturb and correct.

Threshold Variants of Our Building Blocks. Using the above tools, we now give the modifications we need to provide a threshold variant of both the encryption scheme (PK.KeyGen to TBS.KeyGen) and the blind signature primitive of [BCE+20] (BS.KeyGen and BS.Sign to TBS.KeyGen and TBS.Sign resp.).

- **TPK.KeyGen**($1^n, 1^p$). It generates $\mathbf{s} \leftarrow D_{\mathbb{R}^m,\alpha}$ as the secret key in a distributed way using the $\mathcal{F}_{\text{SampZ}}$ algorithm, such that each authority $\mathcal{A}^i, i \in [p]$ gets a share $[\mathbf{s}]^i$. Concerning the public key, it chooses $\mathbf{a} \leftarrow_\$ R_q^m$ uniformly at random. Finally each authority computes and reveals $[u]^i = \mathbf{a}^T[\mathbf{s}]^i \in R_q^m, i \in [p]$ such that u can be recovered and output publicly. The secret keys are then the elements $[e_k]^i = [\mathbf{s}]^i \in R_q^m, i \in [p]$ and the public key is composed of the pair $m_k = (\mathbf{a}, u) \in R_q^m \times R_q$, it outputs (e_k, m_k).

- **TBS.KeyGen**$(1^n, 1^p)$. TBS.KeyGen generates a public polynomial vector $\mathbf{a}$ with a trapdoor $\mathbf{T}$ using a trapdoor generation algorithm in a distributed way using the Threshold Keygen protocol described above. It then generates a random polynomial vector $\mathbf{s} \in R_3^m$ with its image by the hash function such that $\mathrm{p} = h_{\mathbf{a}}(\mathbf{s})$. Concerning $\mathbf{s}$, the algorithm $\mathcal{F}_{\mathrm{SampZ}}$ is executed by each authority, in order to obtain $[\mathbf{s}]^i, i \in [p]$, they each then have to broadcast their public part $\mathbf{a} \cdot [\mathbf{s}]^i, i \in [p]$ to recover and output the public key p. Finally the algorithm outputs the public key $p_k = (\mathrm{p}, \mathbf{a})$ and the private key share $[s_k]^i = ([\mathbf{T}]^i, [\mathbf{s}]^i), i \in [p]$ to each authority $\mathcal{A}^i, i \in [p]$.

- **TBS.Sign**$(\{(\mathcal{A}^i([s_k]^i))\}_{i \in T}, \mathcal{V}(p_k, M))$. Considering a set of T signing authorities $\mathcal{A}^i, i \in [T]$, the signature algorithm is the same as the one in [BCE+20] from the user's side. Concerning the signer's view, firstly the commitment $\mathbf{y}$ is generated in a distributed manner using the algorithm $\mathcal{F}_{\mathrm{SampZ}}$, such that the authorities get a share $[\mathbf{y}]^i$ and distributively output the corresponding element $\mathrm{x} = h_{\mathbf{a}}(\mathbf{y})$ in the same way as it was done in the TBS.KeyGen algorithm for the pair $(\mathbf{s}, \mathrm{p})$. Concerning the signing step, from the signer's view, the first attempt of signature, which is a Fiat-Shamir like signature [Lyu12], is performed between the authorities thanks to the homomorphic property of the Shamir secret sharing, while the GPV-like [GPV08] signature generation is performed in a threshold manner using the SampZ protocol. Finally, the algorithm outputs the signature $\sigma = (M, \mathrm{e}, \mathbf{z})$.

3.3 Our Scheme

As explained above, we chose to modify the [FOO92] framework in order to let voters "Vote and go" and to prevent ballot stuffing by a malicious authority. Instead of committing to their voting choices, voter will have to encrypt them using the public election key. At the end of the election, the decryption key will be disclosed so that anyone will be able to decrypt the ballots and compute the result of the election. To avoid fraud by a malicious authority, we transform the underlying encryption and blind signature schemes considered into threshold variants, so that the corresponding private keys would be shared among several authorities and not a single one.

Considering these modifications of the [FOO92] framework, we describe the complete online voting protocol that we build from the above cryptographic primitives. First, a setup phase generates the parameters of the protocol, including the private and public keys of the used cryptographic schemes. Next the voting phase is composed of two steps: the voter first encrypts his voting option (using the public election key) and then interacts with (at least) t voting authorities to obtain a blind signature on his ciphertext. His ballot b is composed of the ciphertext $\mathbf{c}$ of his voting choice v along with a (blind) signature σ on $\mathbf{c}$ such that $b = (\mathbf{c}, \sigma)$. The Bulletin Board accepts the ballot if σ is a valid signature on **c** and discards it otherwise. In the counting phase, the tallying authorities reveal their share of the private encryption key, so that anyone can recover the corresponding decryption key and decrypt the ballots (the ciphertexts **c**) to compute the result of the election. Auditing the election is easy. For this purpose, an interested voter first has to check that all the ballots collected by the Bulletin Board are valid (i.e. that the signatures σ are valid) and that the decryption key published by the talliers is correct (i.e., corresponds to the public election key). He then has to decrypt all the ballots using the decryption key and computes the result of the election just as the talliers did.

- **Setup**$(1^n, 1^p, 1^N)$. This algorithm has to generate two pairs of secret/public keys, one pair for the encryption scheme and another one for the blind signature scheme. Moreover these keys have to be generated in a threshold manner, for a number p of authorities, with a threshold number of t. Let us denote by $(s_k, p_k) \leftarrow$ **BS.KeyGen**(1^n) and $(e_k, m_k) \leftarrow$ **PK.KeyGen**(1^n), and by $[s_k]^i$ (resp $[e_k]^i$) the shares of the private blind signature key (resp encryption key). Then the setup algorithms outputs $\mathbf{pk} = (p_k, m_k)$ and $\mathbf{sk} = ([s_k]^i, [e_k]^i)_{i \in [p]}$.

- **Vote**$(\mathcal{V}_i(v, \mathbf{pk}), \mathcal{A}^j([s_k]^j)_{j \in \mathrm{T}})$. The voting phase is split in two steps. First, the voter $\mathcal{V}_i$ encrypts his vote $v \in \{0, 1\}^*$ in $\mathbf{c} = $ **PK.encrypt**(v, m_k) in an offline phase. Then in an online phase, he is first authenticated (to check whether he is an eligible voter who has not yet requested a blind signature from the voting authorities). The protocol aborts if the authentication failed or if the voter already requested a blind signature. He then interacts with voting authorities $\mathcal{A}^j$ to get a blind signature $\sigma = $ **BS.Sign**$(\{\mathcal{A}^j([s_k]^j)\}_{j \in \mathrm{T}}, \mathcal{V}_i(p_k, \mathbf{c}))$, with T a set of authorities of size at least t. Finally the voter outputs $(\sigma, \mathbf{c})$ as his ballot and casts it, anonymously, into the bulletin board BB.

- **Validate**$(b, \mathbf{pk})$. On input a ballot $b = (\sigma, \mathbf{c})$, anyone can check its validity by performing the verification algorithm of the blind signature **BS.Verify**$(p_k, \mathbf{c}, \sigma)$, it outputs 0 if the blind signature verification fails and 1 otherwise.

- **Box**(BB, b). It takes as input the current state of the bulletin board BB, along with a ballot b. It first checks the validity of b by performing the algorithm described above: Validate$(b, \mathbf{pk})$. It updates $BB \leftarrow BB \cup \{b\}$ if Validate outputs 1 and remains unchanged if it outputs 0.

- **Tally**$(BB, p_k, \mathcal{E}^j([e_k]^j)_{j \in [p]})$. At the end of the election, at least t (the threshold) authorities $(\mathcal{E}^j)_{j \in [t]}$ holding the shares of the decryption key e_k reveal publicly their share $([e_k]^j)_{j \in t}$, such that anyone can rebuild the decryption key e_k. Then for each ballot $(\sigma, \mathbf{c}) \in BB$, anyone can decrypt **c** and retrieve the vote $v = $ PK.decrypt$(\mathbf{c}, e_k)$ of each voter, after verifying that BS.Verify$(\sigma, p_k) = 1$. Then he/she can tally and outputs the result r, which corresponds to the outcome of the election $\mathbf{r} = \{v_i\}_{i \in k}$ with $k \leqslant N$ the number of voters that output a valid ballot.

- **Verify**$(BB, \mathbf{r}, e_k)$. This algorithm is straightforward. Since the decryption secret key e_k is made public (and since anyone can check that it corresponds to the public election key), anyone can check the validity of the result by decrypting all the ciphertexts **c** contained in valid ballots $(\sigma, \mathbf{c}) \in BB$ (i.e., with a valid blind signature σ) and tally them to compare to the announced result **r**.

302 G. Kaim et al.

3.4 Security of Our Scheme

Theorem 1 (Correctness). *Since the blind signature and public key encryption schemes are correct, then our online voting scheme is correct.*

Proof. According to our definition, our voting protocol is correct if a ballot generated by an honest voter is accepted with overwhelming probability by the BB, and if the result of an election where every party behaves honestly, corresponds to the votes cast by voters. The first condition is fulfilled since the blind signature scheme used to authenticate valid ballots is correct. The second condition is verified since the encryption scheme satisfies the correctness requirement. Since our voting protocol satisfies both conditions it is therefore correct.

Theorem 2 (Verifiability). *Using a strong authentication scheme and a one-more unforgeable blind signature scheme, our voting scheme is verifiable.*

Sketch of Proof. To win the game, the attacker has either to (1) impersonate an honest voter or (2) cast more valid votes (let say $n_C + 1$) than the number n_C of corrupted users. (1) would mean that he has successfully broken the strong authentication scheme used by voters to authenticate to Voting Authorities. (2) would mean that the attacker could generate more valid blind signatures than requested (therefore breaking the one-more unforgeability of the threshold blind signature scheme) or that there exists more dishonest voting authorities than assumed (which could generate as many valid but illegitimate-ballots as they wish). Furthermore, he can not cheat after the end of the election, since the election's tally is made public. We further notice that the tally can not give two different results for two iterations of the Tally algorithm since the decryption mechanism and the blind signature verification algorithm are both deterministic.

Theorem 3 (Ballot anonymity). *Our voting scheme provides perfect (information-theoretic) ballot anonymity.*

Sketch of Proof. In the ballot anonymity game, an attacker $\mathcal{A}^*$ chooses two honest voters $\mathcal{V}_0$ and $\mathcal{V}_1$ and two voting options v_0 and v_1. It then interacts with $\mathcal{V}_0$ and $\mathcal{V}_1$ who then cast, using a perfectly anonymous channel, two ballots b_c (on v_0) and b_{1-c} (on v_1). $\mathcal{A}^*$ has to identify which voter outputs which ballot. We then have to prove that the attacker $\mathcal{A}^*$ has a negligible advantage (compared to random guessing) to win. In our protocol, each ballot does not include any information about the identity of each voter, since the encryption and blind signature schemes are performed only on the voting choices v_0 and v_1. As our blind signature scheme provides perfect blindness and since we assumed that ballots are cast via a perfectly anonymous channel, $\mathcal{A}^*$ cannot find c better than random guessing. Therefore, provided that ballots are cast via a perfectly anonymous channel, our voting protocol provides perfect ballot anonymity.

Partial Results. The encryption scheme prevents any partial result to leak. Indeed the decryption key is shared among several authorities, which cannot open the ballots without at least t shares of it. Then as long as $p - t + 1$ of them remain honest, the ballots cannot be opened before the end of the election.

4   Conclusion

In this paper we presented a new practical lattice-based online voting system. In contrast to traditional schemes, our protocol does not rely on homomorphic aggregation or mix-nets and does not make use of zero-knowledge proofs, which have previously been the main issue in the post-quantum setting. Instead, our scheme extends on an idea first introduced at Auscrypt'92, where the security is (among others) achieved through a blind signature scheme. Compared to the state-of-the art in post-quantum online voting, our system supports complex ballots and provides stronger privacy guarantees (namely everlasting privacy thanks to the perfect blindness provided by the blind signature scheme we used). In a future version of this work, we plan to implement our protocol and present benchmarks of its computational runtime and to develop the intuitive security analysis presented here, using rigorous definitions and formal proofs.

Acknowledgement. The authors wants to thank the anonymous reviewers for their useful comments. This work has been supported by the European Union H2020 PROMETHEUS Innovation Program Grant 780701.

References

[Adi08]   Adida, B.: Helios: web-based open-audit voting. In: USENIX Security Symposium, pp. 335–348. USENIX Association (2008)

[Ajt96]   Ajtai, M.: Generating hard instances of lattice problems (extended abstract). In: STOC, pp. 99–108. ACM (1996)

[Ban93]   Banaszczyk, W.: New bounds in some transference theorems in the geometry of numbers. Math. Ann. **296**(4), 625–636 (1993)

[BCE+20] Bouaziz-Ermann, S., Canard, S., Eberhart, G., Kaim, G., Roux-Langlois, A., Traoré, J.: Lattice-based (partially) blind signature without restart. IACR Cryptology ePrint Archive 2020:260 (2020)

[BCG+15] Bernhard, D., Cortier, V., Galindo, D., Pereira, O., Warinschi, B.: SoK: a comprehensive analysis of game-based ballot privacy definitions. In: IEEE Symposium on Security and Privacy, pp. 499–516. IEEE Computer Society (2015)

[BKP13]   Bendlin, R., Krehbiel, S., Peikert, C.: How to share a lattice trapdoor: threshold protocols for signatures and (H)IBE. In: Jacobson, M., Locasto, M., Mohassel, P., Safavi-Naini, R. (eds.) ACNS 2013. LNCS, vol. 7954, pp. 218–236. Springer, Heidelberg (2013). https://doi.org/10.1007/978-3-642-38980-1_14

[Can01]   Canetti, R.: Universally composable security: a new paradigm for cryptographic protocols. In: FOCS, pp. 136–145. IEEE Computer Society (2001)

[CGGI14] Cortier, V., Galindo, D., Glondu, S., Izabachène, M.: Election verifiability for Helios under weaker trust assumptions. In: Kutyłowski, M., Vaidya, J. (eds.) ESORICS 2014. LNCS, vol. 8713, pp. 327–344. Springer, Cham (2014). https://doi.org/10.1007/978-3-319-11212-1_19

[CGGI16] Chillotti, I., Gama, N., Georgieva, M., Izabachène, M.: A homomorphic LWE based E-voting scheme. In: Takagi, T. (ed.) PQCrypto 2016. LNCS, vol. 9606, pp. 245–265. Springer, Cham (2016). https://doi.org/10.1007/978-3-319-29360-8_16

[CGK+16] Cortier, V., Galindo, D., Küsters, R., Müller, J., Truderung, T.: SoK: verifiability notions for e-voting protocols. In: IEEE Symposium on Security and Privacy, pp. 779–798. IEEE Computer Society (2016)

[dPLNS17] del Pino, R., Lyubashevsky, V., Neven, G., Seiler, G.: Practical quantum-safe voting from lattices. In: ACM Conference on Computer and Communications Security, pp. 1565–1581. ACM (2017)

[FOO92] Fujioka, A., Okamoto, T., Ohta, K.: A practical secret voting scheme for large scale elections. In: Seberry, J., Zheng, Y. (eds.) AUSCRYPT 1992. LNCS, vol. 718, pp. 244–251. Springer, Heidelberg (1993). https://doi.org/10.1007/3-540-57220-1_66

[GGH13] Garg, S., Gentry, C., Halevi, S.: Candidate multilinear maps from ideal lattices. In: Johansson, T., Nguyen, P.Q. (eds.) EUROCRYPT 2013. LNCS, vol. 7881, pp. 1–17. Springer, Heidelberg (2013). https://doi.org/10.1007/978-3-642-38348-9_1

[GKPV10] Goldwasser, S., Kalai, Y.T., Peikert, C., Vaikuntanathan, V.: Robustness of the learning with errors assumption. In: ICS, pp. 230–240. Tsinghua University Press (2010)

[GPV08] Gentry, C., Peikert, C., Vaikuntanathan, V.: Trapdoors for hard lattices and new cryptographic constructions. In: STOC, pp. 197–206. ACM (2008)

[HKLN20] Hauck, E., Kiltz, E., Loss, J., Nguyen, N.K.: Lattice-based blind signatures, revisited. IACR Cryptology ePrint Archive, 2020:769 (2020)

[KKLA01] Kim, K., Kim, J., Lee, B., Ahn, G.: Experimental design of worldwide internet voting system using PKI. In: SSGRR 2001 (2001)

[KR05] Kremer, S., Ryan, M.: Analysis of an electronic voting protocol in the applied pi calculus. In: Sagiv, M. (ed.) ESOP 2005. LNCS, vol. 3444, pp. 186–200. Springer, Heidelberg (2005). https://doi.org/10.1007/978-3-540-31987-0_14

[LM06] Lyubashevsky, V., Micciancio, D.: Generalized compact knapsacks are collision resistant. In: Bugliesi, M., Preneel, B., Sassone, V., Wegener, I. (eds.) ICALP 2006. LNCS, vol. 4052, pp. 144–155. Springer, Heidelberg (2006). https://doi.org/10.1007/11787006_13

[LPR13] Lyubashevsky, V., Peikert, C., Regev, O.: A toolkit for ring-LWE cryptography. In: Johansson, T., Nguyen, P.Q. (eds.) EUROCRYPT 2013. LNCS, vol. 7881, pp. 35–54. Springer, Heidelberg (2013). https://doi.org/10.1007/978-3-642-38348-9_3

[Lyu12] Lyubashevsky, V.: Lattice signatures without trapdoors. In: Pointcheval, D., Johansson, T. (eds.) EUROCRYPT 2012. LNCS, vol. 7237, pp. 738–755. Springer, Heidelberg (2012). https://doi.org/10.1007/978-3-642-29011-4_43

[MP12] Micciancio, D., Peikert, C.: Trapdoors for lattices: simpler, tighter, faster, smaller. In: Pointcheval, D., Johansson, T. (eds.) EUROCRYPT 2012. LNCS, vol. 7237, pp. 700–718. Springer, Heidelberg (2012). https://doi.org/10.1007/978-3-642-29011-4_41

[PR06] Peikert, C., Rosen, A.: Efficient collision-resistant hashing from worst-case assumptions on cyclic lattices. In: Halevi, S., Rabin, T. (eds.) TCC 2006. LNCS, vol. 3876, pp. 145–166. Springer, Heidelberg (2006). https://doi.org/10.1007/11681878_8

[Reg05] Regev, O.: On lattices, learning with errors, random linear codes, and cryptography. In: STOC, pp. 84–93. ACM (2005)

[Rüc10] Rückert, M.: Lattice-based blind signatures. In: Abe, M. (ed.) ASI-
ACRYPT 2010. LNCS, vol. 6477, pp. 413–430. Springer, Heidelberg (2010).
https://doi.org/10.1007/978-3-642-17373-8_24

[Sha79] Shamir, A.: How to share a secret. Commun. ACM **22**(11), 612–613 (1979)

[Sho97] Shor, P.W.: Polynomial-time algorithms for prime factorization and discrete logarithms on a quantum computer. SIAM J. Comput. **26**(5), 1484–
1509 (1997)

Short Paper: Ballot Secrecy for Liquid Democracy

Mahdi Nejadgholi, Nan Yang, and Jeremy Clark[(✉)]

Concordia University, Montreal, Canada
j.clark@concordia.ca

Abstract. Certain advances in election technology, such as online voting, promise to reduce the administrative overhead of running an election. This has breathed new life into the idea of direct democracy, where voters play a more active role in setting legislation. However it is anticipated that a steady stream of referendums would generate voter fatigue. To combat this fatigue, voters could be allowed to delegate their votes to other (more knowledgeable) voters. This idea is old but has been recently reinvented under the name liquid democracy. In this paper, we consider how ballot secrecy should be defined for liquid democracy. We first show that a natural definition of full secrecy leads to several undesirable outcomes. We then show that these are very difficult to address without enabling voter coercion and vote buying. The purpose of the paper is not to affirm liquid democracy; rather, it is to raise awareness of unseen complexity hiding under our initial presumption that liquid democracy could effortlessly support a secret ballot.

1 Introductory Remarks

A *liquid democracy* voting system allows each voter the option of delegating their vote to another voter. This helps offload the burden of informing yourself about every issue and position at stake. While it can be used in any election, it is well-suited in direct forms of democracy, where many or all issues are put to a referendum. In liquid democracy, if Alice and Bob delegate to Carol, Carol's vote carries the weight of three voters. The defining feature of liquid democracy is that Carol can in turn delegate to David. If David votes directly, he can effectively cast four ballots (his own, Carol's, Alice's, and Bob's) in addition to whatever other delegations he has received. In this paper, we note several challenges in defining ballot secrecy for liquid democracy.

2 Preliminaries

2.1 Systems of Democracy

Consider a nation-state where legislation is set through a process of voting on bills. A common system is *representative democracy* where citizens (or legal residents) elect a parliamentary member to represent their region and vote on bills.

M. Bernhard et al. (Eds.): FC 2021 Workshops, LNCS 12676, pp. 306–314, 2021.
https://doi.org/10.1007/978-3-662-63958-0_26

In a system based on *direct democracy*, citizens would vote on the bills themselves. A critical issue with direct democracy is voter fatigue. Given the large number and wide variety of bills, it is difficult for voters to inform themselves on every issue and cast meaningful votes.

One solution to voter fatigue is allowing voters to delegate their votes to someone else (a proxy). Proxy voting is a general term that includes cases where: (a) the voter directs the proxy how to vote, and (b) the voter lets the proxy decide how to vote. Clearly, voter fatigue is only addressed by (b) and not (a). Systems of type (b) are called *delegative democracy*. While forms of delegative democracy have been discussed for centuries, *liquid democracy* is a re-branding of it that has become popular since the late 2000s [3]. We resist calling liquid democracy a 'silicon valley' invention because its early popularity stemmed from Europe, however it has been embraced and amplified by a similar demographic of young technologists. These technologists already advocate for more direct democracy. Complimentary tools include: online voting, which reduces the friction of conducting frequent elections; random sample voting, a competing solution to voter fatigue [1,6]; and blockchain technology (like liquid democracy, proposed in the 2000s), a technological platform for decentralized computation. Liquid democracy is suggested as a governance mechanism for decentralized organizations in the Ethereum whitepaper [4]. Note that experts argue that blockchain offers more hype than merit in the specific case of voting technology for governmental elections [21,22].

Liquid democracy's pseudonymous inventor Sayke maintains that liquid democracy is distinct from delegative democracy. For example, in liquid democracy, a voter could delegate to a set of other voters and have the system cast a ballot in favour of the plurality of opinions [24]. This has been analyzed as *statement voting* in the literature [27]. However all notable software implementations of liquid democracy are limited to delegations only, and that is what we study in this paper.

2.2 Past Experiments and Uses

The open-source *Liquid Feedback* [2] system is likely the best-known Liquid Democracy implementation. It was used by Germany's Pirate Party by 15K members in 2013 [18]. It is still used by Italy's *MoVimento 5 Stelle (M5S)*; a party which received 25% of Italy's parliament seats in 2013. Liquid Feedback is an open vote system and does not implement a secret ballot. Further, despite offering the feature, data from its main trials find less than 5% of voters actually delegated their votes in practice [23].

Google Votes was an experimental implementation of liquid democracy used internally by Google from 2012–2015 through its Google+ social network [15]. The uses were relatively non-significant (*e.g.,* decisions on the Mountain View Microkitchen food fair in California, or the GoogleServe logo). Like Liquid Feedback, there is no ballot secrecy in Google Votes (in fact, voters can do 'biased sharing' by advertising their vote and obtaining delegations on it). Only 3.6% of voters delegated.

Low profile examples include *LiquidFriesland* for voting on municipal initiatives (less than 30 average voters for each initiative) [9], and *Civicracy* whose pilot study for a school council fell through [14]. For more abandoned or unfinished liquid democracy projects, see Paulin's retrospective [23].

Academic contributions from the computer science (and security) community include a coercion-resistant proxy voting scheme [20] that issues voters fake credentials. A second paper introduces statement voting, an end-to-end verifiable voting system that implements a generalization of liquid democracy but does not address coercion [27]. Both of these designs implement *full ballot secrecy* (all votes and delegations are protected). Our paper illustrates several ways in which this level of secrecy is undesirable; unfortunately, relaxing it tends to create coercion issues. This idea is extended for governing decentralized applications running on blockchain technologies like Ethereum [26]. Another blockchain-based solution proposes an efficient algorithm for self-tallying, cycle-resistant liquid democracy for Ethereum, however, the authors do not consider vote secrecy [10]. Another work considers increasing participation in an open liquid democracy system without ballot secrecy [19].

Last, a series of papers from Ford (the most recent and representative work is [11]) dives deeply into different design parameters of liquid democracy, and critically analyzes them. The Ford paper considers many different aspects, technical and social, while our paper does a deep dive on one specific issue: ballot secrecy. Even so, we identify some specific overlaps in Subsect. 4.3.

3   Assumptions

We are interested in what liquid democracy would look like for a governmental election. Most of the systems mentioned in Subsect. 2.2 were developed for transparent, open vote elections with a rolling tally (*i.e.,* realtime updates). It is difficult to imagine all the election law changes that would pave the road for liquid democracy, but we assume two basic principles of elections would still be required: ballot secrecy, and an announcement of the final result only at the conclusion of the election. We also make the following assumptions about a hypothetical liquid democracy system for governmental elections and referendums:

- **Referendums.** Liquid democracy could be used for either elections of individuals or referendums on issues. For simplicity, we will refer to referendums throughout the rest of this paper but it is not without loss of generality.
- **Online.** We assume the referendum is conducted with online voting. Online voting is incredibly problematic from a security perspective, but we will assume that the system has end-to-end verification (E2E), mitigates the untrusted platform problem (*cf.* [5,25]), and provides some basic coercion-resistance (*cf.* [7,8,12,17])—however we will revisit the degree to which such coercion resistance protection is even possible.
- **Phases.** We assume the referendum is conducted in two phases. In phase 1, voters can delegate their votes, change their delegation, or remove their delegation. Phase 1 might happen over the course of weeks or months depending

Table 1. Issues with a full secrecy ballot and proposed features to solve them. In this paper, we evaluate the privacy consequences of these features.

Issue	Proposed feature
Delegation cycle	Real-time cycle detection
Unexpected delegations	Expose incoming weight
Unaccountable or non-responsive delegates	Expose voting action

on the lead-up time to the referendum. In phase 2, voters can cast their ballots, and can no longer delegate or change their delegation. A voter that has delegated in phase 1 can still vote in phase 2 and this action overrides their delegation. We will refer to phase 1 as the delegation phase and phase 2 as the voting phase.

- **Multi-Referendums.** In the case of multiple concurrent referendums, we assume that the delegation phase is on-going but for each specific referendum, the delegation status will freeze at a certain announced time as that referendum moves into the voting stage.

4   Ballot Secrecy for Liquid Democracy

Full Secrecy and Its Shortcomings.
The most natural definition of ballot secrecy for a liquid democracy election is to hide everything except the final tally [20,27]. This includes all votes and all delegations. This approach could however lead to one of three unintended consequences, recapped in Table 1 and explored in each of the following sections of the paper.

4.1   Delegation Cycles

A delegation cycle occurs when Alice delegates to Bob and Bob delegates to Alice (or any longer chain that cycles back to the initial voter). If ballots are secret, there is no directly way for Alice and Bob to discover the cycle within the system. It is important to note that delegation cycles can form without any voter behaving maliciously. If they do not discover the cycle out-of-band, their votes will not be counted. This issue is mentioned without solution by Zhang and Zhou[1] who use full ballot secrecy for their cryptographic design [27].

A straight-forward solution is to offer an 'oracle' in the design that would either (a) answer any voter's query of whether their own vote is in a cycle or not, or (b) prevent a voter from delegating to another voter if that delegation forms a cycle by displaying a failure message to the voter. By the term 'oracle,' we assume this information would be made available only to the voter (or more

---

[1] Authors' note: at our suggestion.

precisely, would only be convincing to the voter and could not be convincingly shown to a coercer; *cf.* designated verifier signatures and proofs [16]).

Consequences for Ballot Secrecy. The security issue with either of these oracles is that their inclusion breaks the *coercion-resistance* of the system. Assume that Mallory, a coercer or vote buyer, uses undue influence to convince Alice to delegate to her. She can check compliance (at any time) by delegating her own vote to Alice and confirming that it forms a cycle. If it does not, Alice did not comply. Alice can try to rush Mallory and undelegate at the last minute, or overwrite the delegation by casting a ballot. In both cases, the coercion evasion strategy is akin to a voting system that lets you vote as many times as you want (revoting or multiple cast). The same simple coercion techniques, such as Mallory retaining Alice's voter ID card, can also thwart these defences in liquid democracy.

Potential Mitigations. A variant on the *fake credential* design pattern—used in many coercion-resistant voting systems [7,8,17], including proxy voting [20]—could be applied here. In these systems, if Alice is coerced, she can make up a fake credential (or have prepared one in advance) to give to the adversary that operates exactly like her real voting credential. During tallying, all votes cast with fake credentials are obliviously removed. This design pattern can work for liquid democracy except that Alice needs to create a fake *identity* or *persona* that can create delegations that are seen by the delegates and are indistinguishable from real identities. One straightforward composition with existing protocols is to consider public keys as identities. Alice can convincingly lie about what public key she registered as her real identity. She use fake keys to cast fake votes or create fake delegations. While this solves the delegation cycle problem by providing a coercion resistance mechanism that is not thwarted by the introduction of a cycle detection oracle, two issues remain: (1) how to cryptographically realize the cycle detection oracle (we do not solve that problem here; this paper is about ideal functionalities), and (2) it does not solve the two additional issues that follow.

4.2   Unexpected Delegations

It seems natural that Alice would like to know if others have delegated to her. For example, knowing that she has a large number of delegations could increase her efforts in informing herself and completing the task of voting. Very popular delegates could find themselves the target of individualized attacks (cybersecurity or otherwise) to modify their vote or to prevent them from voting. First, it seems sensible that serving as a delegate should be opt-in, and that voters who do not want delegations can remain as default voters. A second design feature could offer to each voter an oracle service that reports the number of voters who have delegated to them (*incoming weight oracle*).

Consequences for Ballot Secrecy. Like the cycle-detection oracle, the incoming weight oracle can be used for coercion. Consider Mallory influencing Alice to delegate her vote to her. She checks the incoming weight oracle before and after the purported delegation, which should increase by one delegation, to ensure Alice's compliance.

Potential Mitigations. Weights could be given in ranges and/or with noise added to thwart coercion, however this requires further attention. For instance, if a single delegation (*e.g.,* Alice's delegation is Mallory's 100th) moves the incoming weight from one range (*e.g.,* 10–99) to the next highest range (*e.g.,* 100–999), it can be used for coercion. While noise can provide provable 'differential privacy' when used once, liquid democracy allows the coercer to dynamically add/remove weights and re-query the oracle as many times as she likes, taking statistics over all the results.

The fake persona design pattern suggested for cycle detection can be used to thwart coercion, however it defeats the original goal of providing Alice with a sense of her ballot's weight—while a number can be displayed, there is telling if it consists of real or fake delegations. Delegates can be easily misled in terms of the number of delegations they are actually receiving. Were the design to use both noisy counts and fake personas, providing the coercer with a mechanism to add/remove any number of fake delegations makes it more difficult to disguise the count.

4.3 Unaccountable Delegates

It could be argued that when a voter delegates, there is absolute trust in the delegate. With a secret ballot, if the delegate fails to vote, or purposefully misleads its delegators as to how it will vote, there is no way to hold them accountable. This issue and its consequence for coercion-resistance is already explored by Ford [11], however we include it for completeness.

A *voting action oracle* could be introduced to let voters see the full delegation path to the final vote (Google Votes [15]). Or more simply, the design could make all delegate votes (and further delegations) public information along with the tally (Ford [11]).

Consequences for Ballot Secrecy. As pointed out by Ford, adding accountability harms coercion resistance. If Mallory apply undue influence on Alice, she can have Alice opt-in as a delegate, delegate her own vote to Alice, instruct Alice on how to vote, and then use the voting action oracle to learn if Alice complied.

Potential Mitigations. In the fake persona design pattern, Alice could create a fake identity and give it to Mallory for delegation. First, note that this situation is different from the earlier coercion example in cycle detection. There, Alice was a voter and Mallory was the delegate. Here Alice is the delegate and Mallory is the voter. If fake personas can be created by voters and delegates equally, then the coercion issue here is solved.

However there are good reasons why voters might be allowed to create fake identities, but once a voter opts into becoming a delegate, they can no longer create fake identities. Consider an attack where Mallory becomes a high profile celebrity for having a certain political ideology. In reality, she actually holds a different ideology. If she amasses a large number of delegations from supporters of her fake public ideology, she could decide to cast all the votes in favour of her real ideology, or simply not vote at all—both actions harm the support of her fake public ideology. However if a voting action oracle is provided, both actions will get her caught.

Instead, she could give out a fake identity for other voters to delegate to. She could vote for her fake public ideology using this fake identity to satisfy the voters. In the end, all the votes would be canceled during tallying but the cancelation is done without revealing which votes are being cancelled—therefore, she could avoid getting caught and do this attack indefinitely. For this reason, we consider this issue an open research problem.

5   Concluding Remarks

The problem of defining ballot secrecy for liquid democracy presents a set of four desirable properties with no obvious way of achieving them all: (1) coercion resistance, (2) no cycles, (3) knowledge of incoming weight, and (4) accountability for delegates. Full ballot secrecy alone does not provide any of these [27]. Fake personas have been applied to achieve (1) [20], however we show it can provide both (1) and (2) with a cycle detection oracle.

An alternative to liquid democracy comes close to providing all of (2)–(4). The idea is to restructure the election into multiple rounds. In the first round, voters can only vote directly for issues. In the subsequent rounds, voters can delegate to any voter who has already voted in a prior round (names will be made public) or they can vote directly. This system cannot have cycles by definition (which would require a voter to delegate to someone who has not voted yet). It sidesteps the impact of a delegate receiving a large number of delegations as the delegations are collected only after a ballot is already cast. It is impossible to delegate to someone who will not vote, however it is still possible to delegate to someone who will vote differently from their public political views, leaving the voter with no knowledge or recourse. Finally, if (1) is achieved using fake personas, a malicious delegate could collect delegations using a fake persona knowing these votes will all be discarded during tallying.

A prerequisite to designing an end-to-end verifiable voting system is deciding how the system should operate; more formally captured by defining its ideal functionality. Debates have been had over ideal functionalities for simple first-past-the-post schemes [13] (*e.g.,* should only the winner be declared, or should the final tally of votes be declared?). In this paper, we informally discuss what the ideal functionality of a liquid democracy system should be, particularly as it relates to ballot secrecy. We hope to have demonstrated that it is not a simple or obvious choice, but rather it is an important research question to consider before proposing new designs in this space.

Acknowledgements. We thank the reviewers who helped to improve our paper. J. Clark acknowledges support for this research project from (i) the National Sciences and Engineering Research Council (NSERC), Raymond Chabot Grant Thornton, and Catallaxy Industrial Research Chair in Blockchain Technologies, and (ii) NSERC through a Discovery Grant.

References

1. Basin, D., Radomirovic, S., Schmid, L.: Alethea: A provably secure random sample voting protocol. In: IEEE CSF (2018)
2. Behrens, J., Kistner, A., Nitsche, A., Swierczek, B.: The Principles of LiquidFeedback. Interaktive Demokratie, Berlin (2014)
3. Behrens, J.: The origins of liquid democracy. Liquid Democracy J. 5 (2017)
4. Buterin, V.: Ethereum whitepaper. Technical report, Online (2013)
5. Chaum, D.: SureVote: technical overview. In: WOTE (2001)
6. Chaum, D.: Random-sample voting (2012). Online
7. Clark, J., Hengartner, U.: Selections: Internet voting with over-the-shoulder coercion-resistance. In: FC (2011)
8. Clarkson, M.R., Chong, S., Myers, A.C.: Civitas: toward a secure voting system. In: IEEE Symposium on Security and Privacy, pp. 354–368 (2008)
9. Eisel, S.: Liquidfriesland - ein gescheitertes experiment. https://internet unddemokratie.wordpress.com/2014/05/22/liquidfriesland-ein-gescheitertes-experiment/. Accessed May 2014
10. Fan, X., Li, P., Zeng, Y., Zhou, X.: Implement liquid democracy on Ethereum: a fast algorithm for realtime self-tally voting system. CoRR abs/1911.08774 (2019). http://arxiv.org/abs/1911.08774
11. Ford, B.: A liquid perspective on democratic choice. arXiv:2003.12393 [cs.CY] (2018)
12. Grewal, G.S., Ryan, M.D., Bursuc, S., Ryan, P.Y.A.: Caveat coercitor: coercion-evidence in electronic voting. In: IEEE Symposium on Security and Privacy (2013)
13. Groth, J.: Evaluating security of voting schemes in the universal composability framework. In: Jakobsson, M., Yung, M., Zhou, J. (eds.) ACNS 2004. LNCS, vol. 3089, pp. 46–60. Springer, Heidelberg (2004). https://doi.org/10.1007/978-3-540-24852-1_4
14. Hainisch, R., Paulin, A.: Civicracy: establishing a competent and responsible council of representatives based on liquid democracy. In: 2016 Conference for E-Democracy and Open Government (CeDEM), pp. 10–16 (2016). https://doi.org/10.1109/CeDEM.2016.27
15. Hardt, S., Lopes, L.R.: Google votes: a liquid democracy experiment on a corporate social network (2015)
16. Jakobsson, M., Sako, K., Impagliazzo, R.: Designated verifier proofs and their applications. In: Maurer, U. (ed.) EUROCRYPT 1996. LNCS, vol. 1070, pp. 143–154. Springer, Heidelberg (1996). https://doi.org/10.1007/3-540-68339-9_13

17. Juels, A., Catalano, D., Jakobsson, M.: Coercion-resistant electronic elections. In: Chaum, D., et al. (eds.) Towards Trustworthy Elections. LNCS, vol. 6000, pp. 37–63. Springer, Heidelberg (2010). https://doi.org/10.1007/978-3-642-12980-3_2

18. Kling, C.C., Kunegis, J., Hartmann, H., Strohmaier, M., Staab, S.: Voting behaviour and power in online democracy: a study of LiquidFeedback in Germany's pirate party. http://arxiv.org/abs/1503.07723

19. Kotsialou, G., Riley, L.: Incentivising participation in liquid democracy with breadth-first delegation. arXiv:1811.03710 [cs, econ] (February 2019)

20. Kulyk, O., Neumann, S., Marky, K., Budurushi, J., Volkamer, M.: Coercion-resistant proxy voting. Comput. Secur. 71, 88–99 (2017)

21. Nasser, Y., Okoye, C., Clark, J., Ryan, P.Y.A.: Blockchains and voting: somewhere between hype and a panacea (2017). Online

22. Park, S., Specter, M., Narula, N., Rivest, R.L.: Going from bad to worse: from internet voting to blockchain voting (2020). Online

23. Paulin, A.: An overview of ten years of liquid democracy research. In: The 21st Annual International Conference on Digital Government Research (2020)

24. Sayke: Liquid democracy is not delegative democracy (2006). Blog post

25. Zagórski, F., Carback, R., Chaum, D., Clark, J., Essex, A., Vora, P.L.: Remotegrity: design and use of an end-to-end verifiable remote voting system. In: ACNS (2013)

26. Zhang, B., Oliynykov, R., Balogun, H.: A treasury system for cryptocurrencies: enabling better collaborative intelligence. In: 26th Annual Network and Distributed System Security Symposium, NDSS 2019, San Diego, California, USA, 24–27 February 2019. The Internet Society (2019)

27. Zhang, B., Zhou, H.-S.: Statement voting. In: Goldberg, I., Moore, T. (eds.) FC 2019. LNCS, vol. 11598, pp. 667–685. Springer, Cham (2019). https://doi.org/10.1007/978-3-030-32101-7_38

Shorter Lattice-Based Zero-Knowledge Proofs for the Correctness of a Shuffle

Javier Herranz[✉], Ramiro Martínez, and Manuel Sánchez

Departament de Matemàtiques, Universitat Politècnica de Catalunya,
Barcelona, Spain
{javier.herranz,ramiro.martinez}@upc.edu

Abstract. In an electronic voting procedure, mixing networks are used to ensure anonymity of the casted votes. Each node of the network re-encrypts the input list of ciphertexts and randomly permutes it in a process named shuffle, and must prove (in zero-knowledge) that the process was applied honestly. To maintain security of such a process in a post-quantum scenario, new proofs are based on different mathematical assumptions, such as lattice-based problems. Nonetheless, the best lattice-based protocols to ensure verifiable shuffling have linear communication complexity on N, the number of shuffled ciphertexts.

In this paper we propose the first sub-linear (on N) post-quantum zero-knowledge argument for the correctness of a shuffle, for which we have mainly used two ideas: arithmetic circuit satisfiability results from [6] and Beneš networks to model a permutation of N elements. The achieved communication complexity of our protocol with respect to N is $\mathcal{O}(\sqrt{N}\log^2(N))$, but we will also highlight its dependency on other important parameters of the underlying lattice ingredients.

Keywords: Electronic voting · Verifiable shuffle · Lattice-based cryptography · Zero-knowledge

1 Introduction

E-voting has already been used in real political elections in Norway, Estonia, Switzerland and Australia, among other countries. It could provide voters with the ability to cast votes from anywhere, aid voters with disabilities to cast their votes autonomously, reduce the logistic costs of an election, obtain accurate vote counts faster and in general improve the flexibility of democratic processes. However we can only take advantage of these benefits if the election system is publicly trusted, for which it has to satisfy strong security requirements.

Two key requirements of e-voting are privacy and verifiability. On the one hand each individual voting option has to remain secret, and only the final tally should be revealed. This is usually addressed encrypting votes with an election public key, whose associated secret key is only known by the electoral board and used for the tally. On the other hand, verifiability ensures the integrity of the

© International Financial Cryptography Association 2021
M. Bernhard et al. (Eds.): FC 2021 Workshops, LNCS 12676, pp. 315–329, 2021.
https://doi.org/10.1007/978-3-662-63958-0_27

election. It should be guaranteed that the final result has not been manipulated and corresponds to the options chosen by eligible voters. Whenever a voter wants to remotely cast an encrypted vote she digitally signs it before sending it to the voting server, that verifies the electronic signature before adding it to a virtual ballot box that will be published in a so called *Bulletin Board*, enabling everyone to verify that tallied votes come, with a one to one correspondence, from eligible voters. Systems that allow anyone to verify the integrity of the election using only public information without requiring additional interaction are called universally verifiable.

At this point we have an apparent contradiction, as the link established by the signature between the voter and its encrypted vote seems to prevent the desired level of privacy. A solution called mixing networks (or *mix-nets*) was presented by Chaum in its seminal paper [16] and is currently adopted by all previously mentioned actual elections. A mix-net is composed of a set of mixing nodes (or *mix-nodes*) that consecutively permute and re-encrypt/decrypt the output of the previous mix-node. This operation is called a shuffle. As long as one of these nodes is honest and keeps its permutation secret it should be infeasible to link the identity of the voter that signed one of the input encrypted votes with its value decrypted from the output of the mix-net, thus achieving privacy again. Verifiability can be enforced asking the mix-nodes to publish a zero-knowledge proof of well behaviour, in this case proving that they know a permutation and the randomness used such that their respective output is just a permuted re-encryption of its input, without leaking any additional information.

Since the first universally verifiable mix-net was presented by Sako and Kilian in 1995 [32] many proposals have been published with different kinds of improvements, that will be discussed in detail in the following Subsect. 1.1. However there is still one important issue that has to be addressed, all schemes that guarantee universal verifiability publishing proofs of a shuffle in a Bulletin Board need to ensure the long term security of the information that is being published. This is particularly important as many constructions base their privacy on hardness assumptions about problems such as the Discrete Logarithm problem, that is known to be efficiently solvable by a quantum computer using Shor's algorithm [33]. Even if powerful enough quantum computers are not available now, an adversary could keep this public information until he has the ability to break the security with a quantum computer in the near future. Voting data is specially sensitive information that should remain secret in the long term, while it might still have political and personal implications. Therefore post-quantum hardness assumptions that are believed to hold even against a quantum computer should be used, such as the ones employed by lattice-based, code-based, multivariate polynomials or hash-based cryptography.

The main goal of this article is to present the first post-quantum proof of a shuffle with sub-linear size in the number of inputs, that could be used to build secure mix-nets, guaranteeing long term privacy even in a quantum computing era.

1.1   State of the Art

The structure of a proof of a shuffle heavily depends on the choice of a way of representing a permutation. A great variety of approaches appear in the literature, from applying permutation matrices [21,22,26,35,37], permutation networks [2,3], showing two sets are equal if they are both roots of the same polynomial [7,24,25,31] or using general arithmetic circuits [13]. Most of the work, from the very beginning [1,30], focuses on reducing the size of the proofs for different scenarios. A comprehensive study of mix-nets and proofs of shuffles can be found in [27].

However only a handful of post-quantum e-voting proposals have been recently published. Del Pino *et al.* presented EVOLVE in [19], which uses a somewhat homomorphic encryption scheme to add together several ballots before decrypting them. This alternative can only work with elections where the result can be represented as the addition of individual votes, but it can not implement *write-ins*, that are easily handled by mix-nets. The same limitation applies to the recent work [10], which proposes an elegant way of solving some security issues in [19]. Gjøsteen and Strand also propose the use of fully homomorphic encryption to construct a decryption circuit in [23], but while theoretically interesting it is still far from efficient. The recent work in [5] proposes a practical post-quantum e-voting protocol, but under a very strong trust (perhaps unrealistic) assumption: the shuffle entity has no access to the channels used by voters to cast their votes in the ballot box.

Regarding post-quantum mixnets, the universally verifiable mix-nets of Costa *et al.* and Strand [17,18,34] are both quite impractical, either because of the use of fully homomorphic encryption or because correctness proofs have linear (in N) size, with large constants. The only quantum-safe practical mix-net we are aware of is [11] by Boyen *et al.*, based on a different model that only allows verification by a (temporarily trusted) auditor, making it not universally verifiable.

The construction of an efficient post-quantum universally verifiable mix-net is still an open problem. In this paper we provide a significant step presenting the first such protocol, to shuffle N ciphertexts, with proofs of sub-linear size in N.

A key ingredient for our protocol is the zero-knowledge proof of satisfiability of an arithmetic circuit presented in [6] (and recently improved/generalized in [9]). These proofs achieve post-quantum security properties by using techniques from lattice-based cryptography, and the size of the proofs is sub-linear in the number of gates M of the arithmetic circuit, since it is $\mathcal{O}(\sqrt{M \log^3(M)})$ (in the protocol in [6]). When the soundness property of a zero-knowledge system is satisfied computationally (assuming the hardness of some underlying mathematical problem) then people often refer to such proofs as *arguments* of knowledge. The proofs in [6,9] and consequently the proof for the correctness of a shuffle that we present in this paper are indeed arguments of knowledge, but we use both proofs and arguments to refer to them.

1.2 Arithmetic Circuits for Shuffles

The idea is to use the powerful result of [6], to prove in zero-knowledge that a shuffle (re-encryption and permutation) has been correctly performed. Let $L = \{C_1, \ldots, C_N\}$ be the input list of N ciphertexts for the shuffling node; he is assumed to re-encrypt each ciphertext, which leads to $L' = \{C'_1, \ldots, C'_N\}$ and then to apply a permutation ρ to the list L', which leads to $L'' = \{D_1, \ldots, D_N\}$, where $D_i = C'_{\rho(i)}$, for each $i = 1, \ldots, N$. The list L'' is made public, so the two lists L and L'' are available to the verifier of the zero-knowledge proof of a correct shuffle.

In the case of RLWE-based ciphertexts, the re-encryption step $L \to L'$ can be easily expressed as an arithmetic circuit, where some secret input wires correspond to the (small) random elements used to re-encrypt each ciphertext. The number of gates of this first sub-circuit is $\mathcal{O}(N)$. The challenge is now to express the permutation step, that is the statement that list L'' is a permutation of list L', as an arithmetic circuit with a small enough number of gates. Our solution is to consider the Beneš network that corresponds to that permutation; the circuit that expresses such Beneš network takes as input the N ciphertexts in L' along with a bit $b \in \{0, 1\}$ for each internal 2-in 2-out gate of the Beneš network, indicating if the two input wires must be switched or not, in the output of that gate. The final output of the circuit must be the list of N ciphertexts in L''. The number of gates of such a circuit is $\mathcal{O}(N \log(N))$.

1.3 Our Results

We detail how RLWE ciphertexts must be produced and re-encrypted so that shuffling nodes must prove, in particular, that the noise introduced when re-encrypting each ciphertext is small enough (and thus, in the tally phase, there will not be errors in the decryption of the final ciphertexts). This fact, along with the correct execution of the re-encryption algorithm and the correct execution of a permutation expressed by a Beneš network, constitute the arithmetic circuit to which we apply the results in [6,9]. Since the number of gates of the circuit is $M \in \mathcal{O}(N \log(N))$, the result is a zero-knowledge proof that a shuffle of N ciphertexts has been correctly applied, with post-quantum security based on the hardness of well-known lattice problems, and with size sub-linear on N.

1.4 Organization

In Sect. 2 we review some ingredients of our protocol: RLWE encryption, lattice-based zero-knowledge proofs of satisfiability of arithmetic circuits and Beneš networks. Then in Sect. 3 we propose our protocol, by first describing the arithmetic circuit that represents a shuffle of N RLWE ciphertexts, and then by applying to this circuit the construction in [6]. We analyze our protocol in Sect. 4, in terms of efficiency and security.

2   Preliminaries

2.1   Ideal Lattices: RLWE Problems and Public Key Encryption

Ideal lattices can be seen as ideals in the polynomial ring $\mathcal{R} = \mathbb{Z}[X]/\langle f(X)\rangle$, where the polynomial $f(X) = X^n + f_n X^{n-1} + \cdots + f_2 X + f_1 \in \mathbb{Z}[X]$. Usually, for real cryptographic applications, we will set n a power of 2 and $f(X) = X^n + 1$ and we will consider the quotient ring $\mathcal{R}_q = \mathcal{R}/q\mathcal{R} = \mathbb{Z}_q[X]/\langle X^n + 1\rangle$ since this setting provides several advantages from an implementation point of view.

Let n and q be integers, $\mathcal{R} = \mathbb{Z}[X]/\langle f(X)\rangle$ with $\deg(f) = n$ and $\mathcal{R}_q = \mathcal{R}/q\mathcal{R}$. Let χ_σ be a discrete probability distribution over $\mathcal{R}$ (usually a Gaussian distribution) with parameter σ and a secret polynomial $s \in \mathcal{R}_q$.

Definition 1 (Ring Learning With Errors Distribution). *The RLWE distribution $\mathcal{L}_{s,\chi}$ over $\mathcal{R}_q \times \mathcal{R}_q$ is sampled by choosing a $\overset{R}{\leftarrow} \mathcal{R}_q$, $e \overset{R}{\leftarrow} \chi_\sigma$ and outputting $(a, b = a \cdot s + e \bmod q)$.*

Definition 2 (Search-RLWE Problem). *Given m independent samples $(a_i, b_i) \overset{R}{\leftarrow} \mathcal{L}_{s,\chi}$ for a fixed uniformly random s, find s.*

Definition 3 (Decision-RLWE Problem). *Given m independent samples (a_i, b_i), decide whether these samples are distributed according to $\mathcal{L}_{s,\chi_\sigma}$ for a fixed uniformly random s; or according to a uniform distribution over $\mathcal{R}_q \times \mathcal{R}_q$.*

Hardness of RLWE comes for large enough choices of q. Solving certain instantiations of Search-RLWE is as hard as quantumly solving an approximate Shortest Vector Problem on an ideal lattice.

The problem remains to be hard when the secret s is chosen from the error distribution instead of uniformly at random (see [4] for the reduction).

RLWE Encryption Scheme. This scheme, first proposed by Lyubashevsky, Peikert and Regev in [29], works as follows:

Definition 4 (RLWE encryption scheme). *We consider the ring $\mathcal{R}_q = \mathbb{Z}_q[X]/\langle X^n + 1\rangle$ with n a power of 2 and q a prime. Messages are strings of n bits encoded as a polynomial in $\mathcal{R}_q$. An error distribution χ must be chosen, producing "small" elements of $\mathcal{R}_q$.*

- **$Gen(1^\lambda)$:** *Compute suitable n and q according to λ. Choose a $\overset{R}{\leftarrow} \mathcal{R}_q$ and small $s, e \overset{R}{\leftarrow} \chi$. Output $sk = s$ and $pk = (a, b = a \cdot s + e) \in \mathcal{R}_q \times \mathcal{R}_q$.*
- **$Enc(pk, z, r, e_1, e_2)$:** *To encrypt a message $z \in \{0,1\}^n$ we view it as an element in $\mathcal{R}_q$ by using its bits as the 0-1 coefficients of a polynomial. Then we choose small elements $r, e_1, e_2 \overset{R}{\leftarrow} \chi$ and output $(u, v) = (r \cdot a + e_1, b \cdot r + e_2 + \lfloor \frac{q}{2} \rceil z) \in \mathcal{R}_q \times \mathcal{R}_q$*

- **Dec**$(sk, (u, v))$: *Compute:*

$$
\begin{aligned}
v - u \cdot s &= b \cdot r + e_2 + \left\lfloor \frac{q}{2} \right\rceil z - (r \cdot a + e_1) \cdot s \\
&= (a \cdot s + e) \cdot r + e_2 + \left\lfloor \frac{q}{2} \right\rceil z - r \cdot a \cdot s - e_1 \cdot s \\
&= a \cdot s \cdot r + e \cdot r + e_2 + \left\lfloor \frac{q}{2} \right\rceil z - r \cdot a \cdot s - e_1 \cdot s \\
&= (e \cdot r - e_1 \cdot s + e_2) + \left\lfloor \frac{q}{2} \right\rceil z \\
&\approx \left\lfloor \frac{q}{2} \right\rceil z
\end{aligned}
$$

It has been proved that the RLWE encryption scheme is IND-CPA secure, assuming the hardness of RLWE problems [29]. The usual choice for the error distribution χ consists in running n independent instances (one for each component, if we see elements of $\mathcal{R}_q$ as vectors in $(\mathbb{Z}_q)^n$) of a discrete Gaussian distribution, centered at 0 and with parameter σ, in $\mathbb{Z}_q$.

In this paper we consider *truncated* Gaussian distributions: we fix a positive integer $\hat{k}$ and we check that the output of the Gaussian falls in the set $\{-\hat{k}\sigma, \ldots, -1, 0, 1, \ldots, \hat{k}\sigma\}$; if this is not the case, we reject this sample and do a new one. The statistical distance between the resulting truncated distribution over $\mathcal{R}_q$ and the non-truncated Gaussian distribution over $\mathcal{R}_q$ can be bounded by $n \cdot e^{-\hat{k}^2/2}$ (see for instance [28]). If we take $n, \hat{k}$ such that this value is negligible in the security parameter, then we can safely use truncated Gaussian distributions with the same parameters (q, n, σ) which are considered secure when discrete Gaussian are employed.

The choices of q and σ determine if the encryption scheme works properly: they must be chosen to ensure that all the coefficients of $e \cdot r - e_1 \cdot s + e_2$ can be upper-bounded by less than $\frac{q}{4}$, in this way the message z is recovered by rounding each coefficient of $v - u \cdot s$ to 0 or $\left\lfloor \frac{q}{2} \right\rceil$, whichever is closest modulo q. Also, this scheme allows to define a new algorithm **Re-Enc** to re-encrypt previously encrypted data. This algorithm works as follows:

- **Re-Enc**$(pk, (u, v), r', e_1', e_2')$: To re-encrypt a message z encrypted as (u, v) we choose small $r', e_1', e_2' \xleftarrow{\mathcal{R}} \chi_\sigma$ and output the pair

$$
(u', v') = (u, v) + Enc(pk, 0, r', e_1', e_2') \in \mathcal{R}_q \times \mathcal{R}_q.
$$

Notice that every time we re-encrypt a ciphertext the norm of its noise might grow, and therefore only a limited number of re-encryptions are allowed. Parameters have to be chosen so that the encryption scheme supports at least as many re-encryptions as the number of mix-nodes of the mix-net (which is known in advance). Given that this number is typically a fixed small quantity this requirement is usually already satisfied and has no real impact on the parameter selection.

2.2 Zero-Knowledge Arguments for the Satisfiability of Arithmetic Circuits

An arithmetic circuit over a field $\mathbb{Z}_q$ is a directed acyclic graph whose vertices are called gates and edges are called wires. Gates of in-degree 0 are called input gates and usually are associated to variables or constants. The remaining gates are either multiplication gates or addition gates.

The general idea of the protocol presented by Baum *et al.* [6] to prove the satisfiability of an arithmetic circuit over Z_q is summarized below:

1. the first idea is to arrange the $\mathcal{O}(M)$ wire values of the circuit into a (more or less square) matrix with $\mathcal{O}(\sqrt{M})$ rows and $\mathcal{O}(\sqrt{M})$ columns;
2. using an appropriate lattice-based homomorphic commitment scheme (with outputs being vectors of elements in $\mathbb{Z}_Q$ for some prime number $Q >> q$), one commit to each row of the above-mentioned matrix;
3. using techniques from [8], one reduces the satisfiability of the arithmetic circuit to the satisfiability of linear-algebraic statements over committed matrices;
4. the last step consists in using a new zero-knowledge proof, designed by themselves, to prove the satisfiability of such algebraic statements (products and additions of matrices) in an efficient way, with the proofs being as short as possible.

Authors of [6] show a possible way of choosing the parameters of the lattice, the commitment scheme and the dimensions of the matrix so that the global protocol to prove satisfiability of the arithmetic circuit has communication complexity $\mathcal{O}(\sqrt{M \log^3(M)} \log(Q))$. The protocol involves 9 rounds of interaction between the prover and the verifier. The security (including computational soundness) is based on the hardness of both the Short Integer Solution (SIS) and the Learning With Errors (LWE) problems. For the security proof to be valid, they need $Q \approx q^5$.

2.3 Beneš Networks

We will use as a model a permutation network called Beneš network proposed by Abraham Waksman in [36]. The use of Beneš networks is not new in cryptography, as early results from Masayuki Abe [2] already considered these constructions to apply them to mix-nets. Nevertheless, the asymptotic cost of these solutions were usually worse than others, and they were considered inefficient. In this paper we see that the recent advances in the area of zero-knowledge proofs/arguments for satisfiability of arithmetic circuits may give a new opportunity to this kind of constructions.

Formally, a permutation network is an acyclic graph with N inputs and N outputs where vertices have in-degree and out-degree equal to 2. These vertices are called *switch gates* and each of them has a special input $b \in \{0, 1\}$, which indicates if the two inputs are switched or if they remain in the same order (see Fig. 1).

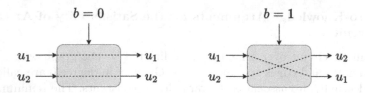

Fig. 1. Switch gate

Beneš networks are constructed recursively. A 2×2 Beneš network is just a switch gate, and it is trivial that a switch gate models every permutation of 2 elements, namely the identity if $b = 0$ and a switch if $b = 1$. Now we can construct a $2^k \times 2^k$ network using two $2^{k-1} \times 2^{k-1}$ Beneš sub-networks and 2^k switch gates, that will be able to perform whichever permutation of 2^k elements.

An easy induction yields that for $N = 2^k$, to craft an $N \times N$ network we will need $2 \log_2(N) - 1$ stages of $N/2$ switch gates each, therefore an $\mathcal{O}(N \log(N))$ amount of switch gates. Beneš networks easily model any of the $N!$ permutations without deadlocks (i.e. for each wire only travels one value). Besides, Beneš networks can be extended to arbitrary sizes, and not just powers of 2 [15].

One could imagine that to perform the permutation the prover could just choose the switch bit of each gate uniformly at random from $\{0,1\}$, and let the circuit apply the resulting permutation. This will not be correct, since in a shuffle every permutation of N elements must have the same probability to appear. The random choosing of the bits implies that some permutation will appear more often than others, so the choice is not uniform, as shown in [3]. Therefore, if we denote by $\mathcal{S}_N$ the set of permutations of N elements, the prover must first choose $\pi \xleftarrow{\mathcal{R}} \mathcal{S}_N$, and then run an algorithm to set the bits accordingly. These algorithms are called *routing algorithms* and have a best known complexity of $\mathcal{O}(N \log(N))$, such as [14], so it does not affect the asymptotic complexity of the prover.

3   The Proposed Protocol

3.1   The Circuit that Encodes a Shuffle

A shuffling node receives as input a list of N ciphertexts $L = \{C_1, \ldots, C_N\}$. He first re-encrypts each ciphertext $C_i = (u_i, v_i)$ using the protocol $C_i' = (u_i', v_i') \leftarrow \mathsf{Re\text{-}Enc}(pk, (u_i, v_i), r_i', e_{1,i}', e_{2,i}')$, which leads to an intermediate list $L' = \{C_1', \ldots, C_N'\}$, and then he applies a random permutation $\rho \in \mathcal{S}_N$ to L', which leads to $L'' = \{D_1, \ldots, D_N\}$, where $D_i = C_{\rho(i)}'$, for each $i = 1, \ldots, N$. The list L'' is the output of the whole shuffling process (along with the correctness proof that we will describe in this section).

The shuffling node computes the Beneš network that represents the secret permutation ρ, that is, an assignment $b_1, b_2, \ldots, b_K$ of bits for each of the K switch gates of the network, where $b_\ell \in \{0,1\}$, for all $\ell = 1, \ldots, K$.

Note that we separate the shuffling in two well-differentiated parts/circuits, one for the re-encryption and one for the permutation. An alternative solution (used for instance in [12]) would be to add a re-randomization step in each switch gate of the Beneš network. However, the size of the global circuit for the shuffle is smaller with our solution: it contains less re-randomization/re-encryption gates, $\mathcal{O}(N)$ than the $\mathcal{O}(N \log N)$ re-randomization gates that would be required in this alternative solution.

All the elements involved in the encryption scheme are polynomials in the ring $\mathcal{R}_q$ of degree at most $n-1$, so we see each element as a tuple of n elements in the field $\mathbb{Z}_q$ underlying the arithmetic circuit that we will consider. For instance, $u_i \leftrightarrow (u_{i,0}, \ldots, u_{i,n-1})$.

The public inputs of the arithmetic circuit are (the $\mathbb{Z}_q$ components of) the N ciphertexts in $L = \{C_1, \ldots, C_N\}$ and the N ciphertexts in $L'' = \{D_1, \ldots, D_N\}$. So, counting elements in the field $\mathbb{Z}_q$ of the circuit, we have $4nN$ public inputs.

The secret inputs of the arithmetic circuit are:

(i) (The $\mathbb{Z}_q$ components of) the N triples of noise $(r'_i, e'_{1,i}, e'_{2,i})$ used to re-encrypt each ciphertext C_i, which means $3nN$ elements in $\mathbb{Z}_q$,

(ii) The K bits $b_1, \ldots, b_K$ for the K switching gates of the Beneš network; we recall that $K \in \mathcal{O}(N \log(N))$.

What does our circuit C_{shuffle} do? Essentially, three different things:

1. Check that the components of the noise are small; for instance, if $r'_i \leftrightarrow (r'_{i,0}, \ldots, r'_{i,n-1})$, then the circuit needs to check that $r'_{i,j} \in \{-\hat{k}\sigma, \ldots, -1, 0, 1, \ldots, \hat{k}\sigma\} \subset \mathbb{Z}_q$, for all $j = 0, \ldots, n - 1$. This checking is encoded as the arithmetic circuit equality $(r'_{i,j} + \hat{k}\sigma) \cdot \ldots \cdot (r'_{i,j} + 1) \cdot r'_{i,j} \cdot (r'_{i,j} - 1) \cdot \ldots \cdot (r'_{i,j} - \hat{k}\sigma) = 0$, in $\mathbb{Z}_q$. Since this has to be done for each $i = 1, \ldots, N$, each $j = 0, \ldots, n - 1$ and each element in the noise triple, we have a circuit with $6\hat{k}\sigma nN$ gates. If some checking fails, the arithmetic circuit is not satisfied.

2. Check that each secret input b_ℓ is a bit, that is, check that $b_\ell \cdot (1 - b_\ell) = 0$ in $\mathbb{Z}_q$, for all $\ell = 1, \ldots, K$. These circuits consist of $2K \in \mathcal{O}(N \log(N))$ gates. If some checking fails, the arithmetic circuit is not satisfied.

3. Check that the Beneš network, when applied to the result of re-encrypting the ciphertexts in L, produces the ciphertexts in L''. This consists in two phases, one for re-encryption and one for permutation:

   (a) re-encryption circuit: each re-encryption $C'_i = (u'_i, v'_i) \leftarrow \mathbf{Re\text{-}Enc}(pk, (u_i, v_i), r'_i, e'_{1,i}, e'_{2,i})$ essentially consists in doing two polynomial multiplications and two polynomial additions, in the ring $\mathcal{R}_q$. If we implement these operations with the classical method, this means $\mathcal{O}(n^2)$ gates for each re-encryption, as an arithmetic circuit over $\mathbb{Z}_q$. The complexity of this circuit can be slightly improved when multiplying polynomials if we use Karatsuba's algorithm. Notice that this would imply that the output is the product of the polynomials over $\mathbb{Z}_q[X]$, which has (at most) $2n - 1$ monomials. We can reduce this resulting polynomial into

$\mathcal{R}_q = \mathbb{Z}_q[X]/\langle X^n + 1\rangle$ again with $n-1$ subtractions, since $X^n = -1$. In this case, if the polynomials have degree a power of 2, the number of integer multiplications becomes $\mathcal{O}(n^{\log_2 3})$.

(b) permutation circuit: the same permutation must be applied to all the n components of each of the two elements (u'_i, v'_i) of a re-encrypted ciphertext C'_i. Inside the Beneš network, each switch gate, with bit input $b \in \{0, 1\}$, couple of inputs $(u_1, u_2) \in (\mathbb{Z}_q)^2$ and couple of outputs $(v_1, v_2) \in (\mathbb{Z}_q)^2$, just consists in applying the following operation

$$v_1 = (1-b) \cdot u_1 + b \cdot u_2 \bmod q$$
$$v_2 = (1-b) \cdot u_2 + b \cdot u_1 \bmod q$$

Therefore, the number of gates of the arithmetic circuit for the global Beneš network is $12nK \in \mathcal{O}(nN \log(N))$.

The outputs of these two phases are then compared with the list L''. If all the elements are equal, then the arithmetic circuit is satisfied.

The number M of gates of the complete arithmetic circuit C_{shuffle} is thus

$$M \in \mathcal{O}\left(N \cdot \left(n\hat{k}\sigma + n^{\log_2 3} + n\log(N)\right)\right)$$

3.2 Non-interactive Proof of Circuit Satisfiability, with Fiat-Shamir

The proof of satisfiability of an arithmetic circuit in [6] is an interactive protocol between the prover (the shuffling node, in our case) and a verifier. The protocol consists in 9 rounds of communication. The amount of information exchanged between the prover and the verifier is $\mathcal{O}(\sqrt{M \log(M)})$ elements of $\mathbb{Z}_Q$, where $Q \approx q^5$, for an arithmetic circuit with M gates operating in the field $\mathbb{Z}_q$.

In our setting of producing a publicly verifiable proof of correctness of a shuffle, interaction is not permitted: the shuffling node must produce a proof π without interacting with the (possibly unknown, yet) verifier.

The standard way of transforming such an interactive protocol into a non-interactive one is to use the Fiat-Shamir paradigm: the challenges sent from the verifier to the prover are replaced with values that are computed by the own prover, applying a secure hash function to the statement of the proof and the values exchanged in the previous rounds of communication. The length of the resulting proof π is thus equivalent to the amount of information exchanged in the interactive version; in our case, π contains $\mathcal{O}(\sqrt{M \log(M)})$ elements of $\mathbb{Z}_Q$.

We emphasize here that relaying in the Fiat-Shamir transformation makes the protocol secure in the ROM, but not in the QROM (that allows oracle queries to be in quantum superposition). This is a common choice in the literature as, at the moment, there has been no natural scheme proven secure in the ROM based on a quantum-safe problem that has later been proven insecure in the QROM. Very recent results have shown how, provided some additional constrains are satisfied, some generic schemes proven secure in the ROM are also secure in the QROM (see [20] and references therein).

3.3   The Resulting Protocol

All in all, our proposed protocol to prove the correctness of a shuffle works as follows. The public input of the shuffling node is a list $L = \{(u_i, v_i)\}$ of N ciphertexts. The node then

1. Chooses noise elements $(r'_i, e'_{1,i}, e'_{2,i})$ using the truncated Gaussian distribution over $\mathcal{R}_q$, and computes re-encryptions $C'_i = (u'_i, v'_i) \leftarrow$ Re-Enc$(pk, (u_i, v_i), r'_i, e'_{1,i}, e'_{2,i})$, for $i = 1, \ldots, N$,
2. Chooses at random a permutation ρ for the set $\{1, 2, \ldots, N\}$ and defines $D_i = C'_{\rho(i)}$, for each $i = 1, \ldots, N$,
3. Finds the bit assignment, $\{b_\ell\}_{1 \leq \ell \leq K}$, for the switch gates of the Beneš network that correspond to permutation ρ,
4. Uses the non-interactive (Fiat-Shamir) version of the satisfiability proof of an arithmetic circuit to compute a proof π for circuit C_{shuffle}.

The shuffling node publishes the list $L'' = \{D_1, \ldots, D_N\}$ of shuffled ciphertexts along with the proof π. Any verifier can take the lists L and L'' and verify the correctness of the non-interactive zero-knowledge proof π.

4   Analysis: Efficiency, Security and Possible Improvements

4.1   Complexity Analysis and Possible Choices of Parameters

The goal of this paper was to design a protocol to prove the correctness of a shuffle of N ciphertexts, with post-quantum security and communication complexity lower than $\mathcal{O}(N)$. The protocol proposed in the previous section achieves this goal.

Regarding communication complexity, the size of the resulting proofs is $\mathcal{O}(\sqrt{M} \log^3(M) \log(Q))$, where Q is a prime number for the commitments needed in the construction of [6], roughly $Q \approx q^5$ and M is the number of gates of the shuffle circuit:

$$M \in \mathcal{O}\left(N \cdot \left(n\hat{k}\sigma + n^{\log_2 3} + n \log(N) \right) \right)$$

Therefore, the dependency of the size of a proof on the number N of shuffled ciphertexts is sub-linear, in the order $\mathcal{O}(\log^2(N)\sqrt{N})$. On the other hand, there are other parameters to be taken into account: the dimension n of the underlying ideal lattice and also the values $\hat{k}$ and σ related to the truncated Gaussian distribution used to produce the (re-encrypted) ciphertexts have an impact on the size of a proof π.

Two possible configurations for these parameters, for a security level of 128 bits, could be

– $n = 128 = 2^7$, $q = 4099 \approx 2^{12}$ (and thus $Q \approx 2^{60}$), $\tilde{k} = 14$, $\sigma = 27$

– $n = 512 = 2^9$, $,q = 1048583 \approx 2^{20}$ (and thus $Q \approx 2^{100}$), $\tilde{k} = 14$, $\sigma = 6$

The length of the proofs in the new protocol starts improving over previous proposals (with linear dependency on N) once N gets big numbers, e.g. one million ciphertexts. For smaller numbers of ciphertexts, i.e. in small elections, the result of our new protocol does not significantly improve over existing solutions.

Possible Improvements. The results in [6] for the zero-knowledge argument of satisfiability of an arithmetic circuit have been improved and generalized in [9]. Authors of this last work give a protocol, for each positive integer $d \geq 1$, where the communication complexity is essentially $\mathcal{O}\left(\log Q \cdot M^{\frac{1}{d+1}} \cdot (d^3 \lambda \log^2(M) d\lambda^2)\right)$. The result in [6] can be seen as the particular case $d = 1$ of the result in [9].

The improvement on the communication complexity with respect to M comes at the cost of a worse (bigger) value needed for the big prime number Q. Roughly speaking, $Q = \mathcal{O}(q^{4+d})$ is required.

Our protocol for the proof of a shuffle can be instantiated by using this zero-knowledge argument, to prove the satisfiability of the shuffle circuit described in Subsect. 3.1. The result are shorter proofs: each time we increase d by one unit, we increase the size of the proof by a factor of $\log(q)$, but we decrease the size of the proof by a more significant factor: from $d = 1$ to $d = 2$, by a factor $\mathcal{O}(M^{1/6})$, from $d = 1$ to $d = 3$ by a factor $\mathcal{O}(M^{1/4})$, etc.

The idea is thus to take the number of votes in the election (i.e. the number N of ciphertexts to be shuffled) and then find a secure configuration for the lattice parameters $(q, n, \sigma, \hat{k})$ and a suitable value for d in order to minimize the size of the produced proofs of a correct shuffle.

4.2 Security Analysis

The security of our proof of correctness of a shuffle follows from the security properties of the zero-knowledge proof systems for arithmetic circuits in [6,9]. On the one hand, the zero-knowledge property of the proof systems implies that an execution of the proof of a shuffle protocol does not leak any information about the secret witness, that is about the randomness employed to re-encrypt each input ciphertext and about the permutation that has been applied (through the corresponding Beneš network) to the list of re-encrypted ciphertexts. Therefore, the proof of a shuffle enjoys privacy.

On the other hand, the (computational) soundness property of the proof systems implies that each accepted execution of the proof of a shuffle protocol must have been produced by a prover (a shuffling node) who knows a valid witness for the considered circuit. In the circuit that we have considered in our protocol, this ensures that:

(i) The noise used for re-encryption is small enough, satisfying the same bound as the truncated Gaussian distribution, because each coefficient of the noise polynomials belongs to the set $\{-\hat{k}\sigma, \ldots, -1, 0, 1, \ldots, \hat{k}\sigma\}$;

(ii) The bits for the Beneš network are actually bits, $b_i \in \{0,1\}$, and so a permutation is applied to the list of re-encrypted ciphertexts.

Therefore, if a dishonest shuffling node wants to fool the election by including false ciphertexts (not coming from a real shuffling of the input ciphertexts) or by adding too much noise to the ciphertexts (in such a way that the final decryption of the encrypted votes, in the tally phase, leads to decryption errors), the proof of correctness of his shuffling will not be accepted, and so this dishonest behaviour will be detected.

Of course, a dishonest shuffling node can use a non-random permutation (for instance, the identity) and can impose all the re-encryption noise to be 0, in such a way that his input list of ciphertexts is exactly equal to the output list of ciphertexts. Such a behaviour can never be avoided, but once again, we insist that the general assumption is that at least one of the shuffling nodes is honest and performs a correct shuffling (re-encryption and permutation), which is enough to provide anonymity to the election.

Putting together the assumptions for the security of the encryption scheme and the assumptions for the security of the proof systems in [6,9], we conclude that our proposed protocol to prove the correctness of a shuffle is secure under the assumption that the SIS and the RLWE problems are hard.

Acknowledgements. The work is partially supported by the Spanish *Ministerio de Ciencia e Innovación (MICINN)*, under Project PID2019-109379RB-I00 and by the European Union PROMETHEUS project (Horizon 2020 Research and Innovation Program, grant 780701).

References

1. Abe, M.: Universally verifiable mix-net with verification work independent of the number of mix-servers. In: Nyberg, K. (ed.) EUROCRYPT 1998. LNCS, vol. 1403, pp. 437–447. Springer, Heidelberg (1998). https://doi.org/10.1007/BFb0054144
2. Abe, M.: Mix-networks on permutation networks. In: Lam, K.-Y., Okamoto, E., Xing, C. (eds.) ASIACRYPT 1999. LNCS, vol. 1716, pp. 258–273. Springer, Heidelberg (1999). https://doi.org/10.1007/978-3-540-48000-6_21
3. Abe, M., Hoshino, F.: Remarks on mix-network based on permutation networks. In: Kim, K. (ed.) PKC 2001. LNCS, vol. 1992, pp. 317–324. Springer, Heidelberg (2001). https://doi.org/10.1007/3-540-44586-2_23
4. Applebaum, B., Cash, D., Peikert, C., Sahai, A.: Fast cryptographic primitives and circular-secure encryption based on hard learning problems. In: Halevi, S. (ed.) CRYPTO 2009. LNCS, vol. 5677, pp. 595–618. Springer, Heidelberg (2009). https://doi.org/10.1007/978-3-642-03356-8_35
5. Aranha, D.F., Baum, C., Gjøsteen, K., Silde, T., Tunge, T.: Lattice-based proof of shuffle and applications to electronic voting. In: Paterson K.G. (eds) Topics in Cryptology – CT-RSA 2021. CT-RSA 2021. LNCS, vol. 12704. Springer, Cham (2021). https://doi.org/10.1007/978-3-030-75539-3_10
6. Baum, C., Bootle, J., Cerulli, A., del Pino, R., Groth, J., Lyubashevsky, V.: Sublinear lattice-based zero-knowledge arguments for arithmetic circuits. In: Shacham, H., Boldyreva, A. (eds.) CRYPTO 2018. LNCS, vol. 10992, pp. 669–699. Springer, Cham (2018). https://doi.org/10.1007/978-3-319-96881-0_23

7. Bayer, S., Groth, J.: Efficient zero-knowledge argument for correctness of a shuffle. In: Pointcheval, D., Johansson, T. (eds.) EUROCRYPT 2012. LNCS, vol. 7237, pp. 263–280. Springer, Heidelberg (2012). https://doi.org/10.1007/978-3-642-29011-4_17

8. Bootle, J., Cerulli, A., Chaidos, P., Groth, J., Petit, C.: Efficient zero-knowledge arguments for arithmetic circuits in the discrete log setting. In: Fischlin, M., Coron, J.-S. (eds.) EUROCRYPT 2016. LNCS, vol. 9666, pp. 327–357. Springer, Heidelberg (2016). https://doi.org/10.1007/978-3-662-49896-5_12

9. Bootle, J., Lyubashevsky, V., Nguyen, N.K., Seiler, G.: A non-PCP approach to succinct quantum-safe zero-knowledge. In: Micciancio, D., Ristenpart, T. (eds.) CRYPTO 2020. LNCS, vol. 12171, pp. 441–469. Springer, Cham (2020). https://doi.org/10.1007/978-3-030-56880-1_16

10. Boyen, X., Haines, T., Mueller, J.: Epoque: practical end-to-end verifiable post-quantum-secure e-voting. To appear in the Proceedings of IEEE EuroS&P 2021 Cryptology ePrint Archive, Report 2021/304 (2021). https://eprint.iacr.org/2021/304

11. Boyen, X., Haines, T., Müller, J.: A verifiable and practical lattice-based decryption mix net with external auditing. In: Chen, L., Li, N., Liang, K., Schneider, S. (eds.) ESORICS 2020. LNCS, vol. 12309, pp. 336–356. Springer, Cham (2020). https://doi.org/10.1007/978-3-030-59013-0_17

12. Boyle, E., Klein, S., Rosen, A., Segev, G.: Securing Abe's mix-net against malicious verifiers via witness indistinguishability. In: Catalano, D., De Prisco, R. (eds.) SCN 2018. LNCS, vol. 11035, pp. 274–291. Springer, Cham (2018). https://doi.org/10.1007/978-3-319-98113-0_15

13. Bünz, B., Bootle, J., Boneh, D., Poelstra, A., Wuille, P., Maxwell, G.: Bulletproofs: short proofs for confidential transactions and more. In: 2018 IEEE Symposium on Security and Privacy, San Francisco, CA, USA, 21–23 May 2018, pp. 315–334. IEEE Computer Society Press (2018)

14. Chakrabarty, A., Collier, M., Mukhopadhyay, S.: Matrix-based nonblocking routing algorithm for Beneš networks. In: 2009 Computation World: Future Computing, Service Computation, Cognitive, Adaptive, Content, Patterns, pp. 551–556 (2009)

15. Chang, C., Melhem, R.: Arbitrary size Benes networks. Parallel Process. Lett. **07**, 05 (1997)

16. Chaum, D.L.: Untraceable electronic mail, return addresses, and digital pseudonyms. Commun. ACM **24**(2), 84–90 (1981)

17. Costa, N., Martínez, R., Morillo, P.: Proof of a shuffle for lattice-based cryptography. In: Lipmaa, H., Mitrokotsa, A., Matulevivcius, R. (eds.) NordSec 2017. LNCS, vol. 10674, pp. 280–296. Springer, Cham (2017). https://doi.org/10.1007/978-3-319-70290-2_17

18. Costa, N., Martínez, R., Morillo, P.: Lattice-based proof of a shuffle. In: Bracciali, A., Clark, J., Pintore, F., Rønne, P.B., Sala, M. (eds.) FC 2019. LNCS, vol. 11599, pp. 330–346. Springer, Cham (2020). https://doi.org/10.1007/978-3-030-43725-1_23

19. del Pino, R., Lyubashevsky, V., Neven, G., Seiler, G.: Practical quantum-safe voting from lattices. In: Thuraisingham, B.M., Evans, D., Malkin, T., Xu, D. (eds.) ACM CCS 2017, Dallas, TX, USA, 31 October–2 November 2017, pp. 1565–1581. ACM Press (2017)

20. Don, J., Fehr, S., Majenz, C.: The measure-and-reprogram technique 2.0: multi-round Fiat-Shamir and more. In: Micciancio, D., Ristenpart, T. (eds.) CRYPTO 2020. LNCS, vol. 12172, pp. 602–631. Springer, Cham (2020). https://doi.org/10.1007/978-3-030-56877-1_21

21. Furukawa, J.: Efficient and verifiable shuffling and shuffle-decryption. IEICE Trans. Fundam. Electron. Commun. Comput. Sci. **88**(1), 172–188 (2005)
22. Furukawa, J., Sako, K.: An efficient scheme for proving a shuffle. In: Kilian, J. (ed.) CRYPTO 2001. LNCS, vol. 2139, pp. 368–387. Springer, Heidelberg (2001). https://doi.org/10.1007/3-540-44647-8_22
23. Gjøsteen, K., Strand, M.: A roadmap to fully homomorphic elections: stronger security, better verifiability. In: Brenner, M., et al. (eds.) FC 2017. LNCS, vol. 10323, pp. 404–418. Springer, Cham (2017). https://doi.org/10.1007/978-3-319-70278-0_25
24. Groth, J.: A verifiable secret shuffe of homomorphic encryptions. In: Desmedt, Y.G. (ed.) PKC 2003. LNCS, vol. 2567, pp. 145–160. Springer, Heidelberg (2003). https://doi.org/10.1007/3-540-36288-6_11
25. Groth, J., Ishai, Y.: Sub-linear zero-knowledge argument for correctness of a shuffle. In: Smart, N. (ed.) EUROCRYPT 2008. LNCS, vol. 4965, pp. 379–396. Springer, Heidelberg (2008). https://doi.org/10.1007/978-3-540-78967-3_22
26. Groth, J., Lu, S.: Verifiable shuffle of large size ciphertexts. In: Okamoto, T., Wang, X. (eds.) PKC 2007. LNCS, vol. 4450, pp. 377–392. Springer, Heidelberg (2007). https://doi.org/10.1007/978-3-540-71677-8_25
27. Haines, T., Müller, J.: SoK: techniques for verifiable mix nets. In: 2020 IEEE 33rd Computer Security Foundations Symposium (CSF), pp. 49–64 (2020)
28. Lyubashevsky, V.: Lattice signatures without trapdoors. In: Pointcheval, D., Johansson, T. (eds.) EUROCRYPT 2012. LNCS, vol. 7237, pp. 738–755. Springer, Heidelberg (2012). https://doi.org/10.1007/978-3-642-29011-4_43
29. Lyubashevsky, V., Peikert, C., Regev, O.: On ideal lattices and learning with errors over rings. J. ACM **60**(6), 1–35 (2013)
30. Markus, J., Ari, J.: Millimix: Mixing in small batches. Technical report (1999)
31. Andrew Neff, C.: A verifiable secret shuffle and its application to e-voting. In: Reiter, M.K., Samarati, P. (eds.) ACM CCS 2001, Philadelphia, PA, USA, 5–8 November 2001, pp. 116–125. ACM Press (2001)
32. Sako, K., Kilian, J.: Receipt-free mix-type voting scheme. In: Guillou, L.C., Quisquater, J.-J. (eds.) EUROCRYPT 1995. LNCS, vol. 921, pp. 393–403. Springer, Heidelberg (1995). https://doi.org/10.1007/3-540-49264-X_32
33. Shor, P.W.: Polynomial-time algorithms for prime factorization and discrete logarithms on a quantum computer. SIAM J. Comput. **26**(5), 1484–1509 (1997)
34. Strand, M.: A verifiable shuffle for the GSW cryptosystem. In: Zohar, A., et al. (eds.) FC 2018. LNCS, vol. 10958, pp. 165–180. Springer, Heidelberg (2019). https://doi.org/10.1007/978-3-662-58820-8_12
35. Terelius, B., Wikström, D.: Proofs of restricted shuffles. In: Bernstein, D.J., Lange, T. (eds.) AFRICACRYPT 2010. LNCS, vol. 6055, pp. 100–113. Springer, Heidelberg (2010). https://doi.org/10.1007/978-3-642-12678-9_7
36. Waksman, A.: A permutation network. J. ACM **15**(1), 159–163 (1968)
37. Wikström, D.: A commitment-consistent proof of a shuffle. In: Boyd, C., González Nieto, J. (eds.) ACISP 2009. LNCS, vol. 5594, pp. 407–421. Springer, Heidelberg (2009). https://doi.org/10.1007/978-3-642-02620-1_28

WTSC – Security and Verification

On-Chain Smart Contract Verification
over Tendermint

Luca Olivieri[1,2](✉) [ID], Fausto Spoto[1] [ID], and Fabio Tagliaferro[1] [ID]

[1] Dipartimento di Informatica, Università di Verona, Verona, Italy
{luca.olivieri,fausto.spoto,fabio.tagliaferro}@univr.it
[2] Corvallis S.r.l, Padova, Italy

Abstract. Smart contracts are computer code that runs in blockchain
and expresses the rules of an agreement among parties. A bug in their
code has major consequences, such as rule violations and security attacks.
Smart contracts are immutable and cannot be easily replaced to patch a
bug. To overcome these problems, there exist automatic static analyzers
that find bugs before smart contracts are installed in blockchain. However, this *off-chain* verification is *optional*: programmers are not forced
to use it. This paper defines *on-chain* verification instead, that occurs
inside the same blockchain nodes, when the code of smart contracts is
installed. It acts as a *mandatory* entry filter that bans code that does
not abide to the verification rules, that are consequently part of the consensus rules of the blockchain. Thus, an improvement in on-chain verification entails a consensus update of the network. This paper provides
an implementation of on-chain verification for smart contracts written
in the Takamaka subset of Java, running as a Tendermint application. It
shows that on-chain verification works, reporting actual experiments.

Keywords: Smart contract · Software verification · Program
analysis · Blockchain · Tendermint

1 Introduction

Blockchain is a distributed ledger that replicates data in a peer-to-peer network
of nodes. Transactions are ledger updates, digitally signed by the users. The
nodes of the network collect broadcasted transactions into a growing cryptogra-
phically-linked chain of blocks. They execute a consensus algorithm to agree
on the ledger evolution. Once consensus is achieved, it is hard, or impossible,
to withdraw transactions from the blockchain. In this sense, blockchains are
immutable. *Smart contracts* specify rules and effects of transactions and can be
either built-in or given as custom code installed inside the same blockchain.

Bitcoin [1,9], in 2008, was the first popular blockchain implementation. It is a
peer-to-peer electronic cash system that stores and transmits value in a currency

Work supported by FSE – Regione del Veneto: DGR N. 1463/2019, *Innovazione e
ricerca per un Veneto più competitivo – Assegni di ricerca anno 2019.*

M. Bernhard et al. (Eds.): FC 2021 Workshops, LNCS 12676, pp. 333–347, 2021.
https://doi.org/10.1007/978-3-662-63958-0_28

called *bitcoin*, using a *Proof of Work* (PoW) consensus algorithm. A Turing-incomplete low-level language specifies Bitcoin's transactions. It can be seen as a limited scripting language for smart contracts. In 2013, *Ethereum* [2, 4] introduced a Turing-complete bytecode for smart contracts, for developing decentralized applications. Ethereum smart contracts can be programmed in high-level languages, with Solidity being the most popular one, and run on the Ethereum virtual machine. Ethereum uses PoW but is currently switching to *Proof of Stake* (PoS), a consensus algorithm with reduced resource consumption [12]. The Tendermint protocol [8] provides a generic and customizable infrastructure for networking and consensus through PoS, with a pseudo-random election of the *validator* node for the next block. Network participants who want to become validators freeze a certain amount of *stake*, that acts as an economic incentive that dissuades from validating or creating fraudulent transactions. If the network detects a fraudulent transaction, the culprit loses part of its stake and the right to act as a validator. Tendermint's protocol tolerates up to $\frac{1}{3}$ of misbehaving nodes. Tendermint leaves the notion of transaction unspecified: programmers can develop an application layer for Tendermint, that specifies which transactions exist and which is their semantics. The application layer can be written in any programming language and can be an actual environment for the execution of Turing-complete smart contracts, similarly to Ethereum.

Not surprisingly, Turing-completeness for smart contracts introduces the risk of all sort of bugs [3, 11]. Since smart contracts deal with money and cannot be replaced, it is paramount to install only *correct* code in blockchain. Thus, there exist many analyzers that verify smart contracts before they get installed in blockchain. For instance, https://mythx.io is an analysis service for Solidity that uses symbolic analysis to detect software vulnerabilities. Echidna [7] uses a fuzzing approach to find a sequence of transactions that violates a given property. Slither [6] uses data-flow and taint analysis to find potential issues. Furthermore, there are companies that provide code audit services, using both automatic tools and human investigation. A limit of these tools and procedures is that they are *optional* and *external* to the blockchain (hence *off-chain*): the latter does not actively protect itself against the deployment of bugged or dangerous code.

This paper makes the following contributions:

- It defines *on-chain* code verification, where the nodes of the blockchain verify the code being deployed. That is, the same network, *internally*, runs a *mandatory* code verification step and rejects code that does not pass it. As a consequence, on-chain verification is a defensive, proactive technique that guarantees that all code executed in blockchain has been successfully verified.
- It describes an actual implementation of a blockchain with on-chain verification, built as a Tendermint application that runs smart contracts written in the Takamaka subset of Java [14]. Note that we have used Tendermint as a third-party tool over which we integrate our code. Nothing has been changed in Tendermint. Our code includes 26 on-chain checks, that mostly verify the correct use of Takamaka's primitives and code annotations and the use of a deterministic subset of Java [15].

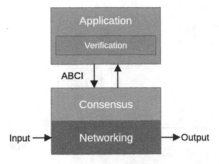

Fig. 1. High-level architecture of an application running on Tendermint Core and performing on-chain verification.

– It describes a lazy re-verification approach that copes with the evolution of the code verification rules. Namely, on-chain verification is part of code deployment transactions, hence its rules are consensus rules whose evolution requires a network update. Moreover, code previously successfully verified with old verification rules might fail to pass new verification rules. The implementation of this last contribution is not available yet.

This paper is organized as follows. Section 2 defines a general architecture for on-chain code verification. Section 3 describes our implementation of on-chain verification, over Tendermint, and shows an on-chain check. Section 4 reports experiments with our implementation and describes how readers and reviewers can validate them. Section 5 shows how the blockchain can cope with the evolution of code verification rules. Section 6 comments on limitations, related and future work.

2   On-Chain Code Verification

This section defines the architecture of a blockchain node with on-chain code verification, built over Tendermint. Following Fig. 1, it consists of three layers:

Networking: discovers and connects nodes with each other, propagates requests for transactions and collects their responses from other nodes.
Consensus: compares and approves/rejects the responses obtained by executing the requests on the nodes.
Application: specifies which requests are valid, how their responses are computed and how the application's state consequently evolves.

Tendermint Core is an implementation of networking and consensus, without any application layer (its distribution includes a few toy applications, irrelevant for our purposes). Programmers develop their own application layer and plug it into Tendermint Core via its Application BlockChain Interface (ABCI). Tendermint Core replicates the application state on each machine of the network.

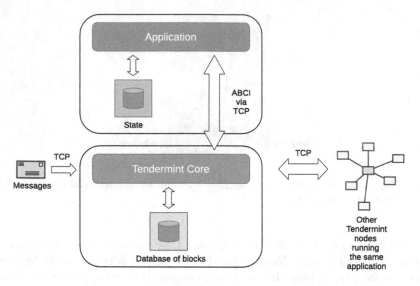

Fig. 2. Tendermint Core and a Tendermint application, with their respective databases.

Figure 2 shows a more detailed picture of Tendermint Core and of an application connected through its ABCI. It shows that Tendermint Core keeps the blocks of the blockchain in its own database, that needn't be the same used to hold the application's *state*. The latter holds, for instance, the code of the smart contracts installed in blockchain and the value of their state variables. Tendermint Core needs only the hash of the application state, for consensus, to ensure that all nodes have reached the same application state.

One can define the application state as a map σ from the hash of the requests that the blockchain has executed to the responses that have been computed for them. The application state contains the full responses, but only the hash of the requests. Hence, it can be implemented as a Merkle-Patricia trie. The full requests are contained in the database of blocks of Tendermint Core instead, since they are needed to replay the transactions in all nodes of the network.

On-chain code verification requires a code verification module (Fig. 1). This is part of the application layer, since it contributes to the execution of the application-specific requests for code installation in blockchain. Assume that a *request*, whose hash is *request$_h$*, reaches the blockchain, requiring to install, in blockchain, the code of some smart contracts, reported inside *request*.

Figure 3 shows the sequence diagram for the execution of *request*. Namely, Tendermint Core routes *request* through networking and consensus up to the application, that uses its verification module to either approve or reject the code. If approved, the application includes the code in a *response* and updates its state σ with a new binding: $\sigma(request_h) = response$. The hash *request$_h$* is an immutable, machine-independent reference to this code, used later to instantiate

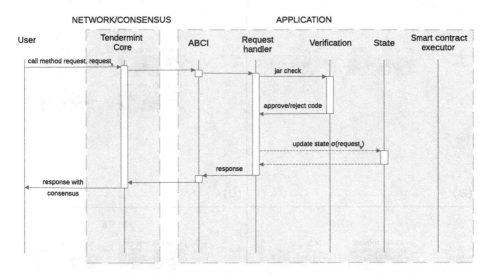

Fig. 3. Sequence diagram for code verification and installation in blockchain.

and execute smart contracts. If the code is rejected, instead, the application state is expanded with a failure response, that does not contain any code.

Figure 4 reports an example of application state evolution. It reports the requests in full, for readability, but remember that only the hash of the requests is kept in the application state. Figure 4(a) shows the application state after the execution of a code installation request for which verification succeeds. The code is Java bytecode, packaged into a *jar*, *i.e.*, a zipped container of Java bytecode. The response contains the same jar (*i.e.*, the same code as the request[1]). In terms of Java, the hash of the request is the *classpath* of subsequent code executions. Figure 4(b) reports, instead, a request whose code fails to verify. The response does not include any code installed in blockchain. This shows that the verification rules are part of the consensus rules that determine which code installation request is valid and which must be rejected instead (Fig. 4(a) and (b)). Hence they must be the same in every node of the network and must be deterministic.

On-chain verification performs code verification statically, only once, when the code is installed in blockchain. For instance, Fig. 4(c) shows a subsequent request that asks to instantiate a smart contract whose code has been installed by the request in Fig. 4(a). The request in Fig. 4(c) uses the hash of the request in Fig. 4(a) as its classpath and contains the parameters for calling the constructor of the smart contract. The execution of the request runs that constructor, without code verification: it has been already performed in Fig. 4(a). The immutable reference *hash of request#0* is used later to refer to the new smart contract

---

[1] The response might also contain an instrumentation of the code, as it is the case for the Java subset for programming smart contracts called Takamaka, that we use in our implementation. This is irrelevant here and we refer the interested reader to [14].

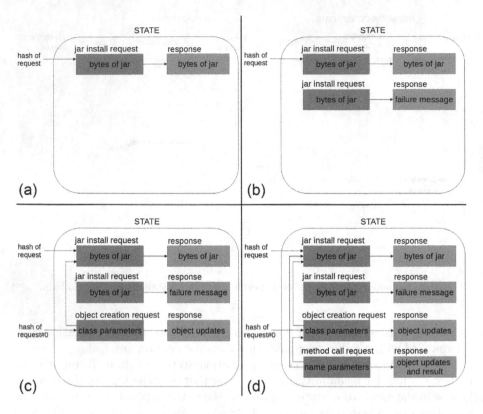

Fig. 4. The evolution of the application state during a sequence of requests.

instance[2]. The state of the new smart contract is reported in the response as a set of *updates*, that is, instance fields modified during the execution of the request, including those of the smart contract instance *hash of request#0* that has been created in blockchain. Finally, Fig. 4(d) shows the execution of a request asking to call a method on the instance of smart contract *hash of request#0*. This last request refers to both the classpath and the target instance smart contract. Its execution, in general, modifies some instance fields of objects in blockchain, that are reported as *updates* in its response. This last request does not verify the code either, since it is not a code installation request.

The rules of on-chain verification are part of the consensus rules of the blockchain, since they determine if the response of a request to install code in the blockchain is successful or failed. Hence, they determine the evolution of the state of the application layer and its hash, that is reported in the blocks of the underlying Tendermint blockchain, that uses it for consensus. This is the

---

[2] The index #0 refers to the first object created during the execution of a request. In general, a request can instantiate many objects, depending on the code that it executes. For simplicity, this example assumes that only one has been instantiated.

standard way of working for Tendermint. Hence, all nodes must use the same verification rules. Nodes that use different rules will be automatically excluded from the Tendermint blockchain.

3 Implementation

We have implemented on-chain verification for smart contracts written in the Takamaka subset of Java [14] (the lazy re-verification technique of Sect. 5 is still under development and we leave it for future work). The goal of Takamaka is to write smart contracts in a well-known programming language, leveraging expertise and existing mature development tools. The application layer of Takamaka is a state machine (the Tendermint *application* in Fig. 2) that executes transactions from request to response. Requests can specify the addition of a jar in the permanent state of the application, or the execution of a constructor, or of an instance or static method of code previously installed in the state. Responses include the effects of the transaction, as a set of field updates (see Fig. 4). Updates can be computed since the jar of the Java code is instrumented before being installed in blockchain, with extra code that keeps track of the affected fields of objects [14]. Determinism is ensured since only a deterministic subset of Java is allowed, restricted to a deterministic API of the Java library [15]. The state machine of Takamaka is implemented in Java and runs on a standard Java virtual machine. The state is kept in a Merkle-Patricia trie that implements a map from hash of requests to their corresponding response (Fig. 4). This trie is kept in the Xodus transactional database by JetBrains[3].

The verification module is implemented as a sequence of *checks* performed on methods and classes. Since the request of installing new code in blockchain contains the compiled bytecode only, such checks run at Java bytecode level, by using the BCEL library for Java bytecode manipulation[4]. The source code is simply not available in blockchain. Currently, Takamaka's on-chain verification performs 26 checks on every jar that gets installed in blockchain. They must all pass, or otherwise the jar will be rejected. Figure 5 describes some of them.

We show a specific example of check now. It verifies that method `caller()` is used in the right context. That method corresponds to `msg.sender` in Solidity: it allows programmers to get a reference to the *contract* that called a method or constructor X.

The method `caller()` can be used inside the code of X only if X satisfies two constraints[5]:

1. X is annotated as `@FromContract(class)`, for some `class`;
2. the invocation of `caller()` occurs on `this`.

---

[3] https://github.com/JetBrains/xodus.

[4] https://commons.apache.org/proper/commons-bcel.

[5] `@FromContract` and, later, `@Payable` are Java *annotations*, that is, a mechanism for adding metadata information to source and compiled code. They are irrelevant for the code executor, but can be used by code analysis and instrumentation tools.

Correct context for @FromContract	@FromContract is only applied to instance methods or to constructors of storage classes (*i.e.*, classes whose instances can be kept in blockchain).
Correct calls to @FromContract	@FromContract methods or constructors are only called from instance methods or constructors of contracts.
Correct context for @Payable	@Payable is only applied to @FromContract methods or constructors of contracts (since only contracts have a balance).
Correct fields in storage classes	Classes whose instances can be kept in blockchain can only have a restricted set of types for their fields.
Correct context for `caller()`	See the description in this paper.
No finalizers	Since their execution is non-deterministic in Java.
Only white-listed Java APIs	To enforce determinism (see [15]).

Fig. 5. Some of the 26 on-chain verifications currently performed by Takamaka.

The rationale of constraint 1 is that @FromContract(class) guarantees that X can *only* be called from a contract of type class, or subclass, or from an external wallet whose paying account has type class, or subclass. Hence the caller exists. For instance, the following contract stores its creator in field owner. The use of caller() is correct here, since it occurs inside a @FromContract constructor:

```
import io.takamaka.code.lang.Contract;
import io.takamaka.code.lang.FromContract;

public class C1 extends Contract {
  private C1 owner;

  public @FromContract(C1.class) C1() {
    owner = (C1) caller(); // ok
  }
}
```

Instead, it is incorrect to invoke `caller()` in a method or constructor not annotated as `@FromContract`, since its caller is not necessarily a contract and `caller()` would be meaningless in that case:

```
import io.takamaka.code.lang.Contract;

public class C2 extends Contract {
  public void m() {
    ... = caller(); // error at deployment time
  }
}
```

The reason of constraint 2 is that its violation lets one access the caller of other contracts, with possible logical inconsistencies and security issues. For the same reason, the use of `tx.origin` is normally an antipattern in Solidity (see *Tx.origin Authentication* in [2]). Constraint 2 holds in classes C1 and C2 above, but is violated below:

```
import io.takamaka.code.lang.Contract;
import io.takamaka.code.lang.FromContract;

public class C3 extends Contract {
  private C3 owner;

  public @FromContract(C3.class) C3() {
    owner = (C3) caller(); // ok
  }

  public @FromContract void m() {
    ... owner.caller() ...; // error at deployment-time
  }
}
```

Figure 6 reports our implementation of a check that verifies if a method satisfies constraints 1 and 2 above. The code has been simplified for readability: its complete version can be found in the repository of the distribution of our implementation of the runtime of Takamaka (see Sect. 4). Full understanding of the code in Fig. 6 requires knowledge about Java bytecode and BCEL, which is outside the scope of this paper. Nevertheless, it is possible to understand the structure of the code: the constructor of the check scans the stream of Java bytecode instructions of the method (`instructions()`), filters those that call a method named `caller` that returns a contract, and checks two conditions for each of them (with the two if's inside the `forEach`): the method must be annotated as `FromContract` (constraint 1 above) and the invocation must be immediately preceded by an `aload_0` bytecode instruction. The latter is Java bytecode for pushing `this` on the stack, as receiver of the call to `caller()` (constraint 2 above). If any of the if's is satisfied, an issue is generated, which will later reject the installation of the code in blockchain.

```
public class CallerIsUsedOnThisAndInFromContractCheck extends Check {

  public CallerIsUsedOnThisAndInFromContractCheck() {
    boolean isFromContract = annotations.isFromContract
      (className, methodName, methodArgs, methodReturnType);

    instructions()
      .filter(this::isCallToCaller)
      .forEach(ih -> {
        if (!isFromContract)
          issue(new CallerOutsideFromContractError(inferSourceFile(), methodName, lineOf(ih)));

        if (!previousIsLoad0(ih))
          issue(new CallerNotOnThisError(inferSourceFile(), methodName, lineOf(ih)));
      });
  }

  private boolean previousIsLoad0(InstructionHandle ih) {
    Instruction ins = ih.getPrev().getInstruction();
    return ins instanceof LoadInstruction && ((LoadInstruction) ins).getIndex() == 0;
  }

  private final static String TAKAMAKA_CALLER_SIG = "()Lio/takamaka/code/lang/Contract;";

  private boolean isCallToCaller(InstructionHandle ih) {
    Instruction ins = ih.getInstruction();
    if (ins instanceof InvokeInstruction) {
      InvokeInstruction invoke = (InvokeInstruction) ins;
      ReferenceType receiver;

      return "caller".equals(invoke.getMethodName())
        && TAKAMAKA_CALLER_SIG.equals(invoke.getSignature())
        && (receiver = invoke.getReferenceType()) instanceof ObjectType
        && classLoader.isStorage(((ObjectType) receiver).getClassName());
    }
    else
      return false;
  }
}
```

Fig. 6. The on-chain check for a correct use of `caller()`.

4   Experiments

We have implemented our on-chain verification for the Takamaka subset of
Java, inside its runtime that works as a Tendermint application. It is an actual
blockchain running on Tendermint, that can be programmed with smart contracts written in Java. Our implementation is part of a larger project, called
Hotmoka, whose long-term goal is to use the Takamaka language for programming both blockchains and IoT devices. We have created three scripts that
request to install in blockchain the examples from Sect. 3. We have also created a test that installs a smart contract and uses it to run many transactions,
to check the scalability of the technique and evaluate the difference when on-
chain verification is on or off. Readers who want to run the experiments and
inspect the results can download the code[6] and follow the instructions in the
WTSC21.txt. That repository contains also the code of the 26 checks of on-chain
verification (including that in Fig. 6).

---

[6] `git clone --branch wtsc21 https://github.com/Hotmoka/hotmoka.git`.

The first experiment starts a blockchain of a single node and runs a script that connects to the node and installs a jar containing class C1 from Sec. 3. The result is successful:

```
Connecting to the blockchain node at localhost:8080... done
Installing the Takamaka runtime in the node... done
Installing C1 in the node... done (on-chain verification succeeded)
C1.jar installed at address ee848b5bc7fd8283ab01b5977970e71f548...
```

The subsequent experiment installs C2 instead. The attempt to install the code in blockchain will fail since on-chain verification fails:

```
Connecting to the blockchain node at localhost:8080... done
Installing the Takamaka runtime in the node... done
Installing C2 in the node...
Exception in thread "main" io.hotmoka.beans.TransactionException:
io.takamaka.code.verification.VerificationException: C2.java:8
caller() can only be used inside a @FromContract method or constructor
```

The third experiment performs the same operation with class C3. This attempt will fail since on-chain verification fails:

```
Connecting to the blockchain node at localhost:8080... done
Installing the Takamaka runtime in the node... done
Installing C3 in the node...
Exception in thread "main" io.hotmoka.beans.TransactionException:
io.takamaka.code.verification.VerificationException: C3.java:14
caller() can only be called on "this"
```

In order to evaluate the scalability of our technique, we have created a smart contract that creates and funds a pool of 500 externally-owned accounts and allows one to determine which is the *richest* among them (has highest balance). We have written a JUnit test that installs that smart contract in blockchain and uses it to create and fund the 500 accounts, execute 1,000 random money transfers between them and ask for the richest. This process is repeated ten times. The execution time of this test is 158.19 s on our machine (Intel Core i3-4150, 16 GB of RAM, running Ubuntu Linux 20.04.1). In total (including code installation and account creation) the test runs 10,020 transactions, that is, it performs 63.34 transactions per second. By turning on-chain verification off, the same test runs in 156.95 s, that is, it performs 63.84 transactions per second. These numbers have been computed as an average over five executions of the test. This shows that on-chain verification increases the execution time of the test by only 0.79%.

5   Evolution of Code Verification

This section shows that a change in the verification rules requires to re-verify all code installed in blockchain and that this can be performed lazily, on-demand.

Section 2 stated that code verification is only performed when code is installed in blockchain. However, that is true only under the unrealistic assumption that the verification module never changes. In practice, that module will be updated eventually, to include new verification rules or to improve the precision of already existing rules. When a new version is deployed, it becomes necessary to update all nodes to that version (or at least all validators), or otherwise consensus might be lost. A change in the verification rules, if deployed on a subset of the network only, entails that the updated nodes might accept a request that the non-updated nodes might reject instead, or vice versa.

All approaches to a network update can be used here. The novelty, however, is that some code that was successfully verified with the previous version of the verification module might be rejected with its current version, or vice versa. Hence, there must be a mechanism that enforces that the execution of some code in blockchain occurs only if that code passes the *current* verification rules. Conceptually, this means that an update of the verification module triggers a re-verification of all code previously successfully installed in blockchain. In practice, this cannot be performed, since it would be extremely expensive and would hang the nodes for a long time. Our solution, that we are going to describe, is to lazily re-verify the code on-demand, when it is asked to run. This amortizes the cost of re-verification. Moreover, [10] shows that only 0.05% of all contracts installed in Ethereum are involved in 80% of the transactions. Hence, a lazy approach avoids the re-verification of code that might actually never run again.

In order to implement this lazy re-verification approach, we expand the information in the *response* of a successful code installation *request* (Fig. 4(a)). Namely, together with the installed code, *response* is enriched with a numerical tag $\tau(response)$, *i.e.*, the version of the verification module that has been used to verify the code inside *response*. The sequence diagram in Fig. 7 shows the workflow for lazy code re-verification. Assume that a request arrives, that requires to run code referred with the hash $request_h$ of a previous, successful code installation *request* (as in Fig. 4(c) and (d)). The node finds out that $\sigma(request_h) = response$ has a verification tag $\tau(response)$ and compares it with the current version τ of the verification module. There are two possibilities:

1. $\tau = \tau(response)$: the code was verified with the current version of the verification module, it does not need re-verification and can be run immediately;
2. $\tau > \tau(response)$: the code was verified with an old version of the verification module; it must be re-verified before being run.

In the second case, the node verifies the code again, using the current version τ of the verification module. This is possible since *response* includes that code (Fig. 4(a)). A new response *response'* will be computed (successful, having τ as verification module version, or failed) and the application state is updated as $\sigma(request_h) = response'$. The use of $request_h$ in future requests will not re-verify the code, until a newer version of the verification module is installed. The update is possible since it occurs in the state, not in the blockchain, whose blocks are immutable.

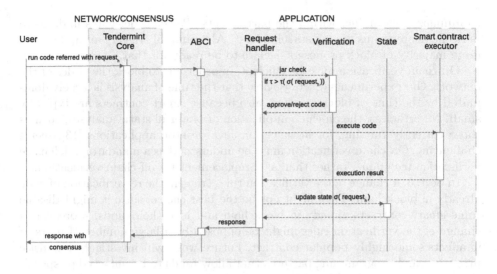

Fig. 7. Sequence diagram for lazy code re-verification.

It is important to note that *response'* might state that reverification failed, because the old code passed the previous verification rules but not the new ones. In that case, the execution of the code will fail, since its classpath is not valid anymore. This means that a smart contract might work today, but might stop working tomorrow, if updated verification rules reject its code. In theory, the converse is also possible: the same contract might be reactivated after tomorrow, if another change in the verification rules replaces a failed response with a successful response. However, we have decided to forbid this second scenario, since it might be surprising for users.

6 Discussion

To our knowledge, this paper defines and implements the first on-chain code verification for smart contracts, that allows the same blockchain to reject the code that does not pass a set of verification rules. From this point of view, the technique is related to continuous integration, that builds and deploys code only if it passes all compilation and testing requirements. The main difference is that smart contracts cannot be replaced or debugged once installed in blockchain.

Some blockchains, such as Ethereum, apply a notion of *transparency* [10], that lets one store in blockchain the source code of the smart contracts, to guarantee that it actually compiles into their bytecode. But this is only an optional technique that ensures that bytecode and source code match: no code verification is applied.

The specific technique for updating the consensus rules of a network, after a change in the verification rules (Sect. 5), is orthogonal to our work. In Cosmos, the government module supports such an update, with (dis-)incentives to minimize misconduct within the participants. *Polkadot* delegates updates to periodic referendums among stakeholders[7]. Algorand [5] triggers an update if a large majority of block proposers declare to be ready for that.

On-chain verification must be efficient, in order not to block the nodes of the network. Our experiments (Sect. 4) show that the time of analysis is largely dominated by the time of block creation, also because smart contracts are typically small. Nevertheless, the on-chain application of powerful static analyses, such as those currently running, for instance, on Java desktop applications [13], seems challenging. On-chain verification must be understood as a mandatory, defensive verification technique, rather than as a replacement for off-chain verification.

In Sect. 5, a change of the verification rules triggers the re-verification of code already in blockchain. This might not be the best choice, since it might disable some smart contracts already in blockchain and lock their funds. Moreover, a change of the verification rules might be opposed by a large number of users, if it affects some highly popular contract. Future work will investigate linguistic primitives and programming patterns that allow funds to be unlocked or specify that some contract should *not* be re-verified after a verification rules change.

References

1. Antonopoulos, A.M.: Mastering Bitcoin: Unlocking Digital Cryptocurrencies, 2nd edn. O'Reilly (2017)
2. Antonopoulos, A.M., Wood, G.: Mastering Ethereum: Building Smart Contracts and Dapps. O'Reilly (2018)
3. Atzei, N., Bartoletti, M., Cimoli, T.: A survey of attacks on ethereum smart contracts (SoK). In: Maffei, M., Ryan, M. (eds.) POST 2017. LNCS, vol. 10204, pp. 164–186. Springer, Heidelberg (2017). https://doi.org/10.1007/978-3-662-54455-6_8
4. Buterin, V.: Ethereum Whitepaper (2013). Available at https://ethereum.org/en/whitepaper/
5. Chen, J., Micali, S.: Algorand: a secure and efficient distributed ledger. Theor. Comput. Sci. **777**, 155–183 (2019)
6. Feist, J., Grieco, G., Groce, A.: Slither: a static analysis framework for smart contracts. In: 2nd International Workshop on Emerging Trends in Software Engineering for Blockchain (WETSEB@ICSE 2019), Montreal, QC, Canada, May 2019, pp. 8–15. IEEE/ACM (2019)
7. Grieco, G., Song, W., Cygan, A., Feist, J., Groce, A.: Echidna: effective, usable, and fast fuzzing for smart contracts. In: 29th ACM SIGSOFT International Symposium on Software Testing and Analysis (ISSTA 2020), USA, July 2020, pp. 557–560. ACM (2020)
8. Kwon, J.: Tendermint: consensus without mining. Available at https://tendermint.com/static/docs/tendermint.pdf (2014)
9. Nakamoto, S.: Bitcoin: a peer-to-peer electronic cash system. Available at https://bitcoin.org/bitcoin.pdf (2008)
10. Oliva, G.A., Hassan, A.E., Jiang, Z.M.: An exploratory study of smart contracts in the ethereum blockchain platform. Empirical Softw. Eng. **25**(3), 1864–1904 (2020)

---

[7] See https://wiki.polkadot.network/docs/en/learn-governance.

11. Popper, N.: A hacking of more than $50 Million dashes hopes in the world of virtual currency. The New York Times, 18 June 2016
12. Sedlmeir, J., Buhl, H.U., Fridgen, G., Keller, R.: The energy consumption of blockchain technology: beyond myth. Bus. Inf. Syst. Eng. **62**(6), 599–608 (2020)
13. Spoto, F.: The Julia static analyzer for java. In: Rival, X. (ed.) SAS 2016. LNCS, vol. 9837, pp. 39–57. Springer, Heidelberg (2016). https://doi.org/10.1007/978-3-662-53413-7_3
14. Spoto, F.: A java framework for smart contracts. In: Bracciali, A., Clark, J., Pintore, F., Rønne, P.B., Sala, M. (eds.) FC 2019. LNCS, vol. 11599, pp. 122–137. Springer, Cham (2020). https://doi.org/10.1007/978-3-030-43725-1_10
15. Spoto, F.: Enforcing determinism of java smart contracts. In: Bernhard, M., et al. (eds.) FC 2020. LNCS, vol. 12063, pp. 568–583. Springer, Cham (2020). https://doi.org/10.1007/978-3-030-54455-3_40

Publicly Verifiable and Secrecy Preserving Periodic Auctions

Hisham S. Galal$^{(\boxtimes)}$ and Amr M. Youssef

Concordia Institute for Information Systems Engineering, Concordia University,
Montréal, Québec, Canada
{h_galal,youssef}@ciise.concordia.ca

Abstract. In lit markets, all the information about bids and offers in
the order book is visible to the public. With this transparency, traders
can discover prices and adjust their strategies accordingly. On the other
hand, submitting a bulk order by a financial institution will have a significant impact on the market price. Therefore, financial institutions prefer
trading on dark pools, which hide order books, to avoid potential losses
from negative market impact. However, the lack of transparency hurts
price discovery, results in poor execution of trades, and promotes illicit
behaviors such as front-running. Hence, several financial regulations have
limited trading on dark pools. Subsequently, periodic auctions, which
are considered regulation-compliant alternatives to dark pools, have witnessed a surge in trading volumes. Unfortunately, similar to dark pools,
there are no guarantees that the operators will neither exploit their exclusive access to the order book nor incorrectly compute the market-clearing
price. In this paper, we build a publicly verifiable and secrecy preserving
periodic auction protocol to address these challenges. We utilize aggregate Bulletproofs to prove the ordering on a vector of commitments. To
alleviate the burden on traders' computation resources and achieve public verifiability, the protocol delegates the verification of the operator's
work to a smart contract. We evaluate the protocol's performance, and
the results show that it is practical and feasible to deploy.

Keywords: Periodic auction · Zero-knowledge arguments · Blockchain

1 Introduction

Investors use financial exchanges to trade equities and securities. Generally, an
exchange is a continuous double-sided auction between buyers and sellers [1].
It records all outstanding limit orders in an order book. A *limit* order consists
of a unit price, a quantity of an asset, and a direction to indicate whether it is
a *bid* by a buyer or an *offer* by a seller. If the order book is transparent and
accessible to the public, the exchange is known as a *Lit market*. On the contrary,
a *dark pool*, which is favored by financial institutions, is an exchange that hides
its order book from traders [1].

© International Financial Cryptography Association 2021
M. Bernhard et al. (Eds.): FC 2021 Workshops, LNCS 12676, pp. 348–363, 2021.
https://doi.org/10.1007/978-3-662-63958-0_29

To understand the main benefit of dark pools, it is worth considering the problem institutional investors face in lit markets. Suppose that Bob is an institutional investor who uses a lit market to buy one million USD worth of an arbitrary asset. The sellers will notice Bob's bid. Hence, they anticipate the increased demand and react by moving their offers to higher prices so that they can gain higher revenue. As a result, Bob will have a hard time trying to fill his order. Thus, he has to either accept the loss in buying the full volume at higher prices, or divide the quantity into smaller batches and buy at different prices. Although the latter approach may seem better, it still incurs high fees and commissions paid to the exchange. Therefore, it is much more convenient for Bob to trade on a dark pool where the market impact will be minimal.

While dark pools provide a better trading platform for financial institutions, they have several issues. Most importantly, they hurt price discovery and put traders on other exchanges at a disadvantage. Furthermore, the lack of transparency could result in poor execution of trades or abuses such as front-running. Conflicts of interest are also a possibility since the operator could trade against pool clients. The U.S. Securities and Exchange Commission has found numerous violations and fined some dark pool operators [2–4]. Accordingly, several recent financial regulations, such as Europe's MiFID-II [5], call for limiting trades on dark pools. Interestingly, post enforcing MiFID-II, periodic auctions, which are considered regulation-compliant alternatives to dark pools, have witnessed a surge in the size of executed trading volumes.

In periodic auctions, the operator matches orders periodically, rather than continuously. Initially, traders submit orders privately to the operator. The submission phase ends at a random time. Next, the operator determines the market clearing price (MCP) and market clearing volume (MCV). Essentially, traders trust the operator to correctly calculate these values since they do not have access to the order book. To counter-balance this trust, regulators must audit the operator's work to reveal malicious behavior. However, the audit process is prohibitively expensive, and it might also be infrequent.

One way to remove trust requirements and reduce costly audits is to utilize the blockchain technology. Clearly, with the advent of the blockchain and Bitcoin [6], mutually distrusting parties can finally make transactions without relying on a trusted third party. Furthermore, complex types of transactions beyond simple payment transfers have quickly emerged due to the rich capabilities of smart contracts on blockchains such as Ethereum [7]. Smart contracts are pieces of data and code deployed on the blockchain. The consensus layer ensures that they execute precisely as their code dictates. Hence, a smart contract can act as a public trusted judge that resolves disputes and verifies the correctness of transactions.

The contributions in this paper are summarized below:

1. We build a protocol to prove that the committed values for a given vector of commitments are in descending order.
2. We utilize the above protocols to build a publicly verifiable and secrecy preserving periodic auction protocol.
3. We implemented a basic prototype to assess the protocol's performance, and released its source code on Github[1].

2   Related Work

Thrope and Parkes [1] proposed a protocol for continuous double-sided auctions. Initially, each trader sends a price, a quantity, and a direction encrypted by the operator's public key of a homomorphic encryption scheme to a bulletin board. Then, the operator decrypts the orders and tries to match them. Once a match is found, the operator executes the matched orders and publishes them in history. The main drawback of this protocol is its heavy computation burden on the operator since it requires ranking all orders and generating proofs of correctness after the execution of every matched order.

Jutla [8] presented a secure five-party computation protocol for periodic auctions. A small number of brokers and a regulatory authority run the protocol. The auction starts with traders sending limit orders to brokers. Next, brokers run the protocol to find MCP and settle matched orders. In each round of this protocol, the regulatory authority must audit extensive computation to ensure the correctness of MCP, which renders the protocol impractical.

Galal and Youssef [9–11] proposed three constructions to build sealed-bid auctions on Ethereum. In the first construction, they utilize Pedersen commitment scheme and an interactive zero-knowledge range argument with high-cost transactions and limited scalability. The second construction uses zkSNARK, which improves the protocol scalability due to the constant proof size and verification cost. However, it requires a trusted setup to generate the proving and verification keys. Finally, the third construction utilizes Intel SGX as a trusted execution environment to determine the auction winner in a full privacy-preserving way with high performance. However, Intel SGX technology is not mature technology yet, and it faces multiple attacks that compromise its security.

Cartlidge et al. [12] utilized SCALE-MAMBA, a multi-party computation (MPC) framework, to emulate a trusted third party. The authors designed three constructions to assess the feasibility of using MPC in stock markets. They argue that it is not practical yet to run continuous double-sided auctions. On the other hand, the periodic auctions and volume matching constructions show promising results. Although this protocol provides strong secrecy, it requires a heavy preprocessing phase in addition to the inherent highly interactive communications between parties.

---

[1] https://github.com/hsg88/PeriodicAuction.

3   Preliminaries

3.1   Assumptions and Notations

Throughout the paper, an adversary $\mathcal{A}$ is a probabilistic interactive Turing Machine that runs in a polynomial time in the security parameter λ. Let $\mathbb{G}$ be a cyclic group of prime order p with generators g and h. Let $\mathbb{Z}_p^*$ denote $\mathbb{Z}_p \backslash \{0\}$, and $x \leftarrow_{\$} \mathbb{Z}_p^*$ denote uniform sampling of an element from $\mathbb{Z}_p^*$. We represent vectors by bold font, e.g. $\boldsymbol{a}$ is a vector with elements $(a_1, \ldots, a_n)$. Finally, let $H : \{0,1\}^* \rightarrow \mathbb{Z}_p^*$ denote a cryptographic collision resistant hash function.

3.2   ElGamal Encryption

We utilize ElGamal encryption scheme where messages are encoded in the exponent. It consists of the following algorithms:

- $(x, y) \leftarrow \mathcal{K}(\mathbb{G}, p, g)$: it samples a secret key $x \leftarrow_{\$} \mathbb{Z}_p$, and generates a public key $y = g^x$.
- $c \leftarrow \mathtt{Enc}_y(m, r)$: it encrypts a message $m \in \mathbb{Z}_p$ using a blinding factor $r \leftarrow_{\$} \mathbb{Z}_p$ by the public key y, and outputs a ciphertext $c = (c_1, c_2) = (g^r, g^m y^r)$.
- $g^m \leftarrow \mathtt{Dec}_x(c)$: it decrypts the ciphertext c by the secret key x, and outputs $g^m \leftarrow c_2 \cdot c_1^{-x}$. One needs to brute-force the discrete log of g^m to recover m which is affordable for small values (e.g., when m is a 32-bit value).

3.3   Pedersen Commitment

Pedersen commitment [13] is a non-interactive commitment scheme that has perfectly hiding and computationally binding properties. It consists of the following algorithms:

- $X \leftarrow \mathtt{Com}(x, r)$: it commits to a message $x \in \mathbb{Z}_p$ using blinding factor $r \leftarrow_{\$} \mathbb{Z}_p$, and outputs $X = g^x h^r$.
- $\{\top/\bot\} \leftarrow \mathtt{Vfy}(X, x, r)$: it verifies whether X commits to x with blinding factor r, and outputs $\top$ on success, otherwise, it outputs $\bot$.

Pedersen commitments are additively homomorphic. For instance, given the commitments $\mathtt{Com}(x_1, r_1)$ and $\mathtt{Com}(x_2, r_2)$, one can compute $\mathtt{Com}(x_1 + x_2, r_1 + r_2) = \mathtt{Com}(x_1, r_2)\mathtt{Com}(x_2, r_2)$ without knowing the committed values.

3.4   Zero-Knowledge Proof of Knowledge

A zero-knowledge proof of knowledge is a protocol that allows a prover to convince a verifier that a certain statement holds without revealing any information beyond that fact. An argument is a proof which only holds if the prover is computationally bounded and certain computational hardness assumptions hold. We consider arguments consisting of three interactive algorithms $(\text{Setup}, \mathcal{P}, \mathcal{V})$ running in probabilistic polynomial time. The Setup algorithm takes 1^λ as input, and produces a common reference string (CRS) denoted by Σ_{cce}. The transcripts produced by $\mathcal{P}$ and $\mathcal{V}$ when interacting on inputs s and t is denoted by $tr \leftarrow \langle \mathcal{P}(s), \mathcal{V}(t) \rangle$. We write $\langle \mathcal{P}(s), \mathcal{V}(t) \rangle = b$ to denote whether the verifier accepts $b = 1$, or rejects $b = 0$. Let $\mathcal{R} \subset \{0,1\}^* \times \{0,1\}^* \times \{0,1\}^*$ be a ternary polynomial-time decidable relation. We call w a witness for a statement x if $(\sigma, x, w) \in \mathcal{R}$. Additionally, we define the CRS-dependent language

$$\mathcal{L}_\sigma = \{x | \exists w : (\sigma, x, w) \in \mathcal{R}\}$$

as the set of statements x that have a witness w in $\mathcal{R}$. Zero-knowledge arguments have the following three properties.

1. *Completeness*: the verifier will always accept a proof generated by an honest prover.
2. *Soundness*: the verifier will not accept a false proof except with a negligible probability.
3. *Zero-knowledge*: the verifier does not learn any information about the witness from the transcripts exchanged with the prover.

Fiat-Shamir heuristic [14] can transform the interactive triple $(\text{Setup}, \mathcal{P}, \mathcal{V})$ to non-interactive zero-knowledge (NIZK) proof in the random oracle model.

3.5   Zero-Knowledge Range Proof

A zero-knowledge range proof allows a prover to convince a verifier that a committed value falls within a given range. One of the recent constructions is Bulletproofs [15], which has a short logarithmic proof size $O(log(n))$ in the bit-width of the range. The proof generation and verification times scale linearly with n. More importantly, it does not require a trusted setup. In particular, given a commitment $X = g^x h^r \in \mathbb{G}$ for a witness $x \in \mathbb{Z}_p$, Bulletproofs allows a prover to generate the following NIZK argument:

$$\{(g, h \in \mathbb{G}, X; x, r) : X = g^x h^r \wedge x \in [0, 2^n - 1]\}$$

Bulletproofs allows the generation of an efficient aggregate argument for a vector of commitments. Specifically, given a vector of m commitments, the aggregate argument is smaller than the total size of m simple arguments. We refer to the protocol generating aggregate range arguments as $\text{BP} = (\text{Setup}, \mathcal{P}, \mathcal{V})$, which consists of the following probabilistic polynomial-time algorithms:

1. $\sigma \leftarrow \mathtt{BP.Setup}(1^\lambda, n, m)$: it takes λ as the security parameter, n as the range bit-width, and m as the vector cardinality; and outputs Σ_{cce} as the CRS.
2. $\pi \leftarrow \mathtt{BP}.\mathcal{P}(\sigma, \boldsymbol{X}, \boldsymbol{x}, \boldsymbol{r})$: it takes a vector of commitments $\boldsymbol{X}$ along with the opening vectors $\boldsymbol{x}$ and $\boldsymbol{r}$; and generates an argument π to prove

$$\{(\boldsymbol{X}; \boldsymbol{x}, \boldsymbol{r}) : X_i = g^{x_i} h^{r_i} \wedge x_i \in [0, 2^n - 1]\}$$

3. $\{\top/\bot\} \leftarrow \mathtt{BP}.\mathcal{V}(\sigma, \boldsymbol{X}, \pi)$: it returns $\top$ if it accepts π; otherwise, it returns $\bot$.

3.6 Evaluator-Prover Model

The evaluator-prover (EP) model [16] provides a practical framework for secrecy preserving proofs of correctness. Involved parties secretly submit input values $(x_1, \ldots, x_n)$ to the EP entity. The EP privately computes a function $y = f(x_1, \ldots, x_n)$, outputs the value y, and generates a proof of the correctness. Parties accept the result on successful verification of the proof of correctness. The EP model is *secrecy preserving* if the proof does not reveal any information about the inputs beyond what is implied by the result.

Note that the EP model does not maintain *strong secrecy* [17], which mandates that the EP cannot disclose information about the inputs. However, the notion of *secrecy preserving* is still useful in the context of periodic auctions. More specifically, at the end of each round, information about the MCP and MCV are published, which gives more hints about the inputs. Hence, the main requirement here is to ensure that the operator cannot exploit this information to its advantage. In particular, the operator must not have access to the submitted orders until the end of the submission phase.

4 Basic Protocols

In this section, we present two zero-knowledge arguments protocols that are utilized to build the periodic auction.

4.1 Zero-Knowledge Proof of Consistent Commitment Encryption

We design an honest-verifier zero-knowledge Σ_{cce}, which is shown in Fig. 1, to prove that an ElGamal ciphertext hides the committed value of a Pedersen commitment. To motivate the need for this protocol, suppose that Alice has sent Bob a commitment $X = g^x h^r$ for an arbitrary value x. Later, she reveals the committed value x to Bob by encrypting it in a ciphertext $c = (c_1, c_2) = (g^r, g^x y^r)$ using Bob's public key y with the same blinding factor r. Alice wants to convince Carol that she has encrypted the committed value x in the ciphertext c using Bob's public key. More precisely, Alice wants to generate the following argument: $\{(g, h, c, X, y; x, r) : c_1 = g^r \wedge c_2 = g^x y^r \wedge X = g^x h^r\}$

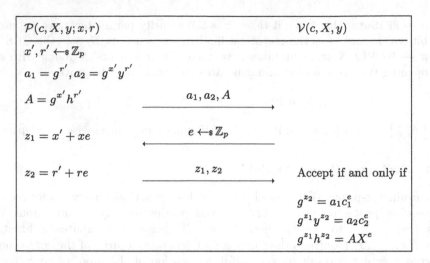

Fig. 1. Σ_{cce} protocol

We utilize Fiat-Shamir heuristic to convert the Σ_{cce} protocol into NIZK argument by using a hash function to get the challenge $e \leftarrow H(c, X, y, a_1, a_2, A)$. We define the following two $\mathcal{PPT}$ algorithms for this protocol:

1. $\pi \leftarrow \Sigma_{cce}.\mathcal{P}(c, X, y, x, r)$. It generates a proof π to prove that the ciphertext c is an encryption of the opening value x for the commitment X.
2. $\{0, 1\} \leftarrow \Sigma_{cce}.\mathcal{V}(c, X, \pi)$. It returns 1 if it has successfully verified the proof π for a ciphertext c and a commitment X; otherwise, it returns 0.

4.2   Zero-Knowledge Argument of Ordering

We build a protocol ProveOrder to prove that the committed values for a vector of Pedersen commitments are in descending order without revealing any information beyond that fact, as shown in Fig. 2. More specifically, given a vector of commitments X of size $m+1$ to a vector of elements x in $[0, 2^n-1]$, we say that x is in descending order if the differences between successive elements x_i, x_{i+1} are non-negative values. Furthermore, since Pedersen commitments are additively homomorphic, one can compute the commitments vector $\hat{X}$ to the differences between successive elements x_i, x_{i+1} given their commitments X_i, X_{i+1}. Now, we can utilize aggregate Bulletproofs to prove that the commitments in $\hat{X}$ are commitments to elements in the range $[0, 2^n - 1]$. Note that we can also prove ascending order by simply reversing the elements in the vectors.

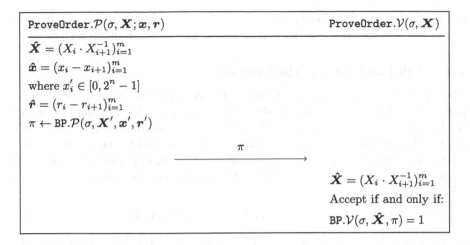

Fig. 2. ProveOrder protocol

By default, this protocol inherits the completeness and zero-knowledge properties of Bulletproofs [15]. To ensure the soundness, we have a condition on the value of 2^n. Specifically, as the operation $x_i - x_{i+1}$ is carried out in $\mathbb{Z}_p$, then, the condition $2^n < \frac{p}{2}$ must hold to ensure that negative differences do not fall in the range $[0, 2^n - 1]$.

It is worth mentioning that the implementation of Fiat-Shamir heuristic can compromise the security of Σ_{cce} and ProveOrder protocols. More precisely, these protocols are susceptible to *replay* attacks by the adversary when they are used with blockchain. For example, the adversary can replay an arbitrary trader's proof to the smart contract without knowing any witness, yet her proof will be successfully accepted. To prevent this attack, we include the *address* of the transaction sender as one of the inputs to the hash function that computes the verifier challenges. Consequently, the adversary's proof will be rejected because the verifier challenges computed by the smart contract will be different from those computed for the replayed proof.

5 Periodic Auction Protocol Design

5.1 System Model

In this protocol, there are three entities, namely, traders, an operator, and a smart contract. The operator and traders interact indirectly through the smart contract using their accounts on the blockchain.

1. Traders are the buyers and sellers who want to exchange their assets through the auction.
2. An operator is the EP entity that privately receives orders and evaluates the MCP and MCV, and proves their correctness to the smart contract.

3. A smart contract publicly verifies the zero-knowledge proofs submitted by traders and the operator, as well as serves as a secure bulletin-board.

5.2 High-Level Flow of the Protocol

The operator deploys the smart contract and initializes it by a set of public parameters. In Appendix A, we show the pseudocode for the smart contract. Each operation performed by the traders or the operator results in a piece of data and zero-knowledge proof, which will be submitted to the smart contract. The smart contract verifies the proof, and upon success, it stores the associated data. A single round of the periodic auction protocol consists of the following three phases:

1. Traders commit to their orders, and utilize Bulletproofs to generate an aggregate range proof.
2. Traders encrypt their orders by the operator's public key, and utilize Σ_{cce} protocol to prove the consistency between ciphertext and commitments.
3. The operator does the following:
   (a) Access price and quantity values in orders.
   (b) Determine the MCP and MCV.
   (c) Generate proof of correctness for MCP and MCV.

6 Protocol Design

6.1 Smart Contract Deployment and Parameters Setup

The protocol starts by the operator Alice generating the public parameter σ by running the setup algorithm of Bulletproofs for a security parameter λ, a bit-width n, and number of commitments m. Then, she generates a key-pair x, y as the secret and public keys for ElGamal encryption scheme, respectively. Additionally, she defines the time-window of each phase by the vector t.

$$
\begin{aligned}
\sigma &\leftarrow \texttt{BP.Setup}(1^\lambda, n, m) \\
x, y &\leftarrow \mathcal{K}(\mathbb{G}, p, g), \\
t &= (t_1, t_2, t_3)
\end{aligned}
$$

Next, she deploys the smart contract and initializes it with the parameters (σ, y, t) and locks a fixed collateral deposit $\mathcal{D}$.

6.2 Phase One: Submission of Orders

Traders submit their orders before the block-height t_1. For example, a trader Bob wants to buy v units of the auctioned asset at a price u. He creates his order as follows:

$$
\begin{aligned}
r &\leftarrow_{\$} \mathbb{Z}_p^2 \\
U &\leftarrow Com(u, r_1) \\
V &\leftarrow Com(v, r_2) \\
\pi &\leftarrow \texttt{BP.}\mathcal{P}(\sigma, (U, V), (u, v), r)
\end{aligned}
$$

First, he creates the commitments U and V for the price and quantity, respectively. Subsequently, the trader generates an aggregate range proof π to assert that the price and quantity values are within the range, i.e. $u, v \in [0, 2^n - 1]$. It is worth mentioning that in the prototype, this phase uses a different Bulletproof setup where $m = 2$ since there are two commitments only. Finally, he sends a transaction that includes the parameters $(\mathtt{dir}, U, V, \pi)$ where $\mathtt{dir}$ indicates whether the order is a bid or an offer.

Upon receiving the transaction, the smart contract checks whether the current block-height is less than t_1, and the transaction has a collateral deposit $\mathcal{D}$. Then, it verifies the aggregate range proof π for the commitments U and V. Finally, it stores the commitments in either the list of $\mathtt{Bids}$ or the list of $\mathtt{Offers}$ based on the value of $\mathtt{dir}$.

It is worth mentioning that front-running has a little impact in periodic auctions in contrast to continuous mainly because orders will be settled at a single MCP regardless of orders sequence. Still, this protocol provides protection against front-running for three main reasons. First, the commitments U and V are perfectly hiding. Second, the aggregate range proof π is zero-knowledge, hence, π does not reveal any information about the witness u and v beyond the fact that they are in range $[0, 2^n - 1]$. Third, there is an idle period between the first and second phases to consider the possibility of revealing orders on minor blockchain forks that will be discarded.

6.3   Phase Two: Revealing Orders

Traders utilize ElGamal encryption to reveal their orders to Alice before the block-height t_2. Therefore, Bob retrieves Alice's public key y from the smart contract and encrypts the opening values (u, r_1) and (v, r_2) as follows:

$$c_u \leftarrow \mathtt{Enc}_y(u, r_1), \ \pi_u \leftarrow \Sigma_{cce}.\mathcal{P}(c_u, U, y, u, r_1)$$
$$c_v \leftarrow \mathtt{Enc}_y(v, r_2), \ \pi_v \leftarrow \Sigma_{cce}.\mathcal{P}(c_v, V, y, v, r_2)$$

Then, he utilizes Σ_{cce} protocol to generate the proofs π_u and π_v to prove that the ciphertext c_u and c_v encrypt the opening values (u, r_1) and (v, r_2) of commitments U and V using Alice's public key y, respectively. Subsequently, he sends a transaction which includes the parameters (c_u, c_v, π_u, π_v).

Initially, the smart contract checks if the transaction is sent within the right time window between t_1 and t_2. Then, it searches for the commitments (U, V) corresponding to transaction $\mathtt{sender}$ in either $\mathtt{Bids}$ or $\mathtt{Offers}$. Subsequently, it verifies the proofs π_u and π_v. Alice can monitor the transactions submitted to the smart contract during this phase to recover the ciphertext c_u and c_v. In practice, Alice can efficiently retrieve the ciphertext by listening to *events* triggered on the smart contract.

6.4   Phase Three: Matching Orders

At the beginning of this phase, Alice instructs the smart contract to find unrevealed orders, remove them, and penalize their owners. Accordingly, she has access to the price and quantity values of revealed orders. She performs the following tasks to determine the MCP and MCV before block-height t_3:

1. Sort the bids descendingly and the offers ascendingly by price.
2. Compute the cumulative quantity in bids and offers.
3. Finds the MCP that clears the highest cumulative quantity, i.e. MCV.
4. Send the MCP and MCV along with proofs of correctness to the smart contract.

She can generate proof of correctness by creating an order with the MCP and MCV values. Then, she inserts that order in the sorted lists of bids and offers consisting of prices and cumulative quantities. Finally, she utilizes `ProveOrder` protocol to prove the sort on price and cumulative quantity commitments. Note that cumulative quantity commitments can be easily computed since Pedersen commitments are additively homomorphic.

Let B and S denote the lists of bids and offers where the numbers of orders in each list are M and N, respectively. Each order in B and S is encoded as a tuple $(U, V, V_c, u, r_1, v, r_2, v_c, r_c)$ of price, quantity, and cumulative quantity commitments and their opening values. Note that, at the beginning, V_c, v_c, r_c are empty. Alice performs the first task as follows:

$$\text{Sort}(B, \text{DESCENDING}), \ \text{Sort}(S, \text{ASCENDING})$$

The `Sort` function sorts the elements in the input list according to the specified criteria on the price values. For example, the elements in B and S are relocated such that:

$$\forall i \in [1, M-1], \ B_i.u > B_{i+1}.u$$
$$\forall j \in [1, N-1], \ S_j.u < S_{j+1}.u$$

Next, for each order in B and S, she computes the cumulative quantities as:

$$\forall i \in [1, M], \ B_i.(V_c, v_c, r_c) \leftarrow B.\left(\prod_{k=1}^{i} V_k, \sum_{k=1}^{i} v_k, \sum_{k=1}^{i} r_{2,k}\right)$$
$$\forall j \in [1, N], \ S_j.(V_c, v_c, r_c) \leftarrow S.\left(\prod_{k=1}^{j} V_k, \sum_{k=1}^{j} v_k, \sum_{k=1}^{j} r_{2,k}\right)$$

Subsequently, she finds the intersection range between prices in B and S. Then, for this range, take the middle point as MCP denoted by p, and the lowest cumulative quantity as MCV denoted by l. After that, she generates an order $\mathcal{M}$ with commitments to p and l as follows:

$$P \leftarrow \text{Com}(p, 0), \ L \leftarrow \text{Com}(l, 0)$$
$$\mathcal{M} = (P, 0, L, p, 0, 0, 0, l, 0)$$

Note that, the blinding values in commitments of $\mathcal{M}$ are set to zero as we want the commitments to be binding only. Moreover, p and l will be posted on the smart contract eventually, we just need them in commitment form to be utilized in the ProveOrder protocol. Finally, she inserts $\mathcal{M}$ in both B and S while preserving the ordering:

$$B.\text{Insert}(\mathcal{M}), \; S.\text{Insert}(\mathcal{M})$$

Now, Alice utilizes ProveOrder protocol to prove the correctness of MCP p and MCV l as follows:

$$\pi_1 \leftarrow \text{ProveOrder}.\mathcal{P}(B.(U, u, r_1), \text{DESCEND})$$
$$\pi_2 \leftarrow \text{ProveOrder}.\mathcal{P}(B.(V_c, v_c, r_c), \text{ASCEND})$$
$$\pi_3 \leftarrow \text{ProveOrder}.\mathcal{P}(S.(U, u, r_1), \text{ASCEND})$$
$$\pi_4 \leftarrow \text{ProveOrder}.\mathcal{P}(S.(V_c, v_c, r_c), \text{ASCEND})$$
$$\boldsymbol{\pi} = (\pi_1, \pi_2, \pi_3, \pi_4)$$

In the smart contract, the indices of orders in Bids and Offers depend entirely on their arrival time. Hence, Alice creates two positioning vectors χ and γ that will be used by the smart contract as proxies to access Bids and Offers in their sorted order, respectively. Finally, Alice sends a transaction which contains the parameters $(p, l, \chi, \gamma, \boldsymbol{\pi})$ to the smart contract.

The smart contract checks that the transaction is sent by Alice between block-heights t_2 and t_3. Then, it checks whether $p, l \in [0, 2^n - 1]$. After that, it appends the order $\mathcal{M}$ in Bids and Offers. Finally, it verifies the proofs $\boldsymbol{\pi}$ before accepting and storing p and l.

Upon successful verification, the smart contract refunds the collateral deposits to Alice and owners of unsettled orders. On the other hand, the smart contract keeps the collateral deposits of owners of executed orders locked for the settlement of the assets exchange phase off-chain. Conversely, if the verification was not successful or the Alice failed to send the proofs $\boldsymbol{\pi}$ before block-height t_3, then the smart contract slashes her deposit and refunds the traders.

7   Performance Evaluation

In this section, we evaluate the performance measurement of the proposed protocol and assess its feasibility.

7.1   Evaluation

We report the measurements of the two main building blocks that constitutes the periodic auction protocol, namely, Σ_{cce} and ProveOrder protocols n Table 1. The proof size is measured by the number of elements in $\mathbb{G}$ and $\mathbb{Z}_p$. For the verifier, we report the number of elliptic curve operations required to verify proofs.

Table 1. Performance of `ProveOrder` and Σ_{cce} protocol.

Performance	#	ProveOrder	Σ_{cce} Protocol
Proof size	$\mathbb{G}$	$2(log_2(n) + log_2(m)) + 4$	3
	$\mathbb{Z}_p$	5	2
Verifier operations	`mul`	$11 + 2n + m$	8
	`add`	$7 + 2n + m$	5

In Ethereum, the point addition and point multiplication operations cost 150 and 6000 gas, respectively. Hence, we can measure the transaction gas cost of verifying the submitted proofs. In Fig. 3, we report the performance measurements: proof size, prover time, and gas cost of proof verification by the smart contract with respect to the total number of orders for the transactions: `SubmitOrder`, `RevealOrder`, and `ClearMarket`. Obviously, the transaction `SubmitOrder` and `RevealOrder` have constant measurements as opposed to `ClearMarket` transaction which scale linearly with the number of orders.

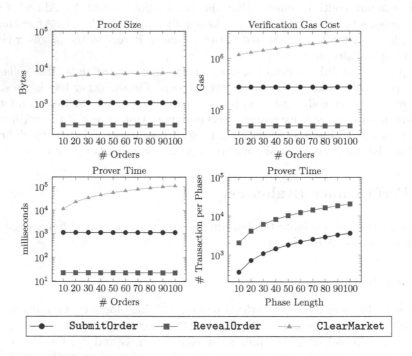

Fig. 3. Performance measurements of the periodic auction protocol

The current block gas limit on Ethereum is roughly 10 M gas. Hence, we can estimate the number of transactions that fit in a single block. More importantly, we can estimate the theoretical number of $\texttt{SubmitOrder}$ and $\texttt{RevealOrder}$ transactions that the smart contract can receive during the first and second phases for different phase lengths as shown in Fig. 3. The $\texttt{SubmitOrder}$ transaction incurs the cost of verifying $\texttt{ProveOrder}$ proof where $n = 16$ and $m = 2$. Similarly, the $\texttt{RevealOrder}$ transaction incurs the cost of verifying Σ_{cce} proof. Accordingly, the transaction cost of $\texttt{SubmitOrder}$ and $\texttt{RevealOrder}$ are roughly 276150 and 48750 gas, respectively. Note that, in practice, the gas cost for each transaction is higher since there are additional operations involving data access and control flow.

Furthermore, we can estimate the highest number of orders that can be processed by a single $\texttt{ClearMarket}$ transaction before exceeding the 10M gas block limit. Typically, the $\texttt{ClearMarket}$ transaction requires verification of two $\texttt{ProveOrder}$ proofs for M bids and two $\texttt{ProveOrder}$ proofs for N offers. For convenience, assume that we have an equal number of bids and offers $M = N$, hence, the $\texttt{ClearMarket}$ transaction incurs the verification cost of four $\texttt{ProveOrder}$ proofs of M commitments. Accordingly, the $\texttt{ClearMarket}$ transaction can theoretically process up to ≈ 728 orders before exceeding the block gas limit. Certainly, in practice, this number is lower due to the gas cost associated with operations other than proof verification.

8 Conclusion

We presented publicly verifiable secrecy preserving periodic auction protocol. The protocol depends on two zero-knowledge proofs, namely, proof of consistent commitment encryption and proof of ordering. Furthermore, we implemented a prototype and evaluated its performance to assess its feasibility. Based on the result, we believe that the periodic auction protocol is a feasible and secure alternative to dark pools.

Appendix A Smart Contract Pseudocode

```
 1: function SUBMITORDER(dir, U, V, π)
 2:     require(msg.value = D)
 3:     require(msg.blockNumber < t₁)
 4:     require(BP.V(σ₂, (U, V), π))
 5:     if dir = BUY then
 6:         Bids[msg.sender] ← (U, V)
 7:     else
 8:         Offers[msg.sender] ← (U, V)
 9:     end if
10: end function
 1: function REVEALORDER(cᵤ, cᵥ, πᵤ, πᵥ)
```

  require($t_1 <$ msg.blockNumber $< t_2$)
  $(U, V) \leftarrow$ FindOrder(msg.sender)
  require($(U, V) \neq$ NULL)
  require($\Sigma.\mathcal{V}(\boldsymbol{c}_u, U, y, \pi_u)$)
  require($\Sigma.\mathcal{V}(\boldsymbol{c}_v, V, y, \pi_v)$)
  emit RevealEvent(msg.sender, $\boldsymbol{c}_u, \boldsymbol{c}_v$)
end function
function ClearMarket($p, l, \boldsymbol{\chi}, \boldsymbol{\gamma}, \boldsymbol{\pi}$)
  require($t_2 <$ msg.blockNumber $< t_3$)
  require(msg.sender = Alice)
  RemoveUnrevealedOrders()
  require($p \in [0, 2^n - 1] \wedge l \in [0, 2^n - 1]$)
  $\mathcal{O} = (g^p, g^l)$
  Bids[Alice] $\leftarrow \mathcal{O}$
  Offers[Alice] $\leftarrow \mathcal{O}$
  Relocate(Bids, $\boldsymbol{\chi}$)
  Relocate(Offers, $\boldsymbol{\gamma}$)
  $U_1 \leftarrow$ Bids.U
  $V_1 \leftarrow$ CumulativeQuantity(Bids.V)
  $U_2 \leftarrow$ Offers.U
  $V_2 \leftarrow$ CumulativeQuantity(Offers.V)
  require(ProveOrder.$\mathcal{V}(\sigma, U_1, \pi_1)$)
  require(ProveOrder.$\mathcal{V}(\sigma, V_1, \pi_2)$)
  require(ProveOrder.$\mathcal{V}(\sigma, U_2, \pi_3,$ ASCEND))
  require(ProveOrder.$\mathcal{V}(\sigma, V_2, \pi_4)$)
  Store p, l
end function

References

1. Thorpe, C., Parkes, D.C.: Cryptographic securities exchanges. In: Dietrich, S., Dhamija, R. (eds.) FC 2007. LNCS, vol. 4886, pp. 163–178. Springer, Heidelberg (2007). https://doi.org/10.1007/978-3-540-77366-5_16
2. Sec charges citigroup for dark pool misrepresentations. https://www.sec.gov/news/press-release/2018-193 (2018)
3. Sec charges itg with misleading dark pool subscribers. https://www.sec.gov/news/press-release/2018-256 (2018)
4. Barclays, credit suisse charged with dark pool violations. https://www.sec.gov/news/pressrelease/2016-16.html (2016)
5. Markets in financial instruments directive ii. https://www.esma.europa.eu/policy-rules/mifid-ii-and-mifir (2018)
6. Nakamoto, S.: Bitcoin: a peer-to-peer electronic cash system (2008)
7. Wood, G.: Ethereum: a secure decentralised generalised transaction ledger. Ethereum Proj. Yellow Pap. **151**, 1–32 (2014)
8. Jutla, C.S.: Upending stock market structure using secure multi-party computation. IACR Cryptology ePrint Arch. **2015**, 550 (2015)

9. Galal, H.S., Youssef, A.M.: Verifiable sealed-bid auction on the ethereum blockchain. In: Zohar, A., et al. (eds.) FC 2018. LNCS, vol. 10958, pp. 265–278. Springer, Heidelberg (2019). https://doi.org/10.1007/978-3-662-58820-8_18

10. Galal, H.S., Youssef, A.M.: Succinctly verifiable sealed-bid auction smart contract. In: Garcia-Alfaro, J., Herrera-Joancomartí, J., Livraga, G., Rios, R. (eds.) DPM/CBT-2018. LNCS, vol. 11025, pp. 3–19. Springer, Cham (2018). https://doi.org/10.1007/978-3-030-00305-0_1

11. Galal, H.S., Youssef, A.M.: Trustee: full privacy preserving Vickrey auction on top of ethereum. In: Bracciali, A., Clark, J., Pintore, F., Rønne, P.B., Sala, M. (eds.) FC 2019. LNCS, vol. 11599, pp. 190–207. Springer, Cham (2020). https://doi.org/10.1007/978-3-030-43725-1_14

12. Cartlidge, J., Smart, N.P., Talibi Alaoui, Y.: MPC joins the dark side. In: Proceedings of the 2019 ACM Asia Conference on Computer and Communications Security, pp. 148–159. ACM (2019)

13. Pedersen, T.P.: Non-interactive and information-theoretic secure verifiable secret sharing. In: Feigenbaum, J. (ed.) CRYPTO 1991. LNCS, vol. 576, pp. 129–140. Springer, Heidelberg (1992). https://doi.org/10.1007/3-540-46766-1_9

14. Bellare, M., Rogaway, P.: Random oracles are practical: a paradigm for designing efficient protocols. In: Proceedings of the 1st ACM Conference on Computer and Communications Security, pp. 62–73 (1993)

15. Bünz, B., Bootle, J., Boneh, D., Poelstra, A., Wuille, P., Maxwell, G.: Bulletproofs: short proofs for confidential transactions and more. In: 2018 IEEE Symposium on Security and Privacy (SP), pp. 315–334. IEEE (2018)

16. Micali, S., Rabin, M.O.: Cryptography miracles, secure auctions, matching problem verification. Commun. ACM **57**(2), 85–93 (2014)

17. Parkes, D.C., Thorpe, C., Li, W.: Achieving trust without disclosure: dark pools and a role for secrecy-preserving verification. In: Proceedings of the Third Conference on Auctions, Market Mechanisms and Their Applications (2015)

EthVer: Formal Verification
of Randomized Ethereum Smart Contracts

Łukasz Mazurek$^{(\boxtimes)}$ (iD)

University of Warsaw, Warsaw, Poland
lukasz.mazurek@crypto.edu.pl

Abstract. Despite the great potential capabilities and the mature technological solutions, the smart contracts have never been used at a large
scale, one of the reasons being the lack of good methods to verify the
correctness and security of the contracts—although the technology itself
(e.g. the Ethereum platform) is well studied and secure, the actual
smart contracts are human-made and thus inherently error-prone. As
a consequence, critical vulnerabilities in the contracts are discovered and
exploited every few months. The most prominent example of a buggy contract was the infamous DAO attack—a successful attack on the largest
Ethereum contract in June 2016 resulting in $70 mln-worth Ether stolen
and the *hard fork* of the Ethereum network (80% of Ethereum users
decided to revert the transaction and hence two parallel transaction his-
tories exist from that event).

The main contribution of this work is the automatic method of formal
verification of randomized Ethereum smart contracts. We formally define
and implement the translation of the contracts into MDP (Markov decision process) formal models which can be verified using the PRISM model
checker—a state of the art tool for formal verification of models. As a
proof of concept, we use our tool, *EthVer*, to verify two smart contracts
from the literature: the *Rock-Paper-Scissors* protocol from *K. Delmolino
et al., Step by step towards creating a safe smart contract: Lessons and
insights from a cryptocurrency lab.* and the *Micropay 1* protocol from *R.
Pass, a. shelat, Micropayments for decentralized currencies.*

Keywords: Cryptocurrencies · Ethereum · Smart contracts ·
Verification · Formal methods · Model checking

1 Introduction

The notion of a *smart contract* was first introduced in 1997 by Nick Szabo [29].
The main idea behind smart contracts is that many contractual clauses (such
as collateral, bonding, delineation of property rights, etc.) can be embedded in
the hardware and software and smart contracts are protocols that can serve
as digital agreements between the users of the network—the fulfillment of the
agreement is automatically guaranteed by the design of the system instead of
some external authority like banks, governments or courts.

© International Financial Cryptography Association 2021
M. Bernhard et al. (Eds.): FC 2021 Workshops, LNCS 12676, pp. 364–380, 2021.
https://doi.org/10.1007/978-3-662-63958-0_30

The first practical implementations of smart contracts emerged together with the introduction of *Bitcoin* in 2009 [23], however they gained their popularity five years later when Ethereum [10] was announced—the first fully operational digital platform dedicated particularly for smart contracts, much more convenient to use and with much larger capabilities than Bitcoin.

Despite their huge potential capabilities, smart contracts have never been adopted on a large scale, one of the reasons being the fact that it is difficult to verify the correctness and security of the contract. As a consequence, critical vulnerabilities are discovered and exploited every few months [1–3]. The most prominent example of a buggy contract was the infamous DAO attack [15]—a successful attack on the largest Ethereum contract in June 2016 resulting in $70 mln-worth Ether stolen and the *hard fork* of the Ethereum network (80% of Ethereum users decided to revert the transaction and hence two parallel Ethereum blockchains exist from that event).

Several approaches to verification of smart contracts have been proposed, including the automatic and semi-automatic tools which analyze the contract code and check if it satisfies some set of predefined security properties [22,24,32] or user-defined properties [8,11,18–20]. The other line of work focuses on providing tools to help creating smart contracts that follow some security patterns by design [25,28,31]. All these approaches suffer from the following limitation: they focus only on the security of the contract code without analyzing the outcome of the scenario of its usage. In other words, the traditional verification tools answer the questions: *Is this contract guaranteed to not "crash"? Can it end up in an unwanted state? Will the contract function be always executed till the end?* In contrast, none of the methods answers the question: *What will be the result if I use the contract in the following way?* Furthermore, we are not aware of any solution which verifies the randomized smart contracts and its probabilistic properties, for example: *Are the chances of winning in that lottery indeed equal to 1/2?*

1.1 Our Contribution

The main contribution of this work is an automatic method for verifying randomized protocols built on top of Ethereum smart contracts. We introduce the ETV language which allows to easily create such protocols using the syntax of Solidity (the main contract language of Ethereum). Furthermore, we formally define the translation of such protocols into the Markov decision processes (MDPs) which can be verified for security and correctness using the PRISM model checker—a state of the art tool for formal verification of models. The formal translation is accompanied by the implementation of *EthVer*—a fully operational compiler that translates an ETV program into a MDP in the PRISM syntax. As a proof of concept we use our tool to compile and verify two protocols from the literature: the Rock-Paper-Scissors protocol from *K. Delmolino et al., Step by step towards creating a safe smart contract: Lessons and insights from a cryptocurrency lab.* [14] and the *Micropay 1* protocol from *R. Pass, a. shelat, Micropayments for decentralized currencies* [26].

What distinguishes our work is that we model not only the smart contract code but also the *scenario* of its execution. The syntax of the contract part of ETV language is a slightly modified syntax of *Solidity* (the programming language of Ethereum smart contracts), while the syntax of the scenario part is very similar to *web3.js* JavaScript library (the library used to execute Ethereum smart contracts). This makes the usage of ETV intuitive to anyone familiar with Solidity and web3.js. We are not aware of any other tool that allows to verify the scenario of smart contract execution in such a way. Also, to the best of our knowledge, our method is the first one that allows to verify the probabilistic properties of randomized smart contracts.

Another novel feature of the ETV language is the abstract construction for cryptographic commitments and digital signatures—the important cryptographic primitives present in many smart contracts. The *EthVer* compiler not only translates these abstract objects into MDP (which allows verification) but also provides the exact implementation of commitments and signatures in Solidity and web3.js. This prevents the user from implementing them by hand, which might me cumbersome and error-prone. We are not aware of any other extension to Solidity which offers such functionality.

The full code of the *EthVer* compiler, as well as the extended version of this paper are available at the *EthVer* project page[1].

1.2   Related Work

Among the existing solutions for verification of smart contracts we can distinguish two main groups which can be summarized as the *verification approach* in which the contract is checked for compliance with some specification or security policy and the *design approach* which simplifies the smart contracts creation process by providing frameworks for their development. Below we analyze the related work falling into these two categories and describe how *EthVer* differs from the existing solutions.

Verification Approach. This group contains static analysis tools for automated bug-finding [22,24,32] that verify the code for satisfying some pre-defined security properties, such as the correct order of transactions, timestamp dependency, prodigality or liveness. The other group of tools [8,18,19] provides semi-automatic methods for proving the contract-specific properties. These tools require some manual interaction from the user, such as specifying the loop invariants in the bytecode. Another work [9] analyzes Ethereum contracts by translating them into a functional language F^*. The language provides verification methods and an interactive proof assistant, however the translation supports only a part of the EVM syntax. Other solutions [12,17] provide dynamic monitoring of the predefined security properties, such as transaction order dependency

---

[1] https://github.com/lukmaz/ethver

or *callback free executions*, a lack of which is claimed to be the source of common bugs. Both of these methods provide the defense from only a subset of the possible vulnerabilities in the contracts.

All the solutions mentioned in the previous paragraph are able to analyze only the Ethereum Virtual Machine (EVM) pre-compiled bytecode. The other tool [20] analyzes the high-level Solidity contract code using symbolic model checking for the user-defined *policies*. However the policies are restricted to quantifier-free first-order logic, so this method can only solve the state reachability problem and hence, e.g., cannot verify probabilistic properties. Another interesting approach [11] provides a game-theoretic framework in which the smart contract is translated into a concurrent game and the properties of this game are further analyzed using the novel method of abstraction-refinement. This method offers much lower computational complexity than the exact model checking of the whole model, however it does not provide the exact result of the verification, but only the lower and upper bound.

There are several other tools that provide static analysis for generic properties [4–7, 30]. None of them is however accompanied by a scientific paper so the full specifications of the actual verification methods are hard to identify.

Design Approach. One example of a high-level language that impose secure design of the smart contract is Simplicity [25]. It is however a general purpose language for smart contracts with no compiler to the EVM bytecode. Another interesting tool allows exporting the compiled code to the intermediate language WhyML[2] which in turn can be checked for security patterns using the program verification platform Why3 [16]. This tool however does not support the full range of properties to verify, in particular it cannot verify probabilistic properties. A slightly different approach [31] introduces *security patterns*—the best practices that must be met while developing the contract code, such as, e.g., performing calls at the end of a function. This approach however does not allow to specify custom properties to be satisfied by the contract.

1.3 EthVer

The *EthVer* compiler falls somehow between the *verification approach* and *design approach*—it is able to verify the actual code of Ethereum smart contract (and also the scenario of its usage), however it requires the contract code to be written in the ETV language which is a slightly modified version of Solidity. Furthermore it allows to verify any custom property written in a dedicated language, including the probabilistic properties.

To the best of our knowledge, none of the solutions described in this section offers the exact model checking of the *probabilistic* properties of the randomized contract. Moreover, the existing approaches focus on verifying the *contract* without taking into account the pattern of execution of the contract by the users.

---

[2] https://why3.lri.fr.

Instead, in *EthVer* we verify the *protocol* which consists of the contract and the *scenario* of usage of the contract by the users. Hence, we are able to verify not only the correctness and security of the contract code, but also the *instructions* on how to use the contract.

It is worth noting here, that the two features of *EthVer* described above allows to perform the full formal verification of the *rock-paper-scissors* protocol [14] and the *Micropay 1* protocol [26], which cannot be done in any of the other tools analyzed in this section. We briefly describe this analysis in Sect. 7.

2   Preliminaries

2.1   Ethereum Languages

The actual code of Ethereum smart contracts is written in the machine code of Ethereum Virtual Machine (EVM). However, the platform provides several high level, user-friendly languages to write the code of a contract with the Solidity language being the most popular among them. The syntax of Solidity is based on JavaScript with some extra features added to handle the flow of money and cryptographic operations. Calling a contract function is realized by sending a special transaction to the contract address. There are several convenient GUI tools to deploy and execute smart contracts, such as, e.g., a desktop application Ethereum Wallet or a web application Remix as well as the console client geth[3]. Under the hood they all use the JavaScript API with the web3.js library[4] which provides the basic functions to interact with the contract as well as some cryptographic functions widely used in smart contracts (such as hash functions and digital signatures). The main web3.js function to interact with a contract is the sendTransaction method which is called on a contract function object and takes as arguments the arguments to the function and the sender address (the from: field) as well as the *value* attached to the transaction. The example usage of the sendTransaction function is listed below:

```
Bank.deposit.sendTransaction(1,
{from: "0x14723a09acff6d2a60dcdf7aa4aff308fddc160c",
  value: web3.utils.toWei("5", "finney")});
```

Note that the transaction value must be passed as an integer number of *wei* (1 *wei* = 10^{-18} *ether*), however, the web3.utils.toWei function can be used to easily convert from different units like *finney* (1 *finney* = 0.001 *ether*).

2.2   The PRISM Model Checker

PRISM is a probabilistic model checker, a tool originally described in [21]. It is designed for formal modeling and analysis of systems which present random or probabilistic behavior. Many smart contracts fit into this category, so we decided

---

[3] http://ethereum.org/.
[4] http://web3js.readthedocs.io/.

to use PRISM as the backbone for our formal verification of Ethereum smart contracts.

PRISM supports different types of models, including discrete-time Markov chains (DTMCs), continuous-time Markov chains (CTMCs), Markov decision processes (MDPs), probabilistic automata (PAs), probabilistic timed automata (PTAs). In *EthVer* we decided to use Markov decision processes, since they allow non-determinism and hence are the best fit for randomized protocols built on top of smart contracts.

The PRISM model is defined as a set of states and transitions between them. Each transition is represented with a *command* of form

$$[\textit{label}] \quad \textit{guards} \; \text{->} \; \textit{updates};$$

where *guards* are the conditions needed to be met in order for the transition to be *enabled*, *updates* represent the probabilistic choices in the algorithm, and *label* is an optional identifier of the transition used for synchronization. The syntax of the updates is as follows:

$$p_1 \; : \; \textit{update}_1 \; + \; p_2 \; : \; \textit{update}_2 \; + \; \ldots \; + \; p_n \; : \; \textit{update}_n$$

The updates list reflects the situation when several transitions are possible from the same state and the choice of the actual transition is probabilistic: the i-th transition happens with probability p_i and results in $\textit{update}_i$ of the model variables.

For more detailed introduction to PRISM please refer to appendix A of the extended version of the paper[5].

2.3 Cryptographic Commitments

A cryptographic commitment scheme is a protocol which consists of two phases: *commit* and *open* (the second phase is also referred to as the *reveal* phase). In the most common implementation during the *commit* phase the user chooses a value r to which they will be committed, chooses a random value s and computes $c = H(r, s)$ where H is a hash function (a collision-resilient function that is hard to invert). Then the user publishes the hash c while keeping r and s secret.

In the *open* phase the user reveals the chosen values r and s and anyone can use c to verify if the author of the commitment didn't change r. The cryptographic commitments are *hiding* and *binding* in the sense that:

− the value of c reveals no information about r,
− once the values of r and c are fixed, it is infeasible to come up with another value of r matching the same c.

---

[5] Recall that the extended version of the paper as well as the code of *EthVer* and example contracts are available at https://github.com/lukmaz/ethver.

Ethereum provides a convenient way to implement the cryptographic commitments using *SHA-3* function (also known as *keccak256*):

```
hash = web3.utils.sha3(web3.utils.
  toHex(r).substr(2)+web3.utils.toHex(s))
```

```
uint8 r; string s; bytes32 c =
  keccak256(abi.encodePacked(48+r,s))
```

Listing 1.1. Computing the commitment in web3.js v1.0.0

Listing 1.2. Computing the commitment in Solidity v0.5.2

Note the different names of the hash function and the subtle differences in passing the arguments. These differences follow from different APIs used by Solidity and web3.js, but the underlying hash function is the same.

2.4 Digital Signatures

Ethereum supports digital signatures based on elliptic curve cryptography implementing the SECP-256k1 standard as described in [13]. The web3.js library provides two useful functions: `web3.eth.accounts.sign(m, sk)` for signing and `web3.eth.accounts.recover(m, signature)` for recovering the public key of the author of the signature. Solidity provides the function `ecrecover` (hash, v, r, s) which takes the hash of the messages and (v, r, s) values, which are the 3 parts of the `signature`[6]. In the most common scenario the signatures are created off-chain in web3.js and then they are later verified by the contract. Due to different APIs of Solidity and web3.js, a special care is needed for the format of numbers passed to the `sign` and `recover` functions. Listings 1.3 and 1.4 show an example code for signing a message in web3.js and verifying the obtained signature in Solidity[7].

```
r2_ = web3.utils.toHex(r2).substr(2);
concat = c + web3.utils.padLeft(r2_, 2)
  + a.toLowerCase().substr(2);
msg = "msg" + web3.utils.sha3(concat);
s = web3.eth.accounts.sign(msg, privKey)
```

Listing 1.3. Signing a message in web3.js v1.0.0

```
string header = "\x19Ethereum
  Signed Message:\n69msg0x";
bytes data = hexToBytes(keccak256(
  abi.encodePacked(c,r2,a)));
bytes32 msgHash = keccak256(
  abi.encodePacked(header, data));
return ecrecover(msgHash,
  s_v, s_r, s_s) == a));
```

Listing 1.4. Verifying the signature in Solidity v0.5.2

3 Interacting with the Contract

The code of a smart contract does not carry all the information needed for verification. Consider a simple Bank contract written in Solidity:

---

[6] Note that we don't describe here how to sign messages in Solidity. In fact, Solidity does not provide convenient API for this. The reason is that a private key is required to sign and we rarely want to do this in the contract code, because we do not want to reveal the private keys to public.

[7] This is the actual code of computing and verifying the signature $\sigma = \text{sig}(c, r_2, a)$ from the Micropay 1 protocol (cf. Sect. 7).

```
contract Bank {
  unit balance;

  function deposit() public payable {
    balance = balance + msg.value;}

  function withdraw(uint amount) public {
    if (amount <= balance) {
      balance = balance - amount;
      msg.sender.transfer(amount);}}}
```

Listing 1.5. A simple Bank contract

Is this a secure smart contract? The answer to this question depends on how we want to use the contract and what behavior of the contract is expected. For example, this contract can be considered secure if we want a bank in which anyone can deposit money and then anyone can withdraw it. On the other hand, if we define the security of the bank with the rule that *only the person who has deposited the money can withdraw it*, then of course this contract is not secure.

In order to concretize the requirements for the contract we must formulate the *scenario* and the *properties* which we want to be satisfied. In case of the Bank contract they can be as follows:

Scenario:

– User A deposits 10 *finney*[8].
– User A withdraws 10 *finney*.

Properties:

– User A gets back his deposited 10 *finney*.

Of course this property is not always satisfied, which can be shown using the *counterexample* scenario in which user A deposits 10 *finney* and then user B withdraws the same 10 *finney*. After that the user A no longer can withdraw 10 *finney*, since the contract account is already empty.

Although this scenario of using the Bank contract may look artificial (why not to use the contract in a different way?), in case of many contracts, the scenario of the proper usage is obvious and well defined. Consider, e.g., a simple lottery in which user A bets 10 *finney* and wins 20 *finney* with probability 1/2 (otherwise loses). In such case, the scenario and the properties for user A are as follows:

Scenario:

– User A deposits 10 *finney*.
– User A waits for the result of the lottery.

Properties:

– With probability 1/2: the user A receives the reward of 20 *finney*.
– With probability 1/2: the user A receives nothing.

---

[8] Recall that 1 *finney* = 0.001 ETH is a denomination of Ether, the currency of Ethereum. For simplicity, we neglect the transaction fees, unless stated otherwise.

4 The ETV Language

To model a contract with its scenario in a verifiable way we introduce the ETV language. The ETV program consists of two parts: the first part is a slightly modified Solidity code of the contract, while the second part represents the scenario using web3.js commands.

4.1 Bounded Integers

The main issue with the verification of smart contracts in PRISM is the usage of *bounded integers* in PRISM. The reason for it is that a new state in the PRISM model is created for every valuation of the variables, and thus increasing the range of variables increases the number of states in the model in the exponential way. On the other hand, in Solidity/web3.js the smallest type for storing integers is uint8 which is capable of storing numbers from the range $[0, 255]$. Frequently we use such type to store the variables which can have only a small number of different values (e.g., only 0, 1 or 2) and we do not need the whole range of uint8.

Because of this limitation we introduce in ETV the *bounded integer* type uint(N) which in practice is the main difference between ETV and Solidity/web3.js.

4.2 Communication

A protocol can contain some operations that are performed directly between the parties of the protocol (without interaction with the blockchain), for example exchanging hash values. We define a dedicated *communication* section for such operations in the ETV language. Such approach allows us to properly model the *adversarial* behavior by allowing the malicious party to also execute the commands from the *communication* section.

4.3 Cryptographic Primitives

The other important feature of the ETV language is the abstract syntax for cryptographic primitives, such as hashes, commitments and signatures. Such primitives can be (a) translated into PRISM which allows to verify the properties of the contract and (b) translated into the actual implementation in Solidity and web3.js which reduces the probability that the user implements it incorrectly. The last feature is especially important because the current versions of Ethereum programming languages (Solidity v0.5.2 and web3.js v1.0.0) present large differences in the API for the cryptographic functions and a special care must be taken to make sure that the Solidity part and the web3.js part of the code operates on the same numbers[9].

---

[9] Examples of the syntax of commitments and signatures in Solidity and web3.js have already been presented in Sect. 2.3 and 2.4.

5   The Compiler

The main practical result of this work is the implementation of *EthVer*—a compiler written in Haskell that takes as the input an ETV file (let us call it `example.etv`) and produces:

- `example.sol`—the contract code in Solidity which can be directly deployed to the Ethereum blockchain,
- `example.scen`—the scenario of the execution of the contract containing the exact JavaScript web3.js commands which can be directly used to execute the contract,
- `example.prism`—the PRISM Markov decision process (MDP), which can be directly used in the PRISM model checker.

While translating ETV code to Solidity and web3.js is straightforward, the translation from ETV to PRISM MDP is highly nontrivial and was the main challenge during creation of *EthVer*. In the next section we describe the core concepts behind this translation and their implementation in *EthVer*.

Furthermore, in the extended version of the paper we formally define the full syntax and the semantics of the ETV language (appendices B and C). In appendix D we formally define the translation from ETV to MDP and prove that it preserves the semantics of ETV.

6   Modeling the Protocol as Markov Decision Process

In this section we present the core concepts of *EthVer*—the way in which we translate an ETV program into a Markov decision process (MDP).

6.1   Modeling the Contract Execution

We model the main part of the contract using 4 PRISM modules[10]: `player0`, `player1`, `contract`, `blockchain`. We show the role of each module on the example of the simple Bank contract (cf. listing 1.5) and the following scenario of its usage:

- User A deposits 10 *finney*.
- User A withdraws 10 *finney*.

We model the honest execution of the scenario with the following commands in the `player0` module:

```
module player0
[broadcast_deposit] (state0 = 1) -> (state0' = 2)
  & (deposit_value0' = 10);
[broadcast_withdraw] (state0 = 2) -> (state0' = 3)
  & (withdraw_amount0' = 10);
endmodule
```

---

[10] A PRISM model can consists of several modules, each corresponding to a different part of the system and each with a separate set of variables.

Each command sets the value as well as all the arguments of the function call and then triggers the corresponding commands in `contract` and `blockchain` modules using the PRISM synchronization mechanism—the command with a non-empty label (the string in square brackets) can be executed only in parallel with the corresponding function with the same label in other modules (as long as such command exists in other modules).

The actual process of calling the contract function consists of two phases: in the first phase, in parallel to `[broadcast_*]` command from `player0` module, PRISM executes the synchronized command from the `blockchain` module which stores the information that this function call is now in the *broadcast* state. Then at some later point PRISM can take one of the function calls from the *broadcast* state and actually execute the corresponding contract code. This is accomplished by another pair of synchronized commands from `blockchain` and `contract` modules[11].

6.2   Modeling the Adversary

Although the verification of the honest execution of the protocol is important, we frequently face vulnerabilities in the contracts which reveal themselves only when one (or more) of the participants misbehave, i.e., deviate from following the scenario. In order to model the adversarial player, we decided to give them the ability to interact with the contract in an arbitrary way. More concretely, the adversary can **call any function of the contract, in any order, with any arguments, as many times as wanted**. With such definition of the adversary we can model any 2-player contract[12] in one of the 3 following *modes*:

– *honest* mode—honest player 0 vs honest player 1
– *adversarial player 0* mode—malicious player 0 vs honest player 1
– *adversarial player 1* mode—honest player 0 vs malicious player 1

6.3   Modeling the Communication

As it was already discussed in Sect. 4.2, some protocols contain phases in which the players do off-chain computation and exchange the computed numbers without calling the contract. Since these procedures do not involve the actual execution of the contract code, they should not be handled in the same way as the

---

[11] The same pattern of a two-phase function execution could be accomplished using only the `player0` and `contract` modules, however because of visibility of the variables in PRISM, the `blockchain` module is needed to correctly pass the arguments of the call.

[12] The current version of *EthVer* is limited to 2-players protocols only. However, all the security claims as well as the formal translation defined in appendix D of the extended version of the paper hold also for protocols with larger number of players. Note that although *EthVer* accepts only 2-player protocols, it verifies the contract also against the attacks in which more adversarial players join the protocol at the same time.

contract calls are. On the other hand, we do not want to limit the capabilities of an adversarial player, and hence we need to give the adversary the possibility of performing these procedures at any time, with any arguments (like in case of contract calls). We model every such action as a *communication function* that are called during honest scenario execution and can also be freely called by the adversary.

These communication functions are stored in the separate `communication` section of the ETV code. The syntax of such functions is very similar to the syntax of contract functions, with the only difference that it cannot handle the money transfers. These functions translate to the `communication` module in the PRISM code which can be triggered using the PRISM synchronization mechanism from the player modules in a similar fashion to the contract function (but without going through the *broadcast* state and without involving the `blockchain` module).

6.4   Modeling the Cryptographic Commitments

Recall that in the standard implementation of random commitments (Sect. 2.3) during the *commit* phase two random numbers (r and s) are generated and then they are later revealed during the *open* phase. Since all variables in PRISM are *public*, we cannot just store r and s as PRISM variables, because it will break the *hiding* property of the commitment. It follows from the fact that MDPs are non-deterministic and for MDPs we always compute the maximal (or minimal) probability `Pmax/Pmin`, where the probability is computed over all the random choices, while the maximum (minimum) is taken over all the non-deterministic choices of the model and hence the non-deterministic choices must be done before the random choices.

To best illustrate the problem, consider a simple game in which A creates a commitment by choosing r and s at random and then B tries to guess r before the revealing phase. If we store the value of r in a variable right after the *commit* phase, then the automaton that models B can non-deterministically choose the correct value of r (since now there is no more randomness in the protocol) and win the game. Hence, in order to properly model the real behavior of keeping r secret, we need to not store the final value of r during the *commit* phase and postpone the actual random choice until the *open* phase.

In our implementation each commitment in PRISM can be in one of the following states: *init*, *committed*, or *revealed*. All the commitments start in the *init* state. During the honest scenario, when the player *creates a random commitment*, the appropriate variable switches to the *committed* state, but no actual choice of the value is made. During the *open* phase, the player needs to call a separate `revealCmt` method which performs the actual random choice. After this call, the commitment variable switches from the *committed* state to the *revealed* state.

Using the same mechanism the adversary can either commit to a random value (by switching to the *committed* state and postponing the actual choice until the revealing phase) or he can immediately commit to the value of his choice by switching directly to the *revealed* state. In both cases he cannot later change the chosen value. This models the real implementation of the commitments in which the chosen value also cannot be changed after the commitment is created.

This approach is realized in *EthVer* by providing the `cmt_uint` type and functions `randomCmt` and `verCmt` which implement directly the described functionality.

6.5   Modeling the Digital Signatures

We introduce a templated type for the signatures: `signature(T1, T2, ...)`. The types `T1`, `T2`, ... are the types of the *fields* of the signature—the values that we want to sign (when we want to sign more than one value, we usually concatenate them before signing). For the signature type we provide two constructions to create and to verify the signature:

```
sigma = sign(c, r2, a);
verSig(verAddress, sigma, (c, r2, a));
```

We model the signatures in PRISM in the following way:

- each signature is initially in the *init* state,
- there is a separate PRISM variable for each *field* of the signature as well as for the address of the author of the signature,
- whenever a signature is created, the fields are assigned with the values being signed (and the author's address); these fields' values cannot be later changed.

The adversary is not allowed to change any field of the existing signature. However to not limit their ability to *interact with the contract in any way at any time*, we allow them to freely create new signatures, i.e., to sign any data at any time with their own key.

6.6   Modeling the Time

Solidity natively supports creating contracts dependent on time using the `now` variable. Moreover, we introduce in ETV the `wait(condition, time)` statement which implements the conditional wait: after reaching that point of the scenario, the party pauses the execution of the protocol until the condition is satisfied or a particular time has passed.

We model the time in PRISM using the `time_elapsed` variable and the synchronized commands labeled `[time_step]`. The `time_elapsed` counter is increased in either of the two cases:

- all the honest parties have finished all of their allowed scenarios steps and are waiting on the `wait` statement,
- the honest party has finished all of their allowed scenarios steps while the adversary decides to not execute any step.

This reflects the assumption that the honest parties always follow the protocol and execute every scenario step within a given time limit while the adversary can interrupt the protocol at any time and refuse to execute a scenario step within the time limit.

7   Case Study: Verification of Two Protocols from the Literature

As a proof of concept we use the *EthVer* compiler to formally verify two protocols from the literature: The Rock-Paper-Scissors protocol from *K. Delmolino et al., Step by step towards creating a safe smart contract: Lessons and insights from a cryptocurrency lab.* [14], and The Micropay 1 protocol from *R. Pass, a. shelat, Micropayments for decentralized currencies* [26]. The results of verification of these protocols are broadly described in appendices E and F of the extended version of this paper.

In the first work [14] the authors analyze the actual smart contract for the Rock-Paper-Scissors game which was created by undergrad students during the cryptocurrency lab. The authors point out several typical mistakes that were made during designing this contract and present a few good programming practices to avoid such bugs in the future. Using *EthVer* we were able to automatically find all the contract bugs and fix all of them. The case study is iterative—after each bug fix we rerun the verification and every time the *EthVer* shows us the next bug of the protocol. Using this iterative method we implement 6 bug fixes in total which finally lead us to the correct version of the contract.

It must be stressed, that in the original paper the authors analyze the contract and fix all the bugs *by hand*. In contrast, in our experiment the only manual action is that we rewrite the original contract to the ETV language (which requires only a few minor tweaks) and then *EthVer automatically* finds all the bugs and provides the *counterexample* for each of them which make it easy to fix the bugs.

In the second paper [26] the authors present the Micropay 1 protocol—a smart contract which can serve as a platform for *micropayments*—fast and cheap off-chain transactions which only occasionally require the interaction with the blockchain. In the original version of the paper [26] (published on the *22nd ACM CCS '15 conference*) the authors describe a buggy version of the protocol—the contract is vulnerable to so called *front-running attack*. After the publication we discovered the bug (it was also discovered independently by Joseph Bonneau) and contacted the authors with our findings. As a result, they published the corrected version of the paper [27]. In case of this protocol we also were able to find and fix the bug using *EthVer*. Again, the *EthVer* has found the bug *automatically*, which means that if the authors verified the protocol before publication using *EthVer* or a similar tool, they would discover the attack and the buggy version of the contract would never be published.

Our case study involved 9 tested models in total (7 versions of the RPS contract and 2 versions of the Micropay contract[13]). The Table 1 shows the performance of all the test runs. Each test was performed on a laptop with Intel Core i7-4750HQ CPU @ 2.00 GHz and 8 GB RAM.

---

[13] The ETV code of all tested models is available in the project repository, https:// github.com/lukmaz/ethver.

Table 1. Performance of all the test runs

Protocol	Number of states	Model checking time
rps v1	1.6M	130 s
rps v1a	1.2M	72 s
rps v1b	1.9M	75 s
rps v2	0.8M	66 s
rps v3	6.6M	470 s
rps v3a	5.3M	264 s
rps v4	5.2M	238 s
micropay v1	16M	24 min
micropay v2	490M	124 min

8   Conclusions

In this work we present the *EthVer* compiler—a novel tool for formal verification of Ethereum smart contracts. We have developed a dedicated ETV language for designing secure and verifiable contracts. We have formally defined and proved the correctness of the translation of this language to Markov decision process (MDP) models in PRISM. This translation has been implemented in Haskell and works as a standalone computer program.

The novelty of our approach lies in the three features: (1) the verification of the whole cryptographic protocol consisting of a smart contract and a scenario of its execution, (2) the verification of probabilistic properties of randomized contracts, and (3) the abstract language construction for cryptographic commitments and signatures, which can be automatically translated into the actual Ethereum code and into the PRISM model. To the best of our knowledge, no other verification approach offers any of these 3 functionalities.

The automatic verification of the model generated by *EthVer* is possible due to our original method of modeling the contract as MDP. Our technique allows to verify the correctness and security of the honest execution of the protocol and also verifies the protocol against the attacks of the adversarial user. Moreover, in case the vulnerability of the protocol is found, our tool returns the *counterexample*—the execution path which leads to the undesired state of the protocol.

As a proof of concept we used *EthVer* to verify two smart contracts from the literature. In both cases *EthVer* was able to automatically find the bugs that were claimed to be found manually by the authors. This means that the vulnerable contracts would not have been created if the authors had used *EthVer* for their verification.

The experiments results show that the verification is practical—it can be performed on a medium-class PC within a reasonable time frame. However, the experiments revealed also the inherent limitation of our method—the size of the model (and hence the verification time) grows exponentially with the number of parameters of the contract. Therefore our method is most suitable for the contracts of a limited size—for larger models the exact model checking is not possible and other verification methods must be used.

References

1. Accidental bug may have frozen $280 million worth of digital coin ether in a cryptocurrency wallet. https://www.cnbc.com/2017/11/08/accidental-bug-may-have-frozen-280-worth-of-ether-on-parity-wallet.html. Accessed 2 Mar 2019
2. How to find $10m just by reading the blockchain. https://coinspectator.com/news/539/how-to-find-10m-just-by-reading-the-blockchain. Accessed 2 Mar 2019
3. An in-depth look at the parity multisig bug. http://hackingdistributed.com/2017/07/22/deep-dive-parity-bug/. Accessed 2 Mar 2019
4. Manticore. https://github.com/trailofbits/manticore
5. Mythril. https://github.com/ConsenSys/mythril
6. Smartcheck. https://github.com/smartdec/smartcheck
7. solgraph. https://github.com/raineorshine/solgraph
8. Amani, S., Bégel, M., Bortin, M., Staples, M.: Towards verifying ethereum smart contract bytecode in Isabelle/HOL. In: Proceedings of the 7th ACM SIGPLAN International Conference on Certified Programs and Proofs, CPP 2018, pp. 66–77. ACM, New York (2018). https://doi.org/10.1145/3167084
9. Bhargavan, K., et al.: Formal verification of smart contracts: short paper. In: Proceedings of the 2016 ACM Workshop on Programming Languages and Analysis for Security, pp. 91–96. ACM (2016)
10. Buterin, V.: Ethereum: a next-generation smart contract and decentralized application platform (2014). https://github.com/ethereum/wiki/wiki/White-Paper. Accessed 22 Aug 2016
11. Chatterjee, K., Goharshady, A.K., Velner, Y.: Quantitative analysis of smart contracts. In: Ahmed, A. (ed.) ESOP 2018. LNCS, vol. 10801, pp. 739–767. Springer, Cham (2018). https://doi.org/10.1007/978-3-319-89884-1_26
12. Cook, T., Latham, A., Lee, J.H.: Dappguard: active monitoring and defense for solidity smart contracts. Retrieved July 18, 2018 (2017)
13. Courtois, N.T., Grajek, M., Naik, R.: Optimizing SHA256 in bitcoin mining. In: Kotulski, Z., Księżopolski, B., Mazur, K. (eds.) CSS 2014. CCIS, vol. 448, pp. 131–144. Springer, Heidelberg (2014). https://doi.org/10.1007/978-3-662-44893-9_12
14. Delmolino, K., Arnett, M., Kosba, A., Miller, A., Shi, E.: Step by step towards creating a safe smart contract: lessons and insights from a cryptocurrency lab. In: Clark, J., Meiklejohn, S., Ryan, P.Y.A., Wallach, D., Brenner, M., Rohloff, K. (eds.) FC 2016. LNCS, vol. 9604, pp. 79–94. Springer, Heidelberg (2016). https://doi.org/10.1007/978-3-662-53357-4_6
15. Falkon, S.: The story of the DAO – its history and consequences (2017). https://medium.com/swlh/the-story-of-the-dao-its-history-and-consequences-71e6a8a551ee
16. Filliâtre, J.-C., Paskevich, A.: Why3 — where programs meet provers. In: Felleisen, M., Gardner, P. (eds.) ESOP 2013. LNCS, vol. 7792, pp. 125–128. Springer, Heidelberg (2013). https://doi.org/10.1007/978-3-642-37036-6_8
17. Grossman, S., et al.: Online detection of effectively callback free objects with applications to smart contracts. In: Proceedings of the ACM on Programming Languages 2(POPL), pp. 1–28 (2017)

18. Hildenbrandt, E., et al.: Kevm: a complete formal semantics of the ethereum virtual machine. In: 2018 IEEE 31st Computer Security Foundations Symposium (CSF), pp. 204–217 (2018). https://doi.org/10.1109/CSF.2018.00022
19. Hirai, Y.: Defining the ethereum virtual machine for interactive theorem provers. In: Financial Cryptography Workshops (2017)
20. Kalra, S., Goel, S., Dhawan, M., Sharma, S.: Zeus: analyzing safety of smart contracts. In: NDSS, pp. 1–12 (2018)
21. Kwiatkowska, M., Norman, G., Parker, D.: PRISM 4.0: verification of probabilistic real-time systems. In: Gopalakrishnan, G., Qadeer, S. (eds.) CAV 2011. LNCS, vol. 6806, pp. 585–591. Springer, Heidelberg (2011). https://doi.org/10.1007/978-3-642-22110-1_47
22. Luu, L., Chu, D.H., Olickel, H., Saxena, P., Hobor, A.: Making smart contracts smarter. In: Proceedings of the 2016 ACM SIGSAC Conference on Computer and Communications Security, pp. 254–269. ACM (2016)
23. Nakamoto, S.: Bitcoin: a peer-to-peer electronic cash system. http://bitcoin.org/bitcoin.pdf
24. Nikolić, I., Kolluri, A., Sergey, I., Saxena, P., Hobor, A.: Finding the greedy, prodigal, and suicidal contracts at scale. In: Proceedings of the 34th Annual Computer Security Applications Conference, pp. 653–663 (2018)
25. O'Connor, R.: Simplicity: a new language for blockchains. In: Proceedings of the 2017 Workshop on Programming Languages and Analysis for Security, pp. 107–120 (2017)
26. Pass, R., Shelat, A.: Micropayments for decentralized currencies. In: Ray, I., Li, N., Kruegel, C. (eds.) ACM CCS 2015: 22nd Conference on Computer and Communications Security, pp. 207–218. ACM Press, Denver (2015). https://doi.org/10.1145/2810103.2813713
27. Pass, R., Shelat, A.: Micropayments for decentralized currencies. Cryptology ePrint Archive, Report 2016/332 (2016). http://eprint.iacr.org/2016/332
28. Pettersson, J., Edström, R.: Safer smart contracts through type-driven development. Master's thesis. Chalmers University of Technology, Sweden (2016)
29. Szabo, N.: Formalizing and securing relationships on public networks. First Monday 2(9) (1997)
30. Tsankov, P., Dan, A., Drachsler-Cohen, D., Gervais, A., Bünzli, F., Vechev, M.: Security: practical security analysis of smart contracts. In: Proceedings of the 2018 ACM SIGSAC Conference on Computer and Communications Security, CCS 2018, pp. 67–82. ACM, New York (2018). https://doi.org/10.1145/3243734.3243780
31. Wohrer, M., Zdun, U.: Smart contracts: security patterns in the ethereum ecosystem and solidity. In: 2018 International Workshop on Blockchain Oriented Software Engineering (IWBOSE), pp. 2–8. IEEE (2018)
32. Zhou, E., et al.: Security assurance for smart contract. In: 2018 9th IFIP International Conference on New Technologies, Mobility and Security (NTMS), pp. 1–5. IEEE (2018)

Absentia: Secure Multiparty Computation on Ethereum

Didem Demirag[(✉)] and Jeremy Clark

Concordia University, Montréal, Canada
d_demira@encs.concordia.ca

Abstract. This paper describes a blockchain-based approach for secure function evaluation (SFE) in the setting where multiple participants have private inputs (multiparty computation) that no other individual should learn. The emphasis of Absentia is reducing the participants' work to a bare minimum, where they can effectively have the computation performed in their absence and they can trust the result. While we use an SFE protocol (Mix and Match) that can operate perfectly well without a blockchain, the blockchain does add value in at least three important ways: (1) the SFE protocol requires a secure bulletin board and blockchains are the most widely deployed data structure with bulletin board properties (immutability and non-equivocation under reasonable assumptions); (2) blockchains provide a built-in mechanism to financially compensate participants for the work they perform; and (3) a publicly verifiable SFE protocol can be checked by the blockchain network itself, absolving the users of having to verify that the function was executed correctly. We benchmark Absentia on Ethereum. While it is too costly to be practical (a single gate costs thousands of dollars), it sets a research agenda for future improvements. We also alleviate the cost by composing it with Arbitrum, a layer 2 'roll-up' for Ethereum which reduces the costs by 94%.

1 Introduction

Consider the traditional setting for multiparty computation (MPC) with a twist: Alice and Bob each have some data, they would like to know the output from running an agreed-upon function on their data, each does not want the other (or anyone else) to learn their data, *and* they want to simply submit their data (*e.g.,* encrypted) to a trustworthy system and come back later for the result, which will always be correct. They are willing to pay for this service and they accept that, only in the worst case of full collusion between the operators of this service (called trustees), their inputs may be exposed—but a single honest trustee protects their privacy.

We assume the reader is familiar with blockchain technology, Ethereum, and smart contracts or decentralized apps (DApps). Can these technologies help? In theory? In practice? We seek to answer these questions through direct experimentation. The abstract above builds the argument for why blockchain can

© International Financial Cryptography Association 2021
M. Bernhard et al. (Eds.): FC 2021 Workshops, LNCS 12676, pp. 381–396, 2021.
https://doi.org/10.1007/978-3-662-63958-0_31

help: (1) it provides an integral point of coordination where trustees can post and track progress on the evaluation; (2) it provides an in-band solution for paying the trustees (in either a cryptocurrency like ETH or in a stablecoin pegged to the value of governmental currency like the USD) in a way that is contingent on their performance; and (3) the blockchain itself can serve as the public verifier and can reject any protocol proof that is not correct. When Alice and Bob retrieve the result (whether in plaintext or individually encrypted under their keys), they know it must be correct—otherwise it would not be there waiting for them.

Our experiments show that while in theory the idea is sound and we are able to successfully perform a secure function evaluation of a single logic gate (NAND gate) on Ethereum, the costs today are too prohibitive for it to be considered practical. We then turn to so-called layer-2 solutions and show that Arbitrum [14] can make Absentia substantially more practical (with room for further improvement).

1.1   Key Design Decisions

Note that we use the more precise term secure function evaluation (SFE) to describe the stateless, one-shot evaluation that Absentia provides. We think of SFE as a subset of secure multiparty computation (MPC)—a more general setting which includes stateful computations performed over time.

Design Decision: Trustee Model. In keeping with our priority for a submit-and-go protocol, someone has to perform the actual evaluation of the function on the inputs. We call these entities *trustees*. We require that the number of trustees (n) can be chosen independently of the number of inputs. In Absentia, we assume all trustees (n-out-of-n) participate (and can identify any that do not). However Absentia could be modified to allow the protocol to proceed if only a threshold (t out of n) of trustees participate—however, also reduces the number of trustees that need to collude to break the privacy of the protocol.

The remaining question is how can Alice and Bob find trustees they assume will not collude? We have several suggestions: (1) it could be based on personal connections; (2) perhaps commercial entities would emerge with either pre-established reputations or earn their reputation over time (similar to oracle providers today); confidence might increase if they offer legally enforceable terms of service; or (3) trustees could be picked at random from a large set of trustees. While (3) may not sound convincing, it is essentially same threat model as the anonymous web-browsing tool Tor which is trusted by many vulnerable users (perhaps Tor also uses flavours of (1) via its Entry Guard program).

Design Decision: Ethereum. While we are not the first to explore multi-party computation and its relationship to blockchain (see Sect. 2.1), we believe we are the first to implement an SFE/MPC protocol on a public, commonly used blockchain; namely, Ethereum. The first research question we ask is whether SFE/MPC is even feasible on Ethereum, given the heavy cryptography it uses.

Our paper establishes a benchmark that we hope to see improved through future research. Ethereum itself has scheduled scalability plans including Ethereum 2.0 (more transactions per second), and a lot of community resources are also being spent examining and implementing *layer 2* solutions that move blockchain functionality off of the main chain without sacrificing many of its security benefits. Technologies include *state channels*, *sidechains*, and *roll-ups* [12]. To experiment with these technologies, we also deploy and benchmark critical components of Absentia on Arbitrum [14], a recently proposed system for optimistic roll-ups (described more in Sect. 4). We now turn to another avenue for improvement, using state-of-the-art MPC protocols.

Design Decision: Mix and Match. Starting with Yao in 1982 [21], the question of how to securely evaluate a general function, when inputs are held by multiple people, has generated a rich body of literature in cryptography. In choosing an SFE/MPC protocol for the basis of Absentia, we looked for one with the following properties:

1. **Trustee model.** As justified above, we seek an SFE/MPC protocol that lets the input holders (*e.g.,* Alice and Bob) offload their inputs to a set of non-colluding trustees for evaluation.
2. **Publicly verifiable** (*a.k.a.* publicly auditable or universally verifiable). Many MPC/SFE protocols are in the semi-honest (*i.e.,* honest-but-curious) model. Some are resilient to covert or malicious adversaries. We require that not only can adversarial behaviour be detected by the participates in the protocol, but that it can be detected by anyone (*i.e.,* the public). This allows (a) Alice and Bob to offload the computational work to the trustees and still ensure the output is correct, even if they did not directly participate, and (b) Alice and Bob can go further and offload the verification itself to someone they trust—the Ethereum network in this case.
3. **Identifiable aborts.** If the protocol does not reach completion, anyone can establish which trustee aborted. Financial incentives can be attached to participation and timeliness.
4. **Elliptic curve operations.** While Ethereum can in theory implement different types of cryptography (RSA groups, integer-based discrete logarithms groups, lattices, *etc.*.), it has native support for its own cryptographic operations (ECDSA signatures) on the elliptic curve secp256k1. For ease of implementation, we prefer a SFE/MPC with the same cryptographic setting.
5. **Circuit type.** When the function to be evaluated is represented as a circuit, the circuit could be based on logic gates (*i.e.,* NAND gates) or arithmetic operations (*e.g.,* additions and multiplications in a modular group). We are indifferent to this design parameter.

One SFE protocol to meet our purposes is Mix and Match [13] and we chose it based on our familiarity with it. We are also aware that the state-of-the-art MPC protocols are based on a different paradigm—based on *Beaver triples* [4]—initiated by the SPDZ protocol [9,10] with many followups (HighGear is a recent example [15]). While SPDZ uses lattice-based somewhat homomorphic encryption (SME), this is during a pre-computation phase and Absentia (for now) assumes all pre-computation has been validated. SPDZ also appears amenable to a trustee model and one paper explores a publicly verifiable variant [3], however since the authors do not compare themselves to Mix and Match, it would be a full research project to determine if it is indeed faster. We note that it is not obviously categorically faster—for example, by not requiring public key operations at all: the publicly verifiable variant uses Pedersen commitments extensively.

We are not aware of an explicit *proof* that Mix and Match is publicly verifiable, however every step of the protocol is covered by a trustee issuing a non-interactive zero knowledge proof and it is later assumed to be by the authors in their auction application [13]. Stated a different way, it appears that even when all trustees fully collude, trustees can only break privacy (and not integrity) with the exception of one sub-protocol, as noted by the authors [13], called the *plaintext equality test* (PET). Despite the caveat, many have used the PET protocol as if it is publicly verifiable (some making justifications based on statistical arguments). Recently it was shown these statistical arguments are not sufficient, but the PET protocol can be made verifiable, even when *all* trustees collude, with a simple additional check on the final output [17].

2   Preliminaries

2.1   Related Work

The blockchain literature has explored SFE and MPC in several regards. Perhaps the closest to Absentia is Enigma [22] which offers stateful MPC as a service. The original academic proposal utilizes a custom blockchain. Now as a commercial project, the emphasis is on providing generic smart contracts with privacy. Enigma runs on a Cosmos/Tendermint-based chain, with an Ethereum bridge contract that allows swapping crypto-assets. Absentia is different in the following regards: (1) users provide the circuit they want evaluated, (2) Absentia does not use trusted execution environments (TEE), and (3) we benchmark running natively on Ethereum. Like Enigma, Hawk also provides a privacy wrapper for contracts [16] based on succinct zero knowledge. A fair MPC is described as an application of Hawk but not implemented.

The literature has also explored moving computation off-chain while not losing privacy or correctness, however from the perspective of a single entity's secret data (*i.e.,* verifiable computing as opposed to SFE/MPC). Examples include Zexe [6], ZkVM [1], and Raziel [19]. Another research direction, initiated by Andrychowicz *et al.* [2], explores how blockchain technologies can support an off-chain MPC to provide fairness. By contrast, Absentia is performing the SFE on the blockchain. Closely related to SFE/MPC are zero knowledge proofs, whose uses in blockchain are now too prolific to adequately summarize here.

2.2   Background

We provide a basic overview of the Mix and Match protocol for secure function evaluation (SFE), while referring the reader to the original paper by Jakobsson and Juels for the full details [13]. Mix and Match uses a partially homomorphic encryption scheme; we instantiate it with additive exponential Elgamal [8]. We implement it over the elliptic curve `secp256k1` which is used natively by Ethereum (we describe later how this results in savings).

Mix and Match: Pre-computation. In a pre-computation stage, the following tasks are completed. First, a set of n trustees, identified by public keys, are chosen. A threshold of trustees needed to complete the protocol can also be chosen, however we implement the simplest case: 2-out-of-2 (we call this *distributed* as opposed to *threshold*). Next, the trustees use a distributed key generation (DKG) protocol for creating n shares of the decryption key, one for each trustee, as well as a single joint public key. Exponential Elgamal supports DKG and threshold decryption [18].

In Mix and Match, a circuit of the function to be evaluated is produced using multi-input and multi-output lookup tables. We evaluate a single binary NAND gate (a universal gate that can create any circuit) which corresponds to a lookup table with two binary inputs (one from Alice and one from Bob) and a single binary output. During a pre-computation stage, the circuit for the function is established as a sequence of lookup tables (the output from one table can be used as an input to another). Each element of each lookup table is individually encrypted under the trustees' public key (we denote an encryption of x as $[\![x]\!]$):

A	B	Out
$[\![0]\!]$	$[\![0]\!]$	$[\![1]\!]$
$[\![1]\!]$	$[\![0]\!]$	$[\![1]\!]$
$[\![0]\!]$	$[\![1]\!]$	$[\![1]\!]$
$[\![1]\!]$	$[\![1]\!]$	$[\![0]\!]$

The encrypted table is then permuted row-wise. Each trustee mixes the rows, rerandomizes each ciphertext, and proves in zero knowledge that the result is correct:

A	B	Out
$[\![0]\!]$	$[\![1]\!]$	$[\![1]\!]$
$[\![1]\!]$	$[\![0]\!]$	$[\![1]\!]$
$[\![1]\!]$	$[\![1]\!]$	$[\![0]\!]$
$[\![0]\!]$	$[\![0]\!]$	$[\![1]\!]$

Complete circuits of such tables can be pre-computed by the trustees before Alice and Bob provide their inputs. Practically speaking, if sets of trustees were pre-established, they could prepare circuits for commonly requested functions and post them publicly. When Alice and Bob decide to do an SFE, they can choose the pre-computed circuit (produced by a specific set of trustees). For the purposes of this paper, we assume circuits have been pre-computed and verified. In the future we may extend Absentia to accept a circuit and complete set of proofs to verify its correct construction, but for this paper, we concentrate on building a verifier for the online phase.

Plaintext Equality Test (PET). Let $\langle [\![x]\!], [\![y]\!] \rangle$ denote two exponential Elgamal ciphertexts; encryptions of x and y respectively. The trustees will first compute $[\![z]\!] = [\![x - y]\!]$ using the additively homomorphic property. If the values are the same, $z = 0$; otherwise $z \neq 0$. Each trustee will choose a random $r_i \neq 0$, compute $[\![\hat{z}_i]\!] = [\![r_i * \hat{z}_{i-1}]\!]$ (where $\hat{z}_0 := z$) and prove correctness in zero knowledge. The resultant $[\![\hat{z}]\!] = [\![\prod r_i * z]\!]$ will still be $[\![0]\!]$ when $x = y$ and will encrypt a randomly distributed non-zero integer otherwise. (The original proposal [13] lets each trustee blind without using the result from the previous trustee—this adds asynchronicity but requires a critical security correction [17]). In the final step, the trustees decrypt and reveal $\hat{z}$. If $\hat{z} = 0$, the equality test returns True; and returns False otherwise.

Mix and Match: Online Phase. At this stage, Alice and Bob provide their inputs $\langle [\![a]\!], [\![b]\!] \rangle$. The trustees can begin with Alice's input $[\![a]\!]$ and they compute a PET between $[\![a]\!]$ and each ciphertext in the column corresponding to Alice's input. They do the same for Bob. They locate the row that returns true for every input column. The encrypted output(s) of this row can then be (1) transferred as an input to the next gate, (2) decrypted publicly if it is a final output, or (3) proxy re-encrypted for Alice (and/or Bob)—meaning it is obliviously and verifiably changed by the trustees from an encryption under the trustees' joint public key to an encryption under Alice's. For simplicity in Absentia, we implement (2). We illustrate for the previous example and $a = 1$ and $b = 0$:

A	B	Out
$\text{PET}([\![a]\!], [\![0]\!]) = F$	$\text{PET}([\![b]\!], [\![1]\!]) = F$	
$\text{PET}([\![a]\!], [\![1]\!]) = T$	$\text{PET}([\![b]\!], [\![0]\!]) = T$	$[\![1]\!]$ is selected
$\text{PET}([\![a]\!], [\![1]\!]) = T$	$\text{PET}([\![b]\!], [\![1]\!]) = F$	
$\text{PET}([\![a]\!], [\![0]\!]) = F$	$\text{PET}([\![b]\!], [\![0]\!]) = T$	

3   Absentia: System Design

High Level Flow. Figure 1 illustrates a high level overview of how participants interact with Absentia. The main contract of the system is the Absentia-DApp (mixmatch.sol), which can create sub-contracts: PET Sub-DApp (PET.sol). Note that Fig. 1 is stylized and the exact implementation might split/join certain function calls but it provides an accurate mental model of participation within the system.

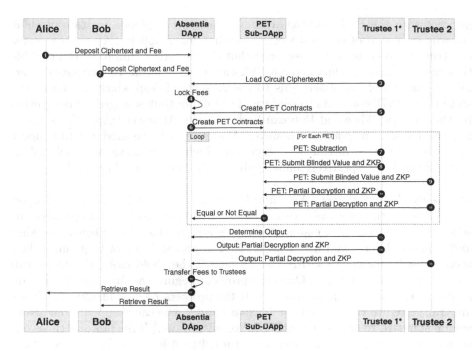

Fig. 1. Overview of Absentia.

At the beginning of the protocol, the contracts are deployed, identifying Alice, Bob, and the trustees (by Ethereum address). Alice and Bob both submit their encrypted input, and deposit fees that will be paid to the trustees for completing the protocol. We consider Absentia *submit-and-go* because Alice and Bob do not have to perform any other functions during the execution of the protocol.

Certain tasks are public operations that can be performed by anyone. For our analysis, we assume that Trustee 1 is the leader (denoted Trustee 1* with an asterisk) and always does these tasks. It is substantially more work, so it might improve the protocol to balance these operations between trustees or to compensate the leader more than the other trustees.

The actual Mix and Match operations done by each trustee is done off-chain using their share of the private key and other secrets (like randomizers) which are always offline. Ethereum is used to record the output of each step, record a zero-knowledge proof that the step was performed correctly, and to actually validate this proof. The DApp will reject any outputs accompanied by invalid or incomplete proofs. All proofs are Σ-protocols (specifically Schnorr [20] or Chaum-Pedersen [7]) made non-interactive with (strong [5]) Fiat-Shamir [11]. As this is not our main contribution, we refer the reader to the original paper by Jakobsson and Juels for the full details how these proofs are used in Mix and Match [13].

For each gate, the Absentia DApp creates enough instances of the PETs (*e.g.*, 8 instances for a binary gate) to perform the evaluation. The trustees then interact with the PET contract, running each to completion (a state machine governs each step of the protocol). Note that for simplicity, Absentia requires the trustees to go in a specified order but the underlying protocol is amenable to some concurrency. Once enough PETs are complete that the output is determined, the leader can assert this to the Absentia DApp which will check the state of the PET contracts to confirm. The final output is staged for decryption by the trustees. Alice and Bob can find it on the Absentia DApp. For simplicity, the result is in plaintext however Absentia could be modified to support proxy re-encryption instead of decryption which would leave two final ciphertexts, encrypted respectively under public keys specified by Alice and Bob.

Payments. Absentia allows Alice and Bob to pay Trustee 1 and Trustee 2 upon completion of the protocol. We implement a simple proof-of-concept payment scheme while noting more elaborate schemes are possible. As implemented, Alice and Bob can deposit and withdraw ETH. The protocol cannot begin until their accounts hold enough to satisfy the fee (and if they hold more, the excess can be withdrawn at any time). Once the protocol begins, the funds for the fee are locked in escrow within the contract. If the protocol reaches finality, the funds are transferred to the accounts of Trustee 1 and 2 who can then withdraw (Note we use standard re-entrancy protection[1] on withdraws.) If the protocol times out without reaching finality, the fees are returned to Alice's and Bob's accounts.

An alternative incentive scheme might pay trustees gradually for each step of the protocol they complete and then a larger bonus for completing. Since Absentia can identify which trustee aborts the protocol (a useful feature that is not always possible in SFE/MPC protocols), trustees could also be required to post a payment (stake) to act as a fidelity bond. They financially commit to completing the protocol in a timely fashion and their stake is taken (slashed) if they do not.

Code Layout. Absentia is implemented in Solidity. All our code and tests are open source.[2] The trustees can perform their operations and generate their proofs in a language of their choice; we implement this in Mathematica (which we also use to generate test vectors for validating the Solidity code). `Mixmatch.sol` and `PET.sol` consists of 214 and 388 lines (SLOC) of Solidity code respectively. We adapt a standard library for elliptic curve operations.[3]

One optimization we implement concerns scalar multiplication over elliptic curves. Since Solidity is verifying proofs in Absentia, it only has to verify multiplications rather than perform them. Put another way, the trustee supplying the proof to Absentia already knows what the result of every multiplication is and can provide these values. As it turns out, it is cheaper to verify a multipli-

---

[1] Open Zeppelin's ReentrancyGuard.sol.
[2] https://github.com/MadibaGroup/2017-Absentia.
[3] Orbs' ECops.sol.

Table 1. Code size for mixmatch.sol

Code	Size (bytes)
Bytecode	27,178
Deployed	26,774
Initialisation and constructor code	404

cation than compute one by 'abusing' Ethereum's relatively inexpensive opcode for validating ECDSA signatures.[4]

Since Absentia generates a lot of PETs to perform the protocol, we implement this aspect with a factory design pattern. In this pattern, each PET is a stand-alone contract. The Mix and Match contract can create instances of these PET contracts and deploy them at new addresses. Our measurements (see below and Table 2) demonstrate that the factory pattern has certain drawbacks. Mixmatch.sol must deploy with a full copy of PET.sol's bytecode in order for it to deploy instances of PET.sol. This results a contract size that is large. Also the function (Create Row) that creates (two) PETs each time it is called is the most expensive function in the system and costs $8,741,453$ gas (gas is Ethereum's metric for the cost of a computation).

All contracts enforce the order in which the functions can execute through state changes maintained within the contract. Key state changes emit events.

3.1 Measurements

Testing Platform. To test Absentia, we use Truffle on a local Ethereum blockchain. Our test files are included on the code repository. We also duplicated Absentia's functionality in Mathematica to help establish correctness.

Code size. The code size for mixmatch.sol is outlined in Table 1. When any Ethereum contract is first deployed, the constructor can only be run once. Thus the constructor code does not need to be referenced for further invocations and is not stored with the deployed bytecode (but can be found in the calldata of the deployment transaction).

When compiled, mixmatch.sol is $26,774$ bytes (plus a constructor of 404 bytes). Because of the factory design, this includes the bytecode to create PET.sol contracts. Ethereum limits contracts to ≈24KB (per EIP170).[5] We simply adjust Truffle's limit to allow us to benchmark it as a single contract. However it cannot be deployed on Ethereum today as is. Straightforward options to bring the code under the limit include: (1) taking PET.sol out of the contract and having the leader deploy each PET contract and load the addresses back

---

[4] V. Buterin, 2018. You can *kinda* abuse ECRECOVER to do ECMUL in secp256 k1 today.

[5] In 2016 when EIP170 was finalized, a 24KB contract could not deploy without crossing the block gas limit, however the gas limit has increased substantially since.

Table 2. Gas costs per function and who runs the function: Alice (A), Bob (B), Trustee 1 as the leader (T1*), or Trustee 2 (T2). Note that many functions are run more than once.

Contract	Function	Gas	Gas cost ($)
ec.sol	Deploy contract	595,517	31.94
Mixmatch.sol (Absentia DApp)	Deploy contract	6,091,398	326.75
	A&B: Load funds	28,040	1.50
	1*: Load outputs	300,798	16.13
	T1*: Create row	8,741,453	468.90
	T1*: Find matching row	37,547	2.01
	T1*: Find matching value	40,868	2.19
	T1*: Create final decryption	4,430,611	237.66
	A&B: Withdraw excess funds	41,110	2.21
	A&B: Withdraw funds	39,221	2.10
PET.sol (PET Sub-DApp)	Deploy Contract	4,681,858	251.14
	A&B or T1*: Load ciphertexts	304,668	16.34
	T1*: Subtraction	242,131	12.99
	T1*: Randomization ZKP	815,340	43.74
	T2: Randomization ZKP	393,561	21.11
	T1*: Partial dec ZKP	364,298	19.54
	T2: Partial cec ZKP	363,612	19.50
	T1*: Full cecryption	107,086	5.74
	T1*: Load final ciphertexts	173,945	9.33

Table 3. Cost for each participant.

	Alice	Bob	Trustee1*	Trustee2
Number of transactions	5	5	44	17
Total gas cost	1,246,712	1,246,712	52,952,603	6,420,996
Total cost in USD	66.87	66.87	2840.41	344.43

into `mixmatch.sol`; (2) move stateless functions to libraries; (3) split the contract up arbitrarily and use `delegatecall` to execute the pieces in a common context; or (4) find ways to optimize the code to reduce its size (it is academic, proof of concept code, and is very close to the limit, so this should be feasible).

Gas Costs. Table 2 provides the cost to deploy Absentia's two contracts and one library, as well as the gas costs of each function. Note that many functions are invoked more than once in a complete run of Absentia. The gas costs are as

Table 4. Cost of scaling absentia

Setting	Total gas
1 gate, 2 trustees	61,867,023
2 gate, 2 trustees	121,240,622
1 gate, 3 trustees	68,288,019

reported in Truffle's local network (Ganache). To convert gas into USD, we use 1 gas = 87 Gwei as recorded on Dec 01, 2020.[6] The price of ETH is \$615.07 for the same date.[7]

As the leader of the protocol, Trustee 1 (T1*) has to perform more operations than the other participants. Table 3 shows the costs per participant. Particularly expensive tasks for the leader is loading all the ciphertexts for the circuit into the contract and initializing the memory needed, in particular for each PET, for the working memory. This is why, for example, Randomization ZKP is so expensive for T1 as compared to T2 (the code of both functions is identical but gas costs are $815, 340$ versus $393, 561$). Trustee 1 initializes many state variables (more expensive in Ethereum) that are not needed once the function completes; while trustee 2 overwrites the variables (less expensive in Ethereum). The next function, Partial Decryption, continues overwriting these variables.

Our design has some room for improvement. For example, in the current implementation, Alice and Bob have to deposit their inputs for each PET contract that is created (8 in total). A better design pattern (more consistent with Fig. 1) would have Alice and Bob deposit once in `mixandmatch.sol` and have the factory contract initialize the PETS with the correct values. Another improvement would aim to reduce the total transaction count for each participant by merging operations that are performed in a sequence by the same participant (we split them into logic blocks to better showcase what the gas was being spent on).

In Table 4, we show how Absentia scales with additional gates and additional trustees. If we want to evaluate a two gate circuit, Alice and Bob still perform the same number of transactions but nearly all of the rest of the functions are run twice as many times. Note that if the output of one gate is fed into the next gate, the leader (T1*) will load the inputs for the second gate. Going back to a single gate, increasing the number of trustees from 2 to 3 is not as expensive. Each additional trustee has a marginal cost equal to Trustee 2's cost in Table 3.

4 Absentia on Layer 2

4.1 Roll-Ups

A loose collection of technologies, called *Layer 2* solutions, have been proposed to address certain shortcomings of operating directly on Ethereum (*Layer 1*)

---

[6] Etherscan.

[7] Coinmarketcap.

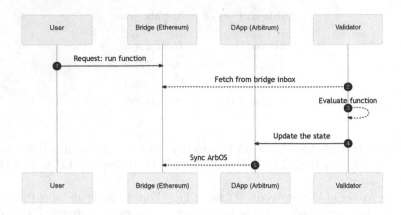

Fig. 2. Overview of arbitrum transaction submission.

or other blockchains [12]. These solutions generally strive for one or more of the following: reducing transaction latency, increasing transaction throughput, or reducing gas costs. In the case of Absentia, reducing gas costs is paramount. However Layer 2 solutions can also change the threat model; for Absentia, we require that Alice and Bob can trust the final output without having to verify any proofs themselves.

The most appropriate layer 2 technology for our requirements is called a *roll-up* which targets gas costs. In Ethereum, every transaction is executed (and thus validated) by every Ethereum node. In a roll-up, transactions are executed by off-chain nodes called *validators*. Validators try to convince the Ethereum network that the result of the transaction execution (*i.e.*, the state change of the EVM) is correct without the Ethereum nodes having to execute it.

Since Ethereum nodes cannot just ignore the Ethereum protocol's specifications for how to validate transactions, the roll-up cannot be implemented on Layer 1. Rather it is implemented inside its own DApp (Layer 2). This Layer 2 DApp is effectively a container, operating by its own custom consensus rules, for DApps that want roll-up functionality. The tradeoff is they are isolated from regular L1 DApps without some additional protocols (*e.g.*, interoperability support for currency/token transfers and external function calls). For Absentia, we do not require interoperability with L1 other than having a currency in L2 to pay the trustees.

There are at least two ways to convince on-chain participants that an off-chain computation was performed correctly. The first is to prove it with a succinct proof. SNARKs are one proof-type for general computations that are more efficient to verify than performing the computation itself. A second approach (called an *optimistic rollup*) is to have a validator assert the result and then allow for anyone to dispute it before finalizing it. Resolving disputes is always possible by having the Ethereum nodes perform the computation itself, but disputes can be settled in a more succinct way (see [14]). If Alice demonstrates that

Table 5. Comparison between deploying a plaintext equality test on Ethereum and deploying on arbitrum (via Ethereum). The links show the reader the actual transactions of a test-run on Kovan/Arbitrum's respective block explorers. Size is the calldata in bytes.

Function	Ethereum		Arbitrum				
	Tx	Gas	L1 Tx	L1 Gas	L2 Tx	L2 ArbGas	Size
Deploy ec	Link	$1,103,372$	Link	80,152	Link	$1,304,481$	4978
Deploy PET	Link	$5,266,352$	Link	386,079	Link	$4,260,273$	24,172
Load Ciphertexts	Link	$305,309$	Link	7869	Link	$820,507$	742
Subtraction	Link	$260,729$	Link	5469	Link	$4,789,799$	550
T1 Randomization ZKP	Link	$819,877$	Link	11,488	Link	$10,972,720$	644
T2 Randomization ZKP	Link	$398,245$	Link	11,440	Link	$11,069,485$	742
T1 Partial Dec ZKP	Link	$366,636$	Link	11,452	Link	$10,692,786$	742
T2 Partial Dec ZKP	Link	$366,089$	Link	11,512	Link	$10,689,113$	742
Full Decryption	Link	$124,816$	Link	6236	Link	$4,258,675$	422

a validator is wrong, the validator is financially punished and Alice is rewarded. Such validators do less work than Ethereum nodes (as well as validators that have to produce SNARKs)—therefore, optimistic rollups enable substantially lower gas costs.

4.2   Arbitrum

Arbitrum is a Layer 2 solution proposed in a *USENIX Security* paper [14] and now maintained as a commercial project by Offchain Labs. Currently, they operate an optimistic rollup on Ethereum. Instead of operating all Arbitrum contracts (called *ArbOS*) in a container DApp on Ethereum, ArbOS instead operates as a side-chain. A *bridge contract* on Ethereum serves as an interface between Ethereum and Arbitrum. Figure 2 shows how function calls work on Arbitrum. A user initiates a transaction on Ethereum to the Bridge Contract with the instruction to deploy a contract or run a function, along with all the data required for Arbitrum to perform this transaction. A validator sees new transactions in the inbox of the bridge, executes one and asserts the result to ArbOS. After a dispute period, the transaction is considered finalized. Periodically, the entire state of ArbOS is committed back to Ethereum. As all Arbitrum transactions are recorded on Ethereum, anyone can compute and compare the current ArbOS state.

4.3   Absentia on Arbitrum

Testing Platform. Arbitrum runs a testnet with a bridge on Ethereum's Kovan testnet. As mentioned above, Absentia is too large to deploy (as a factory contract) within Ethereum's contract size limit. To experiment with Arbitrum, we implement only the PET sub-module as a standalone contract. We run the tests with Truffle. Instead of sending transactions to the Arbitrum bridge (as in Fig. 2), Arbitrum runs a service for developers where transactions are sent (off-chain) to a relay server (called an *Aggregator*) which will batch all pending transactions together as a single Kovan transaction to the bridge (and pay the gas). However we report the measurements as if the participants were sending the transactions themselves.

Gas Costs. Table 5 compares the cost of running a plaintext equality test (PET) on Ethereum (specifically Kovan testnet) and running it on Layer 2 (L2) with Arbitrum. Note the Ethereum numbers differ slightly from Table 2 as it is deployed on a different testnet (Kovan instead of private) and we modified it slightly to be a stand-alone DApp.

Arbitrum creates two transactions (recall Fig. 2): the Ethereum gas cost of relaying the (layer 1 or L1) transaction to the Arbitrum bridge, and the cost for the validator to execute the function, measured in ArbGas. The cost of the first Arbitrum transaction (*L1 Gas*) is paid with ETH but is invariant to its computational complexity. It is essentially only a function of its size (compare *L1 Gas* to *Size*). Note that the gas costs listed on the Kovan block explorer (links under *L1 Tx*) are for aggregated batches of transactions. We report what the cost would be to send it directly (not through an aggregator).

The ArbGas cost on Arbitrum should be similar to the gas cost on Ethereum, however validators do not run EVM bytecode directly. It is translated into Arbitrum virtual machine (AVM) bytecode which has its own opcodes and ArbGas costs. ArbGas has no market price currently. It is expected to be much cheaper than Ethereum's gas. In practice, the trustees could act as validators for Absentia transactions as they have to perform the computation anyways. Therefore we approximate arbgas as free.

A run of PET on Ethereum costs 9,011,425 gas (or 483.38 USD), while on Arbitrum the cost is 531,697 gas (or 28.52 USD). In this use case, Arbitrum reduces Ethereum gas costs by 94%.

5   Concluding Remarks

Ethereum can complement secure function evaluation protocols by enabling coordination, providing incentives, and enforcing correctness. Given recent developments in Ethereum toward performance and scalability, we felt it was an appropriate time to benchmark how expensive SFE is on Ethereum. Even though we expected it to be expensive, we did not imagine a single binary NAND gate would cost thousands of dollars on Ethereum. Most 'interesting' circuits are probably at least hundreds of gates, with many applications that would require many orders of magnitude more.

Despite this, we argue that Absentia is still an important research contribution. It proves the concept works, establishes a lower bound, and it sets a new research challenge: through improvements, how many gates can be evaluated for, say, under $100 USD? Today it might be less than one but we are confident that future research can improve that number substantially. For example, our code can be further optimized; the latest MPC techniques can be applied; and Σ-protocols can be replaced with succinct zero-knowledge proofs. Meanwhile, Layer 1 and Layer 2 technologies will continue progressing.

Acknowledgements. We thank the reviewers who helped to improve our paper. J. Clark acknowledges support for this research project from the National Sciences and Engineering Research Council (NSERC)/ Raymond Chabot Grant Thornton/Catallaxy Industrial Research Chair in Blockchain Technologies and the AMF (Autorité des Marchés Financiers).

References

1. Andreev, O., Glickstein, B., Niu, V., Rinearson, T., Sur, D., Yun, C.: ZkVM: fast, private, flexible blockchain contracts. Technical report, Online (2019)
2. Andrychowicz, M., Dziembowski, S., Malinowski, D., Mazurek, L.: Secure multiparty computations on bitcoin. In: IEEE Symposium on Security and Privacy (2014)
3. Baum, C., Damgård, I., Orlandi, C.: Publicly auditable secure multi-party computation. In: SCN (2014)
4. Beaver, D.: Commodity-based cryptography. In: ACM STOC (1997)
5. Bernhard, D., Pereira, O., Warinschi, B.: How not to prove yourself: Pitfalls of the fiat-shamir heuristic and applications to helios. In: ASIACRYPT (2012)
6. Bowe, S., Chiesa, A., Green, M., Miers, I., Mishra, P., Wu, H.: Zexe: Enabling decentralized private computation. In: IEEE Symposium on Security and Privacy (2020)
7. Chaum, D., Pedersen, T.P.: Wallet databases with observers. In: CRYPTO (1992)
8. Cramer, R., Gennaro, R., Schoenmakers, B.: A secure and optimally efficient multi-authority election scheme. In: EUROCRYPT (1997)
9. Damgård, I., Keller, M., Larraia, E., Pastro, V., Scholl, P., Smart, N.P.: Practical covertly secure mpc for dishonest majority-or: breaking the spdz limits. In: ESORICS (2013)
10. Damgård, I., Pastro, V., Smart, N., Zakarias, S.: Multiparty computation from somewhat homomorphic encryption. In: CRYPTO (2012)
11. Fiat, A., Shamir, A.: How to prove yourself: practical solutions to identification and signature problems. In: CRYPTO, pp. 186–194 (1986)
12. Gudgeon, L., Moreno-Sanchez, P., Roos, S., McCorry, P., Gervais, A.: Sok: Layer-two blockchain protocols. In: Financial Cryptography (2020)
13. Jakobsson, M., Juels, A.: Mix and match: Secure function evaluation via ciphertexts. In: ASIACRYPT (2000)
14. Kalodner, H., Goldfeder, S., Chen, X., Weinberg, S.M., Felten, E.W.: Arbitrum: Scalable, private smart contracts. In: USENIX Security (2018)
15. Keller, M., Pastro, V., Rotaru, D.: Overdrive: Making spdz great again. In: EUROCRYPT (2018)
16. Kosba, A., Miller, A., Shi, E., Wen, Z., Papamanthou, C.: Hawk: The blockchain model of cryptography and privacy-preserving smart contracts. In: IEEE Symposium on Security and Privacy (2016)

17. McMurtry, E., Pereira, O., Teague, V.: When is a test not a proof? In: ESORICS (2020)
18. Pedersen, T.P.: A threshold cryptosystem without a trusted party. In: EURO-CRYPT (1991)
19. Sánchez, D.C.: Raziel: Private and verifiable smart contracts on blockchains. Technical report, arXiv arXiv:1807.09484 (2018)
20. Schnorr, C.P.: Efficient signature generation by smart cards. J. Cryptology **4**(3), 161–174 (1991). https://doi.org/10.1007/BF00196725
21. Yao, A.C.: Protocols for secure computations. In: IEEE FOCS (1982)
22. Zyskind, G., Nathan, O., et al.: Decentralizing privacy: Using blockchain to protect personal data. In: IWPE (2015)

Empirical Analysis of On-chain Voting with Smart Contracts

Robert Muth[✉] and Florian Tschorsch[✉]

Technische Universität Berlin, Berlin, Germany
{muth,florian.tschorsch}@tu-berlin.de

Abstract. Blockchains and smart contracts promise transparency, verifiability, and self-enforcing agreements. Against this background, novel use cases such as decentralized governance platforms that implement voting to collectively manage funds have emerged. While a number of arguments against blockchain-based voting exist, we still see a relevance. In this paper, we therefore present a quantitative analysis of the Ethereum blockchain with respect to voting. To this end, we develop a blockchain analysis toolchain that we use to analyze 3 173 smart contracts on the Ethereum Mainnet with voting functionality. We extract insights on the complexity of deployed voting methods and reveal a trend towards a centralization of funds, i.e., five smart contracts manage 98% of funds comprising more than four million USD. We additionally analyze the feasibility of on-chain voting for Ethereum as well as other well-established blockchains that are used for voting, i.e., Bitcoin and Dash.

Keywords: Blockchain · Analysis · Voting · Smart contract

1 Introduction

The blockchain's integrity and transparent storage space make it tempting to implement blockchain-based online voting [8,10,14] as everyone can verify the correct execution. In particular, blockchains such as Ethereum [27], which provide an opportunity to implement smart contracts [24], inherently allow to verify whether a vote was stored and counted correctly. However, it has been shown and argued that blockchain-based online voting has fundamental issues [8,19], including security [18,23] and privacy [9] problems.

While blockchain-based online voting certainly polarizes, on-chain voting is still being used for reasons such as the decentralized governance of funds. Most prominently, decentralized autonomous organizations (DAOs), e.g., the DAO [11], allow fundraising and enable stakeholders to manage the distribution of funds with on-chain voting. Smart contracts render the decision-making process transparent and self enforcing. Since its debut in 2016, the DAO raised approximately 150 million USD, but at the same time lost about 60 million USD due to an exploit [1]. While we distance ourselves from the idea of blockchain-based online voting, e.g., for official elections, we argue that *on-chain voting* still requires attention and further research.

© International Financial Cryptography Association 2021
M. Bernhard et al. (Eds.): FC 2021 Workshops, LNCS 12676, pp. 397–412, 2021.
https://doi.org/10.1007/978-3-662-63958-0_32

In this paper, we show the relevance of on-chain voting and derive limitations in terms of scalability and transaction costs. To this end, we scan the Ethereum Mainnet for smart contracts with voting functionality and analyze their usage with respect to registered votes, gas costs, and fundings. In order to understand the scalability potential of on-chain voting, we analyze past residual blockchain capacities of Ethereum and evaluate the feasibility of small and large-scale votings. We also look beyond Ethereum and discuss other leading blockchains, including Bitcoin [17] and the governance network of Dash [6]. We provide a publicly available repository with the collected data sets and our analysis pipeline. Our presented database driven analysis approach is compatible with Google BigQuery and therefore does not require any advanced setup.

In our empirical analysis, we found 3 173 deployed Ethereum smart contracts related to voting, which currently hold 11 794 ETH, or more than 4.5 million USD (as of October 30, 2020). From these smart contracts, we identified 88 instances of the DAO (deployed smart contracts that are based on the original DAO source code), which in total received 5 928 votes, so far. Over the past years, voting smart contracts in general accumulated and processed 29 337 ETH. Our analysis suggests a continuously high amount of monetary investments in and interaction with voting smart contracts, indicating a high popularity and relevance. Besides the relevance, we conclude that blockchain voting suffers from scalability issues that render large-scale votings either not feasible in a reasonable time, or very expensive, or both.

The main contributions of this paper can be summarized as follows:

- We develop an analysis pipeline to reveal voting smart contracts on the Ethereum blockchain and present an overview of key metrics, which emphasize the relevance of on-chain voting (see Sect. 3)
- We assess the limitations of on-chain voting with a model-based comparison of blockchain specifications as well as an analysis using historic block data (see Sect. 4)
- We give an outlook on other relevant blockchain with on-chain voting, i.e., Bitcoin and Dash (see Sect. 5)

In addition to our main contributions, we discuss related work in Sect. 2 and conclude the paper in Sect. 6.

2　Related Work

There is a large body of work on blockchain-based voting, proposing various designs to conduct votings using blockchain technologies [5,10,12,16]. Most notably, McCorry et al. [16] developed a smart contract for boardroom voting with maximum voter privacy. Since we do not propose any new voting schemes, these contributions are orthogonal to our work.

In this paper, we analyze the multitude of on-chain voting regardless of any specific use case or property. A series of contributions investigate blockchain data with respect to various other aspects, including privacy [2,22], data storage [15], and smart contract metrics [20]. Moreover, model-based analysis on the security [13] and scalability [4] of blockchains in general exist. Specific to voting, Heiberg et al. [8] evaluate the trade-offs of blockchain-based voting on a qualitative level. They discuss aspects such as complexity, costs, and scale, which go in a similar direction as our paper. We complement their discussion however with an empirical analysis and reveal new insights, for example, on the magnitude of on-chain voting.

Methodically similar to our approach, are [7,20,21,26]. Victor and Lüders [26] inspect the Ethereum blockchain for token implementations, which are managed by the ERC-20[1] smart contract template. While EIP-1202[2] proposes a similar standard for voting smart contracts, it is not as established as the ERC-20 compatible token standards. Fröwis et al. [7] search for token-related behavior with symbolic execution analysis techniques and compare the effectiveness of both methodologies. The diversity of voting schemes, features, and privacy mechanisms make it more difficult to identify voting smart contracts by their bytecode. We therefore propose an analysis pipeline that uses generic voting signatures from other sources in addition to established method signatures. In contrast to automated smart contract inspection, the authors of [20,21] present approaches that are based on manually collected exchange listings and corresponding source code publications on CoinMarketCap and Etherscan.

3   Relevance of On-Chain Voting

In this section, we reveal the magnitude of on-chain voting in Ethereum. We are particularly interested in the diversity of voting smart contracts with respect to cost and fundings.

3.1   Analysis Toolchain and Methodology

Typically, analyzing blockchains requires a synchronized node with all valid transactions. With Geth, the Ethereum foundation provides such a node, which has been optimized to save computational resources and memory. As it turns out, the very data-efficient data structures make it difficult to quickly analyze historic data. For this reason, we instead used Google BigQuery[3] as source to Ethereum Mainnet transactions. BigQuery is a Google Cloud service for big data analysis, which provides a public dataset with all current Ethereum transactions, block details, and smart contracts in a SQL database. As shown in Fig. 1, we use BigQuery as transactions source and to execute complex SQL queries for analysis. The advantage of SQL databases is the ability to index past transactions and query them efficiently (at the cost of additional storage and memory consumption which BigQuery compensates with cloud resources). We

---

[1] https://github.com/ethereum/EIPs/blob/master/EIPS/eip-20.md
[2] https://github.com/ethereum/EIPs/blob/master/EIPS/eip-1202.md
[3] https://cloud.google.com/bigquery

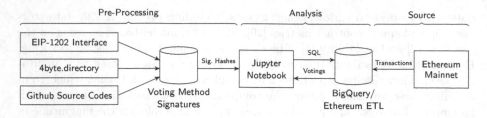

Fig. 1. Our blockchain-based voting analysis toolchain with a Jupyter Notebook and BigQuery (or Ethereum ETL) based on given pre-processed method signatures.

developed a Jupyter Notebook, which manages the analysis process, i.e., preparing input data from pre-processing, compiling SQL statements, monitoring the execution, and preparing the results. Alternatively to our cloud-based approach, the database can be generated locally using a full node and Ethereum ETL[4] without BigQuery.

While smart contracts are generally stored publicly on the Ethereum blockchain, only the compiled bytecode, i.e., EVM code, is available. Similar to high-level programming languages, the original source code compiles to an assembly-style language. To this end, compilers remove comments and substitute identifiers, which render the bytecode difficult to understand without the original source code. In addition, method signatures of smart contracts, i.e., method name and parameter list, are represented by a hash pointer. More specifically, the first for 4 bytes of a method signature's Keccak (SHA-3) hash value are used to point to the respective stack code position. Since Keccak is a cryptographic hash function, it is not possible to infer the method signature from the hash value directly. Hence, it is neither straight forward to search for a certain type of smart contract nor for a partial method signature.

In order to analyze the Ethereum blockchain, we searched for hash values of method signatures that are usually part of voting smart contracts. As shown in Fig. 1 as part of the pre-processing, we collected the hashed method signatures of the EIP-1202 voting interface, which provides a standardized set of methods for voting. In addition, we used the Ethereum Function Signature Database[5], which provides a list of method signatures and their corresponding hash values based on known smart contract source codes and user submissions. We used the database's RESTful API to search for methods containing 'vote', 'voting', or 'ballot'. As a result, we get a list of method signature and hash value tuples, which are related to voting. We use these tuples to retrieve the smart contracts that actually implement the respective method. Finally, we analyzed the source code of the DAO smart contract on Github for identifying transactions to the original instance and deployed copies with them same interface methods.

Inevitably, the approach may lead to some positives as well as false negatives. For example, generic method signatures lead to a false classification of some

---

[4] https://github.com/blockchain-etl/ethereum-etl
[5] https://www.4byte.directory

smart contracts, e.g., `setStatus(...)` of the EIP-1202 or `dropVotes(...)`. We also encountered hash collisions that indicated voting methods in a smart contract but did not belong to voting upon closer inspection. For example, the method signatures `voting_var(address,uint256,int128,int128)` and `totalSupply()` share the same hash value `0x18160ddd` and lead to false-positives. In an attempt of manual inspection, we excluded these instances for our analysis. In order to prioritize precision (over sensitivity), we considered smart contracts that implement at least two method signatures related to voting only. Since the bytecode in the blockchain remains a black box, though, we cannot exclude false classification entirely.

The described methodology enables analyses of Ethereum smart contracts in general and can be used to reveal a multitude statistics. We used it to analyze voting smart contracts with respect to scale and gas cost in general and the interaction with these contracts in particular. We inspected the Ethereum blockchain for the timespan between October 16, 2017 and October 30, 2020. Moreover, we developed a Jupyter Notebook[6] which connects to BigQuery, our own local data records (e.g., historical exchange rates), and other external data sources. A data dump of the following results, the implementation to gather the data set independently, and our full analysis pipeline to reproduce the results is publicly available on GitHub.[7]

3.2 Voting Complexity

In total, we found 1 458 relevant method signatures related to voting, which are implemented in 5 185 smart contracts. Overall, 1 272 059 transactions interacted with these smart contracts and called 129 855 times one of the voting methods. After data cleaning, 3 173 voting smart contracts remain and are subject of the following analysis.

In Table 1, we show the ten most often called voting methods and their average consumed gas. None of the deployed voting smart contracts implemented EIP-1202 completely, but 82 of them implemented at least a subset of its standardized method signatures. While most of the method signatures in Table 1 are not surprising, methods 5, 6, and 9 let us expect a *commit-and-reveal* voting scheme, where voters submit their vote cryptographically concealed, e.g., by using a hash function, and reveal their individual vote later with another transaction. Since such a scheme is more complex, it typically requires more gas.

Method signatures with more than one parameter mostly belong to smart contracts that conduct multiple votings and allow to specify a proposal. For example, most calls with method signature 7 belong to a DAO smart contract that conducts multiple votings, where the `byte32` parameter references the proposal and the `uint256` parameter encodes the user's choice.

In Fig. 2, we compare the complexity of voting methods to the number of method calls. The required gas (on the x axis) is an indicator of the computational complexity. We grouped gas values in buckets of $100 \cdot 10^3$ gas. The

---

[6] https://colab.research.google.com/drive/1oIxMjJu7LQvSMnXiIgC9S_5CgGA_5d2R
[7] https://github.com/robmuth/blockchain-voting-analysis

Table 1. Top ten voting methods with respect to their number of calls.

	Calls	Hash	Signature	∅ Gas	∅ Gas price
1	80 676	0x0121b93f	`vote(uint256)`	71 k	2.4 Gwei
2	6 996	0xb384abef	`vote(uint256,uint256)`	31 k	28.3 Gwei
3	6 420	0xfc36e15b	`vote(string)`	32 k	3.2 Gwei
4	4 534	0xddb6e116	`vote(uint16)`	47 k	3.7 Gwei
5	2 930	0x6cbf9c5e	`commitVote(uint256,bytes32,..`	164 k	3.8 Gwei
6	2 624	0x5e8254ea	`commitVoteOnProposal(bytes32,..`	110 k	7.0 Gwei
7	2 161	0x9ef1204c	`vote(bytes32,uint256)`	151 k	9.6 Gwei
8	2 124	0xcff9293a	`vote(uint32,uint32)`	51 k	12.1 Gwei
9	2 009	0xb11d8bb8	`revealVote(uint256,uint256,..`	62 k	3.4 Gwei
10	1 817	0x3850f804	`castVote(uint256,uint256[],..`	139 k	41.1 Gwei

Table 2. Top four smart contracts with respect to their funds.

	Smart contract	Funds in ETH	
		Received	Balance
1	N/A (Congress Contract) 0x3de0c040705d50d62d1c36bde0ccbad20606515a	5 028	5 010 ($ 1 918 k)
2	Unicorn Token (Congress Contract) 0xfb6916095ca1df60bb79ce92ce3ea74c37c5d359	5 891	4 595 ($ 1 760 k)
3	HONG/hongcoin 0x9fa8fa61a10ff892e4ebceb7f4e0fc684c2ce0a9	3 936	1 003 ($ 384 k)
4	Dogecoin-Ethereum Bounty 0xdbf03b407c01e7cd3cbea99509d93f8dddc8c6fb	6 592	597 ($ 228 k)

consumed gas ranges from 18 120 gas to a maximum of 4 442 268 gas with an average of 82 431 gas. The figure also shows that most voting method calls consume between 100 000 and 200 000 gas (mind the log scale).

3.3   Acquired Funds

Many smart contracts combine one way or another voting with the management of funds. In Table 2, we therefore show the top four deployed voting smart contracts with respect to their funds. We differentiate between the overall received funds and their current balance (as of October 30, 2020). For example, the Unicorn Token uses the Ethereum Foundation DAO Congress contract that allows members to deposit ETH and submit proposals for fundraising; the other members then can vote if the proposal is accepted. After the voting period ends and a pre-defined quorum accepted the proposal, the ETH will be transferred to the proposer automatically.

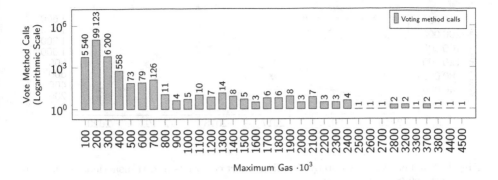

Fig. 2. Complexity of voting methods (measured in gas) in comparison to the number of calls (in total 110 361 calls).

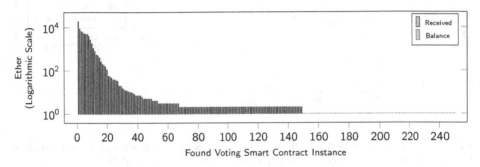

Fig. 3. Received and current balance of ether per voting smart contract, limited to 247 of 3 173 smart contracts in total (as of 2020-10-30).

In Fig. 3, we show the distribution of funds (limited to 247 of 3 173 voting smart contracts which have received ETH). We can clearly observe a long tail distribution (log scale). However, many of the originally acquired funds are already withdrawn. From the overall received funds, 0.05% are still deposited. That is, all analyzed voting smart contracts together have a balance of more than 11 941 ETH, which equals more than 4.8 million USD[8]. The amount of acquired funds can be considered an indicator for the relevance of on-chain voting.

3.4   Trend

In order to get an understanding of the trend, we analyzed the transactions as a time series over the past five years since Ethereum's release in 2015. We particularly focus on the interest and relevance of votings in Ethereum over time.

In Fig. 4, we show the number of voting method calls (left y axis) as well as the number of deployed smart contracts related to voting (right y axis). Once

---

[8] Exchange rate at the time of writing was 407 USD per ETH (source: `coinbase.com`)

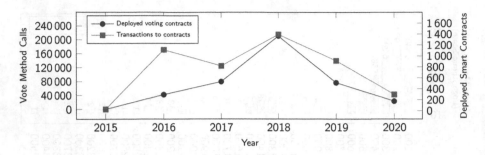

Fig. 4. Number of newly deployed voting smart contracts and transactions to them by year (2015-09-06 – 2020-10-30).

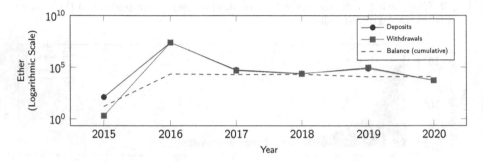

Fig. 5. Ether deposits and withdrawals to voting smart contracts and corresponding balances of voting smart contracts per year (2015-09-06 – 2020-10-30).

deployed, smart contracts remain active and are not counted again in the following years, i.e., the figure shows deployment of new smart contracts. In addition, we analyzed the deposits, withdrawals, and corresponding balances of each voting smart contract over time, which are shown in Fig. 5.

We generally observe that with the debut of the DAO [11] in 2016, the number of smart contracts with voting functionalities as well as the number of transactions that interact with voting contracts increases with a peak in 2018. After 2018, we observe a decline of both metrics. While the trend might suggest a decline in interest, the balances remain stable over time. Upon closer examination, comparing Fig. 3 and Fig. 5, the total balance in 2020 is almost entirely contributed by the top five voting contracts (with more than 500 ETH). That is, while previously the balances were distributed over many smart contracts, we can infer that funds are more centralized now. We conclude that the dynamics and interactions of voting smart contracts declined over time, but on-chain voting has in terms of funding still a relevance.

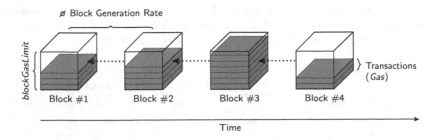

Fig. 6. Blockchain partially filled with transactions, leaving residual gas.

4 Feasibility Analysis

In the following, we present a feasibility analysis of on-chain voting. In particular, we analyze scalability limitations using a model-based analysis as well as an empirical analysis based on historical blockchain data.

4.1 Block Capacities

One of the central scalability parameters is the maximum number of transactions per block interval, i.e., transaction throughput, which eventually also limits the possible number of votes. Ethereum aims for a block generation rate of 15 s and continuously allows miners to agree on a *block gas limit* [27] that limits the size of new blocks. The notion of *gas* was introduced to measure computational complexity of transactions. Ethereum accordingly charges transaction fees based on the transaction's complexity. The sender of a transaction sets a price in ether (ETH), which determines the amount she is willing to pay per computational unit, i.e., the *gas price*.

Depending on the number of transactions per block and their complexity, transactions might not make use of the available block gas limit and leave *residual gas*. In Fig. 6, we visualize the concept of the gas consumption and residual gas. The residual gas determines the space for additional transactions on top of the baseline activities of Ethereum. Later, we make use of the notion of residual gas to evaluate feasibility and scale of on-chain voting.

4.2 Model-Based Scalability Analysis

Our analysis is based on overly optimistic model-based assumptions to reveal upper limits, which enables us to make fundamental statements on the (in)feasibility of on-chain voting. To this end, we start with a number of votes μ that we would like to cast. We are then interested in the number of blocks n that are necessary to cast μ votes. Given the block generation rate, we can approximate the time it takes to mine n blocks, which we denote with Δ. For a block i with a $blockGasLimit(i)$ and a certain $gasCost$ per vote, we can calculate the maximum number of votes per block by $blockGasLimit(i)/gasCost$.

Table 3. Required blocks n and duration Δ [HH:MM] for different voting implementations; median and median absolute deviation (MAD) are based on residual block capacities (monthly intervals between 2015-12-28 and 2020-10-30).

	Implementation	Blocks n			Duration Δ		
		Model	Median	MAD	Model	Median	MAD
Small-scale	Ethereum Naïve	4	18	5	00:01	00:04	00:02
	Ethereum Minimal Voting	7	37	14	00:02	00:09	00:05
	Ethereum *The DAO*	25	118	43	00:07	00:30	00:13
	Bitcoin Naïve	1	3	2	00:10	00:29	00:29
	Dash	1	1	0	00:02	00:02	00:00
Large-scale	Ethereum Naïve	175	783	299	00:44	03:24	01:22
	Ethereum Minimal Voting	350	1 634	677	01:28	06:46	02:56
	Ethereum *The DAO*	1 250	7 320	3 232	05:13	33:46	14:19
	Bitcoin Naïve	3	25	20	00:30	05:12	04:38
	Dash	10	10	0	00:25	00:21	00:05

Based on our blockchain analysis results from Sect. 3, we evaluate two different scales of voting. Since our measurements show that most voting methods were called between 2 k–7 k times, we consider $\mu = 2\,000$ to be a small-scale voting, and $\mu = 100\,000$ to represent future large-scale votings. Moreover, we introduce three on-chain voting "schemes", which are either overly simple or taken from our previous analysis. Please note that these simple voting schemes are not meant to facilitate general voting principles, e.g., anonymity and secrecy.

The *naïve voting* provides different addresses, each representing a voting option. Voters can transfer coins to the respective address until the voting ends, where the balances determine the final voting result. This naïve approach can basically be implemented in every cryptocurrency. In Ethereum, the gas costs are 21 000 gas.

The *minimal voting* uses a smart contract for counting votes. To this end, we implemented a synthetic voting smart contract that only consists of a single method for counting votes (available in our Github repository). We are aware, though, that the Solidity compiler does not generate perfectly optimized bytecode. While an optimized voting smart contract with a completely assembly-style built bytecode would need less gas, we consider the Solidity compiler the most prevalent way to compile smart contract code. After deployment, the minimal voting requires at least 41 897 gas per method call.

For the purpose of more realistic statements, we also analyzed the median gas costs of votes to *the DAO*. To this end, we used our analysis pipeline described in the previous section, which yields 150 k gas per DAO voting call. As expected, this is more complex than our minimal voting as it also manages funds and quorum regulations.

In Table 3, we show the minimum duration of small-scale and large-scale votings for the various voting schemes (see "Model" columns). For Ethereum, we assumed a block gas limit of $12 \cdot 10^6$ gas and a block generation rate of 15 s. For comparability, we also included the naïve voting for Bitcoin and Dash, which we discuss later in Sect. 5. Based on this initial evaluation, we can expect that small-scale on-chain voting is generally feasible in reasonable bounds. At the same time, large-scale votings require under idealistic circumstances more than four hours for the naïve voting scheme, or even about 34 h for the DAO voting smart contract.

4.3   Residual Capacities Analysis

In the following, we enrich our model-based evaluation with historic block-chain data to determine the residual gas limits in Ethereum. This approach provides a more realistic assessment of limitations. More specifically, we define $residualGas(i) = blockGasLimit(i) - usedGas(i)$ for a block i. Please note that in Ethereum the block gas limit is block specific and changes over time. The residual gas is therefore determined by the used gas at a certain point in time.

In Table 3, we show the median number of blocks n as well as the duration Δ for historic data in addition to our model-based evaluation. We calculated n and Δ starting with the last mined block of 2020-10-30 and repeated the process for each preceding month until the genesis block of Ethereum (2015-07-30). In general, our measurements yield values under the (unlikely) condition that all voters submit their votes in a perfectly aligned and coordinated order. We use this approach to provide an (optimistic) understanding for the minimum gas needed to deploy and cast a single vote. Since we repeated the evaluation multiple times by shifting starting points in monthly intervals, we present the median absolute deviation (MAD).

The results show that simple small-scale and large-scale voting yield reasonable performance with approx. 30 min or less for 2 k votes, and between 30–90 min for 100 k votes. The exception is the more complex DAO implementation, which takes more than 5 h.

4.4   Economic Analysis

Since gas cost can be directly translated to ETH, we can also estimate the economic efficiency of on-chain voting. As a first impression, we consider a median gas price 2.0 $\frac{Gwei}{Gas}$ (SD = 5.92) for the 121 980 voting method calls from our data set. We used an exchange rate of 407 USD per ETH as before. Hence, we can approximate the price of a vote for our minimal voting scheme that approximately yields 0.03 USD per vote. For more realistic gas cost, i.e., the most called voting methods require between 100–200 gas, our price approximation ranges between 0.08 USD and 0.16 USD per vote.

Voting costs are a relevant factor for high reachability and inclusive participation. While fees for casting a vote might serve as Sybil protection, they might also deter voters. In general, fees set a higher participation threshold. In order to maximize participation, transaction costs should be as low as possible for submitting votes—or just not be charged, at all. Unfortunately, smart contracts in Ethereum are not able to pay the transaction fees for the senders, e.g., for calling chosen voting methods. It is possible to implement smart contracts that refund transaction fees within the same transaction, but it still requires voters to own initial ETH for paying the transaction fee in advance. Voters who do not own any ETH hence face a greater hurdle to participate.

Interestingly enough, we want to point out an approach that is able to store and release gas to cover some of the gas costs itself. Projects like the GasToken[9] exploit gas reserving opcodes (i.e., `SSTORE` and `CREATE/SELFDESTRUCT`) for saving gas when the gas price is low and releasing it when gas is more expensive. Unfortunately, releasing reserved gas requires gas itself. That is, the transaction costs can be reduced but not covered completely, which leaves us back to the original problem that voters need an initial ETH fund. For enabling future-oriented use cases that require broad involvement, e.g., participatory budgeting or crowd funding, we believe new solutions are required to open on-chain voting.

5   Voting Beyond Ethereum

In the following, we consider other well-established cryptocurrencies, namely Bitcoin [17] and Dash [6], that can also be used for voting one way or another.

5.1   Bitcoin

Several proposals for Bitcoin-based voting exist [3,25,28]. Unfortunately, due do the lack of a full-fledged scripting language, Bitcoin heavily relies on external infrastructure to conduct votings, which makes it difficult to inspect the blockchain and reliably extract information with respect to voting. While we have found indications for on-chain voting, infrastructures have been shut down and therefore prevent analysis. Regardless, it is worth mentioning that Bitcoin miners implement voting functionality directly in the blockchain protocol to agree on improvement proposals.[10]

We can however assume that voting would have at least the same transaction requirements (w.r.t. transaction size and cost) as transferring coins. On this basis, we analyze residual transaction capacities of past blocks and derive the maximum of possible votes over that time span. To this end, we need to consider the specifics and changes of the *segregated witness* proposal,[11] which tackles signature malleability issues and therefore separates signature data from the transaction's hashes. As a result, the maximum block size is then limited by the notion of *block weight*, i.e., *block weight* $< 4 \cdot 10^6$, which corresponds approximately to a block size of 4 MB. A standard Bitcoin transaction for transferring coins from one address to another (P2WSH) with segregated witness requires a block weight of approximately 110 (median over all corresponding transactions until Oct 2020 with a standard deviation of 0.069). Other parameters include a target block generation rate of 10 min.

---

[9] https://github.com/projectchicago/gastoken
[10] https://github.com/bitcoin/bips/blob/master/bip-0009.mediawiki
[11] https://github.com/bitcoin/bips/blob/master/bip-0141.mediawiki

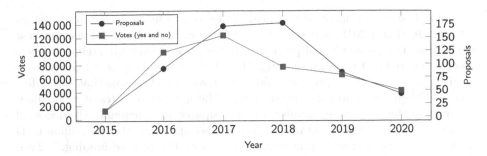

Fig. 7. Dash governance proposals and votes, by year (2015-08-27–2020-10-26).

Evaluation. We analyzed Bitcoin for small-scale and large-scale scenarios with minimal transaction weights, which corresponds to our naïve voting implementation. In addition to a model-based evaluation, we also investigated the residual block capacities. Table 3 shows the minimum amount of blocks as well as the time span it would take to cast μ votes. We assumed a transaction weight of 110 per vote. While Ethereum requires at least 4 min, Bitcoin requires 29 min for small-scale votings. Please note that Bitcoin indicates very high MAD for n and Δ. Hence, Bitcoin's residual capacities fluctuate significantly compared to Ethereum, which makes it more difficult to make predictions. For large-scale voting, Bitcoin requires significantly less blocks (due to the larger block size) and despite its slower block generation rate is faster than Ethereum.

5.2 Dash Governance Platform Analysis

Dash [6] was released in 2014, initially named *Xcoin* and later *Darkcoin*. Dash does not support smart contracts in the same way as Ethereum, but implements dedicated governance mechanisms directly in its protocols. During the mining process new coins will be split and distributed over three stakeholders: master nodes and miners receive each 40%, and the remaining 20% go to Dash's Decentralized Governance by Blockchain (DGBB) funding platform. Master nodes then can vote on public proposals for distributing the collected funds.

The Dash Governance Platform (DGP) is natively implemented in Dash's application protocols and therefore can be monitored by all nodes that have joined the network (also at DashCentral[12]). After a pre-defined voting phase, the number of yes-votes minus the no-votes must exceed 10% of the total number of master nodes for a proposal to pass. Otherwise, the proposal will be rejected.

Evaluation. We analyzed 577 proposals between 2015-08-27 and 2020-10-26. During that time, 379 proposals were funded. In Fig. 7, we show the total number of votes and the number of proposals per year. Dash's governance proposals started at the same year as the first voting smart contracts with Ethereum in

---

[12] https://www.dashcentral.org

2015. Dash shows an increase and peak of newly created proposals and votings between 2016 and 2018, and similar to Ethereum, a steady decrease of interest afterwards. Dash's number of proposals at the peak is approximately 8 times is lower compared to Ethereum (c.f. Fig. 4). Note that the analysis of Dash is more precise and does not suppress any false-positives, which means that the difference to Ethereum is probably even higher. The number of votes at peak times is approximately 1–3 times smaller, when compared to Ethereum. All successful proposals collected 131 453 DASH, which equals approximately 14.7 million USD according to the corresponding exchange rates at the time of funding.[13] Even though the presented votings were not conducted on-chain, the blockchain's protocol automatically pays out fundings with Dash's cryptocurrency and therefore supports the role of on-chain voting.

Additionally, we evaluated the residual capacities of Dash. While Dash is based on Bitcoin, it does not support segregated witness and aims for a block generation rate of 2.5 min with a maximum block size of 2 MB. As shown in Table 3, Dash does not have such a high transaction load as Bitcoin or Ethereum, which directly leads to high residual capacities and therefore better performance for small-scale and large-scale voting. Our measurements show even better results than our model approximation, because the proof-of-work consensus generated new blocks faster than expected. We nevertheless would expect higher durations with the same general load, i.e., residual capacity, as in Bitcoin.

6   Conclusion

In this paper, we have shown that on-chain voting has become a relevant use case in Ethereum, most often, to collectively manage funds. To this end, we presented our blockchain analysis toolchain, that we used to identify and analyze voting smart contracts with respect to their popularity, complexity, and funds. On the one hand, our benchmark of transactions to voting smart contracts and their respective fundings confirm a high relevance. On the other hand, we observed a trend of centralization due to the popularity of DAO contracts.

We further used these insights to assess the feasibility of future large-scale voting on blockchains. Therefore, we also evaluated other well-established blockchains, i.e., Bitcoin and Dash. While small-scale voting scenarios seem feasible on all analyzed blockchains, large-scale voting suffers from severe scalability issues. Although our model-based calculations indicate that large-scale votings can theoretically be conducted in reasonable times under perfect conditions, our measurements on well-established public blockchains show that minimum durations increase significantly due to the limited transaction throughput.

Despite all the flaws of blockchain-based voting, We have shown that on-chain voting has a relevance, e.g., for governance aspects of blockchains. We therefore believe that improving on-chain voting schemes with respect to security, privacy, inclusiveness, and fairness is still necessary and relevant at the same time.

---

[13] http://coinmarketcap.com/en/currencies/dash/historical-data/ (2020-11-16)

References

1. Atzei, N., Bartoletti, M., Cimoli, T.: A survey of attacks on Ethereum smart contracts (SoK). In: Maffei, M., Ryan, M. (eds.) POST 2017. LNCS, vol. 10204, pp. 164–186. Springer, Heidelberg (2017). https://doi.org/10.1007/978-3-662-54455-6_8

2. Béres, F., Seres, I.A., Benczúr, A.A., Quintyne-Collins, M.: Blockchain is Watching You: Profiling and Deanonymizing Ethereum Users. CoRR (2020)

3. Bistarelli, S., Mantilacci, M., Santancini, P., Santini, F.: An end-to-end voting-system based on bitcoin. In: SAC. ACM (2017)

4. Croman, K., et al.: On scaling decentralized blockchains. In: Clark, J., Meiklejohn, S., Ryan, P.Y.A., Wallach, D., Brenner, M., Rohloff, K. (eds.) FC 2016. LNCS, vol. 9604, pp. 106–125. Springer, Heidelberg (2016). https://doi.org/10.1007/978-3-662-53357-4_8

5. Dimitriou, T.: Efficient, coercion-free and universally verifiable blockchain-based voting. Comput. Netw. (2020)

6. Duffield, E., Diaz, D.: Dash: A Payments-Focused Cryptocurrency (2018). https://github.com/dashpay/dash/wiki/Whitepaper. Accessed 26 Oct 2020

7. Fröwis, M., Fuchs, A., Böhme, R.: Detecting token systems on Ethereum. In: Goldberg, I., Moore, T. (eds.) FC 2019. LNCS, vol. 11598, pp. 93–112. Springer, Cham (2019). https://doi.org/10.1007/978-3-030-32101-7_7

8. Heiberg, S., Kubjas, I., Siim, J., Willemson, J.: On Trade-offs of Applying Block Chains for Electronic Voting Bulletin Boards. E-Vote-ID (2018)

9. Henry, R., Herzberg, A., Kate, A.: Blockchain access privacy: challenges and directions. IEEE Secur. Priv. (2018)

10. Hjalmarsson, F.P., Hreioarsson, G.K., Hamdaqa, M., Hjálmtýsson, G.: Blockchain-based e-voting system. In: IEEE CLOUD (2018)

11. Jentzsch, C.: Decentralized Autonomous Organization to Automate Governance. White Paper (2016)

12. Killer, C., Rodrigues, B., Matile, R., Scheid, E.J., Stiller, B.: Design and implementation of cast-as-intended verifiability for a blockchain-based voting system. In: SAC. ACM (2020)

13. Kroll, J.A., Davey, I.C., Felten, E.W.: The economics of bitcoin mining, or bitcoin in the presence of adversaries. In: Proceedings of WEIS (2013)

14. Kshetri, N., Voas, J.M.: Blockchain-enabled e-voting. IEEE Softw. (2018)

15. Matzutt, R., et al.: A quantitative analysis of the impact of arbitrary blockchain content on bitcoin. In: Meiklejohn, S., Sako, K. (eds.) FC 2018. LNCS, vol. 10957, pp. 420–438. Springer, Heidelberg (2018). https://doi.org/10.1007/978-3-662-58387-6_23

16. McCorry, P., Shahandashti, S.F., Hao, F.: A smart contract for boardroom voting with maximum voter privacy. In: Kiayias, A. (ed.) FC 2017. LNCS, vol. 10322, pp. 357–375. Springer, Cham (2017). https://doi.org/10.1007/978-3-319-70972-7_20

17. Nakamoto, S.: Bitcoin: A Peer-to-Peer Electronic Cash System (2008)

18. National Academies of Sciences, Engineering, and Medicine and others: Securing the Vote: Protecting American Democracy, pp. 103–105 (2018)

19. Park, S., Specter, M., Narula, N., Rivest, R.L.: Going from Bad to Worse: From Internet Voting to Blockchain Voting (2020). https://people.csail.mit.edu/rivest/pubs/PSNR20.pdf. Accessed 24 Nov 2020

20. Pinna, A., Ibba, S., Baralla, G., Tonelli, R., Marchesi, M.: A massive analysis of ethereum smart contracts empirical study and code metrics. IEEE Access (2019)

21. Reibel, P., Yousaf, H., Meiklejohn, S.: Short paper: an exploration of code diversity in the cryptocurrency landscape. In: Goldberg, I., Moore, T. (eds.) FC 2019. LNCS, vol. 11598, pp. 73–83. Springer, Cham (2019). https://doi.org/10.1007/978-3-030-32101-7_5

22. Reid, F., Harrigan, M.: An analysis of anonymity in the bitcoin system. In: Social-Com/PASSAT. IEEE Computer Society (2011)

23. Specter, M.A., Koppel, J., Weitzner, D.: The ballot is busted before the blockchain: a security analysis of Voatz, the first internet voting application used in U.S. federal elections. In: 29th USENIX Security Symposium (2020)

24. Szabo, N.: Formalizing and securing relationships on public networks. First Monday **2**(9) (1997)

25. Tian, H., Fu, L., He, J.: A simpler bitcoin voting protocol. In: Chen, X., Lin, D., Yung, M. (eds.) Inscrypt 2017. LNCS, vol. 10726, pp. 81–98. Springer, Cham (2018). https://doi.org/10.1007/978-3-319-75160-3_7

26. Victor, F., Lüders, B.K.: Measuring Ethereum-based ERC20 token networks. In: Goldberg, I., Moore, T. (eds.) FC 2019. LNCS, vol. 11598, pp. 113–129. Springer, Cham (2019). https://doi.org/10.1007/978-3-030-32101-7_8

27. Wood, G.: Ethereum: A Secure Decentralised Generalised Transaction Ledger, Byzantium Revision 7E819EC, 20 October 2019

28. Zhao, Z., Chan, T.-H.H.: How to vote privately using bitcoin. In: Qing, S., Okamoto, E., Kim, K., Liu, D. (eds.) ICICS 2015. LNCS, vol. 9543, pp. 82–96. Springer, Cham (2016). https://doi.org/10.1007/978-3-319-29814-6_8

WTSC – Foundations

Mirroring Public Key Infrastructures to Blockchains for On-Chain Authentication

Ulrich Gallersdörfer[1](✉) ⓘ, Friederike Groschupp[2] ⓘ, and Florian Matthes[1]

[1] Technical University Munich, Munich, Germany
{ulrich.gallersdoerfer,matthes}@tum.de
[2] Department of Computer Science, ETH Zurich, Zurich, Switzerland
friederike.groschupp@inf.ethz.ch

Abstract. In blockchain systems, the lack of established identity management processes pose a problem for applications requiring smart contract owners to be authenticated. One issue that previously proposed solutions face is the accumulation of a critical mass of trusted data that makes the system usable. In this work, we propose an identity assertion and verification framework for Ethereum that overcomes this bootstrapping problem. It achieves this by leveraging TLS certificates, which are part of the established infrastructure that is commonly used for authenticating internet connections. We design and implement an TLS certificate-based authentication framework whose key features are the smart contract-based validation and storage of certificates and address-identity bindings. Looking at the current TLS ecosystem, we find that a large share of all domain certificates is issued by a small number of intermediate and root certificates. Therefore, we decide to store and maintain certificates in one smart contract to minimize processing costs. The evaluation of our prototype implementation shows that the associated cost of our system is within a feasible operating range, with the costs of submitting a new certificate currently averaging around \$1.81 and the cost of creating an address-identity binding averaging around \$1.32. Our system is a pragmatic and, most importantly, quickly bootstrapped method for an identity assertion and verification framework for Ethereum.

Keywords: Blockchain · Authentication · Smart contracts · Ethereum · Certificates

1 Introduction

The world wide web relies on public key infrastructures (PKI) to reliably identify and authenticate remote communication partners, enabling the Internet as we know it. The Domain Name System (DNS) allows users to identify and direct their requests to the respective party behind a domain name (e.g., *example.org*) [22]. TLS/SSL-certificates[1], which are distributed securely through the TLS-PKI, map public cryptographic keys to these domains names to enhance the

---

[1] Often, the terms *TLS* and *SSL* are used interchangeably. In this paper, we only use the term TLS.

© International Financial Cryptography Association 2021
M. Bernhard et al. (Eds.): FC 2021 Workshops, LNCS 12676, pp. 415–430, 2021.
https://doi.org/10.1007/978-3-662-63958-0_33

communication by ensuring the privacy and integrity of messages as well as confirming that a user is talking to the intended party [27]. In contrast, blockchain networks, such as Bitcoin [24] or Ethereum [32], do not currently offer a well-established identity management system with human-friendly names. The native decentralized identity management solely depends on private and public key pairs registered on the blockchain[2]. While this prevents malicious parties from directly interfering with transactions, it does not facilitate the authentication of the counter party, as the public key is not mapped to a real-world identity.

Efforts to bridge this gap currently focus on establishing new identity management solutions which are guided by the blockchain core principles of decentralization and trustlessness: No party should be required to solely run the system or be able to interfere with its operation. A well-known example for such a system is Ethereum Name Service (ENS) [15]. ENS allows for the decentralized registration of domain names with the top level domain .eth to be used within the Ethereum blockchain. However, such newly-established and decentralized systems face huge bootstrapping issues.

Bootstrapping is a serious issue for these projects, as they face lack of adoption from two distinct groups: users and service providers, e.g. companies. First, enterprises need to support these upcoming standards and integrate them in their applications and wallets. Second, users need to install and use these wallets, understand the functionality, and recognize the implications of these specific standards. Both groups are hesitant to invest their time and money in these systems as long as it lacks adoption of the respective counterpart.

For that reason, we explore and evaluate the mirroring of existing, established PKIs and their certificates (alongside unique attributes such as a name) to blockchain networks. We rely on a two-fold approach:

1. Set up an on-chain structure to insert and verify the validity of the certificates managed in the PKI, resulting in the existence of trustworthy certificates and their attributes in the blockchain, and
2. enable the signature verification of these certificates, such that statements signed by the private key of these certificates can be verified on chain.

This system allows us to verify on-chain statements[3] made with certificates that bind the respective unique attribute of the certificate to a smart contract or Externally Owned Account (EOA). Afterwards, third party smart contracts can verify whether the binding is valid and commence interactions with the account.

Several different PKIs are suitable for investigation in our work. Therefore, we allow the usage of any PKI that supports X.509 certificates [7]. In this paper, we evaluate our approach with the broadly used TLS public key infrastructure. Certificates issued via the TLS PKI are bound to fully qualified domain names (FQDNs) as unique attributes. This allows us to bind a smart contracts to FQDNs. As 98% of all website visits rely on TLS [11], bootstrapping issues are eased.

---

[2] Often, a subset of the hash of the public key is used, e.g., 0x42Ff4fa0...89024.

[3] We refer to these statements as *endorsements*. The definition follows in Sect. 2.

In this work, we investigate two questions:

- How can naming attributes of existing PKIs be leveraged in a on-chain blockchain context?
- What are the constraints of leveraging existing PKIs in a blockchain environment?

The paper is organized as follows: Sect. 2 introduces the key concepts of the design and architecture of the on-chain PKI verification system. In Sect. 3, we discuss the suitability of the TLS PKI and evaluate key metrics of the system such as costs and fulfillment of the requirements. In Sect. 4 we compare our approach to related work and conclude the paper in Sect. 5.

We refer readers who are not familiar with the TLS ecosystem to [27] and readers who are not familiar with blockchain technology and Ethereum to [4, 25] for background information on these topics.

2   System Design and Architecture

The aim of our system is to enable users or smart contracts to verify that an Ethereum account (an EOA or a smart contract) is assigned the name attribute of a X.509 certificate. Trusted root certificate authorities sign (indirectly via intermediary certificates when applicable) domain certificates, which we afterward use to create signatures that allow us to verify the assignment of an account to a domain. To verify that such an assignment is created and is valid **on-chain**, we require several components in our system: First, endorsements (Sect. 2.1) contain details about the assignment of an account to a name attribute. The on-chain certificate database (Sect. 2.2) ensures the validity of newly added root-, intermediary- or server-certificates. The on-chain endorsement database (Sect. 2.3) checks the attribution as well as context-dependent properties of the respective certificates such as time or trusted root certificates[4].

2.1   Endorsement

We define the endorsement of an Ethereum address as the signature of the address value together with optional associated data. An endorsement indicates that the endorser claims to own the address, i.e., that they receive ingoing funds, control outgoing funds, vouch for data associated with the address, and are the originator of outgoing transactions. Endorsements need to present some kind of liability and make only sense in scenarios where an adversary cannot gain advantage by signing an address they do not control.

To standardize the endorsement and avoid misuse, we specify the format and content of endorsements. This means the endorsements must be unambiguous. In particular, endorsements need to meet the following requirements:

---

[4] We provide the option to define the set of trusted issuers to keep the system open and flexible for any other X.509-based PKI.

- An endorsement issued for one Ethereum address may not be reused for another Ethereum address because otherwise malicious parties could impersonate the owner of the TLS certificate.
- It must be clear to which web domain an address is linked, as otherwise no clear attribution is available. The situation when this is unclear might arise when a certificate is issued for multiple web domains.
- It must be possible to identify the domain certificate with which the endorsement was created in order to retrieve the public key and to check the validity and revocation status of the certificate.
- It should be possible for the issuer to specify an expiration date of the endorsement, as a service provider might decide to offer a service only for a specific amount of time.

An endorsement comprises a signature and an associated claim. The signature is computed over the hash of the claim. The claim contains the address account $addr$, the web domain ID_{domain}, the unique certificate identifier ID_{cert}, and the optional expiration date $date_{exp}$. We informally characterize the claim C in (1) and the endorsement E in (2).

$$C = \{addr|ID_{domain}|ID_{cert}|date_{exp}\} \tag{1}$$

$$E = \{C, sign(hash(C), key_{priv})\} \tag{2}$$

2.2   On-Chain X.509 Certificate Storage and Validation

There is no absolute truth on the validity of TLS certificates as different entities might trust different root certificate authorities. Therefore, we need to design a mechanism that allows TLS certificate validation solely based on user preferences and in the context of the Ethereum blockchain. Only if this is possible, we can later validate endorsements on-chain.

To remove any dependency on external systems, the information that is required for certification validation needs to reside on-chain. We call this approach mirroring (a part of) the TLS PKI to Ethereum. The information that is required to validate a certificate is the **whole certificate chain** from server to root certificate, the **set of trust anchors** as defined by the verifier, and the **validation procedures**.

The validation procedure for X.509 certificates can be implemented and offered on-chain as an Ethereum library. It is a security-critical component, needs to be carefully implemented, and the source code needs to be openly available to be trusted by users. As the set of trust anchors is specific to the verifier, each contract that acts as verifier needs to declare their own set.

Due to the nature of the TLS-PKI (which we further evaluate in Sect. 3) we store certificate chains in one central contract. Previously added certificates need to be stored only once. Additionally, if the validity of a certificate and its chain is asserted by the database when it is submitted and only valid certificates are accepted, the validation of the certificate needs to be performed only once and can be shared by multiple server certificates. When verifiers are interested in the validity of an endorsement, they are not required to verify the certificate chain again.

A difficulty with the migration approach is the assertion of the revocation status of certificates. Both common revocation mechanisms, namely Certificate Revocation Lists (CRLs) and Online Certificate Status Protocol (OCSP) responses, are documents that are valid for a certain time period and are commonly signed with the issuer private key and can consequently be verified on-chain. The idea is that the database entries of certificates can be updated with the current corresponding revocation information. This needs to be repeated while the certificate is valid and the validity period of the revocation status information expires. If a certificate is revoked, its status cannot be changed anymore.

In the following, we describe the CRUD (create, read, update, delete) operations for certificates stored on the certificate database contract.

Create. Certificates are submitted to the database one-by-one. Anyone can submit certificates. Before a certificate is stored, it is confirmed that it is valid. This check is performed in accordance to RFC 5280 [7]. As the signature of the certificate needs to be verified, the certificate must either be a self-signed certificate or the certificate's issuer's certificate must already be stored in the database. The validity period of the certificate must not be expired. If the certificate validation is successful, the relevant information is retrieved from the certificate and stored in the database. This includes a pointer to the entry of the issuer certificate; in the case of self-signed certificates, it is the certificate itself. The revocation status information is set to *unknown*. If the certificate validation is not successful, the certificate is rejected.

Any self-signed certificate with valid format and content can be added to the database and subsequently act as trust anchor. This enables anyone to create and maintain their own application-specific PKI.

Read. Certificate information can be retrieved from the database with a unique certificate identifier. The certificate chain can be retrieved thanks to the pointers that refer to the issuer of each certificate.

Update. The only information that can be updated is the revocation status of certificates. For this purpose, either the CRL or the OCSP response corresponding to a certificate can be submitted. The submitted information is only used to update the revocation status information if it is valid and signed by the certificate's issuer. For the CRL, the certificate status is considered as *not revoked* when its serial number is not contained in the CRL and considered as *revoked* when it is contained. For OCSP responses, the certificate status is updated to the status that is contained in the response. In both cases, information about the time of the last update and the expiry date are stored. Once a certificate is marked as *revoked* in the database, the state cannot be reversed to *unknown* or *not revoked*.

Other certificate attributes cannot be updated in the database as all information reflects the information of the submitted certificate. If altered information is required, a newly issued certificate must be submitted with a new unique certificate identifier.

Delete. Once submitted, certificates cannot be deleted. This is because other certificates and endorsements may rely on this certificate and their validity and revocation status cannot be verified sufficiently if certificates and their chain of trust are missing.

2.3   On-Chain Endorsement Validation

To make a decision on trust based on an account endorsement, the verifier relies on three components: 1) The validity of the **signer certificate** including its chain, the **validity of the signature in the endorsement**, and the verifier's **trusted root authorities**. The verifier can define its own set of trusted roots, if they want to rely on alternative X.509 based PKIs. We also need to take into account the context, especially the time of the verification. Both certificates and endorsements contain information about their expiry.

The validity of the **signer certificate** and its chain is ensured by the on-chain certificate storage (see Sect. 2.2) which a potential verifier relies on. As the endorsement itself links to the respective certificate, the certificate and its public key can be obtained cost-efficiently. The verifier only needs to verify that the certificate is present in the database, that the root certificate is part of the previously defined trusted roots, that the validity period has not expired, and that the certificate has not been revoked. These operations are significantly cheaper than performing the full validation for a certificate chain.

The validity of the **endorsement** follows a similar approach: Upon retrieval of the public key of the respective certificate, the verifier is able to check if the private key of the respective certificate actually created the signature in the endorsement. Again, they need to validate that the validity period has not expired and that the endorsement has not been revoked. As this signature verification is an expensive operation in blockchains, we further propose a central database for endorsements to execute these operations only once.

Endorsement Database. In addition to the certificate database, we propose a central database for storing endorsements. Besides the cost-reduction of verifying endorsements, providing a central database empowers verifiers to proactively and conveniently search for endorsements. Such a database query can have two distinct goals: The verifier might either be interested whether and by whom a specific Ethereum address was endorsed or whether there exist endorsements for a specific web domain. In addition, a central data base facilitates the revocation of endorsements. Another advantage is that the endorsement can be validated upon submission, subsequent parties interested in the endorsement do not need to perform the validation again.

The external-endorsement database provides the following functionality:

Create. An endorsement E, as defined in Sect. 2.1, is submitted to the database. The validation procedure retrieves the certificate with the certificate ID ID_{cert}, checks that the certificate is issued for the web domain ID_{domain}, and obtains the public key key_{pub}. If the endorsement's signature is valid and not expired, the endorsement it stored in the database.

Read. Endorsements can be retrieved with $addr$ or ID_{domain} as key. As multiple endorsements per account or web domain may exist, the query returns a set of endorsements. The querying party is responsible for checking the endorsements for one that is signed by a certificate whose root certificate they trust.

Update. Endorsements themselves are immutable information. The only associated information that may change is the revocation status. If the original issuer of an endorsement wants to revoke it, they sign the respective information and store it with the endorsement.

Delete. Unexpired endorsements may not be deleted from the database. Some applications might also accept expired endorsements, therefore, expired endorsements should not be deleted while it is allowed to do so. However, if an endorsement was revoked, the revocation information should persist.

Revocation of Endorsements. External endorsements can be revoked by updating their revocation flag. For this purpose, the corresponding certificate owner can create a "revocation signature" which has the following format:

$$R = sign(hash(addr|ID_{domain}|date_{exp}|0xFF), key_{priv}) \qquad (3)$$

This revocation information is submitted to the endorsement database. The smart contract verifies the correctness of the provided signature and, if the signature is valid, marks the endorsement as revoked. Again, a previously revoked endorsement (similar to certificates) can never be valid again. A new endorsement has to be created.

3   Evaluation and Discussion

To assess our system in the context of the TLS-PKI, we first need to understand the structure and organization of the TLS certificate hierarchy. This PKI is a well established system which is omnipresent in today's world wide web. Since 2013, over 3.7 billion certificates have been logged in Certificate Transparency [18]. As this enormous data set is not really accessible[5], we use certificate data provided by Censys [8]. Censys provides a database of certificates that can be conveniently queried online. We define two subsets of certificates: Subset S_1 contains all root, intermediary, and domain certificates that (1) belong to a commonly trusted certificate chain[6] (2) were added to Censys before the 21st of April 2020 and (3) expire after this date. In total, 204,166,070 certificates fulfill these requirements. Subset S_2 contains the domain certificates of the top

---

[5] Assuming conservatively 1500 bytes per certificate, this data set would amount roughly to 5 Tebibyte.

[6] We use the Mozilla NSS root store: https://www.mozilla.org/en-US/about/governance/policies/security-group/certs/, accessed 09/05/2020.

1,000 most visited websites[7]. After eliminating invalid, expired and duplicate certificates and certificates with an invalid trust path, S_2 contains 869 unique domain certificates. We use S_1 for a general understanding of the TLS ecosystem (Sect. 3.1 and use S_2 to test and evaluate compatibility (Sect. 3.2) and costs of our system (Sect. 3.3). Afterwards, we discuss security implications of our system in Sect. 3.4.

3.1   TLS-PKI Structure

Out of the 204,166,070 certificates in S_1, 3,345 are certificate authority (CA) certificates, 204,162,724 are domain certificates, and one certificate is of version X.509 v1 and does therefore not include this information. We define a level-x certificate as a certificate where the shortest trusted path to the root certificate contains x certificates. In S_1, 153 certificates are level-1 certificates (meaning that 153 certificates are in the root store), 2,387 are level-2 certificates, 203,838,127 are level-3-certificates, 325,196 are level-4 certificates, and a negligible number of 207 are level-5 certificates. This means that the most common structure for chains of trust is "domain certificate – intermediate certificate – root certificate". There are no certificates that are level 6 or higher.

It can be expected that each CA certificate is responsible for issuing and maintaining a significant amount of certificates. To find out whether there are differences regarding the number of certificates depending on one CA certificate, we examine S_1 in a bottom-up approach: We group domain certificates by their issuer and count the number of certificates in each group. From the cardinality of the groups, we can derive the number of intermediate and ultimately the number of root certificates required to cover a certain percentage of domain certificates.

At first, we take a look at intermediate certificates that issue domain certificates and order them by how many valid certificates they issued. The by far most prevalent issuer of domain certificates is "Let's Encrypt Authority X3", the currently active intermediate for Let's Encrypt with 123,826,849 issued certificates, a share of over 60%. The top five intermediates together cover over 91% of domain certificates, eight intermediates are required for 95% and 26 for 99%.

Of course, these numbers do not represent the total numbers of CA certificates required to cover the domain certificates as we must take root certificates and, in case of chains containing more than three certificates, additional intermediate certificates in account. A first look at the data shows that root certificates do not scale quite as well as the intermediate certificates: The top six intermediate certificates are all signed by unique roots. This means that in total, $2 \times 6 = 12$ CA certificates are required to cover 93% of certificates. A share of 98% of certificates can be covered by 37 CA certificates, divided in 24 level-2 (intermediate) certificates and 13 level-1 (root) certificates.

The numbers show that it is possible to validate the vast majority of domain certificates even when only a small subset of existing root and intermediate certificates are available. Centralizing the validation and storage of certificates takes

---

[7] https://www.alexa.com/topsites, accessed 09/05/2020.

advantage of this property. The addition of a new certificate only requires the validation of the certificate itself instead of its whole chain if the respective CA certificates already reside in the system. A decentralized approach, where certificate chains are stored and validated by independent smart contracts, cannot take advantage of this. Asymptotically, adding a domain certificate incurs the cost of validating one domain certificate for the centralized approach, while it incurs the cost of validating one root, one intermediate, and one domain certificate in the decentralized approach.

3.2   Compatibility

To test the compatibility of our prototype Solidity implementation[8] of our system and to measure its performance with real and commonly used certificates, we rely on data set S_2. Out of this set, we remove certificates whose certificate chain contains signatures that are using algorithms not yet supported by our implementation, such as ECDSA or SHA-384. Our final testing set is comprised of 576 certificates that serve 660 different domains, in addition to 47 intermediate and 21 root certificates that are required for valid trust chains. This means that our testing set contains 644 certificates in total.

We create a fresh instance of our system and consecutively add all root, intermediate, and domain certificates. All certificates are accepted as valid and added to the database. This complies with the desired behavior, as we have only included valid certificates in this test data set. Furthermore, none of the certificates contains a critical extension that our validation routine does not support (as we describe in Sect. 3.4). Considering the nature of our data set, this is a good indicator that special critical extensions are uncommon for TLS certificates and that our implementation is compatible with most certificates.

3.3   Costs and Performance

The usage cost in form of transaction fees of the Ethereum smart contract is an important factor to the success and viability of our system and demand cost-efficiency especially for the verifier. To gain a perspective on the cost to be expected, we once again consider the modified data set S_2 from Sect. 3.2. Although we outline related in Sect. 4, comparative approaches for gas costs remain complex, as the feature set of our proposed solution does not directly compare to other currently existing systems.

Certificates. We submit all certificates in this set with one certificate per transaction. Figure 1 displays the observed gas usage by transaction, grouped by root, intermediate, and domain certificates. Table 1 displays the concrete

---

[8] An implementation of our prototype is available in [10]. The implementation currently supports the cryptographic algorithms RSA, SHA-1, and SHA-256.

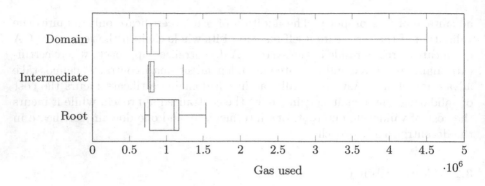

Fig. 1. Amount of gas used for the submission of root, intermediate, and domain certificates in the data set S_2. The graph displays the minimum, median, and maximum value and the first and third quartile of each set.

Table 1. Minimal, first quartile, median, third quartile, and maximum cost of certificate submission in gas usage, ether, and US dollar.

	Root certificate			Intermediate certificate			Domain certificate		
	Gas	Ether	$	Gas	Ether	$	Gas	Ether	$
Min	705,035	0.0078	1.60	750,584	0.0083	1.70	544,777	0.0060	1.23
1st	770,455	0.0086	1.77	762,129	0.0085	1.75	733,073	0.0081	1.66
Med	1,105,114	0.0123	2.53	783,324	0.0087	1.79	793,954	0.0088	1.81
3rd	1,170,981	0.0130	2.67	832,031	0.0092	1.89	903,813	0.0100	2.06
Max	1,537,513	0.0171	3.52	1,233,724	0.0137	2.82	4,503,213	0.0500	10.3

numbers for gas usage, ether and USD cost by transaction[9]. We observe the following results: The median value of the root certificates is the highest. We conclude that this is the case because the majority of root certificate is self-signed using SHA-1, whose computation on Ethereum costs significantly more than SHA-256. The cost for intermediate certificates is quite homogeneous, with some outliers that are signed using SHA-1. For domain certificates the submission cost differs significantly. As domain certificates are commonly issued using the up-to-date SHA-256, the choice of algorithm is not the source of this circumstance. Instead, the reason of this occurrence is the size of domain certificates, especially the number of subject alternative names it specifies. The larger a certificate, the more it costs to parse and validate it, and the larger the SAN field, the more gas is payed for writing it to storage. The most costly certificate specifies 225 subject alternative names.

In Sect. 3.1, we showed that by adding 13 root and 24 intermediate certificates, we can cover 98% of all certificates. Calculating with an average gas usage

---

[9] We assume a gas fee of 11.1 Gwei and a conversion rate of 206 US dollar per ether, as observed on the 30th of April 2020 on https://coinmarketcap.com.

of 1,041,580 for submitting a root certificate and 825,926 for submitting an intermediate certificate, an initial investment of $(1,041,580 \cdot 13) + (825,926 \cdot 24) = 33,362,764$ gas (equivalent to \$75.60) would mean that afterwards 98% of all current certificates can be added and only incur the cost for the domain certificate submission.

Endorsements. The cost of adding an endorsement does not fluctuate as much as for certificates as the only one signature algorithm is used (RSA-SHA256) and endorsements are constant in size except for the length of the domain name. For submitting an endorsement to the external database, we measure a cost of around 577,219 gas (\$1.32).

3.4 Security Considerations

The security of our system relies on three pillars: (i) the implementation of the certificate validation routine and the databases, (ii) the integrity of the TLS system and its certificate authorities, and (iii) the ability of users to map domain names to real-world identities. We briefly discuss these three aspects in this section.

Security of the Certificate and Endorsement Frameworks. We utilized a smart contract engineering process [28] and purposefully designed and implemented our system in a way that does not give one or a number of entities privileges for the system. Once the system is deployed, it is an immutable piece of code. On the one side, this means that our system cannot be subject to any kind of censorship and cannot be influenced by an authorized party. On the other side, this means that errors and vulnerabilities cannot be patched. Therefore, the system must be crafted cautiously.

In the past, the validation of TLS certificates has been a troublesome topic: Many TLS certificate verifier applications have been shown to have critical flaws that lead to invalid certificates being accepted. We aim to minimize the possibility of such critical flaws with two methods. Firstly, we keep the capability of our validation routine purposefully small and support only the most important extension types. Less functionality means less surface for errors and attack vectors. Secondly, we make sure that our implementation does not repeat mistakes that were made in the past [1,6,21]. However, this is no guarantee for correctness and in the future, code audits, further testing, and possibly formal verification should be performed before the system is deployed.

Security of the TLS Ecosystem. In the past, the TLS PKI has been under criticism as all trust is transferred to CAs, which makes them a single point of failure, and CA misbehavior has not been unobserved in the past. However, as the TLS system is widely adopted and "too big to fail", in the past a lot of considerations have been made to improve its security. For example, with the introduction of CT [18], a large step has been made towards the transparency of the TLS PKI and the issuance processes of CAs. It is no longer possible for a CA to issue a fraudulent certificate undetected. Furthermore, due to its wide deployment, the TLS ecosystem has been thoroughly investigated by security researchers in the past and in the present. A system that is set-up newly does not profit from these efforts but still requires trust anchors for bootstrapping and endorsing identity information.

Mapping Domain Names to Real-World Identities. The foundational assumption of using TLS certificates for an authentication framework is that domain names can be linked reliably to real-world identities. This assumes that users have the ability and knowledge to connect a domain name to an organization or person and vice versa. Usually, this is the case as users have experience with using domain names on the internet and as domain names are constructed to be human-friendly, for example by consisting of the company name.

One threat to this approach is *typosquatting*, the intentional registration of slight misspelling of well-known domain names [30]. While these domains are often used to display advertisements on the web [23], they pose a risk to our system. An attacker might use a typosquatting domain and trick users into using their similar domain or count on users accidentally misspelling a domain. However, we deem the chance of mistyping or misreading an Ethereum address higher and the use of domain names as identifying information more reliable.

4   Related Work

In this section we introduce previous work and ongoing efforts with goals or approaches similar to ours. In Subsect. 4.1 we briefly describe several proposals that aim to improve certain properties of PKIs by relying on blockchain technology. We discuss the Ethereum Name Service in Subsect. 4.2.

4.1   Blockchain-Based PKI Solutions

There exist numerous proposals to integrate blockchains and existing PKI infrastructure. However, the focus of these approaches is not to provide identity solutions for blockchain applications, but to leverage the blockchain for improving the properties of (the TLS) PKI. These works are nevertheless relevant as migrating part of the PKI on-chain for Internet purposes has the side effect using the information for on-chain authentication as information is readily available. Giving an overview of all research that has been done in this field is out of the scope of this paper, so we focus on approaches that target Ethereum or Ethereum-like blockchains and include CAs for issuing certificates. Various other approaches [2,3,9,12,26,29,31] do not include CAs in their design and introduce web-of-trust like solutions instead, which means the incompatibility with existing protocols does not solve the inherent bootstrapping problem, or they rely on newly designed blockchains.

CBPKI [16] is a proposal for a cloud blockchain-based public key infrastructure where stateless CAs residing in the cloud are combined with certificate information stored on a blockchain. The approach does not fit our requirements as only the certificate hash is stored on-chain, but not relevant information such as the subject name or the public key, and as it relies on CAs adapting to it and issuing a new type of certificate. CertChain [5], a decentralized and tamper-proof tool for auditing certificates, does not meet our requirements as it is built on a new certificate format, an adapted implementation of Ethereum, and a new type of CAs that also act as miners in the blockchain network. Instant Karma PKI (IKP) [19] is a smart contract-based incentivization platform aiming to prevent fraudulent issuing of TLS certificates: Clients can define policies concerning certificates issued for their domain and CAs can sell insurance against misbehavior. IKP focuses strongly on improving the security of the TLS ecosystem, but does not align with our goals as certificates are not presented to the blockchain unless they are fraudulent and CAs have to take significant action to make the system work. A blockchain-based PKI management framework is presented in [33]. CAs create smart contracts corresponding to store information about the issuance and revocation of certificates. When a verifier receives a certificate, they refer to the smart contract and verify that the hash is contained, that the certificate is not revoked, and that the chain of trust is valid. Just as the approaches before, this proposal relies on proactive CAs. Additionally, a new certificate format is required and only the certificate hash is stored on-chain, which is not sufficient for an on-chain authentication framework. Kubilay et al. introduce CertLedger, a PKI system with the intention of shifting trust from CAs to the blockchain and providing certificate and revocation transparency [17]. CertLedger manages the validation, storing and revocation of certificates. Clients do not validate certificates or maintain their own root store any longer, they simply refer to CertLedger for certificate-related information. In addition, CertLedger provides a transparent revocation system and allows owners of certificates – not just the issuers – to revoke them. While this proposal fulfills many of our goals, it does not allow open participation: The set of trusted CAs is defined by CertLedger board and all validation decisions are made depending on it. This means that (i) the CertLedger board needs to be fully trusted by clients, (ii) clients cannot distrust individual CAs, and (iii) clients cannot add root certificates for specific applications.

4.2   Ethereum Name Service

Ethereum Name Service (ENS) was launched in 2017 and aims to provide a decentralized way to address blockchain resources in a human-friendly way [15] by resolving human-readable names to Ethereum addresses. ENS is curated by the Ethereum Foundation and is described in three Ethereum Improvement Proposals: EIP-137, EIP-162, and EIP-181 [13,14,20]. ENS names are dot-separated hierarchical names called domains; currently, the only supported top-level domain (TLD) is ".eth". TLDs are owned by smart contracts called registrars. The owner of a domain can create subdomains and transfer the ownership of the subdomains to other parties.

The ENS architecture consists of two central components: Registries and resolvers. As ".eth" is currently the only supported TLD, there exists one registry. The ".eth".registry is currently controlled by a 4-of-7 multisig. It is planned to transfer control to a decentralized account in the future [4]. A registry contains a list of all its subdomains and its respective owners, resolvers, and cache expiration. All Ethereum accounts that support the relevant standards can be the owner of a domain. Resolvers are responsible for translating the domain to an actual Ethereum address.

Once ENS is established, it is a cost-efficient and decentralized system providing human-readable identities to Ethereum addresses. One problem, however, remains: Domain ownership can be acquired through auctions and the highest bidder wins. This means that ENS domain names cannot be intuitively mapped to real-world identities. Furthermore, there is no judicial system in place which would allow to redistribute individual domains, for example in the case of impersonation. The decentralization of ENS and the inability to e.g., recover lost domains can be considered as a second nature to blockchain-based applications, however make real-world adoption difficult.

5   Conclusion and Future Work

In this work, we present the conceptual idea, design, and evaluation of a TLS-certificate-based authentication framework for Ethereum. In our framework, identities can be asserted and verified based on TLS certificates that are submitted to and validated by a central database. Identity owners that want to link their identity to an Ethereum account can create endorsements. An endorsement links information about the account address and the domain name, and contains a signature that was created with the certificate's private key and confirms the identity binding. Subsequently, users can obtain this endorsement to authenticate Ethereum accounts they aim to interact with.

The great strength of our system is that it overcomes the bootstrapping problem: Any identity owner can submit their certificate and endorsement without depending on other stakeholders. Under the assumption that certificate authorities are trusted, we can leverage a massive amount of verifiable/verified identity information that is readily available. However, we also acknowledge that our system comes with drawbacks: The TLS system is considered fragmented and not secure enough by some researchers, our system enables authentication only for certificate owners, the on-chain validation of TLS certificates is costly, and storing certificate information increases the size of the Ethereum blockchain. However, we believe that solutions or mitigations can be found to lower the negative impact of these drawbacks. Overall, our framework serves as a pragmatic and feasible approach to establish a system for the identity assertion and verification on Ethereum in a timely manner.

One main goal of future work should be to investigate whether a TLS-certificate-based authentication framework can be used in combination with an identity management system or naming service developed specifically for

Ethereum. A combination of the approaches could utilize the strengths of both: The certificate-based approach can boost the bootstrapping phase of the system. The information acquired in the bootstrapping phase can then be used to populate the system with further, certificate-independent information. The aim is to make the system gradually independent from the TLS ecosystem, thereby improving the security of the framework.

References

1. Akhawe, D., Amann, B., Vallentin, M., Sommer, R.: Here's my cert, so trust me, maybe? Understanding TLS errors on the web. In: Proceedings of the 22nd International Conference on World Wide Web, pp. 59–70 (2013)
2. Al-Bassam, M.: SCPKI: a smart contract-based PKI and identity system. In: Proceedings of the ACM Workshop on Blockchain, Cryptocurrencies and Contracts, pp. 35–40 (2017)
3. Ali, M., Nelson, J., Shea, R., Freedman, M.J.: Blockstack: a global naming and storage system secured by blockchains. In: USENIX Annual Technical Conference, pp. 181–194 (2016)
4. Antonopoulos, A.M., Wood, G.: Mastering Ethereum: Building Smart Contracts and DApps, 1st edn. O'Reilly Media, Beijing (2018)
5. Chen, J., Yao, S., Yuan, Q., He, K., Ji, S., Du, R.: CertChain: public and efficient certificate audit based on blockchain for TLS connections. In: Proceedings - IEEE INFOCOM, October 2018
6. Chen, Y., Su, Z.: Guided differential testing of certificate validation in SSL/TLS implementations. In: 2015 10th Joint Meeting of the European Software Engineering Conference and the ACM SIGSOFT Symposium on the Foundations of Software Engineering, ESEC/FSE 2015 - Proceedings, New York, New York, USA, August 2015. http://dl.acm.org/citation.cfm?doid=2786805.2786835
7. Cooper, D., Santesson, S., Farrell, S., Boeyen, S., Housley, R., Polk, W.: Internet X.509 Public Key Infrastructure Certificate and Certificate Revocation List (CRL) Profile. Technical report (2008)
8. Durumeric, Z., Adrian, D., Mirian, A., Bailey, M., Halderman, J.A.: A search engine backed by internet-wide scanning. In: 22nd ACM Conference on Computer and Communications Security (2015)
9. Fromknecht, C., Velicanu, D.: A decentralized public key infrastructure with identity retention. Cryptology ePrint Archive (2014)
10. Gallersdörfer, U., Groschupp, F., Matthes, F.: Supplementary Material to Mirroring Public Key Infrastructures to Blockchains for On-Chain Authentication (2021). https://github.com/UliGall/paper-mirroring-pki
11. Google: HTTPS encryption on the web (2020). https://transparencyreport.google.com/https/overview
12. Hammi, M.T., Bellot, P., Serhrouchni, A.: BCTrust: a decentralized authentication blockchain-based mechanism. In: 2018 IEEE Wireless Communications and Networking Conference (WCNC), pp. 1–6. IEEE (2018)
13. Johnson, N.: EIP-137: Ethereum Domain Name Service - Specification. https://eips.ethereum.org/EIPS/eip-137
14. Johnson, N.: EIP-181: ENS support for reverse resolution of Ethereum addresses. https://eips.ethereum.org/EIPS/eip-181
15. Johnson, N., Lau, J., Eigenmann, D., Millegan, B.: Ethereum Name Service (2020). https://github.com/ensdomains

16. Khieu, B., Moh, M.: CBPKI: cloud blockchain-based public key infrastructure. In: Proceedings of the 2019 ACM Southeast Conference, ACMSE 2019, New York, New York, USA, pp. 58–63, April 2019

17. Kubilay, M.Y., Kiraz, M.S., Mantar, H.A.: CertLedger: a new PKI model with certificate transparency based on blockchain. Comput. Secur. **85**, 333–352 (2019)

18. Laurie, B., Langley, A., Kasper, E.: Certificate Transparency. Technical report, 6962, RFC Editor (2013)

19. Matsumoto, S., Reischuk, R.M.: IKP: turning a PKI around with decentralized automated incentives. In: Proceedings - IEEE Symposium on Security and Privacy, pp. 410–426. IEEE, May 2017. http://ieeexplore.ieee.org/document/7958590/

20. Maurelian, Johnson, N., Van de Sande, A.: EIP-162: Initial ENS Hash Registrar. https://eips.ethereum.org/EIPS/eip-162

21. Meyer, C., Schwenk, J.: SoK: lessons learned from SSL/TLS attacks. In: Kim, Y., Lee, H., Perrig, A. (eds.) WISA 2013. LNCS, vol. 8267, pp. 189–209. Springer, Cham (2014). https://doi.org/10.1007/978-3-319-05149-9_12

22. Mockapetris, P., Dunlap, K.J.: Development of the domain name system, vol. 18. ACM (1988)

23. Moore, T., Edelman, B.: Measuring the perpetrators and funders of typosquatting. In: Sion, R. (ed.) FC 2010. LNCS, vol. 6052, pp. 175–191. Springer, Heidelberg (2010). https://doi.org/10.1007/978-3-642-14577-3_15

24. Nakamoto, S.: Bitcoin: a peer-to-peer electronic cash system (2008)

25. Narayanan, A., Bonneau, J., Felten, E., Miller, A., Goldfeder, S.: Bitcoin and Cryptocurrency Technologies: A Comprehensive Introduction. Princeton University Press (2016)

26. Patsonakis, C., Samari, K., Roussopoulos, M., Kiayias, A.: Towards a smart contract-based, decentralized, public-key infrastructure. In: Capkun, S., Chow, S.S.M. (eds.) CANS 2017. LNCS, vol. 11261, pp. 299–321. Springer, Cham (2018). https://doi.org/10.1007/978-3-030-02641-7_14

27. Rescorla, E.: The Transport Layer Security (TLS) Protocol Version 1.3. Technical report, 8446, RFC Editor (2018)

28. Sillaber, C., Waltl, B., Treiblmaier, H., Gallersdörfer, U., Felderer, M.: Laying the foundation for smart contract development: an integrated engineering process model. Inf. Syst. e-Bus. Manag. 1–20 (2020). https://doi.org/10.1007/s10257-020-00465-5

29. Singla, A., Bertino, E.: Blockchain-based PKI solutions for IoT. In: Proceedings - 4th IEEE International Conference on Collaboration and Internet Computing, CIC 2018, pp. 9–15. Institute of Electrical and Electronics Engineers Inc., November 2018

30. Spaulding, J., Upadhyaya, S., Mohaisen, A.: The landscape of domain name typosquatting: techniques and countermeasures. In: Proceedings - 2016 11th International Conference on Availability, Reliability and Security, ARES 2016, pp. 284–289. Institute of Electrical and Electronics Engineers Inc., December 2016

31. Wang, Z., Lin, J., Cai, Q., Wang, Q., Zha, D., Jing, J.: Blockchain-based certificate transparency and revocation transparency. IEEE Trans. Dependable Secure Comput. (2020)

32. Wood, D.G.: Ethereum: a Secure Decentralized Generalized Transaction Ledger (2017)

33. Yakubov, A., Shbair, W.M., Wallbom, A., Sanda, D., State, R.: A blockchain-based PKI management framework. In: 2018 IEEE/IFIP Network Operations and Management Symposium, NOMS 2018 (2018)

Reactive Key-Loss Protection
in Blockchains

Sam Blackshear[1], Konstantinos Chalkias[1(✉)], Panagiotis Chatzigiannis[2],
Riyaz Faizullabhoy[1], Irakliy Khaburzaniya[1], Eleftherios Kokoris Kogias[1,3],
Joshua Lind[1], David Wong[1], and Tim Zakian[1]

[1] Novi Financial/Facebook Research, Menlo Park, USA
kostascrypto@fb.com
[2] George Mason University, Fairfax, USA
[3] IST Austria, Klosterneuburg, Austria

Abstract. We present a novel approach for blockchain asset owners to
reclaim their funds in case of accidental private-key loss or transfer to a
mistyped address. Our solution can be deployed upon failure or absence
of proactively implemented backup mechanisms, such as secret sharing
and cold storage. The main advantages against previous proposals is it
does not require any prior action from users and works with both single-
key and multi-sig accounts. We achieve this by a 3-phase $Commit() \rightarrow$
$Reveal() \rightarrow Claim() - or - Challenge()$ smart contract that enables
accessing funds of addresses for which the spending key is not available.
We provide an analysis of the threat and incentive models and formalize
the concept of reactive KEy-Loss Protection (KELP).

Keywords: Blockchain · Smart contracts · Key-loss protection ·
Front-running · Key management · Commitment scheme

1 Introduction

One of the main criticisms over the usability of cryptographic protocols is that of
key-management. This problem is further aggravated in the context of blockchain
systems and decentralized finance, where users need to frequently use their keys
to sign transactions. To add insult to injury, even users that manage to carefully
handle their keys are not fully protected since software bugs or simple human
errors can result in sending funds to the wrong address which might not have a
known associated key.

A side-effect of poor key-management is losing access to the signing key material, without necessarily this being compromised. That can happen for various
reasons, the most common being accidentally deleting a key, forgetting a pass-
word and malfunctioned or even discarded hard disks [27] that make private keys

---

P. Chatzigiannis—Did part of this work during an internship at Novi Financial/Face-
book Research.

M. Bernhard et al. (Eds.): FC 2021 Workshops, LNCS 12676, pp. 431–450, 2021.
https://doi.org/10.1007/978-3-662-63958-0_34

unrecoverable. Several solutions exist towards alleviating this problem, however the vast majority, if not all, are *proactive*. The latter means that users should be educated enough to setup a backup mechanism [6] or to secret-share their key with trusted parties [19] or their social-circle [16]. Unfortunately, these solutions have yet to gain traction, due to the extra steps required, as well as the need to trust someone to hold custody of secret information without abusing them. Additionally, they do not address the second problem of mistyped addresses since such an error is by definition unexpected.

In this paper we address both problems with a single solution, the time-lock based *reactive* KEy-Loss Protection (KELP). On a first glance, reactive recovery looks impossible since by definition the recovering party does not hold a secret to convince the blockchain of being the owner of some locked account. In essence, the rightful owner of that account seems indistinguishable from the adversary.

In KELP, we circumvent this paradox by taking advantage of the fact that there exists information asymmetry, between the account owner and everyone else, on whether a key has actually been lost. Specifically, it is usually the account owner who knows this information first. Based on this assumption, users can claim ownership of any address, but the real owner of such an address has the right within some time to cancel any claim by showing that the secret-key of the address is still available via a proof-of-possession logic, i.e., by signing a new transaction. Thus, a claim can succeed only when the key has indeed been lost, which, the owner of the account is in unique position to know.

A naive protocol, however, is susceptible to two potential attack vectors that should be addressed:

- Front-running: Given the lack of atomicity in blockchains, an adversary can see the pending claim transaction and front-run it by invoking the claim first.
- Random testing: Since a claim transaction does not need approval from the account holder, the adversary can randomly try to claim funds from a large number of accounts.

To address these challenges, KELP employs multiple defensive mechanisms. To protect against front-running attacks, we (a) use a commit-then-reveal scheme and (b) let parties produce *cover traffic* on their accounts [15], by periodically transmitting "fake" lost-key claims, tricking the adversary to front-run them. The cover traffic is then coupled with our protection from random testing, where we automatically require a fee during the claim process which is given to the owner of the challenged address. As a result, an adversary that falsely tries to front-run will be penalized by paying these claim fees, which significantly reduces the incentives and potential rewards of distributed or targeted attacks.

1.1   Background and Related Works

Mistyped Addresses. Due to the irreversible nature of blockchains, transactions can neither be cancelled nor reversed once put in a verified block. Addresses are long enough that many accidental typos have been reported in the past [17], where funds have been sent to accounts for which the private key is unknown. When this happens, it is impossible to reclaim these coins and they are essentially burnt forever. Until now, most of the proposed solutions can only offer proactive defenses and include the following:

- **append a checksum** to the address format. For instance, Bitcoin addresses have an embedded checksum code where mistyping a character would result to another valid address with a very slim probability of about 1 to 4.3 billion. However other blockchains, like Ethereum, do not officially apply checksum protection; but there exist related proposals [11]. A 2018 analysis reported that at least over 12,000 Ether have been lost forever due to typos up to block height 5 million [26];
- **use QR codes**, which have an embedded Reed Solomon error correction to demotivate unfriendly textual copy paste typos [20];
- **address creation with a different script**. Unlike other systems, the account-based Diem blockchain natively supports two different transaction types for (a) generating addresses and (b) sending funds to existing accounts only, similarly to the traditional bank account system [1]. This reduces the probability of accidentally sending coins to mistyped addresses, as the account should already exist to receive funds.

Key-Loss. There exist several different ways to protect blockchain assets against accidental key loss or compromise attacks, but until now there was not a generic solution for users to regain access to accounts for which the key is unrecoverable. Obviously, if the signing key is compromised (or if there is a protocol bug), attackers can directly transfer assets to accounts they own. Pragmatically, there are not a lot of things we can reactively do for the above, apart from initiating a legal investigation or agreeing as a community on forking the blockchain [14]. However, just losing access to the key is a different scenario where although funds remain in the account, nobody can use them. Our KELP approach is probably the first generic reactive solution to cases where the key has not been compromised yet. Before we explain how it works, we need to enlist the current state of the art in key management and account recovering.

Usually, it is a "wallet" that provides the service for users to generate, store and manage private keys of blockchain addresses. These are mainly categorized as software, hardware, paper and website wallets and they provide different functionalities and security threat assumptions. More demanding custodial wallets have also implemented advanced key management and backup processes to a-priori minimize the risk of key loss. On top of that, modern cryptographic and blockchain protocols emerged, such as hierarchical deterministic key generation and efficient secret sharing protocols. Briefly, a list of current key management and recovery techniques is provided below:

- **cold storage**, where the key resides in a medium that is not connected to the internet, thereby protecting the secret from unauthorized access and other vulnerabilities. Examples include writing down the key on a paper and using a safe or offline Hardware Security Module (HSM). Even these however are susceptible to data or hardware degradation under extreme circumstances, and require a secure (and sometimes expensive) process;

– **custodial services**, where one can delegate key management or backup to a third party that safeguards a sealed copy of the signing key. Although, this is similar to the traditional method of using safes or notaries, it requires an interactive (and sometimes slow) process to recover the key, while the maintenance cost might be significant [12];

– **distributed key**, where using Shamir's secret sharing [19], concrete threshold elliptic curve signature schemes or secure multiparty computations (MPC), the key material is distributed to multiple nodes [8]. Most of these solutions are interactive per signing or they are complex in terms of implementation, while some of them do not guarantee accountability on who (from these parties) signed. In [12], a few reasonable enhancements are provided to improve the practicality of these schemes;

– **multi-signatures** *M-of-N*. Some Blockchains like Bitcoin and Diem natively support the so called *multi-sig* or *M-of-N* addresses, a type of signature that combines multiple unique key signatures into one concatenated statement. Although they are easier to implement and solve the accountability issues of other threshold schemes, these transactions are more expensive as they require at least M signatures to be submitted on-chain. Moreover, in blockchains where this functionality is not natively supported, such as Ethereum, problematic smart contract implementations that simulate this logic have caused loss of funds in the past [10];

– **deterministic key generation**, such as the BIP32 [21] protocol, which requires to store or encrypt a single master seed that derives all of the other account keys;

– **social recovery**, like EIP55 [16] where users select a list of Ethereum addresses, called "guardians", which can authorize the recovery of a private key. A similar approach is supported in Diem blockchain [2] via the rotation capability, where an account can delegate the power of its key rotation to another account or smart contract logic;

– **password-derived keys**, usually via the BIP39 protocol which uses a mnemonic phrase, a group of at least 12 easy to remember words, to serve as a back up to regenerate a private key or master seed. In practice though, many wallets recommend writing down and safely store the phrase, and similarly to common passwords, there have been reports of people forgetting their mnemonics [13];

– **biometrics-recovery**. As a solution to weak memorability of passwords, the work in [5] proposes recovery from secret loss by splitting a biometric-encrypted key to multiple nodes. Apart from the limitation of requiring a trusted third party, the recommendation of using fingerprints is questionable, since they are relatively easy to be reconstructed from high resolution images;

– **vault transactions**, a special type of transaction which enforces its output to be locked for a period of time [25]. During the time lock, the legitimate account owner has the option to abort the vault transaction using a secondary recovery key, typically stored offline, providing some form of private key theft protection. In case the recovery key also gets compromised, this effectively blocks the funds from being spent (as both the attacker and the legitimate owner would use the recovery key, aborting all transactions). Fraud proofs [28] also share a similar concept;

- **paralysis proofs** are based on SGX enclaves and smart contracts and focus on threshold or multi-sig keys only [32]. In short, they enable recovery of funds when enough signers become provably unavailable, which results to not being able to satisfy the threshold. To the best of our knowledge, this is the only existing reactive key recovery solution in the literature, however it focuses on a different problem and only works for M-of-N key-structures, but not single keys.

1.2   Our Contributions

We have designed a novel 3-phase time-lock based smart contract that enables key recovery in case of key loss or sending funds to unknown addresses. The major benefits of our approach is that in the best of our knowledge it is the first generic solution that requires *no* prior action from its legitimate holder. Our contract's basic parameters rely on time periods and fees, which need to be carefully selected to mitigate and discourage potential abuse by attackers.

We present our protocol and discuss these considerations in Sect. 2. Section 3 discusses several considerations towards the contract's practical deployment that need to be taken into account for balancing the contract's usability and its attack surface. Finally, in Sect. 4 we show potential contract extensions that are applicable to specific blockchains.

2   KELP Protocol

We provide a description of the time-lock KEy-Loss Protection (KELP) logic, a *three-phase smart contract* that allows reclaiming funds from a locked blockchain address after an account spending-key loss. KELP relies on on-chain time locked commitments, similarly to HTLC smart contracts [29] used in atomic swaps (or layer-2 channel opening/closing) to defend against front-running attacks.

We describe the protocol in two parts: first we present the protocol in terms of generic parameters, and then, in a separate section, we discuss potential appropriate choices for these parameters.

2.1   General Protocol Description

Assuming a hash function h and two time-lock periods t_1 and t_2, a key-loss protection smart contract KELP = (KELP.Commit, KELP.Reveal, KELP.Claim, KELP.Challenge) is a four function logic defined as follows:

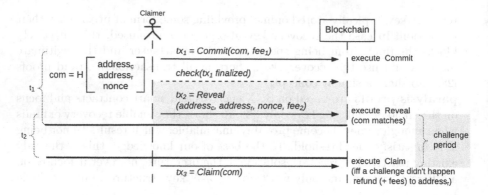

Fig. 1. KELP *Commit*() → *Reveal*() → *Claim*() flow.

KELP.Commit

KELP.Commit($address_c, address_r, nonce$) → com, fee_1 is a transaction which can be executed by any user who wants to claim ownership of $address_c$ for which they believe the spending key has been lost or forgotten. It outputs a commitment value $com = h(address_c || address_r || nonce)$, which is recorded in the blockchain[1] (Fig. 1).

The commitment indicates that, in case of a successful claim, the ownership of $address_c$ will be transferred to the owner of $address_r$. The mechanism of this transfer is blockchain-specific. For example, in some blockchains, funds of $address_c$ can be simply moved to $address_r$. In other blockchains, $address_r$ may specify a new spending key to be associated with $address_c$. In cases when $address_r$ cannot be set to arbitrary values (e.g. when $address_r$ must already exist on chain), an extra *nonce* should be included in the commitment to make guessing of $address_c$ and $address_r$ impractical via brute-force attacks.

For the commitment to be recorded in the blockchain, an extra fee_1 must be included with the Commit transaction. Unlike a regular transaction fee, fee_1 is not paid to miners/validators but to the user who successfully executes one of the Claim or Challenge transactions. The purpose of this fee is to discourage random-testing attacks where malicious actors try to issue claims against a large number of accounts in hopes of randomly finding one for which the key has indeed been lost. The magnitude of fee_1 can be set using a variety of strategies, some of which we discuss in Sect. 2.2.

KELP.Reveal

KELP.Reveal(com) → $address_c, address_r, nonce, fee_2$ is a transaction executed by the user who previously executed a Commit transaction for the specified commitment. The purpose of this transaction is to reveal $address_c$ in the clear

---

[1] Note that *com* can be implemented with any reasonable and efficient commitment scheme i.e., via HMACs, but typically a regular hash function is already available as part of the underlying blockchain's instruction set.

so that, in cases when the account's key has not been lost, the legitimate account owner has an opportunity to challenge the claim.

It is important that the user revealing the claim should wait until their Commit transaction gets finalized to avoid front-running. Specifically, if the Commit transaction has not been finalized, and since $address_c$ is now exposed, someone else (e.g. miner, block producer) could claim its ownership by executing Commit and Reveal transactions of their own ahead of the original Commit.

Before accepting a revealed claim, a KELP contract checks that:

- $h(address_c \| address_r \| nonce)$ is equal to the com value form the corresponding Commit transaction;
- $timeof(\mathsf{Reveal}) - timeof(\mathsf{Commit}) < t_1$, where $timeof()$ is a function which returns time (e.g. as block height) of when a transaction was included into the blockchain;
- Sufficiently large fee_2 was included with the transaction. The appropriate magnitude of fee_2 can be set using a variety of strategies, some of which we discuss in Sect. 2.2.
- There are no active claims against $address_c$, or if there are, the new claim can override the currently active claim. We say that claim A can override claim B if $timeof(\mathsf{Commit}_A) < timeof(\mathsf{Commit}_B)$.

More informally, for a claim to be accepted by the contract, the Reveal transaction must be executed within t_1 period of the corresponding Commit, it must include a large enough fee_2, and it must be able to override other active claims against the account, if any. This way, only one revealed claim is possible against an account at a given point in time.

If a revealed claim is accepted by the contract, both fee_1 and fee_2 are immediately transferred to the account at $address_c$, however, account ownership is not transferred until successful execution of Claim transaction.

KELP.Claim

KELP.Claim$(address_c, address_r, nonce) \rightarrow com$ is a transaction which transfers ownership of $address_c$ to the owner of $address_r$. This transaction is accepted by the contract only if:

- com commitment corresponds to a currently active claim against $address_c$;
- $timeof(\mathsf{Claim}) - timeof(\mathsf{Reveal}) > t_2$. This ensures that the period allotted for the account owner to challenge the claim has elapsed. For practical considerations of choosing the value for t_2 please refer to the following section, but in general it should be on the order of months or even years.

Upon successful execution of a Claim transaction, the ownership of $address_c$ is transferred to the owner of $address_r$. As mentioned earlier, the exact mechanism of ownership transfer is blockchain-specific. In some blockchains this may include transferring balances between the accounts involved, while in other blockchains, it might update spending keys associated with $address_c$.

It is important to note that the cost of a successful claim is negligible. This is because both fee_1 and fee_2 are added to the balance of the account at $address_c$ upon successful execution of the Reveal transaction. Thus, a successful Claim execution has the effect of refunding these fees to the owner of $address_r$.

KELP.Challenge

KELP.Challenge($address_c, signature_c$) → $cancel_{claim}$ is a transaction executed by the owner of $address_c$ to protect the account from malicious claims. This transaction must include a proof that the spending key associated with the account has not been lost - e.g. a $signature_c$ generated with the account's spending key. However, the exact implementation of such transaction is blockchain-specific. For example, in some blockchains, any regular transaction executed from $address_c$ may suffice, while in other blockchains, the Challenge may need to be a special type of transaction.

Executing a Challenge immediately cancels any potential claim (up to that moment) against the account, and, in effect, transfers fee_1 and fee_2 of the unsuccessful claim to the owner of $address_c$. Assuming the value $fee_1 + fee_2$ is significant, this mechanism makes unsuccessful claims very costly, and discourages users from submitting claims unless they are confident that an account's spending key has indeed been lost or forgotten.

All in all, one can compare KELP to legal challenges, where any body can mount a legal case against somebody else but a claim without merit will be quickly rejected and the costs of doing so should be prohibitive.

2.2   Protocol Parameters

This section analyzes the four parameters involved in the KELP protocol:

1. t_1 - time period during which a committed claim must be revealed.
2. t_2 - time period after which a revealed claim can be executed.
3. fee_1 - extra fee included with Commit transaction.
4. fee_2 - extra fee included with Reveal transaction.

Optimal values for these parameters are highly blockchain-specific and depend on such properties as consensus algorithm (e.g. finality times), blockchain structure (e.g. UTXO vs. account-based), degree of centralization etc. We, therefore, leave in-context analysis of these parameters to future research, and provide only general guidelines and considerations as to how they can be chosen.

Parameter t_1. The purpose of this parameter is to set an upper bound on the time a committed claim can remain hidden. To prevent front-running attacks, t_1 should be no shorter than the time it takes for a transaction to be finalized. However, setting t_1 to higher values has an additional benefit as it provides more opportunity for Reveal transactions to be included into the blockchain. This can protect against censorship attacks where a powerful adversary can try to delay block inclusion of Reveal transactions in hopes that t_1 expires and they will be able to execute Commit and Reveal transactions of their own.

At the same time, setting t_1 to very large values (or even to infinity) is not desirable because it would enable malicious actors to issue a large number of Commit transactions against many (or even most) accounts. These commitments will linger in the blockchain, bloating the state and potentially imposing significant burden on node operators. More importantly, a large number of lingering claim commitments makes it risky for a legitimate users to initiate account recovery via the KELP protocol as it increases the probability that there exists a claim commitment against a user's account which predates the Commit transaction which the user could issue.

Given the above considerations, setting t_1 to a period between several hours and several days may be appropriate in most cases.

Parameter t_2. The purpose of this parameter is to provide sufficient time for a legitimate account owner to challenge an adversarial claim. This period should be long enough for the account owner to:

1. Detect a revealed claim against their account;
2. Execute Challenge transaction against the active claim.

Both of these may require significant time. Detecting a claim may be complicated by a number of factors including physical unavailability of the account owner for prolong periods of time. Similarly, executing Challenge transactions may be delayed by the spending key being stored in cold storage or protected by a complicated multi-sig recovery scheme. Moreover, a powerful adversary may try to censor the network and prevent inclusion of Challenge transaction into the blockchain until t_2 elapses. Long t_2 periods would reduce feasibility of such attacks as maintaining complete censorship control over a decentralized network for prolonged periods of time is increasingly difficult.

Thus, depending on the specifics of the underlying blockchain, it may be appropriate to set t_2 to a period of several months or even years.

Parameter fee_1. The purpose of this parameter is to increase the cost of opportunistic Commit transactions and discourage malicious actors from issuing a large number of claim commitments. In this way, this parameter is similar to relatively short t_1 periods. However, whereas short t_1 periods force such actors to periodically renew their opportunistic claims, relatively large fee_1 increases the cost of every such claim.

An important consideration for fee_1 parameter is that it should not reveal any information about the account against which Commit transaction is executed. Otherwise, malicious actors may de-anonymize the account for which the spending key has been lost and attempt to front-run the Commit transaction of the legitimate account owner. Thus, we are not making fee_1 proportional to the balance of the account in question.

However, it is desirable to make fee_1 large enough to make random-testing attacks impractical for the vast majority of accounts. One strategy to achieve this could be to make fee_1 proportional to the balance of an average account on the network. For example, if the average account holds a balance of \$1,000, fee_1 could be set to \$100. This will make opportunistic Commit transactions against most accounts impractical. At the same time, since fee_1 is returned to the account owner upon successful execution of Claim transaction, such a high fee has a negligible impact on the cost of a legitimate claim.

Parameter fee_2. The purpose of this parameter is to increase the cost of opportunistic Reveal transactions and discourage malicious actors from making illegitimate claims. It is similar to fee_1, however, while the magnitude of fee_1 may provide sufficient protection for most accounts, it is disproportionately low as compared to balances of high-value accounts. Thus, a malicious actor may choose to periodically execute Commit transactions against a relatively small set of high-value accounts (and pay the associated fees), in hopes that if a spending key of one such account is lost, they will be able to override the legitimate Reveal transaction and recoup their "investment".

To mitigate this attack, we need to make the cost of an unsuccessful claim unbearably high. However, since imposing outsized fees at Commit time will make the protocol unsuitable for most users, we impose additional fees at Reveal time, when the account becomes publicly known. This allows us to make fee_2 proportional to the balance of the account in question. Such a proportion should be significant, but its exact value could vary based on the specifics of the underlying network, and thus, we leave it to future economic incentives research and analysis.

Assuming fee_2 represents a significant portion of the claimed account's balance (e.g. 10%), to reveal their claim, malicious actors would need to be very confident that their Reveal transaction cannot be overridden by someone else's Reveal with an earlier corresponding Commit. Avoiding such situations would require a very high degree of coordination between all potential adversaries, and may not be feasible in practice.

Moreover, a legitimate account owner can exacerbate this uncertainty by periodically, at random intervals, issuing "fake" Commit and Reveal transactions against their own account. To potential attackers, this would look like an initiation of KELP protocol, implying that the account's owner lost its spending key. Thus, if there is an attacker with a preemptive Commit against the account, they will execute a Reveal transaction of their own to override the Reveal transaction of the legitimate owner. However, since the key is not lost, the legitimate owner can immediately challenge the claims and receive $fee_1 + fee_2$ as a reward.

It is important to note that the cost of a "fake" claim is negligible to the legitimate account owner. This follows from the fact that both fee_1 and fee_2 are returned to the account regardless of whether the claim is overridden by the attacker's claim or not. However, in cases when the original claim is overridden by the attacker, the legitimate account owner will receive an additional reward in the form of fee_1 and fee_2 from the attacker's claim. This may provide a sufficient incentive for owners of high-value accounts to periodically engage in this "bluffing" behavior.

2.3   Considerations for Practical Deployments

Besides selecting values for the four parameters described above, a real-world deployment of KELP protocol will need to address a number of issues which we briefly discuss in this section.

Optionality and Defaults. It is important to understand that the KELP protocol does modify the trust model somewhat (see Sect. 3 for additional discussion). Therefore, we do not recommend it as a mandatory feature for all accounts of a blockchain. Instead, it could be an optional feature which users can freely enable or disable on per-account basis. The exact mechanism of how to do so is blockchain-specific. In some blockchains this could be done via an account-level flag, in others, this would require a new address format. We, therefore, leave a more detailed discussion of the exact mechanism to future in-context research.

Assuming KELP is adapted as an optional account-level feature, the question arises as to whether it should be enabled by default. A conservative approach would be to have it disabled by default, and require users to explicitly opt-in to use the feature. However, this approach has two notable drawbacks:

1. Any funds sent to non-existent addresses become unrecoverable as non-existent addresses would have KELP disabled by default.
2. It could lead to a relatively small number of KELP-enabled accounts, thereby reducing the anonymity set of *Commit* transactions, and in general, making random-testing attacks more viable.

Both of these drawbacks can be mitigated by a number of blockchain-specific strategies. For example, in some blockchains, sending funds to a non-existent address is impossible by design [1]. Similarly, attractiveness of random-testing attacks can be reduced by higher fee_1 and more aggressive "bluffing" strategies as described in the previous section. We, therefore, make no recommendation on whether KELP should be enabled by default, and leave this question to future blockchain-specific analysis. Finally it is made clear that in the case where KELP is optionally enabled, this contradicts to our original statement of offering a completely reactive mechanism. However, even in such a scenario, the actions required are more straightforward than existing proactive practices, mainly because there is no requirement of complex cryptography protocols, storing and/or delegating secrets.

Wallet Support. Before KELP-enabled accounts can be supported by a block-chain, care must be taken to ensure that there is enough support in the entire ecosystem for this feature. Specifically, wallets which desire to support KELP-enabled accounts should be able to provide the following functionality:

1. Implement a proactive claim notification system and detect revealed claims submitted against accounts managed by the wallet;

2. Issue challenge transactions against detected claims;[2]
3. Issue *cover transactions* by faking KELP commits periodically;
4. Execute full key recovery protocol for a user-provided address.

While implementing these may not be overly difficult in software wallets, many custodial services implement their logic in specialized equipment such as HSMs or with multi-signature keys, which may prove non-trivial to update in practice. Thus, to enable KELP on a blockchain in a backward-compatible way, KELP feature should be either disabled by default, or it should be introduced in a way which would make it impossible for legacy wallets to generate KELP-enabled accounts.

KELP.Challenge Transaction. Rather than having the KELP.Challenge transaction be a distinct transaction type, it is desirable to have any regular transaction issued from an account to have the effect of KELP.Challenge transaction, in that it would cancel any revealed claim against the account. In blockchains where this can be implemented, legacy wallets would still be able to defend themselves against attackers attempting to falsely claim their keys, as long as they can monitor the chain and detect adversarial Reveal transactions.

2.4   Reactive Recovery and Synchrony Assumptions

KELP is a construction that can be seen as a simulation of a special layer-2 construction. The two abstract parties transacting are (a) the owner of the account who lost access to the key and (b) the claimer. The goal of the protocol is to securely communicate the knowledge that the *secret* key of (a) has been lost, similarly to opening and closing a layer-2 channel on-chain, which can be challenged. Obviously, in the happy scenario of KELP, the same user has the role of both parties in this hypothetical channel.

Modelling KELP as such, we can investigate the impossibility result introduced by Zyamatin et al. [31], which shows that recovery needs either a time-synchrony assumption (as we do in KELP via periods t_1 and t_2) or some abstract, potentially distributed, trusted third party (as done in proactive recovery mechanisms [19,25]). To the best of our knowledge, the only channel construction that does not assume synchrony employs threshold security assumptions [4], a classic proactive recovery mechanism, which implies that KELP's reactive recovery approach and synchrony assumptions go hand-in-hand.

3   Trust Model and Attack Vectors

In this section we discuss the underlying trust model and potential attack vectors against KELP. It is important to separate potential threats into two broad categories:

---

[2] More proactive ways to issue challenges include for example an *intelligent* wallet that learns its owner's behaviour (frequency of use), so that it can distinguish between the state in which a user simply hasn't logged in for a while, and the state in which they have misplaced their key, automatically issuing challenges in the former state.

1. Attacks against user accounts which are enabled by the KELP protocol. In such cases, we assume that a user has *not* lost their keys, but an attacker is trying to exploit some aspect of the KELP protocol to steal their funds.
2. Attacks against successful execution of the KELP protocol. For these attacks, we assume that a user has lost their key, and the attacker is trying to interfere with the user's ability to reclaim their funds via the KELP protocol.

3.1   New Attacks Against User Accounts

Long-Range Censorship Attack. An adversary which can censor arbitrary transactions on the network for prolonged periods may be able to steal funds from any KELP-enabled account. Such an adversary can issue Commit and Reveal transactions against a target account, and then censor any Challenge transactions from the legitimate account owner. Once t_2 period elapses, the adversary can issue a Claim transaction, thereby completing the attack and taking control of the user's funds.

Therefore, our trust assumption for KELP protocol is that the ability to censor transactions for prolonged periods of time is not feasible in the underlying blockchain. The exact duration of such a period is defined by the t_2 parameter, which can be made excessively large (e.g., months or years). We would argue that if there exists a party which can censor arbitrary transactions on the network for a period of several years, then the network is not secure in the first place.

Key Destruction Attack. An adversary which can destroy a user's key (or delay the user's ability to use their key for a long period of time), can attack the user's account as follows: the adversary destroys the key and immediately executes a Commit transaction against the account with a now destroyed key. Then, once t_1 period elapses, the attacker executes a Reveal transaction, and eventually, a Claim transaction. Since the key is lost, the legitimate account owner has no way of challenging the claim. A potential defence against this threat is presented in Sect. 4, via the so called *dead man's key*. Also, such adversaries might be disincentivised by the fact that they do not have knowledge on whether the key owner makes use of offline backups, possibly handwritten.

3.2   Attacks Against Fund Recovery

Short-Range Censorship Attack. An adversary which can slow down inclusion of transactions into the blockchain, may attempt to do the following: upon seeing a Reveal transaction, the adversary may delay its inclusion into the blockchain, and instead execute their own Commit transaction against $address_c$ specified in the original Reveal transaction. If time t_1 expires before the original Reveal transaction can be included into the blockchain, the adversary will issue their own Reveal transaction followed by a Claim transaction, thereby stealing the funds.

Potential mitigating strategies against this attack are sufficiently long t_1 periods, and periodic *cover transaction* "faking" KELP commits and reveals.

Random Testing Attack. Malicious actors can proactively issue Commit transactions against a large number of accounts in hopes that owners of some of these accounts will eventually lose their keys and try to reclaim their funds via the KELP protocol. Then, upon seeing a Reveal transaction from one such account, the attacker can issue a Reveal transaction of their own against the same account. Assuming that the attacker's proactive Commit transaction predates a Commit transaction of the legitimate account owner, the attacker will override the original Reveal, and once t_2 period elapses, will execute a Claim transaction, thereby receiving control of the funds.

To further increase the effectiveness of this attack, an attacker might issue proactive commits for accounts using heuristic techniques, e.g. focus on high-value accounts which have been dormant for a while.

Potential mitigating strategies against this attack include:

– Relatively short t_1 periods, which would force the attacker to periodically renew their preemptive Commits thereby decreasing the probability that the attacker's Commit would predate the Commit of a legitimate user (or a commit of another malicious actor).
– Relatively high fee_1 and fee_2 to make issuing preemptive Commits against a large number of accounts costly, and to make the cost of an unsuccessful claim unbearably high.
– Periodic *cover transaction* from legitimate account owners "faking" KELP commits and reveals against their accounts, thereby increasing uncertainty of whether a Reveal transaction can be indicative of a key loss.

Side-Channel Attack. Revealing a committer's identity via spending account and/or transactor's IP disclosure will result in a reduced list of potential addresses that the Commit refers to. For instance, the account address that submitted a Commit transaction might leak information about the committed address, enabling bruteforce front-running attacks to be more targeted. Such information can be extracted by analyzing the transaction graph.

There exist tools for hiding sender's identity, here is a short list:

– ZCash [9] provides sender/receiver identity hiding, but unfortunately it does not support arbitrary smart contracts yet;
– Monero [30] does partial identity mixing by creating smaller anonymity sets, but again no custom smart contracts are supported;
– CoinJoin [22] type of mixers could work as intermediate services, but still one needs to trust the mixing third party entity;
– similarly to CoinJoin, third party services can offer such a functionality via non-disclosure agreements and business deals. For instance, associations might undertake this role in permissioned systems like Algorand [24], Corda [18], Hyperledger [3] and Diem [2];
– indistinguishable regular and commit transactions, as discussed in the Extensions section;

– using TOR and/or VPNs could help on obfuscating the committer's IP address;
– using pre-purchased anonymous tokens as shown in Sect. 4;
– using a brand new address, and ensuring this is totally independent from previous transactions made by the same user.

4   Extensions

We already mentioned *cover transactions* and using a regular (transfer coins) script to simulate a Challenge as potential features of KELP. Here we present several useful extensions of the generic KELP protocol, some of them being applicable to specific blockchains only.

Indistinguishable Transactions. As already mentioned, by de-anonymizing a committer's address, the set of address candidates who lost the key can be reduced by transaction graph analysis [23]. One way to circumvent this issue is by making regular and commit transactions indistinguishable. This will make every transaction in the system looking like a potential commit. A simple approach is to expect all of the transactions to carry a 32-byte metadata value, which works as a commitment (i.e., HMAC) to a referred script. Transactions not requiring any commitment can just attach a random nonce, so that any transaction becomes a commit candidate and thus increasing the committers anonymity set. This is not only applicable to KELP, but a generic obfuscation pattern for other *commit - reveal* schemes where hiding committer's identity is important.

Anonymous Commit Tokens. Another option to avoid revealing committer's identity is by using pre-purchased anonymous tokens [7]. In such a model, selected entities can issue tokens which work as anonymous cashier checks. Then, instead of spending from a UTXO or account address, one just submits a purchased token which carries some value and an embedded gas/fee payment logic.

Dead Man's Key. As a defense against key destruction attacks, one could specify a secondary key for the account - a *dead man's key*. This key can have weaker storage restrictions and can be distributed more freely as its only role is to issue Challenge transactions. To execute a successful attack, the adversary would need to destroy both the signing key and all copies of this secondary key.

Key Rotation vs. Claiming Funds. Interestingly, Diem blockchain offers a feature where the address and spending key are decoupled. We can gain advantage of this property and upon a successful Claim, the committer gets a permission to rotate the account's key instead of transferring its funds to a different address. Among the others, this allows for fully controlling the account's state and not just the funds, which is ideal in cases where this address continues to be advertised in QR codes or shared between friends and businesses, and thus might keep receiving assets after the Claim.

Committing to Sequence-ID. Both Ethereum and Diem use a sequence-ID under an account state, which increments on each transaction as a defense against replay attacks. It also works as an indicator on how many transactions an account submitted until the most current block. If KELP was implemented for these blockchains, we should include the current sequence-ID of the account who lost the key as part of the commitment hash. That would allow for an easier implementation logic to check if any transaction occurred after Commit, which would imply that the key was not lost. Thus, regular transactions would invalidate any active Commit, which makes KELP compatible with already up and running custodial wallets that haven't implement the challenge logic yet.

Customizable KELP Parameters. In Sect. 2.3 we discussed if KELP should be an optional feature or the default logic. Going a step further, we could allow custom values for all of the four KELP parameters (t_1, t_2, fee_1, fee_2) at account level. That offers extra flexibility to custodial or unhosted users to control how KELP works for their account in particular. For instance, custodial wallets who can monitor the chain at real-time, might set high fees for important accounts and smaller time periods for faster recovery.

Acknowledgements. The authors would like to thank all anonymous reviewers of FC21 WTSC workshop for comments and suggestions that greatly improved the quality of this paper.

A   KELP Implementation in Diem Blockchain

In this appendix, we present an implementation of the KELP protocol for the Diem Framework v1.2. The code is mostly a straightforward, but has a few Diem-specific features that we will explain here:

Automatic Challenges Using Sequence Numbers. Like many other blockchains, Diem accounts have sequence numbers that are incremented each time a transaction is sent from the account. Our implementation timestamps each reveal on $address_c$ with the sequence number of $address_c$. In the code for claim, we check that no transactions have been sent from $address_c$ since the reveal. This ensures that any transaction sent from $address_c$ is implicitly a challenge.

Reclaiming Entire Accounts with KeyRotationCapability. Diem accounts support key rotation. Each account a has a unique KeyRotationCapability {a: address } resource whose holder has the permission to rotate the authentication key for a. An account that opts in to KELP recovery must give its KeyRotationCapability to the KELP resource. KELP then uses this resource to rotate the key for a in the logic for claim. This allows the claiming party to completely regain control of the account, not just its funds.

Using the signer Type To Avoid Some Uses of $address_r$. The Move language has a type called signer[3] that represents an authenticated user with a specific address. Our implementation leverages this type to omit some uses of $address_r$

---

[3] https://developers.diem.com/docs/move/move-signer.

from the protocol. For example: we don't need to include $address_r$ in the Commit message because we use `signer` to ensure that a commit and reveal transaction originate from the same address.

```
module 0x1::KELP {
    use 0x1::BCS;
    use 0x1::Errors;
    use 0x1::Diem::{Self, Diem};
    use 0x1::DiemAccount::{Self, KeyRotationCapability};
    use 0x1::DiemTimestamp;
    use 0x1::Hash;
    use 0x1::Signer;
    use 0x1::Vector;
    use 0x1::XUS::XUS;

    /// Published under an account that supports KELP recovery
    struct KELP has key {
        /// Key rotation capability for the account that has enabled KELP recovery
        rotate_cap: KeyRotationCapability,
        /// Size of the commit fee
        fee1_amount: u64,
        /// Size of the reveal fee
        fee2_amount: u64,
        /// pooled fees from commit and reveal transactions
        fees: Diem<XUS>,
        /// Length of challenge period between commit and reveal
        t1: u64,
        /// Length of challenge period between reveal and claim
        t2: u64,
    }

    /// Published under an account that has performed a Commit operation to initiate recovery
    struct Commit has key, store {
        /// sha3(KELP address | nonce)
        commit: vector<u8>,
        /// Locked fee to be deposited upon reveal
        fee1: Diem<XUS>,
        /// Time when the commit occurred
        commit_time: u64,
    }

    /// Published under an account that has performed a successful Reveal operation
    struct Reveal has key, store {
        /// Time when the reveal occurred
        reveal_time: u64,
        /// Sequence number of the KELP account at the time of the reveal
        reveal_seq: u64,
    }

    const EBAD_REVEAL: u64 = 0;
    const EBAD_CHALLENGE: u64 = 1;
    const EBAD_CLAIM: u64 = 2;
    const EREVEAL_TOO_SOON: u64 = 3;
    const ECLAIM_TOO_SOON: u64 = 4;

    /// Enable KELP recovery for 'account'
    public(script) fun initialize(
        account_r: &signer, fee1_amount: u64, fee2_amount: u64, t1: u64, t2: u64
    ) {
        let rotate_cap = DiemAccount::extract_key_rotation_capability(account_r);
        let fees = Diem::zero<XUS>();
        move_to(
            account_r,
            KELP { rotate_cap, fee1_amount, fee2_amount, fees, t1, t2 }
        )
    }

    /// Commit to a future claim on a KELP account
    public(script) fun commit(account_r: &signer, commit: vector<u8>, fee1: Diem<XUS>) {
        let commit_time = DiemTimestamp::now_seconds();
        move_to(account_r, Commit { commit, fee1, commit_time })
    }
```

```
/// Reveal a previous claim on a KELP account
public(script) fun reveal(
    account_r: &signer, address_c: address, nonce: vector<u8>, fee2: Diem<XUS>
) acquires Commit, KELP {
    let address_r = Signer::address_of(account_r);
    let Commit { commit, fee1, commit_time } = move_from<Commit>(address_r);
    let message = BCS::to_bytes(&address_c);
    Vector::append<u8>(&mut message, nonce);
    assert(Hash::sha3_256(message) == commit, Errors::invalid_argument(EBAD_REVEAL));

    let kelp = borrow_global_mut<KELP>(address_c);
    let reveal_time = DiemTimestamp::now_seconds();
    assert(reveal_time - commit_time > kelp.t1, Errors::limit_exceeded(EREVEAL_TOO_SOON));

    let reveal_seq = DiemAccount::sequence_number(address_c);
    move_to(account_r, Reveal { reveal_time, reveal_seq });

    // sweep the commit and reveal fees into the KELP resource
    Diem::deposit(&mut kelp.fees, fee1);
    Diem::deposit(&mut kelp.fees, fee2)
}

/// Finalize a claim on a KELP account
public(script) fun claim(
    account_r: &signer, new_key: vector<u8>, address_c: address
): Diem<XUS> acquires Reveal, KELP {
    let address_r = Signer::address_of(account_r);
    let Reveal { reveal_time, reveal_seq } = move_from<Reveal>(address_r);
    let kelp = borrow_global_mut<KELP>(address_c);
    let claim_time = DiemTimestamp::now_seconds();
    // ensure the reveal was not invalidated by a subsequent "challenge" (i.e., a
    //     transaction sent
    // from address_c)
    assert(reveal_seq < DiemAccount::sequence_number(address_c),
        Errors::limit_exceeded(EBAD_CLAIM));
    // ensure the reveal happened afer the conclusion of the challenge period
    assert(claim_time - reveal_time > kelp.t2, Errors::limit_exceeded(ECLAIM_TOO_SOON));

    // successful claim. allower claimer to reclaim account by rotating key
    DiemAccount::rotate_authentication_key(&kelp.rotate_cap, new_key);

    // return fees to the claimer
    Diem::withdraw_all(&mut kelp.fees)
}

/// Collect all commit/reveal fees in the KELP resource under 'account'. This can be called
///      by
/// the owner of the KELP resource at any time. Note: a transaction that calls 'collect_fees'
/// will also (implicitly) issue a challenge by incrementing 'account''s sequence number.
public(script) fun collect_fees(account_c: &signer): Diem<XUS> acquires KELP {
    let address_c = Signer::address_of(account_c);
    let kelp = borrow_global_mut<KELP>(address_c);
    // return fees to the challenger
    Diem::withdraw_all(&mut kelp.fees)
}
}
```

References

1. Diem documentation - accounts (2020). https://developers.diem.com/docs/core/accounts/#creating-accounts
2. Amsden, Z., et al.: The Libra blockchain. Calibra corp, p. 29 (2019)
3. Androulaki, E., et al.: Hyperledger fabric: a distributed operating system for permissioned blockchains. In: Proceedings of the Thirteenth EuroSys Conference, EuroSys 2018, Porto, Portugal, 23–26 April 2018, pp. 30:1–30:15 (2018)

4. Avarikioti, G., Kokoris-Kogias, E., Wattenhofer, R.: Brick: asynchronous state channels. CoRR (2019). http://arxiv.org/abs/1905.11360

5. Aydar, M., Cetin, S.C., Ayvaz, S., Aygun, B.: Private key encryption and recovery in blockchain. arXiv preprint arXiv:1907.04156 (2019)

6. Baldimtsi, F., Camenisch, J., Hanzlik, L., Krenn, S., Lehmann, A., Neven, G.: Recovering lost device-bound credentials. In: Malkin, T., Kolesnikov, V., Lewko, A.B., Polychronakis, M. (eds.) ACNS 2015. LNCS, vol. 9092, pp. 307–327. Springer, Cham (2015). https://doi.org/10.1007/978-3-319-28166-7_15

7. Baldimtsi, F., Lysyanskaya, A.: Anonymous credentials light. In: Proceedings of the 2013 ACM SIGSAC Conference on Computer & Communications Security, pp. 1087–1098 (2013)

8. Battagliola, M., Longo, R., Meneghetti, A., Sala, M.: A provably-unforgeable threshold EdDSA with an offline recovery party (2020)

9. Ben-Sasson, E., et al.: Zerocash: decentralized anonymous payments from bitcoin. In: 2014 IEEE Symposium on Security and Privacy, pp. 459–474. IEEE Computer Society Press, May 2014. https://doi.org/10.1109/SP.2014.36

10. Brenner, M.: How I snatched 153,037 ETH after a bad tinder date (2017). https://eprint.iacr.org/2019/1128

11. Buterin, V., Van de Sande, A.: EIP-55: Mixed-case checksum address encoding (2016). https://eips.ethereum.org/EIPS/eip-55

12. Di Nicola, V., Longo, R., Mazzone, F., Russo, G.: Resilient custody of crypto-assets, and threshold multisignatures. Mathematics 8(10), 1773 (2020)

13. Duncan1949: Lost passphrase for extra account on trezor (2015). https://www.reddit.com/r/TREZOR/comments/33i03g/lost_passphrase_for_extra_account_on_trezor

14. Falkon, S.: The story of the DAO - its history and consequences (2017). https://medium.com/swlh/the-story-of-the-dao-its-history-and-consequences-71e6a8a551ee

15. Grube, T., Thummerer, M., Daubert, J., Mühlhäuser, M.: Cover traffic: a trade of anonymity and efficiency. In: Livraga, G., Mitchell, C. (eds.) STM 2017. LNCS, vol. 10547, pp. 213–223. Springer, Cham (2017). https://doi.org/10.1007/978-3-319-68063-7_15

16. Guilherme Schmidt, R., Mota, M., Buterin, V.: naxe: Secret multisig recovery (2019). https://gitlab.com/status-im/docs/EIPs/blob/secret-multisig-recovery/EIPS/eip-2429.md

17. Haig, S.: Eth community discuss DAO for reversing funds lost to wrong addresses (2020). https://cointelegraph.com/news/eth-community-discuss-dao-for-reversing-funds-lost-to-wrong-addresses

18. Hearn, M.: Corda: A distributed ledger. https://www.r3.com/wp-content/uploads/2019/08/corda-technical-whitepaper-August-29-2019.pdf

19. Jarecki, S., Kiayias, A., Krawczyk, H., Xu, J.: Highly-efficient and composable password-protected secret sharing (or: how to protect your bitcoin wallet online). In: 2016 IEEE European Symposium on Security and Privacy (EuroS P), pp. 276–291 (2016). https://doi.org/10.1109/EuroSP.2016.30

20. Khan, A.G., Zahid, A.H., Hussain, M., Riaz, U.: Security of cryptocurrency using hardware wallet and QR code. In: 2019 International Conference on Innovative Computing (ICIC), pp. 1–10. IEEE (2019)

21. Khovratovich, D., Law, J.: BIP32-Ed25519: hierarchical deterministic keys over a non-linear keyspace. In: 2017 IEEE European Symposium on Security and Privacy Workshops (EuroS&PW), pp. 27–31. IEEE (2017)

22. Maxwell, G.: Coinjoin: Bitcoin privacy for the real world. bitcointalk.org (2013)
23. Meiklejohn, S., et al.: A fistful of bitcoins: characterizing payments among men with no names. In: Proceedings of the 2013 Conference on Internet Measurement Conference, pp. 127–140 (2013)
24. Micali, S.: ALGORAND: the efficient and democratic ledger. CoRR (2016). http://arxiv.org/abs/1607.01341
25. Möser, M., Eyal, I., Gün Sirer, E.: Bitcoin covenants. In: Clark, J., Meiklejohn, S., Ryan, P.Y.A., Wallach, D., Brenner, M., Rohloff, K. (eds.) FC 2016. LNCS, vol. 9604, pp. 126–141. Springer, Heidelberg (2016). https://doi.org/10.1007/978-3-662-53357-4_9
26. Pfeffer, J.: Over 12,000 ether are lost forever due to typos (2018). https://media.consensys.net/over-12-000-ether-are-lost-forever-due-to-typos-f6ccc35432f8
27. Pollock, D.: Infamous discarded hard drive holding 7,500 bitcoins would be worth $80 million today (2017). https://cointelegraph.com/news/infamous-discarded-hard-drive-holding-7500-bitcoins-would-be-worth-80-million-today
28. Ruffing, T., Kate, A., Schröder, D.: Liar, liar, coins on fire! Penalizing equivocation by loss of bitcoins. In: Proceedings of the 22nd ACM SIGSAC Conference on Computer and Communications Security, CCS 2015, pp. 219–230. Association for Computing Machinery, New York (2015). https://doi.org/10.1145/2810103.2813686
29. TierNolan: Bitcoin wiki: Atomic cross-chain trading (2013). https://en.bitcoin.it/wiki/Atomic_swap
30. Van Saberhagen, N.: Cryptonote v 2.0 (2013). https://cryptonote.org/whitepaper.pdf
31. Zamyatin, A., et al.: SoK: communication across distributed ledgers. Cryptology ePrint Archive, Report 2019/1128 (2019). https://eprint.iacr.org/2019/1128
32. Zhang, F., Daian, P., Kaptchuk, G., Bentov, I., Miers, I., Juels, A.: Paralysis proofs: secure access-structure updates for cryptocurrencies and more. Cryptology ePrint Archive, Report 2018/096 (2018). https://eprint.iacr.org/2018/096

Merkle Trees Optimized for Stateless Clients in Bitcoin

Bolton Bailey[✉] and Suryanarayana Sankagiri

University of Illinois Urbana-Champaign, Champaign, IL, USA
boltonb2@illinois.edu

Abstract. The ever-growing size of the Bitcoin UTXO state is a factor preventing nodes with limited storage capacity from validating transactions. Cryptographic accumulators, such as Merkle trees, offer a viable solution to the problem. Full nodes create a Merkle tree from the UTXO set, while stateless nodes merely store the root of the Merkle tree. When provided with a proof, stateless nodes can verify that a transaction's inputs belong to the UTXO set. In this work, we present a systematic study of Merkle tree based accumulators, with a focus on factors that reduce the proof size. Based on the observation that UTXOs typically have a short lifetime, we propose that recent UTXOs be co-located in the tree. When proofs for different transactions are batched, such a design reduces the per-transaction proof size. We provide details of our implementation of this idea, describing certain optimizations that further reduce the proof size in practice. On Bitcoin data before August 2019, we show that our design achieves a 4.6x reduction in proof size vis-a-vis UTREEXO [10], which is a different Merkle-tree based system designed to support stateless nodes.

1 Introduction

Bitcoin and other cryptocurrencies are peer-to-peer systems, designed to maintain an ordered ledger of transactions. Peers participate in a blockchain protocol to come to a consensus on the *state* of the ledger. Roughly speaking, the state specifies the amount of currency each public key has in the system. A peer that stores the state can validate a transaction, i.e., check whether it double spends a coin, or whether it leads to some account balance going negative. In Bitcoin, the state of the system consists of the set of unspent transaction outputs (UTXOs) at any given time. Every transaction spends some UTXOs (except coinbase transactions), and generates new ones in turn. The state is updated after each block by deleting the spent UTXOs and adding the newly generated ones.

The size of the state in any cryptocurrency system can be quite large, making it difficult for peers to store the entire state. For example, in Bitcoin, the state currently contains about 70 million UTXOs, which requires about four gigabytes

© International Financial Cryptography Association 2021
M. Bernhard et al. (Eds.): FC 2021 Workshops, LNCS 12676, pp. 451–466, 2021.
https://doi.org/10.1007/978-3-662-63958-0_35

(GB) to store, and is expected to keep growing with time. This is a major scalability issue for cryptocurrencies. A *stateless cryptocurrency* system, built around a *cryptographic accumulator scheme*, is a promising solution to this issue. It works on the principle that storing the entire state is not a necessity for a peer to verify transactions; it can do so if it is provided with a *proof* that the transaction is consistent with the current state. In such a system, a *stateless client* merely stores an *accumulator*, which is a compact representation of the state. When provided with a *witness* of a particular UTXO, it can prove for itself that the UTXO is part of the state. A computationally bounded adversary cannot generate a witness for a UTXO that is not part of the state.

A cryptographic accumulator scheme can be thought of as a primitive that is a generalization of a hash function. Like a hash, it provides a compact representation of a set of values, which is also binding. In addition, it also provides the means of generating short witnesses for each element in the set (or a subset of elements); a hash function does not have this feature. The witnesses and the accumulator together act as a proof that the element is part of the set. For a formal definition of cryptographic accumulators and a survey of different designs, see [8]. An accumulator scheme is *dynamic* if it supports additions and deletions from the accumulated set. Specifically, given only the witness for a particular element and the accumulator, a party can compute the accumulator of the new set with the element deleted. Moreover, given the accumulator, a party can compute the accumulator of the new set with any element added. To enable a stateless cryptocurrency, we need dynamic accumulators.

In this work, we study the design of Merkle tree based accumulator schemes (henceforth, simply referred to as Merkle trees) for stateless clients in Bitcoin. Here, the accumulated set is the set of UTXOs, i.e., the state of the system. A Merkle tree is (typically) a binary tree, with each tree node containing hash pointers to its children. The leaf nodes contain hash pointers to the UTXOs. The hash of the root node of the tree is the accumulator, which stateless peers store. Any change in the UTXO set is reflected in the accumulator. The witness (or proof) of a UTXO consists of the branch of tree nodes from the corresponding leaf to the root node. A stateless peer verifies the proof of a UTXO by checking that the leaf node has a hash pointer to the UTXO, the root node's hash equals the accumulator, and the internal hashes in the proof are consistent. More generally, the proof for a subset of UTXOs is a sub-tree of the entire Merkle tree. We refer the reader to Chapter 1 of [16] for a detailed description of Merkle trees.

The use of Merkle trees as accumulators is well known, and the idea of using them to enable stateless cryptocurrencies has also been around since at least 2010 [15]. Recently, the UTREEXO project [10] applied this idea to real Bitcoin data. Their proposed system consists of *bridge servers* and *stateless clients*. The bridge servers store the whole Merkle tree, while stateless clients store a small number of hashes of the tree nodes. For every block that arrives in the system, a bridge server provides stateless clients the required sub-tree to prove that the UTXOs consumed by transactions in the block are part of the state. An important aspect of UTREEXO's design is that the size of the witnesses is small enough for it to be viable in practice. This is remarkable given that theoretically speaking, proof sizes for Merkle trees can be quite large; in fact, this is cited as a major drawback of such schemes [3]. The average proof size required per block is an important metric to minimize, as it is a communication and storage overhead for a stateless cryptocurrency system.

1.1 Our Contributions

In this work, we explore whether it is possible to further reduce the proof size required in a stateless Bitcoin system, by altering the construction of the Merkle tree. We identify two factors that influence the batched proof size. The first factor is the height of the Merkle tree. The height of a balanced (binary) tree with n elements is $\Theta(\log n)$. The total proof size for k elements is thus $O(k \log n)$. The design of UTREEXO keeps the tree balanced [10]. The second factor is the location of the UTXOs for which a batch proof is sought. When considering multiple elements, their individual witnesses (proofs) may have some overlapping tree nodes. These nodes need not be repeated in the proof data provided for a single block. The batched proof size is minimized if the leaves whose proof we require are co-located in the tree.

While it is possible to design the Merkle tree such that it is balanced with certainty, one cannot say the same when it comes to co-locating UTXOs that will be spent together. Indeed, when a new UTXO is added to the tree, it may be spent at any time in the future. Thus, the worst-case proof size for proving a batch of k among n UTXOs cannot be better than $\Theta(k \log n)$. The main insight of our work is that if we analyze *average-case proof sizes* instead of worst-case proof sizes, we can build a system that does much better in practice.

Empirical analysis of Bitcoin data reveals that most UTXOs have very short lifetimes (see Fig. 2 in [10]). Stated differently, a large fraction of the UTXOs being spent in a block are likely to be recently added. By arranging UTXOs in the Merkle tree in the same order in which they arrive in the system, it is likely that a large fraction of the UTXOs being spent are co-located. This simple design leads to a significant reduction in the batch proof size, on average.

To elaborate, our contributions are twofold:

- We develop a probabilistic model where the lifetimes of UTXOs have a power-law distribution with index α, consistent with their empirically observed statistics. Under this model, we prove that the batch proof size required per block is $O(d + k^\alpha)$, where d is the depth of the tree, and k is the number of UTXOs added per block. This is proven in Sect. 2.

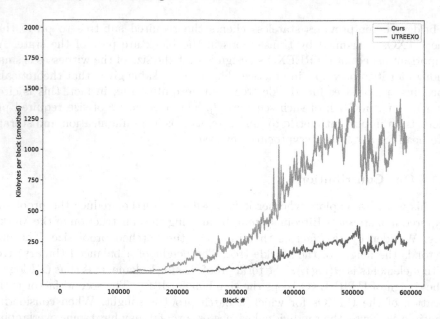

Fig. 1. The size of the proof data required to validate each block in Bitcoin, shown for our implementation and UTREEXO. The plot is smoothed by taking a rolling average over 1000 blocks. The plot is shown for blocks up to height 591,000, which corresponds to August 2019. Totaled over this duration, the UTREEXO proof size is 269.3 GB, whereas ours is 58.2 GB, about a 4.6 factor smaller than UTREEXO. Note that this data does not include hashes of TXOs included in blocks.

- We build a system implementation of our idea in Go, based on the open-source UTREEXO project [10]. In particular, we implement a Merkle Trie, wherein UTXOs are kept in the order in which they arrive. We demonstrate that our design significantly outperforms UTREEXO in terms of the average proof-size required per block (see Fig. 1). The implementation details of our system are given in Sect. 3.

We now take a closer look at the extent to which co-location helps in reducing the batch proof size. Consider the examples given in Fig. 2. Both images highlight the branches of the Merkle tree required to prove the existence of three UTXOs. In the first, the relevant UTXOs are spaced apart, while in the second, they are co-located. One can observe that the total number of nodes to be included in the proof is larger when the UTXOs are spaced farther apart. Indeed, when all k UTXOs being proven are adjacent and the tree is balanced with depth d, the proof size reduces to $O(d + k)$. This is because the smallest sub-tree containing the k pertinent leaves has size $O(k)$, and the branch leading down to the sub-tree is of length at most d. The remarkable and somewhat surprising result of Sect. 2 is that we get nearly the same order complexity even when the UTXOs being proven are randomly chosen (with appropriate assumptions on the distribution).

Remark 1. The term 'node' is reserved for a vertex in the Merkle tree, which contains hash pointers to its children. For individuals participating in the system, we use the terms 'peer', 'server', 'client'.

1.2   Related Work

The concept of a stateless cryptocurrency seems to originate in the bitcointalk.org forum[1]. Miller was the first to suggest red-black Merkle trees as an accumulator for bitcoin state in[2].

The main point of comparison for this paper is UTREEXO [10], the project off of which our code is based. The UTREEXO paper considers a few techniques that we did not, including client-side caching of Merkle tree data to reduce proof size and including the block hash in the leaves to harden against collision attacks. An interesting direction for future work might be to see if these concepts can be ported to our system.

Non-Hash Based Accumulators. Other forms of cryptographic accumulators exist that are not based on Merkle trees. These include hidden order group accumulators, which depend on the RSA assumption or groups of unknown order. This line of work originated with [1]. Progress has been made on these types of accumulators on several fronts: [4] shows how to create dynamic accumulators under this scheme. [13] allowed non-membership proofs. [3] showed how to batch groups of operations on these accumulators to make the proofs smaller. This work, as well as [5], expanded these ideas to vector commitments, which allow for commitments to key-value stores. A downside of many of these constructions is that to instantiate them over an RSA group requires a trusted setup. To avoid this, [14] and [9] show how constructions of class groups can be used that do not require this setup - although operations in class groups use more expensive number-theoretic operations. [6] avoid this in a different way - they show how a multi-party computation to generate an RSA modulus which remains secure if any of the participants are honest.

---

[1] https://bitcointalk.org/index.php?topic=505.0.
[2] https://bitcointalk.org/index.php?topic=101734.0.

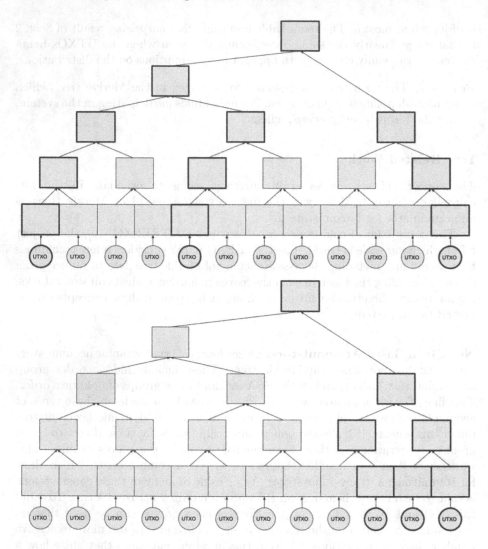

Fig. 2. Two examples, one where we require the proof of three elements that are spread out over the Merkle tree, one where the three elements are close together. The figure demonstrates the value of having proved elements close together in the tree: The total proof size is less for the bottom tree.

Other accumulators are based on bilinear curve pairings [11,17]. These types of accumulators also have very small proof sizes, but they also rely on trusted setups.

Ultimately, these accumulators have benefits over Merkle trees in that they have constant proof sizes, but they have some drawbacks: They require big-integer arithmetic operations that may take time, they are based on more recent cryptographic assumptions, and they are not post-quantum secure.

2   Average-Case Hash Accumulator Complexity

In this section, we will describe constructions for accumulators. We will then introduce an idealized probabilistic model for arrival of and sending of transactions. We will then prove some theorems about the average case performance of various accumulators under this model.

2.1   Accumulators

As stated in the introduction, our approach to constructing practically efficient Merkle tree accumulators is to, as much as possible, cause UTXOs that are spent in the same block to be co-located in the tree. One observation made by UTREEXO was that UTXO durations in the blockchain tend to follow a power-law pattern, which results in the most recently added UTXOs being the most likely to be spent in any block. With this is mind, it is prudent to consider designs that will keep all UTXOs in the tree in the order in which they were inserted, so that the most recently added UTXOs will all be co-located in the right side of the tree. We discuss a few designs for Merkle trees and the extent to which they accomplish this.

UTREEXO. The UTREEXO accumulator maintains a list of at most $\log_2 n$ perfect binary Merkle trees containing the UTXOs. When a batch of elements is removed, each binary tree decomposes into a set of smaller trees, which are then recombined until there is at most one tree of each depth.

   UTREEXO has the benefit that there is no overhead in the form of tree nodes containing further data beyond the hashes of the children. However, it does not keep the hashes of UTXOs in the order in which they are inserted, since the recombination algorithm will necessarily sometimes switch the order of subtrees. It is still the case that the new UTXOs in a block will initially be co-located immediately after being added by virtue of being added in the same tree - but as time goes on, the recombination process may take them apart. How fast this happens depends on the details of the recombination algorithm, which can potentially be implemented in multiple ways, and which is described in the appendix of [10].

Red-Black Merkle Trees. By red-black Merkle tree, we mean a red-black tree [12] in which all references in internal nodes to other nodes are replaced by cryptographic hashes of the contents of those other nodes. The elements of the accumulated set are stored in the leaves of the tree. To use a red-black Merkle tree as an accumulator for the Bitcoin UTXO set, a counter is maintained that tracks the total number of TXOs ever added to the state, and each new TXO is keyed with the next number. To perform a batch addition of k UTXOs to the tree, one first creates a red-black tree out of the k new leaves, then joins this with the existing tree. Note that the time to add a new collection of k elements to the right of an n leaf red-black tree is $O(\log(n))$ (see [2] Lemma 2) and the proof size is therefore also $O(\log(n))$.

As we have mentioned, Miller introduced the idea of using a red-black Merkle tree as an accumulator for Bitcoin UTXOs in a forum post. The benefit of red-black Merkle trees is that they are self-balancing and therefore have depth that is logarithmic in their size. They therefore achieve the worst case bound on batch proof size of $O(k \log n)$, where n is the state size. However, they have some drawbacks. One is that the set of nodes required to prove a collection of members of the accumulator is sometimes less than the set of nodes required to delete those members - the deletion process may require "rotations" which necessitate additional data. Another drawback is that, while the depth of the red-black tree is $O(\log n)$, the number of nodes in a tree of depth d can range from $2^{d/2}$ to 2^d, which makes analysis of the efficiency of the accumulator hard. Merkleizations of other self-balancing trees such as AVL trees could also be considered, but they have many of the same properties we will just focus on red-black trees here. An implementation of red-black Merkle trees exists[3].

Insertion-Order Indexed Merkle Tries. A Merkle trie, or Merkle Patricia tree, is another cryptographic accumulator. Analogous to red-black Merkle trees, a Merkle trie is a trie [7] in which references in internal nodes to other nodes are replaced by hashes.

Merkle tries are used in the Ethereum protocol [18], which, unlike Bitcoin, uses an account model rather than a UTXO model. Nevertheless, we can adapt the data structure for use in tracking UTXOs in the same way as we do for the red-black Merkle tree: We maintain a counter of the number of UTXOs that have been added to the trie and assign numbers to each new UTXO using the counter.

A drawback of this scheme is that we do not have the same guarantee that the depth of the trie will be $O(\log(n))$ where n is the number of elements of the accumulated set as we do for the balanced trees. Instead, we have a max depth of $O(\log(N))$ where N is the total number of elements that have ever passed through the accumulator - for Bitcoin, the difference in these numbers is only about a factor of 10, so there is not a big difference in the logarithms of these values. We will show, under some assumptions, that this difference does not affect the asymptotics of the proof size in the average case. Nevertheless, the trie algorithm is less complex, and the trie seems to be more efficient in practice (see Sect. 3 for details). Tries also have the useful property that the collection of proofs of a batch can be used by a stateless client to delete that batch.

2.2 A Model for Transaction Durations

The theoretical work for this paper will frame a blockchain in terms of a random process of transaction outputs which enter and leave the blockchain at specific

---

[3] https://github.com/amiller/redblackmerkle.

block numbers. Specifically, let $k_{i,t}$ be the number of t-duration-TXOs introduced in block i, (that is, the number of TXOs that were created in block i and spent in block $i + t$. Our theorems will depend on some idealized assumptions about the distribution of $k_{i,t}$:

Assumption 1. *The total number of TXOs entering the blockchain in a given block $k = \sum_{t=1}^{\infty} k_{i,t}$ is constant.*

This assumption reflects that fact that Bitcoin and other cryptocurrencies, by virtue of having a maximum block size, have a fixed cap on the number of TXOs that can be introduced in a block.

Assumption 2. *The duration for an individual TXO within a block is independent of other TXOs and is zeta-distributed. That is, the probability that a TXO will last t blocks is*

$$t^{-\alpha}/\zeta(\alpha)$$

for some $\alpha > 1$ fixed across all TXOs and blocks.

This assumption reflects the observation that there appears to be a power-law effect in the number of t-duration-TXOs [10].

Note that under these assumptions, taking $1 < \alpha < 2$, the state size of the blockchain will grow without bound (but sublinearly).

Theorem 1. *Under Assumptions 1 and 2, the expected size of the state at block height B is $\approx \frac{k}{\zeta(\alpha)(2-\alpha)} \cdot B^{2-\alpha}$*

Proof. The expected size of the state equals the sum of the expected numbers of UTXOs introduced in each block which remain at block B. Equivalently, it is the sum from 1 to B of the number of i duration UTXOs introduced in the last i blocks

$$\sum_{i=1}^{B} i \cdot k \cdot i^{-\alpha}/\zeta(\alpha) = k \cdot \sum_{i=1}^{B} i^{1-\alpha}/\zeta(\alpha)$$

And from Riemann sum approximations, we have

$$\frac{(B+1)^{2-\alpha} - 1}{2 - \alpha} = \int_1^{B+1} i^{1-\alpha} di \le \sum_{i=1}^{B} i^{1-\alpha} \le 1 + \int_1^{B} i^{1-\alpha} di = 1 + \frac{B^{2-\alpha} - 1}{2 - \alpha}$$

$\square$

2.3 Average-Case Asymptotics for Insertion-Order Indexed Merkle Tries

We will first introduce a lemma about the probability of a TXO being spent based on its rank among all TXOs ever added to the blockchain.

Lemma 1. *Consider the blockchain under Assumptions 1 and 2 at some block b. Let x_i be the ith most recently added TXO (including those added then deleted). Then the probability x_i is spent in the current block is $\le \frac{k^{\alpha}}{i^{\alpha}\zeta(\alpha)}$.*

Proof. By Assumption 1, k TXOs are added per block, so x_i was necessarily introduced $\lceil i/k \rceil$ blocks before the current block. By Assumption 2, the probability of such a TXO being spent in the current block is

$$\Pr[x \text{ is spent}] = \frac{\lceil i/k \rceil^{-\alpha}}{\zeta(\alpha)} \leq \frac{(i/k)^{-\alpha}}{\zeta(\alpha)}$$

$\square$

We will now state our main result, which shows that in the limit as the state becomes large, the expected proof size is essentially the same that of a proof of a single element:

Theorem 2. *Let T be the insertion-order indexed Merkle trie (of depth d) of UTXOs in the blockchain just before block B. Then under Assumptions 1 and 2, the expected size of the subtree S consisting of the branches to all TXOs that are spent in block B is $\leq d + O(k^\alpha)$, where the O hides factors that depend on α.*

Proof. As a simplification, consider a trie T' consisting of all UTXOs ever added to the accumulator, without removal. Since every node in S appears in T' at the same location, it suffices to prove the bound on the size of S', the union of branches to spent TXOs in this complete trie.

For $1 \leq i \leq d$ define n_i to be the rightmost node in T' such that the subtree rooted at that node has depth i. Note that there exists such a subtree for every i: By induction on the depth of the tree, n_d is the root of the tree, and either the left or right subtree is depth $d - 1$. The parent of every n_i other than the root is an n_i, since if the subtree rooted at this node has depth j, there cannot be a subtree to the right of it with depth j, or else there would be a subtree of that with depth i, contradicting the fact that n_i is the root of the rightmost depth i subtree.

We can therefore bound the size of S' by splitting T' into disjoint subsets: Consider the partition of T consisting of the set $\{n_i, 1 \leq i \leq d\}$ and then $T_1, T_2, \ldots, T_d$, where T_i is the set of nodes that are in the subtree rooted at n_i, but not in any subtree rooted at n_j for $j < i$.

$$\mathbb{E}[|S|] \leq \mathbb{E}[|S'|]$$

$$\leq d + \sum_{i=1}^{d} \mathbb{E}[|S' \cap T_i|].$$

Since the branches in T_i in the subtree are of height at most the depth of the subtree, we get

$$\leq d + \sum_{i=1}^{d} i \cdot \mathbb{E}[\# \text{ spent leaves in } T_i|].$$

We can loosen this to put it in terms of the maximum number of leaves in T_i and maximum probability of leaf inclusion

$$\leq d + \sum_{i=1}^{d} i \cdot 2^i \cdot \max_{x \in T_i} \Pr[x \text{ is spent in current block}]$$

The leaves of T_i must be entirely to the right of each element of the subtree at n_{i-1}. The left subtree of n_{i-1} has at least 2^{i-2} leaves, since for the node to exist in the complete trie, its left child must be a complete perfect binary tree of depth 2^{i-2}. Therefore, there are at least $\frac{1}{4} \cdot 2^i$ leaves to the right of each leaf in T_i. We can therefore bound the probability of one of these leaves being spent using Lemma 1.

$$\mathbb{E}[|S|] \leq d + \sum_{i=1}^{d} i \cdot 2^i \cdot \max_{x \in T_i} \Pr[x \text{ is spent in current block}]$$

$$\leq d + \sum_{i=1}^{d} i \cdot 2^i \cdot \frac{k^\alpha}{(\frac{1}{4} \cdot 2^i)^\alpha \zeta(\alpha)}$$

$$= d + \frac{4^\alpha k^\alpha}{\zeta(\alpha)} \sum_{i=1}^{d} i \cdot (2^{1-\alpha})^i$$

$$\leq d + \frac{4^\alpha k^\alpha}{\zeta(\alpha)} \sum_{i=1}^{\infty} i \cdot (2^{1-\alpha})^i$$

$$= d + \frac{4^\alpha k^\alpha}{\zeta(\alpha)} \cdot \frac{2^{\alpha+1}}{(2^\alpha - 2)^2}$$

2.4 Mixed Average-Case Adversarial Setting

It is worth asking what happens if the Merkle Trie accumulator is attacked by an adversary who wishes to increase the size of the proofs by spamming the blockchain. To consider this case, we consider a modification of our previous assumptions:

Assumption 3. *In any block, the number of TXOs introduced is $k = k_a + k_r$, where k_r are chosen according to a zeta distribution, and the other k_a are chosen adversarially.*

We see that even if some of the transactions are adversarial, this only hurts the performance of the algorithm by an amount proportional to the amount of adversarial power.

Theorem 3. *Let T be the insertion-order indexed Merkle trie (of depth d) of UTXOs in the blockchain just before block B. Then under Assumption 3, the expected size of the subtree S consisting of the branches to all TXOs that are spent in block B is $\leq d + O(k^\alpha) + dk_a$, where the O hides factors that depend on α.*

Proof. Following the proof of Theorem 2, we see that for the expected size of the subset of S associated with the zeta-distributed TXOs, the same bound of $d + \frac{4^\alpha k^\alpha}{\zeta(\alpha)} \cdot \frac{2^{\alpha+1}}{(2^\alpha-2)^2}$ applies. The only remaining nodes to account for are in the branches associated with adversarial TXOs, which can number at most dk_a, the height of the tree times the number of such branches.

3   Practical Implementation

In this section, we describe the details of our Merkle trie accumulator, to be used in a stateless Bitcoin system. We first specify the exact construction of the trie, and what parts are stored by bridge servers and stateless clients respectively. We then specify the operations performed by servers and clients upon receiving a block. In particular, we specify how the batch proof for a block is constructed.

Construction of a Merkle Trie. In our design, all UTXOs are assigned a unique index, which is a 64-bit unsigned integer. The numbers are assigned to the UTXOs in the order in which they appear in the blockchain starting from 0. Given that the UTXOs are indexed, it is possible to assemble them into a Merkle trie. There are a variety of ways to create the node data structure[4] - our approach is as follows: The Merkle trie is a collection of *tree nodes*, each of which contains a left hash pointer, a right hash pointer, and a *prefix*, which represents the range of indices of all UTXOs below the node. A hash pointer is simply the SHA-256 hash of a piece of data, which serves as a means of recovering the data provided it is stored in a hash map. Tree nodes are either *internal nodes* or *leaf nodes*. For internal nodes, the hash pointers refer to other tree nodes, while for leaf nodes, both the left and right hash pointer refer to the same UTXO. Thus, a leaf node can be distinguished from an internal node by checking if its hash pointers are equal or not. There is a single root node, which does not have a parent. Thus, the collection of tree nodes forms a single binary tree. The total size of a tree node is 72 bytes, with 32 bytes for each of the hash pointers, and 8 bytes for the prefix.

We now elaborate on the role of the prefix, and how it is constructed. The prefix is represented as a 64-bit unsigned integer. For a leaf node, the prefix represents the index of the corresponding UTXO. For an internal node, the prefix represents a range of the form $[k \cdot 2^i, (k+1) \cdot 2^i)$, for any non-negative integer k and positive integer i. The value of the prefix itself is $(2k+1) \cdot 2^i$. For example, the prefix 8 denotes the range $[0, 8)$, while the prefix 10 denotes

---

[4] https://ethresear.ch/t/binary-trie-format/7621/6.

the range $[4, 6)$. Note that any positive integer n can be written in the form $(2k + 1) \cdot 2^i$ for a unique k, i. Furthermore, an internal node must have at least two unique UTXOs among its descendants, and thus covers a range whose width is at least two. Thus, the range of values below an internal node is represented compactly by a single integer, of 8 bytes.

A bridge server stores two hash maps: one that maps the hash of a UTXO to its index, and the other that maps the hash of a tree node to the tree node itself. In order to retrieve the branch of the tree leading to a target UTXO, a bridge server first retrieves the index of the target, and then descends the Merkle trie starting from the root node. At each node, it checks whether the index it is seeking is in the lesser half of the prefix range or the greater half. If the former, it retrieves the left child of the node; else, it retrieves the right child. In our implementation, we use a combination of RAM and disk memory to store both the hash maps. The reading and writing operations from RAM are much faster, but the total amount of RAM available is sometimes insufficient to store the entire tree. We populate the RAM according to a 'least recently used' rule. Whenever a new entry is created, it is written into the RAM portion of the hash map; if space is limited, the least recently used key-value pair is moved to the disk. A stateless client merely needs to store the hashes of the nodes along the right most branch of the Merkle trie, i.e., the branch from the root node to the UTXO with the highest index.

Construction and Verification of a Proof. In order to verify that a particular UTXO is part of the state, a sufficient proof consists of all the tree nodes from the root node to the leaf node corresponding to the target UTXO. A stateless client, which holds the target UTXO and the accumulator, can verify that the leaf node has a hash pointer to the target, and each subsequent node points to the one preceding it, with the hash of the root node matching the accumulator. However, this is overkill; a stateless client does not need to know the hashes of the nodes along the path. It suffices for it to know the hashes of the siblings of all the nodes in the path, along with the prefix lengths of the nodes in the path. The nodes along the path can then be reconstructed based on this information. In particular, to reconstruct the leaf node, the stateless client only needs to know the index of the UTXO from the bridge server. Therefore, in our implementation, the proof consists of the index of the targeted UTXO, the prefix lengths of all nodes in the Merkle tree leading up to the target, and the hashes of the siblings of those nodes. Note that the number of prefixes equals the number of locations, and that they are provided in the same order in the proof. This suffices for a stateless client to reconstruct the whole branch of tree nodes and verify the proof.

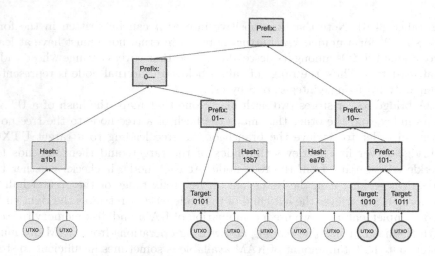

Fig. 3. An example of a batch proof in our implementation. The nodes in the branches leading down to the targets are shown in bold; the prefix lengths and targets from these nodes are given in the proof. In addition, the hashes of the relevant sibling nodes are specified. These nodes are labeled in the figure with their hash. In the real implementation, the hashes are 32 bytes long, and the prefixes/targets are 64 bits long.

Batching the proof for multiple targets provides even greater savings in the proof size. A tree node, which is a sibling of one of the nodes in the proof of a certain target, may lie on the proof branch of another target. In this case, the hash of this node needn't be included as part of the proof. This is best illustrated via the example shown in Fig. 3. If we were only concerned with the proof for target 0101, we would have to include the hash of the right child of the root node. When batched together with additional proofs, this node will be reconstructed by the stateless client, and hence its hash needn't be included. In the example of Fig. 3, the proof needs to include three targets, five prefix lengths and three hashes; without batching, nine prefix lengths and nine hashes would be required (three for each branch). We specify the hashes and the prefix lengths in the order they would be encountered in a depth-first search (DFS) for the targets. Having a specific order allows the stateless clients to reconstruct the tree nodes correctly.

In our design, a further reduction in proof size is achieved by using a standard compression function (we use zlib) to compress the batch proof data. In practice, we observe that this helps compress our proofs by ~20–40%. This reduction is due to the list of targets and prefix lengths in the proof, which are fairly structured strings of bits. In contrast, the hashes in the proof are random strings of bits and cannot be compressed effectively.

Modifying the Merkle Trie. In processing each block, the Merkle trie held by the bridge server is modified by first removing all UTXOs spent during the block, then adding all new UTXOs. Nodes are removed by descending the tree in DFS order, identifying all nodes that will be removed from the tree, removing them, then recomputing the hashes of all nodes whose descendants have changed. Thus, deletion is best implemented as a recursive function. Note that the tree nodes that are modified in the deletion process are exactly the set of tree nodes that are (implicitly) included in the proof. This allows the stateless clients to perform the same set of computations as a bridge server, and compute the intermediate accumulator of the state when UTXOs are deleted.

Nodes are added in a batch by composing new nodes into trees, then adding those trees to the existing trie as subtrees of new nodes. Our technique of indexing UTXOs in an increasing order and ordering them into a trie implies that all new UTXOs get added to the right side of the tree. In fact, while adding UTXOs, only the nodes on the right most branch of the tree are modified. For a stateless client to correctly compute the updated accumulator, it must keep track of the hashes of the right most branch. Thus, strictly speaking, the accumulator is not a single hash, but a set of hashes along a branch. The number of hashes grows as $\log N$, where N is the total number of UTXOs seen until the present moment.

4 Conclusion

This paper presents a new technique for constructing Merkle trees. We have shown, both in a theoretical model and in a practical implementation, that this approach has benefits over existing Merkle accumulator techniques. The code for our project is available on Github[5].

Acknowledgements. This material is based upon work supported by the National Science Foundation under the Graduate Research Fellowship Program with Grant No. DGE – 1746047 and under Grant No. CCF 19-00636. The authors would like to thank Andrew Miller for his advice on the project.

References

1. Benaloh, J., de Mare, M.: One-way accumulators: a decentralized alternative to digital signatures. In: Helleseth, T. (ed.) EUROCRYPT 1993. LNCS, vol. 765, pp. 274–285. Springer, Heidelberg (1994). https://doi.org/10.1007/3-540-48285-7_24
2. Blelloch, G., Ferizovic, D., Sun, Y.: Parallel ordered sets using join. arXiv preprint arXiv:1602.02120 (2016)
3. Boneh, D., Bünz, B., Fisch, B.: Batching techniques for accumulators with applications to IOPs and stateless blockchains. In: Boldyreva, A., Micciancio, D. (eds.) CRYPTO 2019. LNCS, vol. 11692, pp. 561–586. Springer, Cham (2019). https://doi.org/10.1007/978-3-030-26948-7_20
4. Camenisch, J., Lysyanskaya, A.: Dynamic accumulators and application to efficient revocation of anonymous credentials. In: Yung, M. (ed.) CRYPTO 2002. LNCS, vol. 2442, pp. 61–76. Springer, Heidelberg (2002). https://doi.org/10.1007/3-540-45708-9_5

---

[5] https://github.com/surya-sankagiri/utreexo.

466   B. Bailey and S. Sankagiri

5. Campanelli, M., Fiore, D., Greco, N., Kolonelos, D., Nizzardo, L.: Incrementally aggregatable vector commitments and applications to verifiable decentralized storage (2020)
6. Chen, M., Hazay, C., Ishai, Y., Kashnikov, Y., Micciancio, D., Riviere, T.: Diogenes: Lightweight scalable RSA modulus generation with a dishonest majority (2020)
7. De La Briandais, R.: File searching using variable length keys. In: Western Joint Computer Conference, pp. 295–298. IRE-AIEE-ACM 1959 (Western), Association for Computing Machinery, 3–5 March 1959, New York, NY, USA (1959)
8. Derler, D., Hanser, C., Slamanig, D.: Revisiting cryptographic accumulators, additional properties and relations to other primitives. In: Nyberg, K. (ed.) CT-RSA 2015. LNCS, vol. 9048, pp. 127–144. Springer, Cham (2015). https://doi.org/10.1007/978-3-319-16715-2_7
9. Dobson, S., Galbraith, S.D., Smith, B.: Trustless groups of unknown order with hyperelliptic curves (2020)
10. Dryja, T.: Utreexo: a dynamic hash-based accumulator optimized for the bitcoin utxo set. IACR Cryptol. ePrint Arch. 2019, p. 611 (2019)
11. Gorbunov, S., Reyzin, L., Wee, H., Zhang, Z.: Pointproofs: Aggregating proofs for multiple vector commitments. Cryptology ePrint Archive, Report 2020/419 (2020). https://eprint.iacr.org/2020/419
12. Guibas, L.J., Sedgewick, R.: A dichromatic framework for balanced trees. In: 19th Annual Symposium on Foundations of Computer Science, pp. 8–21 (1978)
13. Li, J., Li, N., Xue, R.: Universal accumulators with efficient nonmembership proofs. In: Katz, J., Yung, M. (eds.) ACNS 2007. LNCS, vol. 4521, pp. 253–269. Springer, Heidelberg (2007). https://doi.org/10.1007/978-3-540-72738-5_17
14. Lipmaa, H.: Secure accumulators from Euclidean rings without trusted setup. In: Bao, F., Samarati, P., Zhou, J. (eds.) ACNS 2012. LNCS, vol. 7341, pp. 224–240. Springer, Heidelberg (2012). https://doi.org/10.1007/978-3-642-31284-7_14
15. Miller, A., Hicks, M., Katz, J., Shi, E.: Authenticated data structures, generically. ACM SIGPLAN Not. 49(1), 411–423 (2014)
16. Narayanan, A., Bonneau, J., Felten, E., Miller, A., Goldfeder, S.: Bitcoin and Cryptocurrency Technologies: A Comprehensive Introduction. Princeton University Press, Princeton (2016)
17. Tomescu, A., Abraham, I., Buterin, V., Drake, J., Feist, D., Khovratovich, D.: Aggregatable subvector commitments for stateless cryptocurrencies. IACR Cryptol. ePrint Arch. 2020, p. 527 (2020)
18. Wood, G.: Ethereum: a secure decentralised generalised transaction ledger (2014)

Soft Power: Upgrading Chain Macroeconomic Policy Through Soft Forks

Dionysis Zindros[✉]

University of Athens, Athens, Greece

Abstract. Macroeconomic policy in a blockchain system concerns the algorithm that decides the payment schedule for miners and thus its money mint rate. It governs the amounts, distributions, beneficiaries and conditions required for money supply payments to participants by the system. While most chains today employ simple policies such as a constant amount per block, several cryptocurrencies have sprung up that put forth more interesting policies. As blockchains become a more popular form of money, these policies inevitably are becoming more complex. A chain with a simple policy will often need to switch over to a different policy. Until now, it was believed that such upgrades require a hard fork – after all, they are changing the money supply, a central part of the system, and unupgraded miners cannot validate blocks that deviate from those hard-coded rules. In this paper, we present a mechanism that allows a chain to upgrade from one policy to another through a soft fork. Our proposed mechanism works in today's Ethereum blockchain without any changes and can support a very generic class of monetary policies that satisfy a few basic bounds. Our construction is presented in the form of a smart contract. We showcase the usefulness of our proposal by describing several interesting applications of policy changes. Notably, we put forth a mechanism that makes Non-Interactive Proofs of Proof-of-Work unbribable, a previously open problem.

1 Introduction

At the heart of every blockchain [1] system lives a mechanism that distributes rewards to its validators. The mechanism incentivizes miners to mine in proof-of-work [2] chains and minters to mint in proof-of-stake [3] systems. Additionally, it is an ingenius mechanism to distribute new money when no central bank is present.

Today's blockchain systems employ various policies detailing how exactly the proceeds from mining are distributed to miners. Most of these policies are quite simple. For example, Bitcoin's policy rewards the miner of each block with a *constant* amount of bitcoin, currently 12.5 BTC. This amount is halved every four years. Ethereum miners receive 2 ETH, but the system also rewards uncle blocks [4,5]. A more interesting system is Monero's [6], where a system of *smooth*

© International Financial Cryptography Association 2021
M. Bernhard et al. (Eds.): FC 2021 Workshops, LNCS 12676, pp. 467–481, 2021.
https://doi.org/10.1007/978-3-662-63958-0_36

emission is employed. Instead of *halving* the money supply in a stair function fashion, they slowly decrease the supply block-by-block.

Regardless of what economic policy a chain employs, sooner or later the policy might need to be updated. This becomes necessary as cryptocurrencies are adopted more widely and the community learns about what works better economically. Ethereum's Constantinople hard fork, in which rewards were adjusted [7], constitutes one such example. In fact, as we will showcase in the applications section, some macroeconomic mechanism updates help with incentivizing correct execution of the core consensus protocol.

It is clear that modifying policy is useful and sometimes necessary. But how can policy changes be applied? As the above Ethereum example illustrates, they are easy to do with a hark fork. Indeed, until now, folklore wisdom suggested that any upgrades to the macroeconomics of a chain required a hard fork and were impossible to implement through a soft fork. After all, how can unupgraded miners accept blocks paying according to different rules? One instance illustrating the severity of the problem is a block paying out a higher reward in the new policy than what it used to pay in the old policy. It seems inherently difficult to achieve backwards compatibility when it comes to such drastic changes.

We put forth the first construction which allows policy changes through soft forks. In our path to doing so, we give a definition of what the macroeconomic policy is. Our construction is compatible with the current Ethereum blockchain and is implemented through a smart contract. The mechanism works for any changes in policy, as long as the new policy is *economically compatible* with the old one. It mandates that, in the long run, no more money can be generated by the new policy.

We illustrate the usefulness of our construction by presenting some applications. One notable application is a construction which patches the *bribery* attack on Non-Interactive Proofs of Proof-of-Work (NIPoPoWs). As the patch requires correct incentivization embeded in the consensus mechanism, it is impossible to apply without policy changes. Even though we do it through a soft fork, we are the first to propose a bribery-resilient variant of the NIPoPoWs protocol *in general*, as this attack remained an open problem before this work. The correction of this outstanding issue was an important motivation behind the present work.

Related Work. Forking mechanisms in blockchains have been a topic of contention. A complete overview of hard forks and soft forks is given by Buterin [8] (who also presents some convincing arguments of why hard forks can sometimes be preferable). In addition to soft forks, velvet forks [9,10] present an interesting, and softer, alternative, although they are not always possible and great care must be taken when adopting them [11]. Even in the case of hard forks, core changes to consensus mechanisms must be deployed with prudence [12].

Smart contracts [13] were first used to distribute mining proceeds in the work of Luu et al. [14]. Our construction is inspired by their clever approach. Non-Interactive Proofs of Proof-of-Work (NIPoPoWs) were introduced by Kiayias et al. [9]. The bribing attack against them, which we patch in this work, was discovered by Bünz et al. [15]. Karantias et al. [16] perform convincing measurements that illustrate such attacks have not happened in the wild (yet).

Contributions. In this paper, we make the following key contributions:

- We formally define what a chain macroeconomic policy is. Our definition is generic and can be any algorithm that satisfies certain basic conditions.
- We define the notion of *economic compatibility* between policies, a necessary and sufficient condition for soft fork upgradability between policies.
- We put forth a generic mechanism for upgrading the macroeconomic policy of a chain through a *soft fork* and present it in the form of a *smart contract*.
- We present several applications of our scheme. Notably, we resolve the open problem of Non-Interactive Proof of Proof-of-Work (NIPoPoW) *bribability*.

2 Preliminaries

Blockchain systems maintain consensus through the dissemination of chains. A *chain* C is a finite sequence of *blocks*, and each block B is a triplet (x, s, ctr). A block id is the cryptographically secure hash of the triplet $H(x, s, \mathsf{ctr})$. Here, x denotes the set of confirmed messages (transactions), s denotes the block id of the previous block in the chain, and ctr denotes the *leader election information*, a nonce in the case of proof-of-work systems or a signature in the case of proof-of-stake systems. The first block in the chain is the genesis block $\mathcal{G}$ in which s is taken to be the empty string ϵ by convention. We write $C \preccurlyeq C'$ if C is a (not necessarily strict) prefix of C'. We denote by $C[i]$ the ith block of the chain (zero-based). We use the Python range notation $C[i{:}j]$ to denote the subsequence of blocks, or *subchain*, from i (inclusive) to j (exclusive). Omitting an index takes the subchain from the beginning or to the end respectively.

We denote $\mathcal{E}$ an *execution* of our blockchain protocol [17,18]. The execution captures the messages exchanged by all parties throughout, as well as the random coins produced during the mining process. We use κ to denote the security parameter.

The *block language* $\mathcal{L}_B$ is the set of all syntactically valid blocks and the *chain language* $\mathcal{L}_C \subseteq \mathcal{L}_B^*$ is the set of all valid chains.

Recall that a blockchain can be upgraded with a *soft fork* or a *hard fork*. In both cases, the code of the node is modified and the new software is distributed to the users. Some of the users adopt the new code and those are known as *new* or *upgraded* miners. The ones that do not upgrade are the *old* or *unupgraded miners* who are running the old version of the node. Once downloaded, the new code is activated after a designated *activation block height*. The upgraded software contains new rules that govern the generation and validation of blocks. In both cases, the old rules are *not* forwards compatible with the new rules: If an old node generates an old-style block, it will not be validated by upgraded miners. In the case of a soft fork, the new rules are backwards compatible with the old rules: If a new node generates a new-style block, it will be validated by old miners. Provided the upgraded miners constitute a majority, unupgraded nodes will still follow the longest chain, which will contain only upgraded blocks. Their own blocks will be rejected, so they will be economically pushed to upgrade their software. However, in a hard fork, the new rules are *not* backwards compatible with the old rules: New nodes generate blocks that do not validate according to old rules. As such, the two populations create two distinct chains after the activation block height, which constitutes a chain fork. This is sometimes viewed as dangerous. Nevertheless, even in the case of hard forks, the old population typically eventually upgrades to the new rules and their temporary fork is abandoned.

3   Macroeconomic Policies

A chain policy defines how payouts are given to miners (or minters). While for simple policies it could be a constant, more complex policies may depend on the whole state C of the system.

Definition 1 (Macroeconomic Policy). *Let $\mathcal{L}_C$ be the chain language. We call a function $\pounds : \mathcal{L}_C \times \mathbb{N} \to \mathbb{R}^+$ of the system a* macroeconomic policy *if the function is efficiently computable and for every two chains C, C' such that $C \preccurlyeq C'$, it holds that $\pounds(C, i) \leq \pounds(C', i)$. The system pays out an amount of $\pounds(C, i)$ to the validator of the ith block in C.*

The above definition captures, quite generically, what the rewards of a miner can be. The requirement that the function is monotonic is necessary, as it prescribes that money given out cannot be retroactively taken back. While the rewards can depend just on i, the ability of the function to inspect the whole chain C allows the system to employ complex rules. Additionally, note that it is possible that $|C| > i$. In that case, the policy may decide to pay out rewards to a miner later during the system's execution. We allow the function to output *real* positive amounts payable, even though most systems employ integer outputs to avoid floating-point errors.

Let us look at a couple of typical policies for illustration purposes. Bitcoin's policy is a step function which began at 50 BTC per block and halves every 210,000 blocks. Additionally, rewards cannot be withdrawn for another $c = 100$ blocks, a constraint known as the *maturation time*:

$$\pounds_{\mathrm{BTC}}(C, i) = \begin{cases} 0, \text{ if } |C| + c < i \\ \frac{50}{2^j}, \text{ otherwise} \end{cases} \text{ , where } j = \lfloor \frac{i}{210000} \rfloor$$

Monero's policy emits money *smoothly*, which they argue [6] can help prevent infrastructure problems due to dramatic increases in hashrate when compared to Bitcoin's. Instead, they give out one 2^{18}th of their remaining money supply per block. Their maturation time is $c = 60$ blocks.

$$\pounds_{\text{XMR}}(\mathcal{C}, i) = \begin{cases} 0, \text{ if } |\mathcal{C}| + c < i \\ \frac{2^{64}-1-\sum_{j=0}^{i-1}\pounds_{\text{XMR}}(\mathcal{C},j)}{2^{18}}, \text{ otherwise} \end{cases}$$

Note here that it so happens that an upgrade from Bitcoin's policy to Monero's policy could take place with a soft fork without any special mechanism, as long as Monero's supply is scaled appropriately to be upper bound by Bitcoin's at *every* block (see Fig. 1).

In both systems, the payouts are deterministic (and in the *steady state* do not depend on $\mathcal{C}$), and the total supply at every point in time is $\sum_{i=0}^{|\mathcal{C}|}\pounds(\mathcal{C}, i)$. In fact, the total supply is bounded, and the bound is $\lim_{|\mathcal{C}|\to\infty}\sum_{i=0}^{|\mathcal{C}|}\pounds(\mathcal{C}, i)$. Some systems, such as DOGE do not have a maximum total supply and this limit diverges.

Ethereum's policy is a little trickier. A block can receive a reward even if it does not belong on the adopted chain. Instead, *uncle* blocks are rewarded, too [4,5]. In this system, the function $\pounds$ is defined on *blocktrees* instead of chains. The parameter i is generalized to denote any *path* in the blocktree, and the prefix notation $\preccurlyeq$ must, of course, be amended accordingly to mean *subgraph*. Any chain system whose consensus is based on a DAG [19,20] instead of a tree can be thus augmented. As long as the language $\mathbb{L}_\mathcal{C}$ is appropriately defined, our definition stands, albeit with a more complex interpretation. In this case, as the total supply depends on the execution (and in particular how many uncles it contains), it cannot be calculated exactly.

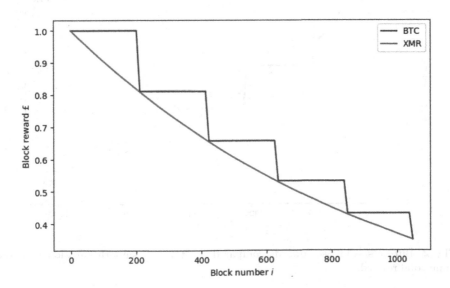

Fig. 1. Bitcoin's staircase rewards compared to Monero's smooth emission with Bitcoin upper bounding Monero.

Let us now determine whether two policies are *backwards compatible*. We begin with a strict definition.

Definition 2 (Economic Compatibility). *A* new *policy* $\mathcal{L}'$ *is* backwards compatible *with an* old *policy* $\mathcal{L}$ with respect to chain $\mathcal{C}$ if

$$\sum_{i=0}^{|\mathcal{C}|-1} \mathcal{L}(\mathcal{C}, i) \geq \sum_{i=0}^{|\mathcal{C}|-1} \mathcal{L}'(\mathcal{C}, i).$$

The two policies are backwards compatible *if they are compatible with respect to every chain.*

Compatibility mandates that the new policy does not pay out more money than the old policy for a particular chain. Note how this requirement is not made *for every block*, but instead *throughout history*. This leniency opens the door for upgrading to quite a wide range of policies. For example, *for the same total supply*, Bitcoin's policy is backwards compatible with Monero's: Bitcoin begins by paying a smaller amount per block than Monero. This money is accumulated. After a while, Monero's supply has dropped and Bitcoin is paying more per block than Monero. However, the accumulated money can make up for the difference at every point in time (see Fig. 2). Our construction in the next section will make it clear how this accumulation can take place in chains with smart contract support.

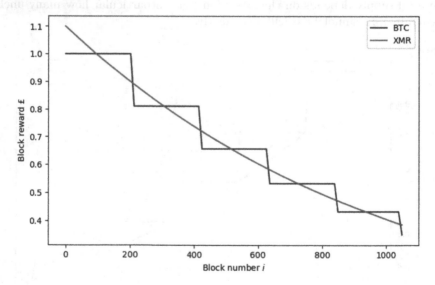

Fig. 2. Bitcoin's staircase rewards compared to Monero's smooth emission with the same total reward.

Generally, our policies will not be required to be *strictly* compatible. Instead, we will only mandate that they are compatible *eventually*.

Definition 3 (Eventual Compatibility). *A new policy $\mathcal{L}'$ is eventually back-wards compatible with an old policy $\mathcal{L}$ with delay d with respect to an execution $\mathcal{E}$ if for every chain $\mathcal{C}$ adopted during the execution, for any $i, j \in \mathbb{N}$ such that $0 \leq i + d < j < |\mathcal{C}|$, there is a $k \in \mathbb{N}$ such that $i \leq k < j$ and $\mathcal{L}'$ is backwards compatible with $\mathcal{L}$ with respect to chain $\mathcal{C}[:k]$.*

Eventual backwards compatibility does not require that the new policy remains solvent *all of the time*. Instead, it promises that the miners will be paid out *eventually*, even though they may have to wait up to time d until the policy becomes solvent and has the money to pay them.

For example, *for the same given total supply*, Monero's policy is *eventually backwards compatible* with Bitcoin's: While initially Monero will require higher payments than Bitcoin, eventually Monero's smooth emission will reduce the supply sufficiently to drop below Bitcoin's reward (see Fig. 2). After this, and when a certain number of blocks have been produced, a sufficient amount of money will have accumulated to be able to pay back the miners who mined more worthy Monero coins in the past. While the miners may have to wait for a delay d for the policy to achieve solvency, they will eventually be paid the correct amount.

To account for unlikely events, we relax this requirement further and require that eventual compatibility is only achieved *with high probability* in the security parameter (over the randomness of the execution). This relaxation enables us to build non-deterministic policies, as long as they are well-behaved with high probability.

It is useful to point out that backwards economic compatibility is a notion useful beyond soft and hard forks. It indicates that the new policy does not generate, in total, more money than the old policy. This implies that any previous assumption on upper bounds in supply is not violated (one such example is any total supply *firewall* limitation in the case of a sidechain [21]). Beyond a useful technical propertly, economic compatibility is primarily an *economic* assumption.

4 Construction

Our construction is based on a simple premise: Instead of paying out the miner directly, we can pay the proceeds of mining into a smart contract beneficiary. Before the soft fork begins, the smart contract is deployed on the old network. This deployment is verified by old and new miners alike. The soft fork then *mandates* that, after a particular activation block height, new blocks always pay into this smart contract's address. Blocks that do not pay into the designated address are rejected as invalid. Old miners accept new blocks because they just have a new valid beneficiary, and it so happens that it is the same for all the blocks they see, but without any notion of its semantics.

Once the beneficiary contract is deployed, it is responsible for managing the policy of the chain. It collects the proceeds of the old policy into its reserves and pays out the miners accordingly. If the new policy is backwards compatible with the old one with respect to every chain, the contract remains solvent. However, if the compatibility is only eventual, the contract will be insolvent at certain points in time. To address this, it gives out *promises to pay* miners, which are assembled in a balance sheet, akin to an ERC-20 [22] smart contract. This money can then be collected at a later time, when the contract becomes solvent again, which is guaranteed to occur after d blocks.

We illustrate our generic construction, parametrized by the new policy $\mathcal{L}$ in Algorithm 1. The contract is initially instantiated to an address as a regular contract. Anyone can do this, but it would typically be done by the cryptocurrency developers. The contract deployment address is noted and embedded into the code of the upgraded node software. The contract has three methods. The default method is paid out when the contract is designated as the beneficiary of any block. At this point, it is unclear what the identity of the miner is. The miner who actually produced the block places their identity in the form of their public key into a designated location within the block. In the case of Bitcoin soft forks, this is typically the *coinbase* transaction, but in a smart-contract-enabled blockchain, which our construction requires, this can be done more cleanly by the call to the identify method of our smart contract, in which the miner creates a transaction calling it and passing their public key pk as an argument to the call. The method call records the identity of the miner. Naturally, the miner must take care to drop from their block transactions of adversarial users calling the identify method, to avoid enterprising usurpers.

After the miner has identified themselves, they can claim the payout from the new policy by invoking the claim function. This function takes a block index i and evaluates the policy $\mathcal{L}$ on the current chain $\mathcal{C}$. Therefore it might need to be called at a later point by the miner to account for, say, maturation constraints. Note here that typically the policy will only depend on a small subset of the blocks in $\mathcal{C}$ and so not all of it needs to be evaluated. While some blockchains allow for access to past blocks liberally [23], the contract can replicate such behavior locally [24] if needed to recreate any portion of the chain required by the policy.

The function records the payout as delivered to the miner so that it cannot be doubly claimed. However, the payment is not actually delivered to the miner beyond a *promise to pay*, recorded in the balance sheet balances of the contract. If and when the contract becomes solvent, the miner can then call withdraw to get their money in the real native currency, such as Ether in our case. This behavior is similar to the balances maintained by an ERC-20 contract. In fact, the beneficiary contract can be a fully fledged ERC-20 contract, in which case the miners will be able to use their promise-to-pay tokens as if it were real ether.

Algorithm 1. The smart contract beneficiary which acts as a decentralized macroeconomic policy manager for policy $\pounds$.

```
 1: contract Policy£
 2:     balances ← ∅
 3:     claims ← ∅
 4:     identities ← ∅
 5:     payable function default()
 6:         ▷ Collect proceeds from this block, but do not pay it out yet
 7:     end function
 8:     function identify(pk)
 9:         identities[block.id] ← pk
10:     end function
11:     function claim(i)
12:         C ← get_chain()
13:         miner ← identities[i]
14:         v ← £(C, i)                        ▷ The particular policy is invoked at this point
15:         D ← v − claims[i]                  ▷ D will be positive due to monotonicity of £
16:         claims[i] ← v
17:         balances[miner] ← balances[miner] + D     ▷ Create a promise to pay later
18:     end function
19:     function withdraw(v)                   ▷ An ERC-20-style withdrawal
20:         require(balances[msg.sender] ≥ v)
21:         require(address(this).balance ≥ v)        ▷ Ensure the contract is solvent
22:         balances[msg.sender] ← balances[msg.sender] − v
23:         msg.sender.send(v)
24:     end function
25: end contract
```

5 Blinded Mining

We have already seen that simple policies such as Bitcoin's and Monero's can be upgraded between one another. It should also be clear that increasing the reward maturation time is easily implementable.

One interesting and more complex policy involves requiring miners to generate and commit to a value χ during their block generation. The commitment $h = H(\chi)$ is placed in the block instead. The value χ is to be kept secret until after k blocks have passed, at which point the value should be revealed soon after, and certainly before $2k$ blocks have passed. This *blinded mining* process can be a useful tool for constructing consensus protocols that can withstand an adaptive adversary or suppression attacks [25].

A cryptoeconomic incentivization of the above protocol can be achieved with the following policy:

$$\mathcal{L}(\mathcal{C}, i) = \begin{cases} c & \text{if } \mathcal{C}[i{:}i+k] \text{ contain no } \chi \\ & \text{but } \mathcal{C}[i+k{:}i+2k] \text{ contains } \chi \\ (1+\epsilon)c & \text{if the above holds, and } \mathcal{C}[i] \text{ is the } \textit{first} \text{ block} \\ & \text{to reveal } \chi' \text{ for block } \mathcal{C}[i-j] \text{ with } j < k \\ 0 & \text{otherwise} \end{cases}$$

where $h = H(\chi), h' = H(\chi')$ are the commitments in $i, i - j$ respectively.

Here, the miner who mined the ith block is rewarded with c only once they reveal the value χ. This revealing can be made in an appropriately structured transaction, even if they do not mine any future blocks. This requirements mandates a sort of *availability* by the miner: They are not paid until they reveal their committed value, and they must ensure they remain online to do so. Additionally, the miner must reveal it before $2k$ blocks, or else their rewards are gone. Lastly, if the value is leaked sooner, i.e., before k blocks have passed, to a different miner, that miner is rewarded with ϵc extra rewards, in addition to their c that they receive for playing fairly. This $0 < \epsilon < 1$ *slashes* the miner who revealed the value too soon. The value ϵ must be large enough $(0 < \epsilon)$ to incentivize competing miners to find the value and reveal it sooner, but small enough to incentivize the miner of i to keep the value secret ($\epsilon \ll 1$ to account for the *time value of money*).

6   Unbribability

A notable achievement possible with a policy upgrade is making NIPoPoWs unbribable. While the precise details of the NIPoPoW protocol are beyond the scope of this work, let us review the essential parts here to motivate the discussion.

In a proof-of-work chain, a block B satisfies the proof-of-work equation $H(B) \leq T$, where T denotes the *mining target* (this can be a constant or a variable). Some blocks satisfy this equation better than others, and specifically achieve $H(B) \leq \frac{T}{2^\mu}$ for some $\mu \in \mathbb{N}$. Such blocks are called μ-superblocks (or superblocks of level μ).

The NIPoPoW protocol posits that a *superlight client*, which functions as an SPV node to the blockchain, can synchronize from a full node by receiving only a small *sample* of superblocks. More concretely, if the full node presents a subsequence of $m \in \mathbb{N}$ superblocks of level μ, then the superlight client is convinced that approximately $m2^\mu$ regular blocks exist in the underlying chain, but these do not need to be sent over the network. Leveraging this basic clever idea, the protocol achieves an exponential improvement in communication complexity compared to legacy SPV clients [9]. The parameter m has a minimum value, but can be increased as needed to ensure security (with a corresponding performance penalty).

A block is a μ-superblock with probability $2^{-\mu}$, so they are exceedingly rare as μ increases. Unfortunately, they are rewarded only as much as regular blocks. As such, an adversary can cheaply *bribe* miners to keep such blocks secret [15]. In this attack, the adversary requests that the miners never broadcast these blocks into the network, and pays the miners behind-the-scenes in exchange for this commitment. In fact, such bribes can even be written in the form of a smart contract, completely removing the need for the adversary and the miners to maintain rogue offchain communication channels. While honest miners will not succumb to such behavior, rational miners might. A rational adversary is also incentivized to give out such bribes if they wish to convince a superlight client that a large amount of money has been transferred to them (the exact amount can be calculated using the methods of Bonneau et al. [26]).

We now put forth a method for defending against this attack. The attack becomes uneconomical if the reward schedule of the chain is modified so that a μ-superblock's worth is proportional to the amount of underlying blocks it captures. More precisely, each μ-superblock must be worth 2^{μ} more than a regular block, provided at least m superblocks of level μ have appeared on the network. In this case, bribing to suppress superblocks capturing a certain amount of proof-of-work requires the same bribe as suppressing the whole underlying chain. As long as such bribes are not economical (an assumption required for the blockchain to function), superblock bribes are not economical either.

To make this new policy backwards compatible with the old policy, the value of regular blocks must be reduced. But how should we ascribe value to these blocks? Suppose the old policy pays out 1 unit of currency per block. If a regular block (which is not a superblock) pays out a value of c and a μ-superblock (which is not a $\mu + 1$ level superblock) pays out a value of $2^{\mu}c$, then we are led to the following paradox: The expected value of the reward diverges:

$$\mathbb{E}[\pounds(\mathcal{C}, i)] = \sum_{\mu=0}^{\infty} c2^{\mu+1} Pr[H(B) \leq \frac{T}{2^{\mu}}] = \sum_{\mu=0}^{\infty} c2^{\mu+1}2^{-\mu} = \infty$$

However, the probability of such divergence is negligible. We will make use of this fact to construct a policy that is eventually backwards compatible with the constant policy with overwhelming probability in the security parameter κ. The policy progresses in epochs. In each epoch j, a constant c_j is adopted as the reward of a 0-level block. Within each epoch, the invariant that each block of level μ is worth 2^{μ} more than each regular block is maintained, i.e., $\pounds(\mathcal{C}, i_1) = 2^{\mu}\pounds(\mathcal{C}, i_2)$ where $\mathcal{C}[i_1]$ is a regular block and $\mathcal{C}[i_2]$ is a μ-superblock (however, this invariant is not maintained *across* epochs). We will now define the lengths of these epochs and the value c_j.

Consider a chain $\mathcal{C}$ with length $|\mathcal{C}|$, a superblock level μ, and a constant m. Observe that the number X of μ-superblocks appearing in $\mathcal{C}$ follows a binomial distribution with a Bernoulli probability of success $p = 2^{-\mu}$ and $|\mathcal{C}|$ trials. As such, $\mathbb{E}[X] = 2^{-\mu}|\mathcal{C}|$. We can now examine whether at least m superblocks of some level μ have appeared in this chain. Call this event DEFAULT. We want our system to avoid this event, as it will imply that our policy will become insolvent.

Let us consider the case when $\mathbb{E}[X] < m$, and so we do not expect the bad event to occur. Still, we wish for the probability of the event occurring to be negligible. Let δ be the value such that $m = (1 + \delta)2^{-\mu}|\mathcal{C}|$, i.e., $\delta = \frac{m}{2^{-\mu}|\mathcal{C}|} - 1 > 0$.

Since the trials are mutually independent Bernoulli trials, we can apply a Chernoff bound to obtain:

$$Pr[\text{DEFAULT}] = Pr[X \geq m] = Pr[X \geq (1 + \delta)\mathbb{E}[X]] < e^{-\delta^2 \frac{\mathbb{E}[X]}{3}}$$

When does this probability attain a value negligible in the security parameter κ? We have:

$$e^{-\delta^2 \frac{\mathbb{E}[X]}{3}} \leq 2^{\kappa} \Leftrightarrow \frac{\delta^2 2^{-\mu}|\mathcal{C}|}{3} \lg e \geq \kappa$$

Replacing δ with its value, we obtain the following sufficient condition for solvency:

$$\left(\frac{m}{2^{-\mu}|\mathcal{C}|} - 1\right)^2 \frac{2^{-\mu}|\mathcal{C}|}{3} \lg e \geq \kappa$$

$$\Leftrightarrow \frac{m^2}{2^{-\mu}} + 2^{-\mu}|\mathcal{C}| \geq \frac{3\kappa}{\lg e} + 2m$$

$$\Leftarrow \frac{m^2}{2^{-\mu}|\mathcal{C}|} \geq \frac{3\kappa}{\lg e} + 2m$$

$$\Leftrightarrow 2^{-\mu}|C| \leq \frac{m^2}{\frac{3\kappa}{\lg e} + 2m}.$$

Observe that the right-hand side is a constant, call it ζ. We can therefore be certain with overwhelming probability in κ that superblocks of levels μ or higher will not appear in chains of length $|\mathcal{C}|$ or less. This immediately leads to an algorithm for epoch evolution: Begin at epoch $j = 1$ in which the reward is $\frac{c_1}{2}$. As long as our chain $|\mathcal{C}|$ has size below $2^{\mu}\zeta$, we treat our system as if superblocks of level μ and above will never appear. Blocks of levels $0, 1, \cdots, \mu-1$ receive pay out rewards of $c_j, 2c_j, \cdots, 2^{\mu-1}c_j$. The expected reward per block in this epoch is $\mathbb{E}[\pounds_j] = \sum_{i=0}^{\mu-1} c_j 2^i / 2^{i+1} = \frac{jc_j}{2}$. Whenever a chain size of $2^{\mu}\zeta$ is reached, the epoch advances to $j + 1$ and the reward is updated so that $\mathbb{E}[\pounds_{j+1}] = \mathbb{E}[\pounds_j]$. Solving for c_{j+1}, the new reward at level 0 then becomes $c_{j+1} = \frac{j}{j+1}c_j$. As you can see, these do not change the reward by much, and the update happens exponentially more rarely as time goes by.

The above construction lets us state the following lemma:

Lemma 1 (Compatibility of NIPoPoW rewards). *The policy $\pounds$ described above is eventually backwards compatible with a policy of constant rewards of amount $(1 + \epsilon)\frac{c_1}{2}$ with overwhelming probability in κ.*

Proof (Sketch). The proof is immediate from the above construction. Each epoch j with maximum chain length $|\mathcal{C}|$ maintains an expected payout per block which is $\mathbb{E}[\mathcal{L}_j] = \frac{c_1}{2}$. This is ensured with overwhelming probability in κ, as it was argued through the above Chernoff bound that superblocks of level $\mu \geq \frac{\zeta}{|\mathcal{C}|}$ appear with only negligible probability. Applying a union bound over all epochs ensures a negligible probability of failure overall in the parameter $\kappa - \log(L)$ where L denotes the total execution time (as the number of epochs grows logarithmically in L). Each block reward is independent from the rest. The deposits available to the policy are the sum of these rewards and are bounded by a Chernoff bound. Thus, this sum will converge with high probability to its expectation after a sufficient number of blocks d. As $(1 + \epsilon)\frac{c_1}{2} > \frac{c_1}{2}$ this ensures eventual compatibility. The delay d depends on the choice of the parameter ϵ. A trade-off exists between lowering the reward slightly to ensure eventual compatibility more quickly. $\qquad\square$

7 More Complex Upgrades

Multiple Upgrades. One outstanding question is how to apply a policy upgrade $\mathcal{L}''$ on top of a chain in which a policy upgrade $\mathcal{L}'$ has already been applied; that is, how to apply multiple policy upgrades in series. The solution is to employ *yet another* smart contract as a second intermediate step between the block reward and the miner.

The approach works by having $\mathcal{L}'$ manage the first policy by receiving the money of the legacy policy $\mathcal{L}$ as before. When the time comes to call the identify function, the second soft fork requires the pk provided to be the second smart contract to which $\mathcal{L}''$ is deployed. As such, the first smart contract always pays out into the second. The miner variable in any valid execution of the first smart contract always takes on the address of the second smart contract after the second soft fork. The second smart contract can then have its own identify function, which uses a different portion of the block to identify the final receipient. The technique can be used repeatedly in series, as illustrated in Fig. 3.

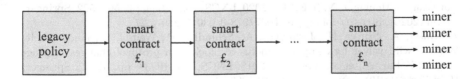

Fig. 3. A series of upgrades $\mathcal{L}_1, \cdots, \mathcal{L}_n$. Each of the contracts maintains its own balance and pays into the next. Only the final contract distributes proceeds to the true miners.

More Complex Policies. For simplicity, our definition of the policy $\mathcal{L}(\mathcal{C}, i)$ returns the amount payable to the miner who mined the block $\mathcal{C}[i]$. It is possible to devise of more complex policies in which the policy pays out multiple people per block or in general does not have just one receipient per block. One such example is a policy that distributes payments to miners who are mining blocks often. It is easy to generalize the definition of policies to allow for such a scenario. The function is defined to be $\mathcal{L}(\mathcal{C})$ and returns a dictionary mapping from address to amount payable. The monotonocity condition is then the obvious generalization of our previous condition: Given two chains $\mathcal{C} \preccurlyeq \mathcal{C}'$, the keys in the dictionary $\mathcal{L}(\mathcal{C})$ must be a subset of the keys in the dictionary $\mathcal{L}(\mathcal{C}')$. Additionally, for every key in both dictionaries, the value in $\mathcal{L}(\mathcal{C})$ must be smaller than or equal to the value in $\mathcal{L}(\mathcal{C}')$.

References

1. Nakamoto S.: Bitcoin: a peer-to-peer electronic cash system. https://bitcoin.org/bitcoin.pdf (2008)
2. Dwork, C., Naor, M.: Pricing via processing or combatting junk mail. In: Brickell, E.F. (ed.) CRYPTO 1992. LNCS, vol. 740, pp. 139–147. Springer, Heidelberg (1993). https://doi.org/10.1007/3-540-48071-4_10
3. Kiayias, A., Russell, A., David, B., Oliynykov, R.: Ouroboros: a provably secure proof-of-stake blockchain protocol. In: Katz, J., Shacham, H. (eds.) CRYPTO 2017. LNCS, vol. 10401, pp. 357–388. Springer, Cham (2017). https://doi.org/10.1007/978-3-319-63688-7_12
4. Kiayias A., Panagiotakos G.: Speed-Security Tradeoffs in Blockchain Protocols. IACR Cryptol. ePrint Arch.: vol. 2015, p. 1019 (2015)
5. Kiayias, A., Panagiotakos, G.: On trees, chains and fast transactions in the blockchain. In: Lange, T., Dunkelman, O. (eds.) LATINCRYPT 2017. LNCS, vol. 11368, pp. 327–351. Springer, Cham (2019). https://doi.org/10.1007/978-3-030-25283-0_18
6. Van Saberhagen, N.: CryptoNote v2.0. https://cryptonote.org/whitepaper.pdf (2013)
7. Schoedon, A.: EIP-1234: Constantinople Difficulty Bomb Delay and Block Reward Adjustment. https://eips.ethereum.org/EIPS/eip-1234 (2018)
8. Buterin, V.: Hard Forks, Soft Forks, Defaults and Coercion. http://web.archive.org/web/20080207010024/www.808multimedia.com/winnt/kernel.htm (2017)
9. Kiayias, A., Miller, A., Zindros, D.: Non-interactive proofs of proof-of-work. In: Bonneau, J., Heninger, N. (eds.) FC 2020. LNCS, vol. 12059, pp. 505–522. Springer, Cham (2020). https://doi.org/10.1007/978-3-030-51280-4_27
10. Zamyatin, A., Stifter, N., Judmayer, A., Schindler, P., Weippl, E., Knottenbelt, W.J.: A wild velvet fork appears! inclusive blockchain protocol changes in practice. In: Zohar, A., et al. (eds.) FC 2018. LNCS, vol. 10958, pp. 31–42. Springer, Heidelberg (2019). https://doi.org/10.1007/978-3-662-58820-8_3
11. Kiayias, A., Polydouri, A., Zindros, D.: The Velvet Path to Superlight Blockchain Clients. IACR Cryptology ePrint Archive: http://eprint.iacr.org/2020/1122 (2020)
12. Ciampi, M., Karayannidis, N., Kiayias, A., Zindros, D.: Updatable blockchains. In: Chen, L., Li, N., Liang, K., Schneider, S. (eds.) ESORICS 2020. LNCS, vol. 12309, pp. 590–609. Springer, Cham (2020). https://doi.org/10.1007/978-3-030-59013-0_29
13. Buterin V., et al.: A next-generation smart contract and decentralized application platform. white paper (2014)

14. Luu, L., Velner, Y., Teutsch, J., Saxena, P.: Smartpool: practical decentralized pooled mining. In: 26th USENIX Security Symposium (USENIX Security 17), pp. 1409–1426 (2017)
15. Bünz, B., Kiffer, L., Luu, L., Zamani, M.: FlyClient: Super-Light Clients for Cryptocurrencies (2020)
16. Karantias, K., Kiayias, A., Zindros, D.: Compact storage of superblocks for NIPoPoW applications. In: Pardalos, P., Kotsireas, I., Guo, Y., Knottenbelt, W. (eds.) Mathematical Research for Blockchain Economy. SPBE, pp. 77–91. Springer, Cham (2020). https://doi.org/10.1007/978-3-030-37110-4_6
17. Garay, J.A., Kiayias, A., Leonardos, N.: The bitcoin backbone protocol: analysis and applications. In: Oswald, E., Fischlin, M. (eds.) EUROCRYPT 2015, Part II: vol. 9057 of LNCS, pp. 281–310. Springer, Heidelberg (2015). https://doi.org/10. 1007/978-3-662-46803-6_10: updated version at http://eprint.iacr.org/2014/765
18. Garay, J., Kiayias, A., Leonardos, N.: The bitcoin backbone protocol with chains of variable difficulty. In: Katz, J., Shacham, H. (eds.) CRYPTO 2017. LNCS, vol. 10401, pp. 291–323. Springer, Cham (2017). https://doi.org/10.1007/978-3-319-63688-7_10
19. Sompolinsky, Y., Lewenberg, Y., Zohar, A.: SPECTRE: A Fast and Scalable Cryptocurrency Protocol. IACR Cryptology ePrint Archive: vol. 2016: http://eprint.iacr.org/2016/1159
20. Sompolinsky, Y., Wyborski, S., Zohar, A.: PHANTOM and GHOSTDAG: A Scalable Generalization of Nakamoto Consensus. IACR Cryptology ePrint Archive: http://eprint.iacr.org/2018/104 (2018)
21. Kiayias, A., Gaži, P., Zindros, D.: Proof-of-stake sidechains. In: IEEE Symposium on Security and Privacy. IEEE (2019)
22. Vogelsteller, F., Buterin, V.: ERC-20 Token Standard, September 2017. https://github.com/ethereum/EIPs/blob/master/EIPS/eip-20-tokenstandard.md (2015)
23. Buterin, V.: Blockhash refactoring. https://github.com/ethereum/EIPs/blob/master/EIPS/eip-210.md (2017)
24. Karantias, K., Kiayias, A., Zindros, D.: Smart contract derivatives. In: Pardalos, P., Kotsireas, I., Guo, Y., Knottenbelt, W. (eds.) Mathematical Research for Blockchain Economy. SPBE, pp. 1–8. Springer, Cham (2020). https://doi.org/10.1007/978-3-030-53356-4_1
25. Zindros, D.: Decentralized Blockchain Interoperability. Ph.D. thesis (2020)
26. Bonneau, J., Clark, J., Goldfeder, S.: On Bitcoin as a public randomness source. IACR Cryptology ePrint Archive: vol. 2015: https://eprint.iacr.org/2015/1015.pdf (2015)

Privacy-Preserving Resource Sharing Using Permissioned Blockchains
(The Case of Smart Neighbourhood)

Sepideh Avizheh(✉), Mahmudun Nabi, Saoreen Rahman, Setareh Sharifian,
and Reihaneh Safavi-Naini

University of Calgary, Alberta, Canada
{sepideh.avizheh1,mahmudun.nabi1,saoreen.rahman,ssharifi,rei}@ucalgary.ca

Abstract. In a resource sharing system users offer goods and services
with specified conditions that if met, the access will be granted. Traditional resource sharing systems use a trusted intermediary that mediates
users' interactions. Our work is motivated by a decentralized resource
sharing platform (proposed in WTSC'20) that uses a permissioned
blockchain to allow users to share their digital items with their specified
attributed-based access policies that are enforced through a set of smart
contracts, and removes the need for a trusted intermediary. The system
however allows users' accesses to be traced, and has limited availability as
access to a resource requires its owner to be on-line. We design a decentralized attribute-based access control system that achieves the same
functionality while preserving the privacy of user's access, and automating access which removes the need for the resource owner to be online.
We use two cryptographic primitives, Ciphertext Policy Attribute-Based
Encryption (CP-ABE), and ring signatures, and design smart contracts
that allow specification and cryptographic enforcement of the users' specified policies. We analyze the security and privacy of the system, provide
the description of smart contracts and give a proof of concept implementation of the smart contracts and cryptographic algorithms that are
used in the system. Our design and implementation are general and can
be used for privacy-preserving resource sharing with fine-grained access
control in other settings including data and information sharing among
collaborating parties.

Keywords: Privacy-preserving resource sharing · Blockchain · Smart
contract · Attribute-based access control · Attribute-based encryption ·
Anonymous authentication · Smart neighborhood

1 Introduction

Resource sharing platforms enable peers to acquire, provide, or share goods
and services through intermediary service providers. Sharing platforms such as
Airbnb [1] and Uber [2] are centralized online platforms that connect resource
owners with resource providers, and manage their interactions and payments.

© International Financial Cryptography Association 2021
M. Bernhard et al. (Eds.): FC 2021 Workshops, LNCS 12676, pp. 482–504, 2021.
https://doi.org/10.1007/978-3-662-63958-0_37

In centralized systems the platform provider is a single Trusted Authority (TA) that mediates all interactions. Centralized designs have the drawback of having a single point of failure and a single TA with full access to users' data. This is not only highly privacy-invasive, but in the case of compromise of TA, reveals all users information and their history of interactions.

In WTSC 2020, a decentralized resource sharing platform for digital items in smart neighbourhoods was proposed [3] that addresses some of the shortcomings of the centralized systems. Authors motivated their work by considering a smart neighbourhood application where an initial trust among parties (and so willingness to share) exists because of the geographic proximity, but there is a need for user control of their sharing so that they are confident about the outcome. Authors proposed a decentralized system that uses a permissioned blockchain that is maintained by a set of Consensus nodes (or C-nodes for short), and enables users to specify conditions of access to their resource and be confident that they will be enforced. Sharing will be among "registered" users of the system that are approved by the C-nodes that use *proof of authority* consensus among themselves to control access to the blockchain. C-nodes verify transactions to ensure they are generated by registered users and publish them on the blockchain. The system uses *attribute-based access control* to allow users to express fine-grained conditions of access to resources by specifying associated *attribute-based access policies*. Resources have certificates for their properties (attributes) that can be verified by users. A resource requester provides their (certified) attributes in their request. The request will be verified by the C-nodes for matching the stated policy. If the request is accepted, the resource owner issues an access token that allows the requester to access the resource. Authors designed a set of smart contracts that automates and implements the system and enforces the stated access policies, effectively removing the need for a single TA. The system however has major drawbacks: it offers no privacy for users and allows their attributes and accesses to be visible by the C-nodes and the resource providers; and it has limited availability: for accessing a resource, the resource provider must be online to issue the access token. We redesign the system to provide privacy for users' access, and automate users' access and remove the need for the resource owner to mediate each request.

1.1   Our Contributions

We use two cryptographic building blocks, a *Ciphertext Policy Attribute-based Encryption (CP-ABE)* [4] to cryptographically enforce access control, and anonymous authentication and access using *ring signature* [5], that together will allow secure private access to resources without the need for the resource owner to be online. Using CP-ABE protects the need to send the requesters' attributes in plaintext to the blockchain, and ring signature enables anonymous authentication and access request validation, preventing traceability of the requests. Effective use of these primitives needs an overhaul of smart contracts in [3] and design of a new set of contracts. We provide a detailed security and privacy analysis of our design, and provide a proof of concept implementation to demonstrate feasibility of using advanced cryptographic primitives in real-life applications.

Although our work is motivated by sharing digital items in smart neighbour-hood, our design and implementation are general and will have wider applications for privacy-preserving sharing of digital items with fine-grained access control, for example, sharing documents among collaborating organizations based on an access policy.

Proposed System. The system consists of a number of entities that interact through the blockchain and smart contracts to publish and access resources according to the stated policies.

Entities. *Users* must register to the system. We consider three types of authorities: (i) *Blockchain Authority (BA)* that consists of the set of C-nodes, and performs user registration, maintain the blockchain and membership of the users, and verify identity of requesters; (ii) *Certificate Authorities (CA)* that are trusted for issuing certificates for attributes of users and shareable digital objects, and certificates will be verifiable by the BAs as well as the users; and (iii) *CP-ABE Attribute Authority (CP-ABE AA)* that is responsible for generating CP-ABE private and public keys for registered users (registration by BA) according to their attributes.

Smart Contracts. We use smart contracts to allow users to advertise their digital objects together with the specified access policy, and securely provide the requested information to the users. We design a set of interconnected smart contracts to achieve these goals with higher privacy.

We consider the following smart contracts:

i. User directory contract (uDir): this contract is deployed by the blockchain authority (BA), and holds the public identity information of the registered users. The shared information of each user consists of a pseudonym and a public key certificate (that includes the user's public key) that has been issued by one of the C-nodes. The information in this contract can be (non-anonymously) requested by users from BA and will be used by users for anonymous authentication and hiding their identity among a group (using ring signature).

ii. Object directory contract (oDir): this contract is deployed by the BA and contains the user information (same as included in uDir) and their shareable items information (one entry per item) including, object Id, description, a link to the objPropRep and objACC contracts.

iii. Object property repository contract (objPropRep) is deployed by the resource owner. It holds the Id and properties of the shareable object.

iv. Object access control contract (objACC) is deployed by the resource owner. It holds the object Id, the access policy and CP-ABE encrypted metadata of the resource.

v. Adjudicator contract (Adj): this contract is deployed by BA, and allows requesters to report misbehaviors. The system can choose a verifier to validate the reports and penalize the misbehaving owners.

The smart contracts and the data stored by them are part of the permissioned blockchain and are accessible to registered users upon making a request.

User Authentication. BA runs an authentication service *AuthServ*, that register users, provide public key certificate, and verify users' requests to access blockchain. We consider that a user access request has the following format: it consists of two parts, (i) the request (e.g., a function call to a smart contract to read some data), and (ii) a signature which endorses the request. In practice, an access request can be simply a transaction or a more complex information unit depending on the implementation and the underlying blockchain system. For privacy, the user identity is verified through an anonymous authentication protocol, and the signature of the request will be based on an anonymous signature.

We use a challenge and response anonymous authentication, where the response is the ring signature [5] of the prover on the challenge sent by the verifier. The challenge in our system is obtained from a randomness beacon service (provided by the BA) that is broadcasted at regular intervals. The random string has length ℓ that is determined by the system security level (we use $\ell = 512$ bits in our implementation). The signature of each request (for e.g. an issued transaction) will include the current value of the challenge, and will be considered valid (after verification of the signature) if it has been generated within a defined interval (timeliness). This effectively combines user authentication and request validation (i.e. request is issued by a registered user within a close time interval). The request that is sent to the BA will be encrypted using the BA's public key.

Processing a Request. There are two types of requests, (i) non-anonymous requests which are used to browse blockchain and obtain information about existing resources and users, and (ii) anonymous requests, which are used for a specific resource. The sequence of steps in making a request to access an item, and its processing are as follows: (i) User B_r authenticates itself to an *AuthServ* using a traditional digital signature, gets the interfaces of uDir and oDir contracts (by issuing non-anonymous requests), and browses oDir and uDir contracts on the blockchain by making another non-anonymous requests; (ii) B_r makes an anonymous request (using ring signature) to the objPropRep contract for an object O that is listed in oDir; *AuthServ* authenticates the (anonymous) request of B_r and passes it to objPropRep contract; (iii) B_r receives the properties of the object O and the corresponding certificates, and if verified, makes an anonymous access request for the object O to the objACC contract; (v) *AuthServ* authenticates the (anonymous) request of B_r and passes it to the objACC contract; (vi) B_r receives the access policies and the CP-ABE encrypted metadata, and decrypts it using its CP-ABE private key. If the private key matches the access policy of CP-ABE encrypted metadata, B_r will obtain the link to the object O. Note that the response to anonymous requests are returned to all ring members that are determined by the requester upon issuing a request.

Security and Privacy. We use a CP-ABE scheme to ensure a requester whose attributes satisfy the item's stated policy is able to decrypt it (security), and use ring signature based authentication protocol to ensure that accesses are by authorized users (security), and the BA and the resource owner cannot link the access requests to the resource requester (privacy). Outsiders will only see encrypted communications. A detailed security and privacy analysis is given in Sect. 4.

Proof of Concept Implementation. We use Ganache [6] to setup the required private (permissioned) Ethereum blockchain infrastructure. Smart contracts are written in *Solidity* language using Remix IDE [7], and *Truffle* is used for contract deployment and run of the experiments. We evaluate computation cost of using cryptographic primitives namely, (CP-ABE) [4], ring signature [5] and AES symmetric key encryption scheme [8], as well as the execution cost of the smart contract functions in Ethereum blockchain. Our results are presented in Sect. 5 and show viability of our system for real-world applications.

Organization. Section 2 reviews preliminaries, Sect. 3 describes the details of our system, assumptions and security goals and user's interaction with the system. Section 4 gives the security and privacy analysis of the proposed system. Section 5 gives the details of the implementation and evaluation result, and finally Sect. 6 concludes the paper.

1.2 Related Work

Anonymous access and participation in system has been used in a variety of applications including electronic voting [9], e-mail [10], and social networking [11]. Access control models have evolved over years and new models that more efficiently capture the requirements have been proposed [12,13]. Attribute-Based Access Control (ABAC) is a more recent model that allows a fine-grained approach to express access control requirements [14,15]. In cryptographic systems, attribute-based encryption (ABE), first proposed by Sahai and Waters [16], are proposed to allow access control based on attributes of decryptor. Goyal et al. [17] introduced ciphertext policy attribute-based encryption (CP-ABE), where each ciphertext is associated with an access structure. A user receives a secret key associated with their set of attributes and is able to decrypt a ciphertext if and only if their attributes satisfy the access structure of the ciphertext. Bethencourt et al. [4] proposed the first CP-ABE construction using the generic bilinear group model [18,19]. CP-ABE is then used in many privacy-preserving resource sharing infrastructures including [20–24].

Using blockchain to store and enforce access control policies are given in [25–27]. In [28], smart contracts are used for enforcing role-based access control policies. The work of [29] uses smart contracts to establish an access control for IoT systems. In [30], a blockchain-enabled decentralized capability-based access control is proposed for propagation and revocation of the access authorization. A multi-authority attribute-based access control scheme is proposed in [31]. The work of [31] uses Ethereum smart contracts to develop an attribute-based access control system. Smart contracts for access control have also been considered in [32–34]. We motivate our work based on [3] and redesign it to ensure privacy of user's access and automating the user's access. The set of smart contracts in our work differs from [3], for example the ACC contract in [3] checks whether the attributes of user match the stated access policy of the resource (enforcement of policy is done on chain) whereas we use CP-ABE to evaluate the access policies (so the enforcement of policy is done off-chain).

2   Preliminaries

In this section, we introduce our notations and the cryptographic primitives that are central to our work.

Ciphertext-Policy Attribute-Based Encryption (CP-ABE). A CP-ABE scheme CP-ABE consists of four algorithms: (i) the setup algorithm CP-ABE.Setup(1^λ) that for a security parameter λ, generates the master secret key msk and the system's public key pk_{abe}; (ii) the key generation algorithm CP-ABE.KGen(1^λ) that generates the CP-ABE private key sk_{abe} for a given attribute set $attr$; (iii) the encryption algorithm CP-ABE.Enc that takes a massage m, and a policy P and produces the ciphertext $c^{CP\text{-}ABE}$; and (iv) the decryption algorithm CP-ABE.Dec that takes a ciphertext $c^{CP\text{-}ABE}$ that is obtained as above and a private key sk_{abe} and outputs m if $attr$, the associated attribute set of sk_{abe}, satisfies the policy P, else returns $\perp$. In our implementation we use Bethencourt et al. CP-ABE scheme [4].

Ring Signature: Ring signature [5] is an anonymous signature scheme that hides a user's public key among a set of N public keys, making the signer of the message the holder of one of the N keys. A ring signature scheme RingS consists of three algorithms: (i) A key generation algorithm RingS.KGen(1^λ) that takes the security parameter λ and produces a set R of N public and private key pairs $R = \{(pk_i, sk_i), i \in \{1, 2 \cdots N\}\}$; (ii) Signature generation algorithm RingS.Sig signs a message m using the signer's private key sk_i, and the public keys in R, and outputs a ring signature σ_R; and (iii) RingS.Vf that takes public keys in R, message m, and the signature σ_R as input and verifies the signature: if valid, returns 1, else 0. A secure ring signature ensures anonymity, unlinkability, and existential unforgeability.

Blockchain and Smart Contracts. A blockchain is a distributed ledger technology which stores data (transactions) in a growing chain of ordered blocks that are securely and irreversibly linked to each other through a cryptographic hash function. All peer nodes who run the system use a consensus algorithm to agree on the validity and the order of blocks [35]. We consider *permissioned blockchains* where the consensus algorithm is run by a set of privileged computing nodes, referred to as *Blockchain Authorities* (BA in this paper)[1], that verify transactions of users, and if verification succeeds, publish the result on the chain based on an agreed consensus algorithm. The consensus algorithm is a *Proof of Authority algorithm* that will be defined and agreed upon by the BAs at the

---

[1] These nodes were referred to as C-nodes in [3].

time of system setup. A permissioned blockchain is only accessible to registered members of the system. In non-permissioned blockchain such as Ethereum [36] anyone can join the blockchain and participate in the consensus algorithm.

Smart contract is a computer program that runs in a blockchain consensus computing network [37]. Each program instruction is agreed upon through the consensus algorithm and so the execution of the program will be trusted.

Randomness Beacon. A randomness beacon is a service that periodically generates and publishes (broadcasts) a random string. Randomness beacons must be *unpredictable, unbiased* and *available* [38]. An additional desirable property of randomness beacon is *public verifiability* that ensure the claimed randomness of the beacon. An example of a randomness beacon is the NIST randomness beacon [39] that uses hardware-generated randomness.

3   System Design

We consider three types of authorities: (i) *Blockchain authorities, BAs*, that register users and issue certificates for users' public keys (for a digital signature algorithm), authenticate users (cf. Sect. 3.2 for more details), and manage interaction of users with the blockchain. Each BA also runs a randomness beacon service that broadcasts random numbers at regular intervals. BA publishes two public keys, one public key is for verifying the signed certificates, and the second public key is for an encryption algorithm that is employed by the users to communicate with blockchain. (ii) *Certificate authorities, CAs*, verify users attributes and objects' properties, and issue the corresponding certificates for them. CA is also responsible for checking the legal restrictions of the objects and only issues certificate for valid objects. (iii) *CP-ABE attribute authority, CP-ABE AA*, generates a master secret key msk and a system public key pk_{abe} for the CP-ABE cryptosystem, and publishes on the blockchain. It also generates private keys for users (corresponding to their certified attributes).

Let A_o be a user who owns object O, and B_r denote a user who makes a request r. The resource owner A_o can deploy contracts for their objects on the blockchain that will be visible to all registered users. A contract can hold the information about multiple objects, and can be updated by A_o.

Owners will be represented by pseudonyms that can be mapped to their identities by the BA who has registered the user and so are traceable by that specific BA when they use their public keys.

User authentication to BA is through a challenge-response authentication protocol between the user and the BA, where BA issues a random challenge, and the user response is the signed challenge, together with the request. A user can use their secret key to sign the request and the challenge, in which case their pseudonym will be known by BA (the BA who has registered the user additionally knows the real identity of the user), or use a ring signature for anonymous authentication. The challenge in both cases is obtained by the latest broadcasted randomness. More details on this protocol in Subsect. 3.2.

We consider five contracts in the system: User directory contract (uDir), Object directory contract (oDir), object property repository contract (objPropRep), object access control contract (objACC) and Adjudicator contract (Adj). uDir, oDir, and Adj are deployed on the blockchain by BA when the system is set up and they hold the information related to all users. objACC and objPropRep are deployed by resource owners, upon sharing a resource. A user B_r who makes a request may receive an object that does not match its advertised properties. In such cases, the requester can report misbehavior to BA that is implemented by the Adjudicator contract. The details of contracts are given in Subsect. 3.3.

3.1 Security Goals

We consider the following entities: (i) users, (ii) BA, (iii) CA and CP-ABE AA, and (iv) outsiders.

Trust Assumptions. We assume BA is semi-honest: they follow the protocol but want to infer information about users and their accesses. For example, BA may link requesters and owners, or link requests of users. CA and CP-ABE AA are fully trusted: they follow the protocol and manage the keys as required. Users can deviate arbitrarily from the protocol: an owner may be unregistered, claim properties that the object does not have, or provide invalid link to the object. Users may be curious about others.

Security. The goal is to ensure that access to an object is only granted if (i) the requester is registered, and (ii) the user's specified access policy is satisfied.

Privacy. We consider two privacy requirements.

i. Registered users, BA, and outsiders cannot link the requester of an object O to the object owner;
ii. Registered users, BA, and outsiders should not be able to link access requests of users.

In our privacy analysis we consider two cases:

i. *Pre-interaction* case, where the system is ready to function (user registration and advertising resources are complete) but no browsing or access request has been made to the BA;
ii. *Post-interaction* case, where some successful interactions to view or access objects have been made.

We define *information leakage (privacy breach) of the system* as the difference between the views of an entity in the above two cases and what can be inferred from it.

3.2 Authentication and Requests

We use $\mathsf{Beacon}(t)$ as the challenge (random value) for user authentication across the system for the time period $[t,\ t+1]$. A user response will be generated using the digital signature scheme $\mathsf{DS} = (\mathsf{DS.KGen},\ \mathsf{DS.Sig},\ \mathsf{DS.Vf})$ and user's private key, on a request that includes $\mathsf{Beacon}(t)$. For anonymous authentication, a ring signature based on this signature scheme will be used. Steps of response generation are as follows.

(i) Get auxiliary information that are required for sending a request to blockchain (e.g. list of registered users for choosing the public key set set_{pk}, the pubic key of *AuthServ* for encryption).

(ii) Use $r_t = \mathsf{Beacon}(t)$ where current time is in $[t,\ t+1]$.

(iii) Sign $(pk_{TYP}||m||r_t)$ where m is the request, r_t is as defined above, and pk_{TYP} is the public key of signature type $TYP \in \{S,\ RS\}$, where S and RS denote traditional digital signature and ring signature, respectively. Let σ denote the signature value. The response is $(m,\ r,\ \sigma,\ pk_{TYP})$.

We consider two types of requests, (i) non-anonymous requests, which are used for browsing the blockchain[2], and (ii) anonymous requests that target a specific resource. For non-anonymous requests, pk_{TYP} is the public key of the user[3]. For anonymous requests, pk_{TYP} is equal to a set set_{pk} of public keys that belong to a set of registered users in the system (it includes the public key of the requester), and will be used in the ring signature.

We require transmitted request to the blockchain be encrypted with the BA's (precisely *AuthServ*) public key Pk_{AS}. Users will use pk_{AS} to encrypt their request to BA, $C = \mathsf{Enc}(pk_{AS},\ (m,\ r,\ \sigma,\ pk_{TYP}))$. Then, *AuthServ* decrypts C, and verifies the requester and request as follows.

(i) Verify that $r = \mathsf{Beacon}(t)$ for the time interval $[t,\ t+1]$ that user is sending the message.

(ii) Verify that pk_{TYP} has been already recorded in uDir contract.

(iii) Verify σ based on the signature type specified by Pk_{TYP}, i.e., $result = \mathsf{DS.Vf}(\sigma,\ pk_{TYP}||m||r,\ pk_{TYP})$. If $result = 1$ send $(m,\ pk_{TYP})$ to blockchain, otherwise send *reject* to the user.

Choosing Ring Members. We assume set_{pk} comprises of two subsets $set_{pk} = set_1 \cup set_2$; set_1 contains public keys that are randomly chosen from the list of registered users, and set_2 is randomly selected public keys from the pk_{set} of last request issued to BA. We assume that the size of ring is determined based on the total number of malicious users in the system such that it can guarantee in each randomly chosen ring at least two parties are honest (the signer and one of the ring members).

Due to the properties of the ring signature and random beacon, our authentication system provides anonymity, unlinkability, existential unforgeability, and real-time authentication (please see Appendix A for more details).

---

[2] We highlight that the requests of resource owner to BA are also non-anonymous.

[3] We can use the ring signature with ring size equal to 1 as a regular signature.

3.3 Smart Contracts

The details of contracts are given below (see Appendix C for abstract of contracts). Note that all the contracts have a *self-destruct* method (to make the contracts inaccessible) which can be called only by the contract owner.

User Directory Contract (uDir): This contract holds a table containing the pseudonym and public key certificate (that includes the public key) of registered users. These information can be browsed by requesters to form the set of public keys set_{pk} for the ring signature. This contract has the following interfaces:

- registerUser(): is used by *AuthServ* to set the information of registered users.
- deleteUser(): is used by Adj contract (if a user misbehaves) or *AuthServ* to delete the information about the user.
- getUsersInfo(): is used by requesters to get the information of registered users in the system.

Object Directory Contract (oDir): This contract holds a table of object Id, pseudonym and public key of the resource owner, description of the object, address of the objACC contract, ABI of objACC contract, address of the objPropRep contract, and ABI of the objPropRep contract (cf. Table 1). This contract has the following interfaces:

Table 1. oDir contract

Oid	pId_o	pk_o	ODesc	objACC address	objACC ABI	objPropRep address	objPropRep ABI
M_i	Alice	0x456ab7	Cartoon, 90 m,	0xfd45322	$[setAccessInfo(M_i), ...]$	0xab49871	$[setPropertyInfo(M_i), ...)]$

- registerResource(): is used by each resource owner to register their objects and provide information for accessing the objects.
- updateResource(): is used by resource owners to update their resources. Only the user whose public key has been stored in the table is able to update the object.
- deleteResource(): is used by resource owners and Adj contract to delete the information of the inaccessible objects.
- getContractInfo(): is used by requesters to retrieve the address and ABI of the objACC and objPropRep for all objects.
- getAdvertiseInfo(): is used by objACC to get the advertisement info for a specific object including the owners information and object description.

Object Property Repository Contract (objPropRep): This contract is deployed by each resource owner and stores the list of objects, their properties, and certificates (cf. Table 2). objPropRep has the following interface:

Table 2. `objPropRep` table

Oid	Properties	Cert
M_i	$prop_1, ..., prop_\nu$	$cert_{CA}^{M_i}$

- `setPropertyInfo()`: is used only by the resource owner to add a new object and its properties and certificates.
- `getPropertyInfo()`: is used by requesters and `objACC` contract to retrieve the information of a specific resource. `objACC` only receives the properties of the object, whereas requesters will receive both the properties and certificates of the requested object.
- `updatePropertyInfo()`: is used only by the resource owner to update the information of a specific object.
- `deletePropertyInfo()`: is used by the resource owner and `Adj` to remove the information of the resources which are no longer accessible or valid.

Access Control Contract (`objACC`): This contract is deployed by each resource owner to upload the ciphertexts (cf. Table 3) and policies that are required for decrypting the CP-ABE ciphertext.

Table 3. `objACC` table

Oid	Ciphertext	Access policies
M_i	$c^{CP-ABE}(M(c_O))$	$Age > 6, Preference = local \lor international, club\ membership = Club2$

- `addAccessInfo()`: is used only by the resource owner to add a CP-ABE encrypted metadata and its access policies.
- `updateAccessInfo()`: is used by the resource owner to update CP-ABE encrypted metadata and policy for an object.
- `deleteAccessInfo()`: is used by the resource owner and `Adj` to remove the information of objects that are not accessible or valid anymore.
- `getAccessInfo()`: is used by requesters to get the CP-ABE encrypted metadata and the access policies to decrypt CP-ABE metadata.
- `setContractAddress()`: is used by the owner to set the address of the `objPropRep` and `oDir` contracts.
- `getRequestHistory()`: is used to retrieve the history of the requests that has been made to the contract. Each `objACC` contract stores the requests, i.e. the authentication information provided by the requester, the Oid of the accessed object, and the time of the request.

Adjudicator Contract (`Adj`): This contract is used to record misbehaviors. It keeps a table containing the Oid of the resource, the public key of the resource owner, the misbehavior, time of report, and state of the complain. Note that since we are ensuring anonymity for requesters `Adj` cannot be used to record the misbehavior of requesters (unlike [3]). However, if a resource owner provides invalid link, a requester can anonymously complain about it for further checks by a trusted entity (verifier) that is determined by BA. (c.f. Table 4)

Table 4. Adj table

Oid	pk_o	Misbehavior	Time	State
M_i	0x4598abc678	Incorrect link	10:05 12/9/2020	Unchecked

- registerVerifier(): is used by BA to set a verifier(s) who can check the complains.
- reportMisbehavior(): is used by requesters to complain about a resource owner and object information.
- setMisbehaviorState(): is used by the specified verifier to set the result of checking the misbehavior. Adj contract calls deleteResource(M_i) of oDir, deletePropertyInfo(M_i) of objPropRep, and deleteAccessInfo(M_i) of objACC contracts to delete the information about the resources that are proved to be incorrect and calls deleteUser(pk_o) of uDir contract to delete the resource owners who are misbehaving.
- getLatestMisbehavior(): is used by users to get the information of the latest misbehavior for a specific resource owner.

3.4   Interactions of Users with System

There are three stages in our scheme (cf. Appendix B for the algorithm).

1. *Registration:*
   (a) Each user with Id_{A_o} (or similarly Id_{B_r} for requester) chooses their pseudonym pId_{A_o} and present it to the blockchain authority (BA) at the time of registration and gets the public-private key pair (Pk_{A_o}, Sk_{A_o}) and a certificate $cert^{BA}_{Pk_{A_o}}$ (corresponding to user's public key). Once the registration is complete, the BA publishes the list $(pId_{A_o}, Pk_{A_o}, cert^{BA}_{Pk_{A_o}})$ to blockchain.
   (b) User A_o contacts the certificate authority and gets certificate for their set of attributes and the properties of the objects they hold.
   (c) The user contacts CP-ABE AA and uses their public key certificate to authenticate themselves, and obtain attribute private keys attached to their pId_{A_o} (or Pk_{A_o}).
2. *Advertising a resource* (please refer to [40] for the flow of advertising a resource):
   (a) User A_o who is the resource owner wants to advertise a digital object $\mathcal{O}$. A_o encrypts the object $\mathcal{O}$ using a symmetric key, $c_{\mathcal{O}} = \text{Enc}(k, \mathcal{O})$ and uploads $c_{\mathcal{O}}$ to the cloud.
   (b) Next, A_o creates CP-ABE metadata $(M(c_{\mathcal{O}}))$. $M(c_{\mathcal{O}})$ consists of (i) additional resource content description, (ii) symmetric key k, and (iii) download link of the resource content (link to encrypted file). A_o then encrypts the $M(c_{\mathcal{O}})$ with policy $P_{\mathcal{O}}$ using CP-ABE encryption scheme and gets the encrypted metadata $c^{CP-ABE}(M(c_{\mathcal{O}}))$.
   (c) A_o deploys two contracts to share their objects: (i)objACC, and (ii)objPropRep.

(d) The blockchain authority (BA) deploys three contracts. (i) `uDir`, (ii) `oDir`, and (iii) `Adj`.

(e) When $\mathcal{A}_o$ adds an object, or updates an object in `objACC` contract, `objACC` retrieves the information of the objects, including objects descriptions and properties, as well as $\mathcal{A}_o$'s information, including its pseudonym and public key from the `oDir` and `objPropRep` contracts and issues an event to all registered users containing the advertisement information.

3. *Request and access* (see Fig. 1 for the flow of request and access):

(a) User $\mathcal{B}_r$ browses `uDir` to obtain the list of registered users and chooses the ring members according to Sect. 3.2. Then, $\mathcal{B}_r$ browses `oDir` to find an object $\mathcal{O}$ that they want to get access to that. User $\mathcal{B}_r$ forms a request (either for getting data from `objPropRep` contract or `objACC` contract) that includes (Oid), signs it using a ring signature and sends it to BA.

(b) BA runs an authentication service ($AuthServ$). $AuthServ$ verifies the signed request, and if valid the respective contract (`objPropRep`$_O$ or `objACC`$_O$) returns the requested data to requester $\mathcal{B}_r$, where $\mathcal{O}$ is the object (note that the response of anonymous requests are returned, in encrypted form, to all ring members determined by $\mathcal{B}_r$ upon making a request). $\mathcal{B}_r$ decrypts the CP-ABE metadata using their CP-ABE private key and gets access to the object.

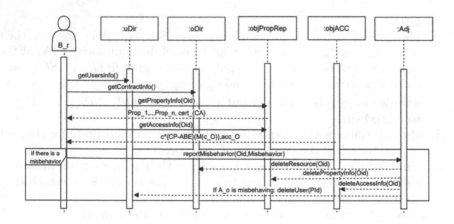

Fig. 1. Sequence diagram of requesting access from a resource requester.

4   Security and Privacy Analysis

For security we need to show that *only registered users whose attributes match the specified access policies of their requested object can obtain access*. For privacy we only consider post-interaction phase, and show that *(i) no registered user or BA is able to link a request to an existing resource owner, (ii) no registered user or BA is able to link the access requests of a resource requester to their previous requests, and (iii) no outsider can link the requests.* For pre-interaction phase, published contracts can be used to develop a profile of a resource owner's resources. Protection of this profile is not a design goal of the system.

Security. We consider four cases: (i) outsiders are not able to access the object, (ii) requesters with attributes different from the access policies cannot get access to the object, (iii) requesters who were a registered user in some point of time but they have been removed from the system (for e.g. because of misbehaving) are not able to get access to any object that matches their attributes later, and (iv) honest requesters with attributes specified in access policies of an object can get access to the object.

Case (i) is true since any entity who issues a request proves to BA that they are a registered user, through the ring signature-based anonymous authentication scheme. Due to the unforgeability of this scheme, an outsider adversary cannot generate a valid ring signature for a new request. If the outsider adversary can successfully capture one of honest user's requests in time t_m (by eavesdropping the communication channel), it cannot use it in a later time $t_r > t_m$. The reason is that the beacon value at time of request t_r is different from the beacon value at time t_m and BA will reject the requests with stale random value.

Case (ii) is ensured because of the security of CP-ABE scheme. All registered users can retrieve the CP-ABE encrypted metadata, but only the users with valid CP-ABE private keys can decrypt it and get access to the object. The CP-ABE private keys are issued by CP-ABE AA who is trusted, and generates private keys after verifying the attribute certificates (which have been issued by trusted CA).

Case (iii) is guaranteed because of the use of beacons in our authentication scheme. Note that we assume the private/public keys never expire, and a CP-ABE encrypted metadata can be decrypted with any valid CP-ABE private key. If we do not use beacon in our authentication scheme, any user who has been removed from the system can capture other users' requests (by eavesdropping on their communication channel to BA) and send it later in time. As the authentication passes, attacker can get access to CP-ABE encrypted metadata (which it can decrypt). However, we protect against this attack by using fresh randomness. The copied requests will not pass the authentication, because we assume the time duration for pulsating a new random value is less than the time required for the attacker to copy a request, and hence the request contains a stale random value, which will be rejected by BA.

Case (iv) is ensured because of the correctness property of the anonymous authentication and CP-ABE scheme. The registered users can pass the authentication and retrieve the CP-ABE encrypted metadata. Users who hold a valid CP-ABE private key can decrypt the CP-ABE encrypted metadata correctly and obtain the link to the object (if the resource owner is malicious and the link is not correct, the requesters can report the misbehavior to `Adj` contract which can be checked by verifiers of the system).

Privacy. We use the users' and the BAs' views to determine the privacy breach. For *pre-interaction privacy analysis*, a registered user can see uDir, oDir, and owners contracts `objPropRep` and `objACC` and can develop a profile of the resource owner only by analyzing the advertisement that is published by the resource owner. As stated earlier we do not seek a solution for owners. We show the privacy only for the post-interaction regime; (i) no registered user and BA are able to link a request to an existing resource owner, (ii) no registered user and BA are able to link the access requests of a resource requester to their previous requests, and (iii) no outsider can link the requests.

Case (i) is guaranteed because resource requesters use anonymous authentication to prove that they are registered users. Due to the anonymity of our authentication scheme (described in Sect. 3.2), the public key of the requester will not be revealed to BA. Additionally, BA only publishes the request of the requester and its ring information to the blockchain. Therefore, other users cannot determine who is the requester. Even if other users know the real identity of a set of public keys in a given ring, since at least two honest parties exist in each ring, for an honest requester the level of anonymity is equal to $\frac{1}{2}$ in the worst case. Malicious users are not able to choose invalid private/public keys in order to break anonymity of the scheme, since we have a registration stage that validates the generation of public keys.

Case (ii) is guaranteed because (a) the attributes of requester are not revealed to BA (requester decrypts the CP-ABE encrypted metadata off-chain), and (b) the unlinkability property of our anonymous authentication scheme (described in Sect. 3.2). BA only sees a set of public keys (a ring) which consists of a subset of public keys chosen from previous requests (rings have intersection) that provides unlinkability for consecutive requests made by a requester.

Case (iii) is ensured since outsiders cannot see the requests sent to BA and received by users (the requests are encrypted using the public key provided by BA and the response messages are encrypted and returned to users that their public keys exist in the issued request).

5 Implementation

In this section, we give details of our implementation for resource sharing in a permissioned Ethereum network. The goal of our proof-of-concept implementation is to analyze the practicality of our proposed model by measuring the cost (in *time*) of the cryptographic operations in our system and the cost (in *gas*) for the blockchain operations.

5.1 System Setup

Actors: We consider users (e.g., resource owner and resource requester), a blockchain authority, a certificate authority and a CP-ABE attribute authority.

Blockchain Setup: For proof of concept implementation, we use a private (permissioned) Ethereum blockchain to set up the required blockchain infrastructure that will be maintained by the blockchain authorities (BA). BA deploys the smart contracts (uDir, oDir and Adj) and A_o deploys the smart contracts (objPropRep and objACC), in the blockchain.

Crypto Tools: We use OpenSSL library [41] for creating certificates, object identifier (*Oid*) (using SHA256), and generating public-private key pairs. In addition, for the symmetric key encryption scheme, we use OpenSSL library supported AES-256-CBC encryption scheme. For the ring signature we use implementation of the original algorithm by Rivest et al. [5] and for CP-ABE we use CP-ABE toolkit supported by advanced crypto software collection service [42].

Device specification: We evaluate the performance of our system on Windows 10 with a 3.60 GHz Intel Core i7 CPU and 8 GB RAM.

Smart contracts in the system: We consider the five smart contracts proposed in Sect. 3.3. All the smart contracts are written in *Solidity* language and developed using the *remix* IDE. Abstracts of these contracts are given in the Appendix C[4].

5.2 Evaluation

To show the practicality of our proposed scheme, we measured the user's cost in different phases: *(i)* registration, *(ii)* resource advertising and *(iii)* resource request. We implemented an example scenario of a movie sharing for our evaluation (see [40] for the example details). We used *Ganache* [6], as a private (permissioned) Ethereum blockchain, Remix IDE [7] for writing the smart contracts in *Solidity* and *Truffle* to deploy and run experiments.

For *registration*, we measure the cost in terms of *time*. Table 5 shows the average time required for each user to generate the RSA keys along with the (fixed) size of the keys.

For *resource advertising*, we used AES-256-CBC encryption scheme on the object "*Tom's Trip to Moon*" of size 16MB and used CP-ABE encryption scheme to get the CP-ABE metadata. Note that the size of the CP-ABE encrypted metadata depends only on the size of the access policies and it is independent of the object size. The reason is that the CP-ABE encrypted metadata contains the symmetric encryption key (e.g., AES 256-bit key) and the link to the object. The encryption and key generation times are shown in Table 5 with size of the outputs for each of these operations. Using the CP-ABE toolkit, it takes 0.023 seconds to generate master and CP-ABE public key. The size of master key is 156 bytes and the size of public key is 888 byte (in total 1044 byte). Moreover, each Ethereum operation is associated with an explicit cost which is expressed in *gas* [37]. We measure the cost (in terms of *gas*) of program execution in Ethereum blockchain by the resource owner for deploying two smart contracts and for executing different functions (e.g., add, update or delete) in the smart contracts. Table 6 shows the gas required for each of the mentioned tasks.

---

[4] The codes of our smart contracts are available in [40].

Table 5. Cost of cryptographic operations

Algorithm	Time (ms.)	Size (bytes)	Actor
Public key generation (RSA)	0.055	451	A_o, B_r
AES Encryption	10.704	6361840	A_o
AES Decryption	5.266	6361816	B_r
CP-ABE private key generation	1.526	71353	A_o
CP-ABE private key generation	2.526	119227	B_r
CP-ABE encryption	75.177	4024	A_o
CP-ABE decryption	0.107	496	B_r
Ring signature generation	2.834	4981	B_r
Ring signature verification	1.513	-	BA
Certificate generation	25.23	1009	BA

Table 6. Cost of blockchain operations (by resource owner)

Tasks	objACC (gas)	objProRep (gas)	oDir (gas)
Deployment	1070938	1064347	NA
Add	1307190	1243438	NA
Update	437233	418354	NA
Delete	159076	151414	NA
RegisterResource	NA	NA	614273

In case of a *resource request*, the costs includes the CP-ABE key generation, ring signature generation and CP-ABE decryption which are shown in Table 5. During this phase, for authentication, the BA sends a challenge (i.e., a random string) of size 512 bits to the requester, and the requester responds with a transaction (signed using ring signature with ring size 10) that includes this challenge value. The requester also needs to make calls to smart contract functions in order to get the required object information (e.g., CP-ABE encrypted metadata, object access policy etc.). Since these function calls does not alter the state of the blockchain (i.e., does not change any variable's value in the contract), there is no cost associated to these calls.

In summary, our proof of concept implementation results in Table 5 shows that the overhead for the cryptographic operations are not high. In addition, it should be noted that, although we measured the gas cost of the smart contract function execution in Table 6, for our model, this cost is not vital as we consider a permissioned blockchain setting. The goal is to estimate the complexity of operations performed on blockchain, provide a benchmark for possible future comparisons, and show the concrete cost in case the smart contracts are deployed on a public blockchain. Overall, the values in the tables indicate that our proposed model is feasible for developing real-world applications.

6   Concluding Remarks

We designed and provided a proof of concept implementation of a blockchain-based privacy-preserving resource sharing platform that enforces user defined attribute-based access policies. Our design uses cryptographic algorithms to provide privacy and direct enforcement of access policies. By leveraging these primitives one needs to balance security and efficiency. For example increasing the level of anonymity will decrease the efficiency of system, since the time required for generating and verifying ring signature will increase with the size of the anonymity set.

There are limitations in our design that can be addressed in future work. Firstly, using CP-ABE for enforcing policies requires users to obtain their private keys from *CP-ABE AA* which results in a single point of trust for the system (allowing *CP-ABE AA* to be able to access all the resources). Distributing this role among multiple authorities using multi-authority ABE schemes [43,44] can significantly improve this limitation. A second challenge in using CP-ABE is the change in the user attributes that will affect their private keys. Efficient updating of users' private keys to reflect their current attribute sets, will be an interesting direction for future research also.

Our work can be extended in a number of ways including, providing anonymity for the resource provider, developing the platform into a marketplace by linking it to a cryptocurrency, providing an effective support for adjudication and handling of complaints, and formal analysis of the system's security and privacy.

A   On the Security of Anyonymous Authentication

We consider a ring signature that provides basic anonymity, unlinkability, and existential unforgeability (for the formal definitions please see [45]). Because we have a registration authority which checks the validity of generated keys, and we assume that there are at least two honest members in the ring, the ring signature is not vulnerable to adversarially-chosen key attacks and basic anonymity is sufficient for our system. Choosing part of the ring randomly prevents the BAs from finding a pattern for the ring used by a particular requester in multiple requests and ensures that anonymity is preserved even in multiple executions of the protocol. Additionally, We assume that the random challenge that is concatenated with the message is unpredictable and unbiasable, and it can provide real-time authentication for users. However, in our authentication scheme, all users that are making request in the same time interval use the same random challenge, this is different from existing point to point authentication schemes. The question is whether the multicast of the challenge random value can give an opportunity to the attacker to break the security of the scheme, specifically, to an outsider to replay the message of an honest user. However, we assume that the time interval for generating a beacon is less than the time that is needed for the attacker to capture and resend the message to BA. So, if attacker sends the copied message the authentication fails. For unlinkability, we consider that the chosen rings by different (or even same) requesters has intersection with each other and provides some level of mixing. This prevents the BAs to link the consecutive requests from a requester.

B   Interactions in Different Phases

The interactions between different entities of our system are shown in the following Algorithm 1 where *the highlighted lines represent the interactions that involve blockchain.*

Algorithm 1. Interactions in proposed resource sharing system.

(Registration) */
1: User $\mathcal{A}$ chooses pseudonym pid_A and (pk_A, sk_A)
2: $\mathcal{A} \rightarrow BA$: $pid_A, (PK_A, SK_A)$
3: $BA \rightarrow \mathcal{A}$: $cert_{BA}^{pk_A}$
4: BA: deploy contract uDir
5: $BA \rightarrow$ uDir: $registerUser\ (pid_A, pk_A, cert_{BA}^{pk_A})$
6: $\mathcal{A} \rightarrow CA$: request certificates
7: $CA \rightarrow \mathcal{A}$: certificate for user attribute and $prop_\mathcal{O}$ ▷ $prop_\mathcal{O}$: properties of object $\mathcal{O}$
8: $\mathcal{A} \rightarrow CP - ABEAA$: $register(cert_{pk_A}^{BA})$
9: $CP\text{-}ABEAA \rightarrow \mathcal{A}$: $(pk_{CP-ABE}^A, sk_{CP-ABE}^A)$

(Advertising resource) */
10: $\mathcal{A}$: get $c_\mathcal{O} = \texttt{Enc}(k, \mathcal{O})$ and upload $c_\mathcal{O}$ to cloud
11: $\mathcal{A}$: create CP-ABE metadata $(M(c_\mathcal{O}))$, and encrypt it to $c^{CP-ABE}(M(c_\mathcal{O}))$
12: $\mathcal{A}$: deploy objPropRep contract with $(\mathcal{O}, prop_\mathcal{O}, cert_\mathcal{O}^{CA})$
13: $\mathcal{A}$: deploy objACC contract with $(\mathcal{O}, acc_\mathcal{O}, c^{CP-ABE}(M(c_\mathcal{O})))$
14: BA: deploy user directory contract (uDir) and object directory contract (oDir)
15: $\mathcal{A} \rightarrow$ oDir: $registerResource(Oid, pid, pk_A, ODesc,$ address and ABI of objACC and objPropRep)

Requesting an access */
16: $\mathcal{A} \rightarrow$ oDir: Oid
17: oDir $\rightarrow \mathcal{A}$: ($object\ description$, address of objACC/objPropRep)
18: $\mathcal{A} \rightarrow$ objACC/objPropRep: Oid
19:      objPropRep $\rightarrow \mathcal{A}$: ($properties, certificate$)
20:      objACC $\rightarrow \mathcal{A}$: encrypted metadata $(c^{CP-ABE}(M(c_\mathcal{O})))$, policies $(acc_\mathcal{O})$
21: $\mathcal{A}$: decrypt $c^{CP-ABE}(M(c_\mathcal{O}))$ using its secret key sk_{CP-ABE}^A

C   Smart Contracts in Our System

We have five smart contracts and the abstract of these contracts are given below (cf. Algorithms 2 to 6).